D1383813

MACROECONOMICS

The McGraw-Hill Economics Series

SURVEY OF ECONOMICS

Brue, McConnell, and Flynn
Essentials of Economics
Third Edition

Mandel
M: Economics—The Basics
Third Edition

Schiller and Gebhardt
Essentials of Economics
Tenth Edition

PRINCIPLES OF ECONOMICS

Asarta and Butters
Connect Master: Economics
First Edition

Colander
Economics, Microeconomics, and Macroeconomics
Tenth Edition

Frank, Bernanke, Antonovics, and Heffetz
Principles of Economics, Principles of Microeconomics, Principles of Macroeconomics
Sixth Edition

Frank, Bernanke, Antonovics, and Heffetz
Streamlined Editions: Principles of Economics, Principles of Microeconomics, Principles of Macroeconomics
Third Edition

Karlan and Morduch
Economics, Microeconomics, Macroeconomics
Second Edition

McConnell, Brue, and Flynn
Economics, Microeconomics, Macroeconomics
Twenty-First Edition

Samuelson and Nordhaus
Economics, Microeconomics, and Macroeconomics
Nineteenth Edition

Schiller and Gebhardt
The Economy Today, The Micro Economy Today, and The Macro Economy Today
Fourteenth Edition

Slavin
Economics, Microeconomics, and Macroeconomics
Eleventh Edition

ECONOMICS OF SOCIAL ISSUES

Guell
Issues in Economics Today
Eighth Edition

Register and Grimes
Economics of Social Issues
Twenty-First Edition

ECONOMETRICS

Gujarati and Porter
Basic Econometrics
Fifth Edition

Hilmer and Hilmer
Practical Econometrics
First Edition

MANAGERIAL ECONOMICS

Baye and Prince
Managerial Economics and Business Strategy
Ninth Edition

Brickley, Smith, and Zimmerman
Managerial Economics and Organizational Architecture
Sixth Edition

Thomas and Maurice
Managerial Economics
Twelfth Edition

INTERMEDIATE ECONOMICS

Bernheim and Whinston
Microeconomics
Second Edition

Dornbusch, Fischer, and Startz
Macroeconomics
Twelfth Edition

Frank
Microeconomics and Behavior
Ninth Edition

ADVANCED ECONOMICS

Romer
Advanced Macroeconomics
Fourth Edition

MONEY AND BANKING

Cecchetti and Schoenholtz
Money, Banking, and Financial Markets
Fifth Edition

URBAN ECONOMICS

O'Sullivan
Urban Economics
Eighth Edition

LABOR ECONOMICS

Borjas
Labor Economics
Seventh Edition

McConnell, Brue, and Macpherson
Contemporary Labor Economics
Eleventh Edition

PUBLIC FINANCE

Rosen and Gayer
Public Finance
Tenth Edition

ENVIRONMENTAL ECONOMICS

Field and Field
Environmental Economics: An Introduction
Seventh Edition

INTERNATIONAL ECONOMICS

Appleyard and Field
International Economics
Ninth Edition

Pugel
International Economics
Sixteenth Edition

MACROECONOMICS

SECOND EDITION

Dean Karlan
Yale University and Innovations for Poverty Action

Jonathan Morduch
New York University

MACROECONOMICS, SECOND EDITION

Published by McGraw-Hill Education, 2 Penn Plaza, New York, NY 10121. Copyright © 2018 by McGraw-Hill Education. All rights reserved. Printed in the United States of America. Previous editions © 2014. No part of this publication may be reproduced or distributed in any form or by any means, or stored in a database or retrieval system, without the prior written consent of McGraw-Hill Education, including, but not limited to, in any network or other electronic storage or transmission, or broadcast for distance learning.

Some ancillaries, including electronic and print components, may not be available to customers outside the United States.

This book is printed on acid-free paper.

1 2 3 4 5 6 7 8 9 LWI 21 20 19 18 17

ISBN 978-1-259-81343-6
MHID 1-259-81343-6

Chief Product Officer, SVP Products & Markets: *G. Scott Virkler*
Vice President, General Manager, Products & Markets: *Marty Lange*
Vice President, Content Design & Delivery: *Betsy Whalen*
Managing Director: *James Heine*
Brand Manager: *Katie Hoenicke*
Director, Product Development: *Rose Koos*
Product Developer: *Alyssa Lincoln*
Lead Product Developer: *Michele Janicek*
Lead Product Developer: *Ann Torbert*
Marketing Manager: *Virgil Lloyd*
Marketing Coordinator: *Dave O'Donnell*
Market Development Manager: *Trina Maurer*
Director of Digital Content Development: *Douglas Ruby*
Director, Content Design & Delivery: *Linda Avenarius*
Program Manager: *Mark Christianson*
Content Project Managers: *Kathryn D. Wright, Kristin Bradley, and Karen Jozefowicz*
Buyer: *Laura M. Fuller*
Design: *Matt Diamond*
Content Licensing Specialists: *Beth Thole and Melissa Homer*
Cover Image: © *Godruma/Getty Images*
Compositor: *SPi Global*
Printer: *LSC Communications*

All credits appearing on page or at the end of the book are considered to be an extension of the copyright page.

Library of Congress Cataloging-in-Publication Data
Names: Karlan, Dean S., author. | Morduch, Jonathan, author.
Title: Macroeconomics / Dean Karlan, Yale University and Innovations for
    Poverty Action, Jonathan Morduch, New York University.
Description: Second edition. | New York, NY : McGraw-Hill Education, [2017]
Identifiers: LCCN 2016034553 | ISBN 9781259813436 (alk. paper)
Subjects: LCSH: Macroeconomics.
Classification: LCC HB172.5 .K374 2017 | DDC 339—dc23 LC record available at
https://lccn.loc.gov/2016034553

The Internet addresses listed in the text were accurate at the time of publication. The inclusion of a website does not indicate an endorsement by the authors or McGraw-Hill Education, and McGraw-Hill Education does not guarantee the accuracy of the information presented at these sites.

www.mhhe.com

dedication

We dedicate this book to our families.

—Dean and Jonathan

Dean Karlan

Dean Karlan is Professor of Economics at Yale University and President and Founder of Innovations for Poverty Action (IPA). Dean started IPA in 2002 with two aims: to help learn what works and what does not in the fight against poverty and other social problems around the world, and then to implement successful ideas at scale. IPA has worked in over 50 countries, with 1,000 employees around the world. Dean's personal research focuses on using field experiments to learn more about the effectiveness of financial services for low-income households, with a focus on using behavioral economics approaches to improve financial products and services. His research includes related areas, such as building income for those in extreme poverty, charitable fundraising, voting, health, and education. Dean is also cofounder of stickK.com, a start-up that helps people use commitment contracts to achieve personal goals, such as losing weight or completing a problem set on time, and in 2015 he founded ImpactMatters, an organization that helps assess whether charitable organizations are using and producing appropriate evidence of impact. Dean is a Sloan Foundation Research Fellow, a Guggenheim Fellow, and an Executive Committee member of the Board of the M.I.T. Jameel Poverty Action Lab. In 2007 he was awarded a Presidential Early Career Award for Scientists and Engineers. He is coeditor of the *Journal of Development Economics* and on the editorial board of *American Economic Journal: Applied Economics.* He holds a BA from University of Virginia, an MPP and MBA from University of Chicago, and a PhD in Economics from MIT. In 2016 he coauthored *Failing in the Field,* and in 2011 he coauthored *More Than Good Intentions: Improving the Ways the World's Poor Borrow, Save, Farm, Learn, and Stay Healthy.*

Jonathan Morduch

Jonathan Morduch is Professor of Public Policy and Economics at New York University's Wagner Graduate School of Public Service. Jonathan focuses on innovations that expand the frontiers of finance and how financial markets shape economic growth and inequality. Jonathan has lived and worked in Asia, but his newest book, *The Financial Diaries: How American Families Cope in a World of Uncertainty* (written with Rachel Schneider and published by Princeton University Press, 2017), follows families in California, Mississippi, Ohio, Kentucky, and New York as they cope with economic ups and downs over a year. The new work jumps off from ideas in *Portfolios of the Poor: How the World's Poor Live on $2 a Day* (Princeton University Press, 2009), which Jonathan coauthored and which describes how families in Bangladesh, India, and South Africa devise ways to make it through a year living on $2 a day or less. Jonathan's research on financial markets is collected in *The Economics of Microfinance* and *Banking the World,* both published by MIT Press. At NYU, Jonathan is executive director of the Financial Access Initiative, a center that supports research on extending access to finance in low-income communities. Jonathan's ideas have also shaped policy through work with the United Nations, World Bank, and other international organizations. In 2009, the Free University of Brussels awarded Jonathan an honorary doctorate to recognize his work on microfinance. He holds a BA from Brown and a PhD from Harvard, both in Economics.

Karlan and **Morduch** first met in 2001 and have been friends and colleagues ever since. Before writing this text, they collaborated on research on financial institutions. Together, they've written about new directions in financial access for the middle class and poor, and in Peru they set up a laboratory to study incentives in financial contracts for loans to women to start small enterprises. In 2006, together with Sendhil Mullainathan, they started the Financial Access Initiative, a center dedicated to expanding knowledge about financial solutions for the 40 percent of the world's adults who lack access to banks. This text reflects their shared passion for using economics as a tool to improve one's own life and to promote better business and public policies in the broader world.

brief contents

We offer the second edition of this text as a resource for professors who, like us, want to show students that *economics can make a positive impact*—in their own lives and in society as a whole. We designed the text with our own version of a "dual mandate":

- to *deliver core economic concepts* along with *exciting new ideas* in economic thought and
- to *keep student learners engaged by confronting issues that are important in the world.*

Our intention is that this approach will help students see economics as a tool to better one's own life, promote better public policies, and run better businesses around the world.

Why Study Economics?

Whenever we've been asked why we teach economics, or why students should study the topic, our answer is simple: *"Economics helps make the world a better place."* It's unfortunate that economics often has a reputation for being the "dismal science." We believe fundamentally that *economics is a good thing.* Economic principles can help students understand and respond to everyday situations. Economic ideas also help us tackle big challenges, such as fixing our health care system and keeping the government fiscally solvent. We show students how economic ideas are shaping their world in important, positive ways, and we provide them with a wide-ranging set of practical insights to help develop their economic intuition.

We have built engagement with real-world problems into the fabric of our chapters, and we present data-driven economic thinking as a way to help solve these problems. Faculty and students will find that our impact-based focus *breaks down barriers* between what goes on in the classroom and what is going on in communities, both at home and around the world.

By keeping the discussion down-to-earth and lively, we aim to make the learning materials easier to use and compelling. The chapters are organized around a familiar curriculum of introductory concepts while adding empirical context for ideas that students often find overly abstract or too simplified. The innovative, empirical orientation of the book enables us to incorporate intriguing findings from recent studies and to address material from such areas as game theory, finance, behavioral economics, and political economy. This approach connects concepts in introductory economics to important *new developments* in economic research, while placing a premium on *easy-to-understand explanations.* In every chapter we fulfill four fundamental commitments:

- **Show how economics connects to important ideas and issues in the world.** This text engages students by approaching economics as a way of explaining real people and their decisions and by providing a set of tools that serve to solve many different types of problems. *We show students that economics can make the world a better place,* while challenging them to reach their own conclusions about what "better" really means.
- **Teach principles as evidence-based tools for dealing with real situations.** The text is centered on examples and issues that resonate with students' experience. Applications come *first,* reinforcing the relevance of the tools that students acquire. Engaging empirical cases are interspersed throughout the content. The applications open up puzzles, anomalies, and possibilities that basic economic principles help explain. The aim is, first and foremost, to ensure that students gain an intuitive grasp of basic ideas.
- **Appeal to today's globally engaged students.** Students today live in a digital, globalized world. We recognize that they are knowledgeable and care about both local and international issues. *Macroeconomics* takes a global perspective, with the United States as a leading example. We draw on a world of examples to bring to life topics like how to encourage

fair competition, create jobs, strengthen markets, protect the environment, engage in international trade, and reduce poverty.

- **Provide a balanced, data-driven view.** Economics provides a way to organize insights, integrate data, and enrich worldviews—no matter one's personal politics. Many topics are uncontroversial; others are hotly debated. Our aim is to provide balanced approaches that help students sharpen and enrich their own understandings of the argument. We do this by focusing on the data and evidence behind the effects we see.

In the second edition of this text, we continue to offer stand-alone chapters that dig into some of the new topics in economics. We've watched as topics like behavioral economics, game theory, political economy, and inequality figure more and more prominently in undergraduate curricula with each passing year. We believe it is important to provide teachers with ways to share new ideas and evidence with their students—important concepts that most nonmajors would usually miss.

At the same time, we realize how selective teachers must be in choosing which material to cover in the limited time available. In light of this, we've been especially glad for the guidance from many teachers in finding ways to present, in a time- and space-efficient way, some of the newer, and most exciting, parts of economics today. We promise you will find the topics, discussions, and writing style of *Macroeconomics* clear, concise, accessible, easy to teach from, and fun to read.

Motivation

Who are we? Why did we write this text?

Macroeconomics draws on our own experiences as academic economists, teachers, and policy advisors. We are based at large research universities and often work with and advise nonprofit organizations, governments, international agencies, donors, and private firms. Much of our research involves figuring out how to improve the way real markets function. Working with partners in the United States and on six continents, we are involved in testing new economic ideas. *Macroeconomics* draws on the spirit of that work, as well as similar research, taking students through the process of engaging with real problems, using analytical tools to devise solutions, and ultimately showing what works and why.

One of the best parts of writing this text, promoting its first edition, and revising for the second edition has been the opportunity to spend time with instructors across the country. We've been inspired by their creativity and passion and have learned from their pedagogical ideas. One of the questions we often ask fellow instructors is why they originally became interested in economics. A common response—one we share—is an attraction to the logic and power of economics as a social science. We also often hear instructors describe something slightly different: the way that economics appealed to them as a tool for making sense of life's complexities, whether in business, politics, or daily life. We wrote this book to give instructors a way to share with their students both of those ways that economics matters.

We also are grateful to the many adopters and near-adopters of the first edition who provided many helpful suggestions for ways to make the second edition an even better resource for instructors and students. As you'll see in the list of chapter-by-chapter changes that starts on page xxiii, we've worked hard to fulfill your expectations and meet that goal.

We hope this product will provide students a solid foundation for considering important issues they will confront in their lives. We hope to inspire students to continue their studies in economics, and we promise this text will give them something useful to take away even if they choose other areas of study. Finally, we hope that, in ways small and large, the tools they learn in these pages and this course will help them to think critically about their environment, to live better lives, and to make an impact on their world.

Dean Karlan
Yale University

Jonathan Morduch
New York University

guided tour of features that benefit student learning

What makes this product different? Here's a quick guided tour of some key features that will engage students as they use the Karlan/Morduch content.

Four questions about how economists think

The text's evidence-based approach is framed by *four questions* that economists ask to break down a new challenge and analyze it methodically. We explore these four questions in Chapter 1 and then carry them throughout. They shape a consistent data-driven and impact-based approach to a wide variety of examples and case studies, demonstrating how the questions can be used to address real issues. By teaching the *right questions to ask,* the text provides students with a method for working through decisions they'll face as consumers, employees, entrepreneurs, and voters. Here are the four questions:

- **Question 1:** *What are the wants and constraints of those involved?* This question introduces the concept of *scarcity.* It asks students to think critically about the preferences and resources driving decision making in a given situation. It links into discussions of utility functions, budget constraints, strategic behavior, and new ideas that expand our thinking about rationality and behavioral economics.
- **Question 2:** *What are the trade-offs?* This question focuses on *opportunity cost.* It asks students to understand trade-offs in any decision, including factors that might go beyond the immediate financial costs and benefits. Consideration of trade-offs takes us to discussions of marginal decision making, sunk costs, nonmonetary costs, and discounting.
- **Question 3:** *How will others respond?* This question asks students to focus on *incentives,* both their incentives and the incentives of others. Students consider how individual choices aggregate in both expected and unexpected ways, and what happens when incentives change. The question links into understanding supply and demand, elasticity, competition, taxation, game theory, and monetary and fiscal policy.
- **Question 4:** *Why isn't someone already doing it?* This question relates to *efficiency.* It asks students to start from an assumption that markets work to provide desired goods and services, and then to think carefully about why something that seems like a good idea isn't already being done. We encourage students to revisit their answers to the previous three questions, to see whether they missed something about the trade-offs, incentives, or other forces at work, or are looking at a genuine market failure. This fourth question links topics such as public goods, externalities, information gaps, monopoly, arbitrage, and how the economy operates in the long run versus the short run.

Unique coverage

Macroeconomics presents the *core principles* of economics but also seeks to present some of the new ideas that are *expanding* the basics of economic theory. The sequence of chapters follows a fairly traditional route through the core principles. By thinking first about the choices faced by individuals, students become better prepared to understand the choices of firms, groups, and governments. The text proceeds step-by-step from the personal to the public, allowing students to build toward an understanding of aggregate decisions on a solid foundation of individual decision making.

Two changes, based on market feedback, took place in the second edition chapter organization:

- We switched the sequence of two macroeconomic chapters, putting the "Unemployment and the Labor Market" chapter before the "Economic Growth" chapter.
- We added a new "Aggregate Expenditure" chapter.

Beyond its basic coverage of macroeconomic principles, *Macroeconomics* offers content that connects the core curriculum to today's macroeconomic concerns:

- Chapter 9, "Unemployment and the Labor Market," and Chapter 13, "Fiscal Policy," relate macroeconomic principles to some of the most-debated policy choices faced by governments.
- Chapter 14, "The Basics of Finance," describes how financial markets fit into the overall economy. The chapter gives an overview of the modern financial system (functions, financial products, and the risk-return trade-off), studies the market for loanable funds, and describes how financial markets connect savers and borrowers. The chapter concludes by locating saving and investment within the national accounts approach.
- Chapter 17, "Financial Crisis," takes a close look at the worst financial crisis in generations. It begins with the economics of financial crises and why things sometimes go wrong in financial markets. The chapter then digs into the details of the Great Recession, including the ways that governments responded through monetary policy and fiscal policy.
- Chapter 19, "Development Economics," written by authors who have devoted much of their careers to studying how to reduce global poverty, examines the relationship between economic growth and economic development. The chapter reviews the current state of research in economic development and assesses promising policies, solutions, and innovations for reducing poverty worldwide.

In addition, because students sometimes need reinforcement with the math requirements of the course, *Macroeconomics* contains five unique math appendixes that explain math topics important to understanding economics. **McGraw-Hill Create**™ enables you to select and arrange the combination of traditional and unique chapters and appendixes that will be perfect for *your* course, at an affordable price for *your* students.

Real Life
Testing models against history

Real Life boxes show how the concept you're reading about relates to the real world. They are your chance to test models against the data. Often these boxes will describe a situation in which people used an economic idea to solve a business or policy question, or they present interesting research ideas or experiences. Watch for links to online content, such as videos or news stories.

Thomas Malthus, an early nineteenth-century economist, created a model that described the relationship between population growth and food production. The model predicted that mass starvation would occur as populations outgrew food supplies. In his famous work *An Essay on*

From Another Angle
Does ice cream cause polio?

From Another Angle boxes show you a different way of looking at an economic concept. Sometimes they will be a humorous story, sometimes a different way of thinking about a situation, and sometimes just an unusual application of a standard idea. We find that a little bit of weirdness goes a long way in helping us to remember things, and we hope it will work for you too.

What Do You Think?
The opportunity cost of a life

Throughout the book, What Do You Think? boxes ask for your opinion about an important policy or life decision. These boxes will present questions that require you to combine facts and economic analysis with values and moral reasoning. They are the sort of tough questions that people face in real life. There are many "correct" answers, depending on your values and goals.

The philosopher Peter Singer writes that opportunity costs can be a matter of life or death. Imagine you are a salesperson, and on your way to a meeting on a hot summer day, you drive by a lake. Suddenly, you notice that a child who has been swimming in the lake is drowning. No one else is in sight.

WHAT DO YOU THINK?

1. In what ways do the two situations presented by Singer—the sales meeting and the drowning child versus the iPod and the unvaccinated child—differ?
2. Singer argues that even something like buying an iPod is a surprisingly serious moral decision. Do you agree? What sort of opportunity costs do you typically consider when making such a decision?

Engaging pedagogical features

Interesting examples open each chapter. These chapter-opening stories, presented in an engaging, journalistic style, feature issues that consumers, voters, businesspeople, and family members face. The examples then take students through relevant principles that can help frame and solve the economic problem at hand.

Boxed features build interest. Four different types of boxed stories add interesting real-world details:

- **Real Life** boxes describe a short case or policy question, findings from history or academic studies, and anecdotes from the field.
- **From Another Angle** boxes show a different way of looking at an economic concept—a different way of

thinking about a situation, a humorous story, or sometimes just an unusual application of a standard idea.

- **What Do You Think?** boxes offer a longer case study, with implications for public policy and student-related issues. They present relevant data or historical evidence and ask students to employ both economic analysis and normative arguments to defend a position. We leave the student with open-ended questions, which professors can assign as homework or use for classroom discussion.

- **Where Can It Take You?** boxes direct students to further classes, resources, or jobs related to the topic at hand, to show students how they might apply economics in their careers and as consumers.

In addition, two other types of boxes—**Potentially Confusing** and **Hints**—offer in-depth explanations of a concept or use of terminology. These boxes call attention to common misunderstandings or provide further explanation of tricky concepts. Students appreciate that rather than smoothing over confusing ideas and language, we offer the support they need to understand economic language and reasoning on a deeper level.

Throughout this book, every chapter contains built-in review tools and study devices for student use. **Concept Check questions tied to learning objectives** appear at the end of each major section and prompt students to make sure they understand the topics covered before moving on. **Conclusions** at the end of each chapter sum up the overall lessons learned. **Summaries** give a deeper synopsis of what each learning objective covered. **Key Terms** provide a convenient list of the economic terminology introduced and defined in the chapter.

Also located at the ends of chapters and smoothly integrated with the chapter text are questions and problems for each learning objective:

- **Review Questions** guide students through review and application of the concepts covered in the chapter. These range from straightforward questions about theories or formulas to more open-ended narrative questions.

- High-quality **Problems and Applications** problem sets provide quantitative homework opportunities.

Both sets of content, plus additional Extra Practice Questions, are **fully integrated with Connect®,** enabling online assignments and grading.

The Karlan and Morduch product was built "from the ground up" with the expectation of *complete digital integration* of the text and related hands-on learning materials. All content in the chapter and online is tagged to the chapter learning objectives. Further, this text comes with a robust line-up of learning and teaching products, built for simple and reliable usability. See below for the highlights of our digital offer within Connect.

McGraw-Hill Connect

Adaptive reading experience. SmartBook contains the same content as the print book, but actively tailors that content to the needs of the individual through adaptive probing. Instructors can assign SmartBook reading assignments for points to create incentives for students to come to class prepared.

Extensive algorithmic and graphing assessment. Robust, auto-gradable question banks for each chapter now include even more questions that make use of the Connect graphing tool. More questions featuring algorithmic variations have also been added.

Interactive graphs. This new assignable resource within Connect helps students see the relevance of subject matter by providing visual displays of real data for students to manipulate. All graphs are accompanied by assignable assessment questions and feedback to guide students through the experience of learning to read and interpret graphs and data.

Videos. New to this edition are videos that provide support for key economics topics. These short, engaging explanations are presented at the moment a student is struggling to help the student connect the dots and grasp challenging concepts.

Math preparedness tutorials. Our math preparedness assignments have been reworked to help students refresh on important prerequisite topics necessary to be successful in economics.

Chapter 0 Orientation Assignments. New video assignments have been added to Connect on topics such as SmartBook, graphing exercises, and the interactive graphs. These videos provide students with information about the different assignment types they will encounter in Connect, to help them be successful on their assignments and ensure a smooth start to the term.

New Student Interface. Connect's new, intuitive interface gives students a view of assignments and deadlines across all courses in Connect, to help them be more organized. Students also have access to a personalized analytics dashboard designed to help them allocate study time appropriately for maximum success in the course.

Supplementary Materials

All supplements accompany this text in a completely seamless integration. The following ancillaries are available for quick download and convenient access via the Online Learning Center at www.mhhe.com/karlanmorduch2e and within Connect. Instructor resources are password protected for security.

Test bank

The test bank has been extensively revised for this edition by Aaron Finkle at University of Maryland and Michael Machiorlatti at Oklahoma City Community College. All test bank items were also thoroughly accuracy-checked by Cindy Clement at University of Maryland and Ida Mirzaie at Ohio State University. The test bank contains thousands of quality multiple-choice questions. Each question is tagged with the corresponding learning objective, level of difficulty, economic concept, AACSB learning category, and Bloom's Taxonomy objective. All of the test bank content is available to assign within Connect.

The test bank is also available in TestGen, a complete, state-of-the-art test generator and editing application software that allows instructors to quickly and easily select test items from McGraw-Hill's test bank content. The instructors can then organize, edit, and customize questions and answers to rapidly generate tests for paper or online administration. Questions can include stylized text, symbols, graphics, and equations that are inserted directly into questions using built-in mathematical templates. TestGen's random generator provides the option to display different text or calculated number values each time questions are used. With both quick-and-simple test creation and flexible and robust editing tools, TestGen is a complete test generator system for today's educators.

PowerPoint presentations

Revised for this edition by Gregory Gilpin at Montana State University, the PowerPoint presentations have been carefully crafted to ensure maximum usefulness in the classroom. Each presentation covers crucial information and supplies animated figures that are identical to those in the book. The presentations also contain sample exercises, instructor notes, and more.

In addition to the instructor PowerPoint presentations, a student version is also provided. The student PowerPoints provide a review of each chapter's main points and graphs in a static, PDF form. Some information is intentionally missing from these PDFs so that students are prompted to follow along with the instructor and fill information in as it is discussed in class.

Instructor's manual

The instructor's manual provides a wealth of resources to help organize and enrich the course. Elements include:

- **Learning Objectives:** Lists the learning objectives for each chapter.
- **Chapter Outline:** Shows an outline of the chapter organization for a quick review.
- **Beyond the Lecture:** Presents ideas and activities you can use to start discussion and engage students in class, along with team exercises and assignments you can use outside of class, revised by Dave Brown, Penn State University.
- **Clicker Questions:** Offer additional opportunities for classroom engagement, created by Dave Brown, Penn State University.
- **End-of-Chapter Solutions:** Provides answers to all end-of-chapter questions and problems, revised for this edition by Nora Underwood at University of Central Florida and Erin Moody at University of Maryland. All end-of-chapter answers and solutions have been accuracy checked by Susan Bell at Seminole State College and Greg Gilpin, Montana State University.

Assurance of Learning Ready

Many educational institutions today are focused on the notion of *assurance of learning,* an important element of some accreditation standards. Karlan and Morduch's *Macroeconomics* is designed specifically to support your assurance of learning initiatives with a simple, yet powerful solution. Each test bank question for *Macroeconomics* maps to a specific chapter learning outcome/objective listed in the text. You can use our test bank software, TestGen, or Connect to easily query for learning outcomes/objectives that directly relate to the learning objectives for your course. You can then use the reporting features to aggregate student results in similar fashion, making the collection and presentation of assurance of learning data simple and easy.

AACSB Statement

McGraw-Hill Education is a proud corporate member of AACSB International. Understanding the importance and value of AACSB accreditation, Karlan and Morduch's *Macroeconomics* recognizes the curricula guidelines detailed in the AACSB standards for business accreditation by connecting selected questions in the text and the test bank to the eight general knowledge and skill guidelines in the AACSB standards.

The statements contained in *Macroeconomics* are provided only as a guide for the users of this textbook. The AACSB leaves content coverage and assessment within the purview of individual schools, the mission of the school, and the faculty. While *Macroeconomics* and the teaching package make no claim of any specific AACSB qualification or evaluation, we have within *Macroeconomics* labeled selected questions according to the eight general knowledge and skills areas.

McGraw-Hill Customer Care Contact Information

At McGraw-Hill, we understand that getting the most from new technology can be challenging. That's why our services don't stop after you purchase our products. You can email our Product Specialists 24 hours a day to get product training online. Or you can search our knowledge bank of Frequently Asked Questions on our support website. For Customer Support, call **800-331-5094**, email hmsupport@mcgraw-hill.com, or visit www.mhhe.com/support. One of our Technical Support Analysts will be able to assist you in a timely fashion.

©Getty Images/iStockphoto

McGraw-Hill Connect®
Learn Without Limits

Connect is a teaching and learning platform that is proven to deliver better results for students and instructors.

Connect empowers students by continually adapting to deliver precisely what they need, when they need it, and how they need it, so your class time is more engaging and effective.

73% of instructors who use Connect require it; instructor satisfaction increases by 28% when Connect is required.

Connect's Impact on Retention Rates, Pass Rates, and Average Exam Scores

Using **Connect** improves retention rates by **19.8%**, passing rates by **12.7%**, and exam scores by **9.1%**.

Analytics

Connect Insight®

Connect Insight is Connect's new one-of-a-kind visual analytics dashboard that provides at-a-glance information regarding student performance, which is immediately actionable. By presenting assignment, assessment, and topical performance results together with a time metric that is easily visible for aggregate or individual results, Connect Insight gives the user the ability to take a just-in-time approach to teaching and learning, which was never before available. Connect Insight presents data that helps instructors improve class performance in a way that is efficient and effective.

Impact on Final Course Grade Distribution

Adaptive

THE **ADAPTIVE** **READING EXPERIENCE** DESIGNED TO TRANSFORM THE WAY STUDENTS READ

More students earn **A's** and **B's** when they use McGraw-Hill Education **Adaptive** products.

SmartBook®

Proven to help students improve grades and study more efficiently, SmartBook contains the same content within the print book, but actively tailors that content to the needs of the individual. SmartBook's adaptive technology provides precise, personalized instruction on what the student should do next, guiding the student to master and remember key concepts, targeting gaps in knowledge and offering customized feedback, and driving the student toward comprehension and retention of the subject matter. Available on tablets, SmartBook puts learning at the student's fingertips—anywhere, anytime.

Over **8 billion questions** have been answered, making McGraw-Hill Education products more intelligent, reliable, and precise.

STUDENTS WANT

SMARTBOOK®

95% of students reported **SmartBook** to be a more effective way of reading material.

100% of students want to use the Practice Quiz feature available within **SmartBook** to help them study.

100% of students reported having reliable access to off-campus wifi.

90% of students say they would purchase **SmartBook** over print alone.

95% of students reported that **SmartBook** would impact their study skills in a positive way.

Mc Graw Hill Education

*Findings based on 2015 focus group results administered by McGraw-Hill Education

www.mheducation.com

detailed content changes

Numerous changes were made to the second edition of this text; this section provides a detailed, chapter-by-chapter list of changes. The hope is that this list will help users of the text quickly see what has changed in each chapter so they can adjust lesson plans as needed.

In all chapters

Throughout all chapters, the authors updated real-world data, reformatted long paragraphs into smaller paragraphs or bulleted lists for easier student reading and learning, and added additional eBook-only box features. They also added more learning objectives (as detailed below) for text subsections, with related new Concept Check questions and end-of-chapter Review Questions and Problems/Applications. The following list does not repeat these bookwide changes, but rather details specific changes made to each chapter.

Chapter 1: Economics and Life

- Added a new paragraph discussing knowledge as a nonscarce good.
- Clarified the example of opportunity cost for self-employed consultants versus factory workers.
- Clarified the presentation of positive and negative incentives.

Chapter 2: Specialization and Exchange

- Changed example in opening story and throughout chapter from China to Bangladesh.
- Moved Learning Objective 2.1 under the "Production Possibilities" header.
- Simplified the chapter by removing the mathematical calculation of the production possibilities frontier.
- Expanded the discussion surrounding Figure 2-7 for better clarity.

Chapter 3: Markets

- Revised the discussion of the defining characteristics of a competitive market, as well as Table 3-1, to make it consistent with the discussion in Chapter 13.
- Slightly expanded the explanation of *ceteris paribus*.

Chapter 4: Elasticity

- Changed the presentation of price elasticity of demand to show only the mid-point method and made more explicit the equations for percentage change in quantity demanded and percentage change in price.
- Added a new table (Table 4-1) to show estimated price elasticities of demand for some common goods.
- Added a new paragraph to further explain nonprice determinants in cross-price elasticity of demand.

Chapter 5: Efficiency

- Clarified and simplified the examples of willingness to pay and willingness to sell.
- Expanded the discussion of total surplus, as shown in Figure 5-5.
- Expanded the discussion of deadweight loss, as shown in Figure 5-8.
- Revised text to clarify the concept of missing markets.
- Added a Concept Check question for Learning Objective 5.6 about how price changes affect the distribution of surplus between consumers and producers.

Chapter 6: Government Intervention

- Changed the sequence of the three reasons to intervene in markets, moving market failures last.
- Introduced the term *welfare effects* in the discussion of deadweight loss.
- Added a new paragraph further explaining the effects of payday lending rates to the "Put a cap on payday lending?" box.
- Added a new Concept Check question for Learning Objective 6.2 about what can cause a price floor to become nonbinding.
- Added a new equation (Equation 6.3) on calculation of government subsidy expenditure.
- Added two new figures: Figure 6-12 shows the deadweight loss from a subsidy and Figure 6-13 shows the effect of a subsidy on surplus.
- Added a new Concept Check question for Learning Objective 6.3 about what determines the incidence of a tax.

Chapter 7: Measuring GDP

- Changed chapter title to "Measuring GDP."
- Tightened introductory section about valuing an economy.
- Moved, to earlier under the "Approaches to Measuring GDP" header, the paragraph discussing why there are three approaches to measuring GDP.
- Slightly expanded the discussion of real versus nominal GDP.
- Added a new Concept Check question for Learning Objective 7.1 about why only final goods and services are counted under GDP and why sales of used goods are not counted.
- Added a new Concept Check question for Learning Objective 7.2 about why total income in a country is equal to total expenditures on goods produced in that country.
- Added a Concept Check question related to Learning Objective 7.3 about how the expenditure approach and the income approach capture two sides of the same transactions.
- Added a new, separate Learning Objective 7.5 about calculating the GDP deflator.

Chapter 8: The Cost of Living

- Slightly expanded the introductory discussion of measuring price changes over time.
- Simplified Learning Objective 8.4 so that it asks students to calculate inflation by just the CPI method and to recognize alternative inflation measures (PPI and GDP deflator).
- Added new Learning Objective 8.5 about using a price index to adjust nominal values into real values.
- Added new Learning Objective 8.6 about how indexing keeps the real value of a payment constant over time.

Chapter 9: Unemployment and the Labor Market

- Changed sequence of two chapters so that "Unemployment and the Labor Market" (now Chapter 9) comes before "Economic Growth" (now Chapter 10).
- Added the formula for computation of the size of the labor force (Equation 9-1).
- Added subheaders to better highlight and differentiate discussions of frictional, structural, and real-wage (classical) unemployment.

Chapter 10: Economic Growth

- Changed sequence of two chapters so that "Economic Growth" (now Chapter 10) follows "Unemployment and the Labor Market" (now Chapter 9).
- Added new text discussion (new Learning Objective 10.4) about the growth accounting framework, including the growth accounting equation (Equation 10-4) and discussion of how technology, labor, and capital contribute to economic growth.
- Added subheaders to better differentiate discussions of domestic savings and foreign direct investment.
- Expanded text discussion of government involvement in R&D and innovation.

Chapter 11: Aggregate Expenditure

- **NEW chapter!** The new chapter "Aggregate Expenditure" introduces the Keynesian approach to addressing business cycles, showing how economies can get stuck due to low aggregate demand. It introduces tools that policy-makers use to try to get economies out of recessions.

Appendix E: Algebra and Aggregate Expenditure

- **NEW appendix!** The new appendix "Algebra and Aggregate Expenditure" shows how to solve for equilibrium AE algebraically.

Chapter 12: Aggregate Demand and Aggregate Supply

- Added new Figure 12-1, which shows how price-driven shifts in planned aggregate expenditure trace out the aggregate demand curve.
- Added new "Hint" box explaining the labeling of the horizontal axis in this chapter as "output," equivalent to aggregate expenditure.
- Added new discussion, including new Figure 12-1, of graphing price-level changes.
- Added new text discussion (new Learning Objective 12.3) section about the differences in the multiplier effects for aggregate demand due to changes in government spending versus changes in taxes.
- Added new Concept Check questions related to Learning Objective 12.6 about shifts in the SRAS and LRAS curves.

- Expanded the discussion of the effect of a decrease in aggregate demand, as shown in Figure 12-11.
- Deleted the "Real Life" box on recessions and remittances.
- Added subheaders to differentiate discussions of temporary supply shocks from permanent supply shocks.
- Added new Learning Objective 12.9 that asks students to use the AD/AS framework to determine whether an observed change in output and prices was due to a demand shock or a supply shock.
- Added new Figure 12-14 showing the different short-run impacts of decreases in aggregate demand versus aggregate supply.

Chapter 13: Fiscal Policy

- Corrected caption for Figure 13-1.
- Added new Learning Objective 13.3 about the effect of time lags on fiscal policy.
- Added subheaders to highlight difference among information lags, formulation lags, and implementation lags.
- Added new Learning Objective 13.4 about how stabilizers can automatically adjust fiscal policy as the economy changes and revised text discussion about automatic stabilizers.
- Added new Learning Objective 13.5, with related text discussion, about the theory and evidence of Ricardian equivalence. The section explains why government policy to lift economies from recessions may be ineffective, highlighting key empirical assumptions and the available evidence.
- Moved section on the multiplier model out of this chapter.
- Slightly expanded discussion of on revenue and spending under "The Government Budget" header.
- Added new Learning Objective 13.8, with related text discussion, about how the government goes into debt and how Treasury securities work.
- Added new Figure 13-7 that shows top foreign holders of U.S. debt.

Chapter 14: The Basics of Finance

- Added new Learning Objective 14.1, with related text discussion, about asymmetry problems that can occur in financial markets.
- Added panel B to Figure 14-2.
- Added new Learning Objective 14.2 about functions of financial markets and banks.

- Added new Learning Objective 14.3 about the market for loanable funds and the difference between savings and investment.
- Highlighted the conceptual difference in economics between savings and investment by formatting discussion as a list and adding a new "Hint" box.
- Added new Figure 14-4 showing how a change in the underlying determinants of investment opportunities shifts the demand curve for loanable funds.
- Added new Learning Objective 14.4 about factors that affect the supply and demand for loanable funds and revised the discussions of the determinants of savings and investment.
- Added new Learning Objective 14.5 about how interest rates on loans vary with the length of the loan and the riskiness of the transaction.
- Added new Learning Objective 14.6 about the key functions of the financial system (intermediating between buyers and sellers, providing liquidity, and diversifying risk).
- Added new discussion of asset bubbles.
- Expanded Learning Objective 14.11 about why savings equals investment in a closed economy and how government spending and foreign capital flows affect the saving-investment relationship.

Chapter 15: Money and the Monetary System

- Replaced old Figure 14-1 of a simple money-creation process with new Table 15-1.
- Revised discussion of money creation in today's economy through bank loans, including new Figure 15-1.
- Revised discussion of measuring money, including change to use of the terminology *monetary base*.
- Clarified discussions of expansionary and contractionary monetary policies.
- Added new paragraph introducing the concept of zero lower bound. The section highlights why policy that depends on reducing interest rates may not work (since the interest rates can't be reduced far enough), leading to a discussion of new tools used by policy-makers like "quantitative easing."
- Added new Figure 15-6, "The Economic Effects of Monetary Policy," showing the effect of the slope of the money demand curve on interest rates.
- Deleted short section from first edition "Coming full circle: Back to the market for loanable funds."

Chapter 16: Inflation

- Added new Learning Objective 16.1 about various definitions of inflation: inflation, deflation, headline inflation, and core inflation.
- Clarified text example of bracket creep, to show how inflation can reduce the resources available to families, even when their income rises with inflation.
- Added subheaders to further highlight sections on disinflation and hyperinflation.
- Added new Learning Objective 16.8 about why policy-makers favor a small amount of inflation

Chapter 17: Financial Crisis

- Revised the chapter-opening story to emphasize how the government's role entails crisis management, not just steering the economy through business cycles.
- Added text discussion of the leverage ratio (part of Learning Objective 17.1).
- Added new Learning Objective 17.2 about the causes of two famous historical financial crises (the South Seas Bubble and the Great Crash of 1929).
- Reformatted discussion of the timeline of the 2007–2008 financial crisis for greater clarity.

Chapter 18: Open-Market Macroeconomics

- Clarified text discussion of the effects of foreign investment.

- Added new Learning Objective 18.7 about the determinants of demand and supply in the forex market and added subheadings under "A model of the exchange-rate market" to clarify discussion.
- Added a "Hint" box to discuss economists' use of the terminology *devalued* and *revalued*.
- Added new Learning Objective 18.9 about why monetary policy is ineffective when maintaining a fixed exchange rate.
- Changed labels on the y-axis in Figures 18-11 and 18-13.
- Fixed label on the x-axis in Figure 18-12, part B.
- Corrected the droplines in Figure 18-16.
- Added new Learning Objective 18.11 about the role of the IMF and how financial crises are created by excessive debt and unsustainable exchange rates.

Chapter 19: Development Economics

- Added new Learning Objective 19.7 about the aims of foreign aid, the role of poverty traps, the main institutions delivering aid, and criticisms of foreign aid.
- Added new Learning Objective 19.8 about how impact investing provides a new tool for creating social impact—the idea that some investors make decisions to earn a financial return while also having social impacts by channeling money to companies with social missions like improving health and reducing poverty.

acknowledgments

Many people helped us create this text. It's said that "it takes a village," but it often felt like we had the benefit of an entire town.

We thank Meredith Startz, Ted Barnett, and Andrew Wright for the foundational work they contributed to the first edition, which still shines through in this edition. Thanks, too, to Victor Matheson (College of the Holy Cross), Diana Beck (New York University), Amanda Freeman (Kansas State University), and John Kane (SUNY--Oswego) for their contributions to and thoughts about early drafts of chapters.

An energetic group of collaborators helped us shape second-edition content in ways that are relevant and engaging for a student audience: David "Dukes" Love (Williams College) steered us through the writing of the macro chapters, helping us revamp our treatment of the aggregate expenditure model and how it leads into the aggregate demand and aggregate supply model. These changes in turn provide simple ways to introduce students to recently added tools of macro policy. Erin Moody (University of Maryland) applied her extensive classroom experience as an essential contributor throughout the micro chapters, ensuring that we addressed the many suggestions we received from users and reviewers of our text since the first edition published. Camille Soltau Nelson (Oregon State University) analyzed Chapter 18, "Externalities," and ensured that this time around the chapter fits the needs of our users. Our IPA team of researchers, Radhika Lokur and Noor Sethi, brought a recent-student perspective to the text and helped us update many of our examples and figures with the most current data.

We couldn't have produced the second edition without all of these talented individuals. We thank them for their expertise and also for their willingness to provide feedback at a moment's notice.

Many other talented individuals contributed on and off throughout this project. We thank Bob Schwab, Kevin Stanley, Ross vanWassenhove, and James Peyton for closely reviewing a draft of our revised Chapter 18 and helping guide us toward a final version. We thank John Neri and Murat Doral for providing detailed feedback on all the macro chapters of the text. We appreciate Jodi Begg's help in providing a base to work from for Chapter 28, "Aggregate Expenditure." We thank Chiuping Chen, Ashley Hodgson, Michael Machiorlatti, and Germain Pichop for reviewing said chapter in its draft stages to ensure we were on the right track.

We thank Nora Underwood (University of Central Florida) and Erin Moody (University of Maryland) for their many and varied contributions to end-of-chapter content, both in the text and in Connect. We are very appreciative of the extensive work done by Susan Bell (Seminole State College) and Greg Gilpin (Montana State University) in accuracy-checking this content. In addition, we thank Russell Kellogg (University of Colorado Denver) for authoring the LearnSmart content.

We also want to share our appreciation to the following people at McGraw-Hill for the hard work they put into creating the product you see before you: Katie Hoenicke, Senior Brand Manager, helped us communicate the overarching vision and promoted our revision. Virgil Lloyd, Marketing Manager, guided us in visiting schools and working with the sales team. Ann Torbert, Lead Product Developer, has been an exemplary editor, improving the exposition on each page and keeping attention on both the big picture and key details. Alyssa Lincoln, Senior Product Developer, and Michele Janicek, Lead Product Developer, managed innumerable and indispensable details—reviews, manuscript, and the many aspects of the digital products and overall package. Kathryn Wright, Core Content Project Manager, helped turn our manuscript into the finished, polished product you see before you. Kristin Bradley, Assessment Content Project Manager, skillfully guided the digital plan. Thanks, too, to Douglas Ruby, Senior Director of Digital Content, and Kevin Shanahan, Senior Product Manager, CPO, for their careful shepherding of the digital materials that accompany the text.

Thank You!

Creating the second edition of a book is a daunting task. We wanted to do everything we could to improve upon the first edition, and we couldn't have done this without professors who told us honestly what they thought we could do better. To everyone who helped shape this edition, we thank you for sharing your insights and recommendations.

Symposia

Luca Bossi
University of Pennsylvania

Regina Cassady
Valencia College

June Charles
North Lake College

Monica Cherry
St. John Fisher College and State University of New York at Buffalo

George Chikhladze
University of Missouri–Columbia

Patrick Crowley
Texas A&M University–Corpus Christi

Attila Cseh
Valdosta State University

Susan Doty
University of Texas at Tyler

Irene Foster
George Washington University

Don Holley
Boise State University

Ricot Jean
Valencia College

Sarah Jenyk
Youngstown State University

Stephanie Jozefowicz
Indiana University of Pennsylvania

Nkongolo Kalala
Bluegrass Community and Technical College

Carrie Kerekes
Florida Gulf Coast University

Brandon Koford
Weber State University

Soloman Kone
City University of New York

W. J. Lane
University of New Orleans

Jose Lopez-Calleja
Miami Dade College

Erika Martinez
University of South Florida–Tampa

Geri Mason
Seattle Pacific University

ABM Nasir
North Carolina Central University

Eric Nielsen
Saint Louis Community College

Rich Numrich
College of Southern Nevada

Michael Polcen
Northern Virginia Community College

Martin Sabo
Community College of Denver

Latisha Settlage
University of Arkansas–Fort Smith

Mark Showalter
Brigham Young University

Warren Smith
Palm Beach State College

Kay Strong
Baldwin Wallace University

Ryan Umbeck
Ivy Tech Community College

Ross VanWassenhove
University of Houston

Terry Von Ende
Texas Tech University

Jennifer Wissink
Cornell University

Focus Groups

Siddiq Abdullah
University of Massachusetts–Boston

Seemi Ahmad
Dutchess Community College

Nurul Aman
University of Massachusetts–Boston

Aimee Chin
University of Houston

Can Erbil
Boston College

Varun Gupta
Wharton County Junior College

Moon Han
North Shore Community College

Hilaire Jean-Gilles
Bunker Hill Community College

Jennifer Lehman
Wharton County Junior College

Mikko Manner,
Dutchess Community College

Nara Mijid
Central Connecticut State University

Shahruz Mohtadi
Suffolk University

Victor Moussoki
Lone Star College

Kevin Nguyen
Lone Star College

Jan Palmer
Ohio University

Julia Paxton
Ohio University

Tracy Regan
Boston College

Christina Robinson
Central Connecticut State University

Rosemary Rossiter
Ohio University

Sara Saderion
Houston Community College

Reviews

Steve Abid
Grand Rapids Community College

Eric Abrams
McKendree University

Richard Ugunzi Agesa
Marshall University

Seemi Ahmad
Dutchess Community College

Jason A. Aimone
Baylor University

Donald L. Alexander
Western Michigan University

Ricky Ascher
Broward College and Palm Beach State College

Shannon Aucoin
University of Louisiana at Lafayette

Gyanendra Baral
Oklahoma City Community College

Klaus Becker
Texas Tech University

Pedro Bento
West Virginia University

Jennifer Bossard
Doane College

Kristen Broady
Fort Valley State University

Gregory Brock
Georgia Southern University

Giuliana Andreopoulos Campanelli
William Paterson University

Joni Charles
Texas State University

Chiuping Chen
American River College

Tom Creahan
Morehead State University

Can Dogan
North American University

Brandon Dupont
Western Washington University

Matthew J. Easton
Pueblo Community College

Linda K. English
Baylor University

Irene R. Foster
George Washington University

Alka Gandhi
Northern Virginia Community College

Soma Ghosh
Albright College

Gregory Gilpin
Montana State University

Lisa Workman Gloege
Grand Rapids Community College

Cynthia Harter
Eastern Kentucky University

Darcy Hartman
Ohio State University

Ashley Hodgson
St. Olaf College

Don Holley
Boise State University

Harvey James
University of Missouri

Sarah Jenyk
Youngstown State University

Russell Kellogg
University of Colorado Denver

Greg Lindeblom
Broward College

Michael Machiorlatti
Oklahoma City Community College

Rita Madarassy
Santa Clara University

Edouard Mafoua
State University of New York at Canton

C. Lucy Malakar
Lorain County Community College

Geri Mason
Seattle Pacific University

Katherine McClain
University of Georgia

Bruce McClung
Texas State University

Robin McCutcheon
Marshall University

Tia M. McDonald
Ohio University

John Min
Northern Virginia Community College

Sam Mirmirani
Bryant University

Ida A. Mirzaie
Ohio State University

Franklin G. Mixon Jr.
Columbus State University

Erin Moody
University of Maryland

Barbara Moore
University of Central Florida

Christopher Mushrush
Illinois State University

Charles Myrick
Oklahoma City Community College

Camille Nelson
Oregon State University

Per Norander
University of North Carolina–Charlotte

Ronald Oertel
Western Washington University

Constantin Ogloblin
Georgia Southern University

Alex Olbrecht
Ramapo College of New Jersey

Tomi Ovaska
Youngstown State University

Jan Palmer
Ohio University

Julia Paxton
Ohio University

James Peyton
Highline College

Germain Pichop
Oklahoma City Community College

Brennan Platt
Brigham Young University

Elizabeth Porter
University of North Carolina–Asheville

Mathew Price
Oklahoma City Community College

Christina Robinson
Central Connecticut State University

Matthew Roelofs
Western Washington University

Randall R. Rojas
University of California–Los Angeles

John Rykowski
Kalamazoo Valley Community College

Robert M. Schwab
University of Maryland

Gasper Sekelj
Clarkson University

James K. Self
Indiana University

Mark Showalter
Brigham Young University

Kevin Stanley
Highline College

Steve Trost
Virginia Polytechnic Institute and State University

Ross S. vanWassenhove
University of Houston

In addition, we continue to be grateful to the first-edition contributors, who over the course of several years of development attended focus groups or symposia or provided content reviews. Thanks to the following, whose insights, recommendations, and feedback helped immeasurably as the project took shape.

Mark Abajian
San Diego Mesa College

Tom Adamson
Midland University

Richard Agesa
Marshall University

Rashid Al-Hmoud
Texas Tech University

Frank Albritton
Seminole State College-Sanford

Terence Alexander
Iowa State University

Clifford Althoff
Joliet Junior College

Diane Anstine
North Central College

Michael Applegate
Oklahoma State University–Stillwater Campus

Ali Ataiifar
Delaware County Community College

Roberto Ayala
California State Polytechnic University–Pomona

Jim Barbour
Elon University

Gary Benson
Southwest Community College

Laura Jean Bhadra
Northern Virginia Community College–Manassas

Prasun Bhattacharjee
East Tennessee State University–Johnson City

Radha Bhattacharya
California State University–Fullerton

Michael Bonnal
University of Tennessee–Chattanooga

Camelia Bouzerdan
Middlesex Community College

Dale Bremmer
Rose-Hulman Institute of Technology

Anne Bresnock
University of California–Los Angeles

Bruce Brown
California State Polytechnic University–Pomona

Ken Brown
University of Northern Iowa

Laura Bucila
Texas Christian University

Andrew Cassey
Washington State University

Kalyan Chakraborty
Emporia State University

Catherine Chambers
University of Central Missouri

Britton Chapman
State College of Florida–Manatee

Sanjukta Chaudhuri
University of Wisconsin–Eau Claire

Chiuping Chen
American River College

Ron Cheung
Oberlin College

Young Back Choi
Saint John's University

Dmitriy Chulkov
Indiana University–Kokomo

Cindy Clement
University of Maryland–College Park

Howard Cochran
Belmont University

Jim Cox
Georgia Perimeter College

Matt Critcher
University of Arkansas Community College–Batesville

Chifeng Dai
Southern Illinois University–Carbondale

Thomas Davidson
Principia College

Rafael Donoso
Lone Star College–North Harris

Floyd Duncan
Virginia Military Institute

David Eaton
Murray State University

Eric Eide
Brigham Young University–Provo

Marwan El Nasser
State University of New York–Fredonia

Harry Ellis
University of North Texas

Maxwell Eseonu
Virginia State University

Brent Evans
Mississippi State University

Russell Evans
Oklahoma State University

Fidelis Ezeala-Harrison
Jackson State University

Chris Fant
Spartanburg Community College

Michael Fenick
Broward College

Abdollah Ferdowsi
Ferris State University

Tawni Ferrarini
Northern Michigan University

Herbert Flaig
Milwaukee Area Technical College

Irene Foster
George Washington University

Joseph Franklin
Newberry College

Shelby Frost
Georgia State University

Fran Lara Garib
San Jacinto College

Deborah Gaspard
Southeast Community College

Karen Gebhardt
Colorado State University

Juan Alejandro Gelves
Midwestern State University

Kirk Gifford
Brigham Young University–Idaho

Otis Gilley
Louisiana Technical University

Gregory Gilpin
Montana State University–Bozeman

Bill (Wayne) Goffe
State University of New York–Oswego

Michael Gootzeit
University of Memphis

George Greenlee
St. Petersburg College

Galina Hale
Federal Reserve Bank of San Francisco

Oskar Harmon
University of Connecticut–Stamford

David Hedrick
Central Washington University–Ellensburg

Dennis Heiner
College of Southern Idaho

Andrew Helms
Washington College

David Hickman
Frederick Community College

Ashley Hodgson
Saint Olaf College

Vanessa Holmes
Pennsylvania State University–Scranton

Scott Houser
Colorado School of Mines

Gregrey Hunter
California Polytechnic University–Pomona

Kyle Hurst
University of Colorado–Denver

Jonathan Ikoba
Scott Community College

Onur Ince
Appalachian State University

Dennis Jansen
Texas A&M University

Shuyi Jiang
Emmanuel College

Barbara Heroy John
University of Dayton

James Johnson
University of Arkansas Community College–Batesville

Mahbubul Kabir
Lyon College

Ahmad Kader
University of Nevada–Las Vegas

John Kane
State University of New York–Oswego

Tsvetanka Karagyozova
Lawrence University

Joel Kazy
State Fair Community College

Daniel Kuester
Kansas State University

Gary Langer
Roosevelt University

Daniel Lawson
Oakland Community College

Richard Le
Cosumnes River College

Jim Lee
Texas A&M University–Corpus Christi

Willis Lewis
Winthrop University

Qing Li
College of the Mainland

Tin-Chun Lin
Indiana University Northwest–Gary

Delwin Long
San Jacinto College

Katie Lotz
Lake Land College

Karla Lynch
North Central Texas College

Arindam Mandal
Siena College

Daniel Marburger
Arkansas State University–Jonesboro

Geri Mason
Seattle Pacific University

Victor Matheson
College of the Holy Cross

Bryan McCannon
Saint Bonaventure University

Michael McIlhon
Century Community and Technical College

Hannah McKinney
Kalamazoo College

Al Mickens
State University of New York–Old Westbury

Nara Mijid
Central Connecticut State University

Martin Milkman
Murray State University

Douglas Miller
University of Missouri–Columbia

Gregory Miller
Wallace Community College–Selma

Edward Millner
Virginia Commonwealth University

Mitch Mitchell
Bladen Community College

Daniel Morvey
Piedmont Technical College

Rebecca Moryl
Emmanuel College

Tina Mosleh
Ohlone College

Thaddaeus Mounkurai
Daytona State College–Daytona Beach

Chris Mushrush
Illinois State University

Muhammad Mustafa
South Carolina State University

Tony Mutsune
Iowa Wesleyan College

Max Grunbaum Nagiel
Daytona State College–Daytona Beach

John Nordstrom
College of Western Idaho

Emlyn Norman
Texas Southern University

Christian Nsiah
Black Hills State University

Jan Ojdana
University of Cincinnati

Ronald O'Neal
Camden County College

Serkan Ozbeklik
Claremont McKenna College

Debashis Pal
University of Cincinnati–Cincinnati

Robert Pennington
University of Central Florida–Orlando

Andrew Perumal
University of Massachusetts–Boston

Steven Peterson
University of Idaho

Brennan Platt
Brigham Young University

Sanela Porca
University of South Carolina–Aiken

Gregory Pratt
Mesa Community College

William Prosser
Cayuga Community College

Gregory Randolph
Southern New Hampshire University

Mitchell Redlo
Monroe Community College

Timothy Reynolds
Alvin Community College

Michael Rolleigh
Williams College

Amanda Ross
West Virginia University–Morgantown

Jason Rudbeck
University of Georgia

Michael Ryan
Gainesville State College

Robert Rycroft
University of Mary Washington

Michael Salemi
University of North Carolina–Chapel Hill

Gregory Saltzman
Albion College

Ravi Samitamana
Daytona State College

Saied Sarkarat
West Virginia University–Parkersburg

Naveen Sarna
Northern Virginia Community College–Alexandria

Jesse Schwartz
Kennesaw State University

Abdelkhalik Shabayek
Lane College

Mark Showalter
Brigham Young University

Cheri Sides
Lane College

Megan Silbert
Salem College

Sovathana Sokhom
Loyola Marymount University

Souren Soumbatiants
Franklin University

Marilyn Spencer
Texas A&M University–Corpus Christi

Brad Stamm
Cornerstone University

Karl Strauss
Saint Bonaventure University

Chuck Stull
Kalamazoo College

Abdulhamid Sukar
Cameron University

Albert Sumell
Youngstown State University

Philip Isak Szmedra
Georgia Southwestern State University

Christine Tarasevich
Del Mar College

Noreen Templin
Butler Community College

Darryl Thorne
Valencia College East

Kiril Tochkov
Texas Christian University

Demetri Tsanacas
Ferrum College

George Tvelia
Suffolk County Community College

Nora Underwood
University of Central Florida

Jose Vazquez
University of Illinois–Champaign

Marieta Velikova
Belmont University

Jeffery Vicek
Parkland College

Jennifer Vincent
Champlain College

Terry von Ende
Texas Tech University

Craig Walker
Oklahoma Baptist University

Jennifer Ward-Batts
Wayne State University

Tarteashia Williams
Valencia College–West Campus

Melissa Wiseman
Houston Baptist University

Jim Wollscheid
University of Arkansas–Fort Smith

Jeff Woods
University of Indianapolis

Ranita Wyatt
Pasco-Hernando Community College–West Campus

Suthathip Yaisawarng
Union College

Jim Yates
Darton College

Daehyun Yoo
Elon University

Ceren Ertan Yoruk
Sage College of Albany

Chuck Zalonka
Oklahoma State University–Oklahoma City

Finally, thanks to the following instructors, and their students, who class-tested chapters of the first edition before publication. Their engagement with the content and their feedback from the "test drive" made this a better product.

Richard Agesa
Marshall University

Anne Bresnock
University of California–Los Angeles

Chiuping Chen
American River College

John Kane
State University of New York–Oswego

Jim Lee
Texas A&M University–Corpus Christi

Martin Milkman
Murray State University

Kolleen Rask
College of the Holy Cross

Jesse Schwartz
Kennesaw State University

Jennifer Vincent
Champlain College

detailed contents

feature boxes

(continued)

WHAT DO YOU THINK?

MACROECONOMICS

Part One

The Power of Economics

The two chapters in Part 1 will introduce you to . . .

the tools and intuition essential to the study of economics. Chapter 1, "Economics and Life," presents four questions that introduce the fundamental concepts of economic problem solving. We also describe how economists think about data and analyze policies: You'll see that we typically separate how one *wants* the world to look ("normative" analysis) from how the world *actually* works ("positive" analysis).

Chapter 2, "Specialization and Exchange," presents the ideas of absolute and comparative advantage, to explain how people (and countries) can most effectively use their resources and talents. Should you hire a plumber or fix the pipes yourself? Should you become a pop star or an economist? We develop these ideas to show how trade can make everyone better off, on both a personal and a national level.

This is just a start. Throughout the book, we'll use these tools to gain a deeper understanding of how people interact and manage their resources, which in turn gives insight into tough problems of all sorts. Economic ideas weave a common thread through many subjects, from the purely economic to political, environmental, and cultural issues, as well as personal decisions encountered in everyday life. Economics is much more than just the study of money, and we hope you'll find that what you learn here will shed light far beyond your economics classes.

Economics and Life

Learning Objectives

LO 1.1   Explain the economic concept of scarcity.

LO 1.2   Explain the economic concepts of opportunity cost and marginal decision making.

LO 1.3   Explain the economic concept of incentives.

LO 1.4   Explain the economic concept of efficiency.

LO 1.5   Distinguish between correlation and causation.

LO 1.6   List the characteristics of a good economic model.

LO 1.7   Distinguish between positive and normative analysis.

MAKING AN IMPACT WITH SMALL LOANS

On the morning of October 13, 2006, Bangladeshi economist Muhammad Yunus received an unexpected telephone call from Oslo, Norway. Later that day, the Nobel committee announced that Yunus and the Grameen Bank, which he founded in 1976, would share the 2006 Nobel Peace Prize. Past recipients of the Nobel Peace Prize include Mother Teresa, who spent over 50 years ministering to beggars and lepers; Martin Luther King Jr., who used peaceful protest to oppose racial segregation; and the Dalai Lama, an exiled Tibetan Buddhist leader who symbolizes the struggle for religious and cultural tolerance. What were an economist and his bank doing in such company?

Grameen is not a typical bank. Yes, it makes loans and offers savings accounts, charging customers for its services, just like other banks. But it serves some of the poorest people in the poorest villages in one of the poorest countries in the world. It makes loans so small that it's hard for people in wealthy countries to imagine what good they can do: The first group of loans Yunus made totaled only $27. Before Grameen came along, other banks had been unwilling to work in these poor communities. They believed it wasn't worth bothering to lend such small amounts; many believed the poor could not be counted on to repay their loans.

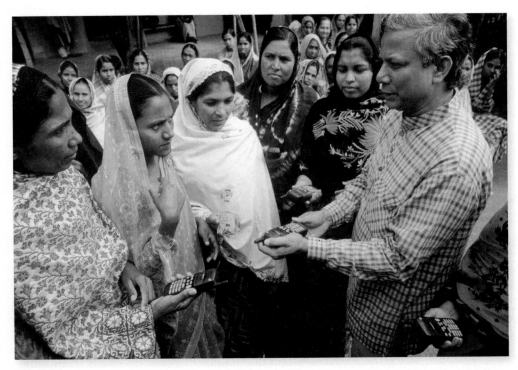

© Karen Kasmauski/Corbis

Yunus disagreed. He was convinced that even small loans would allow poor villagers to expand their small businesses—maybe buying a sewing machine or a cow to produce milk for the local market—and earn more money. Or perhaps a villager wouldn't expand a small business but would instead use the money to pay for a health emergency or to buy food when faced with hunger. Regardless of the way the loans were used, villagers' lives would be more comfortable and secure, and their children would have a better future. Yunus claimed that they would be able to repay the loan and that his new bank would earn a profit.

Yunus proved the skeptics wrong. Today, Grameen Bank serves more than 8 million customers, and it reports that 98 percent of its loans are repaid—a better rate than some banks in rich countries.[1] Grameen also reports steady profits. Such results have inspired other banks to start serving poor communities on nearly every continent, including recent start-ups in the United States in New York City and Omaha, Nebraska.

Muhammad Yunus was trained as an economist. He earned a PhD at Vanderbilt University in Nashville and then taught in Tennessee before becoming a professor in Bangladesh. When a devastating famine struck Bangladesh, Yunus became disillusioned with teaching. What did abstract equations and stylized graphs have to do with the suffering he saw around him?

Ultimately, Yunus realized that economic thinking holds the key to solving hard problems that truly matter. The genius of Grameen Bank is that it is neither a traditional charity nor a traditional bank. Instead, it is a business that harnesses basic economic insights to make the world a better place.

In this book, we'll introduce you to the tools economists are using to tackle some of the world's biggest challenges, from health care reform, to climate change, to lifting people out of poverty. Of course, these tools are not just for taking on causes worthy of Nobel Prizes. Economics can also help you become a savvier consumer, successfully launch a new cell phone app, or simply make smarter decisions about how to spend your time and money. Throughout this book, we promise we'll ask you not just to memorize theories, but also to apply the ideas you read about to the everyday decisions you face in your own life.

The Basic Insights of Economics

When people think of economics, they often think of the stock market, the unemployment rate, or media reports saying things like "the Federal Reserve has raised its target for the federal funds rate." Although economics does include these topics, its reach is much broader.

Economics is the study of how people manage resources. Decisions about how to allocate resources can be made by individuals, but also by groups of people in families, firms, governments, and other organizations. In economics, *resources* are not just physical things like cash and gold mines. They are also intangible things, such as time, ideas, technology, job experience, and even personal relationships.

Traditionally, economics has been divided into two broad fields: microeconomics and macroeconomics. **Microeconomics** is the study of how individuals and firms manage resources. **Macroeconomics** is the study of the economy as a whole, and how policymakers manage the growth and behavior of the overall economy. Microeconomics and macroeconomics are highly related and interdependent; we need both to fully understand how economies work.

Economics starts with the idea that people compare the choices available to them and purposefully behave in the way that will best achieve their goals. As human beings, we have ambitions and we make plans to realize them. We strategize. We marshal our resources. When people make choices to achieve their goals in the most effective way possible given the resources they have, economists say they are exhibiting **rational behavior**. The assumption that people behave rationally isn't perfect. As we'll see later in the book, people can sometimes be short-sighted or swayed merely by the way choices are presented. Nevertheless, the assumption of rational behavior helps to explain a lot about the world.

People use economics every day, from Wall Street to Walmart, from state capitol buildings to Bangladeshi villages. They apply economic ideas to everything from shoe shopping to baseball, from running a hospital to running for political office. What ties these topics together is a common approach to problem solving.

Economists tend to break down problems by asking a set of four questions:

1. What are the wants and constraints of those involved?
2. What are the trade-offs?
3. How will others respond?
4. Why isn't someone already doing it?

Underneath these questions are some important economics concepts, which we will begin to explore in this chapter. The questions and the underlying concepts are based on just a few common-sense assumptions about how people behave, yet they offer a surprising amount of insight into tough problems of all sorts. They are so important to economic problem solving that they will come up again and again in this book. In this chapter we'll take a bird's-eye view of economics, focusing on the fundamental concepts and skimming over the details. Later in the book, we'll return to each question in more depth.

economics
the study of how people, individually and collectively, manage resources

microeconomics
the study of how individuals and firms manage resources

macroeconomics
the study of the economy as a whole, and how policymakers manage the growth and behavior of the overall economy

rational behavior
making choices to achieve goals in the most effective way possible

Scarcity

Question 1: What are the wants and constraints of those involved?

LO 1.1 Explain the economic concept of scarcity.

---

scarcity
the condition of wanting
more than we can get
with available resources

Limited Resource.

For the most part, people make decisions that are aimed at getting the things they want. Of course, you can't always get what you want. People want a lot of things, but they are *constrained* by limited resources. Economists define **scarcity** as the condition of wanting more than we can get with available resources. Scarcity is a fact of life. You have only so much time and only so much money. You can arrange your resources in a lot of different ways—studying or watching TV, buying a car, or traveling to Las Vegas—but at any given time, you have a fixed range of possibilities. Scarcity also describes the world on a collective level: As a society, we can produce only so many things, and we have to decide how those things are divided among many people.

On the other hand, some things are not restricted by resources. Consider, for example, knowledge. The total quantity of available knowledge does not diminish as more and more people acquire it. Similarly, sunlight and air can also be considered nonscarce goods. In economic terms, however, it is safe to say that most goods are considered to be scarce.

The first question to ask in untangling a complex economic problem is, "What are the wants and constraints of those involved?" Given both rational behavior and scarcity, we can expect people to try to get what they want but to be constrained by the limited resources available to them. Suppose you *want* to spend as much time as possible this summer taking road trips around the country. You are *constrained* by the available time (three months of summer vacation) and by the amount of money you have available to pay for gas, food, and places to stay. Behaving rationally, you might choose to work double shifts for two months to earn enough to spend one month on the road. Since you are now *constrained* by having only one month to travel, you'll have to prioritize your time, activities, and expenses.

Now put yourself in Muhammad Yunus's shoes, back in 1976. He sees extremely poor but entrepreneurial Bangladeshi villagers and thinks they could improve their lives with access to loans. Why aren't banks providing financial services for these people? We can apply the first of the economists' questions to start to untangle this puzzle: *What are the wants and constraints of those involved?* In this case, those involved are traditional Bangladeshi banks and poor Bangladeshi villagers.

Let's look at both:

- The banks *want* to make profits by lending money to people who will pay them back with interest. The banks are *constrained* by having limited funds available to lend and needing to pay employees and branch expenses. We can therefore expect banks to prioritize making large loans to customers they believe are likely to pay them back. Before 1976, that meant wealthier, urban Bangladeshis, not the very poor in remote rural villages.
- The villagers *want* the chance to increase their incomes. They have energy and business ideas but are *constrained* in their ability to borrow money because banks believe they are too poor to repay loans.

Analyzing the wants and constraints of those involved gives us some valuable information about why poor Bangladeshis didn't have access to loans. Banks *wanted* to earn profits and managed their *constrained* funds to prioritize those they thought would be profitable customers. Bangladeshi villagers *wanted* to increase their incomes but couldn't follow up on business opportunities due to *constrained* start-up money.

That's good information, but we haven't yet come up with the solution that Dr. Yunus was looking for. To take the next step in solving the puzzle, we turn to another question economists often ask.

Opportunity cost and marginal decision making

Question 2: What are the trade-offs?

LO 1.2 Explain the economic concepts of opportunity cost and marginal decision making.

Every decision in life involves weighing the *trade-off* between costs and benefits. We look at our options and decide whether it is worth giving up one in order to get the other. We choose to do things only when we think the benefits will be greater than the costs. The potential *benefit* of taking an action is often easy to see: You would have fun road-tripping for a month. Bank customers who take out a loan would have the opportunity to expand their businesses or pay for emergency expenses. The *costs* of a decision, on the other hand, are not always clear.

You might think it *is* clear—that the cost of your road trip is simply the amount of money you spend on gas, hotels, and food. But something is missing from that way of thinking. The true cost of something is not just the amount you have to pay for it. Rather, the cost also includes the *opportunity you must now give up for something that you might have enjoyed otherwise.* Suppose if you hadn't gone on your road trip, your second choice would have been to spend that money to buy a big-screen TV and spend that month at home watching movies with friends. The true cost of your road trip is passing up the enjoyment you would have gained from owning the TV and hanging out with friends for a month. Behaving rationally, you should go on the road trip only if it will be more valuable to you than the best alternative use for your time and money. This is a matter of personal preference. Because people have different alternatives and place different values on things like a road trip or a TV, they will make different decisions.

Economists call this true cost of your choice the **opportunity cost**, which is equal to the value to you of what you have to give up in order to get something. Put another way, opportunity cost is the value you could have gained by choosing your next-best alternative—the "opportunity" you have to pass up in order to take your first choice.

Let's return to the road trip. Say you're going with a friend and her plan B would have been buying a new computer, taking a summer class, and visiting her cousins. The opportunity cost of her vacation is different from yours. For her, the opportunity cost is the pleasure she would have gained from owning a new computer, the benefits she would have taken from the course, and the fun she would have had with her cousins. If she's behaving rationally, she will go with you on the road trip only if she believes it will be more valuable to her than what she's giving up.

Opportunity cost helps us think more clearly about trade-offs. If someone asked you how much your road trip cost and you responded by adding up the cost of gas, hotels, and food, you would be failing to capture some of the most important and interesting aspects of the trade-offs you made. Opportunity cost helps us to see why, for example, a self-employed consultant and an equally paid factory worker may face truly different trade-offs when they contemplate taking the same vacation for the same price. The self-employed consultant likely forgoes earning income in order to take a vacation; the factory worker likely gets paid vacation days. The opportunity cost for the consultant includes the value of what he or she would buy with the money earned by working instead of taking the vacation. Thus the opportunity cost of a vacation for the consultant is much higher than it is for the factory worker. That difference makes it much more expensive for the consultant to take a vacation than the factory worker.

Economists often express opportunity cost as a dollar value. Suppose you've been given a gift certificate worth $15 at a restaurant. The restaurant has a short menu: pizza or spaghetti, each of which costs $15. The gift certificate can be used only at this particular restaurant, so the only thing you give up to get pizza is spaghetti, and vice versa. If you didn't have the certificate, you would be willing to pay as much as $15 for the pizza but no more than $10 for the spaghetti. What are your trade-offs?

opportunity cost the value to you of what you have to give up in order to get something; the value you could have gained by choosing the next-best alternative

- What is the opportunity cost of choosing the pizza? Even though the price on the menu is $15, the opportunity cost is only $10—because $10 is the value you place on your best (and only) alternative, the spaghetti.
- What is the opportunity cost of choosing the spaghetti? It's $15, the value you place on the pizza.

Which meal do you choose? One choice has an opportunity cost of $10, the other $15. Behaving rationally, you should choose the pizza because it has the lower opportunity cost. (You give up less by choosing the lower opportunity cost.)

A simpler way of describing this trade-off would be simply to say that you prefer pizza over spaghetti. The opportunity cost of spaghetti is higher because to get it, you have to give up something you like more. But putting it in terms of opportunity cost can be helpful when there are more choices, or more nuances to the choices.

For example, suppose the gift certificate could be used only to buy spaghetti. Now what is the opportunity cost of choosing the spaghetti? It is $0 because you can't do anything else with the gift certificate—your choice is spaghetti or nothing. The opportunity cost of pizza is now $15 because you'd have to pay for it with money you could have spent on $15 worth of other purchases outside the restaurant. So even though you like pizza better, you might now choose the spaghetti because it has a lower opportunity cost in this particular situation.

Once you start to think about opportunity costs, you see them everywhere. For an application of opportunity cost to a serious moral question, read the What Do You Think? box "The opportunity cost of a life."

What Do You Think?
The opportunity cost of a life

Throughout the book, What Do You Think? boxes ask for your opinion about an important policy or life decision. These boxes will present questions that require you to combine facts and economic analysis with values and moral reasoning. They are the sort of tough questions that people face in real life. There are many "correct" answers, depending on your values and goals.

The philosopher Peter Singer writes that opportunity costs can be a matter of life or death. Imagine you are a salesperson, and on your way to a meeting on a hot summer day, you drive by a lake. Suddenly, you notice that a child who has been swimming in the lake is drowning. No one else is in sight.

You have a choice. If you stop the car and dive into the lake to save the child, you will be late for your meeting, miss out on making a sale, and lose $250. The *opportunity cost* of saving the child's life is $250.

Alternatively, if you continue on to your meeting, you earn the $250, but you lose the opportunity to dive into the lake and save the child's life. The *opportunity cost* of going to the meeting is one child's life.

What would you do? Most people don't hesitate. They immediately say they would stop the car, dive into the lake, and save the drowning child. After all, a child's life is worth more than $250.

Now suppose you're thinking about spending $250 on a new iPod. That $250 could instead have been used for some charitable purpose, such as immunizing children in another country against yellow fever. Suppose that for every $250 donated, an average of one child's life ends up being saved. (In fact, $250 to save one child's life is not far from reality in many cases.) What is the opportunity cost of buying an iPod? According to Peter Singer, it is the same as the opportunity cost of going straight to the meeting: a child's life.

These two situations are not exactly the same, of course, but why does the first choice (jump in the lake) seem so obvious to most people, while the second seems much less obvious?

WHAT DO YOU THINK?

1. In what ways do the two situations presented by Singer—the sales meeting and the drowning child versus the iPod and the unvaccinated child—differ?
2. Singer argues that even something like buying an iPod is a surprisingly serious moral decision. Do you agree? What sort of opportunity costs do you typically consider when making such a decision?
3. What might be missing from Singer's analysis of the trade-offs people face when making a decision about how to spend money?

Another important principle for understanding trade-offs is the idea that rational people make decisions *at the margin*. **Marginal decision making** describes the idea that rational people compare the *additional* benefits of a choice against the *additional* costs, without considering related benefits and costs of past choices.

marginal decision making
comparison of additional benefits of a choice against the additional costs it would bring, without considering related benefits and costs of past choices

For example, suppose an amusement park has a $20 admission price and charges $2 per ride. If you are standing outside the park, the cost of the first ride is $22: You will have to pay the admission price and buy a ticket for the ride. Once you are inside the park, the *marginal* cost of each additional ride is $2. When deciding whether to go on the roller coaster a second or third time, you should compare only the benefit or enjoyment you will get from one more ride to the opportunity cost of that additional ride.

This may sound obvious, but in practice, many people don't make decisions on the margin. Suppose you get into the amusement park and start to feel sick shortly thereafter. If doing something else with your $2 and your time would bring you more enjoyment than another roller-coaster ride while feeling sick, the rational thing to do would be to leave. The relevant trade-off is between the *additional* benefits that going on another ride would bring versus the additional costs. You cannot get back the $20 admission fee or any of the other money you've already spent on rides. Economists call a cost that has already been incurred and cannot be recovered a **sunk cost**. Sunk costs should not have any bearing on your *marginal* decision about what to do next. But many people feel the need to go on a few more rides to psychologically justify the $20 admission.

sunk cost
a cost that has already been incurred and cannot be recovered or refunded

Trade-offs play a crucial role in businesses' decisions about what goods and services to produce. Let's return to the example that started this chapter and apply the idea to a bank in Bangladesh: *What are the trade-offs involved in making a small loan?*

- For traditional banks, the opportunity cost of making small loans to the poor was the money that the bank could have earned by making loans to wealthier clients instead.
- For poor borrowers, the opportunity cost of borrowing was whatever else they would have done with the time they spent traveling to the bank and with the money they would pay in fees and interest on the loan. The benefit, of course, was whatever the loan would enable them to do that they could not have done otherwise, such as starting a small business or buying food or livestock.

Based on this analysis of trade-offs, we can see why traditional banks made few loans to poor Bangladeshis. Banks perceived the poor to be risky clients. The opportunity cost of making small loans to the poor seemed to outweigh the benefits—unless the banks charged very high fees. From the perspective of poor rural villagers, high fees meant that the opportunity cost of borrowing was higher than the benefits; they chose not to borrow under the terms offered by banks.

Notice that the answer to this question built off the answer to the first: We had to know the wants and constraints of each party before we could assess the trade-offs they faced. Now that we understand the motivations and the trade-offs that led to the situation Dr. Yunus observed, we can turn to a third question he might have asked himself when considering what would happen when he founded the Grameen Bank.

Incentives

Question 3: How will others respond?

LO 1.3 Explain the economic concept of incentives.

You're in the mood for pizza, so you decide to go back to the restaurant with the short menu. When you get there, you discover that the prices have changed. Pizza now costs $50 instead of $15.

What will you do? Remember that your gift certificate is good for only $15. Unless you can easily afford to shell out $50 for a pizza or you just really hate spaghetti, you probably won't be ordering the pizza. We're sure that you can think of ways to spend $35 that are worth more to you than your preference for pizza over spaghetti. But what if the prices had changed less drastically—say, $18 for pizza? That might be a tougher call.

As the trade-offs change, so will the choices people make. When the restaurant owner considers how much to charge for each dish, she must consider *how others will respond* to changing prices. If she knows the pizza is popular, she might be tempted to try charging more to boost her profits. But as she increases the price, fewer diners will decide to order it.

If a trade-off faced by a lot of people changes, even by a small amount, the combined change in behavior by everyone involved can add up to a big shift. Asking "How will others respond?" to a trade-off that affects a lot of people gives us a complete picture of how a particular decision affects the world. The collective reaction to a changing trade-off is a central idea in economics; it will come up in almost every chapter of this book. You'll see it in questions such as

- What happens when prices change?
- What happens when the government implements a new policy?
- What happens when a company introduces a new product?

Answering any of these questions requires us to consider a large-scale reaction, rather than the behavior of just one person, company, or policy-maker.

In answering this question about trade-offs, economists commonly make two assumptions. The first is that people respond to incentives. An **incentive** is something that causes people to behave in a certain way by changing the trade-offs they face. Incentives can be positive or negative:

> **incentive**
> something that causes people to behave in a certain way by changing the trade-offs they face

- A *positive* incentive (sometimes just called an *incentive*) makes people *more likely* to do something. For example, lowering the price of spaghetti creates a positive incentive for people to order it because it lowers the opportunity cost: When you pay less for spaghetti, you give up fewer other things you could have spent the money on.
- A *negative* incentive (sometimes called a *disincentive*) makes them *less likely* to do it. Charging people more for pizza is a negative incentive to buy pizza because they now have to give up more alternative purchases.

The second assumption economists make about trade-offs is that nothing happens in a vacuum. That is, you can't change just one thing in the world without eliciting a response from others. If you change your behavior—even if only in a small way—that action will change the incentives of the people around you, causing them to change their behavior in response. If you invent a new product, competitors will copy it. If you raise prices, consumers will buy less. If you tax a good or service, people will produce less of it.

Asking *how others will respond* can help prevent bad decisions by predicting the undesirable side-effects of a change in prices or policies. The question can also be used to design changes that elicit positive responses. When Muhammad Yunus was setting up Grameen Bank, he had to think carefully about the incentives that both rural villagers and traditional banks faced; he considered how those incentives could be changed without incurring negative side-effects.

One reason banks saw rural villagers as risky customers is that they were too poor to have collateral to offer the bank. *Collateral* is a possession, like a house or a car, pledged by a borrower to a lender. If the borrower cannot repay the loan, the lender keeps the collateral. The threat of losing the collateral increases the cost of choosing to not repay the loan; collateral gives the borrower a positive incentive to repay. When traditional banks thought about lending to poor Bangladeshis, they believed that without the threat of losing collateral, the villagers would be unlikely to repay their loans.

Yunus needed to think up a different way of creating a positive incentive for poor customers to repay their loans. His best-known solution was to require borrowers to apply for loans in five-person groups. Every person in the group would have a stake in the success of the other members. If one person didn't repay a loan, no one else in the group could borrow from the bank again.

Yunus's idea, called *group responsibility,* was simple but hugely significant. Yunus concluded that borrowers would have a strong incentive to repay their loans: They wouldn't want to ruin relationships with other members of the group—their fellow villagers, with whom they live every day and rely on for mutual support in hard times. This incentive, in turn, changed the trade-off faced by banks; they responded by being more willing to lend to the poor at lower rates. By asking himself how villagers would respond to the new kind of loan and how banks in turn would respond to the villagers' response, Yunus was able to predict that his idea could be the key to spreading banking services to the poor.

Dr. Yunus's predictions proved to be correct. Seeing that poor villagers nearly always repaid their loans under Grameen's system gave other banks confidence that small borrowers could be reliable customers. Banks offering microloans, savings accounts, and other services to the very poor have spread around the world. As a result of Yunus's creativity and thoughtfulness about incentives, the poor have better access to financial services, and banks earn money from providing them. Today, other ideas have proved even more effective in providing the right incentives for small borrowers, continuing in the tradition of experimentation and innovation pioneered by Yunus and Grameen Bank.

Throughout this book, you will see many examples of how the power of incentives can be harnessed to accomplish everything from increasing a company's profits to protecting the environment. But before we get carried away with brilliant economic innovations, we have to ask ourselves one more question, the final test for any ideas that come out of our problem-solving process.

Efficiency

Question 4: Why isn't someone already doing it?

> **LO 1.4** Explain the economic concept of efficiency.

People tend to behave rationally. We clip coupons, compare car models before buying, and think hard about which major to choose in college. Although people are not calculating machines, we usually weigh trade-offs, respond to incentives, and are on the lookout for opportunities to get what we want in the most effective way possible.

The same goes for businesses. There are millions of businesses in the world, each trying to make a profit. When consumers want a good or service, some business will take the opportunity to earn money by providing it. That fact leads to our final assumption: *Under normal circumstances, individuals and firms will act to provide the things people want.* If a genuine profit-making opportunity exists, someone will take advantage of it, and usually sooner rather than later.

This final assumption comes from the idea of **efficiency**. Efficiency describes a situation in which resources are used in the most productive way possible to produce the goods and services that have the greatest total economic value to society. Increasing efficiency means finding a way to better use resources to produce the things that people want.

The definition of efficiency might raise some questions. How do we determine *value,* for example? What exactly do we mean by *resources*? Over the course of the book, we'll dive deeper

efficiency
use of resources in the most productive way possible to produce the goods and services that have the greatest total economic value to society

into these issues. For now, we'll take a broad view: Something is *valuable* if someone wants it. A *resource* is anything that can be used to make something of value, from natural resources (such as water and trees) to human resources (such as talents and knowledge). This broad view leads to an important idea: When the economy is working efficiently, resources are *already* being allocated to valuable ends.

So when you think you see a big, unexploited opportunity—a new product, policy, technology, or business model that could change the world or earn you millions of dollars—ask yourself: If it's such a great idea, *why isn't someone* already *doing it?*

One possible answer is simply that nobody has thought of it before. That's possible. Perhaps you *have* seen an efficient way to allocate resources in a way that produces economic value for society. But if *you* have seen the opportunity, doesn't it seem likely that at least one of the billions of other smart, rational people in the world will have seen it too?

Don't get us wrong: We're not saying there is never an opportunity to do something new in the world. Great new ideas happen all the time—they drive progress. But there's a strong possibility that other people have already thought about the idea, and if they chose not to take advantage of it, that's a hint that you might be missing something. The first thing to do is backtrack to the first three economists' questions:

- Have you misjudged people's wants and constraints?
- Have you miscalculated the trade-offs they face?
- Have you misunderstood how people will respond to incentives?

If you think back through those questions and still think you're on to something, here are some more possibilities to consider. We said that *under normal circumstances,* the economy is operating efficiently and individuals or firms provide the things people want. What are some ways in which circumstances might not be normal?

- *Innovation:* Innovation is the explanation you're hoping is correct. Maybe your idea has not been used yet because it is too new. If you have come up with a truly new idea, whether it is new technology or a new business model, people cannot have taken advantage of it yet because it didn't exist before.

- *Market failure:* Market failures are an important cause of inefficiency. Sometimes people and firms fail to take advantage of opportunities because something prevents them from capturing the benefits of the opportunity, or imposes additional costs on them. For instance, maybe your great new idea won't work because it would be impossible to prevent others from quickly copying it. Or perhaps your great new idea won't work because a few big companies already have the market for it sewn up. Economists call such situations *market failures.* We will discuss market failures in much greater depth later in the book.

- *Intervention:* If a powerful force—often the government—intervenes in the economy, transactions cannot take place the way they normally would. We'll see later in the book that many government economic policies intentionally or unintentionally interfere with people's ability to take advantage of profit-making opportunities.

- *Unprofitable idea:* Maybe your idea won't produce a profit. Individuals and governments have goals other than profit, of course—for example, creating great art or promoting social justice. But if your idea doesn't also generate a profit, then it is less surprising that no one has taken advantage of it.

When Muhammad Yunus asked himself the question "Why isn't someone already lending to the poor?" he first identified a market failure involving lack of collateral. Understanding the market-failure problem enabled him to come up with the idea of group responsibility to fix it.

But then he had to ask himself, "Why aren't other banks already using the group responsibility idea?"

Maybe there was another market failure Yunus hadn't spotted. Maybe some government policy prevented it. Maybe traditional banks had considered it and decided it still wouldn't generate a profit. Yunus wasn't primarily interested in making a profit, of course—he was interested in helping the poor. But if microloans weren't going to earn a profit for the banks even with group responsibility, then that would explain why no one was already doing it.

Fortunately, none of those answers were correct. This was a case in which the answer to *why isn't someone already doing it?* was that the idea was genuinely new. Grameen Bank was able to help very poor people in Bangladesh by lending them money, while making enough profit to expand and serve more customers. Today, over 20 million people in Bangladesh can get small loans from Grameen Bank and other organizations. Around the world, over 200 million low-income customers enjoy the same opportunity. Sometimes, something that seems like a great new idea really *is* exactly that.

✓ CONCEPT CHECK

In every chapter of this book you will find a few Concept Checks. These questions test your understanding of the concepts presented in the preceding section. If you have trouble answering any of the questions, go back and review the section. Don't move forward until you understand these ideas.

- ☐ How do constraints affect decision making? **[LO 1.1]**
- ☐ What do opportunity costs represent? **[LO 1.2]**
- ☐ What is the name for something that changes the trade-offs that people face when making a decision? **[LO 1.3]**
- ☐ Give four reasons that might explain why a product isn't already in the market. **[LO 1.4]**

An Economist's Problem-Solving Toolbox

The four questions we've just discussed are some of the fundamental insights of economics. Using them to understand how the world *might* work is only half the battle. Understanding when and how to apply them is the other half. In the second part of this chapter, we will describe some tools economists use to apply these insights to real situations.

Accurately spotting the fundamental economic concepts at work in the world is sometimes less obvious than you might think. Throughout history, people have observed the world around them and drawn conclusions that have proved hilariously—or sometimes tragically—wrong. We now know that the sun doesn't revolve around the earth. Droughts are not caused by witches giving people the evil eye. Yet, intelligent people once believed these things. It's human nature to draw meaning from the patterns we observe around us, but our conclusions are not always correct.

Economic analysis requires us to combine theory with observations and to subject both to tough scrutiny before drawing conclusions. In this section we will see how to put together theories and facts to determine what causes what. We will also distinguish between the way things are and the way we think they *should be.* You can apply these tools to all sorts of situations, from personal life choices to business decisions and policy analysis.

Correlation and causation

LO 1.5 Distinguish between correlation and causation.

A die-hard sports fan may wear a particular jersey while watching his or her team win the NBA finals or Super Bowl, and then forever insist that jersey is lucky. This is an exaggerated example of a common human tendency: When we see that two events occur together, we tend

Economists try to be particularly careful to differentiate between correlation and causation. *DILBERT © 2011 Scott Adams. Used by permission of UNIVERSAL UCLICK. All rights reserved.*

to assume that one causes the other. Economists, however, try to be particularly careful about what causes what.

To differentiate between two variables that move together and two variables that have a cause-and-effect relationship, we use two different terms. For the instance in which two variables have a consistent relationship, we say there is a **correlation** between them. Correlation can be positive or negative:

correlation
a consistently observed relationship between two variables

- If both variables tend to move in the same direction, we say they are *positively correlated.* For example, wearing raincoats is positively correlated with rain.
- When two variables move in opposite directions, we say they are *negatively correlated.* High temperatures are negatively correlated with people wearing down jackets.

If there is no consistent relationship between two variables, we say they are *uncorrelated.*

causation
a relationship between two events in which one brings about the other

Correlation differs from causation. **Causation** means that one variable causes the other. As the preceding examples show, causation and correlation often go together. Weather and clothing are often correlated because weather *causes* people to make certain choices about the clothing they wear.

Correlation and causation do not *always* go together in a straightforward way. Correlation and causation can be confused in three major ways: coincidence, omitted variables, and reverse causation.

Coincidence

Does the result of the Super Bowl predict the performance of the stock market? A few years ago, some people thought it might. The Super Bowl pits the top team from the American Football Conference against the top team from the National Football Conference. For a long time, when a team from the AFC won, the stock market had a bad year; when a team from the NFC won, the stock market had a great year. In fact, this pattern held true 85 percent of the time between 1967 and 1997.

Would it have been a good idea to base your investment strategy on the results of the Super Bowl? We think not. There is no plausible cause-and-effect relationship here. Stock market outcomes happened to be *correlated with* Super Bowl outcomes for a number of years, but there is no logical way they could be *caused by* them. If you search long enough for odd coincidences, you will eventually find some.

Omitted variables

Consider the following statement: There is a positive correlation between the presence of firefighters and people with serious burn injuries. Does this statement mean that firefighters cause burn injuries? Of course not. We know that firefighters are not burning people; they're trying to save them. Instead, there must be some common underlying variable behind both observed outcomes—fires, in this case.

Sometimes, two events that are correlated occur together because both are caused by the same underlying factor. Each has a causal relationship with a third factor, but not with each other. The underlying factor is called an *omitted variable*—despite the fact that it is an important part of the cause-and-effect story, it has been left out of the analysis. The From Another Angle box "Does ice cream cause polio?" tells the story of an omitted variable that convinced some doctors to mistakenly campaign against a staple of summer fun: ice cream.

From Another Angle
Does ice cream cause polio?

From Another Angle boxes show you a different way of looking at an economic concept. Sometimes they will be a humorous story, sometimes a different way of thinking about a situation, and sometimes just an unusual application of a standard idea. We find that a little bit of weirdness goes a long way in helping us to remember things, and we hope it will work for you too.

A disease called polio once crippled or killed thousands of children in the United States every year. Before it was known what caused polio, doctors observed that polio infections seemed to be more common in children who had been eating lots of ice cream. Observing this *correlation* led some people to assume that there was a *causal* relationship between the two. Some doctors recommended an anti-polio diet that avoided eating ice cream. Many fearful parents understandably took their advice.

We now know that polio is caused by a virus that is transmitted from one person to another. The virus was spread through contaminated food and water—for example, dirty swimming pools or water fountains. It had nothing at all to do with how much ice cream a child ate.

The ice cream confusion was caused by an *omitted variable:* warm weather. In warm weather, children are more likely to use swimming pools and water fountains. And in warm weather, children are also more likely to eat ice cream. Polio was therefore *correlated* with eating ice cream, but it certainly wasn't *caused* by it.

Dr. Jonas Salk developed a polio vaccine in 1952 that stopped the fear of the disease and its spread.

Source: Steve Lohr, "For Today's Graduate, Just One Word: Statistics," *New York Times,* August 5, 2009.

Reverse causation

A third common source of confusion between correlation and causation is *reverse causation: Did A cause B, or did B cause A?* When two events always happen together, it can be hard to say which caused the other.

Let's return to the correlation between rain and raincoats. If we knew nothing about rain, we might observe that it often appears together with raincoats; we might conclude that wearing a raincoat (A) causes rain (B). In this case, we all know that the causation goes the other way, but observation alone does not tell us that.

Looking at the timing of two correlated events can sometimes provide clues. Often, if A happens before B, it hints that A causes B rather than vice versa. But grabbing a raincoat as you leave home in the morning frequently happens *before* it rains in the afternoon. The timing notwithstanding, taking your raincoat with you in the morning clearly does not *cause* rain later in the day. In this case, your *anticipation* of B causes A to happen.

An important lesson for economists and noneconomists alike is never to take observations at face value. Always make sure you can explain *why* two events are related. To do so, you need another tool in the economist's toolbox: a model.

Models

LO 1.6 List the characteristics of a good economic model.

model
a simplified representation of the important parts of a complicated situation

A **model** is a simplified representation of a complicated situation. In economics, models show how people, firms, and governments make decisions about managing resources and how their decisions interact. An economic model can represent a situation as basic as how people decide what car to buy or as complex as what causes a global recession.

Because models simplify complex problems, they allow us to focus our attention on the most important parts. Models rarely include every detail of a given situation, but that is a good thing. If we had to describe the entire world with perfect accuracy before solving a problem, we'd be so overwhelmed with details that we'd never get the answer. By carefully simplifying the situation to its essentials, we can get useful answers that are *approximately* right.

circular flow model
a simplified representation of how the economy's transactions work together

One of the most basic models of the economy is the **circular flow model**. The economy involves billions of transactions every day, and the circular flow model helps show how all of those transactions work together. The model slashes through complexity to show important patterns. Figure 1-1 shows the circular flow of economic transactions in a graphic format called the *circular flow diagram.*

The first simplification of the circular flow model is to narrow our focus to the two most important types of actors in the economy, households and firms:

- *Households* are vital in two ways. First, they supply land and labor to firms and invest capital in firms. (Land, labor, and capital are called the *factors of production.*) Second, they buy the goods and services that firms produce.
- *Firms* too are vital but do the opposite of households: They buy or rent the land, labor, and capital supplied by households, and they produce and sell goods and services.

The circular flow model shows that firms and households are tightly connected through both production and consumption.

In another helpful simplification, the circular flow model narrows the focus to two markets that connect households and firms:

- The *market for goods and services* is exactly what it sounds: It reflects all of the activity involved in the buying and selling of goods and services. In this market, households spend their wages from labor and their income from land and capital, and firms earn revenue from selling their goods and services.
- The second market is the *market for the factors of production.* Here, households supply land, labor, and capital, and firms hire and purchase or rent these inputs.

FIGURE 1-1
Circular flow diagram

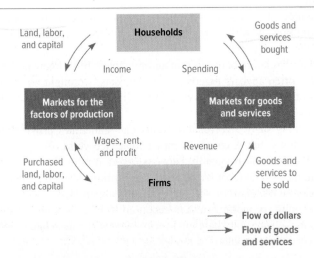

The model puts all of this together. The transactions we have described are part of two loops:

- One is a loop of inputs and outputs as they travel throughout the economy. The *inputs* are the land, labor, and capital firms use to produce goods. The *outputs* are the goods and services that firms produce using the factors of production.

- Another loop represents the flow of dollars. Households buy goods and services using the money they get from firms for using their factors of production. Firms get revenues from selling these goods and services—and, in turn, firms can then use the money to buy or rent factors of production.

You might be a little dizzy at this point, with everything spinning in loops. To help straighten things out, let's follow $5 from your wallet as it flows through the economy. You could spend this $5 in any number of ways. As you're walking down the street, you see a box of donuts sitting in the window of your local bakery. You head in and give the baker your $5, a transaction in the market for goods. The money represents revenue for the baker and spending by you. The donuts are an output of the bakery.

The story of your $5 is not over, though. In order to make more donuts, the baker puts that $5 toward buying inputs in the market for the factors of production. This might include paying rent for the bakery or paying wages for an assistant. The baker's spending represents income for the households that provide the labor in the bakery or rent out the space. Once the baker pays wages or rent with that $5, it has made it through a cycle in the circular flow.

As the circular flow model shows, an economic model approximates what happens in the real economy. Later in the book, we'll discuss other models that focus on specific questions—like how much gasoline prices will go up when the government raises taxes or how fast the economy is likely to grow in the next decade.

The best models lead us to clearer answers about complicated questions. What makes a good economic model? We have already said that good models can leave out details that are not crucial, and they focus on the important aspects of a situation. To be useful, a model *should* also do three things:

1. *A good model predicts cause and effect.* The circular flow model gives a useful description of the basics of the economy. Often, though, we want to go further. Many times we want a model not only to describe economic connections but also to predict how things will happen in the future. To do that, we have to get cause and effect right. If your model says that A causes B, you should be able to explain why. In the "Markets" chapter we'll learn about a central model in economics that shows that for most goods and services, the quantity people want to buy goes down as the price goes up. Why? As the cost of an item rises, but the benefit of owning it remains the same, more people will decide that the trade-off is not worth it.

2. *A good model states its assumptions clearly.* Although models are usually too simple to fit the real world perfectly, it's important that they be clear about their simplifying assumptions. Doing so helps us to know when the model will predict real events accurately and when it will not. For example, we said earlier that economists often assume that people behave rationally. We know that isn't always true, but we accept it as an assumption because it is *approximately* accurate in many situations. As long as we are clear that we are making this assumption, we will know that the model may not be accurate when people fail to behave rationally.

3. *A good model describes the real world accurately.* If a model does not describe what actually happens in the real world, something about the model is wrong. We've admitted that models are not perfectly accurate because they are intentionally simpler than the real world. But if a model predicts things that are not usually or approximately true, it is not useful. How do we tell if a model is realistic? Economists test their models by observing what happens in the real world and collecting data, which they use to verify or reject the

model. In the Real Life box "Testing models against history," take a look at a model that has been tested over and over again in the last few hundred years.

 Real Life

Testing models against history

Real Life boxes show how the concept you're reading about relates to the real world. They are your chance to test models against the data. Often these boxes will describe a situation in which people used an economic idea to solve a business or policy question, or they present interesting research ideas or experiences. Watch for links to online content, such as videos or news stories.

Thomas Malthus, an early nineteenth-century economist, created a model that described the relationship between population growth and food production. The model predicted that mass starvation would occur as populations outgrew food supplies. In his famous work *An Essay on the Principle of Population,* Malthus wrote:

> The power of population is so superior to the power of the earth to produce subsistence for man, that premature death must in some shape or other visit the human race. . . . [G]igantic inevitable famine stalks . . .

Since Malthus wrote these words, famines have in fact killed millions of people. However, they have not been related to population growth in the way that Malthus predicted. Instead, the population of the world has increased from under a billion in 1800 to about 7.4 billion today. At the same time, nutrition standards have risen in almost every country.

Malthus's model left out a crucial part of the story: human ingenuity and technological progress. As the world's population has grown, people have found new ways to grow better food more efficiently and to make more land usable for growing food. They have also found better ways to limit population growth.

Malthus's idea has not died out, though. Today, neo-Malthusian theory predicts that population will still outstrip the world's productive capacity. This theory updates Malthus's model to address more modern concerns, such as increasing environmental degradation that makes land unfit for farming. Others argue that nonrenewable resources, such as oil, will be depleted. Still others warn that even if the world's farmers can produce enough food, unequal access to resources like fresh water will cause local famines and wars.

Critics of these arguments point out that human ingenuity has somehow averted catastrophe at every point in recent history when a Malthusian disaster seemed imminent. The population boom that followed World War II was supposed to lead to starvation, but it was counteracted by the Green Revolution, which increased food production manyfold.

Is the neo-Malthusian model accurate, then, or is it too missing some critical factor? Time will provide the data to answer this question.

Source: T. R. Malthus, *An Essay on the Principle of Population,* 1798.

Positive and normative analysis

LO 1.7 Distinguish between positive and normative analysis.

Economics is a field of study in which people frequently confuse facts with judgments that are based on beliefs. Think about the following example:

- *Statement #1:* Income taxes reduce the number of hours that people want to work.

- *Statement #2:* Income taxes should be reduced or abolished.

Many people have trouble separating these two statements. Some feel that the second statement flows logically from the first. Others disagree with the second statement, so they assume the first can't possibly be true.

If you read carefully, however, you'll see that the first sentence is a statement about cause and effect. Thus, it can be proved true or false by data and evidence. A statement that makes a factual claim about how the world *actually* works is called a **positive statement**.

The second sentence, on the other hand, cannot be proved true or false. Instead, it indicates what *should be* done—but only if we share certain goals, understandings, and moral beliefs. A statement that makes a claim about how the world *should be* is called a **normative statement**.

To see how important the distinction between positive and normative statements can be, consider two claims that a physicist might make:

- *Positive statement:* A nuclear weapon with the explosive power of 10 kilotons of TNT will have a fallout radius of up to six miles.
- *Normative statement:* The United States was right to use nuclear weapons in World War II.

positive statement
a factual claim about how the world actually works

normative statement
a claim about how the world should be

A famous quote makes this point nicely: "Everyone has a right to their own opinion, but not to their own facts." If you search the internet for this quote, you'll see that it has been attributed to many people.
http://www.glasbergen. com/?count=14&s=teaching

Although people could disagree about both of these statements, the first is a question of scientific fact; the second depends heavily on a person's ethical and political beliefs. The first statement may inform your opinion of the second, but you can still agree with one and not the other.

Earlier in this chapter, we introduced a feature called "What Do You Think?" that asks for your opinion about an important policy or life decision. From this point forward, you can use your understanding of the differences between normative and positive analysis to untangle the questions asked in these boxes and combine the two kinds of analysis to arrive at a conclusion. Begin trying your hand at this with the What Do You Think? box "The cost of college cash."

"You're certainly entitled to your opinion."

What Do You Think?
The cost of college cash

In 2012–2013, the average yearly cost of a college education ranged from $15,022 at public universities to $34,483 at private universities. Students have a number of options for paying the bill. They can take out federal loans, private loans, or a combination of the two to defer payments until later, or they can use savings or earnings to foot the bill.

Students who qualify for federal loans enjoy benefits such as limits on the interest rate they can be charged or the total payments they can be expected to make. They also have the possibility of loan forgiveness if they enter certain fields after graduation.

Lending to students is a controversial topic. Some people argue for more controls on private lending institutions, such as interest-rate caps and greater protection for students who default. They reason that lending programs should support students who would not otherwise be able to afford college. Furthermore, they argue, graduating with a lot of debt discourages students from going into lower-paid public service jobs.

Other people maintain that the existing lending system is fine. Getting a college degree, they argue, increases a person's future earning power so much that graduates should be able to handle the debt, even at high interest rates. They worry that overregulation will discourage private lenders from offering student loans, defeating the purpose of giving students better access to financial assistance.

(continued)

WHAT DO YOU THINK?

Use the four basic questions economists ask to break down the problem. Remember that your answer can draw on both positive analysis (what *will* happen if a certain policy is followed) and normative analysis (what *should* be done, given your values and goals). You should be able to say which parts of your answers fall into each category.

1. What motivations and constraints apply to students who are considering different schools and loan options? What motivations and constraints apply to private lenders?
2. What opportunity costs do students face when deciding how to pay for college? Should they avoid loans by skipping college altogether or by working their way through college?
3. How would prospective students respond to government limits on the interest rate on student loans? How would private banks that offer student loans respond?
4. Why do you think the federal government has not yet implemented interest-rate caps on private student loans? Do you anticipate any unintended side-effects of that policy?
5. Consider your arguments in response to questions 1 through 4. Which parts were based on normative statements and which on positive statements?

Sources: National Center for Education Statistics, "Trends in college pricing," http://nces.ed.gov/fastfacts/display.asp?id=76; "How much student debt is too much?" http://roomfordebate.blogs.nytimes.com/2009/06/14/how-much-student-debt-is-too-much/?scp=1&sq=student%20loans&st=cse.

Throughout this book, remember that *you don't have to buy into a particular moral or political outlook in order for economics to be useful to you.* Our goal is to provide you with a toolbox of economic concepts that you can use to engage in positive analysis. We will also highlight important decisions you may face that will require you to engage in normative thinking, informed by economic analysis. You will find that economics can help you to make better decisions and identify the most effective policies, regardless of your goals and beliefs.

✓ CONCEPT CHECK

☐ What does it mean when two variables are positively correlated? **[LO 1.5]**
☐ What are the characteristics of a good economic model? **[LO 1.6]**
☐ What is the difference between a positive statement and a normative statement? **[LO 1.7]**

Conclusion

Economists approach problems differently from many other people. A basic principle of human behavior underlies economics—the idea that people typically make choices to achieve their goals in the most effective way possible, subject to the constraints they face.

In this chapter we have introduced the basic concepts economists use, as well as four questions they ask to break down problems. Throughout this book, you will see these concepts and questions over and over again:

1. Scarcity: *What are the wants and constraints of those involved?*
2. Opportunity cost: *What are the trade-offs?*
3. Incentives: *How will others respond?*
4. Efficiency: *Why isn't someone already doing it?*

In later chapters, as we progress to more complicated problems, try using these four questions to break down problems into manageable pieces. Then you can tackle those smaller pieces using the four fundamental concepts presented in this chapter.

Key Terms

Summary

LO 1.1 Explain the economic concept of scarcity.

Economists usually assume that people behave rationally and live within a condition of scarcity. Answering the question *What are the wants and constraints of those involved?* tells you what to expect from each player in the situation you are analyzing. Given rational behavior and scarcity, you can expect people to work to get what they want (their motivations) using the limited resources at their disposal (their constraints).

LO 1.2 Explain the economic concepts of opportunity cost and marginal decision making.

Trade-offs arise when you must give up something to get something else. Answering *What are the trade-offs?* will tell you about the costs and benefits associated with a decision. The full cost of doing something is its *opportunity cost*—the value to you of what you have to give up in order to get something, or the value you could have gained by choosing the next-best alternative.

Economists assume that rational people make decisions "at the margin," by comparing any additional benefits of a choice to the extra costs it brings. If people are behaving rationally when they face trade-offs, they will always choose to do something if the marginal benefit is greater than the opportunity cost. They will never do it if the opportunity cost is greater than the marginal benefit.

LO 1.3 Explain the economic concept of incentives.

The collective reaction to changing trade-offs is a central idea in economics. Asking *How will others respond?* will give you a complete picture of how a particular decision affects the world. You can assume that any action will bring a response because people react to changes in their incentives.

LO 1.4 Explain the economic concept of efficiency.

Efficiency occurs when resources are used in the most productive way possible to produce the goods and services that have the greatest total economic value to society. In other words, *efficiency* means using resources to produce the things that people want. Under normal circumstances, markets are efficient.

So when you see what seems to be unexploited opportunity, you should ask: If it's such a great idea, *why isn't someone already doing it?* Markets usually allocate resources efficiently. When they don't, other explanations might be in play: a market failure may have occurred; government may have intervened in the economy; there may be goals other than profit involved; or there may be a genuine opportunity for innovation.

LO 1.5 Distinguish between correlation and causation.

When there is a consistently observed relationship between two variables, we say they are *correlated*. This is different from a *causal* relationship, in which one variable brings about the other. Three common ways in which correlation and causation are confused are coincidence, omitted variables, and reverse causation.

LO 1.6 List the characteristics of a good economic model.

A model is a simplified representation of the important parts of a complicated situation. In economics, models usually show how people, firms, and governments make decisions about managing resources and how their decisions interact. The *circular flow model* is a representation of how the transactions of households and firms flow through the economy.

A good economic model should predict cause and effect, describe the world accurately, and state its assumptions clearly. Economists test their models by observing what happens in the world and collecting data that can be used to support or reject their models.

LO 1.7 Distinguish between positive and normative analysis.

A statement that makes a factual claim about how the world actually works is called a *positive* statement. A statement that makes a claim about how the world should be is called a *normative* statement. Economics is a field in which people frequently confuse positive statements with normative statements. You do not have to adopt a particular moral or political point of view to use economic concepts and models.

Review Questions

1. Suppose you are shopping for new clothes to wear to job interviews, but you're on a tight budget. In this situation, what are your wants and constraints? What does it mean to behave rationally in the face of scarcity? **[LO 1.1]**

2. You are a student with a demanding schedule of classes. You also work part time and your supervisor allows you to determine your schedule. In this situation, what is your scarce resource? How do you decide how many hours to work? **[LO 1.1]**

3. Think about the definition of scarcity that you learned in this chapter. Name three ways that you confront scarcity in your own life. **[LO 1.1]**

4. When shopping for your interview clothes, what are some trade-offs you face? What is the opportunity cost of buying new clothes? What are the benefits? How do you balance the two? **[LO 1.2]**

5. You have an 8:30 class this morning, but you are feeling extremely tired. How do you decide whether to get some extra sleep or go to class? **[LO 1.2]**

6. It's Friday night. You already have a ticket to a concert, which cost you $30. A friend invites you to go out for a game of paintball instead. Admission would cost you $25, and you think you'd get $25 worth of enjoyment out of it. Your concert ticket is nonrefundable. What is your opportunity cost (in dollars) of playing paintball? **[LO 1.2]**

7. Suppose you have two job offers and are considering the trade-offs between them. Job A pays $45,000 per year; it includes health insurance and two weeks of paid vacation. Job B pays $30,000 per year; it includes four weeks of paid vacation but no health insurance. **[LO 1.2]**

   a. List the benefits of Job A and the benefits of Job B.

   b. List the opportunity cost of Job A and the opportunity cost of Job B.

8. Your former neighbor gave you his lawnmower when he moved. You are thinking of using this gift to mow lawns in your neighborhood this summer for extra cash. As you think about what to charge your neighbors and whether this idea is worth your effort, what opportunity costs do you need to consider? **[LO 1.2]**

9. Think of a few examples of incentives in your daily life. How do you respond to those incentives? **[LO 1.3]**

10. You supervise a team of salespeople. Your employees already receive a company discount. Suggest a positive incentive and a negative incentive you could use to improve their productivity. **[LO 1.3]**

11. Your boss decides to pair workers in teams and offer bonuses to the most productive team. Why might your boss offer team bonuses instead of individual bonuses? **[LO 1.3]**

12. Think of a public policy—a local or national law, tax, or public service—that offers an incentive for a particular behavior. Explain what the incentive is, who is offering it, and what they are trying encourage or discourage. Does the incentive work? **[LO 1.3]**

13. Why do individuals or firms usually provide the goods and services people want? **[LO 1.4]**

14. You may have seen TV advertisements for products or programs that claim to teach a sure-fire way to make millions on the stock market. Apply the *Why isn't someone already doing it?* test to this situation. Do you believe the ads? Why or why not? **[LO 1.4]**

15. Describe an innovation in technology, business, or culture that had a major economic impact in your lifetime. **[LO 1.4]**

16. Why do people confuse correlation with causation? **[LO 1.5]**

17. Name two things that are positively correlated and two things that are negatively correlated. **[LO 1.5]**

18. Why is it important for a good economic model to predict cause and effect? **[LO 1.6]**

19. Why is it important for a good economic model to make clear assumptions? **[LO 1.6]**

20. Describe an economic model you know. What does the model predict about cause and effect? **[LO 1.6]**

21. Describe an economic model you know. What assumptions does the model make? Are the assumptions reasonable? **[LO 1.6]**

22. What is the difference between disagreeing about a positive statement and disagreeing about a normative statement? **[LO 1.7]**

23. Would a good economic model be more likely to address a positive statement or a normative statement? Why? **[LO 1.7]**

24. Write a positive statement and a normative statement about your favorite hobby. **[LO 1.7]**

Problems and Applications

1. Think about how and why goods and resources are scarce. Goods and resources can be scarce for reasons that are inherent to their nature at all times, that are temporary or seasonal, or that are artificially created. Separate the goods listed below into two groups; indicate which (if any) are artificially scarce (AS) and which (if any) are inherently scarce (IS). **[LO 1.1]**

    a. air of any quality _____
    b. land _____
    c. patented goods _____
    d. original Picasso paintings _____

2. You are looking for a new apartment in Manhattan. Your income is $4,000 per month, and you know that you should not spend more than 25 percent of your income on rent. You have come across the listings for one-bedroom apartments shown in Table 1P-1. You are indifferent about location, and transportation costs are the same to each neighborhood. **[LO 1.1]**

    a. Which apartments fall within your budget? (Check all that apply.)
    b. Suppose that you adhere to the 25 percent guideline but also receive a $1,000 cost-of-living supplement because you are living and working in Manhattan. Which apartments fall within your budget now?

3. Suppose the price of a sweater is $15. Julia's benefit from purchasing each additional sweater is given in

TABLE 1P-1

Location	Monthly Rent
Chelsea	$1,200
Battery Park	2,200
Delancey	950
Midtown	1,500

TABLE 1P-2

	Marginal benefit ($)
1st sweater	50
2nd sweater	35
3rd sweater	30
4th sweater	23
5th sweater	12
6th sweater	8

Table 1P-2. Julia gets the most benefit from the first sweater and less benefit from each additional sweater. If Julia is behaving rationally, how many sweaters will she purchase? **[LO 1.2]**

4. Sweaters sell for $15 at the crafts fair. Allie knits sweaters; her marginal costs are given in Table 1P-3. Allie's costs increase with each additional sweater. If Allie is behaving rationally, how many sweaters will she sell? **[LO 1.2]**

5. Last year, you estimated you would earn $5 million in sales revenues from developing a new product. So far, you have spent $3 million developing the product, but it is not yet complete. Meanwhile, this year you have new sales projections that show expected revenues from the new product will actually be only $4 million. How much should you be willing to spend to complete the product development? **[LO 1.2]**

    a. $0.
    b. Up to $1 million.
    c. Up to $4 million.
    d. Whatever it takes.

TABLE 1P-3

	Marginal cost ($)
1st sweater	5
2nd sweater	8
3rd sweater	12
4th sweater	18
5th sweater	25
6th sweater	32

TABLE 1P-4

		Affected good
a.	A local movie theater offers a student discount.	Movie tickets
b.	A tax on soft drinks passes in your state.	Soft drinks
c.	Subsidies on corn are cut in half.	Corn subsidies
d.	Your student health center begins offering flu shots for free.	Flu shots

6. Consider the following examples. For each one, say whether the incentive is positive or negative. [**LO 1.3**]
    a. Bosses who offer time-and-a-half for working on national holidays.
    b. Mandatory minimum sentencing for drug offenses.
    c. Fines for littering.
    d. Parents who offer their children extra allowance money for good grades.

7. Consider the events that change prices as described in Table 1P-4. For each one, say whether the opportunity cost of consuming the affected good increases or decreases. [**LO 1.3**]

8. Your best friend has an idea for a drive-through bar. Indicate the best explanation for why others have not taken advantage of her idea: true innovation, market failure, government intervention, or unprofitability. [**LO 1.4**]

9. Your best friend has an idea for a long-distance car service to drive people across the country. Indicate the best explanation for why others have not taken advantage of her idea: true innovation, market failure, intervention, or unprofitability. [**LO 1.4**]

10. Determine whether each of the following questionable statements is best explained by coincidence, an omitted variable, or reverse causation. [**LO 1.5**]
    a. In cities that have more police, crime rates are higher.
    b. Many retired people live in states where everyone uses air conditioning during the summer.
    c. More people come down with the flu during the Winter Olympics than during the Summer Olympics.
    d. For the last five years, Punxsutawney Phil has seen his shadow on Groundhog Day, and spring has come late.

11. For each of the pairs below, determine whether they are positively correlated, negatively correlated, or uncorrelated. [**LO 1.5**]
    a. Time spent studying and test scores.
    b. Vaccination and illness.
    c. Soft drink preference and music preference.
    d. Income and education.

12. Each statement below is part of an economic model. Indicate whether the statement is a prediction of cause and effect or an assumption. [**LO 1.6**]
    a. People behave rationally.
    b. If the price of a good falls, people will consume more of that good.
    c. Mass starvation will occur as population outgrows the food supply.
    d. Firms want to maximize profits.

13. From the list below, select the characteristics that describe a good economic model. [**LO 1.6**]
    a. Includes every detail of a given situation.
    b. Predicts that A causes B.
    c. Makes approximately accurate assumptions.
    d. Fits the real world perfectly.
    e. Predicts things that are usually true.

14. Determine whether each of the following statements is positive or normative. (Remember that a positive statement isn't necessarily *correct;* it just makes a factual claim rather than a moral judgment.) [**LO 1.7**]
    a. People who pay their bills on time are less likely than others to get into debt.
    b. Hard work is a virtue.
    c. Everyone should pay his or her bills on time.
    d. China has a bigger population than any other country in the world.
    e. China's One-Child Policy (which limits families to one child each) helped to spur the country's rapid economic growth.
    f. Lower taxes are good for the country.

15. You just received your midterm exam results and your professor wrote the following note: "You received a 70 on this exam, the average score. If you want to improve your grade, you should study more." Evaluate your professor's note. [**LO 1.7**]
    a. Is the first sentence positive or normative?
    b. Is the second sentence positive or normative?

Endnotes

1. Grameen Bank, "Monthly Report 2-2016," http://www.grameen-info.org/monthly-reports-2-2016/.

Specialization and Exchange

Learning Objectives

LO 2.1 Construct a production possibilities graph and describe what causes shifts in production possibilities curves.

LO 2.2 Define absolute and comparative advantage.

LO 2.3 Explain why people specialize.

LO 2.4 Explain how the gains from trade follow from comparative advantage.

THE ORIGINS OF A T-SHIRT

How can we get the most out of available resources? It's one of the most basic economic questions. Factory managers ask it when looking for ways to increase production. National leaders ask it as they design economic policy. Activists ask it when they look for ways to reduce poverty or conserve the environment. And, in a different way, it's a question we all ask ourselves when thinking about what to do in life and how to make sure that we're taking full advantage of our talents.

To get a handle on this question, we start by thinking about resources at the highest level: the logic of international trade and the specialization of production between countries. By the end of the chapter, we hope that you'll see how the same ideas apply to decisions at any scale, right down to whether it makes more sense to fix your own computer or pay a specialist to do it for you.

We'll start with what seems to be a simple question: Where did your T-shirt come from? Look at the tag. We're betting it was made in a place you've never been to, and maybe never thought of visiting. Bangladesh? Honduras? Malaysia? Sri Lanka?

That "made in" label tells only part of the story. Chances are that your shirt's history spans other parts of the globe. Consider a standard T-shirt: The cotton might have been grown in Mali and then shipped to Pakistan, where it was spun into yarn. The yarn might have been sent to Bangladesh, where it was woven into cloth, cut into pieces, and assembled into a shirt. That shirt might then have traveled all the way to the United States, where it was shipped to a store near you. A couple of years from now, when you are cleaning out your closet, you may donate the shirt to a charity, which may ship it to a second-hand clothing vendor in Mali—right back where your shirt's travels began.

Of course, this is not only the story of shirts. It is remarkably similar to the story of shoes, computers, phones, and cars, among many other manufactured goods. Today, the products and services most of us take for granted come to us through an incredibly complex global network of farms, mines, factories, traders, and stores. Why is the production of even a simple T-shirt spread across the world? Why is the cotton grown in Mali and the sewing done in Bangladesh, rather than vice versa? Why isn't the whole shirt made in the United States, so that it doesn't have to travel so far to reach you?

© igor kisselev/Alamy

This chapter addresses fundamental economic questions about who produces which goods and why. The fact that millions of people and firms around the globe coordinate their activities to provide consumers with the right combination of goods and services seems like magic.

This feat of coordination doesn't happen by chance, nor does a super-planner tell everyone where to go and what to do. Instead, the global production line is a natural outcome of people everywhere acting in their own self-interest to improve their own lives. Economists call this coordination mechanism the *invisible hand,* an idea that was first suggested by the eighteenth-century economic thinker Adam Smith.

To get some insight into the *who* and *why* of production, consider how the story of shirts has changed over the last few centuries. For most of the 1800s, Americans wore shirts made in the United States. Today, however, most shirts are made in Bangladesh, China, and other countries where factory wages are low. Have American workers become worse at making shirts over the last two centuries? Definitely not. In fact, as we'll see in this chapter, it doesn't even mean that Bangladeshi workers are better than American workers at making shirts. Instead, each good tends to be produced by the country, company, or person with the lowest opportunity cost for producing that good.

Countries and firms *specialize* in making goods for which they have the lowest opportunity cost. They then trade with one another to get the combination of goods they want to consume. The resulting *gains from trade* can be shared such that everyone ends up better off. It's no surprise that trade has taken off as transportation and communication between countries have become cheaper and better.

The concepts in this chapter apply not just to the wealth of nations and international trade. They also illuminate the daily choices most people face: Who should cook which dishes at Thanksgiving dinner? Should you hire a plumber or fix the pipes yourself? Should you become a rock star or an economist? The concepts these questions raise can be subtle and are sometimes misunderstood. We hope this chapter will provide insights that will help you become a better resource manager in all areas of your life.

Production Possibilities

> **LO 2.1** Construct a production possibilities graph and describe what causes shifts in production possibilities curves.

In Chapter 1, "Economics and Life," we talked about economic models. Good models help us understand complex situations through simplifying assumptions that allow us to zero in on the important aspects. The story of why Bangladesh now produces shirts for Americans that Americans themselves were producing 200 years ago is a complex one, as you'd expect. But by simplifying it into a model, we can reach useful insights.

Let's assume the United States and Bangladesh produce only two things—shirts and, say, bushels of wheat. (In reality, of course, they produce many things, but we're trying not to get bogged down in details right now.) The model uses "wheat" to stand in for "stuff other than shirts," allowing us to focus on what we're really interested in—shirts.

Using this model we'll perform a thought experiment about production using a tool called the *production possibilities frontier*. This tool is used in other contexts as well, many of which have no connection to international trade. Here we use it to show what has changed over the last couple of centuries to explain why Americans now buy shirts from Bangladesh.

Drawing the production possibilities frontier

Let's step back in time to the United States in 1800. In our simple model, there are 2 million American workers, and they have two choices of where to work: shirt factories or wheat farms. In shirt factories, each worker produces 1 shirt per day. On wheat farms, each worker produces 2 bushels of wheat per day.

What would happen if everyone worked on a wheat farm? The United States would produce 4 million bushels of wheat per day (2 bushels of wheat per worker × 2 million workers). This is one "production possibility." Alternatively, what would happen if everyone went to work in a shirt factory? The United States would produce 2 million shirts per day (1 shirt per worker × 2 million workers). Those production possibilities are represented as entries A and E (the top and bottom rows) in panel A of Figure 2-1.

Of course, the United States wouldn't want just shirts or just wheat—and there is no reason that all workers have to produce the same thing. There are many different combinations of shirts and wheat that American workers could produce. Some of these are shown as rows B, C, and D in panel A of Figure 2-1. For example, if one-quarter of the workers go to the shirt factory, they can make 500,000 (0.5 million) shirts (1 shirt per worker × 500,000 workers); the remaining workers can produce 3 million bushels of wheat (2 bushels per worker × 1.5 million workers). This production possibility is represented by row B. Or maybe 1 million workers would make shirts (1 million shirts) and 1 million would produce wheat (2 million bushels). That's row C.

For a graphic look at the production possibilities, we can plot them as points on a graph, as shown in panel B of Figure 2-1. If we fill in enough points, we create the solid green line shown in Figure 2-2. This is the **production possibilities frontier (PPF)**. It is a line or curve that shows all the possible combinations of outputs that can be produced using all available resources. In this case, the frontier plots all combinations of shirts and wheat that can be produced using all available workers in the United States. Points inside the frontier (such as point T) are achievable but don't make full use of all available resources.

The production possibilities frontier helps us answer the first of the economists' questions discussed in Chapter 1, "Economics and Life": *What are the wants and constraints of those involved?* People in the United States *want* to consume shirts and wheat (and other things, of course; remember, we're simplifying). The production possibilities frontier gives us a way to represent the *constraints* on production. The United States cannot produce combinations of shirts

production possibilities frontier (PPF)
a line or curve that shows all the possible combinations of two outputs that can be produced using all available resources

FIGURE 2-1

Possible production combinations

(A)

Production possibilities	Bushels of wheat (millions)	Shirts (millions)
A	4	0
B	3	0.5
C	2	1.0
D	1	1.5
E	0	2.0

(B)

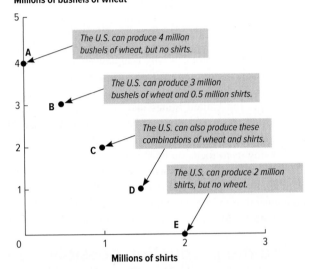

The United States can produce the maximum number of shirts or the maximum amount of wheat by devoting all its resources to one good or the other. But by allocating some resources to the production of each good, the United States can also produce many different combinations of wheat and shirts.

FIGURE 2-2

Production possibilities frontier

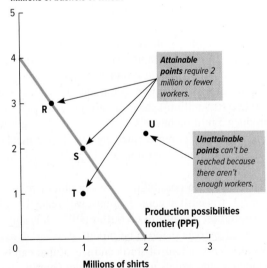

Points on or below the production possibilities frontier, such as R, S, and T, represent combinations of goods that the United States can produce with available resources. Points outside the frontier, such as U, are unattainable because there aren't enough resources.

and wheat that lie outside the frontier—such as point U in Figure 2-2. There just aren't enough workers or hours in the day to produce at point U, no matter how workers are allocated between shirts and wheat.

The production possibilities frontier also addresses the second economists' question: *What are the trade-offs?* Each worker can make *either* 1 shirt *or* 2 bushels of wheat per day. In other words, there is a trade-off between the quantity of wheat produced and the quantity of shirts produced. If we want an extra shirt, one worker has to stop producing bushels of wheat for a day. Therefore, the opportunity cost of 1 shirt is 2 bushels of wheat. Each bushel of wheat takes one worker half a day, so the opportunity cost of a bushel of wheat is half a shirt.

This opportunity cost is represented graphically by the *slope* of the production possibilities frontier. Moving up the frontier means getting more wheat at the cost of fewer shirts. Moving down the frontier means less wheat and more shirts. Looking at Figure 2-2, you'll notice that the slope of the line is −2. This is the same as saying that the opportunity cost of 1 shirt is always 2 bushels of wheat.

For a refresher on calculating and interpreting slopes, see Appendix A, "Math Essentials: Understanding Graphs and Slope," which follows this chapter.

Production possibilities frontiers when opportunity costs differ

So far, we've made the assumption that all workers are able to make the same amount of each good. In reality, some workers will probably be nimble-fingered and great at making shirts; others will be more naturally gifted at farming. What happens if we adjust our simple model to reflect this reality?

Let's start off with all workers producing wheat and nobody making shirts. If we reallocate the workers who are best at making shirts, we can get a lot of shirts without giving up too much wheat. In other words, the opportunity cost of making the first few shirts is quite low.

Now imagine almost all workers are making shirts, so that only the best farmers are left producing wheat. If we reallocate most of the remaining workers to shirt making, we give up a lot of wheat to get only a few extra shirts. The opportunity cost of getting those last few shirts is very high.

We can add a little more nuance to the model, to include land and machinery as resources also needed for production. We would find that the same pattern holds: As more of each resource is allocated to production, the opportunity cost of producing an additional unit of a good typically increases. This happens because we expect producers to always produce as efficiently as they can, which means, all else equal, using the resources with the lowest opportunity cost.

Let's start with everyone producing wheat. With wheat production pushed to the maximum, some farmers probably have to work on land that isn't well-suited to producing wheat. It could be that the land is swampy, or the soil has been overfarmed and depleted of nutrients. When farmers who had been working on this poor land switch over to making shirts, the economy will lose only a little wheat and gain many shirts in return. In contrast, if only a small amount of wheat is being grown using only the best, most fertile land, reallocating the last few farmers will cause a relatively large decrease in wheat production for each additional shirt.

Returning to the simplest model where workers are the only input to production, we can translate this increasing opportunity cost into the production possibilities frontier. Doing so, we get a curve that bows out (a concave curve) instead of a straight line, as shown in Figure 2-3. Panel A shows what happens if we have just three types of workers:

- For every bushel of wheat, some can make 1 shirt; they're the workers between points C_1 and C_2.

- For every bushel of wheat, some can make only $\frac{1}{2}$ of a shirt (between points C_2 and C_3).

- For every bushel of wheat, some can make only $\frac{1}{4}$ of a shirt (between points C_3 and C_4).

In other words, as we go down the curve, we move from those who are better at making shirts to those who are better at producing wheat. As we do so, the opportunity cost of making

FIGURE 2-3
Bowed-out (concave) production possibilities frontier

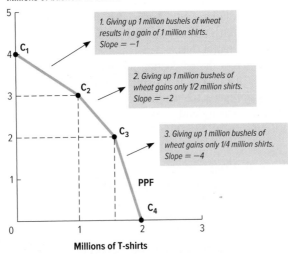

(A) Constructing the PPF

Millions of bushels of wheat

1. Giving up 1 million bushels of wheat results in a gain of 1 million shirts. Slope = −1

2. Giving up 1 million bushels of wheat gains only 1/2 million shirts. Slope = −2

3. Giving up 1 million bushels of wheat gains only 1/4 million shirts. Slope = −4

PPF

Millions of T-shirts

At point C_1, all workers produce wheat, and switching the best sewers to making shirts will result in a big gain in the quantity of shirts. As more and better farmers switch to making shirts, however, the gain in shirts produced decreases relative to the loss in the quantity of wheat. As a result the slope of the PPF is steeper from C_2 to C_3, and again from C_3 to C_4.

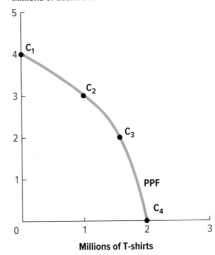

(B) The PPF

Millions of bushels of wheat

PPF

Millions of T-shirts

In reality, each worker has slightly different skills and therefore a slightly different opportunity cost of making shirts in terms of wheat. As a result, we get a smoothly curved production possibilities frontier.

shirts in terms of producing wheat increases. As that happens, the slope of the curve gets steeper (−1 between C_1 and C_2, −2 between C_2 and C_3, and −4 between C_3 and C_4).

In reality there aren't just three types of workers—each of the 2 million workers will have slightly different skills. The many possibilities will result in a curve that looks smooth, as in panel B of Figure 2-3. At each point of the curved production possibilities frontier, the slope represents the opportunity cost of getting more wheat or more shirts, based on the skills of the next worker who could switch.

Choosing among production possibilities

What can the production possibilities frontier tell us about what combination of goods an economy will choose to produce? Earlier, we noted that economies can produce at points inside the frontier, as well as points on it. However, choosing a production point *inside* the frontier means a country could get more wheat, more shirts, or both, just by using all available workers. For instance, in Figure 2-4, the United States can get more wheat without giving up any shirts, by moving from point B_1 to point B_2. It can do the same by moving from point B_2 to B_3.

efficient points
combinations of production possibilities that squeeze the most output possible from all available resources

But once at the frontier, the United States will have to give up some of one good to get more of the other. Points like B_3 that lie *on* the frontier are called **efficient** because they squeeze the most output possible from all available resources. Points *within* (inside) the frontier are *inefficient* because they do not use all available resources.

In the real world, economies aren't always efficient. A variety of problems can cause some workers to be unemployed or other resources to be left idle. We'll return to these issues in detail in future chapters. For now, we'll assume that production is always efficient. People and firms usually try to squeeze as much value as they can out of the resources available to them, so efficiency is a reasonable starting assumption.

FIGURE 2-4

Choosing an efficient production combination

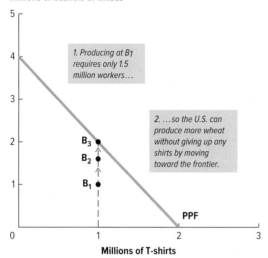

The United States needs only 1.5 million workers to reach point B_1. If the country employs more workers, it can reach point B_2 and get more wheat without giving up any shirts. The country can keep employing more workers until it reaches point B_3 (or any other point on the frontier) and there are no more workers left. Once the frontier is reached, getting more of one good requires giving up some of the other.

FIGURE 2-5

Choosing between efficient combinations

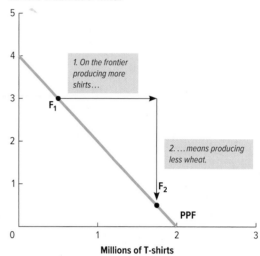

At all points on the production possibilities frontier, the United States employs the entire workforce. Because the country uses all its resources fully at each point, choosing between points on the frontier is a matter of preference when there is no trade with other countries. The United States may choose to produce more wheat and fewer shirts (point F_1) or more shirts and less wheat (point F_2), depending on what its consumers want.

Based on the assumption of efficiency, we can predict that an economy will choose to produce at a point *on* the frontier rather than inside it. What the production possibilities frontier cannot tell us is *which* point on the frontier that will be. Will it be F_1 in Figure 2-5, for example? Or will the United States choose to move down the curve to F_2, producing more shirts at the expense of less wheat? We can't say whether point F_1 or F_2 is better without knowing more about the situation. If the U.S. economy is completely self-sufficient, the decision depends on what combination of shirts and wheat people in the United States want to consume. If trade with other countries is possible, it also depends on consumers and production possibilities in those countries, as we'll see later in the chapter.

Shifting the production possibilities frontier

Thus far, we've built a simple model that tells us what combinations of T-shirts and wheat the United States could produce in 1800. However, a lot of things have changed since 1800, including incredible improvements in technology that improve production possibilities. The production possibilities frontier is a useful tool for illustrating this change and understanding how it affects the constraints and trade-offs the country faces. Two main factors drive the change in U.S. production possibilities: the number of workers and changes in technology.

First, there are more workers. The U.S. population now is about 60 times larger than it was in 1800. Having more workers means more people available to produce shirts and wheat. Graphically, we can represent this change by shifting the entire frontier outward. Panel A of Figure 2-6 shows what happens to the frontier when the U.S. population doubles, with each worker still able to produce 1 shirt or 2 bushels of wheat per day.

FIGURE 2-6

Shifting the production possibilities frontier

(A) Change in resources: Population growth

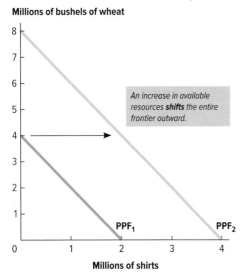

Millions of bushels of wheat

*An increase in available resources **shifts** the entire frontier outward.*

(B) Change in technology: Invention of the power loom

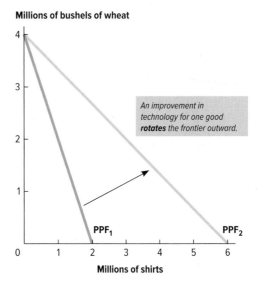

Millions of bushels of wheat

*An improvement in technology for one good **rotates** the frontier outward.*

Production possibilities expand when resources increase. If the working population grows, the country can make more of everything by producing at the same rate as before. *This causes the frontier to shift outward.* If the population doubled, so would the maximum possible quantities of shirts and wheat.

Production possibilities expand when technology improves. If the textile industry adopts the power loom, workers can make more shirts in the same amount of time. *This causes the frontier to rotate outward.* The rate of wheat production remains constant while the rate of shirt production increases, so the slope of the frontier changes.

The real magic of expanded productive capacity lies in the incredible technological advances that have taken place. In 1810, a businessman from Boston named Francis Cabot Lowell traveled to England to learn about British textile factories and to copy their superior technology. He brought back the power loom, which enabled workers to weave much more cotton fabric every day than they could before.[1]

We can model this change in technology through the production possibilities frontier by changing the rate of shirt production from 1 to 3 shirts per day, as shown in panel B of Figure 2-6. As the rate of shirt production increases, while the rate of wheat production remains the same, the shape of the curve changes. In this case, it pivots outward along the *x*-axis: This pivot indicates that for any given number of workers assigned to shirt-making, more shirts are produced than before. At every point except one (where all workers are producing wheat), the country can produce more with the same number of workers, thanks to improved technology.

> For a refresher about shifts and pivots in graphs, see Appendix B, "Math Essentials: Working with Linear Equations," which follows Chapter 3, "Markets."

✓CONCEPT CHECK

☐ Could a person or country ever produce a combination of goods that lies outside the production possibilities frontier? Why or why not? **[LO 2.1]**

☐ Would an increase in productivity as a result of a new technology shift a production possibilities frontier inward or outward? **[LO 2.1]**

Absolute and Comparative Advantage

In 1810, armed with power looms and a growing population, the United States was a highly effective producer of cotton shirts. For more than a century, it was the world's biggest clothing manufacturer. Since then, the U.S. population has grown larger, and manufacturing technology has improved even more. So, why do less than 5 percent of global clothing exports come from the United States?[2]

Up to now, we have worked with a very simple model of production to highlight the key trade-offs faced by individual producers. If there is no trade between countries, then the United States can consume only those goods that it produces on its own. In the real world, however, goods are made all over the world. If Americans want to buy more shirts than the United States produces, they can get them from somewhere else. Under these conditions, how can we predict which countries will produce which goods?

Understanding how resources are allocated among multiple producers is a step toward understanding why big firms work with specialized suppliers. It also helps explain why a wealthy, productive country like the United States trades with much poorer, less-productive countries. In this section we will see that trade actually increases total production, which can benefit everyone involved. To see why, let's turn to the question of why many T-shirts sold in the United States today are made in Bangladesh.

Absolute advantage

LO 2.2 Define absolute and comparative advantage.

Suppose that taking into account all the improvements in shirt-making and wheat-growing technology since 1800, an American worker can now make 50 shirts or grow 200 bushels of wheat per day.[3] A Bangladeshi worker, in comparison, can produce 25 shirts or 50 bushels of wheat. (Why the differences? Perhaps U.S. workers use faster cloth-cutting technology, or maybe because U.S. farmers use fertilizers, pesticides, and irrigation systems that farmers in Bangladesh don't.) In other words, given the same number of workers, the United States can produce twice as many shirts or four times as much wheat as Bangladesh.

If a producer can generate more output than others with a given amount of resources, that producer has an **absolute advantage**. In our simplified model, the United States has an absolute advantage over Bangladesh at producing both shirts and wheat because it can make more of both products than Bangladesh can per worker.

absolute advantage
the ability to produce more of a good or service than others can with a given amount of resources

Comparative advantage

Absolute advantage is not the end of the story, though. If it were, the United States would still be producing the world's shirts. The problem is that for every T-shirt the United States produces, it uses resources that could otherwise be spent growing wheat. Of course, the same could be said of Bangladesh. But in our model of T-shirt and wheat production, the opportunity cost of making 1 shirt in the United States is 4 bushels of wheat (200 bushels ÷ 50 shirts = 4 bushels per shirt). The opportunity cost of making 1 shirt in Bangladesh is only 2 bushels of wheat (50 bushels ÷ 25 shirts = 2 bushels per shirt). The United States has to give up more to make a shirt than Bangladesh does.

When a producer can make a good at a lower opportunity cost than other producers, we say it has a **comparative advantage** at producing that good. In our model, Bangladesh has a comparative advantage over the United States at shirt-making: Its opportunity cost of producing a shirt is only 2 bushels of wheat, compared to 4 bushels of wheat for the United States.

The United States, on the other hand, has a comparative advantage over Bangladesh at producing wheat: Each time the United States produces a bushel of wheat, it gives up the opportunity to

comparative advantage
the ability to produce a good or service at a lower opportunity cost than others

produce one-quarter of a shirt (50 shirts ÷ 200 bushels $= \frac{1}{4}$ shirt per bushel). For Bangladesh, however, the opportunity cost of producing a bushel of wheat is larger: it's one-half of a shirt (25 shirts ÷ 50 bushels $= \frac{1}{2}$ shirt per bushel). The United States has a lower opportunity cost for producing wheat than Bangladesh ($\frac{1}{4}$ shirt is less than $\frac{1}{2}$ shirt). Therefore, we say the United States has a comparative advantage over Bangladesh at wheat production.

A country can have a comparative advantage without having an absolute advantage. In our scenario, the United States has an absolute advantage over Bangladesh at producing both shirts and wheat, but it has a bigger advantage at producing wheat than at making shirts. It can make four times as much wheat per worker as Bangladesh (200 versus 50 bushels) but only twice as many shirts per worker (50 versus 25). It's better at both—but it's "more better," so to speak, at producing wheat. (We know that "more better" is not good grammar, but it nicely expresses the idea.) Likewise, Bangladesh has a comparative advantage at the good it is "less worse" at (producing shirts), even though it does not have an absolute advantage at either compared to the United States.

You may have noticed that for each country, the opportunity cost of growing wheat is the *inverse* of the opportunity cost of producing shirts. (For the United States, $\frac{1}{4}$ is the inverse of 4; for Bangladesh, $\frac{1}{2}$ is the inverse of 2.) Mathematically, this means that it is impossible for one country to have a comparative advantage at producing both goods. Each producer's opportunity cost depends on its *relative* ability at producing different goods. Logic tells us that you can't be better at A than at B and also better at B than at A. (And mathematically, if X is bigger than Y, then $\frac{1}{X}$ will be smaller than $\frac{1}{Y}$.) The United States can't be better at producing wheat than shirts relative to Bangladesh and at the same time be better at producing shirts than wheat relative to Bangladesh. As a result, no producer has a comparative advantage at everything, and each producer has a comparative advantage at something.

We can check this international trade scenario against an example closer to home. When your family makes Thanksgiving dinner, does the best cook make everything? If you have a small family, maybe one person *can* make the whole dinner. But if your family is anything like our families, you will need several cooks. Grandma is by far the most experienced cook, yet the potato peeling always gets outsourced to the kids. Is that because the grandchildren are better potato peelers than Grandma? We think that's probably not the case. Grandma has an absolute advantage at everything having to do with Thanksgiving dinner. Still, the kids may have a *comparative* advantage at potato peeling, which frees up Grandma to make those tricky pie crusts.

We can find applications of comparative advantage everywhere in life. Sports is no exception. Look at the From Another Angle box "Babe Ruth, star pitcher" for another example.

From Another Angle
Babe Ruth, star pitcher

How should baseball managers decide who should play at different positions? One approach is to assign the best player to each position. But the skills required for many positions are similar. What does a manager do when one player has an absolute advantage at multiple positions? One answer is to turn to comparative advantage.

Consider the choice that New York Yankees manager Miller Huggins faced when he acquired a player named Babe Ruth in 1920. Ruth was an excellent pitcher. In 1918 he had set a record for the most consecutive scoreless innings pitched in the World Series—a record that was not broken until 1961. He could easily have become one of the best pitchers of his generation. But Ruth didn't end up as a pitcher. Babe Ruth was both the best pitcher *and* the best hitter on the team. From a practical point of view, he couldn't do both (pitching takes too much energy), so Miller Huggins had to make a choice.

Although Ruth had an *absolute* advantage at both positions, he had a *comparative* advantage as a hitter. The opportunity cost of having Ruth pitch was the number of games the Yankees would win by having him bat. Huggins decided the opportunity cost of Ruth's pitching was higher than the opportunity cost of his batting. Ruth went on to become one of the greatest hitters of all time. In 1920 he hit 54 home runs. That year, only one other *team* collectively hit as many home runs as Ruth *alone* did.

A good manager should, as Miller Huggins did, assign players to positions according to their comparative advantage. The question is not which player is best at a particular position, but which player the team can most afford to lose at any other position. For a player seeking to play a particular position, the right argument may be not that he or she is the best at that position, but that he or she is worth less at any other!

Source: 2016 Family of Babe Ruth and Babe Ruth League c/o Luminary Group LLC.

✓ CONCEPT CHECK

☐ What does it mean to have an absolute advantage at producing a good? **[LO 2.2]**

☐ What does it mean to have a comparative advantage at producing a good? **[LO 2.2]**

☐ Can more than one producer have an absolute advantage at producing the same good? Why or why not? **[LO 2.2]**

Why Trade?

The United States is perfectly capable of producing its own shirts and its own wheat. In fact, in our simple model, it has an absolute advantage at producing both goods. So, why buy shirts from Bangladesh? We are about to see that both countries are actually able to consume more when they specialize in producing the good for which they have a comparative advantage and then trade with one another.

Specialization

LO 2.3 Explain why people specialize.

If you lived 200 years ago, your everyday life would have been full of tasks that probably never even cross your mind today. You might have milked a cow, hauled water from a well, split wood, cured meat, mended a hole in a sock, and repaired a roof.

Contrast that with life today. Almost everything we use comes from someone who specializes in providing a particular good or service. We bet you don't churn the butter you put on your toast. You probably wouldn't begin to know how to construct the parts in your smartphone. We are guessing you don't usually sew your own clothes or grow your own wheat. In today's world, all of us are dependent on one another for the things we need on a daily basis.

In our model, when the United States and Bangladesh work in isolation, each produces some shirts and some wheat—each in the combinations that its consumers prefer. Suppose the United States has 150 million workers and Bangladesh has 80 million. As before,

- each U.S. worker can make 50 shirts or 200 bushels of wheat and
- each Bangladeshi worker can make 25 shirts or 50 bushels of wheat.

TABLE 2-1

Production with and without specialization

When Bangladesh and the United States each specializes in the production of one good, the two countries can produce an extra 0.5 billion T-shirts and 1 billion bushels of wheat using the same number of workers and the same technology.

	Country	Wheat (billions of bushels)	T-shirts (billions)
Without specialization	United States	26	1
	Bangladesh	3	0.5
	Total	**29**	**1.5**
With specialization	United States	30	0
	Bangladesh	0	2
	Total	**30**	**2**

Now, suppose these production combinations occur:

- Based on U.S. consumers' preferences, U.S. workers are split so that they produce 1 billion shirts and 26 billion bushels of wheat.
- In Bangladesh, workers are allocated to produce 0.5 billion shirts and 3 billion bushels of wheat.

Even though Bangladesh's productivity per worker is lower, it has a large number of workers and so is able to produce a large total quantity of goods. (The quantities of shirts and wheat are unrealistically large because we are assuming they are the only goods being produced. In reality, of course, countries produce many different goods, but this simplifying assumption helps us to zero in on a real-world truth.)

We have seen that if the United States and Bangladesh are self-sufficient (each producing what its people want to consume), then together the two countries can make 1.5 billion T-shirts and 29 billion bushels of wheat, as shown at the top of Table 2-1 ("without specialization"). What would happen if, instead, Bangladesh put all its resources into making shirts and the United States put all its resources into producing wheat?

specialization
spending all of your time producing a particular good

If each country focuses on producing the good for which it has a comparative advantage, total production increases. Focusing in this way is called **specialization**. It's the practice of spending all of your resources producing a particular good. When each country specializes in making a particular good according to its comparative advantage, total production possibilities are greater than if each produced the exact combination of goods its own consumers want.

The bottom section of Table 2-1 ("with specialization") shows us:

United States

$$200 \text{ bushels per worker} \times 150 \text{ million workers} = 30 \text{ billion bushels}$$

Bangladesh

$$25 \text{ shirts per worker} \times 80 \text{ million workers} = 2 \text{ billion shirts}$$

By specializing, the two countries together can produce 1 billion bushels of wheat more than before, *plus* 0.5 billion more shirts. Specialization increases total production, using the same number of workers and the same technology.

This rule applies to all sorts of goods and services. It explains why dentists hire roofers to fix a roof leak and why roofers hire dentists to fill a cavity. See the Real Life box "Specialization sauce" for an example of the power of specialization in a setting you are probably somewhat familiar with—McDonald's.

Real Life

Specialization sauce

Henry Ford pioneered the assembly-line method of automobile manufacturing: Each worker does just one small task on each car before it moves down the line to the next worker, who does a different small task. Ford proved that he could build more cars in less time when each employee specialized in this way. Restaurants use the same principle: They can serve more customers faster if they split the work among managers, waitstaff, and chefs. Fast-food restaurants take specialization even further.

Fast food as we know it was born in 1948, when McDonald's founders Dick and Mac McDonald decided to implement a radically new method of preparing food. Inspired by factory assembly lines, they applied Ford's concept of specialization to the restaurant business. Instead of assigning several employees to general food preparation, they split each order into parts, parceling out the steps required to prepare a meal. One employee became the grilling specialist; another added mustard and ketchup. A different employee operated the potato fryer, and yet another mixed the milkshakes.

Any single employee would almost certainly have been able to learn how to grill a hamburger, add condiments, make fries, *and* mix a milkshake. In each restaurant, one particularly skilled employee was probably faster than everyone else at all the steps in making a meal.

Even so, specialization was more efficient. By assigning only one specific task to each employee, the founders of McDonald's revolutionized the speed and quantity of food preparation. Harnessing the power of specialization allowed them to grill more burgers, fry more potatoes, and feed more hungry customers.

Source: Eric Schlosser, *Fast Food Nation* (Boston: Houghton Mifflin, 2002), pp. 19–20.

Gains from trade

LO 2.4 Explain how the gains from trade follow from comparative advantage.

When countries specialize in producing the goods for which they have a comparative advantage, total production increases. The problem with specialization is that each producer ends up with only one good—in our model, wheat in the United States, T-shirts in Bangladesh. If Americans want to wear T-shirts and Bangladeshis want to enjoy wheat, they must trade.

Suppose that Bangladesh and the United States agree to trade 3.5 billion bushels of wheat for 1.5 billion T-shirts. As a result, each country ends up with an additional 0.5 billion bushels of wheat, and the United States also has 0.5 billion more shirts than before. The improvement in outcomes that occurs when specialized producers exchange goods and services is called the **gains from trade**.

gains from trade
the improvement in outcomes that occurs when producers specialize and exchange goods and services

Figure 2-7 shows how the gains from trade affect a country's consumption. Before the trade, it was impossible for the United States and Bangladesh to consume any combination of goods outside their production possibilities frontiers. After the trade between the two specialized producers, each country's consumption increases to a point that was previously unachievable. If Bangladesh consumes the same amount of shirts as before and trades the remaining, both countries are able to consume 0.5 billion bushels more wheat after opening up to trade.

In Figure 2-7, the gains from the U.S.–Bangladesh trade are distributed equally: 0.5 billion bushels more wheat for the United States and 0.5 billion bushels more wheat for Bangladesh. In reality, the distribution can vary. The gains do not have to be equal for the trading arrangement to benefit everyone. If Bangladesh takes an extra 0.25 billion bushels of wheat and the United States an extra 0.75 billion (or vice versa), both countries will still be better off than if they worked alone.

FIGURE 2-7
Specialization and gains from trade

(A) United States' gains from trade

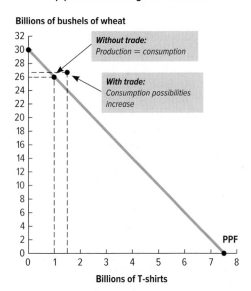

Without trade:
Production = consumption

With trade:
Consumption possibilities
increase

If a country does not specialize and trade, its production and consumption are both limited to points along its production possibilities frontier. By specializing and achieving gains from trading, the United States gains 0.5 million T-shirts and 0.5 billion bushels of wheat.

(B) Bangladesh's gains from trade

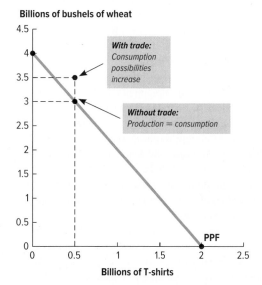

With trade:
Consumption
possibilities
increase

Without trade:
Production = consumption

By opening up to trade, Bangladesh also gains 0.5 billion bushels of wheat compared to what it could produce on its production possibilities frontier.

18 Overall, there is room for trade as long as two things occur: (1) the two countries differ in their opportunity costs to produce a good and (2) they set a favorable trading price. A favorable trading price needs to benefit both parties. If T-shirts from Bangladesh are too expensive, the United States will refuse to buy them. Similarly, if U.S. wheat is too expensive, Bangladesh will not buy it. If the United States agrees to trade 3.5 billion bushels of wheat for 1.5 billion T-shirts, it must be because the United States values 3.5 billion bushels of wheat less than 1.5 billion T-shirts.

To see how much each country values a good, we must look at its opportunity costs. Recall that the opportunity cost of 1 T-shirt for Bangladesh is 2 bushels of wheat. In other words, the value of 1 T-shirt for Bangladesh is at least 2 bushels of wheat. If the United States offered to trade 1 bushel of wheat in exchange for 1 T-shirt, Bangladesh would refuse such a trade; Bangladesh could simply produce the wheat itself. Bangladesh needs to receive at least 2 bushels of wheat in exchange for 1 T-shirt.

To see how many bushels of wheat the United States is willing to give up in exchange for 1 T-shirt, we can look at the United States' opportunity cost. The opportunity cost of 1 T-shirt for the United States is 4 bushels of wheat. Thus, the United States will only trade up to 4 bushels of wheat in exchange for 1 T-shirt. More than 4 bushels of wheat would be worth more than 1 T-shirt. If Bangladesh tries to charge a price greater than the United States' opportunity cost, the United States will choose to make the T-shirts itself. In order for trade to benefit both countries, the trade price of 1 T-shirt must be at least 2 bushels of wheat but less than 4 bushels of wheat.

In general, two countries will benefit from a trade price that falls between their opportunity costs. In our example, the price at which Bangladesh and the United States are willing to trade T-shirts must fall between Bangladesh's opportunity cost for producing T-shirts and the

United States' opportunity cost for producing T-shirts. If Bangladesh is the country that has specialized in T-shirts, it cannot charge a price greater than the United States' opportunity cost. If it does, the United States will simply make the T-shirts itself. Conversely, Bangladesh must receive a price that covers its opportunity costs for making T-shirts or it will not be willing to trade.

Consider the *wants* that drive people to trade. When people specialize and trade, everyone gets more of the things they want than they would if they were self-sufficient. Thus, trade can be driven entirely by self-interest. Just as the United States benefits from trading with Bangladesh (even though the United States may have an absolute advantage at producing both wheat and shirts), an experienced worker or large firm benefits from trading with a less-experienced employee or a small, specialized company.

For example, when Bill Gates was the CEO of Microsoft, he hired recent college graduates to fix bugs in the computer code, even though he might have done it faster himself. Let's say Bill can fix the bug in an hour, but for every hour he's distracted from running Microsoft, the company's profits go down by $1,000. The less-experienced coder earns only $50 an hour, so even if she takes two to three times as long to do the work, it's still worth it for Bill to hire her and spend his own time keeping Microsoft's productivity up. Bill has an absolute advantage at fixing computer bugs, but the opportunity cost in lost profits means the younger coder has a comparative advantage. (Bill's comparative advantage is at running Microsoft.) Everyone ends up better off if they specialize.

In spite of the gains from specializing and trading, not everyone considers this an obvious choice in every circumstance—which brings us to our fourth question from Chapter 1, "Economics and Life": *Why isn't someone already doing it?* In the case of trade, we know that many *are* already doing it. However, some people argue that it's worth giving up the gains from trade for various reasons. For some examples, see the What Do You Think? box "Is self-sufficiency a virtue?"

What Do You Think?
Is self-sufficiency a virtue?

Why should the United States trade with other countries? If every other country in the world were to disappear tomorrow, the United States would probably manage to fend for itself. It has plenty of fertile land, natural resources, workers, and manufacturing capacity. In fact, many observers consider the value Americans place on self-sufficiency to be a cultural trait.

Based on what you now know about specialization and the gains from trade, what do you think about the value of exchange versus the value of self-sufficiency? Economists tend to line up in favor of free international trade; they argue that trade makes both countries economically better off. Serious and worthwhile arguments have also been made on the other side. The following are some reasons that have been proposed for developing national self-sufficiency. When thinking through these questions, remember the answer is rarely simple.

- **National heritage.** Many people feel that a line has been crossed when a country loses its family farms or outsources a historically important industry—for example, auto-making in the United States. Does a country lose its culture when it loses these industries and shifts into other industries instead?
- **Security.** Some people worry that trade weakens a country if it then has to rely on trade for critical goods. If foreign relations sour, wars can result. Is it safe to rely on other countries for your food supply, or does that kind of dependency pose a security risk? For example, what can happen to national security if we rely on other countries entirely for steel or uranium or oil?
- **Quality control and ethics.** When goods are imported from other countries, production standards are harder to control than if the goods are made at home. Some people argue that

(continued)

international trade undermines consumer safety and environmental regulations. Others also say that international trade fosters labor conditions that would be considered unethical or illegal in the United States.

WHAT DO YOU THINK?

1. Do you agree with any of these objections to free trade? Why? When is self-sufficiency more valuable than the gains from trade?
2. Is the choice between trade and self-sufficiency an *either/or* question? Is there a middle-of-the-road approach that would address concerns on both sides of this issue?

Comparative advantage over time

Our simplified model of production possibilities and trade helps us to understand why Americans now buy shirts from other countries. But we noted at the beginning of the chapter that this wasn't always the case: 200 years ago, the United States was selling shirts to the rest of the world. To understand this change, we can apply our model to shifts in comparative advantage over time. These shifts have caused significant changes in different countries' economies and trade patterns.

When the Industrial Revolution began, Great Britain led the world in clothing manufacturing. In the nineteenth century, the United States snatched the comparative advantage through a combination of new technology (which led to higher productivity) and cheap labor (which led to lower production costs). Gradually, the comparative advantage in clothing shifted away from the United States to other countries. Clothing manufacturing moved from country to country, searching for ever-lower costs:

- By the 1930s, 40 percent of the world's cotton goods were made in Japan, where workers from the countryside were willing to work long hours for low wages.
- In the mid-1970s, clothing manufacturing moved to Hong Kong, Taiwan, and Korea, where wages were even lower than those in Japan.
- The textile industry then moved to China in the early 1990s, when millions of young women left their farms to work for wages as much as 90 percent lower than those in Hong Kong. Similar changes happened in Bangladesh.

There's an upside to the progressive relocation of this industry and its jobs: Eventually high-wage jobs replaced low-wage jobs, and these countries experienced considerable economic growth.

Losing a comparative advantage in clothing production sounds like a bad thing at first. But as we know from our model, you can't lose comparative advantage in one thing without gaining it in another. Changes in clothing manufacturing were driven by workers in each country getting more skilled at industries that paid better than making clothes—such as making cars, or programming computers, or providing financial services. This meant the opportunity cost of making clothes increased. The comparative advantage in clothing production shifted to countries where the workers lacked skills in better-paying industries and so were willing to work in textile factories for lower wages.

Most historians would agree that it wasn't a sign of failure when countries lost their comparative advantage in clothing production—it was a sign of success. Former textile producers like Great Britain, the United States, Japan, Korea, and Hong Kong are all much wealthier now than they were when they were centers of clothing manufacturing.

However, these changes probably didn't look or feel like success at the time, especially for workers in textile factories who saw their jobs disappearing overseas. This same tension is arising today in other industries as companies "outsource" tasks that can be done more cheaply in other countries.

✓ CONCEPT CHECK

☐ Why do people or countries specialize? **[LO 2.3]**

☐ How do two countries benefit from trading with each other? **[LO 2.4]**

☐ Is it possible to not have a comparative advantage at anything? Why or why not? **[LO 2.4]**

Conclusion

Specialization and trade can make everyone better off. It is not surprising, then, that in an economy driven by individuals seeking to make a profit or improve their communities, people specialize so as to exploit their comparative advantages. That principle is as true for countries, like the United States and Bangladesh, as it is for individuals picking their careers.

No government intervention is required to coordinate production. The great economic thinker Adam Smith suggested the term *invisible hand* to describe this coordinating mechanism:

> It is not from the benevolence of the butcher, the brewer, or the baker that we expect our dinner, but from their regard to their [self-interest]. . . . he intends only his own gain, and he is in this, as in many other cases, led by an invisible hand to promote an end which was no part of his intention.[4]

The functioning of the invisible hand depends on a lot of other assumptions, such as free competition and full information. Later in the book we will discuss these assumptions, and when they work and when they do not.

Most people take for granted the prevalence of specialization and trade in their everyday lives. Few stop to think about the benefits and where they come from. In this chapter we tried to dig down to the bottom of the assumptions people make and expose the logic behind the gains from trade. As we proceed—especially when we return to topics like international trade and government intervention in the markets—try to remember the underlying incentive that drives people to interact with one another in economic exchanges.

Key Terms

production possibilities frontier (PPF), p. 27

efficient points, p. 30

absolute advantage, p. 33

comparative advantage, p. 33

specialization, p. 36

gains from trade, p. 37

Summary

LO 2.1 Construct a production possibilities graph and describe what causes shifts in production possibilities curves.

A production possibilities graph shows all the combinations of two goods that a person or an economy can produce with a given amount of time, resources, and technology. The production possibilities frontier is a line on that graph that shows all the maximum attainable combinations of goods. Producers of goods and services are not likely to choose a combination of goods inside the production possibilities frontier because they could achieve a higher production level with the same amount of resources. They cannot choose points outside the frontier, which would require more than the available resources. The choice between combinations on the production possibilities frontier is a matter of preference.

Shifts in the production possibilities frontier can be caused by changes in technology, as well as changes in population and other resources. Increases in technological capabilities and population will shift the PPF outward; decreases in these factors will shift the PPF inward.

> **LO 2.2** Define absolute and comparative advantage.

Producers have an absolute advantage at making a good when they can produce more output than others with a given amount of resources. If you put two people or countries to work making the same good, the person or country that is more productive has an absolute advantage.

People or countries have a comparative advantage when they are better at producing one good than they are at producing other goods, relative to other producers. Everyone has a comparative advantage at something, whether or not they have an absolute advantage at anything.

> **LO 2.3** Explain why people specialize.

Specialization means spending all or much of your time producing a particular good. Production is highest when people or countries specialize in producing the good for which they have a comparative advantage. Specialization increases total production, using the same number of workers and the same technology.

> **LO 2.4** Explain how the gains from trade follow from comparative advantage.

The increase in total production that occurs from specialization and exchange is called the gains from trade. With specialization and trade, two parties can increase production and consumption, and each ends up better off.

Shifts in comparative advantage over time have caused significant changes in different countries' economies and trade patterns. These changes signal general economic success, although they can be painful for the individual workers and industries involved.

Review Questions

1. You've been put in charge of a bake sale for a local charity, at which you are planning to sell cookies and cupcakes. What would a production possibilities graph of this situation show? **[LO 2.1]**

2. You manage two employees at a pet salon. Your employees perform two tasks, giving flea baths and grooming animals. If you constructed a single production possibilities frontier for flea baths and grooming that combined both of your employees' work efforts, would you expect the production possibilities

frontier to be linear (a straight line)? Explain why or why not. **[LO 2.1]**

3. You and another volunteer are in charge of a bake sale for a local charity, at which you are planning to sell cookies and cupcakes. What would it mean for one of you to have an absolute advantage at baking cookies or cupcakes? Could one of you have an absolute advantage at baking both items? **[LO 2.2]**

4. You and another volunteer are in charge of a bake sale for a local charity, at which you are planning to sell cookies and cupcakes. What would it mean for you or the other volunteer to have a comparative advantage at baking cookies or cupcakes? Could one of you have a comparative advantage at baking both items? **[LO 2.2]**

5. You and another volunteer are in charge of a bake sale for a local charity, at which you are planning to sell cookies and cupcakes. Suppose you have a comparative advantage at baking cookies, and the other volunteer has a comparative advantage at baking cupcakes. Make a proposal to the volunteer about how to split up the baking. Explain how you can both gain from specializing, and why. **[LO 2.3]**

6. At the flower shop, where you manage two employees, your employees perform two tasks: caring for the displays of cut flowers and making flower arrangements to fill customer orders. Explain how you would approach organizing your employees and assigning them tasks. **[LO 2.3]**

7. Suppose two countries produce the same two goods and have identical production possibilities frontiers. Do you expect these countries to trade? Explain why or why not. **[LO 2.4]**

8. Brazil is the largest coffee producer in the world, and coffee is one of Brazil's major export goods. Suppose that in 20 years, Brazil no longer produces much coffee and imports most of its coffee instead. Explain why Brazil might change its trade pattern over time. **[LO 2.4]**

Problems and Applications

1. Your friend Sam has been asked to prepare appetizers for a university reception during homecoming weekend. She has an unlimited amount of ingredients but only six hours to prepare them. Sam can make 300 mini-sandwiches or 150 servings of melon slices topped with smoked salmon and a dab of sauce per hour. **[LO 2.1]**

   a. Draw Sam's production possibilities frontier.

   b. Now suppose that the university decides to postpone the reception until after the big game, so

Sam has an extra four hours to prepare. Redraw her production possibilities frontier to show the impact of this increase in resources.

c. Now, in addition to the extra time to prepare, suppose Sam's friend Chris helps by preparing the melon slices. Sam can now make 300 mini-sandwiches or 300 melon appetizers per hour. Redraw Sam's production possibilities frontier to show the impact of increased productivity in making melon appetizers.

2. Your friend Sam has been asked to prepare appetizers for the university reception. She has an unlimited amount of ingredients and six hours in which to prepare them. Sam can make 300 mini-sandwiches or 150 servings of melon slices topped with smoked salmon and a dab of sauce per hour. **[LO 2.1]**

   a. What is Sam's opportunity cost of making one mini-sandwich?

   b. What is Sam's opportunity cost of making one melon appetizer?

   c. Suppose the reception has been postponed, so Sam has an extra four hours to prepare. What is the opportunity cost of making one mini-sandwich now?

   d. Suppose the reception has been postponed, so Sam has an extra four hours to prepare. What is the opportunity cost of making one melon appetizer now?

   e. Suppose Sam's friend Chris helps by preparing the melon slices, increasing Sam's productivity to 300 mini-sandwiches or 300 melon appetizers per hour. What is the opportunity cost of making one mini-sandwich now?

   f. Suppose Sam's friend Chris helps by preparing the melon slices, increasing Sam's productivity to 300 mini-sandwiches or 300 melon appetizers per hour. What is the opportunity cost of making one melon appetizer now?

3. Suppose that Canada produces two goods: lumber and fish. It has 18 million workers, each of whom can cut 10 feet of lumber or catch 20 fish each day. **[LO 2.1]**

   a. What is the maximum amount of lumber Canada could produce in a day?

   b. What is the maximum amount of fish it could produce in a day?

   c. Draw Canada's production possibilities frontier.

   d. Use your graph to determine how many fish can be caught if 60 million feet of lumber are cut.

FIGURE 2P-1

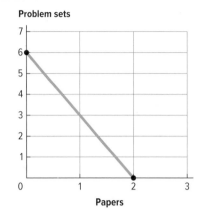

Problem sets

4. The graph in Figure 2P-1 shows Tanya's weekly production possibilities frontier for doing homework (writing papers and doing problem sets). **[LO 2.1]**

   a. What is the slope of the production possibilities frontier?

   b. What is the opportunity cost of doing one problem set?

   c. What is the opportunity cost of writing one paper?

5. Use the production possibilities frontier in Figure 2P-2 to answer the following questions. **[LO 2.1]**

   a. What is the slope of the PPF between point A and point B?

   b. What is the slope of the PPF between point B and point C?

   c. Is the opportunity cost of producing hammers higher between points A and B or between points B and C?

FIGURE 2P-2

Screwdrivers

20

15 A

10   B

5

0   1   2   3

        C

Hammers

FIGURE 2P-3

FIGURE 2P-4

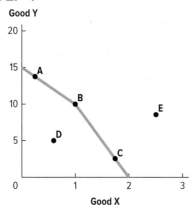

d. Is the opportunity cost of producing screwdrivers higher between points A and B or between points B and C?

6. For each point on the PPF in Figure 2P-3, note whether the point is attainable and efficient, attainable and inefficient, or unattainable. **[LO 2.1]**

7. For each point on the PPF in Figure 2P-4, note whether the point is attainable and efficient, attainable and inefficient, or unattainable. **[LO 2.1]**

8. The Red Cross and WIC (Women, Infants, and Children) program both provide emergency food packages and first-aid kits to New York City homeless shelters. Table 2P-1 shows their weekly production possibilities in providing emergency goods to NYC homeless shelters. NYC homeless shelters need a total of 20 first-aid kits per week. Currently, they get 10 kits from the Red Cross and 10 kits from WIC. With their remaining resources, how many food packages can each organization provide to NYC homeless shelters? **[LO 2.1]**

TABLE 2P-1

	Red Cross	WIC
Food packages	300	200
First-aid kits	50	20

9. Suppose that three volunteers are preparing cookies and cupcakes for a bake sale. Diana can make 27 cookies or 18 cupcakes per hour; Andy can make 25 cookies or 17 cupcakes; and Sam can make 10 cookies or 12 cupcakes. **[LO 2.2]**

a. Who has the absolute advantage at making cookies?

b. At making cupcakes?

10. Paula and Carlo are coworkers. Their production possibilities frontiers for counseling clients and writing memos are given in Figure 2P-5. **[LO 2.2]**

FIGURE 2P-5

a. Which worker has an absolute advantage in counseling clients?

b. Which worker has an absolute advantage in writing memos?

c. Which worker has a comparative advantage in counseling clients?

d. Which worker has a comparative advantage in writing memos?

11. Two students are assigned to work together on a project that requires both writing and an oral presentation. Steve can write 1 page or prepare 3 minutes of a presentation each day. Anna can write 2 pages or prepare 1 minute of a presentation each day. **[LO 2.2]**

a. Who has a comparative advantage at writing?

b. Suppose that Steve goes to a writing tutor and learns some tricks that enable him to write 3 pages each day. Now who has a comparative advantage at writing?

12. Suppose that the manager of a restaurant has two new employees, Rahul and Henriette, and is trying to decide which one to assign to which task. Rahul can chop 20 pounds of vegetables or wash 100 dishes per hour. Henriette can chop 30 pounds of vegetables or wash 120 dishes. **[LO 2.3]**

a. Who should be assigned to chop vegetables?

b. Who should be assigned to wash dishes?

13. The Dominican Republic and Nicaragua both produce coffee and rum. The Dominican Republic can produce 20 thousand tons of coffee per year or 10 thousand barrels of rum. Nicaragua can produce 30 thousand tons of coffee per year or 5 thousand barrels of rum. **[LO 2.3]**

a. Suppose the Dominican Republic and Nicaragua sign a trade agreement in which each country would specialize in the production of either coffee or rum. Which country should specialize in producing coffee? Which country should specialize in producing rum?

b. What are the minimum and maximum prices at which these countries will trade coffee?

14. Eleanor and her little sister Joanna are responsible for two chores on their family's farm, gathering eggs and collecting milk. Eleanor can gather 9 dozen eggs or collect 3 gallons of milk per week. Joanna can gather 2 dozen eggs or collect 2 gallons of milk per week. **[LO 2.3]**

a. The family wants 2 gallons of milk per week and as many eggs as the sisters can gather. Currently, Eleanor and Joanna collect one gallon of milk each and as many eggs as they can. How many dozens of eggs does the family have per week?

b. If the sisters specialized, which sister should collect the milk?

c. If the sisters specialized, how many dozens of eggs would the family have per week?

15. Suppose Russia and Sweden each produces only paper and cars. Russia can produce 8 tons of paper or 4 million cars each year. Sweden can produce 25 tons of paper or 5 million cars each year. **[LO 2.4]**

a. Draw the production possibilities frontier for each country.

b. Both countries want 2 million cars each year and as much paper as they can produce along with 2 million cars. Find this point on each production possibilities frontier and label it "A."

c. Suppose the countries specialize. Which country will produce cars?

d. Once they specialize, suppose they work out a trade of 2 million cars for 6 tons of paper. Find the new *consumption* point for each country and label it "B."

16. Maya and Max are neighbors. They both grow lettuce and tomatoes in their gardens. Maya can grow 45 heads of lettuce or 9 pounds of tomatoes this summer. Max can grow 42 heads of lettuce or 6 pounds of tomatoes this summer. If Maya and Max specialize and trade, the price of tomatoes (in terms of lettuce) would be as follows: 1 pound of tomatoes would cost between _____ and _____ pounds of lettuce. **[LO 2.4]**

Endnotes

1. http://www.encyclopedia.com/topic/Francis_Cabot_Lowell.aspx

2. http://www.economist.com/news/leaders/21646204-asias-dominance-manufacturing-will-endure-will-make-development-harder-others-made

3. http://www.agclassroom.org/gan/timeline/farm_tech.htm

4. Adam Smith, *An Inquiry into the Nature and Causes of the Wealth of Nations*, 1776.

Math Essentials: Understanding Graphs and Slope

Learning Objectives	
LO A.1	Create four quadrants using x- and y-axes and plot points on a graph.
LO A.2	Use data to calculate slope.
LO A.3	Interpret what the direction and steepness of slope indicate about a line.

Graphing is an essential component of economics. We touched on graphs in Chapter 2, "Specialization and Exchange," and we'll only see more graphs from here on out in the course. In order to truly understand the concepts of economics, you'll need to understand the basics of graphing. In this appendix, we'll discuss how to create and interpret different types of graphs.

Creating a Graph

LO A.1 Create four quadrants using x- and y-axes and plot points on a graph.

A graph is one way to visually represent data. In this book, we use graphs to describe and interpret economic relationships. For example, we use a graph called a production possibilities frontier to explore opportunity costs and trade-offs in production. We use graphs of average, variable, and marginal costs to explore production decisions facing a firm. And—the favorite of economists everywhere—we use graphs to show supply and demand and the resulting relationship between price and quantity.

Graphs of one variable

Graphs of a single variable come in three main forms: the bar chart, the pie chart, and the line graph. In school, you've probably made all three and plastered them on science-fair posters and presentations or used them in reports. These graphs are versatile; they can be used to present all sorts of information. Throughout economics, and in this book, you'll come across these graphs frequently.

Probably the most common single-variable graph is the *bar graph,* an example of which is shown in Figure A-1. The bar graph shows the size or frequency of a variable using bars—hence the name. The size of the bar on the y-axis shows the value of the variable, while the x-axis contains the categories of the variables. In Figure A-1, for example, the bar graph shows the number

FIGURE A-1

Top five news websites

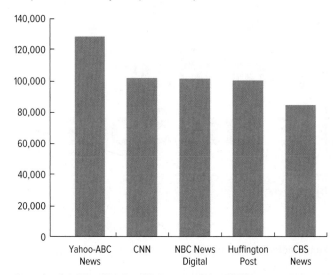

Unique visits for January 2015 (in thousands)

Source: http://www.journalism.org/media-indicators/digital-top-50-online-news-entities-2015/.

of visits received by five major news sites in the month of January 2015. Since the bars stack up next to each other, a bar graph makes it clear exactly where each news site stands in comparison to the others. As you can see, the larger bars for Yahoo-ABC News and CNN mean that these sites get more visits than CBS News.

In general, bar graphs are versatile. You can show the distribution of letter grades in a class or the average monthly high and low temperatures in your city. Any time the size of a variable is important, you are generally going to want to use a bar graph.

Pie charts are generally used to show how much of certain components make up a whole. Pie charts are usually a circle, cut into wedges that represent how much each makes up of the whole. Figure A-2 shows the sales of the 10 largest car manufacturers as a percentage of overall new-car sales (as of April 2016). The large wedges of General Motors and Ford show that these are large automakers compared to the small wedge representing Mercedes-Benz.

The most common use of pie charts is for budgeting. You'll often see government and business income and expenses broken down in a pie chart. Also, come election time, you'll see pie charts all over the news media, representing the percentage of votes in an election each candidate receives.

A final type of graph is called a *line* (or *time-series*) *graph.* This type of graph is helpful when you are trying to emphasize the trend of a single variable. In economics, the most common usage of line graphs is to show the value of a variable over time. Inflation rates, GDP, and government debt over decades are all prime candidates to be presented on a line graph.

Figure A-3 shows the GDP growth rate in Mexico since 1960 on a time-series graph. Presenting the data this way makes it clear that Mexico's GDP growth was strong during the 1960s and 70s (anything above 4 percent growth is very good), dipped below zero in 2009, and rose into positive territory in 2010 and beyond.

Ultimately, single-variable graphs can take us only so far. In order to get at some of the most fundamental issues of economics, we need to be able to plot the values of two variables (such as price and quantity) simultaneously.

FIGURE A-2

Automaker market share

This pie chart shows the relative market share of each automaker. The size of the wedge gives the share of each automaker. General Motors has a large wedge, while Mercedes-Benz has a much smaller share of the market.

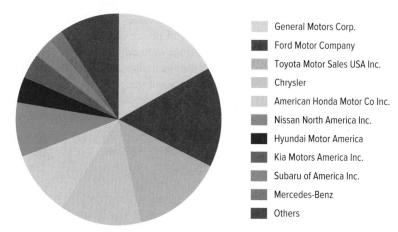

- General Motors Corp.
- Ford Motor Company
- Toyota Motor Sales USA Inc.
- Chrysler
- American Honda Motor Co Inc.
- Nissan North America Inc.
- Hyundai Motor America
- Kia Motors America Inc.
- Subaru of America Inc.
- Mercedes-Benz
- Others

Source: WSJ Markets Data Center, http://online.wsj.com/mdc/public/page/2_3022-autosales.html#autosalesE.

FIGURE A-3

GDP growth in Mexico

A line graph commonly shows a variable over a range of time. This allows the trend in the variable to be clear. In this case, you can see that GDP growth in Mexico has been highly variable, but overall, GDP growth was higher on average before 1980.

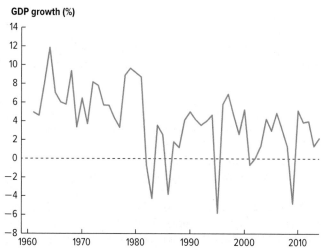

Source: World Bank World Development Indicators.

Graphs of two variables

In order to present two or more variables on a graph, we need something called the *Cartesian coordinate system.* With only two dimensions, this graphing system consists of two axes: the *x* (horizontal) axis and the *y* (vertical) axis. We can give these axes other names, depending on what economic variables we want to represent, such as price and quantity, or inputs and outputs.

In some cases, it doesn't matter which variable we put on each axis. At other times, logic or convention will determine the axes. There are two common conventions in economics that it will be useful for you to remember:

1. **Price on the *y*-axis, quantity on the *x*-axis:** When we graph the relationship between price and quantity in economics, price is always on the *y*-axis and quantity is always on the *x*-axis.
2. **The *x*-axis "causes" the *y*-axis:** In general, when the values of one variable are dependent on the values of the other variable, we put the "dependent" variable on the *y*-axis and the "independent" variable on the *x*-axis. For example, if we were exploring the relationship between test scores and the number of hours a student spends studying, we would place hours on the *x*-axis and test scores on the *y*-axis because hours spent studying affect scores, generally not vice versa. Sometimes, though, the opposite is true. In economics, we often say that price (always the *y*-axis variable) causes the quantity demanded of a good (the *x*-axis variable).

The point where the two axes intersect is called the *origin*. Points to the right of the origin have *x*-coordinates with positive values; points to the left of the origin have *x*-coordinates with negative values. Similarly, points above the origin have *y*-coordinates with positive values and points below the origin have *y*-coordinates with negative values.

To specify a particular point, indicate the *x*- and *y*-coordinates in an ordered pair. Indicate the *x*-coordinate first, and then the *y*-coordinate: (*x,y*). The intersection of the two axes creates four quadrants, as shown in Figure A-4.

Quadrant I: (*x,y*) The *x*- and *y*-coordinates are both positive.

Quadrant II: (−*x,y*) The *x*-coordinate is negative and the *y*-coordinate is positive.

Quadrant III: (−*x,*−*y*) The *x*- and *y*-coordinates are both negative.

Quadrant IV: (*x,*−*y*) The *x*-coordinate is positive and the *y*-coordinate is negative.

Origin: (0,0) The *x*- and *y*-coordinates are both zero at the origin.

FIGURE A-4

The four quadrants

The Cartesian coordinate system is a way to plot values of two variables simultaneously. Different quadrants reflect whether the values of *x* and *y* are positive or negative.

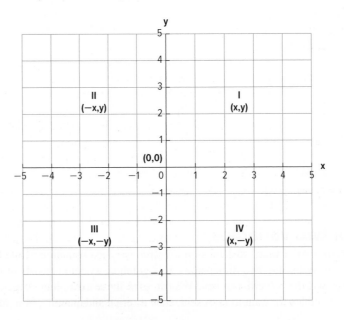

FIGURE A-5

Plotting points on a graph

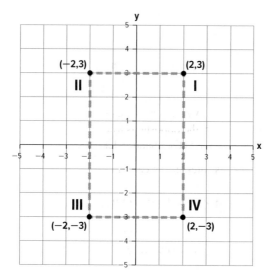

Each set of ordered pairs corresponds to a place
on the Cartesian coordinate system.

Figure A-5 shows the following points plotted on a graph.

Quadrant I: (2,3)

Quadrant II: (−2,3)

Quadrant III: (−2,−3)

Quadrant IV: (2,−3)

In economics, we often isolate quadrant I when graphing. This is because there are many economic variables for which negative values do not make sense. For example, one important graph we use in economics is the relationship between the price of a good and the quantity of that good demanded or supplied. Since it doesn't make sense to consider negative prices and quantities, we show only quadrant I when graphing supply and demand.

Figure A-6 shows a line in quadrant I that represents the relationship between the price of hot dogs at the ballpark and the quantity of hot dogs that a family wants to buy. Price is on the *y*-axis and the quantity of hot dogs the family demands is on the *x*-axis. For instance, one coordinate pair on this line is (3,2), meaning that if the price of hot dogs is $2, the family will want to buy 3 of them.

We could extend this demand curve in ways that make sense graphically but that don't represent logical price-quantity combinations in the real world. For instance, if we extend the demand curve into quadrant II, we have points such as (−2,7). If we extend the demand curve into quadrant IV, we have points such as (6,−1). However, it doesn't make sense to talk about someone demanding negative 2 hot dogs, nor does it make sense to think about a price of negative $1.

Remember that we are not just graphing arbitrary points. Rather, we are illustrating a real relationship between variables that has meaning in the real world. Both (−2,7) and (6,−1) are points that are consistent with the equation for this demand curve, but neither point makes sense to include in our analysis. For graphing this price-quantity relationship, we would limit our graph to quadrant I.

However, some variables you will study (such as revenue) may have negative values that make sense. When this is the case, graphs will show multiple quadrants.

FIGURE A-6

Thinking about the logic behind graphs

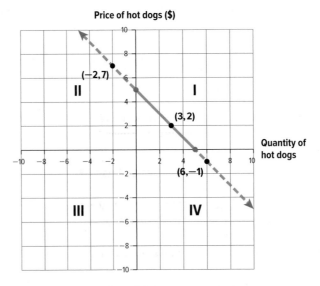

Plotting points in the four quadrants on a graph
gives a line.

Slope

Both the table and the graph in Figure A-7 represent a particular relationship between two variables, *x* and *y.* For every *x,* there is a corresponding *y.* When we plot the points in the table, we see that there is a consistent relationship between the value of *x* and the value of *y.* In this case, we can see at a glance that whenever the *x* value increases by 1, the *y* value increases by 0.5. We can describe this relationship as the *slope* of the line.

FIGURE A-7

The slope of a line

X	Y
−4	2
−2	3
0	4
2	5
4	6

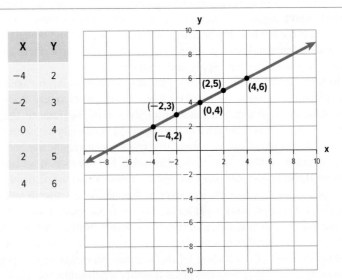

Slope refers to the shape of the line and is
determined by the change in *y* and *x.*

Slope is a ratio of vertical distance (change in y) to horizontal distance (change in x). We begin to calculate slope by labeling one point along the line Point 1, which we denote (x_1, y_1), and another point along the line Point 2, which we denote (x_2, y_2). We can then calculate the horizontal distance by subtracting x_1 from x_2. We calculate vertical distance by subtracting y_1 from y_2.

slope
the ratio of vertical distance (change in y) to horizontal distance (change in x)

EQUATION A-1

$$\text{Horizontal distance} = \Delta x = (x_2 - x_1)$$

$$\text{Vertical distance} = \Delta y = (y_2 - y_1)$$

The vertical distance is sometimes referred to as the **rise**, while the horizontal distance is known as the **run**. "Rise over run" is an easy way to remember how to calculate slope.

rise
vertical distance; calculated as the change in y

EQUATION A-2

$$\text{Slope} = \frac{\text{Rise}}{\text{Run}} = \frac{\Delta y}{\Delta x} = \frac{(y_2 - y_1)}{(x_2 - x_1)}$$

run
horizontal distance; calculated as the change in x

When the relationship between x and y is linear (which means that it forms a straight line), the slope is constant. That is, for each one-unit change in the x-variable, the corresponding y-variable always changes by the same amount. Therefore, we can use any two points to calculate the slope of the line—it doesn't matter which ones we pick because the slope is the same everywhere on the line.

Slope gives us important information about the relationship between our two variables. As you'll see, slope tells us something about both the direction of the relationship between two variables (whether they move in the same direction) and the magnitude of the relationship (how much y changes in response to a change in x).

Calculating slope

LO A.2 Use data to calculate slope.

In Figure A-8, the rise, or vertical distance between point (2,3) and point (4,5), is 5 minus 3, which equals 2. The run, or horizontal distance, is 4 minus 2, which equals 2. Therefore, the slope of the line in Figure A-8 is calculated as:

$$\text{Slope} = \frac{(y_2 - y_1)}{(x_2 - x_1)} = \frac{(5 - 3)}{(4 - 2)} = \frac{2}{2} = 1$$

Let's return to Figure A-7 and apply this same calculation. Because the relationship between x and y is linear, we can use any two points to calculate the slope. Let's pick the point (2,5) to be point 1, which we call (x_1, y_1). Then, pick the point (4,6) to be point 2, which we call (x_2, y_2).

$$\frac{(y_2 - y_1)}{(x_2 - x_1)} = \frac{(6 - 5)}{(4 - 2)} = \frac{1}{2} = 0.5$$

Note that it doesn't matter which point we pick as point 1 and which as point 2. We could have chosen 5 as y_2 and 6 as y_1 rather than vice versa. All that matters is that y_1 is from the same ordered pair as x_1 and y_2 from the same pair as x_2. To prove that this is true, let's calculate slope again using (2,5) as point 2. The slope still comes out to 0.5:

$$\frac{(y_2 - y_1)}{(x_2 - x_1)} = \frac{(5 - 6)}{(2 - 4)} = \frac{(-1)}{(-2)} = \frac{1}{2} = 0.5$$

Use two different points from the table in Figure A-7 to calculate slope again. Try using the points $(-4, 2)$ and $(0, 4)$. Do you get 0.5 as your answer?

FIGURE A-8

Calculating slope

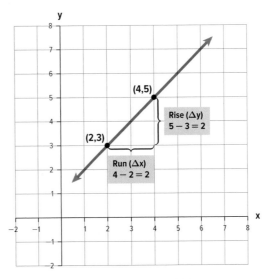

You can calculate the slope by dividing the change in the *y* value over the change in *x*—the rise over the run.

The direction of a slope

LO A.3 Interpret what the direction and steepness of slope indicate about a line.

The direction of a slope tells us something meaningful about the relationship between the two variables we are representing. For instance, when children get older, they grow taller. If we represented this relationship in a graph, we would see an upward-sloping line, telling us that height increases as age increases, rather than decreasing. Of course, it is common knowledge that children get taller, not shorter, as they get older. But if we were looking at a graph of a relationship we did not already understand, the slope of the line would show us at a glance how the two variables relate to one another.

To see how we can learn from the direction of a slope and how to calculate it, look at the graphs in panels A and B of Figure A-9.

In panel A, we can see that when *x* increases from 1 to 2, *y* also increases, from 2 to 4. If we move the other direction down the line, we see that when *x* decreases from 2 to 1, *y* also decreases, from 4 to 2. In other words, *x* and *y* move in the same direction. Therefore, *x* and *y* are said to have a *positive relationship*. Not surprisingly, this means that the slope of the line is a positive number:

$$\text{Slope} = \frac{\Delta y}{\Delta x} = \frac{2}{1} = 2$$

When the slope of a line is positive, we know that *y* increases as *x* increases, and *y* decreases as *x* decreases. If a line leans upward, then its slope is positive.

Now, turn to the graph in panel B. In this case, when *x* increases from 1 to 2, *y* decreases from 4 to 2. Reading from the other direction, when *x* decreases from 2 to 1, *y* increases from 2 to 4.

FIGURE A-9

The direction of a slope

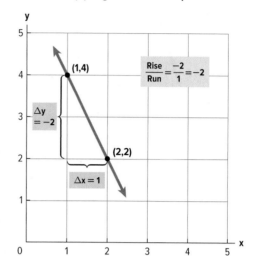

If a line slopes upward, its slope is positive; *y* increases as *x* increases, or *y* decreases as *x* decreases.

If a line slopes downward, its slope is negative: *y* decreases as *x* increases, or *y* increases as *x* decreases.

Therefore, *x* and *y* move in opposite directions and are said to have a *negative relationship.* The slope of the line is a negative number:

$$\text{Slope} = \frac{\Delta y}{\Delta x} = \frac{-2}{1} = -2$$

When the slope of a line is negative, we know that *y* decreases as *x* increases, and *y* increases as *x* decreases. If a line leans downward, then its slope is negative.

In Chapter 3, "Markets," you will see applications of these positive and negative relationships between the variables price and quantity. Here's a preview:

- You will see a positive relationship between price and quantity when you encounter a *supply curve.* You will learn the meaning of that positive relationship: As the price of a good increases, suppliers are willing to supply a larger quantity to markets. Supply curves, therefore, are upward-sloping.

- You will see a negative relationship between price and quantity when you encounter a *demand curve.* You will learn the meaning of that negative relationship: As the price of a good increases, consumers are willing to purchase a smaller quantity. Demand curves are downward-sloping.

From these examples, you can see that two variables (such as price and quantity) may have more than one relationship with each other, depending on whose choices they represent and under what circumstances.

The steepness of a slope

In addition to the *direction* of the relationship between variables, the *steepness* of the slope also gives us important information. It tells us how much *y* changes for a given change in *x*.

FIGURE A-10

The steepness of a slope

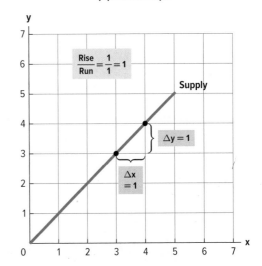

The larger the number representing slope is, the steeper the curve will be. The slope in panel A is steeper than the slope in panel B.

The closer the slope is to zero, the flatter the curve will be. The slope in panel B is flatter than the slope in panel A.

In both panels of Figure A-10, the relationship between x and y is positive (upward-sloping), and the distance between the x values, Δx, is the same. However, the change in y that results from a one-unit change in x is greater in panel A than it is in panel B. In other words, the slope is *steeper* in panel A and *flatter* in panel B.

Numerically, the closer the number representing the slope is to zero, the flatter the curve will be. Remember that both positive and negative numbers can be close to zero. So, a slope of -1 is equally steep as a slope of 1, although one slopes downward and the other upward. Correspondingly, a line with a slope of -5 is steeper than a line with a slope of -1 or one with a slope of 1.

In general, slope is used to describe how much y changes in response to a one-unit change in x. In economics, we are sometimes interested in how much x changes in response to a one-unit change in y. For example, in Chapter 4, "Elasticity," you will see how quantity (on the x-axis) responds to a change in price (on the y-axis).

Key Terms

slope, p. 46G

rise, p. 46G

run, p. 46G

Problems and Applications

1. Create four quadrants using x- and y-axes. Use your graph to plot the following points. **[LO A.1]**
   - a. (1,4)
   - b. (−2,1)
   - c. (−3,−3)
   - d. (3,−2)

2. Create four quadrants using x- and y-axes. Use your graph to plot the following points. **[LO A.1]**
   - a. (0,4)
   - b. (0,−2)
   - c. (1,0)
   - d. (−3,0)

FIGURE AP-1

3. Use the curve labeled "Demand" in Figure AP-1 to create a table (schedule) that shows Price in one column and Quantity in another. What is the slope of the curve labeled "Demand"? **[LO A.2]**

4. Use the curve labeled "Demand" in Figure AP-2 to create a table (schedule) that shows Price in one column and Quantity in another. What is the slope of the curve labeled "Demand"? **[LO A.2]**

FIGURE AP-2

5. Use the information about price and quantity in Table AP-1 to create a graph, with Price on the y-axis and Quantity on the x-axis. Label the resulting curve "Demand." What is the slope of that curve? **[LO A.2]**

6. Use the information about price and quantity in Table AP-2 to create a graph, with Price on the y-axis and Quantity on the x-axis. Label the resulting curve "Demand." What is the slope of that curve? **[LO A.2]**

TABLE AP-1

Price ($)	Quantity
0	120
2	100
4	80
6	60
8	40
10	20
12	0

TABLE AP-2

Price ($)	Quantity
0	5
5	4
10	3
15	2
20	1
25	0

7. Use the curve labeled "Supply" in Figure AP-3 to create a table (schedule) that shows Price in one column and Quantity in another. What is the slope of the curve labeled "Supply"? **[LO A.2]**

8. Use the curve labeled "Supply" in Figure AP-4 to create a table (schedule) that shows Price in one column and Quantity in another. What is the slope of the curve labeled "Supply"? **[LO A.2]**

9. Use the information about price and quantity in Table AP-3 to create a graph, with Price on the y-axis and Quantity on the x-axis. Label the resulting curve "Supply." What is the slope of that curve? **[LO A.2]**

TABLE AP-3

Price ($)	Quantity
0	0
25	5
50	10
75	15
100	20
125	25

TABLE AP-4

Price ($)	Quantity
0	0
2	8
4	16
6	24
8	32
10	40
12	48

FIGURE AP-3

FIGURE AP-4

Price ($)

10. Use the information about price and quantity in Table AP-4 to create a graph, with Price on the y-axis and Quantity on the x-axis. Label the resulting curve "Supply." What is the slope of that curve? **[LO A.2]**

11. What is the direction of slope indicated by the following examples? **[LO A.3]**

    a. As the price of rice increases, consumers want less of it.

    b. As the temperature increases, the amount of people who use the town pool also increases.

    c. As farmers use more fertilizer, their output of tomatoes increases.

12. Rank the following equations by the steepness of their slope from lowest to highest. **[LO A.3]**

    a. $y = -3x + 9$

    b. $y = 4x + 2$

    c. $y = -0.5x + 4$

Part Two

Supply and Demand

The four chapters in Part 2 will introduce you to . . .

the basics of markets, which form the baseline for most economic analysis. Chapter 3, "Markets," introduces supply and demand. Any time we go into the store and decide to buy something, we act on our demand for that good. On the other side, the store figured out that it made sense for them to supply that good to us. The interaction between the forces of demand and supply determines the price we pay and how much gets bought and sold.

Chapters 4, 5 and 6 ("Elasticity," "Efficiency," and "Government Intervention") will use demand and supply to answer a variety of questions: Why do people rush to the store when Apple slashes the price of an iPhone? Why would the government ever want to set limits on prices in the market?

Together with Part 1, the chapters in this part introduce the basic concepts of economic problem solving. To start, we've stripped these ideas down to their simplest form. These same concepts will return throughout the text, and we will build on them as we turn to different problems.

Markets

Learning Objectives

LO 3.1 Identify the defining characteristics of a competitive market.

LO 3.2 Draw a demand curve and describe the external factors that determine demand.

LO 3.3 Distinguish between a shift in and a movement along the demand curve.

LO 3.4 Draw a supply curve and describe the external factors that determine supply.

LO 3.5 Distinguish between a shift in and a movement along the supply curve.

LO 3.6 Explain how supply and demand interact to drive markets to equilibrium.

LO 3.7 Evaluate the effect of changes in supply and demand on the equilibrium price and quantity.

MOBILES GO GLOBAL

For many people, a cell phone is on the list of things never to leave the house without, right up there with a wallet and keys. For better or worse, cell phones have become a fixture of everyday life.

It's hard to believe that as recently as the late 1990s, cell phones were a luxury that only a third of Americans enjoyed. Before that, in the 1980s, they were big, heavy devices, seldom bought for personal use at all. In less than a quarter of a century, this expensive sci-fi technology became a relatively cheap, universal convenience. Today there are approximately 90 cell phones for every 100 people in the United States. In fact, around half of the world's 7.4 billion people have a cell phone subscription.[1] For instance, two-thirds of Africa's 1.13 billion citizens now have cell phones.[2] This phenomenal growth makes it easier to keep up with friends and family. It also connects small-town merchants to businesses in distant cities, opening up new economic possibilities.

How does a product move from expensive to cheap, from rare to commonplace, so quickly? The answer partly lies in the relationship between supply and demand. This chapter shows how

© Tim Robberts/Getty Images

the forces of supply and demand interact to determine the quantities and prices of goods that are bought and sold in competitive markets.

The basic story of how a new product takes hold is a familiar one. In the beginning, cell phones were expensive and rare. Over time, the technology improved, the price dropped, the product caught on, and sales took off. Throughout this process of change, markets allow for ongoing communication between buyers and producers, using prices as a signal. The up-and-down movement of prices ensures that the quantity of a product that is available stays in balance with the quantity consumers want to buy.

To explain the leap in usage that cell phones have made over time, however, we need to go further than just price signals. Outside forces that influence supply and demand, such as changes in technology, fashion trends, and economic ups and downs, have driven that transformation. Markets have the remarkable ability to adjust to these changes without falling out of balance.

In this chapter, we'll step into the shoes of consumers and producers to examine the trade-offs they face. We'll see that the issues that drive supply and demand in the cell phone industry are not unique. In fact, the functioning of markets, as summarized in the theory of supply and demand, is the bedrock of almost everything in this book. Mastering this theory will help you to solve all kinds of problems, from what price to sell your product for as a businessperson, to how to find the cheapest gasoline, to the causes of a shortage of hybrid cars.

Markets

In Chapter 2, "Specialization and Exchange," we discussed the power of the "invisible hand" to coordinate complex economic interactions. The key feature of an economy organized by the invisible hand is that private individuals, rather than a centralized planning authority, make the decisions. Such an economy is often referred to as a **market economy**.

market economy
an economy in which private individuals, rather than a centralized planning authority, make the decisions

What is a market?

What do we mean by a *market*? The word might make you think of a physical location where buyers and sellers come together face-to-face—like a farmers' market or a mall. But people do not have to be physically near each other to make an exchange. For example, think of online retailers like Amazon.com or of fruit that is grown in South America but sold all over the world. The term **market** actually refers to the buyers and sellers who trade a particular good or service, not to a physical location.

Which buyers and sellers are included in the market depends on the context. The manager of a clothing store at your local mall might think about the market for T-shirts in terms of people who live locally and the other places they could buy T-shirts, like competing stores, garage

market
buyers and sellers who trade a particular good or service

sales, or online retailers. The CEO of a major clothing brand, on the other hand, might include garment factories in Bangladesh and the fashion preferences of customers living all over the world in her idea of a market. Which boundaries are relevant depends on the scope of trades that are being made.

What is a competitive market?

LO 3.1 Identify the defining characteristics of a competitive market.

Making simplifying assumptions can help us zero in on important ideas. In this chapter, we will make a big simplifying assumption—that markets are *competitive*. A **competitive market** is one in which fully informed, price-taking buyers and sellers easily trade a standardized good or service. Let's unpack this multipart definition: Imagine you're driving up to an intersection where there is a gas station on each corner. This scenario demonstrates the four defining characteristics of a perfectly competitive market.

First, we bet you'd find that a gallon of gas costs the same in each station at the intersection. Why? Recall the third economists' question from Chapter 1, "Economics and Life": If one station tries to raise its price, *how will others respond?* Assuming the stations are offering standardized gallons of gas, customers should be indifferent between buying from one station or another at a given price. If one raises its price, all the drivers will simply go to a cheaper station instead. The gas station that raised prices will end up losing customers. For this reason, no individual seller has the power to change the market price. In economic terminology, a buyer or seller who cannot affect the market price is called a **price taker**.

The drivers going by are also price takers. If you try to negotiate a discount at one of the gas stations before filling your tank, you won't get far—the owner would rather wait and sell to other customers who will pay more. The price is the price; your choice is to take it or leave it. In competitive markets, both buyers and sellers are price takers.

Second, the gas sold by each station is the same—your car will run equally well regardless of *which* brand you buy. This means that the gas being sold is a **standardized good**—a good or service for which any two units of it have the same features and are interchangeable. In a competitive market, the good being bought and sold is standardized.

Third, the price at each gas station is prominently displayed on a big sign. As you drive by, you can immediately see how much a gallon of each type of gas costs at each station. In a competitive market, you have *full information* about the price and features of the good being bought and sold.

Finally, it's easy for you to choose any of the four gas stations at the intersection. The stations are very near each other, and you don't have to have special equipment to fill up your tank or pay an entrance fee to get into the station. In competitive markets, there are no **transaction costs**—the costs incurred by buyer and seller in agreeing to and executing a sale of goods or services. Thus, in competitive markets, you don't have to pay anything for the privilege of buying or selling in the market. You can easily do business in this four-station market for gasoline.

By thinking about the gas stations at a single intersection, you have learned the four characteristics of perfectly competitive markets. Table 3-1 summarizes the four characteristics of a perfectly competitive market: price-taking participants, a standardized good, full information, and no transaction costs.

In reality, few markets are truly *perfectly* competitive. Even gas stations at the same intersection might not be: Maybe one can charge a few cents more per gallon because it uses gas with less ethanol or offers regular customers an attractive loyalty scheme or has a Dunkin' Donuts to entice hungry drivers. In future chapters, we'll spend a lot of time thinking about the different ways that markets in the real world are structured and why it matters when they fall short of perfect competition.

competitive market
a market in which fully informed, price-taking buyers and sellers easily trade a standardized good or service

price taker
a buyer or seller who cannot affect the market price. In a perfectly competitive market, firms are price takers as a consequence of many sellers selling standardized goods.

standardized good
a good for which any two units have the same features and are interchangeable

transaction costs
the costs incurred by buyer and seller in agreeing to and executing a sale of goods or services

TABLE 3-1
Four characteristics of perfectly competitive markets

Characteristic	Description
Participants are price takers	Neither buyers nor sellers have the power to affect the market price.
Standardized good	Any two units of the good have the same features and are interchangeable.
Full information	Market participants know everything about the price and features of the good.
No transaction costs	There is no cost to participate in exchanges in the market.

The market for cell phones is not perfectly competitive either. Cell phones are not standardized goods—some models look cooler, or have better cameras, or have access to different apps or calling plans. You're unlikely to be completely indifferent between two different cell phones at the same price, as you are between two gallons of gas. Furthermore, the fact that there are a limited number of service providers means that sellers aren't always price takers. If only one network has good coverage in your area or has an exclusive deal with a popular type of phone, it can get away with charging a premium.

So, why *assume* perfect competition if markets in the real world are rarely perfectly competitive? The answer is that the simple model of competitive markets we will develop in this chapter leads us to useful insights, even in markets that aren't perfectly competitive. Taking the time now to make sure you understand perfect competition inside and out will better prepare you to understand why it matters when markets aren't perfectly competitive. As we go through this chapter, we'll note some ways in which the real cell phone market departs from perfect competition. By the end of the chapter, we hope you'll agree that the simple model of perfect competition tells us a lot, if not everything, about how the real cell phone market works.

✓CONCEPT CHECK

☐ What is a market? What are the characteristics of a competitive market? **[LO 3.1]**
☐ Why are participants in competitive markets called *price takers*? **[LO 3.1]**

Demand

Demand describes how much of something people are willing and able to buy under certain circumstances. Suppose someone approached you and asked if you would like a new cell phone. What would you answer? You might think, "Sure," but as a savvy person, you would probably first ask, "For how much?" Whether you want something (or how much of it you want) depends on how much you have to pay for it.

These days most people in the United States have cell phones, but that hasn't been the case for very long. Let's assume for the sake of our model that cell phones are standardized—one model, with given features and calling plans. Now, put yourself in the position of a consumer in the mid-1990s: Maybe you've seen cell phones advertised at $499 and think it's not worth it to you. As the price goes down over time to $399, and $299, you're still not tempted to buy it. At $199, you start to consider it. Then, the first time you see a cell phone advertised for less than $125, you decide to buy.

Different people bought their first cell phone at different prices: At any given time, with any given price, some people in the population are willing and able to buy a phone and others aren't. If we add up all of these individual choices, we get overall *market demand*. The amount of a particular good that buyers in a market will purchase at a given price during a specified period is called the **quantity demanded**. For almost all goods, the lower the price goes, the higher the quantity demanded.

This inverse relationship between price and quantity demanded is so important that economists refer to it as the **law of demand**. The first requirement for the law of demand is the idea sometimes known as *ceteris paribus*, the Latin term for "all other things being the same." In other words, the law of demand says that, when all else is held equal (when all other factors remain the same), quantity demanded rises as price falls.

Economists frequently rely on the idea of *ceteris paribus* to isolate the expected effect of a single change in the economy. For example, suppose you want to predict what would happen next year to cell phone sales if cell phone prices go down. The law of demand tells us that if cell phone prices go down, *holding all else equal*, quantity demanded will go up.

But what if the economy is not doing well next year and consumers hold back on buying new cell phones? In this instance, we *cannot* say in general that "if cell phone prices go down, quantity demanded will go up" because not everything else has been held the same. Instead, the negative impact of the weak economy may offset the positive impact of the reduction in price. We need to be more specific. So, it is critical to "hold all else equal" in order to make clear statements about what we can predict.

The law of demand isn't a made-up law that economists have imposed on markets. Rather, it holds true because it describes the underlying reality of individual people's decisions. The key is to think about the *trade-offs* that people face when making the decision to buy.

What happens when the price of something falls? First, the benefit that you get from purchasing it remains the same because the item itself is unchanged. But the opportunity cost has fallen: When the price goes down, you don't have to give up as many other purchases in order to get the item. When benefits stay the same and opportunity cost goes down, this trade-off suddenly starts to look a lot better. When the trade-off between costs and benefits tips toward benefits, more people will want to buy the good.

Of course, falling prices will not have been the only consideration in people's decisions to buy their first cell phone. Some might have decided to buy one when they got a pay raise at work. Others might have bought one at the point when most of their friends owned one. Incomes, expectations, and tastes all play a role; economists call these factors *nonprice determinants* of demand. We'll discuss their potential effects later in this chapter. First, let's focus on the relationship between price and quantity demanded.

The demand curve

LO 3.2 Draw a demand curve and describe the external factors that determine demand.

The law of demand says that the quantity of cell phones demanded will be different at every price level. For this reason, it is often useful to represent demand as a table, called a **demand schedule**. A demand schedule shows the quantities of a particular good or service that consumers are willing and able to purchase (demand) at various prices. Panel A of Figure 3-1 shows a hypothetical annual demand schedule for cell phones in the United States. (Remember, we're assuming that cell phones are a standardized good. This isn't quite right, but the basic principle holds true: When cell phone prices are lower, you're more likely to buy a new one.) The demand schedule assumes that factors other than price remain the same.

Panel B of Figure 3-1 shows another way to represent demand, by drawing each price-quantity combination from the demand schedule as a point on a graph. That graph, called a **demand curve**, visually displays the demand schedule. That is, it is a graph that shows the quantities of a particular good or service that consumers will demand at various prices. The demand curve also represents consumers' *willingness to buy*: It shows the highest amount consumers will pay for any given quantity.

quantity demanded
the amount of a particular good that buyers will purchase at a given price during a specified period

law of demand
a fundamental characteristic of demand that states that, all else equal, quantity demanded rises as price falls

demand schedule
a table that shows the quantities of a particular good or service that consumers are willing and able to purchase (demand) at various prices

demand curve
a graph that shows the quantities of a particular good or service that consumers will demand at various prices

FIGURE 3-1

Demand schedule and the demand curve

(A) Demand schedule

Cell phones (millions)	Price ($)
30	180
60	160
90	140
120	120
150	100
180	80
210	60
240	40
270	20

This demand schedule shows the quantity of cell phones demanded each year at various prices. As prices decrease, consumers want to purchase more cell phones.

(B) Demand curve

This demand curve is a graphic representation of the demand schedule for cell phones in the United States. Each entry in the demand schedule is plotted on this curve.

Since demand curves and other material in this chapter make extensive use of lines and linear equations, you may want to review those concepts in Appendix B, "Math Essentials: Working with Linear Equations," which follows this chapter.

On the demand curve, quantity goes on the *x*-axis (the horizontal axis) and price on the *y*-axis (the vertical axis). The result is a downward-sloping line that reflects the inverse relationship between price and quantity. The demand curve in Figure 3-1 represents exactly the same information as the demand schedule.

Determinants of demand

The demand curve represents the relationship between price and quantity demanded *with everything else held constant*. If everything else is *not* held constant—that is, if one of the nonprice factors that determines demand changes—the curve will shift.

The downward-sloping demand curve reflects the trade-offs that people face between (1) the benefit they expect to receive from a good and (2) the opportunity cost they face for buying it. Therefore, any factor that changes this balance at a given price will change people's willingness to buy, and thus their purchasing decisions.

The nonprice determinants of demand can be divided into five major categories:

- Consumer preferences.
- The prices of related goods.
- Income of the consumers.
- Expectations of future prices.
- The number of buyers in the market.

Table 3-2 summarizes the impact of each factor on demand. Each of these nonprice determinants affects either the benefits or the opportunity cost of buying a good, even if the price of the good itself remains the same.

TABLE 3-2
Determinants of demand

Determinant	Examples of an increase in demand	Examples of a decrease in demand
Consumer preferences	A "Buy American" ad campaign appeals to national pride, increasing the demand for U.S.-made sneakers.	An outbreak of *E. coli* decreases the demand for spinach.
Prices of related goods	A decrease in the price of hot dogs increases the demand for relish, a complementary good.	A decrease in taxi fares decreases the demand for subway rides, a substitute good.
Incomes	An economic downturn lowers incomes, increasing the demand for ground beef, an inferior good.	An economic downturn lowers incomes, decreasing the demand for steak, a normal good.
Expectations	A hurricane destroys part of the world papaya crop, causing expectations that prices will rise and increasing the current demand for papayas.	An announcement that a new smartphone soon will be released decreases the demand for the current model.
Number of buyers	An increase in life expectancy increases the demand for nursing homes and medical care.	A falling birthrate decreases the demand for diapers.

POTENTIALLY CONFUSING

You may notice that these five factors include price-related issues such as the price of related goods and expectations about future prices. So why do we refer to them as *nonprice determinants*? We do so in order to differentiate them from the effect of the *current price* of the good on demand for that good.

Consumer preferences

Consumer preferences are the personal likes and dislikes that make buyers more or less inclined to purchase a good. We don't need to know *why* people like what they like or to agree with their preferences; we just need to know that these likes and dislikes influence their purchases. At any given price, some consumers will get more enjoyment (i.e., benefits) out of a cell phone than do others. That enjoyment may be based simply on how much they like talking to friends, or whether they use their phones for work, or any number of other personal preferences.

Some consumer preferences are fairly constant across time, such as those that arise from personality traits or cultural attitudes and beliefs. For example, a recluse may have little desire for a cell phone; an on-the-go executive may find a cell phone (or two) to be essential. Other preferences will change over time, in response to external events or fads. For instance, it's more useful to own a cell phone when all your friends already have one. And more people may demand cell phones after a national disaster, knowing they want to be able to reach their families in emergencies.

Prices of related goods

Another factor that affects the demand for a particular good is the prices of related goods. There are two kinds of related goods: substitutes and complements.

We say that goods are **substitutes** when they serve similar-enough purposes that a consumer might purchase one in place of the other—for example, rice and pasta. If the price of rice doubles while the price of pasta stays the same, demand for pasta will increase. That's because the *opportunity cost* of pasta has decreased: You can buy less rice for the same amount of

substitutes
goods that serve a similar-enough purpose that a consumer might purchase one in place of the other

money, so you give up less potential rice when you buy pasta. If the two goods are quite similar, we call them *close substitutes*. Similar fishes, such as salmon and trout, might be considered close substitutes.

For many Americans deciding whether to buy their first cell phone, the nearest substitute would have been a landline phone. Cell phones and landlines are not very close substitutes: You can use them for the same purposes at home or the office, but only one of them can go for a walk with you. Still, if the price of U.S. landline phone service had suddenly skyrocketed, we can be sure that change would have increased the demand for cell phones.

In fact, the very high cost of landline phone services in many developing countries is one reason why cell phones spread very quickly. In the United States, almost every household had a landline phone before it had a cell phone. In many poor countries, landlines are so expensive that very few people can afford one. That's why cell phones are often called a *leapfrog technology*: People go straight from no phone to cell phone, hopping over an entire stage of older technology.

Related goods that are consumed together, so that purchasing one will make a consumer more likely to purchase the other, are called **complements**. Peanut butter and jelly, cereal and milk, cars and gasoline are all complements. If the price of one of the two goods increases, demand for the other will likely decrease. Why? As consumers purchase less of the first good, they will want less of the other to go with it. Conversely, if the price of one of the two goods declines, demand for the other will likely increase. For example, when the prices of new cell phones fall, consumers will be more likely to buy new accessories to go with them.

complements
goods that are consumed together, so that purchasing one will make consumers more likely to purchase the other

Incomes

Not surprisingly, the amount of income people earn affects their demand for goods and services: The bigger your paycheck, the more money you can afford to spend on the things you want. The smaller your paycheck, the more you have to cut back.

Most goods are **normal goods**, meaning that an increase in income causes an increase in demand. Likewise, for normal goods, a decrease in income causes a decrease in demand. For most people, cell phones are a normal good. If someone cannot currently afford a cell phone, she's more likely to buy one when her income rises. If someone already has a cell phone, she's more likely to upgrade to a newer, fancier cell phone when her income rises.

normal goods
goods for which demand increases as income increases

For some goods, called **inferior goods**, the opposite relationship holds: As income increases, demand decreases. Typically, people replace inferior goods with more expensive and appealing substitutes when their incomes rise. For many people, inexpensive grocery items like instant noodles, some canned foods, and generic store brands might be inferior goods. When their incomes rise, people replace these goods with fresher, more expensive ingredients. Decreases in income occur for many people during economic downturns; thus, the demand for inferior goods reflects the overall health of the economy. For an example, see the Real Life box "Can instant-noodle sales predict a recession?"

inferior goods
goods for which demand decreases as income increases

Real Life
Can instant-noodle sales predict a recession?

If you were to open a typical college student's kitchen cupboard, what would you find? Many students rely on a decidedly unglamorous food item: ramen instant noodles. Packed with cheap calories, this tasty snack is famously inexpensive.

Ramen noodles are an example of an inferior good. When people's budgets are tight (as are those of most students), these noodles sell well. When incomes rise, ramen sales drop and more expensive foods replace them.

In Thailand, ramen noodles have even been used as an indicator of overall economic health. The Mama Noodles Index tracks sales of a popular brand of instant ramen noodles. Because the demand for inferior goods increases when incomes go down, an increase in ramen sales could signal a downturn in incomes and an oncoming recession. In fact, observers of the Thai economy say that the Mama Noodles Index does a pretty good job of reflecting changing economic conditions.

Even the demand for inferior goods may decrease during severe economic downturns, however. Although the Mama Noodles Index has risen as expected when the Thai economy falters, the index unexpectedly dropped 15 percent during the deep recession of early 2009.

So are instant noodles an inferior good or a normal good? In Thailand, the answer may depend on who you are or how severely your income has dropped. For the middle class, who choose between ramen and more expensive foods, ramen may indeed be an inferior good. For the poor, whose choice more likely is whether or not they will get enough to eat, ramen may be a normal good. When their incomes rise, they may buy more ramen; when their incomes fall, even noodles may be a luxury.

Sources: "Using their noodles," Associated Press, September 5, 2005, http://www.theage.com.au/news/world/using-their-noodles/2005/09/04/1125772407287.html; Kwanchai Rungfapaisarn, "Downturn bites into instant-noodle market as customers tighten belts," *The Nation,* March 20, 2009, http://www.nationmultimedia.com/business/Downturn-bites-into-instant-noodle-market-as-custo-30098402.html.

Expectations

Changes in consumers' expectations about the future—especially future prices—can also affect demand. If consumers expect prices to fall in the future, they may postpone a purchase until a later date, causing current demand to decrease. If you think cell phones will go on sale in a few months, you might put off your purchase until then. Or you might delay upgrading your smartphone in the hope that when the next model releases, the current model will drop in price. When prices are expected to drop in the future, demand decreases.

Conversely, if consumers expect prices to rise in the future, they may wish to purchase a good immediately to avoid a higher price. This reasoning often occurs in speculative markets, like the stock market or sometimes the housing market. Buyers purchase stock or a house expecting prices to rise, so they can sell at a profit. In these markets, then, demand increases when prices are low and are expected to rise.

Number of buyers

The demand curve represents the demand of a particular number of potential buyers. In general, an increase in the number of potential buyers in a market will increase demand. A decrease in the number of buyers will decrease it. Major population shifts, like an increase in immigration or a drop in the birthrate, can create nationwide changes in demand. As the number of teenagers and college students increases, the demand for cell phones increases too.

Shifts in the demand curve

LO 3.3 Distinguish between a shift in and a movement along the demand curve.

What happens to the demand curve when one of the five nonprice determinants of demand changes? The entire demand curve shifts, either to the right or to the left. The shift is horizontal rather than vertical because nonprice determinants affect the quantity demanded at *each* price. When the quantity demanded at a given price is now higher, the point on the curve corresponding to that price is now further right. When the quantity demanded at a given price is lower, the point on the curve corresponding to that price is now further left.

Consider what happens, for example, when the economy is growing and people's incomes are rising. Let's assume the price of cell phones does not change ("all else held equal"). But with rising incomes, more people will choose to buy a new cell phone at any given price, causing quantity demanded to be higher at every possible price. Panel A of Figure 3-2 shows the resulting shift of the demand curve to the right, from D_A to D_B. In contrast, if the economy falls into a recession and people begin pinching pennies, quantity demanded will decrease at every price, and the curve will shift to the left, from D_A to D_C.

It is important to distinguish between these *shifts* in demand, which move the entire curve, and *movements along* a given demand curve. Remember this key point: *Shifts in the demand curve are caused by changes in the nonprice determinants of demand.* A recession, for example, would lower incomes and move the whole demand curve left. When we say "demand decreases," this is what we are talking about.

In contrast, suppose that the price of phones increases but everything else stays the same—that is, there is no change in the nonprice determinants of demand. Because the demand curve describes the quantity consumers will demand at any possible price, not just the current market price, we don't have to shift the curve to figure out what happens when the price goes up. Instead, we simply look at a different point on the curve to describe what is actually happening in the market right now.

To find the quantity that consumers will want to purchase at this new price, we move along the existing demand curve from the old price to the new one. If, for instance, the price of cell phones increases, we find the new quantity demanded by moving up along the demand curve to the new price point, as shown in panel B of Figure 3-2. The price change does not shift the curve itself because the curve already describes what consumers will do at any price.

FIGURE 3-2

Shifts in the demand curve versus movement along the demand curve

Changes in external factors cause the entire demand curve to shift. The shift from D_A to D_B represents an increase in demand, meaning that consumers want to buy more cell phones at each price. The shift from D_A to D_C represents a decrease in demand, meaning that consumers want to buy fewer cell phones at each price.

A price change causes a movement along the demand curve, but the curve itself remains constant.

To summarize, panel A of Figure 3-2 shows a *shift in demand* as the result of a change in the nonprice determinants; panel B shows a *movement along the demand curve* as the result of a change in price.

Economists use very specific terminology to distinguish between a shift in the demand curve and movement along the demand curve:

- We say that a change in one of the nonprice determinants of demand causes an "increase in demand" or "decrease in demand"—that is, a *shift* of the entire demand curve.
- To distinguish this from *movement along* the demand curve, we say that a change in price causes an "increase in the quantity demanded" or "decrease in the quantity demanded."

Just keep in mind that a "change in demand" is different from a "change in the quantity demanded." Observing this seemingly small difference in terminology prevents a great deal of confusion.

Understanding the effects of changes in both price and the nonprice determinants of demand is a key tool for businesspeople and policy-makers. Suppose you are in charge of an industry group whose members want to spur demand for cell phones. One idea might be to start an advertising campaign to increase the real or perceived benefits of owning a cell phone. If you understand the determinants of demand, you know that the advertising campaign would change consumer preferences. In other words, a successful advertising campaign would shift the demand curve for cell phones to the right. Similarly, if you are a congressional representative who is considering a tax cut to stimulate the economy, you know that a tax cut increases consumers' disposable incomes, increasing the demand for all normal goods. In other words, you are hoping that the resulting increase in incomes will shift the demand curve for cell phones to the right.

✓CONCEPT CHECK

☐ What are the five nonprice determinants of demand? **[LO 3.2]**
☐ What is the difference between a change in demand and a change in quantity demanded? **[LO 3.3]**

Supply

We've discussed the factors that determine how many phones consumers want to buy at a given price. But are cell phone producers necessarily willing to sell that many? The concept of *supply* describes how much of a good or service producers will offer for sale under given circumstances. The **quantity supplied** is the amount of a particular good or service that producers will offer for sale at a given price during a specified period.

As with demand, we can find overall *market supply* by adding up the individual decisions of each producer. Imagine you own a factory that can produce cell phones or other consumer electronics. If the price of cell phones is $110, you might decide there's good money to be made and use your entire factory space to produce cell phones. If the price is only $80, you might produce some cell phones but decide it will be more profitable to devote part of your factory to producing laptop computers. If the cell phone price drops to $55, you might decide you'd make more money by producing only laptops. Each producer will have a different price point at which it decides it's worthwhile to supply cell phones. This rule—all else held equal, quantity supplied increases as price increases—is called the **law of supply**.

(In reality, it's costly to switch a factory from making cell phones to laptops or other goods. However, the simple version illustrates a basic truth: The higher the price of a good, the more of that good producers will want to supply. Similarly, the lower the price of a good, the less of that good producers will want to supply.)

quantity supplied
the amount of a particular good or service that producers will offer for sale at a given price during a specified period

law of supply
a fundamental characteristic of supply that states that, all else equal, quantity supplied rises as price rises

As with demand, supply varies with price because the decision to produce a good is about the *trade-off* between the benefit the producer will receive from selling the good and the opportunity cost of the time and resources that go into producing it. When the market price goes up and all other factors remain constant, the benefit of production increases relative to the opportunity cost, and the trade-off involved in production makes it more favorable to produce more.

For instance, if the price of phones goes up and the prices of raw materials stay the same, existing phone producers may open new factories, and new companies may start looking to enter the cell phone market. The same holds true across other industries. If air travelers seem willing to pay higher prices, airlines will increase the frequency of flights, add new routes, and buy new planes so they can carry more passengers. When prices drop, they cut back their flight schedules and cancel their orders for new planes.

supply schedule
a table that shows the quantities of a particular good or service that producers will supply at various prices

supply curve
a graph that shows the quantities of a particular good or service that producers will supply at various prices

The supply curve

LO 3.4 Draw a supply curve and describe the external factors that determine supply.

Like demand, supply can be represented as a table or a graph. A **supply schedule** is a table that shows the quantities of a particular good or service that producers will supply at various prices. Panel A of Figure 3-3 shows a hypothetical supply schedule for U.S. cell phone providers.

A **supply curve** is a graph of the information in the supply schedule. Just as the demand curve showed consumers' willingness to buy, so the supply curve shows producers' *willingness to sell*: It shows the minimum price producers must receive to supply any given quantity. Panel B of Figure 3-3 shows the supply curve of U.S. cell phone providers—visually representing the supply schedule.

FIGURE 3-3

Supply schedule and the supply curve

(A) Supply schedule

Cell phones (millions)	Price ($)
270	180
240	160
210	140
180	120
150	100
120	80
90	60
60	40
30	20

This supply schedule shows the quantity of cell phones supplied each year at various prices. As prices decrease, suppliers want to produce fewer cell phones.

(B) Supply curve

This supply curve is a graphic representation of the supply schedule for cell phones in the United States. It shows the quantity of cell phones that suppliers will produce at various prices.

Determinants of supply

The law of supply describes how the quantity that producers are willing to supply changes as price changes. But what determines the quantity supplied at any given price? As with demand, a number of *nonprice factors* determine the opportunity cost of production and therefore producers' willingness to supply a good or service. *When a nonprice determinant of supply changes, the entire supply curve will shift.* Such shifts reflect a change in the quantity of goods supplied at *every* price.

The nonprice determinants of supply can be divided into five major categories:

- Prices of related goods.
- Technology.
- Prices of inputs.
- Expectations.
- The number of sellers.

Each of these factors determines the opportunity cost of production relative to a given benefit (i.e., the price) and therefore the trade-off that producers face. Table 3-3 shows how the supply of various products responds to changes in each determinant.

Prices of related goods

Return to your factory, where you can produce either cell phones or laptops. Just as you chose to produce more laptops and fewer cell phones when the price of cell phones dropped, you would do the same if the price of laptops increased while the price of cell phones stayed constant.

The price of related goods determines supply because it affects the opportunity cost of production. When you choose to produce cell phones, you forgo the profits you would have earned from producing something else. If the price of that something else increases, the amount you forgo in profits also increases. For instance, imagine a farmer who can grow wheat or corn (or other crops, for that matter) on his land. If the price of corn increases, the quantity of wheat (the substitute crop) he is willing to grow falls. Why? Because each acre he devotes to wheat is one fewer acre he can use to grow corn.

TABLE 3-3

Determinants of supply

Determinant	Examples of an increase in supply	Examples of a decrease in supply
Price of related goods	The price of gas rises, so an automaker increases its production of smaller, more fuel-efficient cars.	The price of clean energy production falls, so the power company reduces the amount of power it supplies using coal power plants.
Technology	The installation of robots increases productivity and lowers costs; the supply of goods increases.	New technology allows corn to be made into ethanol, so farmers plant more corn and fewer soybeans; the supply of soybeans decreases.
Prices of inputs	A drop in the price of tomatoes decreases the production cost of salsa; the supply of salsa increases.	An increase in the minimum wage increases labor costs at food factories; the supply of processed food decreases.
Expectations	New research points to the health benefits of eating papayas, leading to expectations that the demand for papayas will rise. More farmers plant papayas, increasing the supply.	Housing prices are expected to rise, so builders hold back on new construction projects today (in order to build later when housing prices are higher), decreasing the supply of homes in the near future.
Number of sellers	Subsidies make the production of corn more profitable, so more farmers plant corn; the supply of corn increases.	New licensing fees make operating a restaurant more expensive; some small restaurants close, decreasing the supply of restaurants.

In 1980, this cutting-edge technology cost $4,000.
© C. Borland/Photolink/ Getty Images

Technology

Improved technology enables firms to produce more efficiently, using fewer resources to make a given product. Doing so lowers production costs, increasing the quantity producers are willing to supply at each price.

Improved technology has played a huge role in the changing popularity of cell phones. As technological innovation in the construction of screens, batteries, and mobile networks and in the processing of electronic data has leapt forward, the cost of producing a useful, consumer-friendly cell phone has plummeted. As a result, producers are now willing to supply more cell phones at lower prices.

Prices of inputs

The prices of the inputs used to produce a good are an important part of its cost. When the prices of inputs increase, production costs rise, and the quantity of the product that producers are willing to supply at any given price decreases.

Small amounts of silver and gold are used inside cell phones, for example. When the prices of these precious metals rise, the cost of manufacturing each cell phone increases, and the total number of units that producers collectively are willing to make at any given price goes down. Conversely, when input prices fall, supply increases.

Expectations

Suppliers' expectations about prices in the future also affect quantity supplied. For example, when the price of real estate is expected to rise in the future, more real estate developers will wait to embark on construction projects, decreasing the supply of houses in the near future. When expectations change and real estate prices are projected to fall in the future, many of those projects will be rushed to completion, causing the supply of houses to rise.

Number of sellers

The market supply curve represents the quantities of a product that a particular number of producers will supply at various prices in a given market. This means that the number of sellers in the market is considered to be one of the fixed parts of the supply curve. We've already seen that the sellers in the market will decide to supply more if the price of a good is higher. This does not mean that the number of sellers will change based on price in the short run.

There are, however, nonprice factors that cause the number of sellers to change in a market and move the supply curve. For example, suppose cell phone producers must meet strict licensing requirements. If those licensing requirements are dropped, more companies may enter the market, willing to supply a certain number of cell phones at each price. These additional phones must be added to the number of cell phones existing producers are already willing to supply at each price point.

Shifts in the supply curve

LO 3.5 Distinguish between a shift in and a movement along the supply curve.

Just as with demand, changes in price cause suppliers to move to a different point on the same supply curve, while changes in the nonprice determinants of supply shift the supply curve itself. A change in a nonprice determinant increases or decreases *supply*. A change in price increases or decreases the *quantity supplied*.

FIGURE 3-4

Shifts in the supply curve versus movement along the supply curve

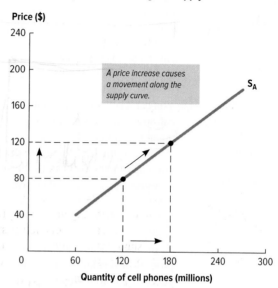

(A) Shifts in the supply curve

When supply decreases, the supply curve shifts to the left.

When supply increases, the supply curve shifts to the right.

Changes in external factors cause the entire supply curve to shift. The shift from S_A to S_B represents an increase in supply, meaning that producers are willing to supply more cell phones at each price. The shift from S_A to S_C represents a decrease in supply, meaning that producers are willing to supply fewer cell phones at each price.

B) Movement along the supply curve

A price increase causes a movement along the supply curve.

A price change causes a movement along the supply curve, but the curve itself remains constant.

A change in one of the nonprice determinants increases or decreases the supply at any given price. These shifts are shown in panel A of Figure 3-4. An increase in supply shifts the curve to the right. A decrease in supply shifts the curve to the left. For instance, an improvement in battery technology that decreases the cost of producing cell phones will shift the entire supply curve to the right, from S_A to S_B; the quantity of phones supplied at every price is higher than before. Conversely, an increase in the price of the gold needed for cell phones raises production costs, shifting the supply curve to the left, from S_A to S_C.

As with demand, we differentiate these shifts in the supply curve from a movement along the supply curve, which is shown in panel B of Figure 3-4. If the price of cell phones changes, but the nonprice determinants of supply stay the same, we find the new quantity supplied by moving along the supply curve to the new price point.

Also, as with demand, economists use very specific terminology to distinguish between a shift in the supply curve and movement along the supply curve:

- We say that a change in one of the nonprice determinants of supply causes an "increase in supply" or "decrease in supply"—that is, a *shift* of the entire supply curve.

- To distinguish this from *movement along* the supply curve, we say that a change in price causes an "increase in the quantity supplied" or "decrease in the quantity supplied."

✓CONCEPT CHECK

☐ What does the law of supply say about the relationship between price and quantity supplied? **[LO 3.4]**

☐ In which direction does the supply curve shift when the price of inputs increases? **[LO 3.5]**

equilibrium

the situation in a market when the quantity supplied equals the quantity demanded; graphically, this convergence happens where the demand curve intersects the supply curve

equilibrium price

the price at which the quantity supplied equals the quantity demanded

equilibrium quantity

the quantity that is supplied and demanded at the equilibrium price

Market Equilibrium

We've discussed the factors that influence the quantities supplied and demanded by producers and consumers. To find out what actually happens in the market, however, we need to combine these concepts. The prices and quantities of the goods that are exchanged in the real world depend on the *interaction* of supply with demand.

Graphically, this convergence of supply with demand happens at the point where the demand curve intersects the supply curve, a point called the market **equilibrium**. The price at this point is called the **equilibrium price** and the quantity at this point is called the **equilibrium quantity**.

Bear with us for a moment as we point out the obvious: There is no sale without a purchase. You can't sell something unless someone buys it. Although this point may be obvious, the implication for markets is profound. When markets work well, the quantity supplied exactly equals the quantity demanded.

We can think of this intersection, where quantity supplied equals quantity demanded, as the point at which buyers and sellers "agree" on the quantity of a good they are willing to exchange at a given price. At higher prices, sellers want to sell more than buyers want to buy. At lower prices, buyers want to buy more than sellers are willing to sell. Because every seller finds a buyer at the equilibrium price and quantity, and no one is left standing around with extra goods or an empty shopping cart, the equilibrium price is sometimes called the *market-clearing price*.

In reality, things don't always work so smoothly: Short-run "friction" sometimes slows the process of reaching equilibrium, even in well-functioning markets. As a result, smart businesspeople may hold some inventory for future sale, and consumers may need to shop around for specific items. On the whole, though, the concept of equilibrium is incredibly accurate (and important) in describing how markets function.

Figure 3-5 shows the market equilibrium for cell phones in the United States. It was constructed by combining the market supply and demand curves shown in Figures 3-1 and 3-3. In this market, the equilibrium price is $100, and the equilibrium quantity supplied and demanded is 150 million phones.

FIGURE 3-5

Market equilibrium in the U.S. market for cell phones

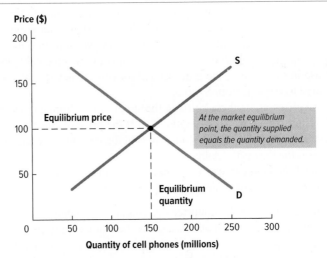

The point where the supply curve intersects the demand curve is called the equilibrium point. In this example, the equilibrium price is $100, and the equilibrium quantity is 150 million cell phones. At this point, consumers are willing to buy exactly as many cell phones as producers are willing to sell.

Reaching equilibrium

LO 3.6 Explain how supply and demand interact to drive markets to equilibrium.

How does a market reach equilibrium? Do sellers know intuitively what price to charge? No. Instead, they tend to set prices by trial and error, by past experience with customers, or by thinking through their costs and adding in a bit of profit. Irrespective of the firm's pricing process, typically the incentives buyers and sellers face naturally drive the market toward an equilibrium price and quantity.

Figure 3-6 shows two graphs, one in which the starting price is above the equilibrium price and the other in which it is below the equilibrium price. In panel A, we imagine that cell phone suppliers think they'll be able to charge $160 for a cell phone, so they produce 240 million phones. They find, though, that consumers will buy only 60 million. (We can read those quantities demanded and supplied at a price of $160 from the demand and supply curves.) When the quantity supplied is higher than the quantity demanded, we say that there is a **surplus** of phones, or an **excess supply**. Manufacturers are stuck holding extra phones in their warehouses; they want to sell that stock and must reduce the price to attract more customers. They have an incentive to keep lowering the price until quantity demanded increases to reach quantity supplied.

In panel B of Figure 3-6, we imagine that cell phone producers make the opposite mistake— they think they'll be able to charge only $40 per phone. They make only 60 million cell phones, but consumers actually are willing to buy 240 million cell phones at that price. When the quantity demanded is higher than the quantity supplied, we say there is a **shortage**, or **excess demand**. Producers will see long lines of people waiting to buy the few available cell phones; they will quickly realize that they could make more money by charging a higher price. They have an incentive to increase the price until quantity demanded decreases to equal quantity supplied, and no one is left standing in line.

surplus (excess supply)
a situation in which the quantity of a good that is supplied is higher than the quantity demanded

shortage (excess demand)
a situation in which the quantity of a good that is demanded is higher than the quantity supplied

---

FIGURE 3-6

Reaching equilibrium in the market for cell phones

When the initial price for cell phones is above the equilibrium point, producers want to supply more cell phones than consumers want to buy. The gap between the quantity supplied and the quantity demanded is called a surplus, or excess supply.

When the initial price for cell phones is below the equilibrium point, consumers want to buy more cell phones than sellers want to produce. The distance between the quantity demanded and the quantity supplied is called a shortage, or excess demand.

Thus, at any price above or below the equilibrium price, sellers face an incentive to raise or lower prices. No one needs to engineer the market equilibrium or share secret information about what price to charge. Instead, money-making incentives drive the market toward the equilibrium price, at which there is neither a surplus nor a shortage. The Real Life box "The Prius shortage of 2003" describes a case in which a producer started out charging the wrong price, but the market solved the problem.

Real Life
The Prius shortage of 2003

In 2003, Toyota introduced the first mainstream "hybrid" car, the Prius, to the U.S. auto market. A hybrid car runs on a combination of gasoline and electric power, using the engine to charge an electric battery in stop-and-go traffic. The Prius got much better gas mileage than its competitors—usually between 40 and 50 miles to the gallon. But for most families the gas savings were more than offset by the car's higher price. The car's main appeal was its environmentally friendly design.

When the Prius hit the U.S. market in October 2003, dealerships sold out immediately. Toyota had significantly underestimated the demand. Prospective buyers had to put their names on a waiting list, often for more than six months. A few years later, when gasoline prices spiked, demand was driven even higher as consumers grew more interested in good gas mileage. In the short run, Toyota could not do much to address the shortage; increasing plant capacity would take time.

Instead, the market found a way to solve the problem. As we know, price acts as a signal between buyers and sellers trying to match demand with supply. When quantity demanded exceeds quantity supplied, the price of the good will rise. As we might expect, Prius buyers began to bid up the price of the car. Dealerships were soon charging thousands of dollars more than the manufacturer's suggested price. For a while, even the price of a *used* Prius was higher than the suggested price for a new car.

Eventually, Toyota responded to the shortage by increasing production capacity of the Prius. The company moved production of the car to progressively larger plants; in 2008, total production topped 1 million. Shortages persisted, however, as increases in demand outstripped the increases in supply. As Toyota scrambled to catch up with demand, sellers happily charged a premium to clear the market.

Source: "Wait time for Prius buyers diminishing," *CNNMoney,* November 6, 2006, http://money.cnn.com/2006/11/06/autos/prius/index.htm.

Changes in equilibrium

LO 3.7 Evaluate the effect of changes in supply and demand on the equilibrium price and quantity.

We've seen what happens to the supply and demand curves when a nonprice factor changes. Because the equilibrium price and quantity are determined by the interaction of supply and demand, a shift in either curve will also change the market equilibrium. Some changes will cause only the demand curve to shift; some, only the supply curve. Some changes will affect both the supply and demand curves.

To determine the effect on market equilibrium of a change in a nonprice factor, ask yourself a few questions:

1. Does the change affect demand? If so, does demand increase or decrease?
2. Does the change affect supply? If so, does supply increase or decrease?
3. How does the combination of changes in supply and demand affect the equilibrium price and quantity?

> **HINT**
> Remember, when we say that supply or demand increases or decreases, we're referring to a *shift in the entire curve*. A change in quantity demanded or supplied would be a *movement* along the curve.

Shifts in demand

We suggested earlier that landline service is a *substitute* for cell phones and that if the price of landline service suddenly skyrockets, then demand for cell phones increases. In other words, the demand curve shifts to the right. The price of landline service probably doesn't affect the supply of cell phones because it doesn't change the costs or expectations that cell phone manufacturers face. So the supply curve stays put.

Figure 3-7 shows the effect of the increase in landline price on the market equilibrium for cell phones. Because the new demand curve intersects the supply curve at a different point, the equilibrium price and quantity change. The new equilibrium price is $120, and the new equilibrium quantity is 180 million.

We can summarize this effect in terms of the three questions to ask following a change in a nonprice factor:

1. *Does demand increase or decrease?* Yes, the change in the price of landline phone service increases demand for cell phones at every price.
2. *Does supply increase or decrease?* No, the change in the price of landline phone service does not affect any of the nonprice determinants of supply. The supply curve stays where it is.
3. *How does the combination of changes in supply and demand affect equilibrium price and quantity?* The increase in demand shifts the demand curve to the right, pushing the equilibrium to a higher point on the stationary supply curve. The new point at which supply and demand "agree"? represents a price of $120 and a quantity of 180 million phones.

FIGURE 3-7

Shift in the demand for cell phones

When an external factor increases the demand for cell phones at all prices, the demand curve shifts to the right. This increase in demand results in a new equilibrium point. Consumers purchase more cell phones at a higher price.

FIGURE 3-8

**Shift in the supply
of cell phones**

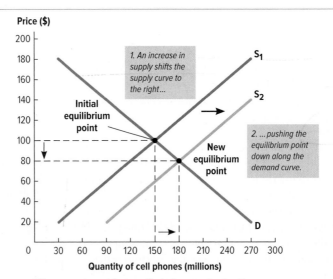

Price ($)

1. *An increase in supply shifts the supply curve to the right...*

2. *...pushing the equilibrium point down along the demand curve.*

Initial equilibrium point

New equilibrium point

Quantity of cell phones (millions)

When an external factor affects the supply of cell phones at all prices, the supply curve shifts. In this example, supply increases and the market reaches a new equilibrium point. Consumers purchase more phones at a lower price.

Shifts in supply

What would happen if a breakthrough in battery technology enabled cell phone manufacturers to construct phones with the same battery life for less money? Once again, asking *How will others respond?* helps us predict the market response. We can see that the new technology does not have much impact on demand: Customers probably have no idea how much the batteries in their phones cost to make, nor will they care as long as battery life stays the same. However, cheaper batteries definitely decrease production costs, increasing the number of phones manufacturers are willing to supply at any given price. So the demand curve stays where it is, and the supply curve shifts to the right.

Figure 3-8 shows the shift in supply and the new equilibrium point. The new supply curve intersects the demand curve at a new equilibrium point, representing a price of $80 and a quantity of 180 million phones.

Once again, we can analyze the effect of the change in battery technology on the market for cell phones in three steps:

1. *Does demand increase or decrease?* No, the nonprice determinants of demand are not affected by battery technology.

2. *Does supply increase or decrease?* Yes, supply increases because the new battery technology lowers production costs.

3. *How does the combination of changes in supply and demand affect equilibrium price and quantity?* The increase in supply shifts the supply curve to the right, pushing the equilibrium to a lower point on the stationary demand curve. The new equilibrium price and quantity are $80 and 180 million phones.

Table 3-4 summarizes the effect of some other changes in demand or supply on the equilibrium price and quantity.

Shifts in both demand and supply

In our discussion so far, we've covered examples in which only demand or supply shifted. However, it's possible that factors that shift demand and supply in the market for cell phones could coincidentally happen at the same time. For example, an increase in landline cost (a demand

TABLE 3-4

Effect of changes in demand or supply on the equilibrium price and quantity

Example of change in demand or supply	Effect on equilibrium price and quantity	Shift in curve
A successful "Buy American" advertising campaign increases the demand for Fords.	The demand curve shifts to the right. The equilibrium price and quantity increase.	
An outbreak of *E. coli* reduces the demand for spinach.	The demand curve shifts to the left. The equilibrium price and quantity decrease.	
The use of robots decreases production costs.	The supply curve shifts to the right. The equilibrium price decreases and the equilibrium quantity increases.	
An increase in the minimum wage increases labor costs.	The supply curve shifts to the left. The equilibrium price increases and the equilibrium quantity decreases.	

factor) could occur simultaneously with an improvement in battery technology (a supply factor). It's also possible that a single change could affect both supply and demand.

For instance, suppose that in addition to reducing the cost of production, the new battery technology makes cell phone batteries last longer. We already know that cheaper batteries will increase supply. As we saw before with increases in supply, price decreases while the quantity increases. Asking *how consumers will respond* allows us to see that the improvement in battery life will also increase demand: Longer-lasting batteries will make a cell phone more valuable to consumers at any given price. As a result, both the demand curve and the supply curve shift to the right. Panels A and B of Figure 3-9 both show that the effect of a double change is a new equilibrium point at a higher price and a higher quantity.

Even without looking at a graph, we could have predicted that in this case the equilibrium *quantity* would rise. Increases in demand and increases in supply both independently lead to a higher equilibrium quantity—and the combination will certainly do so as well.

Without more information, however, we cannot predict the change in equilibrium *price*. Holding all else equal, an increase in demand leads to an increase in price, but an increase in supply leads to a decrease in price. To find the net effect on equilibrium price, we would have to know whether the shift in demand outweighs the shift in supply shown in panel A of Figure 3-9, or vice versa, which is shown in panel B.

FIGURE 3-9

Shifts in both demand and supply

An increase in supply and demand shifts both curves to the right, resulting in a higher quantity traded. However, the direction of the price shift depends on whether supply or demand increases more.

(A) Demand increases more   **(B) Supply increases more**

Sometimes, supply and demand shift together. In this example, both curves shift to the right, but demand increases more. At the new equilibrium point, E_2, consumers purchase more cell phones at a higher price.

Sometimes, supply and demand shift together. In this example, both curves shift to the right, but supply increases more. At the new equilibrium point, E_2, consumers purchase more cell phones at a lower price.

We can state this idea more generally: When supply and demand shift together, it is possible to predict *either* the direction of the change in quantity *or* the direction of the change in price without knowing how much the curves shift. Table 3-5 shows some rules you can use to predict the outcome of these shifts in supply and demand. These rules are:

- When supply and demand move in the *same* direction, we can predict the direction of the change in quantity but not the direction of the change in price.
- When supply and demand move in *opposite* directions, the change in price is predictable, but not the change in quantity.

Thinking about the intuition behind these rules may help you to remember them. Any time you are considering a situation in which supply and demand shift at the same time, ask yourself,

TABLE 3-5

Predicting changes in price and quantity when supply and demand change simultaneously

Supply change	Demand change	Price change	Quantity change
Decrease	Decrease	?	↓
Decrease	Increase	↑	?
Increase	Increase	?	↑
Increase	Decrease	↓	?

"What do buyers and sellers agree on?" For instance, when both supply and demand increase, buyers and sellers "agree" that at any given price, the quantity they are willing to exchange is higher. The reverse is true when both supply and demand decrease: Buyers and sellers agree that at a given price, the quantity they are willing to exchange is lower.

Applying this reasoning to opposite shifts in supply and demand—when one increases but the other decreases—is trickier. To find out what buyers and sellers "agree" on, try rephrasing what it means for demand to increase. One way to say it is that consumers are willing to buy a *higher* quantity at the *same* price. Another way to say it is that consumers are willing to pay a *higher* price to buy the *same* quantity. So, when demand increases and supply decreases, buyers are willing to pay more for the same quantity; also, sellers are willing to supply the same quantity only if they receive a higher price. In other words, they can "agree" on a higher price at any given quantity. We can therefore predict that the equilibrium price will increase.

The opposite is true when demand decreases and supply increases. Buyers are willing to buy the same quantity as before only if the price is lower, and sellers are willing to supply the same quantity at a lower price. Because the two groups can "agree" on a lower price at any given quantity, we can predict that the price will decrease.

Of course, you can always work out the effect of simultaneous shifts in demand and supply by working through the three questions described in the previous section. Draw the shifts in each curve on a graph, as is done in two cases in panels A and B of Figure 3-9, and find the new equilibrium.

Before you finish this chapter, read the Real Life box "Give a man a fish" for some information about how cell phones affected supply and demand in one developing country.

Real Life
Give a man a fish

Are cell phones a technological luxury or a practical necessity? Maybe you can't imagine life without the ability to call or text your friends anywhere, any time. But are cell phones as important as shelter, food, or water? A study in India showed that being able to communicate may help people to meet their basic needs.

In a competitive market, the price of a particular good is found at the point where the quantity supplied equals the quantity demanded. This model assumes that everywhere in the market, buyers and sellers are fully informed about prices and can adjust their behavior accordingly. If buyers and sellers do not have good information about prices, shortages can develop in some locations and surpluses in others.

When the economist Robert Jensen studied the market for fish in Kerala, a state in southwestern India, he found that it did not reach one equilibrium price. Instead, each local fish market has its own equilibrium. In this area, many people rely on fishing for their daily income. Fishermen tend to sell their fish at a single local market; they take the price that prevails at that market on a particular day. If that market has only a few buyers that day, the fishermen end up with too much fish. At the same time, if the fishermen in a neighboring village have a poor catch that day, some buyers at that market will go home empty-handed—even if they are willing to pay a high price. Without a way to know if there is a shortage or surplus in a nearby market, the fishermen can't adjust their prices to reach equilibrium with customers.

Jensen found that the fishermen could solve this problem using cell phones. By communicating with one another and with people on land while out fishing, they were able to find out where their catches would be most profitable that day. They used that information to travel to the right village to sell their fish. Supply began to better match the demand in each village, and

(continued)

prices became more uniform across villages. Access to the right information allowed the market for fish to reach an efficient equilibrium. Sellers earned an average of 8 percent more in profits, and buyers paid an average of 4 percent less for their fish. Fishermen increased their incomes, and consumers stretched their incomes further.

As the saying goes, "Give a man a fish and he will eat for a day. Teach a man to fish and he will eat for a lifetime." To this wisdom, we might add, "Give a man a cell phone. . . ."

Source: R. Jensen, "Give a Man a Fish," *The Quarterly Journal of Economics*, 122, 3, 2007.

✓CONCEPT CHECK

☐ What is the market equilibrium? **[LO 3.6]**

☐ What happens to the equilibrium price and quantity if the supply curve shifts right but the demand curve stays put? **[LO 3.7]**

Conclusion

By the time you reach the end of this course, you'll be quite familiar with the words *supply* and *demand*. We take our time on this subject for good reason: An understanding of supply and demand is the foundation of economic problem solving. You'll be hard-pressed to make wise economic choices without it.

Although markets are not always perfectly competitive, you may be surprised at how accurately many real-world phenomena can be described using the simple rules of supply and demand. In the next chapters we'll use these rules to explain how consumers and producers respond to price changes and government policies.

Key Terms

market economy, p. 50

market, p. 50

competitive market, p. 51

price taker, p. 51

standardized good, p. 51

transaction costs, p. 51

quantity demanded, p. 53

law of demand, p. 53

demand schedule, p. 53

demand curve, p. 53

substitutes, p. 55

complements, p. 56

normal goods, p. 56

inferior goods, p. 56

quantity supplied, p. 59

law of supply, p. 59

supply schedule, p. 60

supply curve, p. 60

equilibrium, p. 64

equilibrium price, p. 64

equilibrium quantity, p. 64

surplus (excess supply), p. 65

shortage (excess demand), p. 65

Summary

LO 3.1 Identify the defining characteristics of a competitive market.

A market is the group of buyers and sellers who trade a particular good or service. In competitive markets, a large number of buyers and sellers trade standardized goods and services. They have full information about the goods, and there is no cost to participate in exchanges in the market. Participants in competitive markets are called price takers because they can't affect the prevailing price for a good.

LO 3.2 Draw a demand curve and describe the external factors that determine demand.

A demand curve is a graph that shows the quantities of a particular good or service that consumers will demand at various prices. It also shows consumers' highest willingness to pay for a given quantity. The law of demand states that for almost all goods, the quantity demanded increases as the price decreases. This relationship results in a downward-sloping demand curve.

Several nonprice factors contribute to consumers' demand for a good at a given price: Consumer preferences, the prices of related goods, incomes, and expectations about the future all affect demand. On a marketwide level, the number of buyers also can increase or decrease total demand. When one of these underlying factors changes, the demand curve will shift to the left or the right.

LO 3.3 Distinguish between a shift in and a movement along the demand curve.

When one of the nonprice factors that drives demand changes, the entire curve *shifts* to the left or the right. With this shift, the quantity demanded at any given price changes. When demand increases, the curve shifts to the right; when demand decreases, it shifts to the left.

When the nonprice determinants of demand stay the same, a change in the price of a good leads to a *movement along* the curve, rather than a shift in the curve.

LO 3.4 Draw a supply curve and describe the external factors that determine supply.

A supply curve is a graph that shows the quantities of a particular good or service that producers will supply at various prices. It shows the minimum price producers must receive to supply any given quantity. The law of supply states that the quantity supplied increases as the price increases, resulting in an upward-sloping supply curve.

Several nonprice factors determine the supply of a good at any given price: They include the prices of related goods, technology, prices of inputs, expectations about the future, and the number of sellers in the market. If one of these underlying factors changes, the supply curve will shift to the left or the right.

LO 3.5 Distinguish between a shift in and a movement along the supply curve.

Just as with demand, a change in the nonprice determinants of supply will cause the entire supply curve to shift to the left or the right. As a result, the quantity supplied is higher or lower at any given price than it was before. When supply increases, the curve shifts to the right; when supply decreases, it shifts to the left.

A shift in the supply curve differs from movement along the supply curve. A movement along the curve happens when the price of a good increases but the nonprice determinants of supply stay the same.

LO 3.6 Explain how supply and demand interact to drive markets to equilibrium.

When a market is in equilibrium, the quantity supplied equals the quantity demanded. The incentives that individual buyers and sellers face drive a competitive market toward equilibrium. If the prevailing price is too high, a surplus will result, and sellers will lower their prices to get rid of the excess supply. If the prevailing price is too low, a shortage will result, and buyers will bid up the price until the excess demand disappears.

LO 3.7 Evaluate the effect of changes in supply and demand on the equilibrium price and quantity.

When one or more of the underlying factors that determine supply or demand change, one or both curves will shift, leading to a new market equilibrium price and quantity.

To calculate the change in the equilibrium price and quantity, you must first determine whether a change affects demand, and, if so, in which direction the curve will shift. Then you must determine whether the change also affects supply, and, if so, in which direction that curve will shift. Finally, you must determine the new equilibrium point where the two curves intersect.

Review Questions

1. Think about a competitive market in which you participate regularly. For each of the characteristics of a competitive market, explain how your market meets these requirements. **[LO 3.1]**

2. Think about a noncompetitive market in which you participate regularly. Explain which characteristic(s) of competitive markets your market does not meet. **[LO 3.1]**

3. Explain why a demand curve slopes downward. **[LO 3.2]**

4. In each of the following examples, name the factor that affects demand and describe its impact on your demand for a new cell phone. **[LO 3.2]**
   a. You hear a rumor that a new and improved model of the phone you want is coming out next year.
   b. Your grandparents give you $500.
   c. A cellular network announces a holiday sale on a data package that includes the purchase of a new smartphone.
   d. A friend tells you how great his new phone is and suggests that you get one, too.

5. Consider the following events:
   a. The price of cell phones goes down by 25 percent during a sale.
   b. You get a 25 percent raise at your job.

Which event represents a shift in the demand curve? Which represents a movement along the curve? What is the difference? **[LO 3.3]**

6. What is the difference between a change in demand and a change in quantity demanded? **[LO 3.3]**

7. Explain why a supply curve slopes upward. **[LO 3.4]**

8. In each of the following examples, name the factor that affects supply and describe its impact on the supply of cell phones. **[LO 3.4]**

   a. Economic forecasts suggest that the demand for cell phones will increase in the future.

   b. The price of plastic goes up.

   c. A new screen technology reduces the cost of making cell phones.

9. Consider the following events:

   a. A fruitworm infestation ruins a large number of apple orchards in Washington state.

   b. Demand for apples goes down, causing the price to fall.

   Which event represents a shift in the supply curve? Which represents a movement along the curve? What is the difference? **[LO 3.5]**

10. What is the difference between a change in supply and a change in quantity supplied? **[LO 3.5]**

11. What is the relationship between supply and demand when a market is in equilibrium? Explain how the incentives facing cell phone companies and consumers cause the market for cell phones to reach equilibrium. **[LO 3.6]**

12. Explain why the equilibrium price is often called the market-clearing price. **[LO 3.6]**

13. Suppose an economic boom causes incomes to increase. Explain what will happen to the demand and supply of phones, and predict the direction of the change in the equilibrium price and quantity. **[LO 3.7]**

14. Suppose an economic boom drives up wages for the sales representatives who work for cell phone companies. Explain what will happen to the demand and supply of phones, and predict the direction of the change in the equilibrium price and quantity. **[LO 3.7]**

15. Suppose an economic boom causes incomes to increase and at the same time drives up wages for the sales representatives who work for cell phone companies. Explain what will happen to the demand for and supply of phones and predict the direction of the change in the equilibrium price and quantity. **[LO 3.7]**

Problems and Applications

1. Consider shopping for cucumbers in a farmers' market. For each statement below, note which characteristic of competitive markets the statement describes. *Choose from:* standardized good, full information, no transaction costs, and participants are price takers. **[LO 3.1]**

   a. All of the farmers have their prices posted prominently in front of their stalls.

   b. Cucumbers are the same price at each stall.

   c. There is no difficulty moving around between stalls as you shop and choosing between farmers.

   d. You and the other customers all seem indifferent about which cucumbers to buy.

2. Suppose two artists are selling paintings for the same price in adjacent booths at an art fair. By the end of the day, one artist has nearly sold out of her paintings while the other artist has sold nothing. Which characteristic of competitive markets has not been met and best explains this outcome? **[LO 3.1]**

   a. Standardized good.

   b. Full information.

   c. No transaction costs.

   d. Participants are price takers.

3. Using the demand schedule in Table 3P-1, draw the daily demand curve for slices of pizza in a college town. **[LO 3.2]**

TABLE 3P-1

Price ($)	Quantity demanded (slices)
0.00	350
0.50	300
1.00	250
1.50	200
2.00	150
2.50	100
3.00	50
3.50	0

4. Consider the market for cars. Which determinant of demand is affected by each of the following events? *Choose from:* consumer preferences, prices of related goods, incomes, expectations, and the number of buyers. **[LO 3.2]**

   a. Environmentalists launch a successful One Family, One Car campaign.

   b. A baby boom occurred 16 years ago.

   c. Layoffs increase as the economy sheds millions of jobs.

   d. An oil shortage causes the price of gasoline to soar.

   e. The government offers tax rebates in return for the purchase of commuter rail tickets.

   f. The government announces a massive plan to bail out the auto industry and subsidize production costs.

5. If a decrease in the price of laptops causes the demand for tablets to increase, are laptops and tablets substitutes or complements? **[LO 3.2]**

6. If rising incomes cause the demand for beer to decrease, is beer a normal or inferior good? **[LO 3.2]**

7. Consider the market for corn. Say whether each of the following events will cause a shift in the demand curve or a movement along the curve. If it will cause a shift, specify the direction. **[LO 3.3]**

   a. A drought hits corn-growing regions, cutting the supply of corn.

   b. The government announces a new subsidy for biofuels made from corn.

   c. A global recession reduces the incomes of consumers in poor countries, who rely on corn as a staple food.

   d. A new hybrid variety of corn seed causes a 15 percent increase in the yield of corn per acre.

   e. An advertising campaign by the beef producers' association highlights the health benefits of corn-fed beef.

8. The demand curve in Figure 3P-1 shows the monthly market for sweaters at a local clothing store. For each of the following events, draw the new outcome. **[LO 3.3]**

   a. Sweaters fall out of fashion.

   b. There is a shortage of wool.

   c. The winter is particularly long and cold this year.

   d. Sweater vendors offer a sale.

FIGURE 3P-1

9. Using the supply schedule found in Table 3P-2, draw the daily supply curve for slices of pizza in a college town. **[LO 3.4]**

10. Consider the market for cars. Which determinant of supply is affected by each of the following events? *Choose from:* prices of related goods, technology, prices of inputs, expectations, and the number of sellers in the market. **[LO 3.4]**

    a. A steel tariff increases the price of steel.

    b. Improvements in robotics increase efficiency and reduce costs.

    c. Factories close because of an economic downturn.

    d. The government announces a plan to offer tax rebates for the purchase of commuter rail tickets.

TABLE 3P-2

Price ($)	Quantity supplied (slices)
0.00	0
0.50	50
1.00	100
1.50	150
2.00	200
2.50	250
3.00	300
3.50	350

e. The price of trucks falls, so factories produce more cars.

f. The government announces that it will dramatically rewrite efficiency standards, making it much harder for automakers to produce their cars.

11. Consider the market for corn. Say whether each of the following events will cause a shift in the supply curve or a movement along the curve. If it will cause a shift, specify the direction. **[LO 3.5]**

   a. A drought hits corn-growing regions.

   b. The government announces a new subsidy for biofuels made from corn.

   c. A global recession reduces the incomes of consumers in poor countries, who rely on corn as a staple food.

   d. A new hybrid variety of corn seed causes a 15 percent increase in the yield of corn per acre.

   e. An advertising campaign by the beef producers' association highlights the health benefits of corn-fed beef.

12. The supply curve in Figure 3P-2 shows the monthly market for sweaters at a local craft market. For each of the following events, draw the new outcome. **[LO 3.5]**

   a. The price of wool increases.

   b. Demand for sweaters decreases.

   c. A particularly cold winter is expected to begin next month.

   d. Demand for sweaters increases.

FIGURE 3P-2

TABLE 3P-3

Price ($)	Quantity demanded (slices)	Quantity supplied (slices)
0.00	350	0
0.50	300	50
1.00	250	100
1.50	200	150
2.00	150	200
2.50	100	250
3.00	50	300
3.50	0	350

13. Refer to the demand and supply schedule shown in Table 3P-3. **[LO 3.6]**

   a. If pizza parlors charge $3.50 per slice, will there be excess supply or excess demand? What is the amount of excess supply or excess demand at that price?

   b. If pizza parlors charge $1.00 per slice, will there be excess supply or excess demand? What is the amount of excess supply or excess demand at that price?

   c. What are the equilibrium price and quantity in this market?

FIGURE 3P-3

FIGURE 3P-4

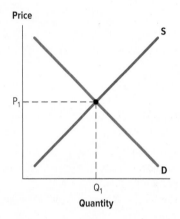

The graph in Figure 3P-3 shows the weekly market for pizzas in a small town. Use this graph to answer Problems 14–16.

14. Which of the following events will occur at a price of $20? **[LO 3.6]**

   a. Equilibrium.

   b. Excess demand.

   c. Excess supply.

   d. No pizzas supplied.

   e. No pizzas demanded.

15. Which of the following events will occur at a price of $10? **[LO 3.6]**

   a. Equilibrium.

   b. Excess demand.

   c. Excess supply.

   d. No pizzas supplied.

   e. No pizzas demanded.

16. What are the equilibrium price and quantity of pizzas? **[LO 3.6]**

17. The graph in Figure 3P-4 shows supply and demand in the market for automobiles. For each of the following events, draw the new market outcome and say whether the equilibrium price and quantity will increase or decrease. **[LO 3.7]**

   a. Environmentalists launch a successful One Family, One Car campaign.

   b. A steel tariff increases the price of steel.

   c. A baby boom occurred 16 years ago.

   d. An oil shortage causes the price of gasoline to soar.

   e. Improvements in robotics increase efficiency and reduce costs.

   f. The government offers a tax rebate for the purchase of commuter rail tickets.

18. Say whether each of the following changes will increase or decrease the equilibrium price and quantity, or whether the effect cannot be predicted. **[LO 3.7]**

   a. Demand increases; supply remains constant.

   b. Supply increases; demand remains constant.

   c. Demand decreases; supply remains constant.

   d. Supply decreases; demand remains constant.

   e. Demand increases; supply increases.

   f. Demand decreases; supply decreases.

   g. Demand increases; supply decreases.

   h. Demand decreases; supply increases.

Endnotes

1. http://www.gsmamobileeconomy.com/GSMA_Global_Mobile_Economy_Report_2015.pdf

2. http://www.ngrguardiannews.com/2015/06/africas-mobile-phone-penetration-now-67/

Math Essentials: Working with Linear Equations

Learning Objectives

LO B.1   Use linear equations to interpret the equation of a line.

LO B.2   Use linear equations to explain shifts and pivots.

LO B.3   Use linear equations to solve for equilibrium.

Relationships between variables can be represented with algebraic equations, as well as graphs and tables. You should be comfortable moving among all three representations. We addressed graphs in Appendix A, "Math Essentials: Understanding Graphs and Slope"; if you didn't read it then, you might want to do so now.

Interpreting the Equation of a Line

LO B.1 Use linear equations to interpret the equation of a line.

If the relationship between two variables is linear, it can be represented by the equation for a line, which is commonly written as:

EQUATION B-1 $y = mx + b$

In this form, called the *slope intercept form, m* is the slope of the line and *b* is the *y*-intercept.

All linear equations provide information about the slope and *y*-intercept of the line. From our discussion in Appendix A, "Math Essentials: Understanding Graphs and Slope," we already know that slope is the ratio of vertical distance (change in *y*) to horizontal distance (change in *x*). So what does the *y*-intercept tell us? It is the point at which the line crosses the *y*-axis. Put another way, it is the value of *y* when *x* is 0. Knowing these values is useful in turning an equation into a graph. Also, as we'll see, they can allow us to get information about the real economic relationship being represented without even having to graph it.

Although you might see the equation for a line rearranged in several different forms, just remember that if *y* is on the left-hand side of the equation, whatever number is multiplying *x* (known as the *coefficient of x*) is your slope. If you don't see a number in front of *x,* the slope is 1. The number being added to or subtracted from a multiple of *x* is a constant that represents the *y*-intercept. If you don't see this number, you know that the *y*-intercept is zero. Take a look at a few examples in Table B-1.

TABLE B-1

Examples of linear equations

The steepness and position of a line in the Cartesian coordinate system is determined by two things: its slope and its intercept. Slope refers to steepness; the intercept determines where the line is positioned.

Equation	Slope	y-intercept
$y = 6x + 4$	6	4
$y = -x - 2$	−1	−2
$y = 10 - 2x$	−2	10
$y = -4x$	−4	0

Turning a graph into an equation

To see how to translate a graph into an algebraic equation, look at Figure B-1. What is the equation that represents this relationship? To derive this equation, we need to find the values of the slope and the y-intercept. We can calculate the slope at any point along the line:

$$\text{Slope} = \frac{\Delta y}{\Delta x} = \frac{(y_2 - y_1)}{(x_2 - x_1)}$$

$$= \frac{(6 - 5)}{(4 - 2)} = \frac{1}{2} = 0.5$$

By looking at the graph to see where the line intersects the y-axis, we can tell that the y-intercept is 4. Therefore, if we write the equation in the form $y = mx + b$, we get $y = 0.5x + 4$. Our table, graph, and equation all give us the same information about the relationship between x and y.

Turning an equation into a graph

Let's work in the opposite direction now, starting with an equation and seeing what information it gives us. The following equation takes the form $y = mx + b$, with P and Q substituted for y and x, respectively.

$$P = -5Q + 25$$

We know from looking at this equation that it represents a line with a slope of −5 and a y-intercept of 25. Suppose that we know this equation represents supply or demand, but we're not sure which. How can we tell whether this is a <u>demand equation or a supply equation</u>? Easy. The slope is negative. We don't need a graph to tell us that the relationship between P and Q is negative and the line will be downward-sloping. Therefore, the equation must represent demand rather than supply.

Because the y-intercept in our equation is 25, we know that the demand curve will cross the y-axis at 25. This tells us that when price is 25, quantity demanded is 0. In order for consumers to demand a positive quantity, price must be lower than 25.

If we need to know more about the relationship represented by the equation, we can graph the demand curve. Since we know that 25 is the y-intercept, we can use the point (0,25) to begin plotting our graph as shown in Figure B-2.

It takes only two points to define a line, and we already have one from the y-intercept. To find a second point, we can plug in any value of Q and solve for the corresponding P (or vice versa). For example, if we let Q = 2 and solve for P, we get:

$$P = -5(2) + 25$$

$$P = -10 + 25$$

$$P = 15$$

We can now plot the point (2,15) and connect it to the y-intercept at (0,25).

FIGURE B-1

Translating a graph into an algebraic equation

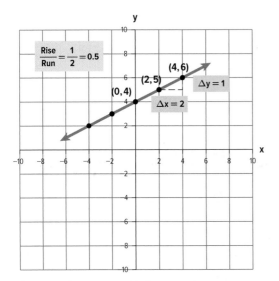

By using information provided on a graph, you can easily construct an equation of the line in the form $y = mx + b$. The slope, m, is calculated by taking the rise of a line over its run. The value of the y-intercept provides the b part of the equation.

FIGURE B-2

Translating an algebraic equation into a graph

The first step in graphing the equation of a line in the form $y = mx + b$ is to plot the y intercept, given by b. Then pick another point by choosing any value of x or y, and solving the equation for the other variable to get an ordered pair that represents another point on the line. Connecting these two points gives the line.

Rather than plugging in random points, though, it is often useful to know the x-intercept as well as the y-intercept. On a demand curve, this will tell us what quantity is demanded when price is 0. To find this intercept, we can let P = 0 and solve for Q:

$$0 = -5Q + 25$$
$$-25 = -5Q$$
$$5 = Q$$

We can now plot the point (5,0) and connect it to (0,25) to graph the demand curve.

Finding intercepts is useful for interpreting other types of graphs as well. In a production possibilities frontier, the intercepts tell you how much of one good will be produced if all resources are used to produce that good and none are used to produce the other good. In the production possibilities frontier shown in Figure B-3, for example, we can find the y-intercept to see that by devoting all workers to making shirts and none to producing wheat, 2 million T-shirts can be produced. Alternatively, we can find the x-intercept to see that if all workers grow wheat and none make shirts, 4 million bushels of wheat can be produced.

We saw in Chapter 2, "Specialization and Exchange," that the slope of the frontier represents the trade-off between producing two goods. We can use our intercepts as the two points we need to calculate the slope.

$$\text{Slope} = \frac{\Delta y}{\Delta x} = \frac{(4 \text{ million} - 0)}{(0 - 2 \text{ million})} = \frac{4}{-2} = -2$$

You know that the slope of the frontier will be negative because it represents a trade-off: You can't make more wheat without giving up some shirts. Because an increase in wheat means a decrease in shirts, the two variables move in opposite directions and have a negative relationship.

FIGURE B-3

Using intercepts to interpret a production possibilities frontier

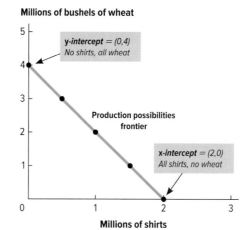

The intercepts of a production possibilities frontier give the maximum amount of a good a country can produce by dedicating all resources in the economy to the production of that good. In this case, with all workers dedicated to the production of one good or the other, the economy can make either 4 million bushels of wheat or 2 million shirts.

This frontier has a constant slope, which means that the trade-off between the two goods—which we can also think of as the opportunity cost of producing shirts in terms of wheat—is also constant.

Equations with *x* and *y* reversed

Thus far, we have represented demand and supply equations with P (or *y*) isolated on the left side of the equation. For example, our demand equation was given as P = −5Q + 25. You may find, however, that in some places, demand and supply equations are given with Q (or *x*) isolated on the left side of the equation instead.

When you see this, you cannot read the equation as giving you the slope and the *y*-intercept. Instead, when an equation is in this form, you have the inverse of slope and the *x*-intercept.

Look at our demand equation again. If we rearrange the equation to solve for Q, we have an equation of the form *x* = *ny* + *a:*

$$P = -5Q + 25$$
$$P - 25 = -5Q$$
$$-\frac{1}{5}P + 5 = Q \quad \text{or} \quad Q = -\frac{1}{5}P + 5$$

We know that the starting equation represents the same underlying relationship as the final equation. For instance, we know that our slope is −5, but in the rearranged form where we have solved for Q, the coefficient multiplying P is the inverse of slope, or $-\frac{1}{5}$. We can generalize this observation to say that when we have an equation of the form $x = ny + a$, $n = \frac{1}{m}$, where *m* is the slope of the line from the same equation expressed in the form $y = mx + b$. We also know that 25 is the *y*-intercept. But in our rearranged form, *a* represents the *x*-intercept,

FIGURE B-4

Same line, different equation forms

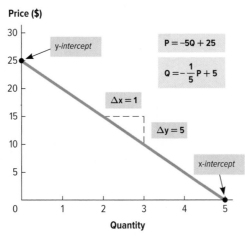

Regardless of whether you solve an equation
for P or Q, the resulting line is the same.

which is 5. The graph in Figure B-4 shows that these two equations represent different aspects of the same line.

Keep in mind that $P = -5Q + 25$ is the same equation as $Q = -\frac{1}{5}P + 5$; we have simply rearranged it to solve for Q instead of P.

Shifts and Pivots

LO B.2 Use linear equations to explain shifts and pivots.

Imagine that your campus cafeteria has a deli with a salad bar and that the price of a salad depends on the number of ingredients you add to it. This relationship is represented by the following equation:

$$y = 0.5x + 4$$

where

y = total price of the salad

x = number of added ingredients

Because our variables are the price of a salad and the number of ingredients, negative quantities do not make sense: You can't have negative carrots in your salad, and we doubt that the cafeteria is paying you to buy salads. Therefore, we can isolate the graph of this equation to the first quadrant, as shown in panel A of Figure B-5.

Our y-intercept of 4 represents the price of a salad if you add zero ingredients. In other words, a plain bowl of lettuce costs $4. The slope of 0.5 represents the cost of adding ingredients to the salad. Each additional ingredient costs 50 cents. The fact that (2,5) is a point along the line shows that the price of a salad with two added ingredients is $5.

FIGURE B-5

Shifting a line to change the intercept

(A) Restrict the graph to Quadrant I

Price of salad ($)

Number of ingredients

In order to easily change the intercept, first restrict the line to values in the first quadrant. This will clearly show the *y*-intercept of the line.

(B) Shift the line upward by moving the intercept

Price of salad ($)

Number of ingredients

Once the *y*-intercept is clear, you can shift the line to the new intercept indicated by the equation of the line.

How much is a salad with six added ingredients?

$$y = 0.5(6) + 4$$
$$y = 3 + 4$$
$$y = 7$$

A salad with six added ingredients is $7, and (6,7) is another point on the graph.

Now, let's see what happens to our graph when the baseline price of a bowl of lettuce without additional ingredients increases to $5. This baseline price is represented by the *y*-intercept, which changes from 4 to 5. The slope of the graph does not change because each additional ingredient still costs 50 cents.

Thus, our equation changes to $y = 0.5x + 5$. Rather than regraphing this new question from scratch, we can simply *shift* the original line to account for the change in the *y*-intercept, as shown in panel B of Figure B-5.

Suppose, instead, that the price of lettuce remains at $4, but the price of additional ingredients increases to $1 each. How will this change the graph and equation?

If the price of lettuce with zero additional ingredients remains at $4, the *y*-intercept will also stay the same. However, the slope will change, increasing from 50 cents to $1. Figure B-6 shows that this change of slope will *pivot* the line in our graph.

Our equation changes as well. This time, we substitute 1 in place of 0.5 for the slope. Thus, $y = x + 4$. (Remember that no coefficient on *x* indicates that the slope is 1.)

What happens if the baseline price of lettuce goes up to $5 *and* the price of toppings goes up to $1? We have to both *shift and pivot* the line to represent the change in the intercept and the slope. (Sounds like a fitness routine, doesn't it?) Figure B-7 shows both changes.

FIGURE B-6

Pivoting a line to change the slope

Changes in slope will pivot the equation of a line. Increases in slope will rotate the line upward; decreases in slope will rotate the line downward.

FIGURE B-7

Shift and pivot

In order to handle a change in slope and intercept, you first shift the line to the new intercept and then pivot the line to reflect the new slope.

You will need to shift and pivot lines in many places throughout this book to represent changes in the relationship between two variables. For instance, we saw in Chapter 3, "Markets," that when a nonprice determinant of demand changes, you need to *shift* the demand curve to show that people demand a higher or lower quantity of a good at any given price. When consumers become more or less sensitive to changes in price, you need to *pivot* the demand curve to represent a change in slope.

Solving for Equilibrium

LO B.3 Use linear equations to solve for equilibrium.

One graph can show multiple relationships between the same two variables. The most frequent case we encounter in this book is graphs showing both the demand relationship and the supply relationship between price and quantity.

Panel A of Figure B-8 shows data from supply and demand schedules. Remember from Chapter 3, "Markets," that as P increases, the quantity *demanded* decreases. Since P and Q are moving in opposite directions, the relationship is negative. When these values are plotted in panel B, we have a downward-sloping line for the demand curve. Conversely, as P increases, the quantity *supplied* increases. Plotting these points yields an upward-sloping supply curve.

When we use one graph to show multiple equations of the same variables, we do so in order to show something meaningful about the relationship between them. For instance, when we show supply and demand on the same graph, we usually want to find the equilibrium point—the point at which the quantity supplied and the quantity demanded are equal to one another at the same price.

FIGURE B-8

Supply and demand

(A) Supply and demand schedules

Price ($)	Q_{demand}	Q_{supply}
20	180	0
30	160	10
40	140	20
50	120	30
80	60	60
90	40	70
100	20	80
110	0	90

The supply and demand schedules show the quantities demanded and supplied for a given price.

(B) Graphing the schedules

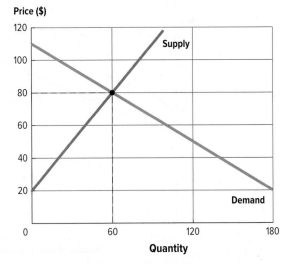

Graphing the values from the schedules gives a downward-sloping demand curve and an upward-sloping supply curve.

We can find the equilibrium point in several ways. If we have schedules showing both demand and supply data, the easiest way to find equilibrium is to locate the price that corresponds to *equal supply and demand quantities*. What is that price in panel A of Figure B-8? At a price of 80, Q is 60 in the demand schedule as well as in the supply schedule.

We can also find the equilibrium point easily by looking at a graph showing both supply and demand. The one-and-only point where the two lines intersect is the equilibrium.

Sometimes, however, it is useful to find equilibrium from equations alone, without having to graph them or to calculate a whole schedule of points by plugging in different prices. Usually you'll want to use this method when you are given equations but no graph or schedule. However, just for practice, let's first derive the supply and demand equations from Figure B-8 and then figure out the equilibrium point.

We want to start by representing supply and demand as equations of the form $y = mx + b$. Let y = price and x = quantity. We need to determine the slope (m) and the y-intercept (b) for each equation.

First, the demand equation: What is the y-intercept? It is the value of y when x is 0. Looking at panel A in Figure B-8, we can see that when Q is zero, P is 110. The y-intercept of the demand equation is 110. Now we need the slope. Because this is a linear relationship and the slope is constant, we can determine the slope using any two points. Let's use the points (180,20) and (160,30).

$$\frac{\Delta y}{\Delta x} = \frac{(P_2 - P_1)}{(Q_2 - Q_1)} = \frac{(20 - 30)}{(180 - 160)} = \frac{-10}{20} = -0.5$$

Thus, our demand equation is: $P = -0.5Q + 110$.

We'll use the same procedure to derive the supply equation. Looking at the supply schedule, we can see that when Q is zero, P is 20. The y-intercept is 20. To determine slope, let's use the points (0,20) and (10,30).

$$\frac{\Delta y}{\Delta x} = \frac{(P_2 - P_1)}{(Q_2 - Q_1)} = \frac{(20 - 30)}{(0 - 10)} = \frac{-10}{-10} = 1$$

Thus, our supply equation is: $P = Q + 20$.

Now that we have our equations, we can use them to solve for equilibrium. Equilibrium represents a point that is on both the demand and supply curves; graphically, it is where the two curves intersect. This means that P on the demand curve must equal P on the supply curve, and the same for Q. Therefore, it makes sense that we find this point by setting the two equations equal to each other.

$$P_D = -0.5Q + 110$$

$$P_S = Q + 20$$

$$P_D = P_S$$

therefore,

$$-0.5Q + 110 = Q + 20$$

This allows us to solve for a numeric value for Q.

$$1.5Q + 20 = 110$$

$$1.5Q = 90$$

$$Q = 60$$

Now that we have a value for Q, we can plug it in either the supply or demand equation to get the value for P. Let's use our supply equation.

$$P = 20 + Q$$

$$P = 20 + 60$$

$$P = 80$$

Solving for equilibrium using the equations gives us the same point we found using the demand and supply schedules: $Q = 60$ and $P = 80$ (60,80).

Problems and Applications

1. Use the demand curve in Figure BP-1 to derive a demand equation. **[LO B.1]**

2. Use the demand schedule in Table BP-1 to derive a demand equation. **[LO B.1]**

3. Use the supply curve in Figure BP-2 to derive a supply equation. **[LO B.1]**

4. Use the supply schedule in Table BP-2 to derive a supply equation. **[LO B.1]**

5. Graph the equation $P = 2Q + 3$. Is this a supply curve or a demand curve? **[LO B.1]**

6. Graph the equation $P = -8Q + 10$. Is this a supply curve or a demand curve? **[LO B.1]**

7. Rearrange the equation $Q = 5 - 0.25P$ and sketch the graph. Is this a supply curve or a demand curve? **[LO B.1]**

8. Rearrange the equation $Q = 0.2P$ and sketch the graph. Is this a supply curve or a demand curve? **[LO B.1]**

TABLE BP-1

Price ($)	Quantity
0	320
10	280
20	240
30	200
40	160
50	120
60	80
70	40
80	0

FIGURE BP-1

FIGURE BP-2

TABLE BP-2

Price ($)	Quantity
100	0
200	25
300	50
400	75
500	100
600	125

9. The entrance fee at your local amusement park is $20 for the day. The entrance fee includes all rides except roller coasters. Roller coasters cost an extra $2 per ride. **[LO B.2]**

    a. Write an equation that represents how much money you will spend on rides as a function of the number of rides you go on: S = total spending on rides; Q = the quantity of roller coaster rides.

    b. What is your total spending on rides if you ride 4 roller coasters?

    c. Draw a graph of the relationship between total spending on rides and the number of roller coaster rides.

    d. Redraw the graph from part (c) to show what changes if the entrance fee increases to $25.

    e. Rewrite the equation from part (a) to incorporate the increased entrance fee of $25.

    f. After the entrance fee increases to $25, what is your total spending on rides if you ride 4 roller coasters?

10. Use the following two equations: **[LO B.3]**
    (1) $P = 12 - 2Q$
    (2) $P = 3 + Q$

    a. Find the equilibrium price and quantity.

    b. Graph the demand and supply equations. Illustrate the equilibrium point.

11. With reference to Table BP-3: **[LO B.3]**

    a. Use the information from the table to create the demand and supply equations.

    b. Use your demand and supply equations to solve for equilibrium.

    c. Graph supply and demand curves. Illustrate the equilibrium point.

TABLE BP-3

Price ($)	Quantity demanded	Quantity supplied
0	12	0
20	10	4
40	8	8
60	6	12
80	4	16
100	2	20
120	0	24

Elasticity

COFFEE BECOMES CHIC

In the 1990s, a coffeehouse craze rippled through middle-class communities in the United States, as a strong economy bolstered sales of high-priced espresso drinks. Soon, Americans were making daily pilgrimages to a place called Starbucks, where a cup of coffee had been transformed into the "Starbucks experience," complete with soundtrack, mints, and charity-themed water bottles. For 15 years the Starbucks business model was highly successful. From 1992 through 2007, the company expanded by over 15,000 stores.

When the U.S. economy stumbled in 2008, however, Starbucks's growth rate dropped to an all-time low. Competitors and customers began to ask, "How much is too much for a cup of coffee?" Presumably, Starbucks executives had asked themselves that very question over the course of more than a decade. Given the company's phenomenal rate of expansion, they must have had the right answer—at least until the economy started having problems.

How do businesses like Starbucks make pricing decisions? How do they anticipate and react to changing circumstances? We learned in the prior chapter that when price changes, quantity demanded changes. If Starbucks raised the price of its lattes—perhaps due to a coffee supply shortage caused by poor weather in Ethiopia—that change would reduce the quantity demanded

© Somsak Sudthangtum/123RF

by consumers. This chapter introduces the idea of elasticity, which describes *how much* this change in prices will affect consumers.

Like the market for cell phones, the market for gourmet coffee is not perfectly competitive. Managers of a big company like Starbucks have some ability to set prices, and they try to choose prices that will earn the largest profits. They also try to respond to changing market conditions: How much will sales fall if the price of coffee beans drives up the cost of a latte? How much will people decrease their coffee consumption during a recession? How many customers will be lost if competitors like Dunkin' Donuts and McDonald's offer less-expensive coffee? Even in perfectly competitive markets, producers want to predict how their profits will change in response to economic conditions and changes in the market price.

Nonprofit service providers also often need to think about price elasticity. For instance, a nonprofit hospital wants to set the price of care so as to cover costs without driving away too many patients. Similarly, colleges and universities want to cover costs and keep education affordable for students.

The ability to address issues like these is critical for any public or private organization. Understanding how to price a Starbucks latte requires the same kind of thinking as figuring out whether to raise entrance fees to national parks to cover the costs of maintaining the wilderness. Solving these challenges relies on a tool called *elasticity,* a measure of how much supply and demand will respond to changes in price and income.

In this chapter, you will learn how to calculate the effect of a price change on the quantity supplied or demanded. You will become familiar with some rules that businesses and policy-makers follow when they cannot measure elasticity exactly. Using what you know about supply and demand, you will be able to categorize different types of goods by noting whether their elasticities are positive or negative. You will also learn how to use a rough approximation of price elasticity to tell whether raising prices will raise or lower an organization's total revenue.

What Is Elasticity?

If Starbucks raises the price of a latte, we can expect the quantity of lattes demanded to fall. But by how much? Although we saw in Chapter 3, "Markets," that price increases cause the quantity demanded to fall in a competitive market, we have not yet been able to say *how big* that movement will be. That question is the subject of this chapter.

Elasticity is a measure of how much consumers and producers will respond to a change in market conditions. The concept can be applied to supply or demand. Also, it can be used to measure responses to a change in the price of a good, a change in the price of a related good, or a change in income.

The concept of elasticity allows economic decision makers to anticipate *how others will respond* to changes in market conditions. Whether you are a business owner trying to sell cars or a public official trying to set sales taxes, you need to know how much a change in prices will affect consumers' willingness to buy.

elasticity
a measure of how much consumers and producers will respond to a change in market conditions

The most commonly used measures of elasticity are *price elasticity of demand* and *price elasticity of supply*. These two concepts describe how much the quantity demanded and the quantity supplied change when the price of a good changes. The *cross-price elasticity of demand* describes how much the demand curve shifts when the price of another good changes. It tells us how much the quantity of coffee demanded changes, for example, when the price of tea increases. Another helpful measure, *income elasticity of demand,* measures how much the demand curve shifts when consumers' incomes change. We'll examine these four elasticity concepts in this chapter. Let's begin with price elasticity of demand.

Price Elasticity of Demand

Price elasticity of demand describes the size of the change in the quantity demanded of a good or service when its price changes. We showed in Chapter 3, "Markets" that quantity demanded generally decreases when the price increases, but so far we have not been able to say *how much* it decreases. Price elasticity of demand fills this gap in our understanding of supply and demand.

price elasticity of demand
the size of the change in the quantity demanded of a good or service when its price changes

Another way to think about price elasticity of demand is as a measure of consumers' sensitivity to price changes. Sensitivity to price changes is measured as more or less elastic:

- When consumers' buying decisions are highly influenced by price, we say that their demand is *more elastic*. By that, we mean that a small change in price causes a large change in the quantity demanded.

- When consumers are not very sensitive to price changes—that is, when they will buy approximately the same quantity, regardless of the price—we say that their demand is *more inelastic*.

Calculating price elasticity of demand

LO 4.1 Calculate price elasticity of demand using the mid-point method.

Consider the challenge Starbucks faced in shoring up falling sales during the recession. In this situation, a business might lower its prices by offering a sale. But would a sale work? How much could Starbucks's managers expect purchases to increase as a result of the sale? In other words, *How will customers respond* to a sale? The ability to answer this question is a critical tool for businesses. To do so, we need to know the price elasticity of demand for Starbucks coffee.

Let's say that Starbucks usually charges $2 for a cup of coffee. What might happen if it offers a special sale price of $1.50? Suppose that before the sale, Starbucks sold 10 million cups of coffee each day. Now, say that consumers react to the sale by increasing the quantity demanded to 15 million cups per day. Figure 4-1 shows the quantity demanded before and after the sale as two points on the demand curve for coffee. Based on the results of this sale, what can we say about consumers' sensitivity to the price of coffee at Starbucks?

Mathematically, price elasticity is the percentage change in the quantity of a good that is demanded in response to a given percentage change in price. The basic formula looks like Equation 4-1.

mid-point method
method that measures percentage change in quantity demanded (or quantity supplied) relative to a point midway between two points on a curve; used to estimate elasticity

EQUATION 4-1
$$\text{Price elasticity of demand} = \frac{\%\ \text{change in Q demanded}}{\%\ \text{change in P}}$$

To calculate percentage change, we will be using the **mid-point method**. The mid-point method measures the percentage change relative to a point *midway between the two points.* The mid-point method can be used to calculate the percentage change in quantity demanded, for example

FIGURE 4-1

Elasticity of the demand for coffee

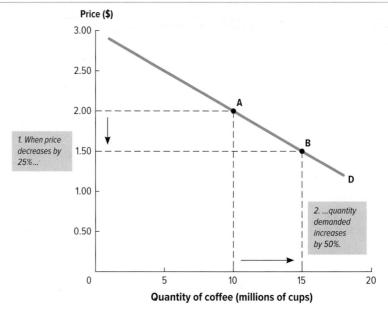

Price ($)

1. When price decreases by 25%...

2. ...quantity demanded increases by 50%.

Quantity of coffee (millions of cups)

When the price of coffee is $2 a cup, consumers demand 10 million cups. If the price falls to $1.50 per cup, the quantity demanded increases to 15 million cups.

(the numerator in Equation 4-1). We do that by dividing the change in quantity demanded by the mid-point (average) quantity, as shown in Equation 4-2.

EQUATION 4-2 $$\% \text{ change in Q demanded} = \frac{Q_2 - Q_1}{\text{Average of Q}} = \frac{Q_2 - Q_1}{\left(\frac{Q_2 + Q_1}{2}\right)}$$

In the denominator of this expression, the mid-point (average) quantity is equal to the sum of the two quantities divided by 2.

We can find the percentage change in price (the denominator of Equation 4-1) in the same way, as shown in Equation 4-3.

EQUATION 4-3 $$\% \text{ change in P} = \frac{P_2 - P_1}{\text{Average of P}} = \frac{P_2 - P_1}{\left(\frac{P_2 + P_1}{2}\right)}$$

? POTENTIALLY CONFUSING

Another way of calculating *percentage change* is to divide the difference between the starting and ending levels by the starting level. Using this method, the percentage change in quantity demanded would be expressed as:

$$\% \text{ change in quantity demanded} = \left[\frac{(Q_2 - Q_1)}{Q_1}\right]$$

Notice that the denominator of this expression is simply the starting value of quantity demanded. While you may have used this method before, this method causes a measurement problem when we use it to calculate elasticity: The elasticity changes depending on which direction we move along the demand curve. To avoid this problem, we will be using the mid-point method for calculating percentage change in this chapter.

Putting Equation 4-2 and Equation 4-3 together, we get Equation 4-4, which is the mid-point method for calculating the price elasticity of demand. This is a fully fleshed-out version of Equation 4-1.

EQUATION 4-4 $$\text{Price elasticity of demand} = \frac{(Q_2 - Q_1)/[(Q_2 + Q_1)/2]}{(P_2 - P_1)/[(P_2 + P_1)/2]}$$

Looking at our example, we find that the demand for coffee went from 10 million cups at $2 to 15 million cups at $1.50. So the average (mid-point) quantity demanded was 12.5 million cups. The average (mid-point) price was $1.75. If we plug the original and sale quantities and prices into Equation 4-4, what do we find? The price was cut by 29 percent and the quantity demanded rose by 40 percent. That tells us that the price elasticity of demand is −1.38.

$$\text{Price elasticity of demand} = \frac{\left(\dfrac{15 \text{ million} - 10 \text{ million}}{12.5 \text{ million}}\right)}{\left(\dfrac{1.50 - 2.00}{1.75}\right)} = \frac{0.40}{-0.29} = -1.38$$

What does it mean for the price elasticity of demand to be −1.38? Remember that the elasticity describes the size of the change in the quantity demanded of a good when its price changes. A measure of −1.38 price elasticity of demand for cups of coffee means that a 1 percent decrease in the price of coffee will lead to a 1.38 percent increase in the quantity of coffee cups demanded. (Alternatively, we could also say that a 1 percent *increase* in the price of coffee will lead to a 1.38 percent *decrease* in the quantity of coffee cups demanded.)

The *price elasticity of demand will always be a negative number*. Why? Because price and quantity demanded *move in opposite directions:*

- A positive change in price will cause a negative change in the quantity demanded.
- A negative change in price will cause a positive change in the quantity demanded.

In our example, the price of coffee decreased and the quantity demanded increased.

However, be aware that economists often drop the negative sign and express the price elasticity of demand as a positive number, just for the sake of convenience. Don't be fooled! Under normal circumstances, price elasticity of demand is always negative, whether or not the negative sign is printed.

POTENTIALLY CONFUSING

Some books include the negative sign, and others drop the negative sign. Another way to think of an elasticity measure is as an absolute value. The *absolute value* of a number is its distance from zero, or its numerical value without regard to its sign. For example, the absolute values of 4 and −4 are both 4. The absolute value of elasticity measures the "size" of the response, while the sign measures its direction. Sometimes only the absolute value will be printed, when it is assumed that you know the direction of the change.

You might be wondering why we work with percentages in calculating elasticity. Why not just compare the change in the quantity demanded to the change in price? The answer is that percentages allow us to avoid some practical problems. Think about what would happen if one person measured coffee in 12-ounce cups, while another measured it by the pot or the gallon. Without percentages, we would have several different measures of price elasticity, depending on which unit of measurement we used. To avoid this problem, economists use the *percentage change* in quantity rather than the *absolute change* in quantity. That way, the elasticity of demand for coffee is the same whether we measure the quantity in cups, pots, or gallons.

Determinants of price elasticity of demand

LO 4.2 Explain how the determinants of price elasticity of demand affect the degree of elasticity.

How would the quantity demanded of lattes (or your drink of choice) change if the price fell from $3 to $1.50? Now, how much would the quantity demanded of cotton socks change if the price fell from $10 per pack to $5? Although both represent a 50 percent price reduction, we suspect that the former might change your buying habits more than the latter. Socks are socks, and $5 savings probably won't make you rush out and buy twice as many. To state this more formally, we would say that the demand for lattes is more elastic than the demand for socks.

The underlying idea here is that consumers are more sensitive to price changes for some goods and services than for others. As said earlier, we can classify the degree of sensitivity to price changes by labeling the demand for a particular good as elastic or inelastic. More rigorous definitions of these terms will be given later, but for now remember this: When consumers are very responsive to price changes for a particular good, we say that the demand for that good is *more elastic*. When consumers are not very responsive to price changes for a particular good, we say the demand for that good is *more inelastic*.

Why isn't price elasticity of demand the same for all goods and services? Many factors determine consumers' responsiveness to price changes. The availability of substitutes, relative need and relative cost, and the time needed to adjust to price changes all affect price elasticity of demand.

Would you expect this price change to reduce the quantity demanded of lobsters? *www.CartoonStock.com*

"Great idea, Pete!"

Availability of substitutes

Recall from Chapter 3, "Markets," that substitutes are goods that are distinguishable from one another but have similar uses. When the price of a good with a close substitute increases, consumers will buy the substitute instead. If close substitutes are available for a particular good, then the demand for that good will be *more elastic* than if only distant substitutes are available. For example, the price elasticity of demand for cranberry juice is likely to be relatively elastic; if the price gets too high, many consumers may switch to grape juice.

Degree of necessity

When a good is a basic necessity, people will buy it even if its price rises. The demand for socks probably is not very elastic, nor is the demand for home heating during the winter. Although people may not like it when the prices of these goods rise, they will buy them to maintain a basic level of comfort. And when prices fall, they probably won't buy vastly more socks or make their homes a lot hotter.

In comparison, the demand for luxuries like vacations, expensive cars, and jewelry is likely to be much more elastic. Most people can easily do without these goods when their prices rise. Note, however, that the definition of a necessity depends on your standards and circumstances. In Florida, air conditioning may be a necessity and heating a luxury; the opposite is likely to be true in Alaska.

Cost relative to income

All else held equal, if consumers spend a very small share of their incomes on a good, their demand for the good will be less elastic than otherwise. For instance, most people can get a year's supply of ballpoint pens for just a few dollars. Even if the price doubled, a year's supply would still cost less than $10, so consumers probably would not bother to adjust their consumption of ballpoint pens.

The opposite is also true: If a good costs a very large proportion of a person's income, like going on a luxury three-week vacation to the beach, the demand for the good will be more elastic. If the price of rooms at high-end beachfront hotels doubles, then a lot of people will decide to do something else with their vacations.

Adjustment time

Goods often have much more elastic demand over the long run than over the short run. Often, adjusting to price changes takes some time. Consider how you might react to an increase in the price of gasoline. In the short run, you might cancel a weekend road trip, but you would still have to do the same amount of driving as usual to school, work, or the grocery store. Over a year, however, you could consider other choices that would further reduce your consumption of gas, such as buying a bus pass or a bicycle, getting a more fuel-efficient car, or moving closer to work or school.

Scope of the market

A major caveat to the determinants just described is that each depends on how you define the market for a good or service. The price elasticity of demand for bananas might be high, but the price elasticity of demand for *fruit* could still be low because there are more substitutes for bananas than for the broader category of fruit. Similarly, although water might have a very low price elasticity of demand as a basic necessity, the demand for *bottled* water could be extremely elastic.

Using price elasticity of demand

When we make decisions in the real world, we often don't know the exact price elasticity of demand. But we don't always need to estimate elasticity precisely to know that consumers will react differently to price changes for lattes than for socks. Instead, businesses and other decision makers often know something general about the shape of the demand curve they are facing. Being able to place goods into several broad categories of elasticity can facilitate real pricing decisions in situations without full information.

At the extremes, demand can be perfectly elastic or perfectly inelastic. When demand is **perfectly elastic**, the quantity demanded drops to zero when the price increases even a minuscule amount. Thus, a perfectly elastic demand curve is horizontal, as shown in panel A of Figure 4-2. This graph indicates that consumers are very sensitive to price. When demand is **perfectly inelastic**, the quantity demanded is the same no matter what the price. Thus, the demand curve is vertical, as shown in panel B of Figure 4-2. These two extremes rarely occur in real life.

perfectly elastic demand
demand for which any increase in price will cause quantity demanded to drop to zero; represented by a perfectly horizontal line

perfectly inelastic demand
demand for which quantity demanded remains the same regardless of price; represented by a perfectly vertical line

---

FIGURE 4-2

Perfectly elastic and perfectly inelastic demand

When demand is perfectly elastic, the demand curve is horizontal. At prices above $5, consumers will not buy any quantity of the good.

When demand is perfectly inelastic, the demand curve is vertical. Consumers will always demand the same quantity of a good, regardless of the price.

Between these two extremes, elasticity is commonly divided into three quantifiable categories: elastic, inelastic, and unit-elastic. When the absolute value of the price elasticity of demand is greater than 1, we call the associated quantity demanded **elastic**. With elastic demand, a given percentage change in the price of a good will cause an even larger percentage change in the quantity demanded. For example, Panel A of Figure 4-3 shows that for elastic demand, an 80 percent change in price could lead to a 150 percent change in the quantity demanded. Remember, we are using the mid-point method to calculate the percentage change here.

elastic
demand that has an absolute value of elasticity greater than 1

When the absolute value of the price elasticity of demand is less than 1, we say that demand is **inelastic**. With inelastic demand, a given percentage change in price will cause a smaller percentage change in the quantity demanded. Panel B of Figure 4-3 illustrates that for inelastic demand, an 80 percent change in price might lead to a 50 percent change in the quantity demanded.

inelastic
demand that has an absolute value of elasticity less than 1

unit-elastic
demand that has an absolute value of elasticity exactly equal to 1

If the absolute value of elasticity is exactly 1—that is, if a percentage change in price causes the same percentage change in the quantity demanded—then we say that demand is **unit-elastic**. Panel C of Figure 4-3 illustrates that for unit-elastic demand, an 80 percent change in price leads to an 80 percent change in the quantity demanded.

The concept of elasticity is not merely a theoretical tool. Businesses and policy decisions often depend on the value of particular elasticities. Table 4-1 displays actual estimates of price elasticities for a selection of goods. You can ask yourself why some price elasticities are larger than others. Why is the quantity demanded of air travel more elastic for leisure travel than business travel? Why is the quantity demanded of gasoline more elastic in the long run than the short run?

As we'll see later in this chapter, the terms *elastic, inelastic,* and *unit-elastic* can be used to describe any sort of elasticity, not just the price elasticity of demand. Although these categories may sound academic, they can have serious implications for real-world business and policy decisions. The Real Life box "Does charging for bednets decrease malaria?" describes a case in which knowing whether the price elasticity of demand is elastic or inelastic is a matter of life and death.

FIGURE 4-3

Elastic, inelastic, and unit-elastic demand

1. After price decreases by 80% under...

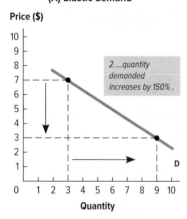

(A) Elastic demand

2. ...quantity demanded increases by 150%.

With an elastic demand curve, a small change in price leads to a big change in the quantity demanded. As a result, the price elasticity of demand is greater than 1.

(B) Inelastic demand

2. ...quantity demanded increases by 50%.

With an inelastic demand curve, even a large price change has a small effect on the quantity demanded. As a result, the price elasticity of demand is less than 1.

(C) Unit-elastic demand

2. ...quantity demanded increases by 80%.

When demand is unit-elastic, the percentage change in price equals the percentage change in quantity, so that the price elasticity of demand is exactly 1.

TABLE 4-1

Estimated price elasticities of demand

Good	Estimated elasticities
Oil in the short run	−0.02
Eggs	−0.27
Gasoline in the short run	−0.05 to −0.6
Water (residential)	−0.41
Alcoholic drinks	−0.44
Gasoline in the long run	−0.25 to −0.7
Electricity	−0.38 to −0.61
Soft drinks	−0.7 to −0.8
Heroin	−0.8
Business air travel	−0.8
Leisure air travel	−1.6
NFL ticket resales	−2.94

Sources: T. Andreyeva, M. W. Long, and K. D. Brownell, "The impact of food prices on consumption: A systematic review of research on the price elasticity of demand for food," *American Journal of Public Health* 100, no. 2 (2010), p. 216; T. Helbling et al., "Oil scarcity, growth, and global imbalances," *in* International Monetary Fund, *World Economic Outlook,* April 2011, ch. 3, https://www.imf.org/external/pubs/ft/weo/2011/01/pdf/c3.pdf; S. M. Olmstead and R. N. Stavins, "Comparing price and nonprice approaches to urban water conservation," *Water Resources Research* 45, no. 4 (2009); T. A. Olmstead, S. M. Alessi, B. Kline, R. L. Pacula, and N. M. Petry, "The price elasticity of demand for heroin: Matched longitudinal and experimental evidence," *Journal of Health Economics* 41 (2015), pp. 59–71; P. Belobaba, A. Odoni, and C. Barnhart, eds., *The Global Airline Industry* (New York: Wiley & Sons, 2015), p. 61; M. A. Diehl, J. G. Maxcy, and J. Drayer, "Price elasticity of demand in the secondary market: Evidence from the National Football League," *Journal of Sports Economics* 16, no. 6 (August 2015), pp. 557–75; A. J. Ros, "An econometric assessment of electricity demand in the United States using panel data and the impact of retail competition on prices," *Insight in Economics,* June 9, 2015, http://www.nera.com/content/dam/nera/publications/2015/PUB_Econometric_Assessment_Elec_Demand_US_0615.pdf; P. Krugman, "Prices and gasoline demand," *The New York Times,* May 9, 2008, http://krugman.blogs.nytimes.com/2008/05/09/prices-and-gasoline-demand/?_r=0; L. Levin, M. S. Lewis, and F. A. Wolak, "High frequency evidence on the demand for gasoline," April 12, 2013, http://web.stanford.edu/group/fwolak/cgi-bin/sites/default/files/files/Levin_Lewis_Wolak_demand.pdf.

Real Life

Does charging for bednets decrease malaria?

Around the world, malaria kills millions of young people every year. There is no vaccine to protect children from malaria. There is a way to escape the disease, though: sleep under a bednet that has been treated with insecticide. Bednets prevent malaria by shielding people from disease-carrying mosquitoes.

Organizations that want to promote the use of bednets to fight malaria face a practical question: Would charging a fee for bednets be more effective in reducing the illness than handing out the nets for free?

Those who advocate charging a fee argue that people who pay for the nets will value them more, and will probably use them more, than those who receive the nets for free. These advocates expect that fewer nets will be wasted on people who don't really want them and that people who do buy them will be more likely to use them. Moreover, if people pay for their bednets, organizations will be able to afford to distribute more of them. On the other hand, the law

(continued)

of demand states that the higher the price, the lower the quantity demanded. Even if charging a fee would make some people more likely to use the nets, it might dissuade others from getting them, thus undermining the aim of the anti-malaria campaign. In particular, it may lead the very poorest to not be able to have a bednet.

To settle this question, health organizations needed to know the price elasticity of the demand for bednets. Working in Kenya, economists Jessica Cohen of the Harvard School of Public Health and Pascaline Dupas of Stanford set up an experiment to try both methods and to measure the price elasticity of demand for bednets. As it turned out, charging a fee greatly reduced the quantity of the nets demanded. In the experiment, the number of people who took bednets dropped by 75 percent when the price increased from zero to $0.75. Furthermore, the people who bought bednets at that price did not use them more effectively than those who received them for free.

If profit were the goal in this campaign, a few bednets sold at $0.75 would generate more revenue than a lot of bednets given away for free. But the goal was to protect people from malaria, not to make a profit. For organizations with a social mission, free distribution of bednets seems more effective than charging a fee.

Source: J. Cohen and P. Dupas, "Free distribution or cost sharing? Evidence from a randomized malaria prevention experiment," *Quarterly Journal of Economics* 125, no. 1 (February 2010), pp. 1–45.

Knowing whether the demand for a good is elastic or inelastic is extremely useful in business. That information allows a manager to determine whether a price increase will cause total revenue to rise or fall. **Total revenue** is the amount that a firm receives from the sale of goods and services, calculated as the quantity sold multiplied by the price paid for each unit. This number is important for an obvious reason: It tells us how much money sellers receive when they sell something.

An increase in price affects total revenue in two ways:

- It causes a *quantity effect,* or a decrease in total revenue that results from selling fewer units of the good.
- It causes a *price effect,* or an increase in total revenue that results from receiving a higher price for each unit sold.

Figure 4-4 shows both the quantity effect and the price effect. When the quantity effect outweighs the price effect, a price increase will cause a drop in total revenue, as it does in Figure 4-4. When the price effect outweighs the quantity effect, a price increase will raise total revenue.

When demand is elastic, a price increase causes total revenue to fall. We already know that when demand is elastic, a change in price will cause a larger percentage change in quantity demanded. Another way of saying this is that the quantity effect outweighs the price effect. So when demand is elastic, a price increase causes a proportionally larger decrease in the quantity demanded, and total revenue falls.

Conversely, when demand is inelastic, the percentage change in price is larger than the percentage change in quantity demanded. The price effect outweighs the quantity effect, and total revenue increases. With inelastic demand, then, consumers will purchase less of a good when its price rises, but the change in the quantity demanded will be proportionally less than the change in price.

Figure 4-5 shows this trade-off between the price and quantity effects. As you can see, panel A shows an elastic demand in which a $1 change in price causes the quantity demanded to increase by 4,000. With the inelastic demand curve in panel B, a $2 decrease in price increases quantity demanded by only 1,000.

total revenue
the amount that a firm receives from the sale of goods and services; calculated as the quantity sold multiplied by the price paid for each unit

FIGURE 4-4

Effect of a price increase on total revenue

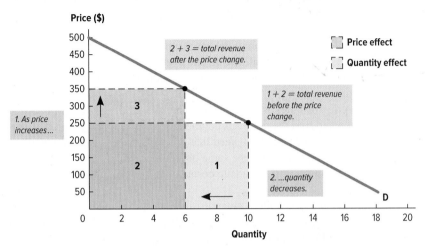

The colored rectangles represent total revenue at two different prices. As the price increases from $250 to $350, total revenue is affected in two ways. The blue rectangle represents the increase in revenue received for each unit sold (the price effect). The yellow rectangle represents the decrease in total revenue as the number of units sold drops (the quantity effect). The elasticity of demand determines which effect is larger. In this case, the yellow area is larger than the blue area, meaning that the quantity effect outweighs the price effect, and total revenue decreases.

FIGURE 4-5

Elasticity and changes in total revenue

In this market, demand is elastic. At a price of $1, 5,000 units are sold for a total revenue of $5,000. If the price increases to $2, only 1,000 units are sold for a total revenue of only $2,000. The quantity effect outweighs the price effect.

In this market, demand is inelastic. At a price of $1, 5,000 units are sold for a total revenue of $5,000. If the price increases to $3, the number of units sold drops by only 1,000, to 4,000 units. Because the price effect outweighs the quantity effect, total revenue climbs to $12,000, an increase of $7,000.

There is one final point to make. So far, everything we've said has described elasticity *at a particular spot on the demand curve.* For most goods, however, elasticity varies along the curve. So when we said that the price elasticity of demand for coffee was −1.38, we meant that it was −1.38 for a price change from $1.50 to $2 a cup. If the price changes from $2 to $2.50, the elasticity will be different.

The reasoning behind this fact is common sense. Imagine that the price of lattes plummets to 10 cents, and you get into the habit of buying one every morning. What would you do if you showed up one morning and found that the price had doubled overnight, to 20 cents? We bet you'd shrug and buy one anyway.

Now, imagine the price of lattes is $10, and you buy them only as occasional treats. If you arrive at the coffee shop and find the price has doubled to $20, what will you do? You'd probably consider very carefully whether you really need that latte. In both cases, you would be responding to a 100 percent increase in price for the same product, but you would react very differently. This makes perfect sense: In one case, the latte costs you only 10 more cents, but in the other, it costs an additional $10.

Your reactions to the latte illustrate a general rule: *Demand tends to be more elastic when price is high and more inelastic when price is low.* This brings us to an important caveat about the three graphs shown in Figure 4-3. Although the example of an elastic demand curve in panel A has a steeper *slope* than the inelastic demand curve in panel B, we now know that slope is not the same as elasticity.

In fact, the elasticity of demand is different at different points along a linear demand curve. The reasoning is nonintuitive, but straightforward when you think about it graphically. Look at Figure 4-6. The line in panel B has a constant slope, but the percentage changes in price and

FIGURE 4-6

Changes in elasticity along the demand curve

(A) Demand and revenue schedule

Price ($)	Quantity	Total revenue ($)
50	0	0
45	1	45
40	2	80
35	3	105
30	4	120
25	5	125
20	6	120
15	7	105
10	8	80
5	9	45
0	10	0

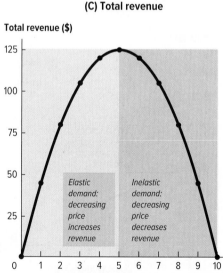

This table lists the data shown in the graphs in panels A and B. Quantity demanded always increases as price falls. Total revenue rises until the price falls to $25, then falls at lower prices.

Price elasticity of demand varies along the demand curve. Above a certain price, demand is elastic; below it, demand is inelastic.

This graph shows total revenue along the demand curve shown above. Total revenue first rises, but then begins to fall as demand moves from elastic to inelastic.

quantity are very different at either end of the curve. For instance, going from $45 to $40 is a much smaller difference (in percentage terms) than from $10 to $5, but the slope of the curve is the same between both sets of points.

The result is that as we move along a linear demand curve starting from a price equal to zero, revenue first increases as the price increases, and then decreases with higher prices. (You can see this result in the "Total revenue" column in panel A.) The maximum revenue occurs where demand is unit-elastic.

Panel C of Figure 4-6 graphs out the total revenue curve associated with the demand curve in panel B, using calculations from the schedule in Panel A. Note that when the price is high, lowering the price will increase revenue. For example, when the price decreases from $45 to $40 (see the schedule), total revenue almost doubles, from $45 to $80. When the price is low, however, lowering it further decreases total revenue. Moving from $10 to $5, for example, decreases total revenue from $80 to $45.

Price elasticity of demand has all sorts of real-world applications. See, for example, the issue discussed in the What Do You Think? box "Should entrance fees at national parks be raised?"

> For a refresher on slope versus elasticity, see Appendix C, "Math Essentials: Calculating Percentage Change, Slope, and Elasticity," which follows this chapter.

What Do You Think?
Should entrance fees at national parks be raised?

The National Park Service is the steward of 84 million acres of America's most famous natural spaces, including Yellowstone, the Grand Canyon, and the Everglades. In 2008, the Park Service proposed higher fees at some parks. Writer John Krist argued in favor of the price increases:

> A day at Disneyland costs a family of four at least $232, not counting Mickey Mouse ears. At Six Flags Magic Mountain, the admission price would be at least $180. A seven-day pass to enter Yellowstone National Park costs $25 per car, which means that the same family spending a week among bison, elk, geysers and grizzlies would pay the equivalent of 89 cents per person, per day.

> Which is why it's perplexing to see such an outcry over news that the Park Service wants to raise entrance fees at 135 sites over the next two years. . . . Their principal arguments are economic: Tourism-dependent communities fret that higher fees will reduce visitation and cut into profits, while others argue that the increases will keep out those of limited financial means. It's true, in theory at least, that raising the price of something should decrease demand for it.* . . .

> On the other hand, it's absurd to expect a finite amount of parkland to accommodate a continually increasing number of people. Anyone who has driven into Yosemite Valley on a holiday weekend is unlikely to regard a drop in park visitation as entirely a bad thing.

> Slightly higher user fees are unlikely to have much effect on park use, but they could have a significant effect on the quality of the park experience. Most of that money will stay at individual parks, where it can be spent on upkeep and repairs—the sort of unglamorous expenditures that typically get shortchanged in the politically driven federal budget process. Smaller crowds and plumbing that works—what's not to like?

*You can tell that the author of this piece hadn't read this book. If he had, he would have been careful to say that raising the price decreases the *quantity demanded,* rather than saying it decreases *demand.*

WHAT DO YOU THINK?

1. Do you agree with Krist's argument that the demand for national park visits is inelastic at current price levels, so that higher fees are "unlikely to have much effect on park use"? Think about the factors that affect price elasticity, such as the availability and price of substitutes.

(continued)

2. How would you weigh the following trade-offs?

   a. Should the Park Service intentionally try to shrink the demand for visits in order to reduce crowding? In order to protect parks from environmental damage?

   b. Does the Park Service have a responsibility to keep national parks accessible to families who cannot afford to pay higher fees?

   c. Should the Park Service be concerned about the economic impact of a reduced demand for visits on surrounding communities?

Source: John Krist, "So what if park fees go up?," *High Country News*, July 16, 2008.

✓ CONCEPT CHECK

□ What is the formula for calculating the price elasticity of demand? **[LO 4.1]**

□ Why should you use the mid-point method to calculate the price elasticity of demand? **[LO 4.1]**

□ If demand is inelastic, will an increase in price lead to more, less, or the same amount of revenue **[LO 4.2]**

□ If demand is elastic, will an increase in price lead to more, less, or the same amount of revenue? **[LO 4.2]**

□ If demand is unit-elastic, will an increase in price lead to more, less, or the same amount of revenue? **[LO 4.2]**

Price Elasticity of Supply

What happens when an increase in coffee consumption drives up the price of coffee beans? *How will the coffee market respond* to the price change? We can predict, based on the law of supply, that coffee growers will respond to an increase in price by increasing their production. But by how much will they increase production? The concept of price elasticity of supply can help us answer that question.

price elasticity of supply
the size of the change in the quantity supplied of a good or service when its price changes

Price elasticity of supply is the size of the change in the quantity supplied of a good or service when its price changes. Price elasticity of supply measures producers' responsiveness to a change in price, just as price elasticity of demand measures consumers' responsiveness to a change in price.

Chapter 3, "Markets," showed that when prices rise, producers supply larger quantities of a good; when prices fall, they supply smaller quantities. Just as the price elasticity of demand for a good tells us how much the quantity demanded changes as we move along the demand curve, the price elasticity of supply tells us how much the quantity supplied changes as we move along the supply curve.

Calculating price elasticity of supply

LO 4.3 Calculate price elasticity of supply using the mid-point method.

Price elasticity of supply, shown in Equation 4-5, is measured in the same way as price elasticity of demand: as the percentage change in quantity divided by the percentage change in price.

EQUATION 4-5
$$\text{Price elasticity of supply} = \frac{\% \text{ change in quantity supplied}}{\% \text{ change in price}}$$

To ensure that elasticity will be the same whether you move up or down the supply curve, you should use the mid-point method, as in Equation 4-6.

EQUATION 4-6 $\qquad$ Price elasticity of supply $= \dfrac{(Q_2 - Q_1)/[(Q_1 + Q_2)/2]}{(P_2 - P_1)/[(P_1 + P_2)/2]}$

Suppose that when the price of coffee beans goes from \$1 to \$1.20 per pound, production increases from 90 million pounds of coffee beans per year to 100 million pounds. Using the mid-point method, the percentage change in quantity supplied would be:

$$\% \text{ change in quantity supplied} = \dfrac{(100 \text{ million} - 90 \text{ million})}{95 \text{ million}} = 11\%$$

The percentage change in price would be:

$$\% \text{ change in price} = \dfrac{1.2 - 1}{1.1} = 18\%$$

So the price elasticity of supply at this point on the supply curve is:

$$\text{Price elasticity of supply} = \dfrac{11\%}{18\%} = 0.6$$

As with the price elasticity of demand, we can describe the price elasticity of supply using three categories:

- *Elastic,* if it has an absolute value greater than 1.
- *Inelastic,* if it has an absolute value less than 1.
- *Unit-elastic,* if it has an absolute value of exactly 1.

We can also describe the extreme cases: Supply is *perfectly elastic* if the quantity supplied could be anything at a given price, and is zero at any other price. At the other extreme, supply is *perfectly inelastic* if the quantity supplied is the same, regardless of the price.

Going back to our example, an elasticity of 0.6 tells us that the supply of coffee beans is relatively inelastic, at least in the short run. Does this result make sense? As it turns out, coffee takes a long time to grow. Coffee plants don't produce a full yield for four to six years after they are planted. Because coffee growers can't increase production quickly, it makes sense that the supply of coffee would be inelastic. (What if prices had fallen from \$1.20 to \$1, instead of rising from \$1 to \$1.20? Using the mid-point method, the elasticity would be the same.)

! HINT

- Remember that the elasticity of *demand* is calculated by dividing a positive number by a negative number, or by dividing a negative number by a positive number, so the answer is always negative.
- The elasticity of *supply,* on the other hand, is calculated by dividing either a positive number by another positive number or a negative number by another negative number. In either case, the answer is always positive.

Remembering this rule can help you to check your arithmetic.

There is one important difference between the elasticities of supply and demand: The price elasticity of demand is always negative and the price elasticity of supply is always positive. The reason is simple: The quantity demanded always moves in the *opposite direction* from the price, but the quantity supplied moves in the *same direction* as the price.

Determinants of price elasticity of supply

LO 4.4 Explain how the determinants of price elasticity of supply affect the degree of elasticity.

Whether supply is elastic or inelastic depends on the supplier's ability to change the quantity produced in response to price changes. Three factors affect a supplier's ability to expand production: the availability of inputs, the flexibility of the production process, and the time needed to adjust to changes in price. Recall that this last factor—time—is also a determinant of the elasticity of demand. Just as consumers take time to change their habits, suppliers need time to ramp up production.

Availability of inputs
The production of some goods can be expanded easily, just by adding extra inputs. For example, a bakery can easily buy extra flour and yeast to produce more bread, probably at the same cost per loaf. Increasing the supply of other goods is more difficult, however, and sometimes is impossible. If the price of Picasso paintings goes up, there isn't much anyone can do to produce more of them.

In other words, the elasticity of supply depends on the elasticity of the supply of inputs. If producing more of a good will cost a lot more than the initial quantity did because the extra inputs will be harder to find or more costly, then the producer will be reluctant to increase the quantity supplied. Higher and higher prices will be needed to convince the producer to go to the extra expense.

Flexibility of the production process
The easiest way for producers to adjust the quantity supplied of a particular good is to draw production capacity away from other goods when its price rises, or to reassign capacity to other goods when its price falls. Farmers may find this sort of substitution relatively simple: When corn prices are high, they will plant more acres with corn; when corn prices are low, they will reassign acres to more profitable crops. Other producers have much less flexibility. If you own a company that manufactures specialized parts for Toyota, you might need to buy new machinery to begin making parts for Ford, let alone switch to another type of product entirely.

Adjustment time
As with demand, supply is more elastic over long periods than over short periods. That is, producers can make more adjustments in the long run than in the short run. In the short run, the number of hotel rooms at Disneyland is fixed; in the medium and long run, old rooms can be renovated and new hotels can be built. Production capacity can also increase or decrease over time as new firms start up or old ones shut down.

✓ CONCEPT CHECK
☐ How would you calculate the price elasticity of supply? **[LO 4.3]**
☐ What are the three determinants of the price elasticity of supply? **[LO 4.4]**

Other Elasticities

The demand for a good is sensitive to more than just the price of the good. Because people are clever, flexible, and always on the lookout for ways to make the most of opportunities, demand also responds to changing circumstances, such as the prices of other goods and the incomes consumers earn. Let's consider two other demand elasticities, the *cross-price elasticity of demand* and the *income elasticity of demand*.

Cross-price elasticity of demand

LO 4.5 Calculate cross-price elasticity of demand, and interpret the sign of the elasticity.

Earlier we noted that price elasticities are affected by the availability of alternative options. For example, we might expect a Starbucks latte to have relatively price-elastic demand because some people will shift to buying coffee from Dunkin' Donuts when the price of a Starbucks latte rises. Once again, recalling the four economists' questions we presented in Chapter 1, "Economics and Life," asking *How will others respond?* is the key to understanding the situation.

What happens if the price of Dunkin' Donuts regular coffee falls but the price of a Starbucks latte stays the same? **Cross-price elasticity of demand** describes how much demand changes when the price of a *different* good changes. For example, because lattes and regular coffee are substitutes, we expect the demand for lattes to decrease when the price of regular coffee falls (as some people switch from lattes to coffee). The reverse also holds: If the price of a cup of Dunkin' Donuts coffee rises, while the price of a Starbucks latte remains the same, we expect the demand for lattes to increase (as some people switch from coffee to the relatively cheaper latte). Equation 4-7 gives the formula for the cross-price elasticity of demand.

cross-price elasticity of demand a measure of how the demand for one good changes when the price of a different good changes

EQUATION 4-7

$$\text{Cross-price elasticity of demand between A and B} = \frac{\% \text{ change in quantity of A demanded}}{\% \text{ change in price of B}}$$

Remember that nonprice determinants (like income or tastes) will shift a demand curve. In the case of cross-price elasticity, the price of a substitute or a complement is a nonprice determinant. Thus, the entire demand curve shifts. However, we still measure this change in demand by observing the change in the quantity demanded. But in this case, the initial quantity demanded is on one demand curve and the final quantity demanded is on another demand curve.

When two goods are substitutes, we expect their cross-price elasticity of demand to be positive. That is, an increase in the price of one will cause an increase in the quantity demanded of the other. On the other hand, a decrease in the price of one good will cause a decrease in the quantity demanded of the other. Just how elastic the demand is depends on how close the two substitutes are: If they are very close substitutes, a change in the price of one will cause a large change in the quantity demanded of the other, so that cross-price elasticity will be high. If they are not close substitutes, cross-price elasticity will be low.

Cross-price elasticity can also be negative. We saw that the price elasticity of demand is always negative and can be expressed as an absolute value. In contrast, cross-price elasticity can be positive or negative. Its sign tells us about the relationship between two goods:

- When two goods are substitutes, their cross-price elasticity will be positive.
- When two goods are complements (that is, when they are consumed together), cross-price elasticity will be negative.

For example, when people drink more coffee, they want more cream to go with it. Coffee and cream are complements, not substitutes. So when the demand for coffee increases, the demand for cream will increase, all else held equal. When two goods are linked in this way, their cross-price elasticity will be negative: an increase in the price of one good will decrease the quantity demanded of both goods. Again, the relative size of the elasticity tells us how strongly the two goods are linked. If the two goods are strong complements, their cross-price elasticity will be a large negative number. If the two goods are loosely linked, their cross-price elasticity will be negative but not far below zero.

Income elasticity of demand

LO 4.6 Calculate income elasticity of demand, and interpret the sign of the elasticity.

People buy some goods in roughly the same amounts, no matter how wealthy they are. Salt, toothpaste, and toilet paper are three examples. These are not the sort of products people rush out to buy when they get a raise at work. Other goods, though, are very sensitive to changes in income. If you got a raise, you might splurge on new clothes or a meal at a fancy restaurant.

The **income elasticity of demand** for a good describes how much demand changes in response to a change in consumers' incomes. Similar to cross-price elasticity, a change in income causes the demand curve to shift. We measure this change in demand by observing the change in the quantity demanded. As Equation 4-8 shows, the income elasticity of demand is expressed as the ratio of the percentage change in the quantity demanded to the percentage change in income:

income elasticity of demand
a measure of how much the demand for a good changes in response to a change in consumers' incomes

EQUATION 4-8 $$\text{Income elasticity of demand} = \frac{\%\text{ change in quantity demanded}}{\%\text{ change in income}}$$

Recall from Chapter 3, "Markets," that increases in income raise the demand for normal goods and lower the demand for inferior goods. Income elasticity tells us how much the demand for these goods changes.

For example, a Starbucks Frappuccino® is a normal good that might be fairly responsive to changes in income. When people become wealthier, they will buy more of a small luxury item like this. Therefore, we would guess that the income elasticity of demand for fancy iced coffee drinks is positive (because the drink is a normal good) and relatively large (because the drink is a nonnecessity that has many cheaper substitutes).

Regular coffee is also generally a normal good, so its income elasticity should be positive. However, we might guess that it will be less elastic than a Frappuccino's. Many people consider their standard cup of coffee every day before work to be more of a necessity than a luxury and will buy it regardless of their incomes. Another way to put it is that the demand for Frappuccinos is income-elastic, while the demand for plain coffee is relatively income-inelastic.

For normal goods like these, income elasticity is positive because as incomes rise, demand increases. This then leads to an increase in quantity demanded. Both necessities and luxuries are normal goods, and although their income elasticities are positive, their sizes vary:

- If the good is a necessity, income elasticity of demand will be positive and less than 1.
- If the good is a luxury, income elasticity will be positive and greater than 1.

As with the cross-price elasticity of demand, the income elasticity of demand can be negative as well as positive. The income elasticity of demand is negative for inferior goods because quantity demanded decreases as incomes increase.

In 2009 Starbucks introduced a new retail product, VIA® Ready instant coffee. Although some coffee enthusiasts sneered, others thought it was a shrewd move at a time of economic hardship. Instant coffee mix may be an inferior good in some places: As incomes increase, people will drink more expensive beverages and *decrease* their consumption of instant coffee. During a recession, however, budgets tighten and people may increase their consumption of instant coffee as they cut back on more expensive drinks. At least, that is what Starbucks was hoping. In this scenario, the income elasticity of instant coffee would be small and negative. A less-appealing inferior good that people quickly abandon as they grow richer would have a large, negative income elasticity.

Once again, the sign and size of a good's elasticity tell us a lot about the good. Table 4-2 summarizes what we have learned about the four types of elasticity.

If you find this discussion particularly interesting, you might want to consider work as a pricing analyst. You can read more about this in the Where Can It Take You? box "Pricing analyst."

TABLE 4-2
Four measures of elasticity

Study   *Good To Know* *Familiar*

Measure	Equation	Negative	Positive	More elastic	Less elastic
Price elasticity of demand	$\dfrac{\text{\% change in quantity demanded}}{\text{\% change in price}}$	Always	Never	Over time, for substitutable goods and luxury items	In the short run, for unique and necessary items
Price elasticity of supply	$\dfrac{\text{\% change in quantity supplied}}{\text{\% change in price}}$	Never	Always	Over time, with flexible production	In the short run, with production constraints
Cross-price elasticity	$\dfrac{\text{\% change in quantity demanded of A}}{\text{\% change in price of B}}$	For complements	For substitutes	For near-perfect substitutes and strong complements	For loosely related goods
Income elasticity	$\dfrac{\text{\% change in quantity demanded}}{\text{\% change in income}}$	For inferior goods	For normal goods	For luxury items with close substitutes	For unique and necessary items

Where Can it Take You?
Pricing analyst

A major task in most industries is to keep an eye on competitors' prices and respond accordingly. Large businesses hire *pricing analysts* to perform this critical function. Pricing analysts use their knowledge of elasticity and markets to help businesses determine the right price to charge for their products.

Some businesses have especially complicated pricing problems. Think about airlines, which charge different prices for every flight on every route, every day. Moreover, airlines frequently charge different prices for economy, business-class, and first-class tickets. How will air travelers respond to a change in ticket prices? What will happen if the price of a ticket to New York goes up, while tickets to Las Vegas go on sale? How will customers respond to a change in competitors' ticket prices? How will they respond to a booming economy or a recession?

The answers to these questions may differ for every type of ticket. To respond to changing market conditions in the airline industry, pricing analysts need to understand all types of elasticity.

✓ CONCEPT CHECK

☐ Why is the cross-price elasticity of demand positive for substitutes? **[LO 4.5]**

☐ Why does the income-elasticity of demand depend on whether a good is normal or inferior? **[LO 4.6]**

Conclusion

Supply and *demand* may be the most common words in economics, but applying these concepts to the real world requires a bit of elaboration. Elasticity is the first of several concepts we will study that will help you to apply the concepts of supply and demand to business and policy questions. In this chapter we saw how elasticity can be used to predict how price changes will influence revenue. In the coming chapters we will use elasticity to predict the effects of government intervention in the market, and we will dig deeper into the consumer and producer choices that drive elasticity.

Key Terms

elasticity, p. 80

price elasticity of demand, p. 81

mid-point method, p. 81

perfectly elastic demand, p. 85

perfectly inelastic demand, p. 85

elastic, p. 85

inelastic, p. 85

unit-elastic, p. 86

total revenue, p. 88

price elasticity of supply, p. 92

cross-price elasticity of demand, p. 95

income elasticity of demand, p. 96

Summary

LO 4.1 Calculate price elasticity of demand using the mid-point method.

Elasticity is a measure of consumers' and producers' responsiveness to a change in market conditions. Understanding the elasticity for a good or service allows economic decision makers to anticipate the outcome of changes in market conditions and to calibrate prices so as to maximize revenues.

Price elasticity of demand is the size of the change in the quantity demanded of a good or service when its price changes. Elasticity should be calculated as a percentage using the mid-point method to avoid problems with conflicting units of measurement and with the direction of a change.

Price elasticity of demand is almost always negative because the quantity demanded falls as the price rises. It is usually represented as an absolute value, without the negative sign.

LO 4.2 Explain how the determinants of price elasticity of demand affect the degree of elasticity.

In general, demand is inelastic for goods that have no close substitutes, are basic necessities, or cost a relatively small proportion of consumers' income. Demand is also inelastic over short periods and for broadly defined markets.

When demand is elastic, a percentage change in the price of a good will cause a larger percentage change in the quantity demanded; the absolute value of the elasticity will be greater than 1. When demand is inelastic, a percentage change in price will cause a smaller percentage change in the quantity demanded; the absolute value of the elasticity will be less than 1. When demand is unit-elastic, the percentage changes in price and quantity will be equal, and the elasticity will be exactly 1.

LO 4.3 Calculate price elasticity of supply using the mid-point method.

Price elasticity of supply is the size of the change in the quantity supplied of a good or service when its price changes. Price elasticity of supply is almost always positive because the quantity supplied increases as the price increases.

LO 4.4 Explain how the determinants of price elasticity of supply affect the degree of elasticity.

Supply is generally inelastic when additional inputs to the production process are difficult to get and the production process is inflexible. Supply is also inelastic over short periods.

Supply is considered elastic when the absolute value of its price elasticity is greater than 1, inelastic when the absolute value is less than 1, and unit-elastic when it is exactly 1.

LO 4.5 Calculate cross-price elasticity of demand, and interpret the sign of the elasticity.

Cross-price elasticity of demand is the percentage change in the quantity demanded in response to a given percentage change in the price of a *different* good. The cross-price elasticity of demand between two goods will be positive if they are substitutes and negative if they are complements.

LO 4.6 Calculate income elasticity of demand, and interpret the sign of the elasticity.

Income elasticity of demand is the percentage change in the quantity of a good demanded in response to a given percentage change in income. Income elasticity of demand will be positive for normal goods and negative for inferior goods.

Review Questions

† 1. You are advising a coffee shop manager who wants to estimate how much sales will change if the price of a latte rises. You tell him that he should measure the change in sales using the percentage change in quantity of coffee sold rather than the number of cups of coffee or the total ounces of coffee sold. Similarly, you tell him that he should measure the price increase in percentage terms rather than in terms of absolute dollars. Explain why he should measure elasticity in percentage terms rather than in terms of dollars and cups. **[LO 4.1]**

╀ 2. Explain why the coffee shop manager should calculate elasticity using the mid-point method. **[LO 4.1]**

╀ 3. You are working as a private math tutor to raise money for a trip during spring break. First explain why the price elasticity of demand for math tutoring might be elastic. Then explain why the price elasticity of demand for math tutoring might be inelastic. **[LO 4.2]**

╀ 4. You are working as a private math tutor to raise money for a trip during spring break. You want to earn as much money as possible, and you think the demand for math tutors is currently inelastic. Should you increase or decrease the price you charge? Explain. **[LO 4.2]**

╀ 5. You have been hired by the government of Kenya, which produces a lot of coffee, to examine the supply of gourmet coffee beans. Suppose you discover that the price elasticity of supply is 0.85. Explain this number to the Kenyan government. **[LO 4.3]**

╀ 6. You have noticed that the price of tickets to your university's basketball games keeps increasing, but the supply of tickets remains the same. Why might supply be unresponsive to changes in price? **[LO 4.3]**

⇠ 7. Which will have a more price-elastic supply over six months: real estate in downtown Manhattan or real estate in rural Oklahoma? Explain your reasoning. **[LO 4.4]**

↗ 8. Certain skilled labor, such as hair cutting, requires licensing or certification, which is costly and takes a long time to acquire. Explain what would happen to the price elasticity of supply for haircuts if this licensing requirement were removed. **[LO 4.4]**

9. Although we could describe both the cross-price elasticity of demand between paper coffee cups and plastic coffee lids and the cross-price elasticity of demand between sugar and artificial sweeteners as highly elastic, the first cross-price elasticity is negative and the second is positive. What is the reason for this? **[LO 4.5]**

10. Name two related goods you consume that would have a positive cross-price elasticity. What happens to your consumption of the second good if the price of the first good increases? **[LO 4.5]**

11. Name two related goods you consume that would have a negative cross-price elasticity. What happens to your consumption of the second good if the price of the first good increases? **[LO 4.5]**

12. In France, where cheese is an important and traditional part of people's meals, people eat about six times as much cheese per person as in the United States. In which country do you think the demand for cheese will be more income-elastic? Why? **[LO 4.6]**

13. Name a good you consume for which your income elasticity of demand is positive. What happens when your income increases? **[LO 4.6]**

14. Name a good you consume for which your income elasticity of demand is negative. What happens when your income increases? **[LO 4.6]**

Problems and Applications

1. When the price of a bar of chocolate is $1, the quantity demanded is 100,000 bars. When the price rises to $1.50, the quantity demanded falls to 60,000 bars. Calculate the price elasticity of demand using the mid-point method. **[LO 4.1]**

   a. Suppose the price increases from $1 to $1.50. Calculate the price elasticity of demand.

   b. Suppose the price decreases from $1.50 to $1. Calculate the price elasticity of demand.

2. If the price elasticity of demand for used cars priced between $3,000 and $5,000 is −1.2 (using the mid-point method), what will be the percent change in quantity demanded when the price of a used car falls from $5,000 to $3,000? **[LO 4.1]**

3. Three points are identified on the graph in Figure 4P-1. **[LO 4.2]**

   a. At point A, is demand inelastic, elastic, or unit-elastic?

FIGURE 4P-1

b. At point B, is demand inelastic, elastic, or unit-elastic?

c. At point C, is demand inelastic, elastic, or unit-elastic?

4. Which of the following has a more elastic demand in the short run? **[LO 4.2]**

    a. Pomegranate juice or drinking water?

    b. Cereal or Rice Krispies®?

    c. Speedboats or gourmet chocolate?

5. In each of the following instances, determine whether demand is elastic, inelastic, or unit-elastic. **[LO 4.2]**

    a. If price increases by 10 percent and quantity demanded decreases by 15 percent, demand is _____.

    b. If price decreases by 10 percent and quantity demanded increases by 5 percent, demand is _____.

6. In each of the following instances, determine whether quantity demanded will increase or decrease, and by how much. **[LO 4.2]**

    a. If price elasticity of demand is −1.3 and price increases by 2 percent, quantity demanded will _____ by _____ percent.

    b. If price elasticity of demand is −0.3 percent and price decreases by 2 percent, quantity demanded will _____ by _____ percent.

Problems 7 and 8 refer to the demand schedule shown in Table 4P-1. For each price change, say whether demand is **elastic,** **unit-elastic,** *or* **inelastic,** *and say whether total revenue* **increases, decreases,** *or* **stays the same.**

7. Consider each of the following price increase scenarios. **[LO 4.2]**

    a. Price increases from $10 to $20. Demand is _____ and total revenue _____.

    b. Price increases from $30 to $40. Demand is _____ and total revenue _____.

    c. Price increases from $50 to $60. Demand is _____ and total revenue _____.

8. Price decreases from $70 to $60. Demand is _____ and total revenue _____. **[LO 4.2]**

Problems 9–12 refer to Figure 4P-2.

9. Draw the price effect and the quantity effect for a price change from $60 to $50. Which effect is larger? Does total revenue increase or decrease? No calculation is necessary. **[LO 4.2]**

10. Draw the price effect and the quantity effect for a price change from $30 to $20. Which effect is larger? Does total revenue increase or decrease? No calculation is necessary. **[LO 4.2]**

11. Draw the price effect and the quantity effect for a price change from $60 to $70. Which effect is larger? Does total revenue increase or decrease? No calculation is necessary. **[LO 4.2]**

12. Draw the price effect and the quantity effect for a price change from $10 to $20. Which effect is larger? Does total revenue increase or decrease? No calculation is necessary. **[LO 4.2]**

TABLE 4P-1

Price ($)	Quantity demanded
80	0
70	50
60	100
50	150
40	200
30	250
20	300
10	350
0	400

FIGURE 4P-2

FIGURE 4P-3

13. Use the graph in Figure 4P-3 to calculate the price elasticity of supply between points A and B using the midpoint method. **[LO 4.3]**

14. If the price of a haircut is $15, the number of haircuts provided is 100. If the price rises to $30 per haircut, barbers will work much longer hours, and the supply of haircuts will increase to 300. What is the price elasticity of supply for haircuts between $15 and $30? **[LO 4.3]**

15. Which of the following has a more elastic supply in the short run? **[LO 4.4]**

    a. Hospitals or mobile clinics?

    b. Purebred dogs or mixed-breed dogs?

    c. On-campus courses or online courses?

16. In each of the following instances, determine whether supply is elastic, inelastic, or unit-elastic. **[LO 4.4]**

    a. If price increases by 10 percent and quantity supplied increases by 15 percent, supply is

    _____.

    b. If price decreases by 10 percent and quantity supplied decreases by 5 percent, supply is

    _____.

17. In each of the following instances, determine whether quantity supplied will increase or decrease, and by how much. **[LO 4.4]**

    a. If price elasticity of supply is 1.3 and price increases by 2 percent, quantity supplied will _____ by _____ percent.

    b. If price elasticity of supply is 0.3 and price decreases by 2 percent, quantity supplied will _____ by _____ percent.

18. Suppose that the price of peanut butter rises from $2 to $3 per jar. **[LO 4.5]**

    a. The quantity of jelly purchased falls from 20 million jars to 15 million jars. What is the cross-price elasticity of demand between peanut butter and jelly? Are they complements or substitutes?

    b. The quantity of jelly purchased increases from 15 million jars to 20 million jars. What is the cross-price elasticity of demand between peanut butter and jelly? Are they complements or substitutes?

19. For each of the following pairs, predict whether the cross-price elasticity of demand will be positive or negative: **[LO 4.5]**

    a. Soap and hand sanitizer.

    b. CDs and MP3s.

    c. Sheets and pillowcases.

20. Suppose that when the average family income rises from $30,000 per year to $40,000 per year, the average family's purchases of toilet paper rise from 100 rolls to 105 rolls per year. **[LO 4.6]**

    a. Calculate the income-elasticity of demand for toilet paper.

    b. Is toilet paper a normal or an inferior good?

    c. Is the demand for toilet paper income-elastic or income-inelastic?

21. In each of the following instances, determine whether the good is normal or inferior, and whether it is income-elastic or income-inelastic. **[LO 4.6]**

    a. If income increases by 10 percent and the quantity demanded of a good then increases by 5 percent, the good is _____ and _____.

    b. If income increases by 10 percent and the quantity demanded of a good decreases by 20 percent, the good is _____ and _____.

Math Essentials: Calculating Percentage Change, Slope, and Elasticity

Learning Objectives

LO C.1 Understand how to calculate percentage changes.

LO C.2 Use slope to calculate elasticity.

The math associated with the concept of elasticity covers a wide variety of topics. In order to be able to calculate elasticity, you need to be able to calculate percentage changes. In order to talk about shape of a line, and its elasticity, you need to be able to understand slope and the relationship between variables, particularly price and quantity.

Percentage Change

LO C.1 Understand how to calculate percentage changes.

In Chapter 4, "Elasticity," we calculated elasticity in all its forms. If you're not entirely comfortable calculating percentage change, though, elasticity can be a daunting idea. Percentage changes represent the relative change in a variable from an old value to a new one. In the chapter, and in this appendix, we use the mid-point method to calculate percentage change. The mid-point method measures the percentage change relative to a point *midway between the two points*.

Equation C-1 shows how to calculate percentage change using the mid-point method. There, X_1 represents the original value of any variable X, and X_2 is the new value of this variable.

EQUATION C-1
$$\text{Percentage change} = \left[\frac{(X_2 - X_1)}{\left(\frac{X_2 + X_1}{2} \right)} \right] \times 100$$

Notice that the denominator is the *mid-point* between X_1 and X_2. In other words, it is the average of X_1 and X_2. Overall, you can use this method to calculate the percentage change in variables of various kinds. A percentage change in quantity, for example, would be expressed as:

EQUATION C-1A $$\text{Percentage change in quantity} = \left[\frac{(Q_2 - Q_1)}{\left(\frac{Q_2 + Q_1}{2} \right)} \right] \times 100$$

where Q_2 represents the new value of quantity demanded and Q_1 the original quantity demanded.

Similarly, a percentage change in price would be expressed as:

EQUATION C-1B $$\text{Percentage change in price} = \left[\frac{(P_2 - P_1)}{\left(\frac{P_2 + P_1}{2} \right)} \right] \times 100$$

Let's try an example for practice: For weeks, you have been watching the price of a new pair of shoes. They normally cost $90, but you see that the store has a sale and now offers them for $70. You find the percentage change in the price of the shoes by first subtracting the old price ($90) from the new one ($70) to find the change in price, which is −$20. To find how much of a change this is, you take this −$20 price change and divide it by the price midway between $70 and $90 ($80).

$$\frac{\$70 - \$90}{\left(\frac{\$70 + \$90}{2} \right)} = \frac{-\$20}{\$80} = -0.25$$

You then multiply by 100 to get the percentage change: $-0.25 \times 100 = -25\%$. In this case, the $20 price reduction was a 25 percent decrease in price. Not a bad sale!

Notice that in this case, the percentage change is negative, which indicates that the new value is less than the original. If the prices of shoes had increased instead, the associated percentage change would be a positive value.

The best way to do get comfortable with calculating percentage changes is through lots of practice. You can find a few extra problems to try on your own at the end of this appendix, and you also could challenge yourself to calculate price changes you see in your everyday life.

Slope and Elasticity

LO C.2 Use slope to calculate elasticity.

In Appendix A, "Math Essentials: Understanding Graphs and Slope," we showed that the direction of a slope tells us something meaningful about the relationship between the two variables we are representing:

- When x and y move in the *same direction,* they are said to have a *positive* relationship. Not surprisingly, this means that the slope of the line is a positive number. When the slope of a line is positive, we know that y increases as x increases, and y decreases as x decreases.
- Similarly, when x and y move in *opposite directions,* they are said to have a *negative* relationship. The slope of the line is a negative number. When the slope of a line is negative, we know that y decreases as x increases, and y increases as x decreases.

In Chapter 3, "Markets," we saw a positive relationship between price and quantity in the supply curve. We saw a negative relationship between price and quantity in the demand curve. Two variables (such as price and quantity) may have more than one relationship to each other, depending on whose choices they represent and under what circumstances.

The steepness of a slope is also important. Numerically, the closer the number representing the slope is to zero, the flatter the curve will be. Remember that both positive and negative numbers can be close to zero. So, a slope of −1 is equally steep as a slope of 1, although one slopes downward and the other upward. Correspondingly, a line with a slope of −5 is steeper than a line with a slope of −1 or one with a slope of 1.

You can tell just from looking at an equation how steep the line will be. If this idea is still a little hazy, you might want to page back to Appendix A, in the "Steepness of a slope" section, to refresh your memory. The steepness of slope is important to understanding the concept of elasticity.

Although the ideas of slope and elasticity are related, there are two basic mathematical distinctions between them:

1. Slope describes the change in y per the change in x, whereas elasticity measures are based on the change in x per the change in y.

2. We usually measure elasticity in terms of *percentage changes,* rather than absolute (unit-based) changes.

Why would we be interested in how much x changes in response to a one-unit change in y? To get at this difference, let's look at Figure C-1. It is similar to Figure A-10 (in Appendix A) but replaces the variables x and y with the quantity of a good (Q) and its price (P).

In Chapter 4, "Elasticity," you learned that *price elasticity* is a measure of the responsiveness of supply (or demand) to changes in price. In other words, it is a measure of how quantity (on the x-axis) responds to a change in price (on the y-axis). So this time, let's make the change in price (vertical distance) the same and look at how much quantity changes (horizontal distance).

Looking at Figure C-1, we can see that when price moves from P_1 to P_2, quantity supplied changes by less in panel A than it does in panel B. When price increases from P_1 to P_2 in panel A, quantity increases by 1 unit, from Q_1 to Q_2. In contrast, panel B shows an increase of 2 units from Q_1 to Q_2 for the same change in P. This means supply is less responsive to a price change in panel A compared to panel B.

FIGURE C-1

Measuring a change in Q in response to a change in P

(A) Steeper slope

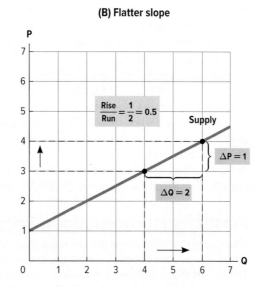

(B) Flatter slope

The steeper slope in panel A indicates that price changes less in panel A than in panel B in response to a change in quantity demanded.

The flatter slope in panel B indicates that price changes more in panel B than in panel A in response to a change in quantity demanded.

FIGURE C-2

Slope versus elasticity of horizontal and vertical lines

When a line is horizontal, the slope is zero and the associated elasticity is infinite. In other words, demand or supply only occurs at a single price.

When a line is vertical, the slope is infinite and the elasticity is zero. Regardless of the price, quantity supplied or demanded is going to be the same.

X over Y, or Y over X?

We have noted that slope is indicated by $\frac{\Delta y}{\Delta x}$. In contrast, elasticity is commonly indicated by $\frac{\%\Delta Q}{\%\Delta P}$, which corresponds to $\frac{\Delta x}{\Delta y}$. In some sense, then, *elasticity is computed as the mirror image of slope.* The easiest way to picture this is to see the difference between slope and elasticity for vertical and horizontal lines.

In Figure C-2, the horizontal line pictured in panel A has a slope of zero. This is because a one-unit change in *x* results in zero change in *y*. Therefore, slope is calculated as $\frac{0}{\Delta x}$. Zero divided by any number is zero. If we think of the horizontal line as a demand curve mapping price to quantity demanded, however, the price elasticity is infinity.

How can slope be zero and elasticity infinity? Remember that slope measures how much *y* changes in response to a change in *x*. Elasticity, however, measures the sensitivity of P (on the *y*-axis) to a change in Q (on the *x*-axis). Whereas *x* is in the denominator when calculating slope, it is in the numerator when calculating elasticity. For a horizontal line, then, elasticity will be %ΔQ/0 since there is no change in P. Division by 0 is mathematically undefined, or known as infinity.

The reverse is true when we look at a vertical line. When a graph is vertical, there is zero change in *x* for any change in *y*. Therefore, slope is calculated as $\frac{\Delta y}{0}$. In this case, slope is undefined (infinity). But elasticity will be 0/%ΔP. Again, zero divided by any number is zero.

Elasticity changes along lines with constant slope

The second important mathematical difference between slope and elasticity is that we usually measure slope in terms of absolute changes, but we measure elasticity in terms of percentage changes. This means that at different points along a straight line, slope is constant, but elasticity varies.

As an example, take a look at the demand schedule in Table C-1. First, let's calculate the slope between two different sets of points. Using the first two prices and quantities at the top of the demand schedule, we see that the slope between these points is −1.

TABLE C-1
Demand schedule

Price ($)	Quantity
80	0
70	10
60	20
50	30
40	40
30	50
20	60
10	70
0	80

$$\text{Slope } \#1 = \frac{\Delta P_1}{\Delta Q_1} = \frac{(0-10)}{(80-70)} = \frac{-10}{10} = -1$$

Then, pick another two points. Using the quantities 30 and 20 and their respective prices, we can calculate that the slope is still −1.

$$\text{Slope } \#2 = \frac{\Delta P_2}{\Delta Q_2} = \frac{(30-20)}{(50-60)} = \frac{10}{-10} = -1$$

No matter what two points along the demand curve we choose, the slope is the same. *Slope is constant because the demand curve is linear.*

Now let's calculate elasticity between these same two sets of points. We will use the mid-point method described in Chapter 4, "Elasticity," to calculate elasticity:

$$\text{Elasticity} = \frac{\%\Delta Q}{\%\Delta P} = \frac{\Delta Q/Q_{midpoint}}{\Delta P/P_{midpoint}}$$

Let's start with the top of the demand curve and calculate the price elasticity of demand for a price change from 80 to 70. Using the mid-point method, we have:

$$\frac{\Delta Q/Q_{midpoint}}{\Delta P/P_{midpoint}} = \frac{(0-10)/5}{(80-70)/60} = \frac{-10/5}{10/60} = \frac{-2}{0.17} = -11.8$$

Now let's calculate the price elasticity of demand at the bottom of the demand curve for a price change of 30 to 20.

$$\frac{\Delta Q/Q_{midpoint}}{\Delta P/P_{midpoint}} = \frac{(50-60)/55}{(30-20)/25} = \frac{-10/55}{10/25} = \frac{-0.18}{0.4} = -0.45$$

Even though both of these calculations represented a 10-unit change in quantity in response to a $10 change in price, along a linear demand curve, elasticity changes. Moving down along the demand curve means less elasticity. This is because the same change in Q or P is a different *percentage* of the midpoint at different points on the line.

Problems and Applications

1. Calculate the percentage change in each of the following examples using the mid-point method. **[LO C.1]**
    a. 8 to 12.
    b. 18 to 14.
    c. 130 to 120.
    d. 95 to 105.

2. Find the percentage change in price in each of the following examples using the mid-point method. **[LO C.1]**
    a. The price of a $4.50 sandwich increases to $5.50.
    b. A sale discounts the price of a sofa from $750 to $500.

3. Use the demand curve in Figure CP-1 to answer the following questions. Use the mid-point method in your calculations. **[LO C.2]**
    a. What is the price elasticity of demand for a price change from $0 to $20?
    b. What is the price elasticity of demand for a price change from $20 to $40?
    c. What is the price elasticity of demand for a price change from $40 to $60?

4. Use the demand schedule in Table CP-1 to answer the following questions. Use the mid-point method in your calculations. **[LO C.2]**
    a. What is the price elasticity of demand for a price change from $4 to $8?
    b. What is the price elasticity of demand for a price change from $8 to $16?
    c. What is the price elasticity of demand for a price change from $20 to $24?

FIGURE CP-1

TABLE CP-1

Price ($)	Quantity
0	60
4	50
8	40
12	30
16	20
20	10
24	0

TABLE CP-2

Price ($)	Quantity
0	56
1	48
2	42
3	35
4	28
5	21
6	14
7	7
8	0

5. Use the demand schedule in Table CP-2 to answer the following questions. Use the mid-point method when calculating elasticity. **[LO C.2]**
    a. What is the price elasticity of demand for a price change from $2 to $3? What is the slope of the demand curve for a price change from $2 to $3?
    b. What is the price elasticity of demand for a price change from $3 to $5? What is the slope of the demand curve for a price change from $3 to $5?
    c. What is the price elasticity of demand for a price change from $6 to $7? What is the slope of the demand curve for a price change from $6 to $7?

Efficiency

Learning Objectives

LO 5.1   Use willingness to pay and willingness to sell to determine supply and demand at a given price.

LO 5.2   Calculate consumer surplus based on a graph or table.

LO 5.3   Calculate producer surplus based on a graph or table.

LO 5.4   Calculate total surplus based on a graph or table.

LO 5.5   Define efficiency in terms of surplus, and identify efficient and inefficient situations.

LO 5.6   Describe the distribution of surplus, or benefits to society, that results from a policy decision.

LO 5.7   Calculate deadweight loss.

LO 5.8   Explain why correcting a missing market can make everyone better off.

A BROKEN LASER POINTER STARTS AN INTERNET REVOLUTION

In 1995, a young software developer named Pierre Omidyar spent his Labor Day weekend building a website he called AuctionWeb. His idea was to create a site where people could post their old stuff for sale online and auction it off to the highest bidder. Soon after, he sold the first item on AuctionWeb for $14.83. It was a broken laser pointer, which he had posted on the site as a test, never expecting anyone to bid on it. When Pierre pointed out that the pointer was broken, the bidder explained that he was "a collector of broken laser pointers."

As you might have guessed, AuctionWeb became the wildly successful company we now know as eBay. In 2015, 20 years after the site was first conceived, the total value of items sold on eBay was $82 billion and 162 million people around the world were active buyers.[1]

Like many creation stories, the tale of eBay's first sale gives us insight into what makes it tick. People are interested in some pretty odd things (like broken laser pointers), but given a big enough crowd, matches usually can be made between buyers and sellers. When buyers and

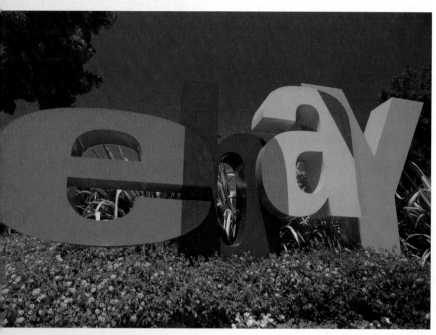
© David Paul Morris/Bloomberg/Getty Images

sellers are matched up and they trade, each is made better off. The buyer gets an item he wants, and the seller gets money. Because both parties are willing participants, they benefit from engaging in such transactions. In fact, they even are willing to pay eBay to provide the marketplace where they can find one another. How else is someone with a broken laser pointer going to find an eager buyer?

eBay's success is based on one of the most fundamental ideas in economics: *Voluntary exchanges create value and can make everyone involved better off.* The importance of that idea stretches far beyond eBay. This principle drives a range of businesses—from grocery stores, to investment banks, to online retailers—that do not manufacture or grow anything themselves. Instead, they facilitate transactions between producers and consumers.

But this principle raises a question: How do we know that people are better off when they buy and sell things? Can we say anything about *how much* better off they are?

To answer these questions, we need a tool to describe the *size of the benefits* that result from transactions and who receives said benefits. In this chapter we will introduce the concept of *surplus*. It can measure the benefit that people receive when they buy something for less than they would have been willing to pay. It also can measure the benefit that people receive when they sell something for more than they would have been willing to accept. *Surplus* is the best way to look at the benefits people receive from successful transactions.

Surplus also shows us why the equilibrium price and quantity in a competitive market are so special: They maximize the total well-being of those involved. Even when we care about outcomes other than total well-being (like inequality in the distribution of benefits), surplus gives us a yardstick for comparing different ideas and policies. For instance, calculations of surplus can clearly show who benefits and who loses from policies such as taxes and minimum wages. As we'll see, maximizing total surplus—an idea called *efficiency*—is one of the most powerful features of a market system. Even more remarkable is that it is achieved without centralized coordination.

Surplus also shows us how simply enabling people to trade with one another can make them better off. Often, creating a new market for goods and services (as the Grameen Bank did in Bangladesh, in the example in Chapter 1, "Economics and Life") or improving an existing market (as eBay did on the Internet) can be a good way to help people. Knowing how and when to harness the power of economic exchanges to improve well-being is an important tool for businesspeople and public-minded problem solvers alike.

Willingness to Pay and Sell

> **LO 5.1** Use willingness to pay and willingness to sell to determine supply and demand at a given price.

eBay is an online auction platform that allows people to post items for sale that anyone else online can buy. People who want to buy the item make bids offering to pay a particular price. This decentralized marketplace supports all sorts of transactions: from real estate, to used cars, to rare books, to (in one extraordinary case) a half-eaten cheese sandwich said to look like the Virgin Mary (which sold for $28,000).[2]

Who uses eBay? What do they want? At the most basic level, they are people who want to buy or sell a particular good. We're not sure how many people want broken laser pointers or decade-old cheese sandwiches, so let's stick with something a little more typical. How about digital cameras? Just as we did in Chapter 3, "Markets," we'll make the simplifying assumption that there is just one kind of digital camera rather than thousands of slightly different models.

Imagine you see a digital camera posted for sale on eBay. Who might bid on it? What are their *wants and constraints*? Most obviously, people who bid will be those who *want* a camera. But they will also care about the price they pay: Why spend $200 for a camera if you can get it for $100 and spend the other $100 on something else? Potential buyers *want* to pay as little as possible, but on top of this general preference, each buyer has a maximum price she is willing to pay.

Economists call this maximum price the buyer's **willingness to pay** or the *reservation price*. Economists use these two terms interchangeably; in this book, we'll stick with "willingness to pay." This price is the point above which the buyer throws up her hands and says, "Never mind. I'd rather spend my money on something else." Each potential buyer wants to purchase a camera for a price that is as low as possible and no higher than her maximum *willingness to pay*.

On eBay, we can see willingness to pay in action. When the price of a product remains below a bidder's willingness to pay, he'll continue to bid on it. When the going price passes his willingness to pay, he'll drop out.

Of course, buyers are only half the story. Who posted the camera for sale on eBay in the first place? To create a functioning market for digital cameras, someone has to want to sell. Whereas buyers want to buy a camera for as low a price as possible, sellers want to sell for as high a price as possible. Why take less money if you could get more? Just as each potential buyer has a willingness to pay, each potential seller has a *willingness to sell*. **Willingness to sell** is the minimum price that a seller is willing to accept in exchange for a good or service. A seller always wants to sell for a price that is as high as possible, but never lower than his minimum.

We can see willingness to sell in action on eBay through the "reserve price" that sellers can set when they post an item. This reserve price sets a bar below which the seller will not accept any bids. If she doesn't get any higher bids, she simply keeps the item.

So far, so good: Buyers want to buy low; sellers want to sell high. What does this have to do with markets? We're about to see that willingness to pay and willingness to sell are actually the forces that drive the shape of demand and supply curves.

willingness to pay (reservation price) *Know* the maximum price that a buyer would be willing to pay for a good or service

willingness to sell the minimum price that a seller is willing to accept in exchange for a good or service

Willingness to pay and the demand curve

Let's return to potential camera buyers and take a closer look at how they choose to bid on the camera posted on eBay. To keep things simple, let's imagine that there are five potential buyers who are considering bidding on this particular camera.

- Bidder #1 is a bird watcher who cares passionately about having a good camera to document the rare birds she finds. She is willing to pay up to $500 for the camera.
- Bidder #2 is an amateur photographer. He has an outdated camera and is willing to pay $250 for this newer model.

- Bidder #3 is a real estate agent who will be willing to pay $200 or less to be able to take better pictures of her properties.
- Bidder #4 is a journalist. She wouldn't mind having a newer camera than the one her newspaper provided but would pay no more than $150 for it.
- Bidder #5 is a teacher who will spend no more than $100—the amount of the eBay gift certificate given to him by appreciative parents for his birthday.

We can plot on a graph each potential buyer's willingness to pay. In panel A of Figure 5-1, we've graphed possible prices for the camera against the number of buyers who would be willing to bid that price for it. Remember that each person's willingness to pay is a *maximum*—he or she would also be willing to buy the camera at any lower price. Therefore, at a price of $100, all five buyers are willing to bid; at $350, only one will bid.

If you squint a bit, you might notice that the graph in panel A looks a lot like a demand curve: Price is on the *y*-axis, quantity is on the *x*-axis, and there's a line showing that quantity demanded increases as price decreases. In fact this *is* a demand curve, although it represents only five potential buyers. We could conduct the same exercise in a bigger market and plot out the willingness to pay of millions of people rather than just five. In that case, we'd get a smooth demand curve, as shown in panel B of Figure 5-1. The individual steps that we see in panel A get smaller and smaller over the millions of cameras demanded, resulting in the smoothed-out curve.

Notice that although each buyer's willingness to pay is driven by different factors, we can explain the motivations behind all of their decisions by asking, *What are the trade-offs?* Money that is spent to buy a camera on eBay cannot be spent on other things. Willingness to pay is the point at which the benefit that a person will get from the camera is equal to the benefit of

FIGURE 5-1

Willingness to pay and the demand curve

(A) Willingness to pay with few buyers

At any given price, buyers with a higher willingness to pay will buy and those with a lower willingness to pay will not. If the price were $350, only one buyer would buy. If it were $50, all five people would buy. This demand curve has a step-like shape rather than a smooth line because there are a limited number of buyers whose prices are expressed in round dollar amounts.

(B) Willingness to pay with many buyers

In the real market for a particular model of a digital camera, there are millions of cameras demanded at a particular price. The steps that we see in panel A get smaller and smaller until they disappear into a smooth curve.

spending the money on another alternative—in other words, the opportunity cost. For instance, $250 is the point at which the enjoyment that the amateur photographer gets from a camera is the same as the enjoyment he would get from, say, buying $250 worth of stamps for his stamp collection instead.

Since everyone has things they want other than cameras, the same opportunity cost logic applies to each of the potential buyers represented in the demand curve. At prices above the maximum willingness to pay, the opportunity cost is greater than the benefits. At lower prices, the benefits outweigh the opportunity cost.

To figure out which of our five individual buyers will actually purchase a camera, we have to know the market price. To find the market price, we have to know something about the supply of digital cameras. Therefore, we turn next to investigating the supply curve.

Willingness to sell and the supply curve

As you may have guessed, just as the shape of the demand curve was driven by potential buyers' willingness to pay, the shape of the supply curve for digital cameras is driven by potential sellers' *willingness to sell.* To simplify things, let's imagine five prospective sellers who have posted their cameras for sale on eBay.

- Seller #1 is a comic book collector. He was given a camera as a birthday present, but all he really cares about is having money to spend on comic books. He's willing to part with his camera for as little as $50.
- Seller #2 is a sales representative for a big company that makes digital cameras. She's authorized to sell a camera for $100 or higher.
- Seller #3 is a professional nature photographer who owns several cameras but won't sell for anything less than $200. At a lower price he'd rather give the camera as a gift to his nephew.
- Seller #4 is a sales representative for a small company that is just starting up in the camera industry and has much higher costs of production than the larger company; it can make money only by selling its cameras for $300 or more.
- Seller #5 is an art teacher who is sentimentally attached to her camera, given to her by a friend. She won't give it up unless she can get at least $400.

We can represent these five individuals by plotting on a graph their willingness to sell. Panel A of Figure 5-2 shows a graph of potential prices and the number of cameras that will be up for bid at each price. This graph is a supply curve representing only five potential sellers. As with the demand curve, if we added all of the millions of digital cameras that are actually for sale in the real world, we see the smooth supply curve we're accustomed to, as in panel B.

Sellers' willingness to sell is determined by the *trade-offs* they face, and, in particular, the opportunity cost of the sale. The opportunity cost of selling a camera for sellers #1, #3, and #5 is the use or enjoyment that the seller could get from keeping the camera. In the case of the two camera manufacturers, sellers #2 and #4, the opportunity cost is whatever else the firm would do with the money that would be required to manufacture the camera—say, marketing the camera or researching new technology. The opportunity cost of each of the five sellers will be determined by different factors—not all of them strictly monetary, as in the case of the teacher, who is sentimentally attached to her camera.

For an item that a seller just wants to get rid of (like the broken laser pointer mentioned at the start of the chapter), the starting price might be one cent. If opportunity cost is zero, anything is better than nothing!

On the other hand, in a market where manufacturers are producing and selling new products, the minimum price will have to be high enough to make it worth their while to continue making new products. This would be the case for the two camera manufacturers. If the selling price didn't cover the costs of production, the manufacturers would simply stop making the item—otherwise,

FIGURE 5-2

Willingness to sell and the supply curve

(A) Willingness to sell with few sellers

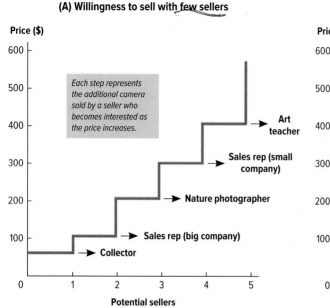

Each step represents the additional camera sold by a seller who becomes interested as the price increases.

(B) Willingness to sell with many sellers

At any given price, sellers with a lower willingness to sell will sell, while those with a higher willingness to sell will not. At a price of $400, all five people will sell their cameras, while at a price of $200, only three sell. This rough supply curve would look smooth if there were many sellers, each with a different willingness to sell.

In the real market for a particular model of a digital camera, there are millions of cameras supplied at a particular price. The steps that we see in panel A get smaller and smaller until they disappear into a smooth curve.

they would actually lose money every time they made a sale. (Occasionally, we do see manufacturers selling below the cost of production, but only when they've made a mistake and have to get rid of already-produced goods.)

Having met five potential buyers and five potential sellers, we're now in a position to understand what happens when the two groups come together in the market to make trades. But first, take a look at the Real Life box "Haggling and bluffing" to consider how buyers' willingness to pay interacts with sellers' willingness to sell in the real world.

Real Life
Haggling and bluffing

If you've ever visited a flea market or bought a used car, you have probably haggled over price. In much of the world, haggling for goods is an integral part of daily life. Even in wealthy countries, bargaining over salaries and promotions is commonplace—employees offer to sell their time and skills, and employers offer to buy them. In any bargaining situation, the seller wants to sell for as high a price as possible, and the buyer wants to buy for as low a price as possible. How do they reach an agreement?

The idea of willingness to pay explains a lot of bargaining strategies. Usually, the seller will start with a price much higher than the minimum she is actually willing to accept. Likewise, the

✓ CONCEPT CHECK

☐ What consumer surplus is received by someone whose willingness to pay is $20 below the market price of a good? **[LO 5.2]**

☐ What is the producer surplus earned by a seller whose willingness to sell is $40 below the market price of a good? **[LO 5.3]**

☐ Why can total surplus never fall below zero in a market for goods and services? **[LO 5.4]**

Using Surplus to Compare Alternatives

In a competitive market, buyers and sellers will naturally find their way to the equilibrium price. In our eBay example, we expect that buyers and sellers of digital cameras will bargain freely, offering different prices until the number of people who want to buy is matched with the number of people who want to sell. This is the invisible hand of market forces at work. It doesn't require any eBay manager to coordinate or set prices. But as we're about to see, the magic of the invisible hand doesn't stop there.

Market equilibrium and efficiency

LO 5.5 Define efficiency in terms of surplus, and identify efficient and inefficient situations.

The concept of surplus lets us appreciate something very important about market equilibrium: Not only is it the point at which transactions occur between the buyers willing to pay the most and sellers able to produce at the lowest cost. It also is the point at which total surplus is maximized. In other words, equilibrium maximizes the total well-being of the participants in the market.

To see why this is so, let's look at what would happen to surplus if, for some reason, the market moved away from equilibrium. Suppose an eBay manager decides to set the price of cameras so that people don't have to go to the trouble of bidding. He decides that $300 seems like a reasonable price. How will potential buyers and sellers *respond* to this situation? Figure 5-6 shows us:

- There are now 10 million fewer cameras sold (the quantity sold falls from 30 million to 20 million). Buyers who wanted 10 million cameras at the equilibrium price of $200 are no longer willing to buy at $300, reducing their consumer surplus to zero.
- That means that sellers who would have sold those 10 million cameras to buyers also miss out and get producer surplus of zero.
- For the 20 million cameras that still are sold, buyers pay a higher price and lose surplus.
- The sellers of those 20 million cameras benefit from the higher price and gain the surplus lost by consumers.

Overall, total surplus in the market is lower than it was at the equilibrium price because 10 million fewer cameras are sold.

What happens if the interfering eBay manager instead decides to sell digital cameras for $100? As Figure 5-7 shows:

- Buyers are willing to purchase 40 million cameras at a price of $100. Sellers are willing to sell only 15 million at $100.
- Since 15 million fewer cameras sell (that is, 15 million instead of 30 million at equilibrium), buyers and sellers lose the surplus that would have been gained through their sale.
- For the 15 million transactions that still take place, consumers gain surplus of $1.5 billion ($100 × 15 million) from buying at a lower price (area 2). That consumer surplus is exactly equal to the surplus the remaining sellers lose from selling at a lower price.

FIGURE 5-6

Changing the distribution of surplus

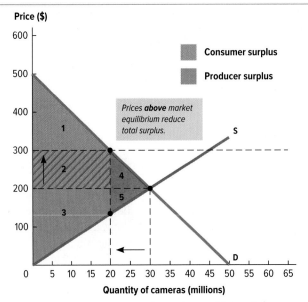

When the price rises above the market equilibrium, fewer transactions take place. The surplus shown in area 2 is transferred from consumers to producers as a result of the higher price paid for transactions that do still take place. The surplus in areas 4 and 5 is lost to both consumers and producers as a result of the reduced number of transactions.

FIGURE 5-7

Surplus when price is below equilibrium

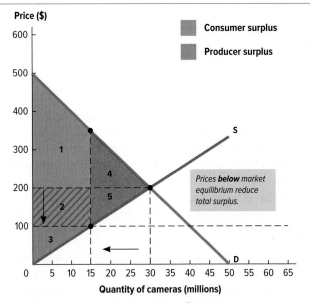

When the price of cameras drops to $100, buyers are willing to purchase 40 million, but sellers want to sell only 15 million. For those who do trade, successful buyers gain surplus of $1.5 billion (area 2) from buying at the lower price, while the sellers lose surplus of that same amount. The buyers and sellers who would have traded at equilibrium but no longer do so lose $1.875 billion of combined surplus. The surplus in areas 4 and 5 is lost to both consumers and producers as a result of the reduced number of transactions. Total surplus falls from $7.5 billion to $5.625 billion.

- The buyers and sellers who would have traded at equilibrium but no longer do so lose $1.875 billion of combined surplus. Breaking this down, we find that the 15 million buyers no longer in the market lose $1.125 billion (area 4), and sellers lose $0.75 billion (area 5) in surplus.
- This $1.875 billion total (areas 4 + 5) in lost surplus is subtracted from the amount of total surplus before the price ceiling. Overall, total surplus falls from $7.5 billion to $5.625 billion.

In both cases—when the price is $300 (above the equilibrium price) or when it is $100 (below the equilibrium price)—total surplus decreases relative to the market equilibrium. In fact, we find this same result at *any price* other than the equilibrium price. The key is that a higher or lower price causes fewer trades to take place because some people are no longer willing to buy or sell. The value that would have been gained from these voluntary trades no longer exists. As a result, *the equilibrium in a perfectly competitive, well-functioning market maximizes total surplus.*

Another way to say this is that the market is **efficient** when it is at equilibrium: There is no exchange that can make anyone better off without someone becoming worse off. Efficiency is one of the most powerful features of a market system. Even more remarkable is that it is achieved without centralized coordination.

efficient market an arrangement such that no exchange can make anyone better off without someone becoming worse off

Changing the distribution of total surplus

LO 5.6 Describe the distribution of surplus, or benefits to society, that results from a policy decision.

A reduction in total surplus was not the only interesting thing that happened when the meddling eBay manager moved the price of digital cameras away from equilibrium. Another outcome was *reassignment of surplus* from customers to producers, or vice versa, for the transactions that did take place:

- When the price was raised, sellers gained some well-being at the expense of buyers.
- When the price was lowered, buyers gained some well-being at the expense of sellers.

In both cases, achieving this transfer of well-being from one group to the other came at the expense of *reduced total surplus.*

When an artificially high price is imposed on a market, it's bad news for consumer surplus. Consumers lose surplus due to the reduced number of transactions and the higher price buyers have to pay on the remaining transactions.

The situation for producers, though, is more complex. At the artificially high price, producers lose some surplus from the transactions that would have taken place under equilibrium and no longer do. On the other hand, they gain more surplus from the higher price on the transactions that do still take place. These two effects will compete with one another. Whichever effect "wins" will determine whether the producer surplus increases or decreases overall.

To see why, let's go back to Figure 5-6. Area 2 is surplus that is transferred from consumers to producers. Areas 4 and 5 represent surplus lost to consumers and producers, respectively, from transactions that no longer take place. Whether area 2 is bigger or smaller than area 5 will indicate whether producer surplus increases or decreases. That result depends on the shape of the demand curve and the supply curve. In this case, we can see that area 2 is bigger than area 5. The effect of the artificially high price was to make sellers better off (at the expense of making buyers even more worse off).

The opposite situation occurs when prices are lower than the market equilibrium, which you can see by looking again at Figure 5-7. Fewer transactions take place (because fewer producers are willing to sell), and so both producers and consumers lose some surplus from missed transactions. For the transactions that do still take place, consumers pay less and gain surplus at the expense of producers. Producers get paid less and lose surplus. Thus, a price below the market equilibrium will always reduce producer surplus. That price might increase or decrease consumer surplus: The outcome depends on how much surplus is gained by those who buy at a lower price compared to what is lost to those who can no longer buy at all.

We don't expect eBay managers to start imposing their own prices any time soon—that would be contrary to the whole idea of eBay as a decentralized virtual marketplace. But there are times when governments or other organizations do decide to impose minimum or maximum prices on markets. That happens because efficiency is not the only thing we care about. Many fundamental public policy questions revolve around possible trade-offs between economic efficiency and other concerns such as fairness and equity. We'll look in much more detail at this idea in the next chapter.

Deadweight loss

> **LO 5.7** Calculate deadweight loss.

deadweight loss
a loss of total surplus that occurs because the quantity of a good that is bought and sold is below the market equilibrium quantity

An intervention that moves a market away from equilibrium might benefit either producers or consumers, but it always comes with a decrease in total surplus. Where does that surplus go? It disappears and becomes what is known as a **deadweight loss**. Deadweight loss is the loss of total surplus that occurs when the quantity of a good that is bought and sold is below the market equilibrium quantity. Any intervention that moves a market away from the equilibrium price and quantity creates deadweight loss. Fewer exchanges take place, so there are fewer opportunities for the generation of surplus.

We can calculate deadweight loss in two ways: One way is to subtract total surplus *after* a market intervention from total surplus at the market equilibrium *before* the intervention. Or we can calculate deadweight loss directly by determining the area of the triangle on a graph. This second method is usually the easiest.

Figure 5-8 shows what happens in the eBay camera market when the price is too low at $100. Only 15 cameras are exchanged at this price, but the efficient quantity is 30. For the units between 15 and 30, consumers have a willingness to pay that is higher than producers' costs. Thus, exchanging the units would create surplus, but because the units are not exchanged, this potential surplus is lost. To calculate the exact size of this deadweight loss, we calculate the area between supply and demand for those units that aren't exchanged. The "base" of this triangle is measured

FIGURE 5-8

Deadweight loss

Deadweight loss represents the surplus that is lost to both producers and consumers as a result of fewer transactions taking place when the price moves away from equilibrium. Here, deadweight loss is equal to the gray shaded area.

along the *y*-axis from \$100 to \$350. The "height" is measured along the *x*-axis from 15 to 30. Then, using the formula for the area of a triangle, the deadweight loss is $\frac{b \times h}{2} = \frac{250 \times 15}{2} = 1{,}875$.

We'll see in the next chapter that deadweight loss is an incredibly important concept for understanding the costs of government intervention in markets, through mechanisms such as taxes and controls on the prices of goods.

Missing markets

LO 5.8 Explain why correcting a missing market can make everyone better off.

When there are people who would like to make exchanges but cannot, for one reason or another, we miss opportunities for mutual benefit. In this situation, we say that a market is "missing": Buyers and sellers would like to make a trade but for some reason cannot. The term "missing" can be misleading. Sometimes a market exists, so it is not literally missing, but, rather, not all trades are happening as potential buyers and sellers would together like to have happen. Asking why a market is missing is important; the answer can provide guidance to policies and businesses that can make the world a better place by allowing more people to engage in trade for mutual benefit.

Markets can be missing for a variety of reasons. Sometimes public policy prevents the market from existing—for instance, when the production or sale of a particular good or service is banned. Or sometimes a particular good or service is taxed; the tax doesn't eliminate the market but does add a cost, which leads to fewer transactions. Markets can also be missing or shrunk due to other types of holdups: a lack of accurate information or communication between potential buyers and sellers, or a lack of technology that would make the exchanges possible.

eBay and newer companies such as Airbnb, Uber, and Lyft are examples of how technology can generate new value by creating or expanding a market. Prior to the existence of such companies, people who wanted to offer a service or product, and people who wanted to buy it, often never found each other. For example, before eBay you could hold a garage sale to get rid of your extra stuff; you could go to your local stores or post an ad in a newspaper if you were looking to buy an unusual item. But it was quite difficult to find out if someone on the other side of the country was offering a rare product or a better price. eBay allows more buyers to find sellers and vice versa, encouraging more mutually beneficial trades.

The idea that we can increase total surplus by creating new markets and improving existing ones has important implications for public policy. Policies and technologies that help people share information and do business more effectively can increase well-being. For instance, ideas like creating a market for small loans by the Grameen Bank (see Chapter 1, "Economics and Life") or expanding access to cell phones in Indian fishing villages (see Chapter 3, "Markets") don't just redistribute pieces of the pie to help the poor. Instead, they make the whole pie bigger.

Think about the many situations in the world in which new technology, new strategies, and outreach to new clients have created a market that brings value to people. Also think about some controversial situations in which markets don't exist but could be created, as described in the What Do You Think? box "Kidneys for sale."

What Do You Think?
Kidneys for sale

When buyers and sellers come together to participate in voluntary transactions, the resulting markets create value that would not otherwise exist. The idea that well-functioning markets maximize surplus is an important descriptive fact.

(continued)

But people may have moral and political priorities that go beyond maximizing surplus. In fact, many important public policy questions revolve around trade-offs between economic efficiency and other goals.

For instance, the law in the United States (and many other countries) prohibits certain types of market transactions. Consider the following cases:

- It's illegal to buy or sell organs for medical transplants.
- It's illegal to buy or sell certain drugs, such as cocaine and heroin.
- It's illegal to buy or sell children for adoption.
- It's illegal to buy or sell certain types of weapons, such as nuclear devices.

Looking at it from one angle, these are all examples of missing markets. You now know that when markets are missing, we miss opportunities to create surplus by enabling voluntary transactions to take place. For instance, a market for organs could make a lot of people better off. Some healthy people would gain surplus by selling their kidneys: They would rather have money and one remaining kidney than two kidneys and no money. Meanwhile, some people with kidney disease would happily pay for the donation of a healthy kidney. Because the law prevents this transaction from happening, both miss out on surplus.

If maximizing surplus is our highest goal, it's plausible that we should allow organs and other such goods to be traded on the market. But allowing markets for organs goes against many people's moral instincts—perhaps because they hold other goals higher than maximizing surplus.

WHAT DO YOU THINK?

1. Do you agree that the law should prevent trade in organs?
2. How about drugs, children, and nuclear weapons?
3. Are there any reasons that markets for these goods might not end up maximizing surplus?
4. What values and assumptions are driving your answers?

✓ CONCEPT CHECK

☐ What can we say about the size and distribution of total surplus in an efficient market? **[LO 5.5]**

☐ How do price changes affect the distribution of surplus between consumers and producers? **[LO 5.6]**

☐ Why does an intervention that moves a market away from the equilibrium price and quantity create a deadweight loss? **[LO 5.7]**

☐ What does it mean to say that a market is "missing"? **[LO 5.8]**

Conclusion

In this chapter we've introduced the concepts of willingness to pay and willingness to sell, which help explain when individual buyers and sellers will choose to make a trade. We've also discussed what it means to measure consumer and producer surplus and shown that the market equilibrium is efficient because it maximizes total surplus.

As we'll see in the next chapter, surplus and deadweight loss are powerful tools for understanding the implications of business ideas and public policies. Who will benefit from the policy? Who will be harmed by it? What effect will it have on the economy overall? The language of surplus, efficiency, and distribution of benefits is particularly helpful for getting to the bottom of controversial decisions.

Later in the book, we will describe important cases in which the efficiency rule about market equilibrium does not always hold true, and we'll see how surplus can also help us understand these cases.

Key Terms

willingness to pay (reservation price), p. 105

willingness to sell, p. 105

surplus, p. 109

consumer surplus, p. 109

producer surplus, p. 112

total surplus, p. 113

zero-sum game, p. 114

efficient market, p. 117

deadweight loss, p. 118

Summary

LO 5.1 Use willingness to pay and willingness to sell to determine supply and demand at a given price.

Willingness to pay and willingness to sell describe the value that an individual places on a particular good or service. Willingness to pay (also sometimes known as the reservation price) is the maximum price that a buyer would be willing to pay for a particular good or service. Willingness to sell is the lowest price a seller is willing to accept in exchange for a particular good or service.

Consumers will buy only if the price is lower than their willingness to pay. Producers will sell only if the price is higher than their willingness to sell.

LO 5.2 Calculate consumer surplus based on a graph or table.

Surplus is a way of measuring who benefits from transactions and how much. Consumer surplus is the net benefit that consumers receive from purchasing a good or service, measured by the difference between each consumer's willingness to pay and the actual price. Graphically, it is equal to the area below the demand curve and above the market price.

LO 5.3 Calculate producer surplus based on a graph or table.

Producer surplus is a measure of the net benefits that a producer receives from the sale of a good or service, measured by the difference between the producer's willingness to sell and the actual price. Graphically, it is equal to the area above the supply curve and below the market price.

LO 5.4 Calculate total surplus based on a graph or table.

Total surplus is a measure of the combined benefits that everyone receives from participating in an exchange of goods or services. It is calculated by adding consumer surplus and producer surplus. Graphically, it is equal to the total area between the supply and demand curves, to the left of the equilibrium quantity.

LO 5.5 Define efficiency in terms of surplus, and identify efficient and inefficient situations.

A market is *efficient* if there is no exchange that can make anyone better off without someone becoming worse off. An efficient market maximizes total surplus but doesn't tell us how the surplus is distributed between consumers and producers. In a competitive market, efficiency is achieved only at the market equilibrium price and quantity; higher prices and lower prices will both decrease the quantity bought and sold and reduce total surplus.

LO 5.6 Describe the distribution of surplus, or benefits to society, that results from a policy decision.

Prices above or below the market equilibrium reduce total surplus but also redistribute surplus between producers and consumers differently. A price above the equilibrium always decreases consumer surplus. Also, at a price above equilibrium, some producers win and others lose; the overall effect on producer surplus depends on the shape of the supply and demand curves. A price below the equilibrium always decreases producer surplus; some consumers win and others lose.

LO 5.7 Calculate deadweight loss.

Deadweight loss is the loss of total surplus that occurs when the quantity of a good that is bought and sold is below the market equilibrium quantity. Any intervention that moves a market away from the equilibrium price and quantity causes deadweight loss. Fewer exchanges take place, so there are fewer opportunities for the generation of surplus.

LO 5.8 Explain why correcting a missing market can make everyone better off.

A market is "missing" when there is a situation in which people would like to engage in mutually beneficial trades of goods and services but can't because no market for them exists. A missing market is a special case of a market in which quantity is held below the equilibrium—in this case, at or close to zero. Missing markets can occur for many reasons, including government intervention or a lack of information or technology. When missing markets are filled, people are able to trade, which generates surplus.

Review Questions

1. Bill is a professional photographer. His camera is broken and he needs a new one within the next hour, or he will miss an important deadline. Lisa is a high-school student who doesn't have a camera but wants to get one to take pictures at her prom next month. Who do you think would have a higher willingness to pay for a particular camera today? Why? **[LO 5.1]**

2. You are in the market for a new couch and have found two advertisements for the kind of couch you want to buy. One seller notes in her ad that she is selling because she is moving to a smaller apartment, and the couch won't fit in the new space. The other seller says he is selling because the couch doesn't match his other furniture. Which seller do you expect to buy from? Why? (*Hint:* Think who would be the more motivated seller.) **[LO 5.1]**

3. Suppose you are at a flea market and are considering buying a box of vintage records. You are trying to bargain down the price, but the seller overhears you telling a friend that you are willing to pay up to $50. Why is your consumer surplus now likely to be lower than it would have been if the seller hadn't overheard you? **[LO 5.2]**

4. Consider a market in equilibrium. Suppose supply in this market increases. How will this affect consumer surplus? Explain. **[LO 5.2]**

5. You currently have a television that you want to sell. You can either pick a price and try to sell it at a yard sale or auction it off on eBay. Which method do you think will yield a higher producer surplus? Why? **[LO 5.3]**

6. Consider a market in equilibrium. Suppose demand in this market decreases. How will this affect producer surplus? Explain. **[LO 5.3]**

7. Consider the market for plane tickets to Hawaii. A bad winter in the mainland United States increases demand for tropical vacations, shifting the demand curve to the right. The supply curve stays constant. Does total surplus increase or decrease? (*Hint:* Sketch out a generic supply and demand curve and look at what happens to the size of the triangle that represents total surplus when the demand curve shifts right.) **[LO 5.4]**

8. You need to paint your fence, but you really hate this task. You decide to hire the kid next door to do it for you. You would be willing to pay him up to $100, but you start by offering $50, expecting to negotiate. To your great surprise, he accepts your $50 offer. When you tell your friend about the great deal you got, she is shocked that you would take advantage of someone. What can you tell your friend to assure her that you did not cheat the kid next door? **[LO 5.4]**

9. New York City has a long-standing policy of controlling rents in certain parts of the city—in essence, a price ceiling on rent. Is the market for apartments likely to be efficient or inefficient? What does this imply for the size of total surplus? **[LO 5.5]**

10. Total surplus is maximized at the equilibrium price and quantity. When demand increases, price increases. Explain how total surplus is still maximized if price increases due to an increase in demand. **[LO 5.5]**

11. When the price of gasoline was very high in the summer of 2008, several U.S. presidential candidates proposed implementing a national price ceiling to keep fuel affordable. How would this policy have affected producer and consumer surplus? How would it have affected total surplus? **[LO 5.6]**

12. Consider a policy to help struggling farmers by setting a minimum trade price for wheat. Will this be an effective way to increase their surplus? Explain. **[LO 5.6]**

13. If rent control creates deadweight loss for both consumers and suppliers of housing, why are consumers often in favor of this policy? **[LO 5.7]**

14. Suppose price is 5 percent above equilibrium in two markets: a market for a necessity and a market for a luxury good. All else equal (including supply conditions), in which market do you expect deadweight loss to be greater? Explain. **[LO 5.7]**

15. Your grandmother likes old-fashioned yard sales and doesn't understand why everyone is so excited about eBay. Explain to her why the creation of a market that enables people who don't live in the same town to buy and sell used goods increases total surplus over the yard-sale market. **[LO 5.8]**

16. At Zooey's elementary school, children are not allowed to trade lunches or components of their lunches with other students. Lunchroom monitors watch closely and strictly enforce this policy. Help Zooey make an argument about the inefficiency of this policy to her principal. **[LO 5.8]**

Problems and Applications

1. Use the information in Table 5P-1 to construct a step graph of the six consumers' willingness to pay. **[LO 5.1]**

TABLE 5P-1

Buyer	Willingness to pay for one unit ($)
Fred	8
Ann	2
Morgan	16
Andre	12
Carla	2
Hanson	4

TABLE 5P-2

Seller	Willingness to sell one unit ($)
Joseph	25
Juan	20
Kristin	60
Peter	10
Candice	25
Solomon	50

2. Use the information in Table 5P-2 to construct a step graph of the six sellers' willingness to sell. **[LO 5.1]**

3. Answer the following questions based on Tables 5P-3 and 5P-4. **[LO 5.1]**
   a. What is the quantity demanded at $10? What is the quantity supplied at $10?
   b. What is the quantity demanded at $25? What is the quantity supplied at $25?

4. Based on Table 5P-5, calculate consumer surplus for each consumer when the price is $17. What is the total consumer surplus at this price? **[LO 5.2]**

TABLE 5P-3

Buyer	A	B	C	D	E	F	G	H	I
Willingness to pay for one unit	$35	$33	$27	$22	$21	$13	$13	$12	$6

TABLE 5P-4

Seller	A	B	C	D	E	F	G	H	I
Willingness to sell for one unit	$4	$9	$12	$14	$15	$21	$23	$30	$51

TABLE 5P-5

Buyer	A	B	C	D	E	F	G	H	I
Willingness to pay for one unit	$6	$27	$13	$21	$33	$35	$12	$13	$22

FIGURE 5P-1

FIGURE 5P-2

5. Use the demand curve represented in Figure 5P-1 to draw the consumer surplus when the market price is $8. What is the value of consumer surplus at this price? **[LO 5.2]**

6. Based on Figure 5P-2, consumer surplus is $0 when price is greater than or equal to what price? **[LO 5.2]**

7. Use the market represented in Figure 5P-2 to plot the equilibrium price and quantity and to draw the consumer surplus when the market is in equilibrium. What is the value of consumer surplus at the equilibrium price? **[LO 5.2]**

8. Use the market represented in Figure 5P-2 to draw the consumer surplus when the price is $5. What is the value of consumer surplus at this price? **[LO 5.2]**

9. Based on Table 5P-6, calculate producer surplus for each producer when the price is $20. What is total producer surplus at this price? **[LO 5.3]**

10. Use the supply curve represented in Figure 5P-3 to draw the producer surplus when the market price is $5. What is the value of producer surplus at this price? **[LO 5.3]**

11. Based on Figure 5P-2, producer surplus is $0 when price is less than or equal to what price? **[LO 5.3]**

FIGURE 5P-3

12. Use the market represented in Figure 5P-2 to plot the equilibrium price and quantity and to draw the producer surplus when the market is in equilibrium. What is the value of producer surplus at the equilibrium price? **[LO 5.3]**

TABLE 5P-6

Buyer	A	B	C	D	E	F	G	H	I
Willingness to pay for one unit	$21	$4	$30	$14	$12	$15	$51	$9	$23

FIGURE 5P-4

FIGURE 5P-6

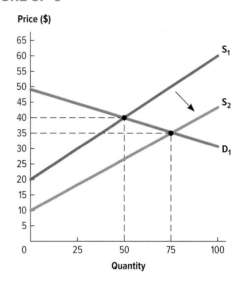

13. Use the market represented in Figure 5P-2 to draw the producer surplus if the price is $9. What is the value of producer surplus at this price? **[LO 5.3]**

14. Use the market represented in Figure 5P-4 to draw the consumer and producer surplus when the market is in equilibrium. What is the value of total surplus at equilibrium? **[LO 5.4]**

15. Consider the market represented in Figure 5P-5. **[LO 5.4]**
    a. Calculate total surplus when demand is D_1.
    b. Calculate total surplus when demand decreases to D_2.

16. Consider the market represented in Figure 5P-6. **[LO 5.4]**
    a. Calculate total surplus when supply is S_1.
    b. Calculate total surplus when supply increases to S_2.

17. Consider the market represented in Figure 5P-7. **[LO 5.5]**
    a. Draw the consumer surplus and the producer surplus at the equilibrium price and quantity. What is the value of total surplus at equilibrium?
    b. Draw the consumer surplus and the producer surplus if the price is $30. What are the values of consumer surplus, producer surplus, and total surplus at this price?
    c. Draw the consumer surplus and the producer surplus if the price is $10. What are the values of consumer surplus, producer surplus, and total surplus at this price?

FIGURE 5P-5

FIGURE 5P-7

18. Assume the market for wine is functioning at its equilibrium. For each of the following situations, say whether the new market outcome will be *efficient* or *inefficient*. **[LO 5.5]**

    a. A new report shows that wine is good for heart health.

    b. The government sets a minimum price for wine, which increases the current price.

    c. An unexpected late frost ruins large crops of grapes.

    d. Grape pickers demand higher wages, increasing the price of wine.

19. Based on Figure 5P-8, choose all of the following options that are true. **[LO 5.5, 5.6]**

    a. The market is efficient.

    b. Total surplus is higher than it would be at market equilibrium.

    c. Total surplus is lower than it would be at market equilibrium.

    d. Producer surplus is lower than it would be at market equilibrium.

    e. Consumer surplus is lower than it would be at market equilibrium.

20. In which of the following situations can you say, without further information, that consumer surplus decreases relative to the market equilibrium level? **[LO 5.6]**

    a. Your state passes a law that pushes the interest rate (i.e., the price) for payday loans below the equilibrium rate.

    b. The federal government enforces a law that raises the price of dairy goods above the equilibrium.

    c. Your city passes a local property tax, under which buyers of new houses have to pay an additional 5 percent on top of the purchase price.

    d. The government lowers the effective price of food purchases through a food-stamp program.

21. Use the areas labeled in the market represented in Figure 5P-9 to answer the following questions. **[LO 5.6]**

    a. What area(s) are consumer surplus at the market equilibrium price?

    b. What area(s) are producer surplus at the market equilibrium price?

    c. Compared to the equilibrium, what area(s) do consumers lose if price is P_2?

    d. Compared to the equilibrium, what area(s) do producers lose if the price is P_2?

    e. Compared to the equilibrium, what area(s) do producers gain if the price is P_2?

    f. Compared to the equilibrium, total surplus decreases by what area(s) if the price is P_2?

22. Figure 5P-10 shows a market for cotton, with the price held at $0.80 per pound. Draw and calculate the deadweight loss caused by this policy. **[LO 5.7]**

23. Consider the market represented in Figure 5P-11. **[LO 5.7]**

    a. Suppose the government sets a minimum price of $25 in the market. Calculate the deadweight loss.

    b. Suppose the government sets a maximum price of $25 in the market. Calculate the deadweight loss.

24. What is the value of the existence of the market represented in Figure 5P-12? **[LO 5.8]**

FIGURE 5P-8

FIGURE 5P-9

FIGURE 5P-10

Price ($)

Quantity (millions of lb.)

FIGURE 5P-11

Price ($)

Quantity

FIGURE 5P-12

Price ($)

Quantity

FIGURE 5P-13

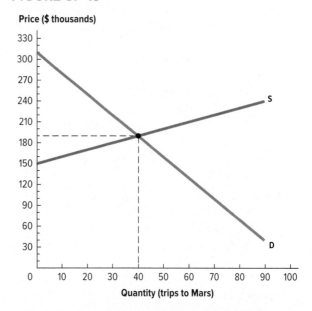

Price ($ thousands)

Quantity (trips to Mars)

25. We can consider the market for traveling to Mars to be missing because no technology exists that allows this service to be bought and sold. Suppose that someone has invented space-travel technology that will enable this service to be provided. Figure 5P-13 shows the estimated market for trips to Mars. Calculate the surplus that could be generated by filling in this missing market. **[LO 5.8]**

Endnotes

1   https://investors.ebayinc.com/releasedetail. cfm?ReleaseID=952024

2   http://news.bbc.co.uk/2/hi/4034787.stm

Math Essentials: The Area under a Linear Curve

Learning Objective

LO D.1 Calculate surplus by finding the area under a linear curve.

Chapter 5 introduced you to the concept of surplus. Surplus measures the gains or losses in well-being resulting from transactions in a market. You will often need to calculate a numerical value for surplus. To do that, you need to know how to find the area under a linear curve, and, therefore, we will review a little geometry.

The Area under a Linear Curve

LO D.1 Calculate surplus by finding the area under a linear curve.

Graphically, surplus is represented as the area between a supply or demand curve and the market price. The area between these curves and the market price will take the form of a triangle. In order to find surplus, you are going to need to be able to calculate the area of a triangle:

EQUATION D-1 $\text{Area of triangle} = \frac{1}{2} \times \text{Base of triangle} \times \text{Height of triangle} = \frac{1}{2}bh$

The key, then, is to figure which length to use as the base and which as the height.

In panel A of Figure D-1, consumer surplus is the shaded triangle below the demand curve and above the market price. The base of this triangle is the *horizontal distance* from the equilibrium point to the y-axis, $(12 - 0) = 12$. The height is the *vertical distance* from the equilibrium price to the y-intercept of the demand curve, $(50 - 20) = 30$. Therefore, the area of the triangle—and the consumer surplus—is:

$$\frac{1}{2} \times (12 \times 30) = \$180$$

Producer surplus is the shaded area below the market price and above the supply curve in panel B of Figure D-1. The base of the triangle is again the *horizontal distance* from the equilibrium point to the y-axis, $(12 - 0) = 12$. The height is the vertical distance from the equilibrium

FIGURE D-1

Measuring the area under a curve

(A) Measuring consumer surplus

Consumer surplus is found by taking the area of the triangle above the market price and below the demand curve.

(B) Measuring producer surplus

Measuring producer surplus, on the other hand, is found by taking the area of the triangle below the market price and above the supply curve.

price to the y-intercept of the supply curve, $(20 - 0) = 20$. Therefore the area of the triangle—and the producer surplus—is:

$$\frac{1}{2} \times (12 \times 20) = \$120$$

You learned in Chapter 5 that total surplus is consumer surplus plus producer surplus:

$$\text{Total surplus} = \$180 + \$120 = \$300$$

We can also calculate total surplus directly by calculating the area of the larger triangle that encompasses both. This time, the calculation of this triangle is slightly different. The base is the amount of space in between the y-intercept of the supply and demand curves. This gives a base of 50. The height of the triangle, on the other hand, is the distance from the y-axis to the equilibrium point. The area is thus $\frac{1}{2} \times 50 \times 12 = \$300$, the same result as before.

Occasionally, you will see oddly shaped surplus areas. You can always calculate these by breaking them down into familiar rectangles and triangles. Then calculate the area of each using length times width (for a rectangle) and $\frac{1}{2}$bh (for a triangle), and add the results to find the total area.

Problems and Applications

1. Use the graph in Figure DP-1 to answer the following questions. **[LO D.1]**

   a. What is the amount of consumer surplus?

   b. What is the amount of producer surplus?

   c. What is the amount of total surplus?

FIGURE DP-1

2. Use these two supply and demand equations to answer the following questions. **[LO D.1]**

$$P = 50 - 4Q$$

$$P = 2 + 2Q$$

   a. What is the equilibrium price? What is the equilibrium quantity?

   b. Draw a graph of supply and demand and illustrate the equilibrium.

   c. What is the amount of consumer surplus?

   d. What is the amount of producer surplus?

   e. What is the amount of total surplus?

Government Intervention

Learning Objectives

LO 6.1   Calculate the effect of a price ceiling on the equilibrium price and quantity.

LO 6.2   Calculate the effect of a price floor on the equilibrium price and quantity.

LO 6.3   Calculate the effect of a tax on the equilibrium price and quantity.

LO 6.4   Calculate the effect of a subsidy on the equilibrium price and quantity.

LO 6.5   Explain how elasticity and time period influence the impact of a market intervention.

FEEDING THE WORLD, ONE PRICE CONTROL AT A TIME

In the spring of 2008, a worldwide food shortage caused food prices to skyrocket. In just a few months, the prices of wheat, rice, and corn shot up as much as 140 percent. In the United States, the number of people living on food stamps rose to the highest level since the 1960s. By June, low-income Americans were facing tough choices, as the prices of basics like eggs and dairy products rose. Many reported giving up meat and fresh fruit; others said they began to buy cheap food past the expiration date.[1]

Rising food prices caused trouble all over the world. The *Economist* magazine reported on the political fallout:

> [In Côte d'Ivoire,] two days of violence persuaded the government to postpone planned elections. . . . In Haiti, protesters chanting "We're hungry" forced the prime minister to resign; 24 people were killed in riots in Cameroon; Egypt's president ordered the army to start baking bread; [and] the Philippines made hoarding rice punishable by life imprisonment.[2]

Faced with hunger, hardship, and angry outbursts, many governments felt obliged to respond to the crisis. But what to do? Responses varied widely. Many countries made it illegal to charge high prices for food. Other countries subsidized the price of basic necessities. In the United

© Abdurashid Abdulle/AFP/Getty Images

States and Europe, policy-makers tried to alleviate the shortage by paying farmers to grow more food. Were these responses appropriate? What, if anything, *should* governments do in such a situation?

Food is a tricky issue for policy-makers because it's a basic necessity. If prices rise too high, people go hungry. If prices fall too low, farmers go out of business, which raises the risk of food shortages in the future. So, while policy-makers aren't too concerned if the prices of many goods—like digital cameras or lattes—jump up and down, they often do care about food prices. But attempts to lower, raise, or simply stabilize prices can backfire or create unintended side effects. Sometimes the cure ends up being worse than the problem itself.

In this chapter, we'll look at the logic behind policies that governments commonly use to intervene in markets. There are often both intended and unintended consequences—and economic models and data can help think through both. We will start with *price controls,* which make it illegal to sell a good for more or less than a certain price. Then we will look at *taxes* and *subsidies,* which discourage or encourage the production of particular goods. These tools are regularly applied to a broad range of issues, from unemployment to home ownership, air pollution to education. For better or worse, they have a huge effect on our lives as workers, consumers, businesspeople, and voters.

Why Intervene?

In Chapter 3, "Markets," we saw that markets gravitate toward equilibrium. When markets work well, prices adjust until the quantity of a good that consumers demand equals the quantity that suppliers want to produce. At equilibrium, everyone gets what he or she is willing to pay for. In Chapter 5, "Efficiency," we saw that equilibrium price and quantity also maximize total surplus. At equilibrium, there is no way to make some people better off without harming others.

So, why intervene? Why not let the invisible hand of the market determine prices and allocate resources? Some would argue that's exactly what should be done. Others believe the government has to intervene sometimes—and the fact is that every single government in the world intervenes in markets in some fashion.

Three reasons to intervene

The arguments for intervention fall into three categories: changing the distribution of surplus, encouraging or discouraging consumption of certain goods, and correcting market failures. As we discuss different policy tools throughout the chapter, ask yourself which of these motivations is driving the intervention.

Changing the distribution of surplus

Efficient markets maximize total surplus, but an efficient outcome may still be seen as unfair. For example, even if the job market is efficient, wages can still drop so low that some workers fall below the poverty line while their employers make healthy profits. In such cases, some may argue for intervention in markets in order to change the distribution of surplus. The government might respond by intervening in the labor market to impose a minimum wage. This policy will change the distribution of surplus, reducing employers' profits (which may lead to higher prices) and lifting workers' incomes.

Of course, the definition of fairness is up for debate. Reasonable people can—and often do—argue about whether a policy that benefits a certain group (such as minimum-wage workers) is justified or not. Our focus will be on accurately describing the benefits and costs of such policies. Economics can help us predict whose well-being will increase, whose well-being will decrease, and who may be affected in unpredictable ways.

Encouraging or discouraging consumption

Around the world, many people judge certain products to be "good" or "bad" based on culture, health, religion, or other values. At the extreme, certain "bad" products are banned, such as many addictive drugs.

More often, governments use taxes to discourage people from consuming "bad" products, rather than simply banning them. Common examples are cigarettes and alcohol. Furthermore, in some cases consumption of a good imposes costs on others, such as second-hand smoke from cigarettes. In such cases the government may add a tax so that consumers or producers of the good have to pay more of the cost to society of consuming or producing that good. (Figuring out exactly what that cost is can be quite difficult, by the way.)

On the other hand, governments use *subsidies* to encourage people to consume "good" products or services. For instance, many governments provide public funding for schools to encourage education and for vaccinations to encourage parents to protect their children against disease.

Correcting market failures

Our model of demand and supply has so far assumed that markets work efficiently. In the real world, though, that's not always true. For example, sometimes there is only one producer of a good, who faces no competition and can charge an inefficiently high price. In other cases, one person's use of a product or service imposes costs on other people that are not captured in prices paid by the first person; an example is the pollution that others experience when smoke is ejected by your car (that is, the price you pay for the gas that is burned in your car imposes a cost on others when they must experience the pollution).

Situations in which the assumption of efficient, competitive markets fails to hold are called **market failures**. When there is a market failure, intervention can actually increase total surplus. We'll have much more to say about market failures in future chapters. In this chapter, we will stick to analyzing the effect of government interventions in efficient, competitive markets.

market failures
situations in which the assumption of efficient, competitive markets fails to hold

Four real-world interventions

In this chapter we'll look at four real-world examples of how governments have intervened or could intervene in the market for food. For each, we'll consider the motives for the intervention and what its direct and indirect consequences were or could be. These four interventions are:

1. For many Mexican families, tortillas are an important food. What happened when the Mexican government set a *maximum price* for tortillas, in an effort to keep them affordable?
2. To ensure supplies of fresh milk, the U.S. government wanted to protect dairy farmers. What happened when the government set a *minimum price* for milk?
3. Many Americans struggle with health problems caused by overeating and poor nutrition. Several states have responded by banning the use of certain fats in food products; others require that restaurants post nutritional information about the foods they serve. What would happen if governments *taxed* high-fat or high-calorie foods?
4. What would happen if, instead of setting a maximum price for tortillas, the Mexican government *subsidized* tortillas?

As we walk through these examples of real policies, we want you to apply both positive and normative analysis. Remember the difference:

- *Positive analysis* is about facts: Does the policy actually accomplish the original goal?
- *Normative analysis* is a matter of values and opinions: Do you think the policy is a good idea?

Few policies are all good or all bad. The key question is, *What are the trade-offs* involved in the intervention? Do the benefits outweigh the costs?

✓**CONCEPT CHECK**

☐ What are three reasons that a government might want to intervene in markets?

Price Controls

Suppose you are an economic policy advisor, and food prices are rising. What should you do? If you live in a region with many low-income consumers, you might want to take action to ensure that everyone gets enough to eat. One policy tool you might consider using is a **price control**—a regulation that sets a maximum or minimum legal price for a particular good. The direct effect of a price control is to hold the price of a good up or down when the market shifts, thus preventing the market from reaching a new equilibrium.

price control
a regulation that sets a maximum or minimum legal price for a particular good

Price controls can be divided into two opposing categories: *price ceilings* and *price floors*. We met this idea already in Chapter 5, "Efficiency," when we imagined an interfering eBay manager setting prices for digital cameras. In reality, eBay would never do such a thing, but governments often do, particularly when it comes to markets for food items. What are the effects of using price controls to intervene in a well-functioning, competitive market?

Price ceilings

LO 6.1 Calculate the effect of a price ceiling on the equilibrium price and quantity.

A **price ceiling** is a maximum legal price at which a good can be sold. Many countries have price ceilings on staple foods, gasoline, and electricity because policy-makers try to ensure everyone can afford the basic necessities.

Here, we come to the first of the real-world interventions in the chapter: Historically, the government of Mexico has set a price ceiling for tortillas. The intent is to guarantee that this staple food will remain affordable. Panel A of Figure 6-1 illustrates a hypothetical market for tortillas without a price ceiling. The equilibrium price is $0.50 per pound and the equilibrium quantity is 50 million pounds.

Let's say that the government of Mexico responded to rising tortilla prices by setting a price ceiling of approximately $0.25 per pound, as shown in panel B of Figure 6-1. How would we expect consumers to respond to this intervention? When the price falls, consumers will want to buy more tortillas. In this example, the price fell from $0.50 to $0.25, and as a result, quantity demanded increased from 50 million to 75 million pounds. How would we expect producers to respond to this intervention? Predictably, a lower price means fewer producers will be willing to supply tortillas. In this example, when the price fell to $0.25, the quantity supplied dropped from 50 million to 25 million pounds.

The lower price imposed by the price ceiling means higher quantity demanded but lower quantity supplied. Supply and demand were no longer in equilibrium. The price ceiling created

price ceiling
a maximum legal price at which a good can be sold

FIGURE 6-1

A market with and without a price ceiling

Without government intervention, the market for tortillas in Mexico would reach equilibrium at a price of $0.50 per pound and a quantity of 50 million pounds.

After government intervention, a price ceiling of $0.25 keeps the price of tortillas below the equilibrium point. At this new price, consumers want to buy more tortillas (75 million pounds) than producers want to supply (25 million pounds), resulting in a shortage of tortillas.

a *shortage* of tortillas, equal to the 50-million-pound difference between the quantity demanded (75 million) and the quantity supplied (25 million).

Did the price ceiling meet the goal of providing low-priced tortillas to consumers? Yes and no. Consumers were able to buy *some* tortillas at the low price of $0.25 a pound—but they *wanted* to buy three times as many tortillas as producers were willing to supply. We can assess the full effect of the price ceiling by looking at what happened to consumer and producer surplus. Even without looking at the graph, we already know that a price ceiling will cause producer surplus to fall: Sellers are selling fewer tortillas at a lower price.

We also know that total surplus—that is, producer and consumer surplus combined—will fall because the market has moved away from equilibrium. Some trades that would have happened at the equilibrium price do not happen. Also, the surplus that would have been generated by those mutually beneficial trades is lost entirely. This area is known as *deadweight loss* and is represented by area 1 in Figure 6-2. As discussed in Chapter 5, "Efficiency," **deadweight loss** represents the loss of total surplus that occurs because the quantity of a good that is bought and sold is below the market equilibrium quantity. Economists refer to changes in the economic well-being of market participants, as measured by changes in consumer surplus or producer surplus like deadweight loss, as *welfare effects*.

deadweight loss
a loss of total surplus that occurs because the quantity of a good that is bought and sold is below the market equilibrium quantity

What we can't tell without looking at the graph is whether consumer surplus will increase or decrease; that response depends on the shape of the supply and demand curves. In this instance, consumers lose surplus from trades that no longer take place (from the 25 million pounds of tortillas no longer supplied). But for the trades that still do take place, consumers gain surplus from paying $0.25 instead of $0.50. In those trades, producers lose the same amount of surplus from receiving the lower price. This direct transfer of surplus from producers to consumers is represented by area 2 (the cross-hatched area) in Figure 6-2.

Did consumer surplus increase or decrease? Because area 2 in Figure 6-2 is larger than half of area 1 (the portion of deadweight loss that would have gone to consumers at equilibrium), we

FIGURE 6-2

Welfare effects of a price ceiling

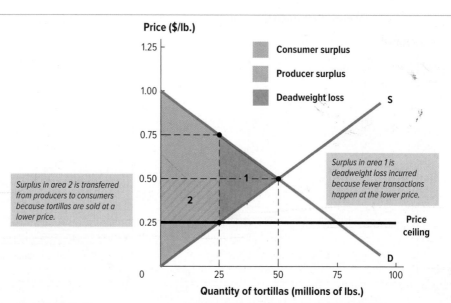

The price ceiling causes the total quantity of tortillas traded to fall by 25 million (from equilibrium at 50 million to 25 million). This results in deadweight loss. The price ceiling also causes surplus to be transferred from producers to consumers: Consumers win because they pay a lower price, and producers lose because they sell at a lower price ($0.25 instead of $0.50).

know that the intended goal of the price ceiling was achieved: a net increase in the well-being of consumers.

Was the policy worthwhile? On the one hand, consumers gained surplus. On the other hand, the surplus lost by producers was greater than that gained by consumers, meaning that total surplus decreased. Is it a price worth paying? That is a normative question about which reasonable people can disagree.

Another factor we may want to consider in our overall analysis of the price ceiling is how the scarce tortillas are allocated. Because a price ceiling causes a shortage, goods must be rationed. Rationing could be done in a number of ways. One possibility is for goods to be rationed equally, with each family entitled to buy the same amount of tortillas per week. This is what happened when food was rationed in the United States during World War II. Another possibility is to allocate goods on a first-come, first-served basis. This mode of rationing forces people to waste time standing in lines.

In still other cases, rationed goods might go to those who are given preference by the government, or to the friends and family of sellers. Finally, shortages open the door for people to bribe whoever is in charge of allocating scarce supplies. Rationing via bribery results in even more deadweight loss than in the example shown in Figure 6-2. Economists call this *rent-seeking behavior,* and it is often cited as an argument against imposing price ceilings.

The What Do You Think? box "Put a cap on payday lending?" asks you to weigh the costs and benefits of a controversial price ceiling on the interest rates of payday loans.

What Do You Think?
Put a cap on payday lending?

After the global financial crisis that began in 2008, policy-makers considered many proposals to reform financial practices. Small loans to consumers got a lot of attention because some people felt that irresponsible borrowing—through credit cards, mortgages, and consumer loans—was in part to blame for the crisis.

One of the most controversial types of borrowing is the *payday loan,* a short-term cash loan—usually for less than $1,000—that is intended to be repaid with the borrower's next paycheck. Many borrowers like these loans because they can walk out of the loan center with cash in their pockets in 30 minutes or faster. Payday loan centers tend to be located in low-income neighborhoods, where people have few other options for borrowing.

Because people with poor credit often use payday loans, lenders often charge high fees or interest rates (reflecting the higher risk of loan default). The fees also tend to be modest relative to the labor cost for the lender, but quite high relative to the amount borrowed. For example, you might not see a problem with a retailer earning a $20 profit on the sale of a $100 jacket. But if an individual must pay a $20 fee for a $100 one-week loan, that person will be paying a very high interest rate on an annualized basis.

In 2008, the U.S. Congress considered putting a price ceiling of 36 percent per year on the interest rates lenders could charge for payday loans. Since the interest rate is effectively the "price" of taking out a loan, this measure amounted to a price ceiling on a certain sort of loan service. Supporters of the proposed price ceiling argued that limiting interest rates would protect vulnerable consumers from "predatory" lenders who offer loans people can't afford. Those loans often trap borrowers in a cycle of taking out loans simply to repay prior loans.

Critics of the price ceiling countered that capping interest rates would force many payday lenders out of business. Consumers who make informed decisions to take out payday loans would be hurt by the resulting loss of credit. Those borrowers who have no other options could be driven to stop paying their bills or overdraw their checking accounts. This could lead to utilities

(continued)

being cut off or even eviction—consequences likely far worse than the fee on the payday loan. Ultimately, as expensive as payday loans are, they may be better than the next-best alternative.

Currently, 18 states (as well as the District of Columbia) have banned payday loans or set a ceiling on the interest rates that are charged for them. In 2008, for example, Ohio capped payday loan rates at 28 percent per year. Other states still allow less-restricted payday loans. In Missouri, lenders can charge up to 75 percent over a short loan period. You can learn about short-term loan regulations in your state by visiting http://www.paydayloaninfo.org/state-information.

WHAT DO YOU THINK?

1. An Internet search for *payday loan* turns up dozens of websites that promise "instant," "easy," or "no-hassle" loans. What's the cheapest rate you can find in your state? Would you consider borrowing at this price?
2. Price ceilings hold down prices, but also cause shortages and transfer surplus from payday-loan store owners to borrowers. Knowing that, would you support a cap on payday loan interest rates?
3. What would you expect the outcome of such a policy to be for buyers (borrowers) and sellers (lenders)?
4. Can you think of a way to protect potential victims of high interest rates without hurting borrowers who make informed borrowing decisions?

Source: "Payday loan consumer information," Consumer Federation of America's PayDay Loan website, http://www.paydayloaninfo.org.

Nonbinding price ceilings

A price ceiling does not always affect the market outcome. If the ceiling is set above the equilibrium price in a market, it is said to be *nonbinding*. That is, the ceiling doesn't "bind" or restrict buyers' and sellers' behavior because the current equilibrium is within the range allowed by the ceiling. In such cases, the equilibrium price and quantity will prevail.

Price ceilings are usually binding when they are first implemented. (Otherwise, why bother to create one?) Over time, though, shifts in the market can render the ceilings nonbinding. Suppose the price of corn decreases, reducing the cost of making tortillas. Figure 6-3 shows how the supply curve for tortillas would shift to the right (from S_1 to S_2) in response to this change in the market (a change in the price of inputs). This shift causes the equilibrium price to fall below the price ceiling. The new equilibrium is 80 million pounds of tortillas at $0.20 a pound, and the price ceiling becomes nonbinding.

Price floors

> **LO 6.2** Calculate the effect of a price floor on the equilibrium price and quantity.

price floor
a minimum legal price at which a good can be sold

A **price floor** is a minimum legal price at which a good can be sold. The United States has a long history of establishing price floors for certain agricultural goods. The rationale is that farming is a risky business—subject to bad weather, crop failure, and unreliable prices—but also an essential one, if people are to have enough to eat. A price floor is seen as a way to guarantee farmers a minimum income in the face of these difficulties, keeping them in business and ensuring a reliable supply of food.

We now come to the second of our four real-world interventions: The United States has maintained price floors for dairy products for over 65 years; the Milk Price Support Program began with the Agricultural Act of 1949. What effect has this program had on the market for

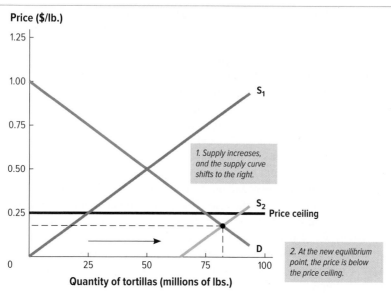

FIGURE 6-3

Nonbinding price ceiling

Price ($/lb.)

A price ceiling is intended to keep prices below the equilibrium level. However, changes in the market can reduce the equilibrium price to a level below the price ceiling. When that happens, the price ceiling no longer creates a shortage because the quantity supplied equals the quantity demanded.

milk? In panel A of Figure 6-4, we show a hypothetical unregulated market for milk in the United States, with an annual equilibrium quantity of 15 billion gallons and an equilibrium price of $2.50 per gallon.

Now suppose the U.S. government implements a price floor, so that the price of milk cannot fall below $3 per gallon, as shown in panel B of Figure 6-4. How will producers and

(A) Market without price floor   **(B) Market with price floor**

FIGURE 6-4

A market with and without a price floor

Without government intervention, the equilibrium point in the market for milk would be 15 billion gallons at a price of $2.50 per gallon.

A price floor raises the price of milk above the equilibrium point. At the new price of $3 per gallon, consumers want to buy less than suppliers want to produce, resulting in a 10-billion-gallon surplus.

consumers respond? At \$3 per gallon, dairy farmers will want to increase milk production from 15 to 20 billion gallons, moving up along the supply curve. At that price, however, consumers will want to decrease their milk consumption from 15 to 10 billion gallons, moving up along the demand curve. As a result, the price floor creates an excess supply of milk that is equal to the difference between the quantity supplied and the quantity demanded—in this case, 10 billion gallons.

Has the government accomplished its aim of supporting dairy farmers and providing them with a reliable income? As with price ceilings, the answer is yes and no. Producers who can sell all their milk will be happy: They are selling more milk at a higher price. However, producers who cannot sell all their milk, because demand no longer meets supply, will be unhappy. Consumers will be unhappy because they are getting less milk at a higher price.

Again, we can apply the concept of surplus to formally analyze how this change in total surplus is distributed between consumers and producers. Before the price floor, 15 billion gallons of milk were supplied and bought; after the price floor, this number is only 10 billion. Five billion gallons of milk that could have been traded were not, reducing total surplus. This deadweight loss is represented by area 1 in Figure 6-5.

Like price ceilings, price floors change the distribution of surplus; in this case, producers win at the expense of consumers. When the price floor is in effect, the only consumers who buy are those whose willingness to pay is above \$3. Their consumer surplus falls because they are buying the same milk at a higher price. Consumers' lost surplus is transferred directly to the producers who sell milk to them. This transfer of consumer surplus is represented by area 2 (the cross-hatched area) in Figure 6-5.

Did producers gain or lose overall? The answer depends on whether the area of transferred consumer surplus is bigger or smaller than the producers' share of the deadweight loss. Area 2 (the transfer of consumer surplus) is larger than the section of area 1 lost to producers; in this case, the price floor policy increased well-being for producers.

FIGURE 6-5

Welfare effects of a price floor

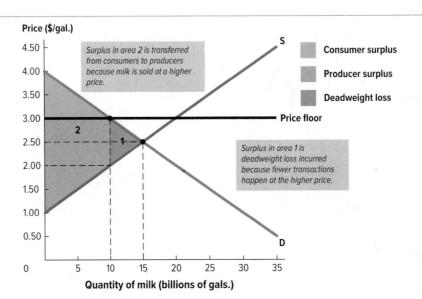

The price floor causes the total quantity of milk traded to fall by 5 billion gallons relative to equilibrium. This results in deadweight loss. The price floor also causes surplus to be transferred from consumers to producers: In this example, producers win because they sell at a higher price, and consumers lose because they pay a higher price.

Is the price of reduced total and consumer surplus worth paying to achieve increased producer surplus? One factor to consider is how the extra surplus is distributed among producers. Producers who are able to sell all their milk at the higher price will be happy. But producers who do not manage to sell all of their goods will be left holding an excess supply. They may be worse off than before the imposition of the price floor. With excess supply, customers may choose to buy from firms they like based on familiarity, political preference, or any other decision-making process they choose.

To prevent some producers from being left with excess supply, the government may decide to buy up all the excess supply of milk, ensuring that *all* producers benefit. In fact, that is how the milk price support program works in the United States. The Department of Agriculture guarantees producers that it will buy milk at a certain price, regardless of the market price. Of course, paying for the milk imposes a cost on taxpayers and is often cited as an argument against price floors. How much milk will the government have to buy? The answer is the entire amount of the excess supply created by the price floor. In the case of the hypothetical milk price floor, the government will have to buy 10 billion gallons at a price of $3. The cost to taxpayers of maintaining the price floor in this example would be $30 billion each year.

Nonbinding price floors

Price floors are not always binding. In fact, in recent years, the market prices for dairy products in the United States have usually been above the price floor. The price floor may become binding, however, in response to changes in the market. Figure 6-6 shows how such a decrease in supply could render a price floor nonbinding. Consider the effect of the increased demand for ethanol in 2007 on the market for milk. Ethanol is a fuel additive made from corn. The sudden rise in demand for ethanol pushed up the price of corn, which in turn pushed up the cost of livestock feed for dairy farmers. As a result of this change in the price of inputs, the supply curve for milk shifted to the left (from S_1 to S_2 in Figure 6-6). This shift pushed the equilibrium price for milk above the $3 price floor to $3.50.

FIGURE 6-6

Nonbinding price floor

Although a price floor is usually set so as to raise prices above the equilibrium level, changes in the supply can raise the equilibrium price above the price floor. When that happens, the surplus that was created by the price floor disappears and the quantity supplied equals the quantity demanded.

✓ CONCEPT CHECK

□ Why does a price ceiling cause a shortage? **[LO 6.1]**

□ What can cause a price ceiling to become nonbinding? **[LO 6.1]**

□ Explain how a government can support a price floor through purchases. **[LO 6.2]**

□ What can cause a price floor to become nonbinding? **[LO 6.2]**

Taxes and Subsidies

Taxes are the main way that governments raise revenue to pay for public programs. Taxes and subsidies can also be used to correct market failures and encourage or discourage production and consumption of particular goods. However, like price floors and price ceilings, they can have unintended consequences.

Taxes

LO 6.3 Calculate the effect of a tax on the equilibrium price and quantity.

We began this chapter by discussing hunger, which is usually a minor problem in wealthy countries. Indeed, the United States has the opposite problem: diseases associated with overeating and poor nutrition such as obesity, heart disease, and diabetes. How can policy-makers respond to this new type of food crisis? This issue is the third of the real-world interventions in this chapter.

In 2008, the state of California banned the use of trans fats in restaurants in an effort to reduce heart disease and related problems. Trans fats are artificially produced ("partially hydrogenated") unsaturated fats. Used in many fried and packaged foods because they extend products' shelf lives, they are believed to be unhealthy if consumed in excess. For decades, trans fats have been the key to making commercially produced french fries crispy and pastries flaky.

Rather than banning trans fats, what would happen if California taxed them? When a good is taxed, either the buyer or seller must pay some extra amount to the government on top of the sale price. How should we expect people to *respond* to a tax on trans fats? Taxes have two primary effects: First, they discourage production and consumption of the good that is taxed. Second, they raise government revenue through the fees paid by those who continue buying and selling the good. Therefore, we would expect a tax both to reduce consumption of trans fats and to provide a new source of public revenue.

Figure 6-7 illustrates this scenario by showing the impact of a trans-fat tax on the market for Chocolate Whizbangs. A delicious imaginary candy, Chocolate Whizbangs are unfortunately rather high in trans fats. Suppose that, currently, 30 million Whizbangs are sold every year, at $0.50 each. To discourage consumption, a tax on Whizbangs has been proposed; the new tax could be imposed either on sellers or on buyers.

A tax on sellers

Let's say that the government of California enacts a trans-fat tax of $0.20, which the seller must pay for every Whizbang sold. *How will buyers and sellers respond?* The impact of a tax is more complicated than the impact of a price control, so let's take it one step at a time.

1. **Does a tax on sellers affect supply? *Yes, supply decreases.***

   When a tax is imposed on sellers (producers), they must pay the government $0.20 for each Whizbang sold. At any market price, sellers will behave as if the price they are receiving is actually $0.20 lower. Put another way, for sellers to be willing to supply any given quantity, the market price must be $0.20 higher than it was before the tax.

FIGURE 6-7

Effect of a tax paid by the seller

A tax levied on the seller adds a new supply curve that is $0.20 higher than the original, which is the amount of the tax. As a result, the equilibrium quantity decreases and the equilibrium price increases. At the equilibrium quantity, the price paid by buyers is now different from the amount received by sellers after the tax is paid. This "tax wedge" is equal to the amount of the tax, or $0.20.

Figure 6-7 shows this change in supply graphically, by adding a new supply curve (S₂). (Technically, this "shift" isn't really a shift of the curve but a way of showing the new equilibrium price; see the nearby Potentially Confusing box.) The new supply curve is $0.20 higher, the exact amount of the tax. At any given market price, sellers will now produce the same quantity as they would have at a price $0.20 lower before the tax: At $0.60 on curve S₂ the quantity supplied will be the same as at a price of $0.40 on curve S₁. At a price of $0.50 on curve S₂ the quantity supplied will be the same as at a price of $0.30 on curve S₁, and so on.

2. **Does a tax on sellers affect demand?** *No, demand stays the same.*

Demand remains the same because the tax does not change any of the nonprice determinants of demand. At any given price, buyers' desire to purchase Whizbangs is unchanged. Remember, however, that the *quantity demanded* does change, although the curve itself doesn't change.

3. **How does a tax on sellers affect the market equilibrium?** *The equilibrium price rises and quantity demanded falls.*

The new supply curve causes the equilibrium point to move up along the demand curve. At the new equilibrium point, the price paid by the buyer is $0.60. Because buyers now face a higher price, they demand fewer Whizbangs, so the quantity demanded falls from 30 million to 25 million. Notice that at the new equilibrium point, the quantity demanded is lower and the price is higher. Taxes usually reduce the quantity of a good or service that is sold, shrinking the market.

? POTENTIALLY CONFUSING

In Chapter 3, "Markets," we distinguished between a curve *shifting* to the left or right and *movement along* the same curve. A shift represents a fundamental change in the quantity demanded or supplied at any given price; a movement along the same curve simply shows a switch to a different quantity and price point. The question here is, does a tax cause a *shift* of the demand or supply curve or a *movement along* the curve?

The answer is neither, really. Here's why: When we add a tax, we're not really shifting the curve; rather, we are adding a second curve. We still need the original curve to understand what is happening. This is because the price that sellers receive is actually $0.20 lower than the price at which they sell Whizbangs, due to the tax. So we need one curve to represent what sellers receive and another curve to represent what buyers pay.

Notice in Figure 6-7 that the price suppliers receive is on the original supply curve, S_1, but the price buyers pay is on the new supply curve, S_2. The original curve *does not actually move,* but we add the second curve to indicate that because of the tax, buyers face a different price than what the sellers will get. In order for the market to be in equilibrium, the quantity that buyers demand at $0.60 must now equal the quantity that sellers supply at $0.40.

Now let's look at the new equilibrium price in Figure 6-7. The price paid by buyers to sellers is the new market price, $0.60. However, sellers do not get to keep all the money they receive. Instead, they must pay the tax to the government. Since the tax is $0.20, the price that sellers receive once they have paid the tax is only $0.40. Ultimately, sellers do not receive the full price that consumers pay; the tax creates what is known as a *tax wedge* between buyers and sellers. A **tax wedge** is the difference between the price paid by buyers and the price received by sellers, which equals the amount of the tax. In Figure 6-7, the tax wedge is calculated as shown in Equation 6-1.

tax wedge
the difference between the price paid by buyers and the price received by sellers in the presence of a tax

EQUATION 6-1 $$\text{Tax wedge} = P_{\text{buyers}} - P_{\text{sellers}} = \text{Tax}$$

For each Whizbang sold at the new equilibrium point, the government collects tax revenue, as calculated in Equation 6-2.

EQUATION 6-2 $$\text{Government tax revenue} = \text{Tax} \times Q_{\text{post-tax}}$$

Specifically, the government receives $0.20 for each of the 25 million Whizbangs sold, or $5 million total. Graphically, the government revenue equals the green-shaded area in Figure 6-8.

Just like a price control, a tax causes deadweight loss and redistributes surplus. We can see the deadweight loss caused by the reduced number of trades in Figure 6-8. It is surplus lost to buyers and sellers who would have been willing to make trades at the pre-tax equilibrium price.

The redistribution of surplus, however, is a little trickier to follow. Under a tax, *both* producers and consumers lose surplus. Consumers who still buy pay more for the same candy than they would have under equilibrium, and producers who still sell receive less for the same candy. The difference between this lost surplus and deadweight loss, however, is that it doesn't "disappear." Instead, it becomes government revenue. In fact, the area representing government revenue in Figure 6-8 is exactly the same as the surplus lost to buyers and sellers still trading in the market after the tax has been imposed. This revenue can pay for services that might transfer surplus back to producers or consumers, or both, or to people outside of the market.

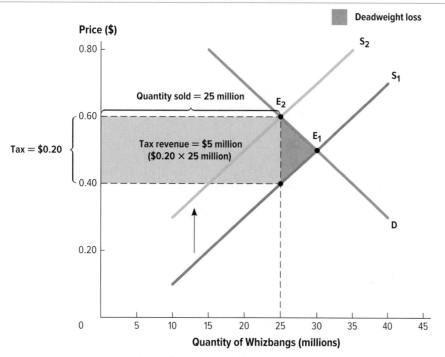

FIGURE 6-8

Government revenue and deadweight loss from a tax

The revenue from a per-unit tax is the amount of the tax multiplied by the number of units sold at the post-tax equilibrium point. The amount of tax revenue directly corresponds to the surplus lost to consumers and producers. The trades that no longer happen under the tax represent deadweight loss.

A tax on buyers

What happens if the tax is imposed on buyers instead of sellers? Surprisingly, the outcome is exactly the same. Suppose California enacts a sales tax of $0.20, which the buyer must pay for every Whizbang bought. In this case, as Figure 6-9 shows, the demand curve (rather than the supply curve) moves by the amount of the tax, but the resulting equilibrium price and quantity are the same.

To double-check this result, let's walk step by step through the effect of a tax levied on buyers.

1. **Does a tax on buyers affect the supply curve?** *No, supply stays the same.*

   The supply curve stays the same because the tax does not change the incentives producers face. None of the nonprice determinants of supply are affected.

2. **Does a tax on buyers affect the demand curve?** *Yes, demand decreases.*

   Demand decreases because the price buyers must pay per unit, including the tax, is now $0.20 higher than the original price. As Figure 6-9 shows, we take the original demand curve D_1 and factor in the amount of the tax; the result is a second demand curve D_2, which represents the price buyers pay under the tax. At any given price, buyers will now behave as if the price were actually $0.20 higher. For example, at $0.40 on curve D_2, the quantity demanded is as if the price were $0.60 on curve D_1. At $0.30 on curve D_2, the quantity demanded is as if the price were $0.50.

3. **How does a tax on buyers affect the market equilibrium?** *The equilibrium price and quantity both fall.*

   As a result, the equilibrium point with the new demand curve is further down the supply curve. The equilibrium price falls from $0.50 to $0.40 and the quantity demanded and

FIGURE 6-9

Effect of a tax paid by the buyer

A tax levied on the buyer adds a new demand curve $0.20 below the original curve. As a result, the equilibrium quantity decreases and the equilibrium price paid by the buyer increases. These results are the same as those of a tax levied on the seller.

supplied falls from 30 million to 25 million. Although the market equilibrium price goes down instead of up, as it does with a tax on sellers, the actual amount that buyers and sellers pay is the same no matter who pays the tax. When buyers pay the tax, they pay $0.40 to the seller and $0.20 to the government, or a total of $0.60. When sellers pay the tax, buyers pay $0.60 to the seller, who then pays $0.20 to the government. Either way, buyers pay $0.60 and sellers receive $0.40.

As Figure 6-9 shows, a tax on buyers creates a tax wedge just as a tax on sellers does. At the new equilibrium point, the price sellers receive is $0.40. The buyer pays $0.40 to the seller and then the $0.20 tax to the government, so that the total effective price is $0.60. Using Equation 6-1, once again the tax wedge is $0.20, exactly equal to the amount of the tax.

$$\text{Tax wedge} = \$0.60 - \$0.40 = \$0.20$$

Furthermore, the government still collects $0.20 for every Whizbang sold, just as under a tax on sellers. Again, using Equation 6-2, the post-tax equilibrium quantity is 25 million, and the government collects $5 million in tax revenue.

$$\text{Government tax revenue} = \$0.20 \times 25 \text{ million} = \$5 \text{ million}$$

What is the overall impact of the tax on Whizbangs? Regardless of whether a tax is imposed on buyers or sellers, there are four effects that result from all taxes:

1. Equilibrium quantity falls. The goal of the tax has thus been achieved—consumption of Whizbangs has been discouraged.

2. Buyers pay more for each Whizbang and sellers receive less. This creates a tax wedge, equal to the difference between the price paid by buyers and the price received by sellers.

3. The government receives revenue equal to the amount of the tax multiplied by the new equilibrium quantity. In this case, the California state government receives an additional $5 million in revenue from the tax on Whizbangs—which could be used to offset the public health expenses caused by obesity-related diseases.

4. The tax causes deadweight loss. The value of the revenue the government collects is always less than the reduction in total surplus caused by the tax.

In evaluating a tax, then, we must weigh its goal—in this case, reducing the consumption of trans fats—against the loss of surplus in the market.

Who bears the burden of a tax?

We've seen that the outcome of a tax does not depend on who pays it. Whether a tax is levied on buyers or on sellers, the cost is shared. But which group bears more of the burden?

In our example, the burden was shared equally:

- Buyers paid $0.50 for a Whizbang before the tax; after the tax, they pay $0.60. Therefore, buyers bear $0.10 of the $0.20 tax burden.

- Sellers received $0.50 for each Whizbang before the tax; after the tax, they receive $0.40. Therefore, sellers also bear $0.10 of the $0.20 tax burden.

The shaded rectangles in panel A of Figure 6-10 represent graphically this 50-50 split. The relative tax burden borne by buyers and sellers is called the **tax incidence**.

Often, however, the tax incidence is not split equally. Sometimes one group carries much more of it than the other. Compare the example just given to another possible market for Whizbangs,

> **tax incidence**
> the relative tax burden borne by buyers and sellers

FIGURE 6-10

Tax incidence and relative elasticity

In all panels, the supply curve S₂ lies $0.20 above the original curve.

☐ Sellers' tax burden

☐ Buyers' tax burden

(A) Equal incidence

When supply and demand have the same relative elasticity, buyers and sellers share the tax burden equally.

(B) Sellers pay more

When demand is more elastic than supply, sellers shoulder more of the tax burden than buyers.

(C) Buyers pay more

When supply is more elastic than demand, buyers shoulder more of the tax burden than sellers.

represented in panel B of Figure 6-10. In this case, buyers paid $0.50 before the tax. After the tax, they pay $0.54, so their tax burden is $0.04 per Whizbang. Sellers, on the other hand, receive only $0.34 after the tax, so their tax burden, at $0.16 per Whizbang, is four times as large as that of buyers.

Panel C of Figure 6-10 shows the opposite case, in which buyers bear more of the burden than sellers. Thus, buyers pay $0.66 and sellers receive $0.48.

What determines the incidence of a tax? The answer has to do with the relative elasticity of the supply and demand curves. Recall from Chapter 4, "Elasticity," that price elasticity describes how much the quantity supplied or demanded changes in response to a change in price. Since a tax effectively changes the price of a good to both buyers and sellers, the relative responsiveness of supply and demand will determine the tax burden. Essentially, *the side of the market that is more price elastic will be more able to adjust to price changes and will shoulder less of the tax burden.*

Panel B of Figure 6-10 imagines a market in which demand is more elastic: Many consumers easily give up their Whizbang habit and buy healthier snacks instead. In that case, Whizbang producers pay a higher share of the tax. Panel C imagines a market in which demand is less elastic: Consumers are so obsessed with Whizbangs that they will buy even at the higher price. In that case, buyers pay a higher share of the tax.

Recall that the market outcome of a tax—the new equilibrium quantity and price—is the same regardless of whether a tax is imposed on buyers or on sellers. Thus, the tax burden will be the same no matter which side of the market is taxed. Note in panel C of Figure 6-10 that buyers bear the greater part of that burden, even though the tax is imposed on sellers. The situation in panels B and C shows there can be a difference between *economic incidence* (the economic effect of a tax on either buyers or sellers) and *statutory incidence* (the person who is legally responsible for paying the tax). The actual economic incidence of a tax is unrelated to the statutory incidence.

This is an important point to remember during public debates about taxes. A politician may say that companies that pollute should be held accountable for the environmental damage they cause, through a tax on pollution. Regardless of how you may feel about the idea of taxing pollution, remember that levying the tax on companies that pollute does not mean that they will end up bearing the whole tax burden. Consumers who buy from those producers will also bear part of the burden of the tax, through higher prices. Policy-makers have little control over how the tax burden is shared between buyers and sellers.

Subsidies

LO 6.4 Calculate the effect of a subsidy on the equilibrium price and quantity.

subsidy
a requirement that the government pay an extra amount to producers or consumers of a good

A **subsidy** is the reverse of a tax: It is a requirement that the government pay an extra amount to producers or consumers of a good. Governments use subsidies to encourage the production and consumption of a particular good or service. They can also use subsidies as an alternative to price controls to benefit certain groups without generating a shortage or an excess supply.

Let's return to the Mexican dilemma—what to do when hungry people cannot afford to buy enough tortillas. This is the last of the four real-world interventions in the chapter, and here we ask a different question: What would happen if the government *subsidized* tortillas rather than imposed a price ceiling on them?

Figure 6-11 shows the tortilla market we discussed earlier in the chapter. The figure shows that before the subsidy, the market is in equilibrium at a price of $0.70 per pound and a quantity of 50 million pounds. Now suppose the government offers tortilla makers a subsidy of $0.35 per pound. *How will buyers and sellers respond to the subsidy?* They will respond in the opposite way that they respond to a tax:

- With a tax, the quantity supplied and demanded decrease, and the government collects revenue.
- With a subsidy, the quantity supplied and demanded increase, and the government spends money.

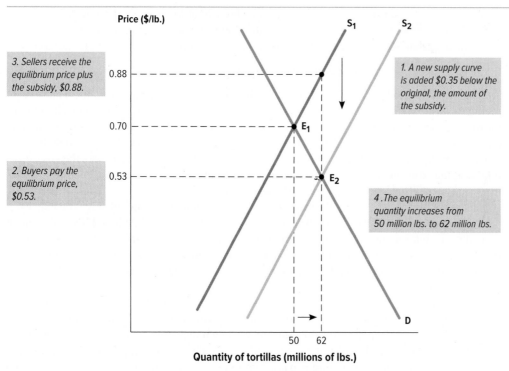

FIGURE 6-11
Effect of a subsidy to the seller

3. Sellers receive the equilibrium price plus the subsidy, $0.88.

1. A new supply curve is added $0.35 below the original, the amount of the subsidy.

2. Buyers pay the equilibrium price, $0.53.

4. The equilibrium quantity increases from 50 million lbs. to 62 million lbs.

Price ($/lb.)

S_1 S_2

0.88

0.70 E_1

0.53 E_2

D

50   62

Quantity of tortillas (millions of lbs.)

A subsidy has the opposite effect of a tax. A new supply curve is added $0.35 below the original supply curve. This decreases the equilibrium price and increases the equilibrium quantity supplied and demanded.

We can calculate the effect of a $0.35 tortilla subsidy by walking through the same three steps we used to examine the effect of a tax.

1. **Does a subsidy to sellers affect the supply curve?** *Yes, supply increases.*

   When producers receive a subsidy, the real price they receive for each unit sold is higher than the market price. At any market price, therefore, they will behave as if the price were $0.35 higher. Put another way, for sellers to supply a given quantity, the market price can be $0.35 lower than it would have to be without the subsidy. As a result, the new supply curve is drawn $0.35 below the original. In Figure 6-11, S_2 shows the new supply curve that is the result of the subsidy.

2. **Does a subsidy to sellers affect the demand curve?** *No, demand stays the same.*

   The demand curve stays where it is because consumers are not directly affected by the subsidy.

3. **How does a subsidy to sellers affect the market equilibrium?** *The equilibrium price decreases and the equilibrium quantity increases.*

   The equilibrium quantity with the new supply curve increases as consumers move down along the demand curve to the new equilibrium point. At the new, post-subsidy equilibrium, the quantity supplied increases from 50 million pounds of tortillas to 62 million pounds. As with a tax, the price buyers pay for tortillas differs from the price sellers receive after the subsidy because the subsidy creates a wedge between the two prices. This time, however, sellers receive a *higher* price than the pre-subsidy equilibrium of $0.70, and buyers pay a *lower* one. Buyers pay $0.53 per pound and sellers receive $0.88 per pound. The government pays the $0.35 difference.

The government subsidizes each pound of tortillas sold at the new equilibrium point. To calculate the total amount of government expenditure on a subsidy, we can use Equation 6-3. The government spends $0.35 for each of the 62 million pounds of tortillas sold, or $21.7 million total.

EQUATION 6-3   Government subsidy expenditure = Subsidy × $Q_{\text{post-subsidy}}$

Like taxes, subsidies also cause deadweight loss and redistribute surplus. Panel A of Figure 6-12 shows the deadweight loss caused by the overproduction and overconsumption of tortillas. If there is no subsidy, 50 million pounds is the equilibrium quantity. Any more, and the cost to produce them would be higher than the benefit to consumers. Thus, it would be inefficient to exchange more than 50 million pounds of tortillas. The subsidy lowers the cost to the producer, thus causing producers and consumers to exchange 12 million more pounds of tortillas than is efficient. This leads to a deadweight loss.

Panel B of Figure 6-12 shows the total government expenditure on the subsidy. You may wonder why only part of the government expenditure is counted as deadweight loss. If the government is funding 12 million more pounds of tortillas than is efficient, shouldn't the entire expenditure be deadweight loss? The answer is no, because the government is increasing both consumer and producer surplus with its expenditures. However, the deadweight loss arises because not all of the expenditure becomes surplus.

Figure 6-13 shows the consumer surplus and producer surplus from a subsidy. Notice that both consumer surplus and producer surplus increase with a subsidy. However, recall that the increase in surplus is funded by the government, as shown in panel B of Figure 6-12. Notice that the amount of government expenditure is less than the total increase in producer and consumer surplus. Ultimately, that expenditure is passed on to taxpayers (both producers and individuals) in the form of more taxes.

FIGURE 6-12

Deadweight loss from a subsidy

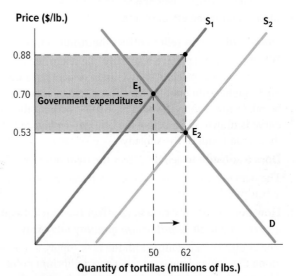

(A) Deadweight loss from tortilla subsidy

(B) Government spending on tortilla subsidy

For the 12 million pounds of tortillas produced due to the subsidy, supply exceeds demand. Thus, the exchange of these tortillas causes deadweight loss.

The government subsidy expenditure is the amount of the subsidy multiplied by the post-subsidy equilibrium quantity. The subsidy increases both consumer surplus and producer surplus but imposes a cost on the government, which ultimately is paid for by taxes on consumers and producers.

FIGURE 6-13

Effect of a subsidy on surplus

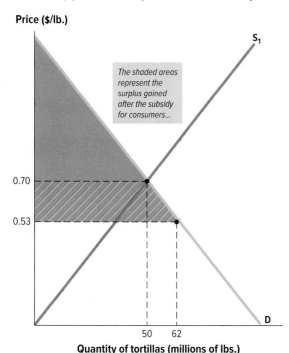

(A) Consumer surplus from tortilla subsidy

Price ($/lb.)

S₁

The shaded areas represent the surplus gained after the subsidy for consumers...

0.70

0.53

D

50   62

Quantity of tortillas (millions of lbs.)

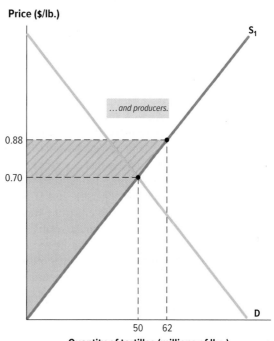

(B) Producer surplus from tortilla subsidy

Price ($/lb.)

S₁

...and producers.

0.88

0.70

D

50   62

Quantity of tortillas (millions of lbs.)

The post-subsidy price paid by consumers ($0.53) is lower than the initial equilibrium price ($0.70), and the post-subsidy quantity (62 million pounds) is higher than the initial equilibrium quantity (50 million pounds). This results in an increase in consumer surplus.

The post-subsidy price received by sellers ($0.88) is higher than the initial equilibrium price ($0.70), and the post-subsidy quantity (62 million pounds) is higher than the initial equilibrium quantity (50 million pounds). This results in an increase in producer surplus.

Are the benefits to consumers and producers worth the cost? That depends on how much we value the increased production of tortillas and their reduced cost to consumers versus the opportunity cost of the subsidy—that is, whatever other use the government or taxpayers might have made of that $21.7 million.

In addition, as the Real Life box "The unintended consequences of biofuel subsidies" shows, the obvious benefits of a subsidy can sometimes be swamped by unexpected costs.

Real Life

The unintended consequences of biofuel subsidies

The United States subsidizes the production of "biofuels" such as ethanol, a cleaner fuel than gasoline. Ethanol is fermented from many sources of starch, though it is most typically created from corn in the United States. The professed goal of the push towards biofuels such as ethanol—and thus the subsidy—is to reduce pollution. As hoped, the subsidy has caused a huge increase in the production of ethanol. Unfortunately, it has also had some unintended effects. Michael Grunwald, a journalist for *Time* magazine, argues that, indirectly, biofuels can actually increase pollution.

(continued)

Grunwald claims that the problem is simple, and yet something policy-makers didn't antici-pate. In order to grow the products that ethanol is created from, farmers need land—which can lead to the destruction of forests, wetlands, and grasslands. This can lead to the opposite effect of the hoped-for reduction in air pollution. Unfortunately, unintended consequences aren't always just a postscript to market interventions. Sometimes, they can change the whole story.

Source: M. Grunwald, "The clean energy scam," *Time,* March 27, 2008, http://www.time.com/time/magazine/article/0,9171,1725975,00.html. The *New York Times* had a follow-up in its environmental blog: http://green.blogs.nytimes.com/2008/11/03/the-biofuel-debate-good-bad-or-too-soon-to-tell/.

As with a tax, the effect of a subsidy is the same regardless of whether it is paid to producers or consumers. If consumers received a $0.35 subsidy for every pound of tortillas they bought, their demand curve would be $0.35 above the original, and the supply curve would remain unchanged. In that case, the equilibrium outcome would be the same as if producers received the subsidy: Quantity increases from 50 million pounds to 62 million pounds, buyers pay $0.53 per pound, and sellers receive $0.88 per pound.

Also as with a tax, the way in which the benefits of a subsidy are split between buyers and sellers depends on the relative elasticity of the demand and supply curves. *The side of the market that is more price elastic receives more of the benefit.* In our example, both have almost the same benefit: Buyers are better off by $0.17 per pound of tortillas, and producers by $0.18.

As with taxes, it is important to note that who gets what share of benefit from the subsidy does not depend on who receives the subsidy. Sometimes in debates about subsidies you will hear someone argue that a subsidy should be given either to buyers or sellers because they "deserve it more." This argument doesn't make much sense in a competitive market (although it might in a noncompetitive market).

In sum, a subsidy has the following effects, regardless of whether it is paid to buyers or sellers:

1. Equilibrium quantity increases, accomplishing the goal of encouraging production and consumption of the subsidized good.
2. Buyers pay less and sellers receive more for each unit sold. The amount of the subsidy forms a wedge between buyers' and sellers' prices.
3. The government has to pay for the subsidy, the cost of which equals the amount of the subsidy multiplied by the new equilibrium quantity.

✓CONCEPT CHECK

☐ What is a tax wedge? **[LO 6.3]**
☐ What determines the incidence of a tax? **[LO 6.3]**
☐ How does a subsidy affect the equilibrium quantity? How does it affect the price that sell-ers receive and the price that buyers pay? **[LO 6.4]**
☐ Does it matter whether a subsidy is paid to buyers or sellers? Why or why not? **[LO 6.4]**

Evaluating Government Interventions

LO 6.5 Explain how elasticity and time period influence the impact of a market intervention.

We began this chapter with a discussion of three reasons why policy-makers might decide to intervene in a market: to change the distribution of surplus, to encourage or discourage consump-tion, and to correct market failures. To decide whether policy-makers have achieved their goals

TABLE 6-1

Government interventions: a summary

Intervention	Reason for using	Effect on price	Effect on quantity	Who gains and who loses?
Price floor	To protect producers' income	Price cannot go below the set minimum.	Quantity demanded decreases and quantity supplied increases, creating excess supply.	Producers who can sell all their goods earn more revenue per item; other producers are stuck with an unwanted excess supply.
Price ceiling	To keep consumer costs low	Price cannot go above the set maximum.	Quantity demanded increases and quantity supplied decreases, creating a shortage.	Consumers who can buy all the goods they want benefit; other consumers suffer from shortages.
Tax	To discourage an activity or collect money to pay for its consequences; to increase government revenue	Price increases.	Equilibrium quantity decreases.	Government receives increased revenue; society may gain if the tax decreases socially harmful behavior. Buyers and sellers of the good that is taxed share the cost. Which group bears more of the burden depends on the price elasticity of supply and demand.
Subsidy	To encourage an activity; to provide benefits to a certain group	Price decreases.	Equilibrium quantity increases.	Buyers purchase more goods at a lower price. Society may benefit if the subsidy encourages socially beneficial behavior. The government and ultimately the taxpayers bear the cost.

by implementing a price control, tax, or subsidy, we need to assess the effects of each intervention, including its unintended consequences.

We've established a few rules about the expected outcomes of market interventions. Table 6-1 summarizes the key effects of price controls, taxes, and subsidies. In general, we can say the following:

- Price controls have opposing impacts on the quantities supplied and demanded, causing a shortage or excess supply. In contrast, taxes and subsidies move the quantities supplied and demanded in the same direction, allowing the market to reach equilibrium at the point where the quantity supplied equals the quantity demanded.
- Taxes discourage people from buying and selling a particular good, raise government revenue, and impose a cost on both buyers and sellers.
- Subsidies encourage people to buy and sell a particular good, cost the government money, and provide a benefit to both buyers and sellers.

In the following sections we will consider some of the more complicated details of market interventions. These details matter. Often the details of an intervention make the difference between a successful policy and a failed one.

How big is the effect of a tax or subsidy?

Regardless of the reason for a market intervention, it's important to know exactly *how much* it will change the equilibrium quantity and price. Can the effect of a tax or subsidy on the equilibrium quantity be predicted ahead of time? The answer is yes, *if* we know the price elasticity of supply and demand. A general rule applies: *The more elastic supply or demand is, the greater the change in quantity.* This rule follows directly from the definition of price elasticity, which measures buyers' and sellers' responsiveness to a change in price—and a tax or subsidy is effectively a change in price.

Figure 6-14 shows the effect of a $0.20 tax on the quantity demanded under four different combinations of price elasticity of supply and demand—again, for Whizbangs. It's worthwhile to walk through each combination, one by one:

- In panel A, both supply and demand are *relatively inelastic:* In this case the tax causes the equilibrium quantity to decrease, but not by much. Both buyers and sellers are willing to continue trading, even though they now must pay the tax.
- In panel B, *demand is more elastic than supply:* When the supply curve is $0.20 higher, the change in quantity is much larger than in panel A.
- In panel C, *supply is elastic but demand is relatively inelastic:* Again, because suppliers are highly responsive to the cost of the tax, the quantity changes more than in panel A.
- In panel D, *supply and demand are both elastic:* In this case, the quantity goes down even more than in the second and third examples.

To predict the size of the effect of a tax or subsidy, then, policy-makers need to know the price elasticity of both supply and demand. As we have seen, they can also use that information to determine who will bear more of the burden or receive more of the benefit.

If you are interested in the role of government in the economy, read the Where Can It Take You? box "Public economics" to learn more about the field.

FIGURE 6-14

Price elasticity and the effect of a $0.20 tax

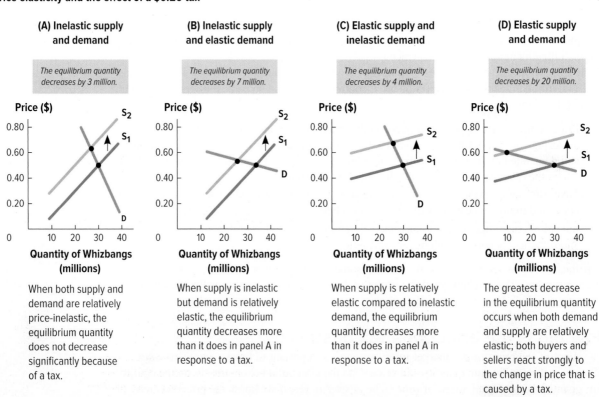

(A) Inelastic supply and demand

The equilibrium quantity decreases by 3 million.

When both supply and demand are relatively price-inelastic, the equilibrium quantity does not decrease significantly because of a tax.

(B) Inelastic supply and elastic demand

The equilibrium quantity decreases by 7 million.

When supply is inelastic but demand is relatively elastic, the equilibrium quantity decreases more than it does in panel A in response to a tax.

(C) Elastic supply and inelastic demand

The equilibrium quantity decreases by 4 million.

When supply is relatively elastic compared to inelastic demand, the equilibrium quantity decreases more than it does in panel A in response to a tax.

(D) Elastic supply and demand

The equilibrium quantity decreases by 20 million.

The greatest decrease in the equilibrium quantity occurs when both demand and supply are relatively elastic; both buyers and sellers react strongly to the change in price that is caused by a tax.

Where Can it Take You?

Public economics

Are you more interested in elections and legislation than in how to run a business? If so, we hope you are beginning to realize that understanding the economics behind public policy is incredibly important. Although well-designed policies can accomplish great things, well-intentioned but poorly designed policies can backfire badly.

To learn more about the economics of public policy, consider taking a *public economics* course. We will discuss policy issues throughout this book, but there is a lot more to learn, whether you want to be a politician, an analyst at a think tank, or just an informed voter.

Long-run versus short-run impact

We have seen that in addition to changing the price of a good or service, price controls cause shortages or excess supply. Because buyers and sellers take time to respond to a change in price, sometimes the full effect of price controls becomes clear only in the long run.

Suppose the U.S. government imposes a price floor on gasoline in an attempt to reduce air pollution by discouraging people from driving. Panel A of Figure 6-15 shows the short-run impact of a price floor in the market for gasoline. In the short run, the quantity of gas demanded might not change very much. Although people would cut down on unnecessary driving, the greater part of demand would still be based on driving habits that are difficult to change, such as commuting to school or work or going to the grocery store. And unless gasoline producers have a lot of unused oil wells sitting around, sellers might have trouble ramping up production quickly. In the short run, demand and supply are not very elastic, so the price floor results in only a small excess supply.

FIGURE 6-15

Government intervention in the long and short run

In the short run, neither the supply nor the demand for gasoline is very elastic, so the effect of a price floor on the quantity supplied is relatively small.

In the long run, both the supply and the demand for gasoline will change in response to price controls. As a result, the long-run effect on the quantity supplied is much greater than the short-run effect.

Recall that for both supply and demand, one of the determinants of price elasticity is the period over which it is measured. On both sides of the market, elasticity is often greater over a long period than over a short one:

- On the demand side, consumers might make small lifestyle changes over the medium term, such as buying a bus pass or shopping closer to home. Over the long run, they might make even bigger changes. When they need to buy a new car, for example, they will be inclined to buy a model that offers high gas mileage. If they move to a new job or home, they may place more weight than in the past on commuting distance.

- Supply will also be more elastic over the long run. Because a higher price gives suppliers an incentive to produce more, they may invest in oil exploration, dig new wells, or take steps to increase the pumping capacity of existing wells. Panel B of Figure 6-15 shows the long-run impact of a price floor in the market for gasoline. Because both supply and demand are more elastic in the long run than in the short run, the excess supply of gasoline is much larger in the long run than in the short run.

If the goal of the price floor was to reduce air pollution by giving consumers an incentive to cut down on driving, the impact might look disappointing in the short run: The quantity of gas burned will decrease very little. Over the long run, however, the quantity of gas burned will decrease further, and the policy will look more successful.

If, on the other hand, the reason for the price floor was to support gasoline suppliers, the short-run response would look deceptively rosy because suppliers will sell almost the same quantity of gas at a higher price. As the quantity falls over the long run, however, more producers will be stuck with an excess supply and the policy will start to look less successful.

In the European Union and the United States, farmers are given very generous subsidies. Without these subsidies, many farmers would be forced to quit farming. Critics argue that subsidies distort the market by keeping prices of certain foods much higher than they would be without subsidies. Read the full debate in the What Do You Think? box "Farm subsidies."

What Do You Think?
Farm subsidies

Many wealthy countries spend a lot of money on price floors and subsidies that encourage domestic agricultural production. For instance, the costs associated with Europe's Common Agricultural Policy (CAP) currently account for almost half the European Union's budget, or approximately $50 billion per year.

CAP was established in 1957 with the following objectives:

1. To increase agricultural productivity by developing technical progress and by ensuring the rational development of agricultural production and the optimum utilization of the factors of production, particularly labor.
2. To ensure thereby a fair standard of living for the agricultural population, particularly by the increasing of the individual earnings of persons engaged in agriculture.
3. To stabilize markets.
4. To guarantee regular supplies.
5. To ensure reasonable prices in supplies to consumers.

Supporters believe that these are important and worthwhile policy goals. However, CAP has come under heavy criticism for many reasons. Critics say that CAP imposes a huge cost on taxpayers; creates excess supplies of crops by distorting farmers' incentives; hurts farmers in poor countries, whose produce must compete with Europe's subsidized crops; and channels public funds to big agribusinesses.

The European Union is not alone in its policies. Every year the U.S. farm bill allocates many billions of dollars to crop price supports. Japan also intervenes heavily in agricultural markets.

WHAT DO YOU THINK?

1. Do you approve of the stated objectives of Europe's Common Agricultural Policy? Which, if any, do you think merit the market distortions they may create?
2. Do wealthy nations have a responsibility to consider the impact of their agricultural policies on poorer countries, or are domestic farming interests more important?

Source: European Commission, "The Common Agricultural Policy: A Partnership between Europe and Farmers" (2012), http://ec.europa.eu/agriculture/cap-overview/2012_en.pdf.

✓ CONCEPT CHECK

☐ If the demand for a good is inelastic, will a tax have a large or small effect on the quantity sold? Will buyers or sellers bear more of the burden of the tax? **[LO 6.5]**

☐ Would you expect a tax on cigarettes to be more effective over the long run or the short run? Explain your reasoning. **[LO 6.5]**

Conclusion

If you listen to the news, it might seem as if economics is all about business and the stock market. Business matters, but many of the most important, challenging, and useful applications of economic principles involve public policy.

This chapter gives you the basic tools you need to understand government interventions and some of the ways they can affect your everyday life. Of course, the real world is complicated, so this isn't our last word on the topic. Later, we discuss how to evaluate the benefits of both markets and government policies. We'll also discuss market failures and whether and when governments can fix them.

Key Terms

market failures, p. 132

price control, p. 132

price ceiling, p. 133

deadweight loss, p. 134

price floor, p. 136

tax wedge, p. 142

tax incidence, p. 145

subsidy, p. 146

Summary

LO 6.1 Calculate the effect of a price ceiling on the equilibrium price and quantity.

The government usually intervenes in a market for one or more of the following reasons: to change the distribution of a market's benefits, to encourage or discourage the consumption of particular goods and services, or to correct a market failure. Governments may also tax goods and services in order to raise public revenues.

A price ceiling is a maximum legal price at which a good can be sold. A binding price ceiling causes a shortage because at the legally mandated price, consumers will demand more than producers supply. This policy benefits some consumers because they are able to buy what they want at a lower price, but other consumers are unable to find the goods they want. Producers lose out because they sell less at a lower price than they would without the price ceiling.

LO 6.2 Calculate the effect of a price floor on the equilibrium price and quantity.

A price floor is a minimum legal price at which a good can be sold. A price floor causes an excess supply because at the minimum price, sellers will supply more than consumers demand. This policy benefits some producers, who are able to sell their goods at a higher price, but leaves other producers with goods they can't sell. Consumers lose because they buy less at a higher price. Maintaining a price floor often requires the government to buy up the excess supply, costing taxpayers money.

LO 6.3 Calculate the effect of a tax on the equilibrium price and quantity.

A tax requires either buyers or sellers to pay some extra price to the government when a good is bought and sold. A tax shrinks the size of a market, discouraging the consumption and production of the good being taxed. The effect is the same regardless of whether the tax is levied on buyers or sellers. The tax burden is split between consumers and producers, and the government collects revenues equal to the amount of the tax times the quantity sold.

LO 6.4 Calculate the effect of a subsidy on the equilibrium price and quantity.

A subsidy is a payment that the government makes to buyers or sellers of a good for each unit that is sold. Subsidies increase the size of a market, encouraging the consumption and production of the good being subsidized. The effect is the same regardless of whether the subsidy is paid to buyers or sellers. Both consumers and producers benefit from a subsidy, but taxpayers must cover the cost.

LO 6.5 Explain how elasticity and time period influence the impact of a market intervention.

In evaluating the effects of a government intervention in the market, it is important to consider both the intended and unintended consequences of the policy. The size of the impact of a tax or subsidy and the distribution of the burden or benefit will depend on the price elasticities of supply and demand. Furthermore, the impact of a government intervention is likely to change over time, as consumers and producers adjust their behavior in response to the new incentives.

Review Questions

1. You are an advisor to the Egyptian government, which has placed a price ceiling on bread. Unfortunately, many families still cannot buy the bread they need. Explain to government officials why the price ceiling has not increased consumption of bread. **[LO 6.1]**

2. Suppose there has been a long-standing price ceiling on housing in your city. Recently, population has declined and demand for housing has decreased. What will the decrease in demand do to the efficiency of the price ceiling? **[LO 6.1]**

3. Suppose the United States maintains a price floor for spinach. Why might this policy decrease revenues for spinach farmers? **[LO 6.2]**

4. Suppose Colombia maintains a price floor for coffee beans. What will happen to the size of the deadweight loss if the price floor encourages new growers to enter the market and produce coffee? **[LO 6.2]**

5. Many states tax cigarette purchases. Suppose that smokers are unhappy about paying the extra charge for their cigarettes. Will it help smokers if the state imposes the tax on the stores that sell the cigarettes rather than on smokers? Why or why not? **[LO 6.3]**

6. Consider a tax on cigarettes. Do you expect the tax incidence to fall more heavily on buyers or sellers of cigarettes? Why? **[LO 6.3]**

7. In the United States, many agricultural products (such as corn, wheat, and rice) are subsidized. What are the potential benefits of subsidizing these products? What are the costs? **[LO 6.4]**

8. A subsidy will increase consumer and producer surplus in a market and will increase the quantity of trades. Why, then, might a subsidy (such as a subsidy for producing corn in the United States) be considered inefficient? **[LO 6.4]**

9. Suppose the government imposes a price ceiling on gasoline. One month after the price ceiling, there is a shortage of gasoline, but it is much smaller than critics of the policy had warned. Explain why the critics' estimates might still be correct. **[LO 6.5]**

10. A state facing a budget shortfall decides to tax soft drinks. You are a budget analyst for the state. Do you expect to collect more revenue in the first year of the tax or in the second year? Why? **[LO 6.5]**

Problems and Applications

1. Many people are concerned about the rising price of gasoline. Suppose that government officials are thinking of capping the price of gasoline below its current

FIGURE 6P-1

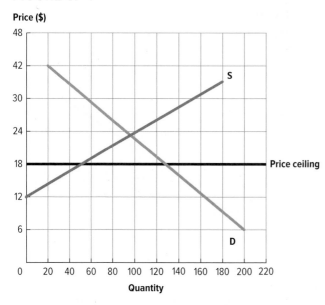

Price ($)

FIGURE 6P-3

Market for farmed halibut

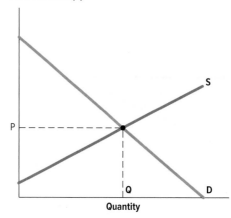

Price of halibut ($)

price. Which of the following outcomes do you predict will result from this policy? Check all that apply. **[LO 6.1]**

   a.   Drivers will purchase more gasoline.

   b.   Quantity demanded for gasoline will increase.

   c.   Long lines will develop at gas stations.

   d.   Oil companies will work to increase their pumping capacity.

2.   Consider the market shown in Figure 6P-1. The government has imposed a price ceiling at $18. **[LO 6.1]**

   a.   At a price ceiling of $18, what is quantity demanded? Quantity supplied?

   b.   At this price ceiling, is there a shortage or a surplus? By how many units?

3.   Figure 6P-2 shows a market in equilibrium. **[LO 6.1]**

FIGURE 6P-2

Price ($)

   a.   Draw a price ceiling at $12. What is the amount of shortage at this price? Draw and calculate the deadweight loss.

   b.   Draw a price ceiling at $4. What is the amount of shortage at this price? Draw and calculate the deadweight loss.

4.   Decades of overfishing have dramatically reduced the world supply of cod (a type of whitefish). Farm-raised halibut is considered a close substitute for ocean-fished cod. Figure 6P-3 shows the market for farm-raised halibut. **[LO 6.1]**

   a.   What effect will overfishing cod have on the price of cod? On the graph, show the effect of overfishing cod on the market for farmed halibut.

   b.   A fast-food chain purchases both cod and halibut for use in its Fish 'n' Chips meals. Already hurt by the reduced supply of cod, the fast-food chain has lobbied aggressively for price controls on farmed halibut. As a result, Congress has considered imposing a price ceiling on halibut at the former equilibrium price—the price that prevailed before overfishing reduced the supply of cod. What will happen in the market for farmed halibut if Congress adopts the price control policy? Draw and label the price ceiling, quantity demanded, quantity supplied, and deadweight loss.

5.   Consider the market shown in Figure 6P-4. The government has imposed a price floor at $36. **[LO 6.2]**

   a.   At a price floor of $36, what is quantity demanded? Quantity supplied?

   b.   At this price floor, is there a shortage or a surplus? By how many units?

FIGURE 6P-4

FIGURE 6P-5

6. The Organization for the Promotion of Brussels Sprouts has convinced the government of Ironia to institute a price floor on the sale of brussels sprouts, at $8 per bushel. Demand is given by $P = 9 - Q$ and supply by $P = 2Q$, where Q is measured in thousands of bushels. **[LO 6.2]**

   a. What will be the price and quantity of brussels sprouts sold at market equilibrium?

   b. What will be the price and quantity sold with the price floor?

   c. How big will be the excess supply of brussels sprouts produced with the price floor?

7. The traditional diet of the citizens of the nation of Ironia includes a lot of red meat, and ranchers make up a vital part of Ironia's economy. The government of Ironia decides to support its ranchers through a price floor, which it will maintain by buying up excess meat supplies. Table 6P-1 shows the supply and demand

TABLE 6P-1

Price ($)	Quantity demanded (thousands of lbs.)	Quantity supplied (thousands of lbs.)
6	5	80
5	20	70
4	35	60
3	50	50
2	65	40
1	80	30

schedule for red meat; quantities are given in thousands of pounds. **[LO 6.2]**

   a. How many thousands of pounds of meat would you recommend that the government purchase to keep the price at $4/pound?

   b. How much money should the government budget for this program?

8. The market shown in Figure 6P-5 is in equilibrium. Suppose there is a $15 per unit tax levied on sellers.

   a. Draw the after-tax supply curve.

   b. Plot the after-tax price paid by consumers and the after-tax price paid by sellers.

9. The market shown in Figure 6P-6 is in equilibrium. Suppose there is a $1.50 per unit tax levied on sellers. **[LO 6.3]**

   a. Draw the after-tax supply curve.

   b. Plot the after-tax price paid by consumers and the after-tax price paid by sellers.

   c. Draw consumer surplus, producer surplus, tax revenue, and deadweight loss after the tax.

   d. Calculate deadweight loss.

   e. Calculate total surplus.

10. Suppose the government is considering taxing cigarettes. Because it is often politically more popular to tax the producers of cigarettes than the consumers of cigarettes, the government first considers the impact on the market as a result of taxing the producers of cigarettes. Figure 6P-7 shows the market in equilibrium. **[LO 6.3]**

FIGURE 6P-6

FIGURE 6P-7

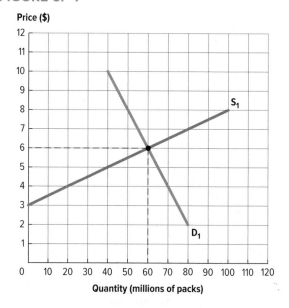

a. Draw the after-tax supply curve if the government chooses to tax cigarette producers $2.50 per pack of cigarettes.

b. Plot the after-tax price paid by consumers and the after-tax price received by sellers.

c. Do consumers or producers bear the greater burden of this tax?

d. Now suppose the government considers taxing the consumers of cigarettes instead of the producers of cigarettes. Draw the after-tax supply curve if the government chooses to tax cigarette consumers $2.50 per pack of cigarettes.

e. Plot the after-tax price paid by consumers and the after-tax price received by sellers.

f. Do consumers or producers bear the greater burden of this tax?

g. Is the price sellers receive when the government taxes consumers of cigarettes more than, less than, or the same as the price sellers receive when the government taxes producers of cigarettes?

h. Is the price buyers pay when the government taxes consumers of cigarettes more than, less than, or the same as the price buyers pay when the government taxes producers of cigarettes?

11. Suppose you have the information shown in Table 6P-2 about the quantity of a good that is supplied and demanded at various prices. **[LO 6.3]**

   a. Plot the demand and supply curves on a graph, with price on the *y*-axis and quantity on the *x*-axis.

   b. What are the equilibrium price and quantity?

   c. Suppose the government imposes a $15 per unit tax on sellers of this good. Draw the new supply curve on your graph.

   d. What is the new equilibrium quantity? How much will consumers pay? How much will sellers receive after the tax?

   e. Calculate the price elasticity of demand over this price change.

   f. If demand were less elastic (holding supply constant), would the deadweight loss be smaller or larger? **[LO 6.5]**

TABLE 6P-2

Price ($)	Quantity demanded	Quantity supplied
45	10	160
40	20	140
35	30	120
30	40	100
25	50	80
20	60	60
15	70	40
10	80	20
5	90	0

FIGURE 6P-8

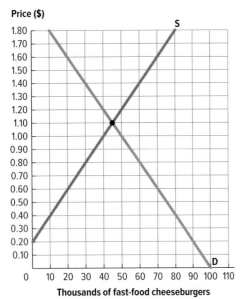

Thousands of fast-food cheeseburgers

FIGURE 6P-9

12. The weekly supply and demand for fast-food cheese-burgers in your city is shown in Figure 6P-8. In an effort to curb a looming budget deficit, the mayor recently proposed a tax that would be levied on sales at fast-food restaurants. **[LO 6.3]**

   a. The mayor's proposal includes a sales tax of 60 cents on cheeseburgers, to be paid by consumers. What is the new outcome in this market (how many cheeseburgers are sold and at what price)? Illustrate this outcome on your graph.

   b. How much of the tax burden is borne by consumers? How much by suppliers?

   c. What is the deadweight loss associated with the proposed tax?

   d. How much revenue will the government collect?

   e. What is the loss of consumer surplus from this tax?

13. The market shown in Figure 6P-9 is in equilibrium. Suppose there is a $15 per unit subsidy given to buyers. **[LO 6.4]**

   a. Draw the after-subsidy demand curve.

   b. Plot the after-subsidy price paid by consumers and the after-subsidy price paid by sellers.

14. The market shown in Figure 6P-10 is in equilibrium. Suppose there is a $15 per unit subsidy given to sellers. **[LO 6.4]**

   a. Draw the after-subsidy supply curve.

   b. Plot the after-subsidy price paid by consumers and the after-subsidy price paid by sellers.

FIGURE 6P-10

Quantity

15. Demand and supply of laptop computers are given in Figure 6P-11. The quantity of laptops is given in thousands. Suppose the government provides a $300 subsidy for every laptop computer that consumers purchase. **[LO 6.4]**

   a. What will be the quantity of laptops bought and sold at the new equilibrium?

   b. What will be the price consumers pay for laptops under the subsidy?

FIGURE 6P-11

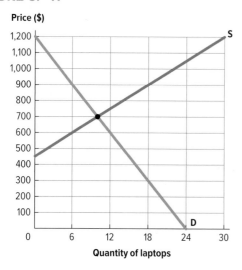

Quantity of laptops

c. What will be the price that sellers receive for laptops under the subsidy?

d. How much money should the government budget for the subsidy?

16. The market shown in Figure 6P-12 is in equilibrium. Suppose there is a $1.50 per unit subsidy given to buyers. **[LO 6.4]**

   a. Draw the after-subsidy demand curve.

   b. Plot the after-subsidy price paid by consumers and the after-subsidy price paid by sellers.

   c. Draw government expenditures for the subsidy.

   d. Calculate government expenditures.

FIGURE 6P-12

Quantity (millions)

FIGURE 6P-13

Quantity (millions)

17. The market shown in Figure 6P-13 is in equilibrium. Suppose there is a $3 per unit subsidy given to buyers. **[LO 6.4]**

   a. Draw the after-subsidy demand curve.

   b. Plot the after-subsidy price paid by consumers and the after-subsidy price paid by sellers.

   c. Draw the deadweight loss after the subsidy.

   d. Calculate deadweight loss.

18. Suppose government offers a subsidy to laptop sellers. Say whether each group of people gains or loses from this policy. **[LO 6.4]**

   a. Laptop buyers.

   b. Laptop sellers.

   c. Desktop computer sellers (assuming that they are different from laptop manufacturers).

   d. Desktop computer buyers.

19. Suppose that for health reasons, the government of the nation of Ironia wants to increase the amount of broccoli citizens consume. Which of the following policies could be used to achieve the goal? **[LO 6.1, 6.4]**

   a. A price floor to support broccoli growers.

   b. A price ceiling to ensure that broccoli remains affordable to consumers.

   c. A subsidy paid to shoppers who buy broccoli.

   d. A subsidy paid to farmers who grow broccoli.

20. The following scenarios describe the price elasticity of supply and demand for a particular good. In which scenario will a subsidy increase consumption the most? Choose only one. **[LO 6.5]**

    a. Elastic demand, inelastic supply.

    b. Inelastic demand, inelastic supply.

    c. Elastic demand, elastic supply.

    d. Inelastic demand, elastic supply.

21. The market shown in Figure 6P-14 is in equilibrium. **[LO 6.5]**

    a. If a tax was imposed on this market, would buyers or sellers bear more of the burden of the tax? Why?

FIGURE 6P-14

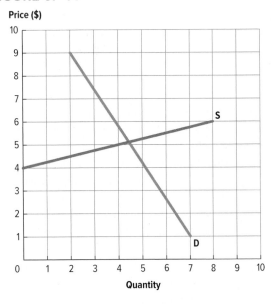

22. The following scenarios describe the price elasticity of supply and demand for a particular good. All else equal (equilibrium price, equilibrium quantity, and size of the tax), in which scenario will government revenues be the highest? Choose only one. **[LO 6.5]**

    a. Elastic demand, inelastic supply.

    b. Inelastic demand, inelastic supply.

    c. Elastic demand, elastic supply.

    d. Inelastic demand, elastic supply.

Endnotes

1. http://www.time.com/time/magazine/article/0,9171,1727720,00.html and http://www.nytimes.com/2008/06/22/nyregion/22food.html.

2. "The new face of hunger," *The Economist,* April 17, 2008.

Part Three

The Data of Macroeconomics

The two chapters in Part 3 will introduce you to . . .

the topic of macroeconomics and two important macroeconomic concepts: gross domestic product and consumer prices.

How well off do you think you will be in 10 years? In 20 years? Your answers probably depend on choices that you may already be considering—especially choices about where to live, family plans, and your career.

Of course, your future financial position will also depend on forces outside of your control. Some of those forces will be economic, like how many jobs are available, how housing prices change, and how fast prices rise over time. These forces are the focus of macroeconomics, the study of how billions of daily decisions made by individuals add up to shape the overall economy. It's the study of economic growth, inflation, booms and busts, and unemployment.

Chapter 7, "Measuring GDP," covers the calculation of gross domestic product (GDP), the most useful metric of macroeconomics, which sums up the amount of economic activity in a country. It's the first number economists look at when tracking overall economic growth and the ups and downs of the economy.

Chapter 8, "The Cost of Living," covers another important part of macroeconomic record-keeping: consumer prices. A century ago, a bottle of Coke cost a nickel and and a brand-new car could be purchased for hundreds of dollars. Both items cost a lot more today, but that doesn't mean that we're worse off—our incomes have risen along with prices. As you'll see, accounting for consumer prices gives an important part of the macro picture.

As we progress through the study of macroeconomics, the concepts of GDP and changing price levels will come up over and over again; they are useful tools for answering questions about the health and direction of the economy. These two chapters offer insight into forces that will affect your job and income, as well as the wealth and well-being of the whole country.

Measuring GDP

Learning Objectives

LO 7.1   Understand the importance of using the market value of final goods and services to calculate GDP and explain why each component of GDP is important.

LO 7.2   Explain the equivalence of the expenditure and income approaches to valuing an economy.

LO 7.3   Explain the three approaches that are used to calculate GDP and summarize the categories of spending that are included in the expenditure approach.

LO 7.4   Explain the difference between real and nominal GDP.

LO 7.5   Calculate the GDP deflator.

LO 7.6   Use GDP per capita to compare economies and calculate the real GDP annual growth rate.

LO 7.7   Discuss some limitations to GDP, including its measurement of home production, the underground economy, environmental degradation, and well-being.

IT'S MORE THAN COUNTING PEANUTS

If we made a list of the economic changes that are most dramatically reshaping the world, the rapid growth of China's economy would likely top it. In 1978, when China's leaders moved to open up its economic system, it was the world's 15th-largest economy. The size of China's economy doubled. Then it doubled, and doubled, and doubled again. By 2011, China's economy clocked in at about $6 trillion, passing Japan's to become the second-largest economy in the world. Rapid economic growth can create jobs, reduce poverty, and improve standards of living. In China, the fraction of the population living below the international poverty line ($1.90 per person per day) fell from 88 percent in 1981 to 6.5 percent in 2012.[1]

Economic growth has increased living standards all over the world in recent decades, although typically in less dramatic fashion than in China. The health of the national economy has a powerful effect on everyday life in any country. When the economy is doing well, jobs are plentiful and most people can live well and securely. When the economy does poorly, jobs are

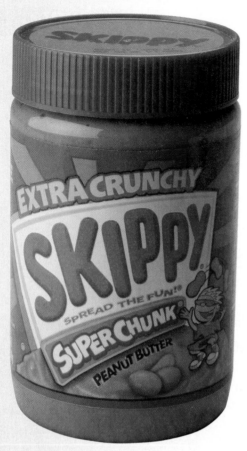

© The McGraw-Hill Companies, Inc./Elite Images

scarce, businesses close down, and people struggle. It's no wonder that politicians spend a lot of energy debating the best plan to expand the economy. Over the next few chapters, we'll discuss many of the ideas and terms used in those debates.

But, first, we need to answer a basic question: How do we measure the "size" of an economy? If we can answer that, we can compare China's economy to economies of other nations. We also can determine whether an economy is growing or not over time. What does it really *mean* to say that China has a $6 trillion economy?

The answers to these questions require some careful accounting. As a start, think about just one of the many transactions that take place in the U.S. economy. Say you bought a jar of peanut butter when you went to the grocery store. Although you may not have thought beyond your next peanut butter and jelly sandwich, your purchase contributed to the size of the economy.

Consider some of the things that happened before that jar of peanut butter made it into your shopping cart: A farmer grew the peanuts, perhaps on a small farm in Georgia. The farmer sold his peanuts to a wholesaler in Atlanta. The wholesaler then sold the peanuts to a peanut butter factory in Ohio, which combined the peanuts with other ingredients to produce a jar of peanut butter. The factory then sold that jar to a grocery store chain, which delivered it to your neighborhood store.

Many people were employed to produce that peanut butter: farmers, accountants, truck drivers, custodians, and grocery-store cashiers. Many firms earned profits from the jar of peanut butter, too: the peanut farm, the wholesaler, the factory, the shipping company, and your local store. Clearly, the activities that went into making and buying the jar of peanut butter added value to the economy. Can we measure how much?

The peanuts passed through many stages: from seed, to harvested nut, to peanut butter, to a jar on the grocery store shelf. At each stage, the peanuts were sold as an *output* of one firm and purchased as an *input* by another firm. Should we add up all of these sales individually to calculate the value the jar of peanut butter added to the economy? No—if we did that, we'd be overcounting the value of the peanuts. All of the sales were just steps toward one end product: your peanut butter. How then *do* we calculate the total value of your jar of peanut butter to the economy?

This is the problem that economists faced in the 1920s and 1930s when they first attempted to calculate the value of the U.S. economy. How can you add up all economic activity to arrive at an overall value for the economy, *without double-counting* items that are resold more than once before they reach the consumer?

The solution is a system called *national income accounting,* created by Nobel Prize winners Simon Kuznets and Richard Stone. In this chapter, we'll see how to use this system to calculate the value of a national economy. We'll see why it's so useful to measure a country's total output and also why gross domestic product (GDP), the most commonly used measure, has some limitations. In later chapters, we'll put these ideas to work to explain economic growth, unemployment, and economic booms and slowdowns.

Valuing an Economy

Economics has traditionally been divided into two broad fields, microeconomics and macroeconomics. *Microeconomics* is the study of how individuals and firms manage resources. In microeconomics, we zero in on a single person's budget, or one firm's cost of production, or the price of a particular good.

Macroeconomics, on the other hand, is the study of the economy on a broad scale, focusing on issues such as economic growth, unemployment, and inflation. In macroeconomics, we talk about consumption, production, and prices in the *aggregate,* on a national level, and we look at the effects of those aggregate forces on the whole economy.

Compared to microeconomics, the concepts of macroeconomics may seem distant from decisions we make and challenges we face. But macroeconomic issues can have profound impacts on our daily lives. Everyone tends to do better when there are steady economic growth, stable prices, and low unemployment. On the flip side, long periods of stagnation, inflation, and high unemployment can do great damage to families and communities.

At the start of the chapter, we introduced one of the most important macroeconomic issues of our time: the incredible growth of the Chinese economy. Thinking about the Chinese economy raises some questions:

- How do we know how big the Chinese economy is?
- How do we know that it is larger than Japan's but smaller than the United States's?
- What does it mean to say that the size of China's economy doubled?

To talk about these critical issues, we need a tool for measuring the "size" or "value" of a national economy. Based on the kind of questions that metric lets us answer, you can see why it is one of the most important and commonly used data points in macroeconomics. It gives us a sense of the well-being of the average person in a country. It also allows us to gauge the direction an economy is headed, by looking at changes over time.

The most commonly used metric for measuring the value of a national economy is gross domestic product, or GDP. Gross domestic product is the sum of the market values of all final goods and services produced within a country in a given period of time. That's a mouthful of a definition. Before we look at how economists calculate GDP, let's unpack the component parts of the definition.

> **macroeconomics**
> the study of the economy as a whole, and how policy-makers manage the growth and behavior of the overall economy

> **gross domestic product (GDP)**
> the sum of the market values of all final goods and services produced within a country in a given period of time

Unpacking the definition of GDP

LO 7.1 Understand the importance of using the market value of final goods and services to calculate GDP and explain why each component of GDP is important.

The definition of GDP has four important pieces:

- the *market value*
- of *final goods and services*
- produced *within a country*
- in a *given period of time.*

Let's take each piece one at a time and explain its importance.

Market values

If we measured the output of economies by simply listing every single good and service, we wouldn't learn much—680 million jars of peanut butter, 103 million copies of Microsoft Word, 421 million haircuts, and so on. The list would go on for thousands of pages. It wouldn't be very interesting. Nor would it be useful for comparing the overall size of national economies, which tend to make different things. For example, how would we compare the U.S. economy, which produces lots of peanut butter, with the Mexican economy, which produces lots of tortillas?

Clearly, we need to translate the production of peanut butter, tortillas, software, haircuts, and all the other goods and services into a common unit so we can add them up. That common unit is their *market value*—which in the United States is measured in dollars. So we know from this part of the definition that GDP is going to be a number measured in the local currency.

Final goods and services

Consider the 800 or so peanuts that end up in your jar of peanut butter. Suppose our Georgia peanut farmer sells them to the Atlanta wholesaler for 12 cents. The wholesaler sells them to the Ohio peanut butter factory for 24 cents. The peanut butter factory sells the jar of peanut butter to the grocery store for $1.85. Finally, the grocery store sells it to you for $3.40 in an 18-ounce jar. How much does this process contribute to GDP?

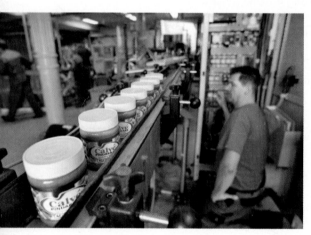

If we simply add up all the transactions, we might think that the jar of peanut butter contributed $5.61 to GDP ($0.12 + $0.24 + $1.85 + $3.40). But, if that were true, producing the jar of peanut butter would contribute more to GDP than its final selling price. That can't be right. If it were, we could grow the economy just by trading the same jar of peanut butter for the same dollar, over and over again, and adding up each "transaction."

The problem here is that by adding each of the transactions, we are double-counting, giving us too big a total. To avoid double-counting, we should ignore the price of *intermediate* goods and services—that is, goods and services used only to produce something else, like the raw peanuts that were sold to the peanut butter factory.

Instead, we want to count only expenditures on *final goods and services*—those that get sold to the consumer. In this case, the only final good was the jar of peanut butter you bought at the store. Its price was $3.40—so that is how much your purchase contributed to GDP.

Inge van Mill/Hollandse Hoogte/Redux

Produced within a country

The goods and services that count toward GDP are defined in terms of the *location of production,* not the citizenship of the producer. So:

- If a U.S. company owns a factory in Mexico, the value of the goods produced in that factory will count toward Mexican GDP, not U.S. GDP.
- A U.S. citizen working in France will contribute to French GDP.
- Likewise, a French or Mexican citizen working in the United States will contribute to U.S. GDP.

gross national product (GNP)
the sum of the market values of all final goods and services produced and capital owned by the permanent residents of a country in a given period of time

What if we want to measure the value of what is produced by all U.S. companies regardless of their location? In this case, we use a different metric, called **gross national product (GNP)**. GNP is the sum of the market values of all final goods and services produced and capital owned *by the permanent residents* of a country in a given period of time. GNP measures those market values no matter where in the world the production occurs. It is similar to GDP except that it

1. includes *worldwide* income earned by a country's enterprises and permanent residents and
2. excludes production by foreign nationals working domestically.

Given period of time

In theory, we could calculate the output of the economy over any time period—a day, a month, a year. When you hear people talking about GDP, they're often referring to an annual figure. However, a year is a long time to wait for an update on how the economy is doing, so GDP is usually calculated on a *quarterly* basis—that is, four times a year.

Typically, what we really want to know is an estimate of annual GDP, using the most recent quarterly information. We can't just multiply this quarter's GDP by four, however, because the economy seldom rolls along at the same pace all year. For instance, December usually has more economic activity than other months due to people buying presents and traveling. Therefore, we need to adjust quarterly GDP estimates to account for these seasonal patterns. That's why quarterly GDP is typically shown as a *seasonally adjusted estimate at an annual rate*. By taking account of predictable seasonal patterns, we can have a good guess at what annual GDP will be if the economy continues at its current pace.

Production equals expenditure equals income

LO 7.2 Explain the equivalence of the expenditure and income approaches to valuing an economy.

Now that we have defined the term *gross domestic product,* how do we go about measuring it? First of all, let's zero in on what we really mean when we talk about the size of an economy: the amount of "stuff" people in the economy are making.

Economists refer to this "stuff" as either *output* or *production,* and it includes both goods and services. Indeed, about three-quarters of U.S. output is services, not goods. As we've seen, though, there's not much point in simply listing thousands of pages of goods and services. So how do we put a dollar value on it? There are three ways of approaching this problem. We'll look at the first two ways briefly here (and then look at all three in the next section). The first is called the *expenditure approach.* The second is called the *income approach.*

The market value of a good or service is the price at which it is bought and sold. If we add up all the money people spend buying final goods and services—being careful to omit spending on intermediate goods so as not to double-count—the sum will be the market value of all output sold in the economy. In other words, we can use the expenditure approach to measure total output by *measuring total expenditure.*

Every transaction, of course, has not only a buyer who spends on a good or service but also a seller who earns income from the sale. Thus, expenditures by one person translate directly into *income* for someone else. So, we can also measure production using the income approach by *adding up everyone's income.* This may sound familiar if you remember the *circular flow model* of the economy that was presented in Chapter 1, "Economics and Life," and is repeated here in Figure 7-1.

Households buy things from firms in the market for goods and services. Firms then use some of the money they earn in revenue to pay wages to workers and rent to landowners in the market for the factors of production. In each of these transactions, expenditures by one party are income for another.

The circular flow model is a major simplification of the economy. (We're ignoring, for now, the money paid in taxes or the money that is saved instead of spent, for example.) Yet it shows that we should get to the same figure for GDP regardless of whether we measure expenditure or income in an economy:

National production = National expenditure = National income

This equality is a crucial idea in the study of macroeconomics.

FIGURE 7-1

Circular flow diagram

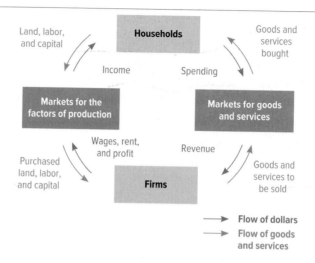

CONCEPT CHECK

☐ Why are only final goods and services counted under GDP? Why are sales of used goods not counted? **[LO 7.1]**

☐ Why is total income in a country equal to total expenditures on goods produced in that country? **[LO 7.2]**

Approaches to Measuring GDP

LO 7.3 Explain the three approaches that are used to calculate GDP and summarize the categories of spending that are included in the expenditure approach.

We just saw that national production equals national expenditure equals national income. The equality of production, expenditure, and income would hold true in a literal, straightforward way if we lived in a *closed economy*—an economy in which all goods were produced and sold domestically and everything was consumed as soon as it was made. The actual economy is more complicated, but the basic equality still holds—as long as we're a little more careful about how we define each part.

One complication is international trade. Once we start to consider imports and exports, we see that expenditure in one country can translate into income in *another* country. Also, what happens when goods are produced but not sold? In this section, we will consider three approaches to measuring GDP—the expenditure approach, the income approach, and the value-added approach. Looking at the different approaches, we will see how economists deal with the complications of international trade and unsold inventories.

Why are there three approaches—and how do you know when to use one instead of another? It turns out that all three approaches end up with the same GDP number, but each provides a slightly different picture of how the different pieces make up the big picture. You'll understand the details after reading the next three sections. For now, it's enough to give this broad overview of the differences:

- The *expenditure approach* highlights the importance of consumer spending versus government purchases.

- The *income approach* emphasizes information about the relative importance of different factors of production.
- The *value-added approach* is especially useful for tracking how goods are sold and resold.

Many countries use all three approaches to calculate GDP so that policy-makers and researchers can get a full picture of economic activity.

The expenditure approach

To measure output using the *expenditure method*, we start by breaking down expenditure into categories. We don't want to double-count, so we *don't* include intermediate products, like raw peanuts and the labor of peanut factory workers, which firms buy only to transform into final goods and services. But we *do* include the following:

- *Final goods and services*. Most final goods and services are bought by people who intend to *consume* them, such as a family buying groceries or clothes or haircuts.
- *Goods bought as investment*. Firms buy some goods as an *investment* in future production, such as a farmer buying a new tractor to help him grow peanuts or a peanut butter factory buying new peanut-grinding machinery. The reason we count these is that the tractor and the machinery are not "used up" in producing a jar of peanut butter in the same way that raw peanuts are.
- *Government purchases*. We also want to count *government* purchases, which includes everything from fighter planes, to asphalt for road repair, to those plastic bins that go through the scanner at airport security checkpoints.
- *Net exports (exports minus imports)*. If we're interested in the output of the U.S. economy, then clearly we want to count goods and services produced in the United States and bought by foreigners, which are called *exports*. But we *don't* want to count expenditures by Americans on items produced outside of the United States, which are called *imports*. For that reason, we subtract the amount of imports from the amount of exports and use the result—*net exports*—to calculate expenditures.

To find total expenditure we add together these four categories: consumption, investment, government purchases, and net exports. Let's look at each in more detail.

Consumption

The first category, **consumption**, measures spending on goods and services by private individuals and households. It includes almost anything you'd buy for yourself, from basic, nondurable goods (like food and clothing), to durable goods (like computers and cars), to services (like tutoring and plumbing). If you pay rent or college tuition, those expenses are also included in consumption.

Note that what is consumed has to be *new*. This requirement avoids the illogical conclusion that we could grow the economy simply by reselling the same jar of peanut butter over and over again. If you buy a used camera on eBay, for example, the camera itself is not counted toward the size of the economy; the original purchase of the camera was already recorded in GDP when it was sold new. However, the fee the seller pays to eBay *is* counted as consumption and so is the price the seller pays FedEx to deliver the camera to you.

consumption
spending on goods and services by private individuals and households

Investment

The second category, **investment**, includes spending on productive inputs, such as factories, machinery, and inventories. That means goods bought by people or firms who plan to use those purchases to produce other goods and services in the future, rather than consuming them. It includes *capital goods,* which are items like machines or tools that will be used for production

investment
spending on productive inputs, such as factories, machinery, and inventories

of other goods or services. It also includes buildings and structures, like warehouses, that will be involved in providing goods and services.

It's worth noting that newly built houses are also counted as investment. In contrast, if you rent a house, the expenditure falls under consumption. Why the difference? A newly built house will provide a place to live (or to rent out) now and for years to come, just as a newly built factory will generate output now and in future years. But when you *rent* a house, you are paying its owner for the service of letting you live there. You are consuming "place-to-live" services, but you're not making an investment because the house belongs to someone else and won't generate future revenues for you.

Again, note that investment goods are counted only if they are *new*. We don't count buying an existing factory or secondhand tools as investment. Nor do we count an individual's purchase of an existing house. The services of the Realtor selling you the house, though, would be counted toward consumption.

? POTENTIALLY CONFUSING

You may have heard people talk about their "investments"—stocks, bonds, mutual funds, and other products bought and sold in the financial markets. While it may seem as if these financial products should be counted under the "I" (investment) term in GDP, *they do not get counted as a part of GDP.* There are two reasons for that:

- First, if you buy a share of General Motors stock through the New York Stock Exchange, your money does not go to General Motors. Instead, you are buying stock from some other investor who has decided to sell her stock in General Motors. (We'll cover how economists think about buying stocks and making other financial "investments" in Chapter 14, "The Basics of Finance.")
- Second, including stock purchases in GDP calculations would be another type of double-counting. If we added to GDP every time someone bought shares, we could make the economy seem to be growing simply by having people resell the same shares over and over again—just like selling the same jar of peanut butter multiple times.

Finally, our definition of investment also includes a less-obvious type of "purchase": spending on inventories. When we equated production, income, and expenditure, we raised the question of how to deal with goods that are produced but not sold. **Inventory** is the answer: It's the stock of goods that a company produces now but keeps to sell at a future time. If Ford manufactures a car this year, but the car sits on the lot until next year, the car becomes part of Ford's inventory. If Apple makes a batch of iPhones but keeps them in a warehouse until it's time to release the new model for public sale, they become part of Apple's inventory.

inventory
the stock of goods that a company produces now but does not sell immediately

When a good is added to a company's inventory, we treat it as if the *producing company* has "bought" it to keep in stock for the future. The value of that "sale" is included in our calculation of investment for the year. What happens next year when a consumer buys the new-model iPhone? We don't want to count the same iPhone toward GDP in two different years. So, its value will be subtracted from Apple's inventory at the same time as it is counted as consumption. These two transactions cancel out, meaning the purchase results in no net increase in GDP.

Government purchases

government purchases
spending on goods and services by all levels of government

The next category of spending, **government purchases**, represents goods and services bought by all levels of government. This includes both

- "Consumption"-type purchases of goods (for instance, buying new bulbs to go in streetlights) and services (buying the labor of government workers who repair streetlights).

- "Investment"-type purchases (for instance, buying a truck that government workers will use to repair streetlights in the future).

In fact, the technical name for this category of spending is "government consumption expenditures and gross investment." We'll stick with the term *government purchases* because it's less of a mouthful.

However, one important category of government spending does *not* count as a government purchase: spending that simply *transfers* resources to individuals, through Social Security or similar programs. The Social Security payment to an elderly person from the government does not count toward government purchases. When that person spends money from his Social Security check to buy groceries, the spending will then be counted as private consumption.

Net exports

The three categories of spending we've considered—consumption, investment, and government purchases—include spending on goods and services produced abroad as well as those produced domestically. Let's think about the GDP of the United States. Our calculation of consumption will include instances when people in the United States buy goods made abroad—say, a sweater imported from Scotland. If we're trying to measure the value of the goods produced *within the United States,* we don't want to count this spending. On the flip side, we don't want to miss spending by people in other countries on goods or services made in the United States and exported for sale abroad.

These two forces work in opposite directions: Domestic spending on imports should get subtracted from our GDP calculations, while international spending on exports should get added. We can simplify these international transactions by combining exports and imports into one term, called **net exports** or **NX**. Net exports represent the value of goods and services produced domestically and consumed abroad minus the value of goods and services produced abroad and consumed domestically. If exports are higher than imports, NX will be positive. If imports are higher than exports, NX will be negative. Figure 7-2 shows how we can think about the role of net exports using a visual tool.

net exports (NX) exports minus imports; the value of goods and services produced domestically and consumed abroad minus the value of goods and services produced abroad and consumed domestically

---

FIGURE 7-2

Adding up expenditures when there are imports and exports   Everything that is produced domestically is added to GDP, whether it is purchased for consumption, for investment, by the government, or by people abroad (exports). Goods that are produced internationally but bought domestically, otherwise known as imports, are subtracted from GDP because they represent expenditures leaving the country. Transactions between foreign producers and foreign buyers do not involve domestic production or expenditure and therefore do not figure into GDP calculations.

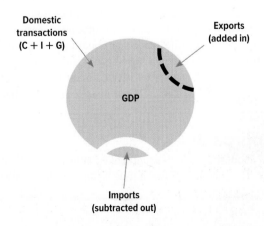

FIGURE 7-3

U.S. GDP breakdown   This figure shows the *expenditure method* of calculating GDP, which adds together consumption, investment, government purchases, and net exports (exports minus imports). In the United States, imports are currently higher than exports, so the value of net exports is negative and is subtracted from the total.

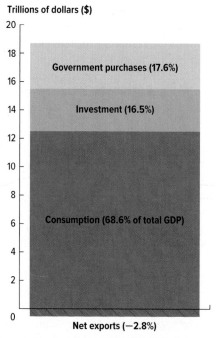

Trillions of dollars ($)

- Government purchases (17.6%)
- Investment (16.5%)
- Consumption (68.6% of total GDP)
- Net exports (−2.8%)

Sources: Bureau of Economic Analysis, Table 1.10, Gross Domestic Income by Type of Income (percent of GDP, 2016), and Table 1.1.5, Gross Domestic Product (USD, 2016), http://www.bea.gov/iTable/iTable.cfm?ReqID=9&step=1#reqid=9&step=1&isuri=1.

Summing spending categories

When we add together spending in all four categories—consumption, investment, government purchases, and net exports—the total will be equal to expenditures on all goods and services produced in a country. As we learned in the previous section, the total of those national expenditures is equal to the value of national production. This equation is represented as follows.

EQUATION 7-1   Expenditure = C + I + G + NX = Production

As you can see in Figure 7-3, consumption is by far the largest single category of expenditure in the United States, but investment and government purchases are also significant. We can also see that U.S. residents *buy* more goods from abroad than they *sell* to people abroad. That's why the value for net exports is a negative number, −2.8 percent of total 2016 GDP. In other words, in 2016 U.S. consumers spent more abroad than U.S. producers earned from foreigners buying U.S.-made goods, and the size of that difference was equal to 2.8 percent of GDP. If exports had been higher than imports, this number would have been positive.

Figuring out what goes into GDP and what isn't counted in the expenditure method takes a little practice. To help you keep track, Table 7-1 summarizes some of the examples presented in this chapter.

The income approach

A different way to think about the value of a national economy is to add up the *income earned by everyone in the country*. The income approach thus brings together information on the different factors of production.

TABLE 7-1

Is it GDP?

Know

Situation	GDP Category	Why?
Buying a new digital camera	Consumption	Purchasing a *new* good or service always counts toward GDP.
Buying a used camera on eBay	Not counted	As a used good, the camera does not count toward GDP as it was already counted when new. The fees paid to eBay for selling the camera count as consumption, though.
Buying a new house	Investment	Since the house can increase or fall in value, it makes sense to think of it as an investment.
Renting an apartment	Consumption	You are paying the owner of the house for a service, so it is counted as consumption.
Apple makes a new batch of iPhones but doesn't sell them until next year	Investment	Counted as a part of investment as Apple is holding these phones as a part of its inventory.
Buying shares of General Motors stock	Not counted	Shares of stock are a transfer of money from one owner of the stock to another. Including stocks would cause a double-counting problem.
TSA buys plastic bins for airport security	Government spending	Any consumption or investment purchases made by the government are counted in GDP as government spending.
Babysitting for your neighbor	Not counted	In principle, it should be included in GDP, but such income is often not reported to the IRS, and thus it can't be included in official statistics.

To value an economy using the income approach, we add up

- wages earned by workers,
- interest earned on capital investments,
- rents earned on land and property, and
- profits earned by firms (plus a couple of additional technical adjustments).

These cover all the types of income earned by people in a country. National income can be shown in an equation as:

EQUATION 7-2   Income = Wages + Interest + Rental income + Profits

This *income approach* will give us the same result as the expenditure approach in an economy without any imports and exports. Why? Because in every transaction, there is not only a buyer who spends but also a seller who earns the same amount in income. If you spend $20 on gasoline, that same $20 is both expenditure to you and income to the owner of the gas station. The expenditure approach added up everything on one side of this transaction. Now, the income approach adds up everything on the *other side* of the transaction, which comes out to the same amount.

What happens with foreign trade? When goods produced in the United States are exported, that's expenditure by other countries and income for the United States. When people in the United States spend money on goods made in another country, that's expenditure in the United States and income for the other country.

The "value-added" approach

Finally, we come to the third approach that economists sometimes use to measure economic output: the *value-added approach*. We have seen that the expenditure approach solves the double-counting problem by considering only transactions that represent final, and not intermediate, goods and services. For example, we count a consumer's purchase of a jar of peanut butter from a store but not a peanut butter factory's purchase of peanuts from a peanut wholesaler. What if, instead, we looked at *all* transactions, but counted only the *value they add* to the economy?

To see the reasoning behind this approach, let's stick with peanut butter. At each stage of the peanut butter production process, let's look at the difference between the sale value of the product and the value of the inputs that went into it. This difference represents the "value added" at that stage of production. For instance:

- The farmer *adds value* to the economy by taking seeds, land, and water and growing peanuts. Just for simplicity, imagine the farmer didn't pay anything for his inputs. The value added to the economy is the $0.12 the farmer gets from selling his peanuts to the wholesaler, minus the value of the inputs, which we are imagining to be zero.
- If the wholesaler buys those $0.12 in peanuts and sells them to a peanut butter factory for $0.24, then the wholesaler has added $0.12 ($0.24 − $0.12) in value to the economy by helping to link up farmers and factories.
- The peanut butter factory adds value by pressing the peanuts into butter and putting it into jars. If the factory is able to get $1.85 per jar, it has added $1.61 ($1.85 − $0.24) in value to the economy.
- The grocery store adds value by transporting jars to a convenient location in your neighborhood, where clerks are on hand to allow you to purchase it for the final price of $3.40 per jar, a value added of $1.55 ($3.40 − $1.85).

To see the final value added, simply sum up the value added at each stage of the process: $0.12 + $0.12 + $1.61 + $1.55 = $3.40. You'll notice that this is the same as the final price of the peanut butter in the store—the amount that is counted in the expenditure method. The value-added approach is an alternative, and equally valid, way of avoiding the problem of double-counting the peanuts. It lets us break down the total value paid and see how much value was created at each step of the production process.

The value-added approach is especially useful when thinking about services involved in the resale of existing goods. We've already seen, for example, that resale of used cameras, existing houses, and shares of company stock do not count toward GDP—but the related services provided by eBay, Realtors, and stockbrokers do. Added value helps us to think about why this is so. A stockbroker adds value by handling the paperwork associated with purchasing shares of stock. A Realtor adds value by publicizing the fact that a house is for sale, showing potential purchasers around, and helping negotiate a sale. eBay adds value by connecting buyers with sellers.

In general, any intermediary involved in the sale of used goods adds value by sourcing those goods and making them available for sale in a convenient way.

✓CONCEPT CHECK

- ☐ What is the difference between consumption spending and investment spending? **[LO 7.3]**
- ☐ Under which category of expenditure do inventories fall? **[LO 7.3]**
- ☐ Does the sale of intermediate goods count toward GDP in the expenditure approach? **[LO 7.3]**
- ☐ How do the expenditure approach and income approach capture two sides of the same transactions? **[LO 7.3]**
- ☐ How do GDP calculations account for the value added in the sale of an existing house by a realtor? **[LO 7.3]**

Using GDP to Compare Economies

U.S. GDP increased from $12.5 trillion in 2005 to over $18 trillion in 2016. Does this mean that people in the United States produced more goods and services in 2016 than in 2005? Or does it mean that we just paid more for the same things because prices were higher? GDP is a function of both the quantity of goods and services produced (output) and their market value (prices).

Often, an increase in GDP is the result of growth in *both* components—an increase in output *and* an increase in prices. If we want to use GDP to compare the health of a national economy over time or to compare economies of different countries, we need to know how much of the growth to attribute to each factor.

Real versus nominal GDP

LO 7.4 Explain the difference between real and nominal GDP.

GDP enables us to track changes in the value of output over time. But if you compare levels of just GDP in different years, you can't be sure whether differences are due to changes in production, or prices, or both. To zero in on changes in production, we need a new measure. We use the term *real GDP* to refer to GDP measurement that focuses *solely on output,* controlling for price changes. Formally, **real GDP** is calculated based on goods and services valued at *constant prices.* Those constant prices are given for a specific year. We might, for example, measure real GDP by valuing output in 2016 at the prices that prevailed in 2010.

If we report GDP *without controlling for price changes,* we are talking about *nominal GDP.* **Nominal GDP** is calculated based on goods and services valued at *current prices* (current at the time they are produced). Thus, in nominal GDP measurement, output for 2016 would be valued in 2016 prices.

real GDP
GDP calculation in which goods and services are valued at constant prices

nominal GDP
GDP calculation in which goods and services are valued at current prices

Calculating nominal and real GDP

To see the difference between real and nominal GDP measures in practice, let's imagine an economy with only two goods: pizza and spaghetti. For ease of discussion, let's call this fictional economy "Pizzetta."

Suppose that in 2013, Pizzetta produced 5 million pizzas at a price of $10 each and 20 million plates of spaghetti at a price of $8. Table 7-2 shows this output. In 2014, the number of pizzas and plates of spaghetti increased to 6 million and 22 million, respectively; prices stayed the same. In 2015, Pizzetta produced the same number of pizzas and plates of spaghetti, but prices increased. In 2016, both quantity and prices increased.

In order to calculate nominal GDP, we simply multiply the quantity of each good produced in a given year by its price in that year, as shown in column 6 of Table 7-2. We can see that Pizzetta's nominal GDP increased between 2013 and 2014 and again in 2015 and 2016.

What doesn't nominal GDP tell us? If we looked just at nominal GDP, we couldn't tell the cause of the increase. We wouldn't see that in 2014 the increase was due to larger output, or that in 2015 the increase was due only to an increase in prices with no increase in output. Looking at real GDP helps us see the different causes of the changes in GDP in the two years.

To calculate real GDP (GDP valued at constant prices), we have to choose a *base year.* In the base year, nominal GDP and real GDP are equal. In every other year, we multiply the quantity of a good produced in that year by its price in the base year. In essence, we are holding prices constant while allowing quantities to rise and fall. This method isolates increases in output from increases in prices.

Looking at the Pizzetta example, suppose we pick 2013 as our base year. We can see in Table 7-2 that in 2014, the increase in real GDP is actually the same as the increase in nominal

TABLE 7-2
Calculating real versus nominal GDP growth

Nominal GDP is the sum of the market values of all final goods and services, which we calculate by multiplying the quantity of each output by its market price in the current year. To calculate *real GDP,* we want to value those goods and services at their prices in the base year. When prices stay the same, nominal GDP and real GDP increase at the same rate. If prices rise, nominal GDP will be higher than real GDP.

(1)	(2)	(3)	(4)	(5)	(6)	(7)	(8)
Year	Pizzas (millions)	Price of pizza ($)	Spaghetti (millions)	Price of spaghetti ($)	Nominal GDP (millions of $)	Real GDP in 2010 prices (millions of $)	What's happening
2013 (base year)	5	10	20	8	(5 × $10) + (20 × $8) = **$210**	(5 × $10) + (20 × $8) = **$210**	In the base year, nominal GDP and real GDP are equal by definition.
2014	6	10	22	8	(6 × $10) + (22 × $8) = **$236**	(6 × $10) + (22 × $8) = **$236**	When output rises and prices stay constant, nominal and real GDP rise at the same rate.
2015	6	12	22	10	(6 × $12) + (22 × $10) = **$292**	(6 × $10) + (22 × $8) = **$236**	When prices rise and output stays constant, nominal GDP rises, but real GDP does not.
2016	7	13	25	11	(7 × $13) + (25 × $11) = **$366**	(7 × $10) + (25 × $8) = **$270**	When both output and prices rise, nominal and real GDP rise at different rates.

GDP ($236 million). That makes sense: Prices didn't change between the two years, so base-year prices are the same as current-year prices.

Between 2014 and 2015, however, the difference between nominal and real GDP shows up. Nominal GDP increases because prices increased. (Prices of pizza and spaghetti increased by $2 each.) But real GDP stays constant because output stayed constant.

Between 2015 and 2016, both nominal *and* real GDP increase because both prices *and* output increased. However, the increase in real GDP ($34 million) is smaller than the increase in nominal GDP ($74 million). What does that tell us? It indicates that only $34 million of the $74 million growth in nominal GDP is due to rising output; the rest is due to rising prices.

In summary:

- Real GDP isolates changes in an economy's output.
- Nominal GDP encompasses changes in both output and prices.

As a result, because economists and policy-makers are often most interested in changes in output, they typically use real GDP numbers as a reference point. When economists and policy-makers do want to focus on changes in prices, they turn to another measure—the GDP deflator.

The GDP deflator

LO 7.5 Calculate the GDP deflator.

We just saw that the difference between nominal and real GDP is the difference between current prices and base-year prices. If we want to know about how prices have changed, we *could* directly compare the price of each good in the current and base years. But that would be much like listing every good and service instead of reporting total GDP: It's not incorrect, but it's long and boring and doesn't do much to summarize what's going on in the economy as a whole. The GDP deflator is one way of summarizing how prices have changed across the entire economy.

The **GDP deflator** is a measure of the overall change in prices in an economy, using the ratio between real and nominal GDP. To compute the index, we first need to have measures of nominal GDP and real GDP from the current year. Then, we calculate the GDP deflator as follows:

GDP deflator
a measure of the overall change in prices in an economy, using the ratio between real and nominal GDP

EQUATION 7-3

$$\text{GDP deflator} = \frac{\text{Nominal GDP}}{\text{Real GDP}} \times 100$$

The GDP deflator equation gives us the ratio between the base-year value of current output (the real GDP number) and the current-year value of current output (the nominal GDP number). The equation has three direct implications:

- In the base year, the GDP deflator is always equal to 100 because current prices *are* base-year prices. Thus, in the base year, nominal GDP equals real GDP.
- If prices have risen such that nominal GDP is now higher than real GDP, the deflator will be greater than 100. So, for example, if the GDP deflator is 115 in a given year, we infer that the overall price level is 15 percent higher than it was in the base year.
- If prices have fallen such that nominal GDP is now lower than real GDP, the deflator will be less than 100. Similarly, if we are looking at a year before the base year, when prices were lower, the deflator will be less than 100.

Table 7-3 shows the GDP deflator for the imaginary country Pizzetta in 2013–2016.

The GDP deflator gets its name from its relationship to inflation. *Inflation* is an idea we'll discuss at length in future chapters; in fact, Chapter 16, "Inflation," is entirely devoted to the topic. For now, it's enough to note that inflation describes how fast the overall level of prices is changing. Inflation is defined in terms of a year-to-year increase in prices, rather than an increase over a base year.

Year	Nominal GDP (millions of $)	Real GDP (millions of $)	Deflator	Inflation
2013	210	210	$\frac{\$210}{\$210} \times 100 = \mathbf{100}$	—
2014	236	236	$\frac{\$236}{\$236} \times 100 = \mathbf{100}$	(100 − 100)/100 = 0%
2015	292	236	$\frac{\$292}{\$236} \times 100 = \mathbf{124}$	(124 − 100)/100 = 24%
2016	366	270	$\frac{\$366}{\$270} \times 100 = \mathbf{136}$	(136 − 124)/124 = 9.7%

TABLE 7-3
Calculating the GDP deflator and inflation rates
Using the values of nominal and real GDP, we can calculate the GDP deflator, a measure of price changes over time. It is set to 100 for a base year; as prices increase, the value of the deflator increases as well. With the GDP deflator we can calculate inflation, the percentage change of prices.

We can calculate inflation by looking at the increase in the GDP deflator between any two years using the equation below:

EQUATION 7-4

$$\text{Inflation rate} = \left[\frac{\text{Deflator}_{\text{Year 2}} - \text{Deflator}_{\text{Year 1}}}{\text{Deflator}_{\text{Year 1}}}\right] \times 100$$

For instance, as shown in Table 7-3, the inflation rate in Pizzetta between 2015 and 2016 is:

$$\text{Inflation rate} = \left[\frac{\text{Deflator}_{2016} - \text{Deflator}_{2015}}{\text{Deflator}_{2015}}\right] \times 100$$

$$= \frac{136 - 124}{124} \times 100$$

$$= 9.7\%$$

The GDP deflator is one simple way of measuring changes in the price level. It allows us to "deflate" nominal GDP by controlling for price changes. In official government statistics, the GDP deflator is actually calculated using a somewhat more elaborate method called a *chain-weighted index*. The basic intuition is the same as the simpler approach we've described here.[2] We'll return to the idea of changes in the overall price level in Chapter 8, "The Cost of Living."

Using GDP to assess economic health

LO 7.6 Use GDP per capita to compare economies and calculate the real GDP annual growth rate.

How do we use GDP to compare economies? We could, of course, simply look at the GDPs of two countries side by side to see their relative sizes. High GDP means a big economy. Figure 7-4 shows the GDPs of a number of countries around the world. As you can see, the United States has the largest economy by far, followed by China.

However, if what we really want to know is the income of an *average individual* in these countries, GDP will paint a misleading picture. The reason is that the populations of the countries are quite different sizes. China's GDP is just over one-third as high as that of the United States, but its population is more than four times as large. India has just under four times as many people as the United States but only one-tenth the GDP. The total income earned in China and India is spread across far more people, so the average person has a lower income. Meanwhile, Norway has a much smaller economy than the United States, but because its population is also much smaller, the average Norwegian is actually richer than the average American. To compare average income across countries, we need to know GDP per capita.

GDP per capita

GDP per capita
a country's GDP divided by its population

If we want get an idea of how much is produced *per person* in a country, we need to divide GDP by population size. This measure is called **GDP per capita**. ("Per capita" simply means per person.) Figure 7-5 shows GDP per capita in each country in the world. When we compare this map to Figure 7-4, the most noticeable pattern is that the wealthy but small countries of Europe and the Middle East rise to the top, while populous countries like China, Brazil, and India move down.

GDP per capita is a useful measure. Knowing, for example, that GDP per capita in Switzerland is $58,087 while in Haiti it is only $1,750 suggests a lot about differences in life in these two countries.

FIGURE 7-4

GDP around the world (2016)

The top 10 countries in terms of overall nominal GDP include rich countries—with both large populations (the United States) and small (the United Kingdom)—as well as some poorer countries with large populations (China and India).

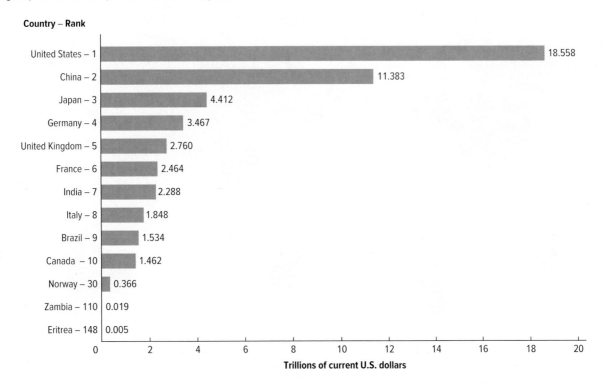

Source: http://statisticstimes.com/economy/countries-by-projected-gdp.php.

However, GDP per capita doesn't tell us everything. First, it is a measure of *average* income; it doesn't tell us anything about how that income is distributed. A country with deep poverty and a rich elite could have higher GDP per capita than a country where everyone has a moderate standard of living.

Second, it doesn't tell us what you can buy with a given amount of money in that country. The same goods might be more expensive in some countries than in others. For instance, GDP per capita in the United States and Hong Kong are both about $58,000, but many goods and services are more expensive in Hong Kong than in the United States. A dollar in Hong Kong won't buy you as much as it would in the United States. When we account for this difference in the cost of living, the real value of GDP per capita in Hong Kong falls to about $52,000, which is *lower* than in the United States.[3]

Conversely, many poor countries are cheaper to live in than rich ones. This doesn't mean that every single thing costs less but that, overall, the cost of living is lower. Looking at GDP per capita without accounting for differences in the cost of living makes poor countries look even poorer than they really are. In the United States or Hong Kong, for example, it would be almost impossible to survive on an income of $3,000 per year. In parts of Tanzania or Bangladesh, on the other hand, it would buy you a decent basic lifestyle. We will return to the subject of how to account for these differences in price levels in the next chapter. For now, just remember that GDP per capita is only a start in understanding people's real ability to consume goods and services.

FIGURE 7-5
Global GDP per capita (in 2015 U.S. dollars)

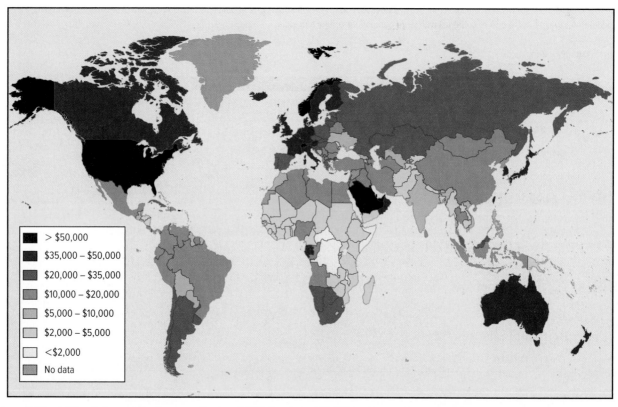

■	> $50,000
■	$35,000 – $50,000
■	$20,000 – $35,000
■	$10,000 – $20,000
■	$5,000 – $10,000
■	$2,000 – $5,000
□	<$2,000
■	No data

Source:Ali Zifan, via Wikimedia Commons, https://commons.wikimedia.org/wiki/File:Countries_by_GDP_(PPP)_Per_Capita_in_2015.svg. Uses IMF data.

GDP growth rates

One of the most common uses of GDP is to track changes in an economy over time. We usually talk about changes in GDP in terms of the *growth rate*. This is often measured as the percent change in real GDP from one time period to the next, typically annually or quarterly at an annual rate:

EQUATION 7-5
$$\text{GDP growth rate} = \left[\frac{\text{GDP in Year 2} - \text{GDP in Year 1}}{\text{GDP in Year 1}} \right] \times 100$$

For instance, if U.S. real GDP grew from $14 trillion in one year to $14.5 trillion (in constant dollars) the next, the annual growth rate would be:

$$\text{GDP growth rate} = \left[\frac{\$14.5 \text{ trillion} - \$14 \text{ trillion}}{\$14 \text{ trillion}} \right] \times 100 = 3.6\%$$

If the economy shrinks, the growth rate will be negative. For instance, the U.S. economy shrunk between 2008 and 2009, with a negative annual real GDP growth rate of −2.4 percent.

We can think about GDP growth rates in several ways. Let's think first about how economic growth changes year to year for the same country. A shrinking economy is a big deal. It means that people are actually producing less than they did the year before.

We have special terms for a period in which the economy contracts:

- A **recession** is a period of significant decline in economic activity. There is no hard-and-fast rule about what constitutes a "significant decline," but a recession is usually marked by falling GDP, rising unemployment, and an increased number of bankruptcies.

- A **depression** is a severe or extended recession. Again, there is no hard-and-fast rule about when a recession becomes a depression.

recession
a period of significant economic decline

depression
a particularly severe or extended recession

An old joke, heard from both Harry Truman and Ronald Reagan, says that a recession is when your neighbor loses his job; a depression is when you lose yours.

In the United States, a recession or depression is considered "official" when a committee of economists at an organization called the National Bureau of Economic Research (NBER) calls it one. The country often feels the effects of a recession long before they register in government statistics: People start losing their jobs and businesses experience falling sales. In the 2008 recession, for instance, the news media were using the word "recession" for almost a year before the NBER confirmed it.

Recessions are actually not as uncommon as you might think. Figure 7-6 shows that there were eight periods of recession in the United States in the 56 years between 1960 and 2016. You can also see that, overall, U.S. real GDP grew significantly and quite steadily over this same period. The 1990s and early 2000s were particularly recession-free decades, with only two brief and relatively mild dips in GDP. The 2008 recession involved a much deeper dip in GDP and lasted much longer.

Another way we can look at economic growth is to compare how fast different countries are growing. High growth rates are not necessarily associated with high total GDP or high GDP per capita, as Figure 7-7 shows. We can see that real GDP growth in the world's rich countries, such as the United States and Europe, has been relatively slow in recent years (albeit from a much higher starting level). Much more rapid growth has occurred in middle-income and poorer countries, led by China and followed by South Asia and East Africa.

FIGURE 7-6

U.S. real GDP over time   Real GDP has been steadily rising since 1960, and has more than quadrupled in value over the past 56 years. The gray bars show recessions, when economic activity slows.

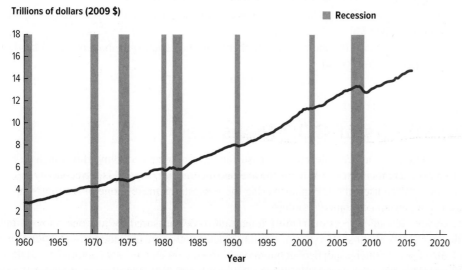

Sources: Federal Reserve Bank of St. Louis, **https://research.stlouisfed.org/fred2/series/GDPC1#** (quarterly real GDP); and NBER, **http://www.nber.org/cycles/cyclesmain.html**(recession dates).

FIGURE 7-7

Global real GDP growth rates (2014)   In contrast with the map of overall income, poorer countries grew faster than more developed countries, on average.

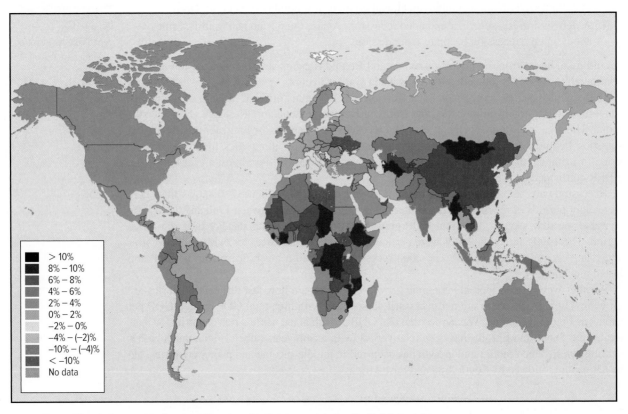

⬛	> 10%
⬛	8% − 10%
⬛	6% − 8%
⬛	4% − 6%
⬛	2% − 4%
⬛	0% − 2%
⬛	−2% − 0%
⬛	−4% − (−2)%
⬛	−10% − (−4)%
⬛	< −10%
⬛	No data

Source: Ali Zifan, via Wikimedia Commons, **http://www.statsilk.com/maps/world-stats-open-data.** Uses The World Factbook data.

✓**CONCEPT CHECK**

☐ What is the difference between real and nominal GDP? **[LO 7.4]**

☐ To calculate the GDP deflator, why do we divide nominal GDP by real GDP from the *same* year? **[LO 7.5]**

☐ What does it mean if country A has higher GDP than country B, but country B has higher GDP per capita? **[LO 7.6]**

Limitations of GDP Measures

GDP is a powerful and versatile way of measuring the size of an economy. How much do people produce in different countries? What is the average income per person? Is the economy growing? How quickly? The uses of GDP in answering these questions make it one of the most important measures in a macroeconomist's toolbox.

However, we can't expect *everything* important to be measured by just one number. In this section, we'll talk about some types of economic activity that are excluded from GDP by design. We'll also look at which aspects of economic well-being are and are not captured by GDP. With GDP, we get a powerful start on describing the health and direction of an economy, but we can get an even richer picture by supplementing it with other metrics.

Data challenges

LO 7.7 Discuss some limitations to GDP, including its measurement of home production, the underground economy, environmental degradation, and well-being.

When critics argue that we should look beyond GDP, they point out that GDP calculations leave out some important types of economic activity. GDP measures the market value of final goods and services, but it doesn't include anything that is not traded in a market or that isn't reported to the government. That means that three major categories of economic activity are not counted as part of GDP: home production, the underground economy, and nonmarket externalities such as environmental degradation.

Home production

Goods and services that are both produced and consumed within one household are called *home production*. In general, home production goods and services are not included in GDP:

- If you eat out, your meal is part of GDP. If you eat at home, it's not.
- If you hire a cleaning service to clean your home, that's part of GDP. If you clean your own home, it's not.

Similarly, the same goods might or might not be part of GDP, depending on whether you sell them or consume them yourself:

- If you grow vegetables in your garden and sell them at a farmers' market, that's part of GDP. If you eat them yourself, it's not.
- If your grandmother knits a sweater and gives it to you for your birthday, that's not part of GDP. If your grandmother sells her knitting on eBay or Etsy, it is.

Home production is a major component of economic activity in most places. Because of that, it can change how one country compares to another. In relatively poor countries, many people grow their own food on small farms and may make their own tools and clothes. In these instances, the official GDP measure may be missing a significant percentage of real production. Even in wealthy countries, much of the value of caretaking work—raising children or caring for elderly parents—is uncounted.

Some economists have made efforts to quantify the value of this work. For more detail, read the From Another Angle box "Valuing homemakers."

From Another Angle

Valuing homemakers

If you were to compare the GDP growth of the United States and Germany between the 1970s and the 1990s, you'd find that the U.S. economy grew more than Germany's. Does this mean that life got better in the United States during that period relative to life in Germany? Estimates of home production cast an interesting light on this question.

One major difference between the United States and Germany over those three decades is the change in the number of people in the workforce. In the 1970s, comparable proportions of Germans and Americans were in paid employment; by the 1990s, a higher proportion of Americans had jobs. This difference can be largely explained by the rising rate of female participation in the U.S. labor force. A larger workforce makes for a larger GDP.

(continued)

But the larger GDP does not necessarily mean that the United States is better off. The women who stayed at home in the 1970s weren't sitting around doing nothing. They were running households and raising families, growing and making goods for home consumption, doing volunteer work in their communities, and so on. Although these are valuable activities, a mother or father who stays home to look after children and bake cookies contributes nothing to GDP. But when she or he goes out to work, hires someone to look after the children, and buys cookies at the store, that adds to GDP.

Therefore, we can't automatically conclude from the rise in U.S. GDP relative to Germany's that more goods and services were being produced in the United States in the 1990s. Could it be that some goods and services simply moved from the uncounted area of home production to the documented area of GDP?

Studies suggest this may, in fact, be the case. When you add up paid work, home production, and volunteer work, Americans and Germans put in about the same number of hours per week, but workers in Germany spend 5.3 hours less on paid work and 6 hours more on household production than do Americans. Estimating home production suggests that a lower German employment rate does not necessarily imply lower overall production or a lower standard of living.

Consideration of home production can also change the way we view recessions. U.S. GDP dropped in 2008, but home production went up. Feeling a financial squeeze, people substituted home-cooked meals for restaurant meals, planted vegetable gardens, and did their own repairs rather than hire someone. When the economy was doing well, people's choices suggest that they preferred to hire others to do these tasks. So the recession clearly reduced people's well-being. But economist Nancy Folbre, who has led efforts to quantify the value of home production, argues that it might not have reduced well-being by nearly as much as official GDP statistics suggest.

Sources: http://economix.blogs.nytimes.com/2009/05/04/including-home-production-gdp-might-not-look-so-bad; http://www.nber.org/papers/w8797.pdf; http://scholar.harvard.edu/files/alesina/files/work_and_leisure_in_the_u.s._and_europe.pdf.

The underground economy

Many goods and services are sold below the radar, outside of official records. These transactions make up the *underground economy*.

On the extreme end, there is trade in goods and services that are themselves illegal—banned drugs, restricted weapons, endangered animals and plants, and so on. Sales of illegal goods and services are part of what is called the *black market*. Because black-market transactions are illegal, they are, of course, not reported to the government or tax authorities. As a result, they don't show up in government statistics, and they don't get counted as part of the official GDP. In principle, though, black-market activities belong in the GDP calculation.

At the less-extreme end are economic transactions that are otherwise legal but are sometimes not reported to the government. Failure to report can be either accidental or deliberate (to avoid paying taxes). For instance, were you ever hired to mow a neighbor's lawn, or babysit, or run errands for a few bucks when you were in high school? If you didn't report those amounts to the IRS,[4] you were participating in what's known as the *gray market*—so called because it sits somewhere between the black market and the documented economy.

Gray-market transactions aren't counted in GDP for the same reason that black-market transactions aren't counted: If it's not reported, it doesn't show up in government statistics. And, if it doesn't show up in government statistics, it can't be counted in GDP.

Even though black- and gray-market transactions don't get reported, researchers try to quantify them to get a sense of what's missing in our GDP calculations. It turns out that the underground economy accounts for a significant portion of the total economy in many countries. On average across the world, the underground economy is worth about one-third of GDP. This average hides wide variations, though:

- In the United States, for example, the underground economy has been valued at only around 7 or 8 percent of GDP.
- It is estimated at more than half of GDP in Nigeria and more than two-thirds in some Latin American countries.[5]

The typical explanation for this pattern reflects the cost of doing business legally. In some countries you have to pay extremely high taxes or pay bribes to officials to cut through bureaucratic red tape. When the cost of doing business legally is high, people are much more likely to conduct their business through other channels. In such countries, GDP may significantly underestimate the true size of the economy. In the case of Nigeria, it would mean increasing the official GDP figure by 50 percent.[6]

Environmental externalities

Suppose an electricity company causes air pollution by burning coal. The electricity generated ends up being counted in GDP. It may appear in the price paid by households for their electricity. Or it may be wrapped up in the price of goods and services that other firms make using the electricity as an input.

Some economists feel that GDP, as a metric, is missing the costs associated with pollution. They argue that we need to account for the *negative externalities* of economic activities. In a sense, we can think of the value of negative externalities as *negative output.* They are final "goods" that do harm to people, and therefore have negative value, but don't otherwise get counted in production or expenditure measures.

Increasingly, those who deal with economic statistics are trying to incorporate the value of negative externalities into GDP. Some countries have tried to calculate **green GDP**. This alternative measure of GDP subtracts the environmental costs of production from the positive outputs normally counted in GDP.

In some countries that are growing rapidly, such as China and India, there are few regulations to guard against environmental degradation. When the Chinese government attempted to calculate green GDP in 2007, it came up with some shocking results. Once adjusted for pollution, the soaring GDP growth rates in many provinces in China dropped to almost zero. This was such an inconvenient finding that the government abandoned the green-GDP project.[7]

The Chinese government is not alone in its concerns about the political implications of GDP measures. For more about the intersection of politics and national accounting, read the From Another Angle box "The politics of green GDP."

green GDP
an alternative measure of GDP that subtracts the environmental costs of production from the positive outputs normally counted in GDP

From Another Angle
The politics of green GDP

Since GDP is widely viewed as the measure of the overall health of the economy, politicians have an incentive to make GDP numbers look as strong as possible. Strong numbers help their reelection chances. As a result, the question of what is the best way to measure the economy isn't left to number-crunching economists—it can also be deeply political.

A perfect example of this is green GDP. Recognizing that GDP may not capture the negative externalities of environmental production, officials in the U.S. Bureau of Economic Analysis (BEA) started to work on how to calculate a more "complete" measure of economic activity.

(continued)

This idea started off with the typical GDP equation: $C + I + G + NX$. What made the new GDP calculation "green" was that it would weigh the value of this production against its overall environmental costs. Included in those costs would be the consumption of nonrenewable resources—such as pumping oil and mining coal—and some of the costs from pollution.

You may have noticed that we don't see this figure reported in the news. Why not? The BEA needed funding to continue the project, which needed the approval of Congress. The National Academy of Science supported the proposal, but members of Congress nixed it. It seems they were worried that measuring green GDP might suggest the economy was shrinking rather than growing, and that industry—which has powerful lobbies—would get the blame.

By contrast, a similar French effort had top-level support. Former President Nicolas Sarkozy recruited several prominent economists—including two Nobel laureates, Amartya Sen and Joseph Stiglitz—to serve on the grandly named "Commission on the Measurement of Economic and Social Progress."

The commission published a 300-page report in September 2009 outlining 12 recommendations. These included measures of the state of health, education, the environment, and income inequality that could be used to build a more inclusive measure of overall well-being. This measure was never officially calculated. We can guess roughly what it might show by seeing how France scored in other, already-crafted measures such as the Better Life Index from the OECD (Organisation for Economic Co-operation and Development): France ranked 18th among 34 OECD member countries. That ranking is seven positions *lower* than how France stood when the same countries were ranked by the size of their GDP per capita.

If President Sarkozy had been hoping for a new metric that would make the French feel good about their country on the world stage, then this type of calculation would have fallen far short. As we have seen, the traditional measurement of GDP is more than just a metric favored by economists—it can be quite useful for politicians as well.

Sources: http://www.oecdbetterlifeindex.org/; http://www.nytimes.com/2010/05/16/magazine/16GDP-t .html?pagewanted=all; http://www.insee.fr/fr/publications-et-services/default.asp?page=dossiers_web/stiglitz/ documents-commission.htm.

GDP vs. well-being

GDP tells us a lot about the living standards in a country, but it can't tell us everything. Suppose you are offered the chance to live in a country that you know nothing about. You could quickly learn more by finding out the country's average income as measured by its GDP per capita. Which data would you turn to next to find out about the quality of life there? Quality of life is a nuanced idea, and it's hard to capture perfectly with any number. However, metrics like infant or child mortality (how many babies and children die), literacy rates (how many people can read), and life expectancy (how long people live) can give us a fuller picture of the well-being of a country's inhabitants.

You might assume that countries with high GDP per capita are likely to do well on these other metrics. The wealthier a country is, the more easily it can afford good health care and education for its people. Broadly speaking, you would be right. As Table 7-4 shows, GDP per capita *is* highly correlated with these quality-of-life measures. However, the correlation is not perfect: Look at Equatorial Guinea in Africa. Countries that are much poorer than Equatorial Guinea— such as Brazil, Bulgaria, and China—nonetheless seem to do a much better job of caring for the health of their children and elderly.

There are good reasons to expect that GDP per capita might not perfectly correlate with people's well-being. Let's take an obvious example: Equatorial Guinea is relatively rich on average (thanks to having important oil reserves), but its income is distributed very unequally. While the

TABLE 7-4 GDP compared with other measures of well-being

While GDP is commonly used to measure average income in a country, it can't capture all aspects of quality of life. Overall, metrics of well-being and quality of life like infant mortality, literacy, and life expectancy are correlated with GDP per capita, but in extreme cases, like that of Equatorial Guinea, they can diverge dramatically.

Country	GDP per capita (Current U.S. $)	Literacy rate (% of population over 15)	Life expectancy at birth (Years)	Child mortality (Deaths per 1,000 under age 5)	Life Satisfaction Index (0 to 10)
Norway	97,299	[No data]	82	3	7.5
United States	54,629	[No data]	79	7	7.1
Equatorial Guinea	18,918	95.3	58	94	[No data]
Brazil	11,726	92.6	74	16	6.9
Bulgaria	7,851	98.4	75	10	4.2
China	7,590	96.4	76	11	5.1
Mali	704	38.7	58	115	3.9

Sources: World Bank WDI, 2014, http://data.worldbank.org/indicator (GDP per capita, Life expectancy, Child mortality); CIA World Factbook, 2015 https://www.cia.gov/library/publications/the-world-factbook/fields/2103.html (Literacy Rate); World Happiness Report 2015 http://worldhappiness.report/wp-content/uploads/sites/2/2015/04/WHR15.pdf (Life Satisfaction Index);

country's elite are rich, more than three out of four citizens live on under $2 a day.[8] In this sense, pursuing GDP growth as the highest priority can be in opposition to improving quality of life in other ways, at least in the short term.

If what we care about is not so much the output of an economy but the happiness of the people who comprise it, can we measure happiness directly? Economists and others are trying to do this in a systematic way. These efforts are recent, and nobody is suggesting that such measures replace GDP. One of the measures they've developed is the Life Satisfaction Index. (See the final column in Table 7-4.) It suggests that the correlation between GDP per capita and happiness is, indeed, far from perfect. For example, people in Bulgaria seem to be less happy than we might expect from their average income; people in Mali seem to be happier. For more on measuring happiness, read the Real Life box "Can money buy you happiness?"

Real Life

Can money buy you happiness?

Everyone has heard the saying, "Money can't buy you happiness." But is that actually true? The answer turns out to depend on how much money and how you define happiness.

First, how can we tell whether someone is happy? Researchers have generally relied on just asking people how they feel. Studies show consistently that people who are married tend to be happier, as do people who are religious and people who are in good health. Income seems to matter a lot, too.

However, we need to remember the difference between *causation* and *correlation*. The fact that wealth and life satisfaction are correlated doesn't mean that having more money *causes* happiness. In fact, when you look at the same country over time, people don't necessarily get happier as the country they live in gets richer.

(continued)

For instance, the United States has a much higher GDP per capita now than it did 50 years ago, but researchers have found that Americans are not noticeably happier than they were 50 years ago. One possible explanation for this puzzle is that people naturally tend to compare their lifestyles and material wealth to those of their peers, rather than to their parents or grandparents.

How about the relationship between money and happiness for individuals within a country? Research in the United States has found that there *is* a correlation between happiness and money—up to a point. That point happens to be an income level of about $75,000 per year. Below that income level, more money appears to be related to higher levels of happiness on average. Above that income level, it's much less clear—whether money buys happiness seems to depend on the way in which you ask people if they're happy.

Typically, researchers use two distinct methods. One is to ask something like, "How satisfied are you with your life as a whole these days?" This measure, usually called *life satisfaction*, continues to rise with income. In other words, someone earning $750,000 is likely to tell a researcher that she is more satisfied than someone earning $75,000.

The other method is to ask people about the emotions they felt *on the previous day*. For example, did you feel happiness yesterday? Enjoyment? Anger? Stress? Worry? Here, we find that overall someone earning $75,000 is more likely to have experienced positive emotions than someone earning $25,000. But despite what you would think, someone earning $750,000 did not report more positive emotions, and less negativity, than someone earning $75,000. Although money doesn't always buy happiness, it seems to help up to a certain point.

Sources: Angus Deaton, "Income, Health, and Well-Being around the World: Evidence from the Gallup World Poll," *Journal of Economic Perspectives* 22, no. 2 (2008), pp. 53–72; http://economix.blogs.nytimes .com/2009/03/10/the-happiest-states-of-america/; http://www.princeton.edu/~deaton/downloads/deaton_kahneman_high_income_improves_evaluation_August2010.pdf.

✓ CONCEPT CHECK

- ☐ What is home production? **[LO 7.7]**
- ☐ Why might GDP fall if environmental damages caused by production were taken into account? **[LO 7.7]**
- ☐ What supplemental metrics are commonly used to measure quality of life alongside GDP per capita? **[LO 7.7]**

Conclusion

GDP is a powerful and versatile metric. There are good reasons that it is one of the most commonly used tools in macroeconomics. It gives a simple measure of the size of an economy and the average income of its participants. It also allows us to make comparisons over time or across countries. The system of national income accounts gives us a picture of how output, expenditure, and income are linked, and a framework for adding up the billions of daily transactions that occur in an economy.

Comparing nominal and real GDP allows us to disentangle the role of increasing prices versus increasing output in a growing economy. The GDP deflator and the inflation rate track changes in overall price levels over time—which, as we'll see in the next chapter, is a major task in macroeconomics.

GDP per capita gives us a sense of the average income within a country, although it doesn't tell us about the distribution of income or quality of life. Finally, calculating real GDP growth rates shows us in which direction the economy is moving, and is an important indicator of recession or depression.

In the next chapter, we'll dig deeper into the tools that economists use to measure price changes and the cost of living. When we combine these tools with GDP, we have a menu of macroeconomic metrics that will allow us to describe and analyze national and international economies.

Key Terms

macroeconomics, p. 167

gross domestic product (GDP), p. 167

gross national product (GNP), p. 168

consumption, p. 171

investment, p. 171

inventory, p. 172

government purchases, p. 172

net exports (NX), p. 173

real GDP, p. 177

nominal GDP, p. 177

GDP deflator, p. 179

GDP per capita, p. 180

recession, p. 183

depression, p. 183

green GDP, p. 187

Summary

LO 7.1 Understand the importance of using the market value of final goods and services to calculate GDP and explain why each component of GDP is important.

Most goods and services go through several production steps and may pass through multiple firms before ending up in the hands of the consumer. However, when calculating GDP, we should consider only the value of the final good or service, in order to avoid double-counting. The value added by each step of the production process will be included in the price of the final product.

The most commonly used variable for measuring the value of a national economy is gross domestic product, or GDP. GDP is the sum of the market values of all final goods and services produced within a country in a given period of time. The goods and services that count toward GDP are defined in terms of the location of production, not the citizenship of the producer. GDP is usually calculated on both annual and quarterly (three-month) bases; only new goods and services being produced within that time period are counted. Quarterly GDP estimates are typically given as a seasonally adjusted annual rate, which projects what annual GDP will be based on the current quarter's output if the economy continues to follow expected seasonal patterns.

LO 7.2 Explain the equivalence of the expenditure and income approaches to valuing an economy.

Economists can think about the size of a national economy in three different ways: how much is produced (output), how much is spent (expenditure), and how much income is earned (income). All three of these methods add up to the same thing. Total output is the *value* of the things produced in an economy in dollar terms, which is

the same as the price for which those outputs sell, which is the same as what people spent to buy those outputs. Therefore, the value of output is equal to expenditures. Every transaction has both a buyer and a seller, so expenditures by one person translate directly into income for someone else; therefore, income equals expenditure.

LO 7.3 Explain the three approaches that are used to calculate GDP and summarize the categories of spending that are included in the expenditure approach.

The *expenditure* approach of calculating the size of an economy involves adding up all spending on goods and services produced in an economy and subtracting spending on imports. We can break expenditures into four categories: *Consumption* (C) measures spending on goods and services to be consumed by private individuals and families. *Investment* (I) includes any goods that are bought in order to produce other goods and services in the future. *Government purchases* (G) are goods and services bought by all levels of government, for either consumption or investment. Finally, *net exports* (NX) are foreign spending on domestically produced goods and services minus domestic spending on foreign-produced goods and services. The sum of these categories and the equivalence of income (Y) and expenditure gives us the equation $Y = C + I + G + NX$.

The *income* approach adds up the income earned by everyone in a country—including wages (earned by workers), interest (earned on capital investments), rental income (earned on land and property), and profits (earned by firms).

The *value-added* approach accounts for the value that is added at each stage of production in the economy. This approach allows economists to investigate the contribution of each transaction in the economy to overall GDP.

It also solves the double-counting problem because only part of the value of each transaction is registered, and it does not register the total price of intermediate goods and services.

Many countries use all three approaches to calculate GDP so that policy-makers and researchers can get a full picture of economic activity.

LO 7.4 Explain the difference between real and nominal GDP.

GDP is a function of both the quantity of goods and services produced (output) and their market value (prices); an increase in GDP can result from growth in either or both components. To isolate the role of growing output, we can control for price changes. *Real GDP* is calculated based on goods and services valued at constant prices. *Nominal GDP* is calculated based on goods and services valued at current prices.

LO 7.5 Calculate the GDP deflator.

One way to measure price changes is by calculating the GDP deflator. The GDP deflator summarizes the overall increase in prices in an economy using the ratio between real and nominal GDP in a given year. If prices have risen such that nominal GDP is now higher than real GDP, the deflator will be greater than 100. If prices have fallen such that nominal GDP is now lower than real GDP, the deflator will be less than 100. The GDP deflator allows us to "deflate" nominal GDP by controlling for price changes.

LO 7.6 Use GDP per capita to compare economies and calculate the real GDP annual growth rate.

GDP per capita is total GDP divided by the population of a country. It tells us the average income or productivity per person in the economy. To track changes in an economy over time, we can calculate the real GDP growth rate, measured as the percent change in real GDP from one time period to the next, typically annually or quarterly at an annual rate. When the economy shrinks, the growth rate is negative and is one of the major indicators used to determine whether the economy is in a recession or depression.

LO 7.7 Discuss some limitations to GDP, including its measurement of home production, the underground economy, environmental degradation, and well-being.

GDP is a rough measure of the average standard of living in a country, but it does not tell us about the distribution of wealth. Furthermore, three important segments of the economy are not included in GDP by design:

home production (goods and services that are produced and consumed within a household), the underground economy (illegal transactions, or legal transactions that simply aren't reported to the government), and externalities (such as pollution) that are not fully accounted for in regular production or consumption measures. Higher GDP is often associated with other indicators of higher well-being, such as health, education, and life satisfaction, but does not guarantee those things.

Review Questions

1. U.S. car dealers sell both used cars and new cars each year. However, only the sales of the new cars count toward GDP. Why does the sale of used cars not count? **[LO 7.1]**

2. There is an old saying, "You can't compare apples and oranges." When economists calculate GDP, are they able to compare apples and oranges? Explain. **[LO 7.1]**

3. When Americans buy goods produced in Canada, Canadians earn income from American expenditures. Does the value of this Canadian output and American expenditure get counted under the GDP of Canada or the United States? Why? **[LO 7.2]**

4. Economists sometimes describe the economy as having a "circular flow." In the most basic form of the circular flow model, companies hire workers and pay them wages. Workers then use these wages to buy goods and services from companies. How does the circular flow model explain the equivalence of the expenditure and income methods of valuing an economy? **[LO 7.2]**

5. In 2011, the average baseball player earned $3 million per year. Suppose that these baseball players spend all of their income on goods and services each year, and they save nothing. Argue why the sum of the incomes of all baseball players must equal the sum of expenditures made by the baseball players. **[LO 7.2]**

6. Determine whether each of the following counts as consumption, investment, government purchases, net exports, or none of these, under the expenditure approach to calculating GDP. Explain your answer. **[LO 7.3]**
   a. The construction of a court house.
   b. A taxicab ride.
   c. The purchase of a taxicab by a taxicab company.
   d. A student buying a textbook.
   e. The trading of municipal bonds (a type of financial investment offered by city or state governments).
   f. A company's purchase of foreign minerals.

7. If car companies produce a lot of cars this year but hold the new models back in warehouses until they release

them in the new-model year, will this year's GDP be higher, lower, or the same as it would have been if the cars had been sold right away? Why? Does the choice to reserve the cars for a year change which category of expenditures they fall under? **[LO 7.3]**

8. The value-added method involves taking the cost of intermediate outputs (i.e., outputs that will in turn be used in the production of another good) and subtracting that cost from the value of the good being produced. In this way, only the value that is added at each step (the sale value minus the cost of the goods that went into producing it) is summed up. Explain why this method gives us the same result as the standard method of counting only the value of final goods and services. **[LO 7.3]**

9. Imagine a painter is trying to determine the value she adds when she paints a picture. Assume that after spending $200 on materials, she sells one copy of her painting for $500. She then spends $50 to make 10 copies of her painting, each of which sells for $100. What is the value added of her painting? What if a company then spends $10 per copy to sell 100 more copies, each for $50? What is the value the painter adds then? If it's unknown how many copies the painting will sell in the future, can we today determine the value added? Why or why not? **[LO 7.3]**

10. In a press conference, the president of a small country displays a chart showing that GDP has risen by 10 percent every year for five years. He argues that this growth shows the brilliance of his economic policy. However, his chart uses nominal GDP numbers. What might be wrong with this chart? If you were a reporter at the press conference, what questions could you ask to get a more accurate picture of the country's economic growth? **[LO 7.4]**

11. Suppose that the GDP deflator grew by 10 percent from last year to this year. That is, the inflation rate this year was 10 percent. In words, what does this mean happened in the economy? What does this inflation rate imply about the growth rate in real GDP? **[LO 7.5]**

12. An inexperienced researcher wants to examine the average standard of living in two countries. In order to do so, he compares the GDPs in those two countries. What are two reasons why this comparison does not lead to an accurate measure of the countries' average standards of living? **[LO 7.4, 7.6]**

13. In 2010, according to the International Monetary Fund, India had the world's 10th-highest nominal GDP, the 135th-highest nominal GDP per capita, and the 5th-highest real GDP growth rate. What does each of these indicators tell us about the Indian economy and how life in India compares to life in other countries? **[LO 7.6]**

14. China is a rapidly growing country. It has high levels of bureaucracy and business regulation, low levels of environmental regulation, and a strong tradition of entrepreneurship. Discuss several reasons why official GDP estimates in China might miss significant portions of the country's economic activity. **[LO 7.7]**

15. Suppose a college student is texting while driving and gets into a car accident causing $2,000 worth of damage to her car. Assuming the student repairs her car, does GDP rise, fall, or stay constant with this accident? What does your answer suggest about using GDP as a measure of well-being? **[LO 7.7]**

Problems and Applications

1. Suppose a gold miner finds a gold nugget and sells the nugget to a mining company for $500. The mining company melts down the gold, purifies it, and sells it to a jewelry maker for $1,000. The jewelry maker fashions the gold into a necklace that it sells to a department store for $1,500. Finally, the department store sells the necklace to a customer for $2,000. How much has GDP increased as a result of these transactions? **[LO 7.1, 7.3]**

2. Table 7P-1 shows the price of inputs and the price of outputs at each step in the production process of making a shirt. Assume that each of these steps takes place within the country. **[LO 7.1, 7.3]**

   a. What is the total contribution of this shirt to GDP, using the standard expenditure method?

   b. If we use a value-added method (i.e., summing the value added by producers at each step of the production process, equal to the value of output minus the price of inputs), what is the contribution of this shirt to GDP?

   c. If we mistakenly added the price of both intermediate and final outputs without adjusting for value added, what would we find that this shirt contributes to GDP? By how much does this overestimate the true contribution?

3. The U.S. government gives income support to many families living in poverty. How does each of the following aspects of this policy contribute to GDP? **[LO 7.2]**

TABLE 7P-1

	Cotton farmer ($)	Fabric maker ($)	Sewing and printing ($)
Inputs	0	1.10	3.50
Value of output	1.10	3.50	18.00

a. Does this government's expenditure on income support count as part of GDP? If so, in which category of expenditure does it fall?

b. When the families buy groceries with the money they've received, does this expenditure count as part of GDP? If so, in which category does it fall?

c. If the families buy new houses with the money they've received, does this count as part of GDP? If so, in which category does it fall?

4. Given the following information about each economy, either calculate the missing variable or determine that it cannot be calculated. **[LO 7.2, 7.3]**

   a. If C = $20.1 billion, I = $3.5 billion, G = $5.2 billion, and NX = −$1 billion, what is total income?

   b. If total income is $1 trillion, G = $0.3 trillion, and C = $0.5 trillion, what is I?

   c. If total expenditure is $675 billion, C = $433 billion, I = $105 billion, and G = $75 billion, what is NX? How much are exports? How much are imports?

5. Using Table 7P-2, calculate the following. **[LO 7.2, 7.3]**

   a. Total gross domestic product and GDP per person.

   b. Consumption, investment, government purchases, and net exports, each as a percentage of total GDP.

   c. Consumption, investment, government purchases, and net exports per person.

6. Determine which category each of the following economic activities falls under: consumption (C), investment (I), government purchases (G), net exports (NX), or not included in GDP. **[LO 7.3]**

   a. The mayor of Chicago authorizes the construction of a new stadium using public funds.

   b. A student pays rent on her apartment.

   c. Parents pay college tuition for their son.

TABLE 7P-2

Sector	Value (millions)
Consumption	$770,000
Investment	$165,000
Government spending	$220,000
Net exports	−$ 55,000
Population	50

d. Someone buys a new Toyota car produced in Japan.

e. Someone buys a used Toyota car.

f. Someone buys a new General Motors car produced in the United States.

g. A family buys a house in a newly-constructed housing development.

h. The U.S. Army pays its soldiers.

i. A Brazilian driver buys a Ford car produced in the United States.

j. The Department of Motor Vehicles buys a new machine for printing drivers' licenses.

k. An apple picked in Washington in October is bought at a grocery store in Mississippi in December.

l. Hewlett-Packard produces a computer and sends it to a warehouse in another state for sale next year.

7. Table 7P-3 shows economic activity for a very tiny country. Using the expenditure approach, determine the following. **[LO 7.3]**

   a. Consumption.

   b. Investment.

TABLE 7P-3

Activity	Total value (thousands of $)
Families buy groceries	600
Electronics company sells HD projectors to households	100
Personal trainer gives Zumba class	5
Custard stand sells pistachio ice cream	2
Police department buys new cars	500
Mayor leads creation of new education budget	300
Elevator construction company builds new factory	600
Local businessperson purchases corn from Mexico	400
Sports-gear company sells hockey gloves to Canadian team	200
Bike store sells used carbon-fiber bikes	200
Local stockbroker executes trades for clients	2,000

TABLE 7P-4

Category	Value (billions of $)
Wages	8.3
Interest	0.7
Total business expenditures	21.0
Total business revenues	30.0

c. Government purchases.

d. Net exports.

e. GDP.

8. During the recent recession sparked by financial crisis, the U.S. economy suffered tremendously. Suppose that, due to the recession, the U.S. GDP dropped from $14 trillion to $12.5 trillion. This decline in GDP was due to a drop in consumption of $1 trillion and a drop in investment of $500 billion. The U.S. government, under the current president, responded to this recession by increasing government purchases. **[LO 7.3]**

   a. Suppose that government spending had no impact on consumption, investment, or net exports. If the current presidential administration wanted to bring GDP back up to $14 trillion, how much would government spending have to rise?

   b. Many economists believe that an increase in government spending doesn't just directly increase GDP, but that it also leads to an increase in consumption. If government spending rises by $1 trillion, how much would consumption have to rise in order to bring GDP back to $14 trillion?

9. Assume Table 7P-4 summarizes the income of Paraguay. **[LO 7.3]**

   a. Calculate profits.

   b. Calculate the GDP of Paraguay using the income approach.

c. What would GDP be if you were to use the value-added approach?

d. What would GDP be if you were to use the expenditure approach?

10. Table 7P-5 provides information about the cost of inputs and the value of output for the production of a road bike. Note there are four different stages of production. **[LO 7.3]**

   a. What value is added by the supplier of the raw materials?

   b. What value is added by the tire maker?

   c. What value is added by the maker of the frame and components?

   d. What value is added by the bike mechanic?

   e. What value is added by the bike store?

   f. What is the total contribution of the bike to GDP?

11. Imagine that the United States produces only three goods: apples, bananas, and carrots. The quantities produced and the prices of the three goods are listed in Table 7P-6. **[LO 7.4]**

   a. Calculate the GDP of the United States in this three-goods version of its economy.

   b. Suppose that a drought hits the state of Washington. This drought causes the quantity of apples produced to fall to 2. Assuming that all prices remain constant, calculate the new U.S. GDP.

   c. Assume, once again, that the quantities produced and the prices of the three goods are as listed in Table 7P-6. Now, given this situation, carrot sellers decide that the price of carrots is too low, so they agree to raise the price. What must be the new price of carrots if the U.S. GDP is $60?

TABLE 7P-6

Goods	Quantities produced	Prices ($)
Apples	5	2.00
Bananas	10	1.00
Carrots	20	1.50

TABLE 7P-5

Raw materials	Manufacturing	Construction	Sale by the retailer
• Rubber for one tire ($20) • Aluminum for the frame ($80) • Other component materials ($70)	• Tire maker sells tires for $30 each • Frame maker sells bike frame and components for a total of $250	• Bike mechanic puts everything together and sells the bike for $350	• Retailer sells the bike for $500

12. Based on Table 7P-7, calculate nominal GDP, real GDP, the GDP deflator, and the inflation rate in each year, and fill in the missing parts of the table. Use 2014 as the base year. **[LO 7.4, 7.5]**

13. Suppose that the British economy produces two goods: laptops and books. The quantity produced and the prices of these items for 2015 and 2016 are shown in Table 7P-8. **[LO 7.4, 7.5]**

    a. Let's assume that the base year was 2015, so that real GDP in 2015 equals nominal GDP in 2015. If the real GDP in Britain was $15,000 in 2015, what was the price of books?

    b. Using your answer from part *a*, if the growth rate in nominal GDP was 10 percent, how many books must have been produced in 2016?

    c. Using your answers from parts *a* and *b*, what is the real GDP in 2016? What was the growth rate in real GDP between 2015 and 2016?

14. Based on Table 7P-9, calculate nominal GDP per capita in 2015 and 2016, and the real GDP growth rate between the two years. Which countries look like they experienced recession in 2015–2016? **[LO 7.6]**

TABLE 7P-7

Year	Quantity of oranges	Price of orange ($)	Quantity of beach balls	Price of beach ball ($)	Nominal GDP ($)	Real GDP ($)	GDP deflator	Inflation rate (%)
2014	500	1.00	850	5.00				
2015	600	1.50	900	7.50				
2016	750	1.65	1,000	8.25				

TABLE 7P-8

Year	Quantities produced	Price ($)
2015	Laptops = 50 Books = 1,000	Laptops = 200 Books = ?
2016	Laptops = 100 Books = ?	Laptops = $150 Books = 10

TABLE 7P-9

	2015			2016		
	Nominal GDP (billions of $)	Real GDP (billions of $)	Population	Nominal GDP (billions of $)	Real GDP (billions of $)	Population
Argentina	328.03	383.48	39,746,000	310.17	386.68	40,134,000
Egypt	162.44	123.21	75,200,000	188.61	128.97	76,800,000
Germany	3,651.62	2,100.54	82,013,000	3,338.68	2,002.46	81,767,000
Ghana	28.53	11.27	22,532,000	26	11.8	23,108,000
United States	14,319	13,228.65	304,718,000	14,119	12,880.53	307,374,000

15. Table 7P-10 describes the real GDP and population of a fictional country in 2015 and 2016. **[LO 7.6]**
    a. What is the real GDP per capita in 2015 and 2016?
    b. What is the growth rate in real GDP?
    c. What is the growth rate in population?
    d. What is the growth rate in real GDP per capita?

16. Table 7P-11 shows data on population and expenditures in five countries, as well as the value of home production, the underground economy, and environmental externalities in each. **[LO 7.6, 7.7]**
    a. Calculate GDP and GDP per capita in each country.
    b. Calculate the size of home production, the underground economy, and environmental externalities in each country as a percentage of GDP.
    c. Calculate total and per capita "GDP-plus" in each country by including the value of home production, the underground economy, and environmental externalities.

TABLE 7P-10

Year	Real GDP (billions of $)	Population (millions)
2015	10	1.0
2016	12	1.1

d. Rank countries by total and per capita GDP, and again by total and per capita "GDP-plus." Compare the two lists. Are the biggest and the smallest economies the same or different?

17. Suppose a parent was earning $20,000 per year working at a local firm. The parent then decides to quit his job in order to care for his child, who was being watched by a babysitter for $10,000 per year. Does GDP rise, fall, or stay constant with this action, and how much does GDP change (if at all)? **[LO 7.7]**

TABLE 7P-11

Country	C ($)	I ($)	G ($)	Net exports ($)
Bohemia	9,800,000,000	230,000,000	950,000,000	−120,000,000
Silesia	450,000,000	78,000,000	100,000,000	13,000,000
Bavaria	2,125,000,000	319,000,000	597,000,000	134,000,000
Saxony	2,750,000,000	75,000,000	1,320,000,000	−45,000,000
Ottoman Empire	6,225,000,000	567,000,000	1,435,000,000	1,000,000

Country	Population	Home production ($)	Underground economy ($)	Environmental externalities ($)
Bohemia	1,200,000	1,250,000,000	5,770,000,000	−1,560,000,000
Silesia	160,000	75,000,000	128,000,000	−45,000,000
Bavaria	425,000	386,000,000	1,450,000,000	−523,000,000
Saxony	760,000	146,000,000	250,000,000	−820,000,000
Ottoman Empire	800,000	432,000,000	654,000,000	−396,300,000

Endnotes

1. http://databank.worldbank.org/data/reports.aspx?source=2&country=CHN&series=&period=, http://www.bjreview.com/Opinion/201510/t20151016_800040481.htm, and http://www.nytimes.com/2010/08/16/business/global/16yuan.html?_r=0.

2. To find out more about the chain-weighted index, see this explanation from the Federal Reserve: http://www.frbsf.org/publications/economics/letter/2002/el2002-22.pdf.

3. http://www.tradingeconomics.com/hong-kong/gdp-per-capita-ppp.

4. Below certain thresholds, some earnings from self-employment don't need to be reported, so failure to report isn't necessarily against the tax laws. In any case, if they're not reported, those activities are not captured in GDP calculations.

5. https://openknowledge.worldbank.org/bitstream/handle/10986/3928/WPS5356.pdf?sequence=1.

6. Ibid.

7. http://www.nytimes.com/2007/08/26/world/asia/26china.html?pagewanted=2.

8. http://data.worldbank.org/country/equatorial-guinea.

The Cost of Living

Learning Objectives

LO 8.1 Understand the importance of a market basket in tracking price changes.

LO 8.2 Calculate and use a price index to measure changes in the cost of living over time.

LO 8.3 Name the two main challenges the BLS faces when measuring price changes and outline how it responds to these challenges.

LO 8.4 Calculate the inflation rate and recognize alternative measures.

LO 8.5 Use a price index to adjust nominal variables into real variables.

LO 8.6 Understand how indexing keeps the real value of a payment constant over time.

LO 8.7 Explain what purchasing power parity is.

LO 8.8 Use a price index to calculate PPP-adjusted variables and compare the cost of living across different places.

THANK YOU FOR NOT SMOKING

Tucked in among the signs and ads on commuter trains in Massachusetts is a small notice that says, "No smoking—General Laws Chapter 272, Sec 43A—Punishable by imprisonment for no more than 10 days or a fine of no more than one hundred dollars." It's the kind of sign that you'd glance at and quickly forget. But when you think about the crime and the two possible punishments (10 days in jail or paying $100 cash), it's a pretty imbalanced trade-off. Surely, most people would choose to pay $10 a day to avoid jail. What is the point of giving both options when one is clearly worse than the other?

To understand the reasoning behind the two punishments, it helps to know one fact: The no-smoking law was written in 1968. Back then, a Hershey Bar cost 5 cents and a box of cornflakes cost 29 cents. Today a box of cornflakes costs $3.79. Back then, it would take nearly eight days working at McDonald's to earn $100. Today it would take about two days at the current federal minimum wage of $7.25 per hour.

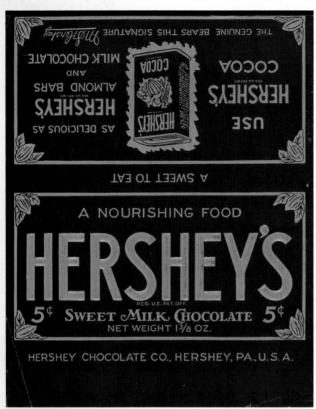

Courtesy of Hershey Community Archives, Hershey, PA

Clearly, prices and wages are much higher today than they were in 1968. When the fine was originally set, $100 went a long way. It also took a long time to earn. As prices increased over time, $100 bought less and less, and the opportunity cost of paying the $100 fine fell. In contrast, 10 days is still 10 days. As a result, what might have been a tough choice when the law was written—the fine or the jail time—now seems an easy trade-off.

The smoking fine draws our attention to an important idea: A dollar now is very different from a dollar in the past. More generally, it reminds us that a "dollar" is just a word or a piece of paper. What really matters is what we can buy with the dollar—and what we can buy with a dollar changes over time.

When we talk about what a dollar actually buys, we are talking about the *cost of living*. When we say the cost of living has gone up, we mean that, looking broadly over a range of goods and services, a dollar buys less today than it used to buy.

In this chapter we'll describe the most important measures of changing prices. In the first part of the chapter, you'll see how to measure changes of prices over time. In the second part, you will see why prices differ among countries and how to measure these differences. Along the way, you'll get a sense of how the cost of living factors into everything from how far your paycheck will stretch, to debates over the size of Social Security, to how many poor people live on the planet.

The Cost of Living

In Chapter 7, "Measuring GDP," we discussed how to measure output on a national level. Now we turn our attention to the second pillar of macroeconomic data: prices. Before, we calculated real GDP to see how output increases over time, independent of price changes. Now, we want to focus on the price changes themselves.

Measuring prices in a national economy helps us answer the question, "What's a dollar (or euro or yen or peso) worth?" This question is trickier than it might sound. What a dollar will buy you changes from year to year as the prices of goods rise or fall (but usually rise) over time. It also changes as you go from place to place. In general, a dollar will get you a lot more in Iowa City, Iowa, than in New York City, New York.

Of course, people earn more money now than they used to. And, on average, people earn more in New York City than they do in Iowa City. If higher income goes with higher prices, people's actual ability to consume the things they want may remain the same. The key to understanding the cost of living is to look at the full picture.

If all prices and incomes rose at the same rate everywhere in the world, tracking the cost of living would be a simple accounting question. What makes it an interesting and important macroeconomic topic is the fact that, in the real world, prices change at different speeds across time and place. Those differing speeds have effects on people's economic behavior. For example:

- At any given time, wages might be rising more slowly than the price of consumer goods. That difference effectively shrinks your ability to buy things.
- Or if you have $5,000 in student debt, rising price levels mean that the real value of that debt (in terms of the quantity of goods and services you have to give up in order to pay back the loan) is getting smaller over time.
- Or suppose you have competing job offers in New York City and Iowa City, Iowa. You will want to consider not only the salaries offered but also the costs of living in both places.

The cost of living can differ greatly, even for two cities in the same country, as shown in the Real Life box "The costs of living in New York City vs. Iowa City."

Real Life

The costs of living in New York City vs. Iowa City

"I want to wake up in that city that doesn't sleep," sang Frank Sinatra. "I want to be a part of it, New York, New York."

Waking up in the city that doesn't sleep isn't cheap, though. Today, New York City is the most expensive city in America. A simple one-bedroom apartment can cost thousands of dollars a month in rent. In fact, the median price of homes in Manhattan exceeds $485,000; the U.S. median is about $222,700. Other things are quite expensive as well. According to online price-tracker Numbeo, "cheap" eats in New York City will cost you about $18. A swankier three-course dinner is going to cost at least $80 per person.

Using the same price-tracker, we can compare the relative expense of living in different U.S. cities. It turns out that groceries in Manhattan cost 32 percent more on average than in Iowa City, and rent costs about 200 percent more. You can rent a one-bedroom apartment in Iowa City for about $600, less than you would pay for a walk-in-closet-sized apartment in Manhattan.

As you would expect, though, people also get paid more in New York City. The latest data from the U.S. Census show the median NYC household income is $52,737. Iowa City has a median income of $42,119. That's a difference in incomes of 20 percent.

The income difference is pretty substantial, but it's less than half of the difference in prices. In other words, the median household in Iowa City is substantially better off than the median household in New York City, at least in terms of the quantity of goods and services they can afford to buy.

Why, then, do people choose to live in New York City? Why doesn't everyone prefer to move to places like Iowa City? We can deduce that people who choose to live in Manhattan get some kind of additional utility from their choice, worth many thousands of dollars a year to them. But if living in a "city that doesn't sleep" isn't your thing, you're likely to find greater happiness—and cheaper meals—in another part of the country.

Sources: www.numbeo.com; http://www.bestplaces.net/col; http://www.dailymail.co.uk/news/article-2971028/Life-90-square-foot-box-Woman-s-apartment-takes-cramped-New-York-living-extreme-does-pay-750-West-Village.html; http://factfinder.census.gov/faces/nav/jsf/pages/index.xhtml.

As these examples show, changing price levels can have real effects on people's incentives and choices. They determine the relative value of your salary, of saving or borrowing, of living in one city or another, and a multitude of other decisions. When you add up all of these microeconomic choices, you can get big macroeconomic effects.

Measuring Price Changes over Time

What does it mean to track how "prices" change? After all, people buy many different goods and services, and each has its own price. For the things you routinely buy, some prices go up and some go down. Some prices move a lot, while some don't budge. For example:

- Perhaps your rent went up over the past year, but the price of gasoline held steady.
- Maybe it became cheaper to buy an older iPhone once the new iPhone came out.
- Maybe the price of clothing rose only slightly since last year, but cable bills went through the roof.

Some of these price changes will matter more to a given consumer than other price changes. The most important factors are how much the price changed (and in what direction) and whether the item is a big part of their total budget. A 10 percent increase in rent (often a big budget item) hurts much more than a 10 percent jump in the price of your favorite shampoo. Consumers can get a rough sense of how changes in prices affect them overall by:

- First considering how much of their spending goes to which items.
- Then using that knowledge to weigh the importance of individual price changes.

The same idea translates to thinking about changes in prices in the overall economy: The idea is to track how individual prices move over time, giving the most weight to the items that account for the biggest shares of a typical consumer's budget. That process can give a measure of how the *overall* cost of living has changed. The aim is a single number that summarizes changes in the prices of many goods, not just one at a time.

But how do we know which goods and services to look at in the first place? How do we weigh the importance of rent versus shampoo for the whole economy? The idea of a "market basket" gives us a method for comparing prices over time and locations.

The market basket

> **LO 8.1** Understand the importance of a market basket in tracking price changes.

When comparing the cost of living across time and place, we have to consider the prices of many different goods and services—housing, food, clothing, transportation, entertainment, and so on. To accomplish this, we construct something that looks like a really long shopping list, called a **market basket**. The list includes specific goods and services in fixed quantities that roughly correspond to a typical consumer's spending. (Who's a "typical" consumer? Good question. We'll come back to that later.)

The goal of creating the market basket is to see how the cost of buying the goods and services on the list changes over time. By keeping goods and quantities constant, we can be sure that any change in the total cost of the basket is caused by a change in prices, rather than the type or amount of things being consumed.

To see how this method works, imagine that you noticed changes from last year to this year in the prices of four items you typically buy at the grocery store:

market basket
a list of specific goods and services in fixed quantities

	Price last year ($)	Price this year ($)
Bread (per loaf)	3.00	3.15
Milk (per gallon)	2.50	2.55
Beef (per pound)	3.50	3.64
Carrots (per pound)	1.00	1.25

How much did the price of groceries increase since last year? It depends on which type of food you look at. The price of bread rose by 5 percent, milk by 2 percent, beef by 4 percent, and carrots by a whopping 25 percent.

Suppose we want to know how much the *overall cost of your groceries* rose—a very reasonable and practical question. To answer it, we have to know how much of each food you typically buy. For instance, if you typically buy a loaf of bread, a gallon of milk, three pounds of beef, and a pound of carrots, then:

(*Remember:* The formula for calculating a percentage change is $\left[\frac{(X_2 - X_1)}{X_1}\right] \times 100$.)

$$\text{Cost last year} = (\$3.00 \times 1) + (\$2.50 \times 1) + (\$3.50 \times 3) + (\$1.00 \times 1) = \$17.00$$

$$\text{Cost this year} = (\$3.15 \times 1) + (\$2.55 \times 1) + (\$3.64 \times 3) + (\$1.25 \times 1) = \$17.87$$

$$\text{Price increase from last year to this year} = \left[\frac{(\$17.87 - \$17)}{\$17}\right] \times 100 = 5.1\%$$

This is the *basket approach.* It measures changes in the cost of your shopping basket, assuming that you buy the same items in the same quantities. This approach gives us a *single number* to measure how much your total costs rise over time.

Someone might ask, "Why not just average the increase in the price of each grocery item (bread, 5%; milk, 2%; beef, 4%; carrots, 25%)?" If we did that, we would get a completely different—and wrong!—answer:

$$= \frac{(5\% + 2\% + 4\% + 25\%)}{4}$$

$$= 9\% \text{ (Remember, } this\ answer\ is\ wrong!)$$

Why would this calculation be wrong? You don't spend nearly as much on carrots as you do on beef or milk or bread. Therefore, the relatively big increase in the price of carrots doesn't affect you as much as the average of the percentage increases would suggest. After all, we want a meaningful answer to the original question, "How much did the price of groceries increase since last year?" To get that answer, what we really want to know is how much more it will cost when you take your usual basket of groceries to the store checkout.

Of course, most people don't buy exactly the same thing all the time, especially when they see that prices are changing. In fact, we know that when prices rise, quantity demanded usually falls. In reality, you might decide to buy less beef and switch from carrots to potatoes. If we allowed your basket to change, though, we'd be capturing both the change in prices and the change in your behavior. To focus on the price change alone, we have to keep the basket fixed, even though we know that is not an entirely realistic simplification.

We'll come back to ways of dealing with this challenge later in the chapter. For now, the basket approach gives us a way to capture lots of different price changes in a single number that (approximately) represents the purchases of a typical consumer.

Consumer Price Index

LO 8.2 Calculate and use a price index to measure changes in the cost of living over time.

The basket approach allows us to track changes in the cost of living. To summarize these changes, we construct a **price index**. It measures how much the cost of a market basket has risen or fallen relative to the cost in a base time period or location.

The most commonly used index tool for tracking changes in the cost of living in the United States is the **Consumer Price Index, or CPI**. The CPI tracks changes in the cost of a basket of goods and services purchased by a typical U.S. household. It is calculated by the Bureau of Labor Statistics (BLS), a statistical agency in the U.S. federal government.

The method for calculating the CPI is relatively simple. First, the BLS comes up with a basket of goods and services purchased by a typical household. Then, every month it collects data on the prices of those goods and services in a variety of places around the country. Using these data, the BLS calculates the cost of buying that market basket.

The CPI measures the increase in the cost of the market basket relative to the cost in a given base year. For instance, suppose that the cost of the market basket was $40,000 in 2015 (the base year) and $40,400 in 2016. To find the index for 2016 relative to 2015, we use the following formula:

price index
a measure showing how much the cost of a market basket has risen or fallen relative to the cost in a base time period or location

Consumer Price Index (CPI)
a measure that tracks changes in the cost of a basket of goods and services purchased by a typical U.S. household

EQUATION 8-1

$$\text{CPI} = \frac{\text{Cost of desired-year basket in base-year prices}}{\text{Cost of base-year basket in base-year prices}} \times 100$$

$$= \left(\frac{\text{Basket}_{\text{desired-year}}}{\text{Basket}_{\text{base-year}}}\right) \times 100$$

$$= \left(\frac{\text{Basket}_{2016}}{\text{Basket}_{2015}}\right) \times 100$$

$$= \left(\frac{\$40,400}{\$40,000}\right) \times 100 = 101$$

In the base year, by definition, the index will always be 100. In future years:

- If the cost of the basket rises higher than the base-year cost, the index will be more than 100.
- If the cost of the basket falls below the base-year cost, the index will be less than 100.

In our example, with 2015 as the base year, the CPI increases from 100 to 101. This change implies a 1 percent increase in the basket of consumer goods. That 1 percent increase also means a 1 percent increase in the cost of living for a typical household.

The BLS's stated goal for the CPI is to answer the question, "What is the cost, at this month's market prices, of achieving the standard of living attained in the base period?" In other words, the CPI helps us understand how the cost of living today compares with the cost of living at some time in the past. In the (hypothetical) example above, the CPI tells us that the cost of living in 2016 was 1 percent higher than it was in 2015. As Figure 8-1 shows, the CPI has risen consistently over the last hundred years.

FIGURE 8-1

CPI from 1913 to 2015 Prices increased more dramatically in the second half of the last century than they did in the first half. Over the first 50 years, prices tripled. In 2015, prices were approximately eight times greater than they were in 1963.

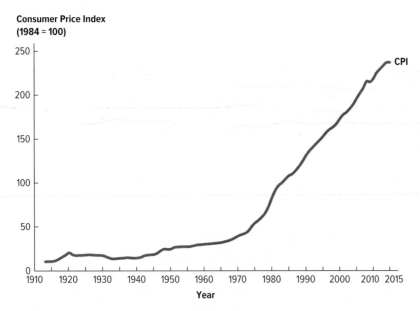

Source: http://inflationdata.com/Inflation/Consumer_Price_Index/HistoricalCPI.aspx?reloaded=true

> **! HINT**
>
> Figure 8-1 happens to use 1984 as the base year. In other words, the index for 1984 was 100, and the indexes for other years are numbers relative to 1984. An index of 105, for example, means prices were 5 percent higher than in 1984.
>
> What would happen to the graph if a different base year had been chosen? The shape of the graph would be exactly the same, though the index numbers would be scaled to a different base year.

The challenges in measuring price changes

LO 8.3 Name the two main challenges the BLS faces when measuring price changes and outline how it responds to these challenges.

The idea behind the CPI is straightforward, but turning that idea into reality requires addressing two big challenges:

- The first is to figure out which goods should go into the market basket so that the CPI reflects the average purchases of the widest group of people.
- The second is how to measure changes over time. Take this simple question as an example: Is it a price increase if a computer costs 10 percent more but is also 10 percent faster?

In this section, we'll address both of these challenges in turn.

Which goods?

The first question is, *which goods* should go into the market basket to measure price changes? Your next-door neighbor may love carrots, and you may love beef. As a result, your grocery bills will probably look very different, and they will increase at different rates as the prices of carrots and beef change. There is no way to have a single number that perfectly describes changes in the cost of living for everyone because people buy different things. The best we can do is to come up with a basket that tries to represent a "typical" household.

Who is typical? The CPI is based on an average of the goods and services purchased by "urban consumers"—anyone living in a city of 2,500 or more. This accounts for 81 percent of the U.S. population; it includes people in all sorts of jobs as well as unemployed and retired people. It doesn't, however, include people living in rural areas, members of the military, or the "institu-tionalized" population (mostly people living in prisons or mental hospitals).

The CPI tries to balance out the consumption of different types of people in different life stages and situations. Rather than representing the exact consumption of any particular house-hold, it is an average across a very large group of U.S. consumers. A particular family's cost of living might increase more or less than the CPI, depending on exactly how much of which things the family buys. Figure 8-2 shows the breakdown of spending in 2015 in the average urban-consumer household across eight major categories.

Changes over time: Substitution and innovation

Earlier, we noted that a price index like the CPI measures pure price changes only if the types and quantities of goods in the market basket remain constant. However, there is an accuracy trade-off involved: Keeping the basket fixed accurately isolates price changes from behavior changes. However, when real people's behavior has changed enough, keeping the basket fixed also means that it will no longer accurately represent the consumption of a typical household.

Price indexes have to deal with the fact that as tastes and prices change, households tend to buy different goods and services. There are two main reasons for changes in consumption pat-terns over time—substitution and innovation.

FIGURE 8-2

Spending by urban consumers represented in the CPI   This bar chart shows how much prices in certain sectors are weighted in the calculation of the Consumer Price Index. By far, the largest component of the Consumer Price Index is housing costs, at over 40 percent. The next two largest components are transportation, followed by food and beverage, which together make up about a third of the CPI. The rest of the categories together comprise the final quarter.

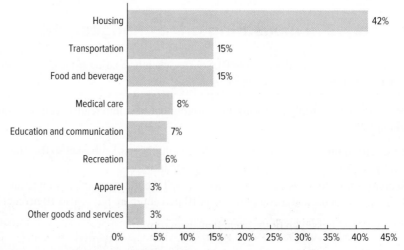

Source: U.S. Bureau of Labor Statistics, http://www.bls.gov/cpi/cpiri_2015.pdf

Substitution is the idea that people switch between similar goods and services when relative prices shift. For example:

- If the price of carrots goes up by 25 percent while the prices of other vegetables increase by a smaller amount, people will tend to buy fewer carrots and more other vegetables.
- If the price of going out to the movies goes up and the price of streaming video goes down, people will tend to watch more videos at home and fewer at the movie theater.

If the market basket doesn't reflect the fact that people buy less of particular goods as they get more expensive, it will overstate actual changes in the cost of living.

The second reason why the market basket has to change over time is *innovation:* As new goods and services become available, people change what they consume. When the CPI was first calculated during World War I, for example, it did not include refrigerators, washing machines, telephones, computers, and many other goods that almost all households today purchase at one time or another. Some of these things couldn't be bought at any price because they hadn't been invented. Others existed but hadn't made it into the general consumer market yet.

The BLS does occasionally update the basket used to calculate the CPI, to account for both substitution and new products. These updates undermine the idea of comparing a *constant* basket of goods and services. But the underlying aim is to capture the cost of achieving a certain *standard of living.* Creating a basket that balances these competing goals requires some tricky judgment calls.

Similar judgment calls are required when products get better. For example, cars today are far safer, are more reliable, and offer more features than did those in the 1950s. So if cars are more expensive now than they were in the 1950s, how do we tease apart the fact that the price of the basic product has increased from the fact that car quality is now higher? If a higher price represents higher quality, the true cost of living may not actually have increased.

Think about the reverse situation: Suppose that the price of a car stayed the same, but its features improved. We would say that the cost of living has fallen because you are able to achieve higher well-being for the same price. In the same sense, if the price of the car increases as its features improve, the cost of living may actually be constant, as you pay more but also achieve greater well-being.

The question is how we weigh the quality change against the price change. In trying to make these judgment calls, the BLS has to attempt something called *hedonic quality adjustment:* It tries to estimate what the price of the item would be *without* the improved features.

✓CONCEPT CHECK

- ☐ What is the purpose of a market basket? **[LO 8.1]**
- ☐ What is a price index? **[LO 8.2]**
- ☐ Does the CPI show price changes for people living in rural areas? **[LO 8.3]**
- ☐ Name the two challenges that complicate the calculation of inflation. **[LO 8.3]**

Using Price Indexes

Now that we know how to measure price changes over time, what do we *do* with that knowledge? As we saw with GDP in Chapter 7, "Measuring GDP," many economic variables give an incomplete picture when expressed in nominal terms—that is, without accounting for price differences. To solve this problem, we can use price indexes to turn nominal variables into real ones.

Using price indexes, we can isolate changes in prices from changes in fundamentals like income and output and can express those changes in constant dollars relative to a base year. Those changes are captured in the **inflation rate**, which represents the size of the change in the overall price level. The inflation rate is one of the central concepts in macroeconomics. In this section we'll discuss how to calculate the inflation rate and how to use it.

inflation rate
the size of the change in the overall price level; the percent change in a price index such as the CPI from year to year

The inflation rate

LO 8.4 Calculate the inflation rate and recognize alternative measures.

The inflation rate is the percent change in the CPI from year to year, calculated as follows:

EQUATION 8-2 $$\text{Inflation rate} = \left[\frac{(\text{CPI}_{year2} - \text{CPI}_{year1})}{\text{CPI}_{year1}}\right] \times 100$$

Table 8-1 shows increases in the CPI from 2005 to 2015, using an average of prices in 1982–84 as the base period (when the CPI = 100). If we want to know how much prices have increased since the base period, the change in the CPI provides a direct answer. For instance, the 2005 CPI of 195.3 means that price levels in 2005 were 95.3 percent higher than they were in the base period, 1982–84.

When you read about inflation in the news, it is typically expressed as an increase over the *previous year*. For example, what if we want to compare 2006 to 2005, rather than to 1982–84? We can calculate the percent increase in prices from year to year as follows:

$$\text{Inflation rate}_{2006} = \left(\frac{\text{CPI}_{2006} - \text{CPI}_{2005}}{\text{CPI}_{2005}}\right) \times 100$$

$$= \left(\frac{201.6 - 195.3}{195.3}\right) \times 100 = 3.2\%$$

An inflation rate of 3.2 percent means that the overall price level increased at that rate between 2005 and 2006.

If you follow news reports on the economy, you may hear discussion of two different inflation measures:

- *Headline inflation* measures the changes in prices for the entire market basket of the average urban consumer. It's simply another term for inflation measured using the CPI.

- *Core inflation* measures price changes with food and energy costs taken out of the market basket.

TABLE 8-1

Calculating the inflation rate

To calculate the inflation rate, subtract the CPI of the previous year from the current year and then divide by the CPI of the previous year. In most years, prices have increased, but in 2009, there was negative inflation, or deflation.

Source: The base period (when the CPI = 100) is 1982–1984. U.S. Bureau of Labor Statistics and http://inflationdata.com/ Inflation/Consumer_Price_Index/ HistoricalCPI.aspx? reloaded=true.

Year	CPI	Calculation	Inflation rate(%)
2005	195.3	—	
2006	201.6	$\frac{201.6 - 195.3}{195.3} \times 100$	3.2
2007	207.3	$\frac{207.3 - 201.6}{201.6} \times 100$	2.8
2008	215.3	$\frac{215.3 - 207.3}{207.3} \times 100$	3.9
2009	214.5	$\frac{214.5 - 215.3}{215.3} \times 100$	−0.4
2010	218.1	$\frac{218.1 - 214.5}{214.5} \times 100$	1.7
2011	224.9	$\frac{224.9 - 218.1}{218.1} \times 100$	3.1
2012	229.6	$\frac{229.6 - 224.9}{224.9} \times 100$	2.1
2013	233.0	$\frac{233.0 - 229.6}{229.6} \times 100$	1.5
2014	236.7	$\frac{236.7 - 233.0}{233.0} \times 100$	1.6
2015	237.0	$\frac{237.0 - 236.7}{236.7} \times 100$	0.1

Why have two different measures? Compared to many goods, energy and food prices go up and down a lot. Because they might be very high or very low at the time the CPI is calculated, including them might over- or understate the real change in overall prices. On the other hand, most Americans spend a large part of their income on food and gas. Any basket that does not include these goods is missing a large part of the cost-of-living picture. Looking at both headline and core inflation can give us a more accurate sense of what's really happening in the economy.

Alternative inflation measures

The difference between headline and core inflation suggests a more general idea: We can measure inflation using *any* basket of goods or price index we want. The resulting measures of inflation will reflect changes in the prices of different sets of goods. The CPI focuses on prices *paid by consumers.*

What if we are more interested in the costs that businesses, rather than consumers, are facing? An alternative price index, the *Producer Price Index (PPI),* measures the prices of goods and services purchased *by firms.* The PPI includes things that are not part of the typical person's consumption basket, such as industrial machinery. Because increases in input prices eventually make it to consumers when they buy the final product, the PPI is considered a good predictor of *future* consumer prices. Regardless of whether we use the CPI or the PPI, inflation is measured as a *percent increase in the index from one year to the next.*

Another alternative is to calculate the inflation rate using the *GDP deflator,* as we did in Chapter 7, "Measuring GDP." The GDP deflator measures price changes for *everything produced in the country.* It doesn't, though, include goods produced abroad that might have a real effect on the typical household's cost of living, such as oil. Another key difference is that the GDP deflator is computed using the actual quantities that are produced in the economy each year, rather than using a "fixed" basket of goods.

All three measures of inflation—CPI, PPI, and GDP deflator—are useful; they simply measure different things. In practice, inflation rates calculated using the three methods track each other quite closely. Figure 8-3 shows inflation rates in the United States using each measure over the last 55 years.

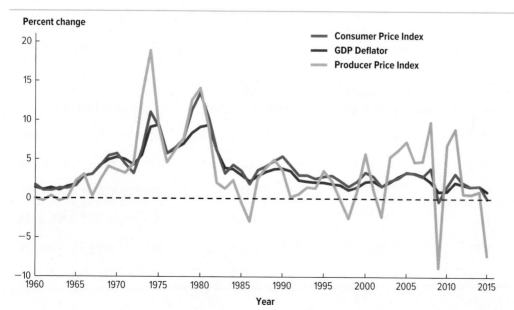

FIGURE 8-3

U.S. inflation rates, as measured by the CPI, PPI, and GDP deflator, 1960–2015

This graph shows the three main measures of inflation over the past 55 years. All three show similar trends in the rise and fall of prices. The Producer Price Index shows the most dramatic ups and downs, while the GDP deflator shows more restrained changes.

Source: U.S. Federal Reserve Bank of St. Louis—FRED, http://research.stlouisfed.org/fred2/.

Deflating nominal variables

LO 8.5 Use a price index to adjust nominal variables into real variables.

Often, we want to study how the real value of a variable, such as income, has changed over time. To do this, we can use the CPI (or another price index) to "deflate" the nominal variable and state it in constant, real terms.

You might be surprised, or even shocked, if your grandparents told you how much money they made in their younger days. For instance, in 1969, a salary of $20,520 would have allowed your grandparents to live a comfortable life, send their kids to college, and put away a little for retirement. When your grandparents retired 45 years later, in 2014, that income would have been below the federal poverty line for a family of four.

Suppose we want to know how much money your grandparents would have to earn now to have purchasing power equivalent to their income in 1969. To compare changes in purchasing power over time, we can translate nominal income in any past year into constant, real dollars. Equation 8-3 shows how any dollar amount from the past can be translated into its current value.

EQUATION 8-3   Value of year-X income in year-Y dollars

$$\text{Real value}_{\text{yearY}} = \text{Nominal value}_{\text{yearX}} \times \left(\frac{\text{CPI}_{\text{yearY}}}{\text{CPI}_{\text{yearX}}} \right)$$

Let's apply this equation to find the purchasing power of $20,520 in 2014 dollars. We multiply $20,520 by the ratio of the CPI in 2014 and 1969:

$$\text{Real value}_{2014} = \text{Nominal value}_{1969} \times \left(\frac{\text{CPI}_{2014}}{\text{CPI}_{1969}} \right)$$

$$= \$20,520 \times \left(\frac{236.7}{36.7} \right)$$

$$= \$132,346$$

What does this result mean? It means that in 2014 you would have needed $132,346 to buy the amount of goods and services your grandparents would have been able to buy with $20,520 in 1969. It turns out that they were doing pretty well, after all.

We can make this same calculation with any base year and any nominal variable. For instance, suppose we want to know how much of the increases in the incomes of the wealthy are attributable to inflation and how much they represent an increase in real wealth. The first two columns of Table 8-2 show average income for the top 20 percent of the population in nominal terms. The

TABLE 8-2

Calculating the deflation of nominal variables

At first glance, the average income of those living in 1969 looks much lower than in 2014. When 1969 incomes are inflated so that the value of these dollars is the same between the two decades, the gap decreases.

Sources: Income data from the U.S. Census, https://www.census.gov/hhes/www/income/data/historical/families; CPI data from http://inflationdata.com/Inflation/Consumer_Price_Index/HistoricalCPI.aspx?reloaded=true.

Year	Average income of top 20 percent ($)	CPI (1982–84 = 100)	Value in 2014 dollars
1969	20,520	36.7	$20,520 \times \left(\frac{236.7}{36.7}\right)$ = **$132,346**
1979	43,265	72.6	$43,265 \times \left(\frac{236.7}{72.6}\right)$ = **$141,058**
1989	85,529	124.0	$85,529 \times \left(\frac{236.7}{124.0}\right)$ = **$163,263**
1999	135,250	166.6	$135,250 \times \left(\frac{236.7}{166.6}\right)$ = **$192,158**
2009	170,844	214.5	$170,844 \times \left(\frac{236.7}{214.5}\right)$ = **$188,526**
2014	217,021	236.7	217,021

third column shows the CPI for each decade. The fourth column uses the CPI to translate income into a direct comparison of purchasing power in 2014 dollars. These data show that although the cost of living has increased, the income of the wealthiest 20 percent of Americans has increased faster. (How do we know that? We can see that real—inflation-adjusted—income of the group has grown steadily, except in 2009. So, income must have grown faster than prices. If they had grown at exactly the same rate, real income in 1969 would equal real income in 2014.) In other words, increased nominal incomes are partly due to inflation but also partly due to a real increase in purchasing power.

Inflation adjustment can make a huge difference in how we perceive things that happen *now* relative to things that happened *in the past,* as discussed in the From Another Angle box "The wealthiest American?"

From Another Angle
The wealthiest American?

Who would you say is the richest American in history? Bill Gates, maybe? Gates created the first computer operating system, which eventually bloomed into software giant Microsoft. At his wealthiest, he was worth over $101 billion—more dollars than any other individual in U.S. history. Whether that makes him the richest American, though, all depends on how you look at it.

Going backward through history, we find that the nominal wealth of the richest people in a generation keeps shrinking:

- At his death in 1937, John D. Rockefeller's wealth was a puny-sounding $1.4 billion.
- Cornelius Vanderbilt, famous for wealth gained through railroads and shipping, finished with a fortune of $100 million in 1877.
- John Jacob Astor, who had a virtual monopoly on the fur trade, had a final wealth of $20 million in 1848.

If all we did was consider *nominal* dollar amounts, Bill Gates looks vastly wealthier than all of them.

If we adjust those fortunes for inflation, we get a different picture. It's not exactly easy to compare the cost of living of today's multibillionaires with those of yesteryear. Technically, we'd need a constant basket of the kind of goods a typical multibillionaire might purchase. But we can't ask how much it might have cost Astor to buy a Bugatti sports car in 1848 or what Vanderbilt might have paid for a private jet in 1877. Those things didn't exist.

Still, some economists took a stab at translating the fortunes of history into constant 2006 dollars. The result?

- Rockefeller tops the inflation-adjusted list, by a lot. He would have been able to buy $305 billion worth of Cristal champagne and private Caribbean islands had he been alive in 2006.
- Not far behind, at $281 billion, is steel magnate Andrew Carnegie.
- Vanderbilt comes in third at $168 billion.
- Astor's $20 million in 1848 money would buy him $110 billion worth of luxury if he could have spent it in 2006.

As it turns out, Bill Gates doesn't tower over the super-rich from previous eras after all.

Sources: http://www.forbes.com/2007/09/14/richest-americans-alltime-biz_cx_pw_as_0914ialltime_slide_2.html; http://archive.fortune.com/magazines/fortune/fortune_archive/2007/03/05/8401299/index.htm.

Adjusting for inflation: Indexing

> **LO 8.6** Understand how indexing keeps the real value of a payment constant over time.

How can we be sure that wages will keep up with inflation? One fundamental theory in macroeconomics says that, with enough time, wages should naturally rise to offset the effects of inflation, so in the end inflation should not matter to people's well-being and their choices. However, most economists agree that there are times when some prices are changing so fast that the rest of the economy struggles to keep up.

If prices increase faster than wages, for instance, people will experience a drop in their standard of living. Everyone will face a very strong incentive to buy things *now* if they are afraid prices will be higher next week or next month. In that economic environment, inflation can distort economic choices. We'll talk a lot more about problems like these in later chapters, particularly in Chapter 16, "Inflation." For now, let's look at how *measuring* inflation can be an important step toward solving problems that inflation causes.

One very practical application of the CPI is to index payments to inflation. Ida May Fuller was the first-ever recipient of monthly Social Security benefits. When she retired in 1940, she received a check for $22.54. For the next decade, her benefits stayed constant, at $22.54 every month. By 1950, the real value of her Social Security check had fallen by almost half, due to inflation. In 1950, her $22.54 check could buy only $13.37 worth of goods and services, when translated into the purchasing power of 1940.

In the early years of Social Security, no accommodation was made for inflation. Retirees expected to receive the same nominal dollar amount monthly for the rest of their lives. In 1950, Congress looked at the problem faced by elderly people like Ms. Fuller. In signing the Social Security Act in 1935, President Franklin D. Roosevelt had expressed his intent that the law would "give some measure of protection to the average citizen . . . against poverty-ridden old age." With the real value of benefits dwindling every year as the cost of living rose, Social Security's success in protecting the elderly against poverty and hardship was limited. In response, Congress revised the law, to nearly double the value of monthly benefits.[1]

From 1950 to 1974, Congress amended the Social Security Act every few years. Each time, it increased the level of benefits in accord with the cost of living. However, these increases were sporadic and required a concerted effort on the part of lawmakers.

Starting in 1975, Congress implemented a different solution: indexing. **Indexing** automatically increases payments in proportion to the cost of living. Such payments are said to be *indexed to inflation.* Congress indexed Social Security benefits directly to the CPI: If the CPI increases 5 percent, so does the nominal value of monthly benefits. As a result, the dollar amount of benefits has increased most years since 1975, keeping pace with changes in the cost of living.

Indexed payments are usually referred to as *cost-of-living adjustments,* or *COLAs.* In the United States, few salaries or income payments are indexed to inflation (except for those with union contracts, where they are more common). Social Security does have a COLA and affects millions of retirees. Indexing is much more common in other countries. In much of Europe, government employees' salaries receive automatic COLAs, as do retirees' pensions.

The reasoning behind indexing is straightforward: If you want the real value of a payment to stay constant over time, make the adjustment for inflation automatic. The alternative is to rewrite a law or a contract every year—a process that involves more work and less certainty.

However, indexing is not without controversy. To consider some reasons why COLAs can be a mixed blessing, read the What Do You Think? box "COLAs for better or worse."

indexing
the practice of automatically increasing payments in proportion to the cost of living

What Do You Think?

COLAs for better or worse

Cost-of-living adjustments (COLAs) provide increases in payments to offset inflation that occurred in the past year. Without an adjustment for the cost of living, what you could buy with a given wage or Social Security check would shrink steadily. Inflation would eat away at the value of these payments.

Traditionally, COLAs for the 59 million people who receive Social Security have been pegged to the *CPI-W.* This is a version of the Consumer Price Index that registers prices for urban and clerical workers. Some argue that the government should shift to a method more sensitive to the actual spending patterns of the elderly, who buy different things than urban and clerical workers. For example, in 2010 and 2011, retirees did not receive a COLA because the CPI-W stayed constant. However, health care costs increased by over 5 percent in both years. As a result, for the elderly the real value of Social Security payments fell.

One proposed alternative is a measure that uses a price basket geared to elderly consumers. In this alternative, for example, medical costs would represent 11 percent of the total, compared with 5 to 6 percent of the total in the traditional CPI-W.

There often are calls for COLAs to be applied to the minimum wage. Although the cost of living goes up every year, the federal minimum wage is not changed unless Congress decides to do so—which happens rarely. As you can see in Figure 8-4, increases in the minimum wage have not kept up with prices. The result is that the real value of the minimum wage has declined since the 1960s. Overall, the real value of the current minimum wage is about $3.00 per hour less than it was in 1968, although it is almost double the original minimum wage set in 1938.

(continued)

FIGURE 8-4

The real value of the minimum wage   Since the 1940s, the real value of the minimum wage has fluctuated as Congress has adjusted its nominal value to try to keep pace with inflation. Overall, the real value of the minimum wage climbed steadily between 1938 and the 1960s but has generally fallen since that time.

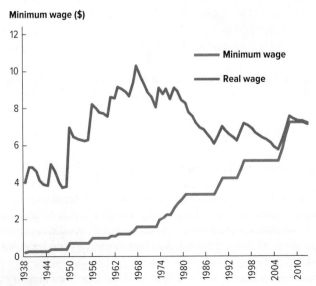

Source: https://www.dol.gov/featured/minimum-wage/chart1.

Some states, such as Washington, Vermont, and Colorado, have set a minimum wage above the federal level, which they adjust for inflation. While this ensures that the real value of the minimum wage stays the same in those states, opponents say that it's unwise to lose the flexibility to adjust the minimum wage as economic conditions change over time. When times are tough, requiring increases in the minimum wage could drive businesses to hire fewer workers.

WHAT DO YOU THINK?

1. Are COLAs an appropriate tool for Social Security? Are they appropriate for the minimum wage?
2. Returning to the chapter-opening example, should COLAs be used to determine fines for breaking laws like the no-smoking regulation on Massachusetts trains? How should the fines be calculated?

Source: http://www.nytimes.com/2011/03/27/opinion/27sun2.html?_r=1; https://www.ssa.gov/news/press/basicfact.html; http://oregonstate.edu/instruct/anth484/minwage.html.

✓**CONCEPT CHECK**

☐ What is the role of the base period when measuring inflation? **[LO 8.4]**
☐ When is PPI, rather than CPI, the appropriate measure of inflation? **[LO 8.4]**
☐ How do differences between real and nominal variables reveal changes in prices over time? **[LO 8.5]**
☐ How does Social Security adjust payments based on changes to the cost of living? **[LO 8.6]**

Accounting for Price Differences across Places

So far, we've seen how to capture the fact that our grandparents paid less for a loaf of bread than we do today. Now, how do we capture the fact that a loaf of bread *today* costs less on average in Mexico than in the United States? Or, indeed, that a loaf of bread might cost less on average in Iowa City than in New York City? Just as we need to adjust economic variables for price changes over time, we sometimes need a tool that allows us to adjust for differences in prices across locations.

In Chapter 7, "Measuring GDP," we mentioned an idea called *purchasing power parity* that enables us to compare the true cost of living in various locations. Here, we explain how it works.

Purchasing power parity

LO 8.7 Explain what purchasing power parity is.

In theory, goods ought to cost the same everywhere, once they have been translated into a common currency using foreign exchange rates. To see why, imagine a pair of jeans that costs less in Mexico than in the United States. Given the difference in price, wouldn't entrepreneurs travel from the United States to Mexico, convert their dollars into pesos, buy the jeans, take them back to the United States, and sell them for a profit?

In principle, yes. These entrepreneurs will continue until the increased quantity of jeans supplied in the United States and the increased quantity demanded in Mexico cause the prices in the two countries to equalize. At that point, no one has an incentive to buy jeans abroad. The result is that purchasing power should theoretically be the same everywhere, when stated in a common currency. This idea is called **purchasing power parity (PPP)**.

purchasing power parity (PPP) the theory that purchasing power in different countries should be the same when stated in a common currency

In reality, PPP almost never holds exactly. Overall price levels are lower in Mexico. For most goods, $100 exchanged into pesos buys you more in Mexico than $100 would buy you in the United States. Why? There are three main factors: transaction costs, non-tradable goods and services, and trade restrictions. Let's briefly consider them.

- **Transaction costs:** One reason that PPP doesn't hold is transportation costs: It costs money to move goods from place to place. However, the difference in PPP is usually larger than what would be explained by transport costs alone; there are other transaction costs also. For example, it costs time and money to find sellers in another country. If the price difference is small and the costs of making transactions in another country are high, the *trade-off* involved may not be worth it. As a result, the entrepreneurs will decide not to bring in less-expensive jeans from Mexico.

- **Non-tradables:** Some goods and services just can't be taken from place to place very easily, or at all. For instance, you can't buy an apartment in Iowa City and transport it to Manhattan. You can't buy a pizza in Italy and transport it to North Dakota. (Well, you could, but it wouldn't be worth eating when you got it there.) You can't buy a haircut in India if you live in New Orleans. (Of course, you could fly to India to get your hair cut, but the transaction costs would be extremely high relative to the few dollars you'd save.) These types of goods and services are called *non-tradables*.

- **Trade restrictions:** Finally, international trade isn't free. There are often tariffs and trade restrictions that increase the cost or difficulty of making exchanges across national borders. Such restrictions discourage people from fully taking advantage of lower prices in other countries.

For these three reasons, we frequently see substantially different prices for individual goods and services, as well as different overall price levels, across countries or locations within a country. For example, the purchasing power of a dollar is higher in Mexico than in the United States and lower in Switzerland. If we want to compare incomes or costs across different countries, we're going to need to adjust nominal prices in different places. This is similar to what we do when comparing standards of living in different time periods. To compare prices in different places, economists have developed the idea of *purchasing power indexes*.

Purchasing power indexes

> **LO 8.8** Use a price index to calculate PPP-adjusted variables and compare the cost of living across different places.

Just as we can use a price index to account for changes in prices over time, we can also construct a price index that describes differences in prices across locations. The methodology is quite similar:

- First, we need to find a market basket of goods and services that we can compare across countries.
- Next, we measure the price of the goods in the basket in each country and calculate the overall cost of purchasing it in each country.
- Then, we build an index showing how much the basket costs in each country relative to some base.

For a simple example, let's think about the price of Big Macs around the world. The *Economist* magazine measures these prices in 120 countries in what it calls the Big Mac Index. The Big Mac isn't a basket that represents the full cost of living, of course. But it has the advantage of being similar in each country, due to McDonald's international production and sourcing policies. It also requires a variety of inputs, such as beef, bread, lettuce, labor, advertising, and real estate.

The Big Mac Index uses the United States as the base country and compares the cost of a Big Mac there to the cost in another country. In the United States, the price of a Big Mac in

January 2016 was \$4.93; in Mexico it was 49 pesos. Remember the theory of purchasing power parity—that purchasing power in different countries should be the same when stated in a common currency. If that theory holds true, Big Macs would have the same real price in the United States and Mexico. In that case, the exchange rate between dollars and pesos should be 9.93 pesos per dollar (49 pesos ÷ \$4.93).

In reality, the official exchange rate between pesos and dollars in January 2016 was 18.02 pesos per dollar. We can calculate the Big Mac Index by comparing the official exchange rate (18.02) to the exchange rate predicted by PPP (9.93):

$$\text{Big Mac Index for Mexico} = \frac{(9.93 - 18.02) \times 100}{18.02}$$

$$= \frac{-8.09 \times 100}{18.02} = -45\%$$

What does a negative Big Mac Index for Mexico tell us? It means that price levels in Mexico are lower than we'd expect if PPP held true. As a result, real purchasing power is higher in Mexico than it is in the United States. That is, if you exchange your dollars for pesos, they'll go further at a McDonald's in Mexico than one in the United States.

A positive Big Mac Index (as in expensive countries like Sweden and Switzerland) would imply that price levels are higher than predicted by PPP. Therefore, real purchasing power is lower in such places than in the United States.

Figure 8-5 shows how price levels differ across a number of countries, using the Big Mac Index and with the United States as the base level.

FIGURE 8-5

The Big Mac Index   The Big Mac Index is one way to measure differences in purchasing power across countries. According to the index, China and other countries in Asia, including Malaysia and Thailand, have a low cost of living. Rich countries generally have costs of living that are similar to that in the United States or even higher.

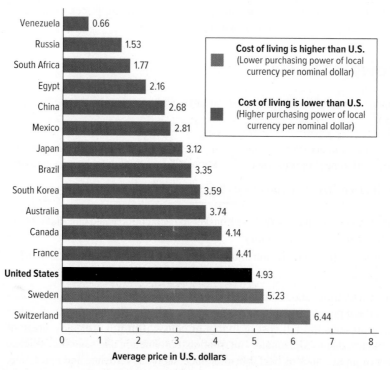

The Big Mac Index is a simple way of looking at price differences. The main measure actually used for international price comparisons is the World Bank's *International Comparison Program (ICP) index.* It uses a broad market basket that tries to represent the full cost of living across countries. The question is how to construct that market basket. People in different places consume different things depending on their culture, climate, religion, and so on. As a result, it's impossible to create a market basket that is "typical" everywhere. The methods behind the idea of PPP are still being improved, but for now, even imperfect PPP data are better than no data at all.

PPP-adjustment

Suppose that we are comparing GDP per capita around the world. What we want from this statistic is some sense of the differences in the average standard of living across countries. If the cost of living varies, the nominal level of GDP per capita will actually mean very different things in different countries.

PPP-adjustment involves recalculating economic statistics to account for differences in price levels across countries. When we do this, we say that we are calculating *PPP-adjusted* variables. PPP-adjustment using a price index is quite similar to adjusting for cost of living increases using a price index like the CPI.

For example, let's calculate PPP-adjusted GDP per capita in the United States and Mexico. In 2014, nominal GDP per capita in the United States was $54,629; in Mexico it was $10,325.[2] The U.S. figure is about five times larger than that for Mexico. But because prices are generally lower in Mexico, we turn to data from the World Bank's International Comparison Program to account for differences in how much one's income can purchase in the two economies. According to the World Bank's PPP index, the purchasing power of a given amount of dollars was about 20.7 percent lower in the United States. In other words, on average, in Mexico goods and services cost about 20.7 percent less than they do in the United States. (Notice that this number differs from that found using the Big Mac Index. This is mainly because the PPP index considers much more than the price of Big Macs. Also, the PPP data are from 2014 and the Big Mac Index is from 2016.)

To find PPP-adjusted GDP per capita of any country relative to the United States, we can use Equation 8-4.

> **PPP-adjustment**
> recalculating economic statistics to account for differences in price levels across countries

EQUATION 8-4   PPP-adjustment

$$\text{PPP-adjusted GDP} = \text{Nominal dollars}_{countryA} \times \left(\frac{1}{1 - \text{Price-level adjustment}_{countryA}} \right)$$

We can plug the numbers for Mexico into this equation:

$$\text{PPP-adjusted GDP} = \$10,325 \times \left(\frac{1}{1 - 0.207} \right)$$

$$= \$10,325 \times 1.2610 = \$13,019.83$$

If we look only at the nominal figure ($10,325), we might think that the average person in Mexico has a standard of living comparable to someone earning that amount in the United States. In reality, as the PPP-adjusted figure shows us, the average Mexican lives about as well as someone who earns $13,019 in the United States.

PPP-adjustment gives us a more realistic sense of differences in living standards around the world. In general, price levels are lower in poorer countries, so PPP-adjustment lets us see that poorer countries are not quite so poor as suggested by their nominal GDP per capita.

✓CONCEPT CHECK

☐ How can transaction costs partially explain differences in purchasing power parity? **[LO 8.7]**

☐ What does the Big Mac Index show? **[LO 8.7]**

☐ Why do economists adjust international statistics based on purchasing power? **[LO 8.8]**

Conclusion

What can a dollar buy? The answer today is not the same as it will be next year, and it's not the same in New York City as it is in Iowa City. The result is that a nominal dollar amount in a particular time or place is just part of the answer. What we really care about is the *purchasing power* of that dollar amount. That's what determines how much you can buy at the store.

In this chapter, we've developed tools that allow us to track changes in the overall price level. These tools help us understand how the purchasing power of a dollar changes over time and across locations. Using the cost of a constant market basket allows us to construct a price index that shows relative price levels over time, such as the CPI. It also allows us to construct price indexes that show relative purchasing power in different places, such as the World Bank's International Comparison Program (ICP) index.

Using price indexes, we can adjust economic variables such as wages, income, GDP, and interest rates to see the difference between their nominal and real values. This lets us answer questions like "What would today's salaries have bought in our grandparents' time?" or "How rich are people in other countries relative to the United States?" It can also help us make better choices when deciding how to invest money, write contracts, or set up policies that account for the effects of inflation.

This chapter and the previous one have introduced the basic language and metrics of macroeconomics. We've discussed output and prices, and how to measure both the size of an economy and the cost of living there. In the next chapter, we'll move to another fundamental economic concern: how to maintain steady employment levels and avoid periods of high unemployment.

Key Terms

market basket, p. 202

price index, p. 204

Consumer Price Index (CPI), p. 204

inflation rate, p. 207

indexing, p. 212

purchasing power parity (PPP), p. 214

PPP-adjustment, p. 216

Summary

LO 8.1 Understand the importance of a market basket in tracking price changes.

To understand how the overall cost of living has increased, we need a way to measure the combined change in the prices of multiple goods, whose individual prices may be changing at different rates. To accomplish this, we can construct a market basket that includes specific goods and services in fixed quantities. By keeping goods and quantities constant, we can be sure that any change in the total cost of the basket is caused by a change in prices, rather than the type or amount of things being consumed.

LO 8.2 Calculate and use a price index to measure changes in the cost of living over time.

To summarize changes in price levels, we can construct a price index, which measures how much the cost of a market basket has risen or fallen relative to the cost in the base year or location. The most commonly used tool for measuring the cost of living in the United States is the Consumer

Price Index, or CPI. It tracks the cost of a basket of goods and services that is representative of the purchases of U.S. households. The price index in a given year is equal to the ratio of the cost of the market basket in that year to the cost in the base year, multiplied by 100. In the base year, the index will always be 100. In future years, if the price of the basket rises, the index will be more than 100. If the price of the basket falls below that in the base year, the index will be less than 100. An index of 120 implies a 20 percent increase in price levels over the base year.

LO 8.3 Name the two main challenges the BLS faces when measuring price changes and outline how it responds to these challenges.

The BLS faces two major challenges in constructing a basket: how to decide which consumption should be measured and how to account for changes in consumption over time. To deal with the first challenge, the CPI is based on an average of the goods and services purchased by "urban consumers," which ends up representing

81 percent of the U.S. population. It also presents two broad measures of this basket, headline inflation (another term for the CPI) and core inflation. Core inflation measures price changes for the CPI market basket, but with food and energy costs taken out. Removing those costs may miss a large part of the inflation picture.

The second challenge comes from changes to consumption and products over time. If the market basket doesn't change to reflect the substitutions consumers make as prices change, it will overstate the effect due to the rising prices. Finally, in trying to measure changes in the standard of living, economists need to tease out differences between mere changes in prices of products versus changes in quality as a result of innovation and technological advances.

LO 8.4 Calculate the inflation rate and recognize alternative measures.

The inflation rate describes the size of changes in the overall price level year to year. It is calculated by measuring the percent change in a price index from one year to the next. *Headline inflation* measures the changes in prices for the entire market basket of urban consumers. *Core inflation* measures price changes with food and energy taken out.

Inflation estimates based on the CPI measure price changes paid by consumers. Estimates based on the Producer Price Index (PPI) measure the prices of goods and services purchased by firms. Estimates based on the GDP deflator measure price changes for everything produced within a country (and thus exclude imports). Unlike the CPI and PPI, estimates based on the GDP deflator do not use a "fixed" basket of goods. In practice, inflation rates based on the CPI, PPI, and GDP deflator track each other quite closely.

LO 8.5 Use a price index to adjust nominal variables into real variables.

One of the most important applications of price indexes is the ability to be able to determine the purchasing power of money from a different time period. This gives the power to see the value of what a certain amount of dollars from the past could buy today, or how much a certain amount of dollars today would be worth in the past. To translate a nominal amount from year X into a constant, real amount in year Y, multiply the nominal value for year X times the ratio of the CPI of year Y divided by the CPI of year X.

LO 8.6 Understand how indexing keeps the real value of a payment constant over time.

Indexing is an important application of the need to adjust nominal values into their real purchasing power.

Recognizing that the purchasing power of money changes over time, payments and paychecks can be automatically indexed to inflation, so that their purchasing power stays equal even as prices change. Indexed payments are often referred to as cost-of-living adjustments.

LO 8.7 Explain what purchasing power parity is.

Purchasing power parity (PPP) is the idea that price levels in different countries should be the same, once they have been stated in a common currency. For a number of reasons—including transaction costs, non-tradable goods and services, and trade restrictions—PPP doesn't typically hold true; the real purchasing power of a dollar differs from place to place.

LO 8.8 Use a price index to calculate PPP-adjusted variables and compare the cost of living across different places.

When we recalculate economic variables to account for differences in purchasing power across countries, we say that we are calculating PPP-adjusted variables. To measure this difference in purchasing power, we can calculate a price index by comparing the cost of purchasing a market basket in each country. If the cost of living is lower than the base country, then PPP-adjusted GDP will be higher than nominal GDP. If the cost of living is higher than the base country, then PPP-adjusted GDP will be lower than nominal GDP.

Review Questions

1. If we want to measure changes in the cost of living, why don't we track differences in each household's *actual* expenditures from one year to the next, rather than the difference in the cost of a market basket? Offer several reasons why this method would fail to capture changes in the overall price level accurately. **[LO 8.1]**

2. There are many different types of market baskets that economists measure. For example, the market basket for consumers—called the Consumer Price Index—tracks the prices associated with the typical consumer's purchases of goods and services. The Producer Price Index tracks the prices of the goods and services purchased by firms. A third type of market basket is the Home Price Index, which tracks the value of residential housing. In what scenarios would each of these market baskets be useful? **[LO 8.1]**

3. Why is the list of the highest-grossing films of all time dominated by movies made within the last 10 years? (*Hint:* Did *Star Wars: The Force Awakens,* released in 2015, really sell considerably more movie tickets than the classic *Gone with the Wind,* or is something else going on?) **[LO 8.2]**

4. How would you use the concept of the Consumer Price Index to compare prices across different locations? **[LO 8.2]**

5. What types of goods and services would a basket measuring the inflation rate for farmers include? Why doesn't the BLS calculate the price levels for a market basket approximating the purchases of farmers? **[LO 8.3]**

6. Does the CPI represent the actual change in the cost of living for any given household? Explain why or why not. **[LO 8.3]**

7. Suppose wages rise in China, leading to an increase in the price of toys imported from China. How would this change affect the CPI, PPI, and the GDP deflator in the United States? **[LO 8.4]**

8. If the growth rate in nominal income is larger than the inflation rate (as measured by the change in the CPI or the GDP deflator), has the real value of income grown? **[LO 8.4]**

9. What is the better measure of inflation to determine how much should be paid to employees for cost-of-living adjustments: the Producer Price Index (PPI) or the CPI? Why? **[LO 8.5]**

10. Why are people unlikely to buy Big Macs in the places where they are relatively cheap according to purchasing power parity and sell them where they are relatively more expensive, in order to make a profit? **[LO 8.4, 8.6]**

11. In many poor countries, even middle-class families may have full-time servants, a luxury reserved for only the very wealthiest households in rich countries like the United States. How does the existence of low-cost domestic help affect PPP-adjusted GDP statistics in poor countries? **[LO 8.7, 8.8]**

12. Would Kentucky, a state with a very low cost of living, have a PPP-adjusted GDP higher or lower than its GDP calculated without PPP-adjustment? Why? **[LO 8.8]**

Problems and Applications

1. Subscribing to the theory that life is indeed a beach, the residents of La Playa spend all of their money on three things: Every year, they collectively buy 250 bathing suits, 600 tubes of sunscreen, and 400 beach towels. Using the data in Table 8P-1, calculate the following. **[LO 8.1]**

   a. The total cost of this basket each year from 2013 through 2016.

   b. How much the price of this basket has changed from year to year in percentage terms.

2. Suppose a typical American consumer purchases three goods, creatively named good A, good B, and good C. The prices of these goods are listed in Table 8P-2. **[LO 8.1]**

   a. If the typical consumer purchases two units of each good, what was the percentage increase in the price paid by the consumer for this basket between 2015 and 2016?

   b. If the typical consumer purchases 10 units of good B and 2 units of both good A and good C, what was the percentage increase in the price paid by the consumer for this basket?

   c. Given your answers to parts a and b, what is the relationship between the market basket and the percentage price change?

3. Using the data in Table 8P-3, calculate the CPI and the inflation rate in each year, using 2010 as a base year. **[LO 8.2]**

4. Table 8P-4 lists the prices and quantities consumed of three different goods from 2014–2016. **[LO 8.2]**

   a. For 2014, 2015, and 2016, determine the amount that a typical consumer pays each year to purchase the quantities listed in the table.

   b. Using the amounts you found in part a, calculate the percentage change in the amount the consumer paid from 2014 to 2015, and from 2015 to 2016.

   c. Why is it problematic to use your answers to part b as a measure of inflation?

   d. Suppose we take 2014 as the base year, which implies that the market basket is fixed at the 2014 consumption levels. Using 2014 consumption levels, now find the rate of inflation from 2014 to 2015 and from 2015 to 2016. (*Hint:* First calculate the cost of the 2014 market basket using each year's prices and then find the percentage change in the cost of the basket.)

TABLE 8P-1

Item (amount purchased)	Price 2013 ($)	Price 2014 ($)	Price 2015 ($)	Price 2016 ($)
Bathing suits (250)	10.00	12.00	15.00	18.00
Sunscreen (600)	4.00	5.00	5.00	6.00
Beach towels (400)	5.00	5.50	7.00	9.00

TABLE 8P-2

Good	Price in 2015 ($)	Price in 2016 ($)
A	10	15
B	5	4
C	1	2

TABLE 8P-3

Year	Price of basket ($)	CPI	Inflation rate
2010	20,000	100	—
2011	21,500		
2012	22,800		
2013	26,150		
2014	28,825		
2015	32,700		

    e. Repeat the exercise from part *d,* now assuming that the base year is 2015.

    f. Why were your answers from parts *d* and *e* different?

5. Which of the following goods have likely required hedonic quality adjustment over time if they were included in the Consumer Price Index (CPI)? **[LO 8.3]**

    a. Laptop computers.

    b. Cellphones.

    c. Salt.

    d. Televisions.

    e. Housing.

    f. Tennis rackets.

6. Use Table 8P-5 to calculate core and headline inflation in each time frame relative to the base year, assuming that each category is weighted equally in the calculation of headline inflation. **[LO 8.2, 8.4]**

    a. 2012 to a base year.

    b. 2016 to a base year.

    c. 2012 to 2016.

7. Table 8P-6 shows the GDP deflator and the CPI over five recent years. By what percent did prices change between years for each measure? Calculate the annual inflation rate and then the inflation rate across the entire time period. **[LO 8.4]**

8. The median American household earned $9,387 in 1973 and $53,657 in 2014. During that time, though, the CPI rose from 44.4 to 236.7. **[LO 8.5]**

    a. Calculate the total growth rate in nominal median household income from 1973 to 2014.

    b. Calculate the total growth rate in real median household income from 1973 to 2014.

TABLE 8P-5

	Food and energy	Other goods and services
2012	120	102
2016	105	107

TABLE 8P-6

Year	GDP deflator	Change in GDP deflator	CPI	Change in CPI
2012	100		100	
2013	105		104	
2014	112		110	
2015	123		113	
2016	127		120	
2012–2016	—			

TABLE 8P-4

	2014		2015		2016	
Good	Price ($)	Quantity	Price ($)	Quantity	Price ($)	Quantity
A	10	10	15	8	20	5
B	5	18	3	30	4	25
C	1	10	2	5	5	10

9. Using Table 8P-7, find the real value of a $1,000 payment to be received each year given the following CPI values. Next, find the amount that this $1,000 should be adjusted to, in order to keep its real value at $1,000. **[LO 8.5, 8.6]**

10. Suppose General Electric paid its line workers $10 per hour in 2015 when the Consumer Price Index was 100. Suppose that deflation occurred and the aggregate price level fell to 80 in 2016. **[LO 8.5, 8.6]**

    a. What did GE need to pay its workers in 2016 in order to keep the real wage fixed?

    b. What did GE need to pay its workers in 2016 if it wanted to increase the real wage by 10 percent?

    c. If GE kept the wage fixed at $10 per hour in 2016, in real terms, what percentage increase in real wages did its workers get?

11. Suppose Table 8P-8 shows the prices of a tall Starbucks latte in countries around the world. Using the data, and the fact that a latte costs $3 in the United States, calculate how much a country's currency is under- or overvalued according to purchasing power. First, calculate the implied exchange rate for each country. Next, calculate the "latte index" for each country using the Big Mac index formula from the chapter. **[LO 8.7]**

TABLE 8P-7

Year	CPI	Real value of $1,000	Cost-of-living adjusted payment
2013	100	1,000	0
2014	103		
2015	105		
2016	110		

TABLE 8P-8

Country	Price	Official exchange rate
Thailand	60 baht	30 baht/dollar
Argentina	15 pesos	6 pesos/dollar
United Kingdom	2 pounds	0.5 pound/dollar
Japan	450 yen	80 yen/dollar

TABLE 8P-9

Office location	Salary ($)	CPI
Cleveland	80,000	100
Miami	120,000	155
New York City	150,000	210

TABLE 8P-10

Country	GDP ($)	Price level (%)
Ona	10,000	6
Rye	12,700	−27
Zolfo	14,100	−10
Avon	23,400	20

12. An employee asks her boss whether she can transfer offices so that she can work in a different part of the country. The boss responds positively and says that the employee can choose to work in Cleveland, Miami, or New York City. The boss then hands the employee a list, as shown in Table 8P-9, of the salaries that she would earn in the different cities and the average price levels in those same cities. **[LO 8.7, 8.8]**

    a. From a standpoint of maximizing the employee's consumption possibilities, which office should she choose?

    b. What would be the minimum salary in New York City the boss could offer the employee to make the employee indifferent between moving to Cleveland and to New York City?

13. Calculate the PPP-adjusted GDP for each of four countries, using the information found in Table 8P-10. **[LO 8.8]**

Endnotes

1. https://www.ssa.gov/history/briefhistory3.html.

2. http://data.worldbank.org/indicator/NY.GDP.PCAP.CD?order=wbapi_data_value_2014+wbapi_data_value+wbapi_data_value-last&sort=desc.

Part Four

Labor Markets and Economic Growth

The two chapters in Part 4 will introduce you to . . .

labor markets and economic growth. As we explore labor markets, we turn to the forces that shape employment patterns in both the long run and the short run. Moving on to economic growth, we turn to the forces that determine why some countries are richer and others are poorer.

Chapter 9, "Unemployment and the Labor Market," discusses how the unemployment rate reflects the struggles of individuals looking for work and why it is considered to be an important barometer of the overall health of the economy. A strong economy has many benefits: Factories and business create new jobs, people find it relatively easier to get work, and unemployment is usually low. But when the economy falters, firms lay off workers to cut production and unemployment is high. Because it acts as a signal of the state of the economy, the unemployment rate is tracked closely from month to month and is influential in government policy and political debates.

Chapter 10, "Economic Growth," focuses on one of the great challenges in economics: How can policy and resources be combined to create healthy economic growth? Growth increases economic opportunities, creates a dynamic business environment, and generates new wealth that allows people to lead more comfortable, secure lives. In recent years, economic growth has lifted hundreds of millions of people around the world out of poverty. In the search for the combination of policies that will lead to economic growth, we look to success stories like the astounding advances in China in the last few decades, and we take cautionary lessons from countries that still search for ways to lift living standards.

Unemployment and the Labor Market

Learning Objectives

LO 9.1   Explain how economists measure employment and unemployment.

LO 9.2   Explain how wage rates above equilibrium cause unemployment.

LO 9.3   Explain why there is a natural rate of unemployment in an economy.

LO 9.4   Explain why there is a cyclical component of unemployment.

LO 9.5   Identify factors that may stop wages from falling to the equilibrium level.

LO 9.6   Describe the challenges policy-makers face when designing unemployment insurance and understand how this and related policies can affect rates of unemployment.

WHAT DOES IT MEAN TO BE UNEMPLOYED?

Rick Alexander is a master builder who spent three decades running a successful home-restoration business in Connecticut. When his elderly parents fell ill in 2008, he gave up his business and moved to Florida to help them. He thought it would be easy to find work—after all, he had a certified trade and many years of experience. He looked first for a job as a supervisor at construction sites but didn't find anything. Lowering his sights, he next looked for work at wholesalers and lumberyards, and then he applied for any job at hardware stores. Still, he experienced a constant stream of rejections. He tried to start his own business, but in the struggling housing market in Florida, he couldn't generate enough sales to make it profitable. Tired of the search, Rick Alexander gave up looking for work.[1]

Alexander's story is frustratingly common, especially during a recession. In tough times, jobs are hard to find. In October 2009, four months after the official end of the "Great Recession," the unemployment rate in the United States rose to close to 10 percent. Unemployment was even higher for certain groups of the population. For young men without a high-school degree, the unemployment rate was close to 30 percent.[2] Even many college graduates struggled to find work and ended up living back at home with their parents.

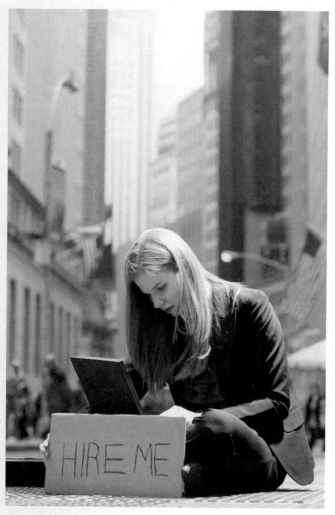
© Sean De Burca/Getty Images

Of course, unemployment exists even when the economy is not in a recession. The natural churning of the labor market causes people to be unemployed for short periods as they move between jobs. That churn is a normal part of economic life. Even when there's no recession, regional unemployment occurs as factories close and when the needs of local employers shift. Such unemployment is made worse when laid-off workers find that their skills no longer match the jobs that are available. Ironically, policies designed to protect workers—like minimum wage laws and unionization—also can lead to unemployment. Although they help existing workers, they often make it harder for those out of work to find jobs.

Some unemployment may be unavoidable, but too much of it can have serious consequences, both for the economy as a whole and on a personal level. One consequence of unemployment is that some of the productive potential of the economy—the time and skills of the unemployed—is not being put to use.

Another consequence is much more personal. Rick Alexander's story shows how prolonged unemployment can be one of the most difficult experiences that a person suffers. It creates uncertainty about the future and can bring on feelings of hopelessness, especially when trying to support oneself and one's family. Studies show that being unemployed is correlated with higher rates of depression and lower assessments of self-worth. Unemployment is an economic problem with potentially serious social and psychological consequences.

Being unemployed can take a mental toll, but the reality is that the difficulties of finding a job are in large part shaped by macroeconomic forces outside of an individual's control. What are these forces? Why does unemployment exist in the first place? These questions pose a puzzle for economists.

We start by assuming that a market reaches an equilibrium where quantity demanded is equal to quantity supplied at the prevailing price. Applying that idea to labor demand and labor supply, the fact that unemployment exists suggests that people want to supply more labor at the prevailing wage than firms are demanding. Why don't wages drop until unemployment is eliminated? In this chapter, we'll investigate the reasons why wages might not drop to an equilibrium level. We'll also see why some unemployment will exist even when the labor market is in equilibrium. As we distinguish between different sources of unemployment, we'll see the logic of different strategies to address the underlying problems.

Defining and Measuring Unemployment

LO 9.1 Explain how economists measure employment and unemployment.

Measuring unemployment turns out to be more complicated than simply counting those who aren't working. The chapter-opening story illustrates some of the complexity: On the one hand, we want to count Rick Alexander as unemployed when he's actively searching for a job. On the other hand, Alexander's retired parents don't have jobs, but they're not interested in getting them. How do we differentiate those two forms of being unemployed? And how do we represent the situation when someone like Alexander gets so discouraged that he stops looking for work? Defining unemployment in a clear and consistent way is an important step toward getting a handle on the underlying issues. In general, **unemployment** occurs when someone wants to work but cannot find a job.

People are unemployed for many reasons:

- Job seekers may be holding out for high salaries.
- Job seekers may lack relevant skills.
- Sometimes job seekers have the right skills and appropriate ambitions but still can't land a job in the current market.

The government's definition of unemployment attempts to capture all of these situations. The Bureau of Labor Statistics, the government agency in charge of collecting employment statistics, defines unemployment in this way:

> Persons aged 16 years and older who had no employment during the reference week, were available for work, except for temporary illness, and had made specific efforts to find employment sometime during the 4-week period ending with the reference week.[3]

This definition means that the United States counts people as being unemployed *only if they meet three criteria:*

1. They didn't work at all in the prior week.
2. They were available to work if they had been offered a job.
3. They were making efforts to look for a job.

Measuring unemployment

In this section, we will put together all the pieces you need to understand the sort of unemployment figures you might see or hear in a news report or a Bureau of Labor Statistics (BLS) official report. These reports are extremely influential in the worlds of business and politics. Everyone wants to know what the latest information about unemployment says about the health of the economy.

First, we need to define some key groups of people. The *working-age population* is the civilian, noninstitutional population aged 16 and over. This category means all adults except those who are in the armed forces (such as soldiers) or who are inmates in an institution (such as prisons or mental facilities).

However, not everyone who is over 16 *wants to work*. In the official definition of unemployment, we want to count only those people who are "available for work" and "making specific efforts to find employment." That means we don't count as unemployed the following categories of people:

- Full-time students.
- Parents who are staying home to look after their children.
- People who cannot work because of a disability.
- People who have inherited wealth and choose to live off that wealth rather than work.
- Retirees. (Some countries define the "working-age population" as 16 to 64, but the BLS does not impose an upper age limit.)

unemployment
situation in which someone wants to work but cannot find a job in the current market

When we want to refer to people of working age excluding those in the categories listed above (full-time students, stay-at-home parents, retirees, and so on), we instead talk about the *labor force.*

labor force
people who are in the working-age population and are either employed or unemployed; people who are currently working or who are actively trying to find a job

The **labor force** consists of people in the working-age population who are either currently working ("employed") or who would like to work and are actively trying to find a job ("unemployed"). That is,

EQUATION 9-1   Labor force = Employed + Unemployed

(The labor force does not include those people in the categories listed above who are in the working-age population but not wanting to work.)

The unemployment rate

unemployment rate
the number of unemployed people divided by the number of people in the labor force

We now have the numbers we need to define the **unemployment rate**, which is the number of unemployed people divided by the labor force:

EQUATION 9-2 $\text{Unemployment rate} = \dfrac{\text{Number of unemployed}}{\text{Labor force}} \times 100$

$$= \dfrac{\text{Unemployed}}{\text{Employed} + \text{Unemployed}} \times 100$$

Table 9-1 shows the official unemployment and employment numbers for the U.S. economy for December 2006 and December 2015. The first date, December 2006, is just before the start of a large economic downturn. The data for nine years later show the lingering effects that a deep recession can have on a labor market. Over this nine-year period, there was an increase in the number of unemployed people, from 6,762,000 to 7,904,000.

Table 9-1 also shows the number of people in the labor force. Dividing the number of unemployed by the size of the labor force gives us the unemployment rate at both dates:

Unemployment rate, December 2006:

$$\frac{6,762,000}{152,732,000} \times 100 = 4.4 \ \text{percent}$$

Unemployment rate, December 2015:

$$\frac{7,904,000}{157,833,000} \times 100 = 5.0 \ \text{percent}$$

TABLE 9-1

U.S. employment statistics

With increases in the working-age population and the number of people in the labor force, the overall number of people employed—as well as those unemployed—increased from 2006 to 2015.

Source: Bureau of Labor Statistics, Table A-1, Employment Status of the Civilian Population by Sex and Age, seasonally adjusted (accessed May 19, 2016), http://www.bls.gov/news.release/empsit.t01.htm#cps_empsit_a01.f1.

The December 2015 unemployment rate tells us that at the end of 2015, approximately 5 percent of Americans who wanted to work couldn't find work.

The unemployment rate describes what is going on in the national economy as a whole but doesn't tell us much about *who* is affected. In general, the unemployment rate varies greatly by educational status, gender, age, and race. On average, younger people have higher unemployment rates than older people, and people with less education are more likely to be unemployed than people with more education. Figure 9-1 shows some comparisons of unemployment among different types of people in the years 2003–2015.

Month	Working-age population (noninstitutionalized)	Labor force	Employed	Unemployed
December 2006	230,108,000	152,732,000	145,970,000	6,762,000
December 2015	251,936,000	157,833,000	149,929,000	7,904,000

FIGURE 9-1
Unemployment rates by demographic group

(A) Unemployment rate by sex

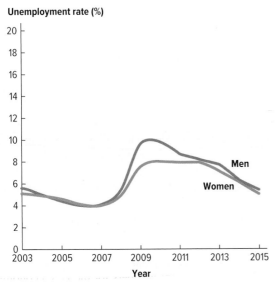

Until the start of the great recession, unemployment rates were the same for men and women. Afterwards, men were far more likely to be unemployed, although this has stabilized in recent years.

(B) Unemployment rate by age

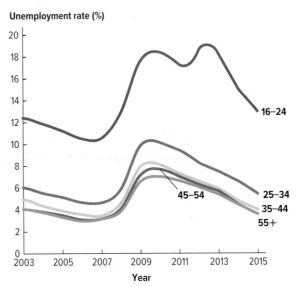

In general, younger people are more likely to be unemployed.

(C) Unemployment rate by race

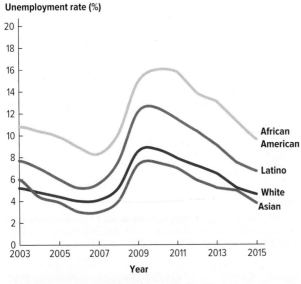

Although the overall trend is the same for all races, African Americans have a much higher rate of unemployment.

(D) Unemployment rate by education level

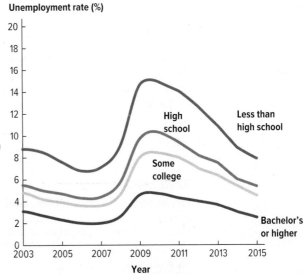

The more education a person has, the more likely he or she is to have a job.

Source: Bureau of Labor Statistics, Table A-2 Employment Status of the Civilian Population by Race, Age, and Sex (accessed April 16, 2013), http://www.bls.gov/cps/tables.htm.

The labor-force participation rate

labor-force participation rate
the number of people in the labor force divided by the working-age population

We can also learn something interesting about the state of the economy by looking at the **labor-force participation rate**, which is the number of people in the labor force divided by the working-age population:

EQUATION 9-3

$$\text{Labor-force participation rate} = \frac{\text{Labor force}}{\text{Working-age population}} \times 100$$

This figure tells us what fraction of the population *wants* to be working, whether or not they actually have a job.

During recessions we usually see the labor-force participation rate fall. Some people who are unemployed eventually give up looking for work, like Rick Alexander in our chapter-opening example. Once these people stop actively looking for work, they are no longer considered part of the labor force. Other people may drop out of the labor force in a recession because they choose to go back to school, or take early retirement, or become homemakers instead of looking for work.

Based on Table 9-1, we can compute the labor-force participation rate in December 2006:

$$\frac{152,732,000}{230,108,000} \times 100 = 66.4 \ \text{percent}$$

This means that 66.4 percent of the total working-age population was in the labor force in December 2006. In December 2015 the labor-force participation rate was:

$$\frac{157,833,000}{251,936,000} \times 100 = 62.6 \ \text{percent}$$

Over the nine-year period, 3.8 percent of the working-age population stopped participating in the labor force. It is likely that at least some of these people would have been unemployed if they had stayed in the labor force. So the unemployment rate of 5 percent in December 2015 may understate the effect of the recession on employment.

Table 9-2 summarizes the two different measures of the U.S. labor market in 2006 and 2015.

TABLE 9-2

Employment in the United States, 2006 and 2015

The unemployment rate in 2015 was higher than in 2006, but the 2015 unemployment rate signaled a big improvement over conditions during the Great Recession (the unemployment rate had hit 10 percent in October 2009). At the same time, however, the percentage of the population participating in the labor force fell between 2006 and 2015.

	Unemployment rate (%)	Labor-force participation rate (%)
December 2006	4.4	66.4
December 2015	5.0	62.6
Change	+0.6	−3.8

Source: Bureau of Labor Statistics (accessed June 22, 2016), http://www.bls.gov/cps/tables.htm.

? POTENTIALLY CONFUSING

When discussing unemployment, people often talk about *percentage point* changes—such as the unemployment rate increasing by 0.6 percentage *point,* from 4.4 percent to 5 percent. Sometimes people talk loosely about unemployment, referring to such a change as unemployment going up by "0.6 percent" rather than by "0.6 percentage point." There is a big difference, although people may guess what is meant by the loose talk.

If we want to, we could, of course, talk about changes in unemployment in terms of percent, rather than percentage points. For example, from 4.4 to 5 is an increase of 13 percent. That would be technically accurate, but you rarely hear economists talk this way.

Talking in percentage *points* makes a change easier to conceptualize: If you hear that the unemployment rate increased by "0.6 percentage point," for example, it means that 6 people out of every 1,000 in the labor force have lost their jobs.

On the other hand, if you hear that an economy's unemployment rate increased by "13 percent," you have no way of knowing how bad the change really is. Maybe the increase was from 1 percent unemployment to 1.13 percent, which would be considered a small change. Or maybe unemployment went from 10 percent to 11.3 percent, which would be considered a more substantial change.

This is why statisticians and economists report changes in percentage points, not percentages, when discussing unemployment.

Beyond the unemployment rate

People often use the unemployment rate to summarize the state of the labor market, but it has significant limitations. Most obviously, it doesn't include people like Rick Alexander, introduced at the start of the chapter. While Alexander was actively looking for work, he was counted as unemployed. Once he gave up hope of finding a job, he was deemed to have dropped out of the labor force and was no longer counted as unemployed.

This seems like a semantic trick. Why should we count Alexander as unemployed when he's feeling optimistic and spends his days sending out résumés, but not when he turns pessimistic and gives up the search? In fact, the Bureau of Labor Statistics (BLS) has a term for people like Alexander: **discouraged workers**. Discouraged workers are people who have looked for work in the past year but have given up looking because of the condition of the labor market. Thinking about discouraged workers gives a broader view of who is affected by a recession.

What about people who have part-time jobs but would like to work full time? Such people are defined as being **underemployed**. So are workers who are in jobs that are not suited to their skill level—for example, a law-school grad who can't get a job in law and reluctantly takes work as a barista at Starbucks. The BLS collects data on the first kind of underemployment (working fewer hours than you would like), but unfortunately not on the second kind (working in a job for which you are overqualified).

In fact, the BLS collects *six* different measures of unemployment, as shown in Table 9-3:

- The first two are "narrow" unemployment rates, counting only people who have been unemployed for a long time (U1) and those who have recently lost their jobs or done temporary work (U2).

discouraged workers people who have looked for work in the past year but have given up looking because of the condition of the labor market

underemployed workers who are either working less than they would like to or are working in jobs below their skill level

Discouraged workers are not counted as unemployed.
© Tony Biddle, Perfect World Design.

TABLE 9-3

Six measures of unemployment

Total unemployment in an economy can be measured using narrower or broader definitions. The BLS reports six main measures, ranging from the narrowest (U1), which includes only those who are chronically unemployed, to the broadest (U6), which includes everyone from the chronically unemployed to those who are already working part time but want to be working full time. The "official" unemployment rate typically cited in the news media is U3.

Category of unemployment	Rate in December 2006 (%)	Rate in December 2015 (%)
U1: Long-time unemployed (more than 15 weeks)	1.4	2.1
U2: Job losers + those who completed temporary work	2.1	2.4
U3: Unemployed	4.4	5.0
U4: Unemployed + discouraged workers	4.6	5.4
U5: Unemployed, discouraged workers + marginally attached workers	5.2	6.1
U6: Unemployed, discouraged workers, marginally attached workers + underemployed	7.9	9.9

Source: BLS Table A-15, Alternative Measures of Unemployment and Underemployment, seasonally adjusted (accessed May 19, 2016), http://www.bls.gov/news.release/empsit.t15.htm.

- The "official" unemployment rate is the one shown in the table as U3.
- The fourth measure combines unemployed plus discouraged workers.
- The fifth measure adds "marginally attached" workers. These people are like discouraged workers in some respects—they would *like* to work, and they have looked for work at some point in the last year. But they don't meet the strict definition of unemployed because, for whatever reason, they haven't looked for a job in the last four weeks.
- The final definition, U6, includes underemployed people with part-time work who seek full-time jobs.

Adding extra dimensions to unemployment measures helps to paint a fuller picture of the labor market. Taking the broadest measure (U6)—which includes discouraged and marginally attached workers and the underemployed—almost 10 percent of the labor force was considered to not be working as much as they would like to in 2015, compared with under 8 percent in 2006.

The other notable change that occurred during the recession is the increasing percentage of people who were unemployed for a long stretch of time:

- In 2006, people unemployed for more than 15 weeks made up only 1.4 percent of the labor force, or approximately a third of all unemployed people.
- In 2015, this number rose to 2.1 percent of the labor force, or more than 40 percent of all unemployed people.

This change shows that unemployment during the recession wasn't just about short stints of joblessness between positions, but also about long-term inability to find work.

Where do the data come from?

The main source of information on unemployment in the United States is a household survey that asks people if they are working and how much they are earning. This survey, performed by the Bureau of Labor Statistics, is called the Current Population Survey. Every month, employees of the BLS survey about 60,000 households. It's not exact—it would be prohibitively expensive to survey every single U.S. household every month—but the sample size is big enough to give a reliable estimate for the economy as a whole.

The survey is collected year-round, allowing the BLS to analyze and adjust for changes in unemployment that are due to the season. If you're a trained ski instructor, for example, you'll more easily find work in February than in August. Farm workers and construction workers are also affected by seasonal changes. The BLS publishes statistics that are *seasonally adjusted* in order to help distinguish these expected seasonal patterns from deeper shifts in economic conditions. The data we show in the tables here are all seasonally adjusted.

✓CONCEPT CHECK

☐ How is the labor-force participation rate calculated? **[LO 9.1]**
☐ Are discouraged workers counted as being unemployed? **[LO 9.1]**
☐ How is underemployment different from unemployment? **[LO 9.1]**

Equilibrium in the Labor Market

LO 9.2 Explain how wage rates above equilibrium cause unemployment.

The existence of *any* amount of unemployment is a bit of a puzzle. Labor is bought and sold in a market, just like other goods and services. There is demand for labor (from firms wanting to hire workers), a supply of labor (from individuals looking for jobs), and a price (called the wage). In most markets, we expect the price to adjust until the market reaches equilibrium, a point at which the quantity supplied equals the quantity demanded. The existence of unemployment suggests that this simplest of models can't fully explain what goes on in the labor market. In this section, we explore the predictions of the simple model. In the next section, we'll add nuance to show that unemployment can arise when the wage is held above the equilibrium level or when real-world frictions prevent labor supply or labor demand from adjusting perfectly to changes in the economy.

As in any other market, the labor market features a demand curve and a supply curve. The demand for labor comes from firms, who need labor to produce output. The **labor demand curve**, depicted in panel A of Figure 9-2, shows the relationship between the total quantity of

labor demand curve
a graph showing the relationship between the total quantity of labor demanded by all the firms in the economy and the wage rate

---

(A) Firms and the labor market

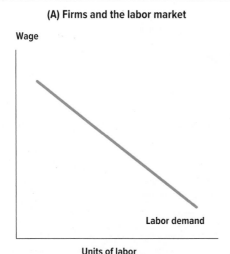

As the price of labor, or the wage, decreases, the amount of labor demanded by firms increases. This relationship is shown by the curve above.

(B) Workers and the labor market

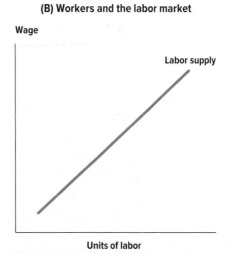

Conversely, as the wage rate increases, workers are increasingly willing to supply labor. This relationship is shown by the curve above.

FIGURE 9-2

Labor demand and labor supply

labor demanded by all the firms in the economy and the wage rate. All things being equal, firms will want to hire more labor when wages are lower and less labor when wages are higher.

The supply of labor comes from people who are able to work and who choose to participate in the labor market. As we have seen, not everyone who could potentially work wants to work. Other things being equal, we expect that across the economy as a whole, people will be willing to supply more labor at higher wage rates and less labor at lower wage rates. The **labor supply curve**, pictured in panel B of Figure 9-2, shows the relationship between the total quantity of labor supplied in the economy and the wage rate.

Together, the labor demand and labor supply curves describe the national labor market, as shown in Figure 9-3. As in any other market, equilibrium occurs at the intersection of the supply and demand curves. At the equilibrium wage, quantity demanded equals quantity supplied: Everyone who wants to work at prevailing wages and has the required skills is able to find a job. Our definition of unemployment—people wanting to work but being unable to find a job at the prevailing wage—is easy to rephrase in the language of supply and demand. The quantity of labor supplied at the prevailing wage (people wanting to work at that wage) is greater than the quantity of labor demanded (jobs offered by firms wanting to hire at that wage). In other words, there is a *surplus* of labor.

Surplus arises in a market when the prevailing price is higher than the equilibrium price. (Look back to Chapter 6, "Government Intervention," if you need to confirm this statement.) Figure 9-4 shows how unemployment occurs when the wage rate is W_1—that is, higher than the equilibrium level of W^*. In this very simple model, unemployment is the gap between the number of people who want to work and the number of jobs offered at the prevailing wage. (However, we'll see in a minute that when a little nuance is added to the model, we can get unemployment even when the wage is not above the equilibrium level.)

Here's the puzzle: Why would wages remain above the equilibrium level? We know what *should* happen in a market when the price is too high: The price should fall until the market reaches equilibrium. Why don't firms offer lower wages, or unemployed people offer to work for lower wages, until the equilibrium wage is reached? In the next section we'll look at several reasons why this might not happen, as well as reasons unemployment occurs even at the equilibrium wage.

labor supply curve
a graph showing the relationship between the total labor supplied in the economy and the wage rate

---

FIGURE 9-3

The labor market in equilibrium

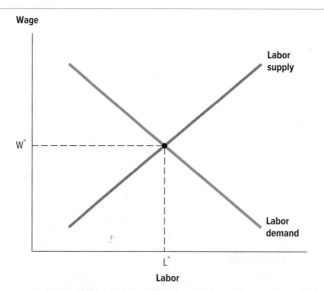

When the labor demand and labor supply curves are put together, this forms a labor market of people willing to buy and sell labor. Like any other market, where the two curves intersect, the market is at an equilibrium, with a stable wage (price) and amount of labor bought and sold.

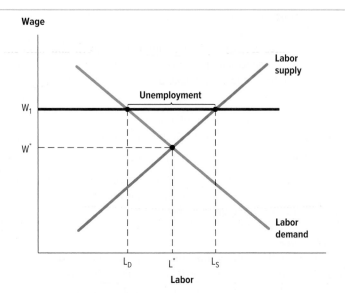

FIGURE 9-4
The labor market with unemployment

When people are willing to supply more labor than firms are willing to hire, the labor market has a surplus of workers, which is also known as unemployment.

✓CONCEPT CHECK

☐ What is the equilibrium price of labor also called? **[LO 9.2]**
☐ What two curves intersect at the labor market equilibrium? **[LO 9.2]**

Categories of Unemployment

To start understanding the causes of unemployment, it's helpful to separate out two categories of unemployment:

- First is unemployment explained by the *natural* rate of unemployment. This is the normal level of unemployment that persists in an economy in the long run.
- Second is *cyclical* unemployment, which describes short-term fluctuations around this long-run norm.

We'll see that some unemployment is an unavoidable part of a dynamic economy, but also that the amount of unemployment is affected by public policy.

Natural rate of unemployment

LO 9.3 Explain why there is a natural rate of unemployment in an economy.

The simplified model of the labor market described in Figure 9-3 suggests that we might reasonably expect to see *zero* unemployment when the market is in long-run equilibrium. The data in the first half of the chapter, however, showed that this is never the case (even when the economy is doing well, as it was around 2005).

Instead, all economies experience some level of unemployment, regardless of how well or badly the economy is doing in the short term. We refer to this normal level of unemployment that persists in an economy in the long run as the **natural rate of unemployment**. The natural rate of unemployment is also sometimes called the *equilibrium rate of unemployment*. Three contributors lead to the natural rate of unemployment: frictional, structural, and real-wage (classical) unemployment.

natural rate of unemployment the normal level of unemployment that persists in an economy in the long run

Frictional unemployment

frictional unemployment
unemployment caused by workers who are changing location, job, or career

19

The first contributor to the natural rate of unemployment is **frictional unemployment**. It is unemployment caused by workers who are changing their location, job, or career. When people search for new jobs, it takes time to search for openings, submit applications, interview, move to a new city, and so on. How long it takes to make a job transition can depend on a lot of factors. These include things like:

- how well-informed workers are about job openings,
- how picky workers are about waiting to find the job that is the best possible match, and
- what resources workers can draw on to support them while they search.

Some amount of frictional unemployment is unavoidable—it's a natural and healthy part of life in a dynamic economy. Jobs in one company open up while others close, and ambitious workers leave their jobs to seek out better positions.

Structural unemployment

structural unemployment
unemployment that results from a mismatch between the skills workers can offer and the skills in demand

The second contributor to the natural rate of unemployment is **structural unemployment**. It is unemployment that results from a mismatch between the skills workers can offer and the skills that are in demand. Consumer preferences are constantly shifting, and new technologies are being invented all the time. As a result, skills that are in demand today may not be in demand next year.

If people could switch effortlessly from a job in a shrinking industry (like auto manufacturing) to one in a booming industry (like online services), then structural unemployment wouldn't exist. However, the reality is that people have educational qualifications, job experiences, and family and community ties that are hard to change in the short run. These qualifications and ties make them better suited for jobs in some sectors and locations than others. A changing economy can lead to a mismatch between the types of jobs that firms are offering and the types of jobs for which people are qualified.

For example, consider the job of travel agent. If you want to book a flight, you probably just go online, right? A couple of decades ago, you would have gone to a travel agent, who would have used a special database of routes and prices to propose an itinerary. The advent of websites such as Travelocity, Kayak, Priceline, and Expedia allows customers to do the travel agent's job for themselves easily and quickly. As a result, demand for the services of travel agents has plummeted; people who trained as travel agents lost their jobs and couldn't find new ones using the same knowledge and skills.

Some degree of structural unemployment is inevitable in an ever-changing economy, but governments can take steps to minimize it. One way is to provide information to unemployed people about which professions are experiencing rising demand for labor. Another way is to subsidize retraining programs for unemployed workers to learn new skills, improving their chances of finding work.

These programs can help, but the changes can take years. If you were a middle-aged, unemployed auto worker, could you imagine moving to a different part of the country to start a new career from scratch?

Real-wage (classical) unemployment

real-wage or classical unemployment
unemployment that results from wages being higher than the market-clearing level

The third contributor to the natural rate of unemployment is **real-wage** or **classical unemployment**. This idea captures the effect of wages remaining persistently above the market-clearing level. It's what we saw in Figure 9-4: Anything that acts like a price floor in the labor market will create surplus labor, which we call unemployment. Explanations include minimum wage laws, bargaining by unions, and strategic choices by employers to pay wages above the equilibrium rate. We'll explore each of these possible explanations later in the chapter.

The common thread in these three different contributors to the natural rate of unemployment is that they reflect underlying features of the economy. As you'd guess, the features can change over time, which can raise or lower the natural rate. For instance, a new policy dramatically raising the minimum wage by $10 an hour would surely raise the natural rate of unemployment. An educational system that retrains laid-off workers could lower the natural rate.

The natural rate of unemployment, however, doesn't go up and down with every boom and bust in the economy. Those short-term fluctuations in unemployment need a different explanation, which we turn to next.

Cyclical unemployment

LO 9.4 Explain why there is a cyclical component of unemployment.

The economy goes through ups and downs over time, which are reflected by changes in GDP growth. Economists call this pattern of ups and downs the *business cycle,* a topic we'll discuss further in Chapter 12, "Aggregate Demand and Aggregate Supply." The business cycle matters for unemployment because it affects the demand for labor:

- When the economy is going strong, demand for workers increases as firms expand their operations.
- When the economy slows down, demand for workers decreases as firms downsize.

Cyclical unemployment is unemployment caused by these short-term economic fluctuations. Because GDP growth tends to go in *cycles,* speeding up and slowing down in a regular pattern, we call the related unemployment *cyclical,* too.

cyclical unemployment
unemployment caused
by short-term economic
fluctuations

Imagine the effect of an economic slowdown as a reduction in the total demand for labor at any wage. In other words, the labor demand curve shifts to the left. In the simple labor-market model, this change would cause the equilibrium to move down along the supply curve, reaching a new equilibrium at a lower quantity of labor and lower wage. Why don't wages simply fall during a cyclical slowdown, so that the market still clears and cyclical unemployment is zero? The typical explanation is that wages are "sticky" in the real world, meaning that they are slow to respond to shifts in the economy.

There are many possible reasons for wage stickiness: Some workers may be on contracts that are difficult to change, or employers may choose not to raise and lower wages all the time because it will upset workers and cause them to not work as hard. The degree of wage stickiness in the real world is a controversial topic, even among economists.

The result of wage stickiness is that actual wages are temporarily above the market-clearing level, which causes cyclical unemployment. When the economy swings back toward the boom part of the business cycle, labor demand will recover and cyclical unemployment will decrease.

Figure 9-5 shows the relationship between GDP and unemployment in the U.S. economy over the last 35 years. When growth goes down, unemployment tends to go up shortly after, and vice versa.

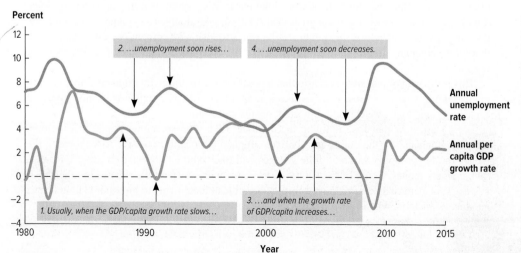

FIGURE 9-5

Cyclical unemployment in the United States   In general, unemployment tends to be higher when GDP growth is low, although this is not always true. Unemployment tends to lag behind overall GDP growth, meaning it will change soon after, but not at the same time as, GDP growth changes.

Source: BEA and BLS, accessed on the FRED (accessed on May 19 2016).

The slight delay, or time lag, makes unemployment what we call a *lagging* or *trailing* indicator. It takes time for changes in the economy to translate into changes in employment. Employers wait to see how bad a recession looks before making the difficult decision to lay off workers. They also wait to see how solid a recovery looks before committing to take on new employees. While playing wait-and-see, firms may first try to decrease or increase the hours of existing employees.

✓ CONCEPT CHECK

☐ What is the natural rate of unemployment? **[LO 9.3]**

☐ Contrast frictional and structural unemployment. **[LO 9.3]**

☐ With what measure does cyclical unemployment tend to move? **[LO 9.4]**

Public Policies and Other Influences on Unemployment

Addressing issues relating to unemployment can be tough. Unemployment is an important indicator of the overall health of the economy. It is also a very personal issue for those who experience it. As a result, discussions about the causes of unemployment—particularly those that have implications for public policy—can get heated.

In this section, we'll break down some of the policies and other factors in the economy that can influence the level of unemployment. Before we get into the details, consider one example of a controversial unemployment-related debate: Do immigrants cause unemployment by taking jobs? See the From Another Angle box "Immigration's effects on the labor market" to see why economists generally disagree that this is the case.

From Another Angle
Immigration's effects on the labor market

Imagine an American worker—we'll call him John. John lives in Charlotte, North Carolina. He's 35 years old and works as a bus driver. Now, imagine a would-be immigrant—we'll call him José. José is a 35-year-old bus driver who lives in Lima, Peru; he makes about a quarter of what John earns.

José decides to move to Charlotte and knocks on the door of the local bus company. He offers to drive John's bus for half of what John earns. It's a great deal for the company since it will save money on wages. It's a great deal for José, who doubles his salary. Unfortunately, it's lousy for John, who loses his job unless he wants to take a 50 percent pay cut. (We assume that John's company doesn't have a union and that the company can hire and fire drivers when it wants.)

This is the kind of plausible scenario that lies behind the rhetoric you often hear about immigrants taking American jobs. It looks like a straightforward case, right? Well, no. Applying some economic logic, we can add important details to the story.

For a start, now that José is living in Charlotte, he is also spending money in Charlotte, increasing demand for the goods and services supplied by local businesses. Also, some of the money the bus company saves on John's wages will likely end up reflected in lower bus fares, saving riders money. Some of the money riders save will get spent elsewhere, in other businesses. This increased demand from consumers will lead local firms to hire more labor. That's good news for John, who is now looking for work.

Of course, this simplified example hides a good deal of complexity in the real-world effects of immigration on labor markets. Transition is painful, and businesses do not always have so much flexibility. And it's not easy for someone like John to get fired and then have to try to find a new job.

The point is that immigration can cause disruptions. But, over time, immigration also can expand the economy, rather than just steal jobs from current workers. The arrival of new workers increases the size of the labor force. It also contributes to economic growth by reducing the costs of production and increasing demand for goods and services. Immigration is a political hot potato for many reasons. Still, our simple example helps to illustrate why economists generally reject the simple assertion that immigration necessarily causes unemployment.

There are winners and losers, as immigrants tend to compete for some kinds of jobs more than others. Let's say there's an influx of new immigrants, many of whom want to find jobs as construction workers. How you see the situation depends on your personal situation. For example:

- It's bad news if you're an American looking for construction work: You face more competition for jobs, driving down wages.
- But it's good news if you're an American who runs a construction company: You now have more candidates to choose from, some of whom might be willing to accept a lower wage. You might earn higher profits, which you will then spend in other parts of the economy, creating demand for labor elsewhere.
- It's also good news if you're an American looking to buy or renovate a house or store, allowing you to get the same services at lower cost.

Rhetoric and emotion can get in the way of seeing the full picture. The political debate more readily focuses on immediate job losses, like the one suffered by John, the bus driver. And it's often hard to put numbers on society's longer-term gains, which tend to be diffuse. Economists see their role as trying to assess all of these trade-offs with as much balance as possible.

Source: Michael Clemens et al., "The Place Premium: Wage Differences for Identical Workers across the U.S. Border" (Center for Global Development Working Paper, 2008).

Factors that may stop wage rates from falling

LO 9.5 Identify factors that may stop wages from falling to the equilibrium level.

In the previous section, we noted that unemployment can be influenced by forces that prevent wages from falling to the market-clearing level, either in the long run (through the natural rate of unemployment) or in response to short-term economic fluctuations (though cyclical unemployment). Why don't wages fall so that everyone with the skills and desire gets a job? In this section we will look at three possible explanations:

- The government might prevent it, through minimum-wage legislation.
- Labor unions might prevent it, through bargaining backed by the threat to strike.
- Firms themselves might prevent it, by voluntarily choosing to pay higher wages than necessary.

Let's consider these three explanations in turn.

Minimum wage

A *minimum wage* is the lowest wage that a firm is legally allowed to pay its workers. In the United States, the federal minimum wage in 2016 was $7.25 per hour. Some states mandate a higher minimum wage. Individual cities, including Los Angeles, California, and Seattle, Washington, have passed laws to raise the minimum wage to $15 by 2020.[4]

The $7.25 per hour wage is approximately the wage that entry-level workers at a fast-food restaurant earn.[5] A worker who earns $7.25 an hour and works 40 hours a week earns just over $15,000 a year, before taxes. In 2016, that annual wage was not enough to keep a two-person household above the poverty line.

Supporters of minimum-wage legislation argue that workers deserve a basic standard of living. They say it is not fair to allow firms to pay workers a wage that would leave them struggling to escape poverty. But even those who support the idea of a higher minimum wage do not agree on the optimal level: $12 per hour? $15 per hour? Lower? Higher?

Opponents of minimum wage legislation point to graphs like the one we showed in Figure 9-4, which suggests that if the minimum wage is higher than the equilibrium wage, then we would expect unemployment to result. Of course, if the minimum wage is set at a level *below* the equilibrium wage, it will have no effect; this is called a *nonbinding* minimum wage.

Does a minimum wage cause unemployment? The question can't be resolved by a theoretical analysis alone. We need to look at data. Economists have found evidence both for and against the idea that a minimum wage causes unemployment:

- Evidence from fast-food restaurants in different U.S. states indicates that raising the state minimum wage did not cause fast-food chains to lay off employees. This implies that the real-world labor market does not work exactly like the model shown in Figure 9-4.

- In other cases, economists have found that minimum wages do appear to cause a small amount of unemployment or a change in *who* is employed, as firms substitute more skilled, older workers for unskilled, younger workers.

Another possibility some economists raise, given that the minimum wage applies only to people hired legally, is that it could drive jobs "under the table." That is, firms might respond to minimum-wage legislation by employing undocumented migrants at below-minimum wages or paying workers cash without telling the government.

Views on minimum wages vary greatly. If the minimum wage does indeed cause unemployment, people who can't find jobs will lose out, while people lucky enough to be in jobs will benefit. If it *doesn't* cause unemployment, then all workers will benefit, while firms lose out by making lower profits. The debate rages on.

Unions and bargaining

In 2007, television and screenplay writers went on strike. They picketed outside the major Hollywood studios and Broadway theaters, refusing to work until they were offered a bigger share of the profits from the shows they worked on. The writers' strike meant that production had to shut down for many TV shows; the writers gave up $285 million in lost wages. The strike was resolved after 100 days, with the writers gaining a pay increase and a bigger share of profits, especially from TV shows streamed over the Internet and mobile devices.

Strikes like this are made possible by the existence of labor unions. In this case the writers were part of a union called the Writers' Guild. **Labor unions** are groups of employees who join together to bargain with their employer(s) over salaries and working conditions.

labor unions
groups of employees who join together to bargain with their employer(s) over salaries and work conditions

Unions benefit their members by being able to bargain as a group. If just a few disgruntled writers had gone on strike, then other writers could easily have been brought in to cover for them. But if workers strike together, they can bring an industry to a halt. This threat enables workers to drive a harder bargain with employers on wages and working conditions, such as benefits like health insurance, pension plans, and vacation time.

In the United States, the power of unions is falling. In the 1950s, about one-third of U.S. workers were in unions. The proportion is far lower today: As of 2015, about 11.1 percent of all wage and salary workers, or just under 15 million Americans, are in unions. About 35 percent of these union members work for government entities.[6] In some countries independent unions are restricted or banned altogether.

What does the existence of labor unions mean for the labor market and for unemployment? If labor unions drive a hard enough bargain, wage rates can rise above the equilibrium level. Then, the effect of labor unions is the same as with the minimum wage. To the extent that the labor market behaves like any other market, when unions manage to negotiate higher wages for their members, employers will in theory respond by employing fewer people. That means that being in a union is good for its own members but can be harmful for the unemployed looking for work. There's some evidence, though, that the presence of unions pushes wages upward even for workers who are not in a union (if they work in a sector with a strong union presence). One reason is that employers with nonunion workers want to keep their employees happy enough that they do not feel the need to form a union.

Opinions about the role of unions on wages depend on whether you think that labor markets do a good job of determining fair wages, and how much weight you put on the well-being of unemployed people versus people with jobs.

Efficiency wages

Another reason why wages might be above the market-clearing level is that some firms may *want* to pay their workers more than the going wage. Why would they do this? There are two related reasons:

- First, paying a higher wage will make workers less likely to quit, saving the expense of advertising for, interviewing, and training new people.
- Second, workers are more likely to fear losing their jobs and might work harder to keep the jobs they have.

Thus, it could be efficient for a firm to pay workers more than the going wage rate, especially in sectors where skills are scarce and worker motivation really matters. The idea is to give positive incentives to maximize productivity: Job transitions, from one worker to another, harm productivity. Also, workers exerting more effort to keep their jobs obviously also improves productivity. Paying wages above market-clearing levels may simply be a smart decision by firms.

The idea of deliberately setting wages above the market rate in order to increase productivity is captured by the term **efficiency wages**. Henry Ford is famous for instituting an efficiency wage at the Ford car factories in Detroit. He doubled his workers' wages in 1914 in order to reduce costly turnover and absenteeism, a move that turned out to be quite profitable.

efficiency wages
wages that are deliberately set above the market rate to increase productivity

How might efficiency wages prevent wages from falling in a recession? Imagine that you are running a firm with 10 employees, and a recession causes the wage rate for labor to drop by 10 percent. Which would you rather do: force all your employees to take a 10 percent pay cut or fire one employee?

You might calculate that the latter option is better. Sure, it would leave you with one fewer employee, but all nine remaining employees would be highly motivated to work hard and keep their jobs, knowing they are earning above the going rate. Among them, the nine employees may even end up producing more for the firm than 10 employees, disgruntled because of a pay cut, would have produced.

In addition, the fact that efficiency wages can create unemployment can strengthen their impact. When employers fire workers (rather than cut pay), the rising level of unemployment worsens the consequence of losing a job. When workers fear an extended period of unemployment (rather than just having to work at a lower wage), they are likely to push themselves that much harder.

There is little clear evidence so far about how much of unemployment can be explained by efficiency wages. Some economists think that it's a key feature of labor markets; others argue that simply raising wages is unlikely to increase productivity.

Recently economists have built on the efficiency-wage idea that workers' effort is also determined by whether wages are seen as being "fair." Needing to maintain "fair" wages might also limit employers' flexibility in cutting wages. The idea has support from laboratory-style economic experiments that explore made-up situations, and the idea awaits rigorous study in the real labor market.

Unemployment insurance

LO 9.6 Describe the challenges policy-makers face when designing unemployment insurance and understand how this and related policies can affect rates of unemployment.

unemployment insurance
money paid by the government to people who are unemployed

Frictional and structural unemployment are part of the normal working of the economy. Most economists, though, believe that some government policies can affect the level of these kinds of unemployment. One such policy is unemployment insurance. **Unemployment insurance** is money that is paid by the government to people who are unemployed. There are usually certain conditions that determine eligibility—such as actively looking for work and reporting work-related activities.

Unemployment insurance doesn't directly affect the wage rate, so it is not an explanation for why wages do not reach equilibrium. Rather, unemployment insurance can affect *how quickly* people find jobs. That factor will affect the natural rate of unemployment—that is, both frictional and structural unemployment. Unemployment insurance makes joblessness less painful by giving people income while they look for work.

The effect of unemployment insurance on unemployment is ambiguous:

- On one hand, if unemployment insurance is generous, then people might not look as hard for work. People may be more likely to take their time and wait for a better job, rather than accepting the first job offered. This suggests that unemployment insurance could increase the equilibrium level of unemployment.

- On the other hand, if people don't have to rush into taking the first job they're offered, they are more likely to find the right job for them. Having employers and employees "better matched" may mean that fewer people leave their jobs, which may reduce the level of frictional unemployment.

Which effect will be greater is up for debate. Also up for debate is the "right" level of unemployment insurance to offer if we want the two effects to balance out: We want to give people enough breathing space to find a suitable job, but not so much that they become unrealistic perfectionists.

The amount and duration of unemployment insurance vary widely across countries. In the United States, unemployment insurance is based on how much an individual earned over the previous year, up to a maximum level. The standard duration of unemployment benefits is 26 weeks. However, this time period can be extended in times of unusually high unemployment. For example, during the recession of 2008–2009, the maximum limit was extended to 99 weeks for most states.

What happens if you don't have a job when your unemployment insurance runs out? In the United States, people can move onto other government welfare programs such as food and housing assistance. In European countries, unemployment benefits typically last longer and replace a greater percentage of average work income.

Not all countries offer unemployment insurance. For more on how such countries help those who are out of work, see the Real Life box "Unemployment and developing countries."

Real Life
Unemployment and developing countries

Some developing countries have very high levels of unemployment. In South Africa, for example, more than 26 percent of the labor force is unemployed, even by the most narrowly defined measures. In developing countries, unemployment insurance is not the norm, and low-income countries must often devote government budgets to more pressing needs. Where does this leave the unemployed?

Governments in some low-income countries have implemented measures to help those without work. India, for example, has a program called the National Rural Employment Guarantee Act, which is meant to guarantee adults 100 days of work per year. The work usually is at the minimum wage on low-skilled projects such as building roads, but it's a job nonetheless. By December 2013, the program had provided work for adults from over 300 million households.

Two survival options for those without a job are much more common in low-income countries than in the United States. One is the *informal sector.* The informal sector provides jobs without formal contracts and legal protections. These jobs include street-sellers, maids, taxi drivers, weavers, and small-scale factory workers. The organization "Women in Informal Employment: Globalizing and Organizing" (WIEGO) has teamed up with the International Labor Organization to collect data about informal job activity. They estimate that, outside of agriculture, about one-half to three-quarters of workers in low-income economies are informally employed. If you include workers in agriculture (most of whom are farmers), the fraction can be as high as 90 percent, especially in South Asia and sub-Saharan Africa. The informal sector tends to offer lots of part-time, temporary jobs, and that makes it easier for people who lose one job to patch together income by taking other short-term jobs.

The other survival option is to rely on extended family. Studies like *Portfolios of the Poor: How the World's Poor Live on $2 a Day* (co-authored by one of the authors of this book) show that in Bangladesh and South Africa, where there is not much government support available, people in need often turn to their extended families in hard times.

In short, unemployment is a global problem—but like many problems, the solutions depend a lot on the resources available to address it within each country.

Sources: Government of India, Ministry of Rural Labor, Mahatma Gandhi National Rural Employment Guarantee Act, 2005: Report to the People, 2014, http://vikaspedia.in/agriculture/policies-and-schemes/nrega-report-to-people;Mari Megias, "Policy Matters: The Informal Economy," Harvard Kennedy School, 2012, http://www.hks.harvard.edu/news-events/news/articles/policy-matters-the-informal-economy;and Daryl Collins, Jonathan Morduch, Stuart Rutherford, and Orlanda Ruthven, *Portfolios of the Poor: How the World's Poor Live on $2 a Day* (Princeton, NJ: Princeton University Press, 2009).

Other factors: Taxes and worker rights

Unemployment insurance is just one policy we can expect to affect rates of unemployment. What are some others?

Taxes on wage income are important as well. We would expect, all else equal, that lower taxes would reduce unemployment. Why? The reasoning is that lower taxes give people more incentive to find a job, knowing they will keep more of the income they earn from the job. The magnitude of the impact taxes have on job-search effort, however, is inconclusive.

Another important factor is the ease with which employers can fire employees. In some countries, firing can be done on a whim, without explanation. In other countries, workers are legally protected, and employers have to prove they have a good reason. We would expect that policies to protect workers would lead to greater unemployment. Why? Because employers would be reluctant to hire people if they know that it will be difficult to get rid of them. A particular aspect of this debate is explored in the What Do You Think? box "Youth employees on trial."

What Do You Think?
Youth employees on trial

When you start looking for your first professional job, you often hit a big challenge: Without work experience, it can be tough to find a job. But how do you get work experience without

(continued)

having a job? This is one reason why young people typically have a higher unemployment rate than older workers. If you look back at Figure 9-1, panel B, you'll see that youth unemployment peaked close to 20 percent during the recent recession, compared with around 7-10 percent for the whole population.

At the root of this issue lies a communication problem: Young people looking for their first job lack ways to credibly demonstrate to employers that they will be good employees. Why should employers take a chance on a young person who has no job experience, when they could instead choose to employ someone with proven skills in the workplace? Of course, a particular young person with no job experience might turn out to be a great employee. But until you've employed the person, you have no way of knowing that. And once you've employed someone, it can often be expensive, time-consuming, and even legally problematic to fire that person.

This is the thinking that led New Zealand to implement a policy allowing employers to fire new employees during their first 90 days at work—without the workers having any right to file legal action for unfair dismissal. Supporters of this policy say it helps young people to find jobs by removing some risk for the employer. The employer can test a new employee for 90 days and, if it doesn't work out, can simply offload him or her.

Not everyone is happy with the idea. Some critics argue that the trial period is a way for firms to exploit young people, employing them without the same benefits and protections that other workers take for granted. Some worry that firms might never actually hire *any* permanent workers, instead relying on constant turnover of employees under the trial period.

WHAT DO YOU THINK?

1. Is this policy a smart way to solve this information problem, or is it just a license to exploit young people?
2. What would keep employers from hiring and firing new workers every 90 days?

Source: New Zealand Institute of Economic Research, Inc., "90-Day Trial Periods Appear Successful—NZIER Insight 25," http://nzier.org.nz/publications/90-day-trial-periods-appear-successful-nzier-insight-25 (accessed November 28, 2012).

✓ CONCEPT CHECK

☐ Why do some governments set a minimum wage? **[LO 9.5]**
☐ Why would an employer pay an efficiency wage? **[LO 9.5]**
☐ What are the trade-offs in the effect of unemployment insurance? **[LO 9.6]**

Conclusion

Most of our adult lives are spent working, and finding a great job can be a key to happiness. At the same time, not being able to find the right job—or not being able to find any job at all—can be one of the toughest life experiences.

The labor market is in many ways like any other market. It's driven by the forces of supply and demand, and we can describe an equilibrium wage rate at which the quantity of labor supplied equals the quantity of labor demanded. But there are differences too: Minimum wages, bargaining by labor unions, and efficiency wages can all cause the wage rate to be above the market-clearing level for extended periods, which leads to unemployment.

We've discussed how the official unemployment rate is measured. Since the unemployment rate doesn't always give a full picture of labor-market conditions, economists and policy-makers often pore over other measures, such as the labor-force participation rate.

We've described the main reasons for unemployment. Frictional and structural unemployment occur naturally; they will exist in any labor market regardless of policy. They are caused by people switching between jobs or shifting from one sector to another.

Another type of unemployment, cyclical unemployment, mirrors the overall health of the economy and the business cycle. In boom times, jobs get created and cyclical unemployment is small. But jobs are lost when the economy weakens, and cyclical unemployment rises.

Economists debate how much the rules of the labor market affect the overall rate of unemployment. We've seen that labor-market policies often come with important trade-offs:

- Policy-makers have to decide how generous to make unemployment benefits. Providing more support for the unemployed may be desirable from a social perspective, but when benefits are *too* generous, incentives to actively search for a job are diminished.

- Similarly, raising minimum wages helps workers on the bottom rungs of the labor market, but raising minimum wages can also make it harder for unemployed workers to find jobs.

Unemployment is not something that occurs in isolation from the rest of the economy. In fact, one of the most powerful ways to reduce unemployment is to generate sustained economic growth in the overall economy. In the next chapter, we focus on this important economic challenge: How can policy and resources be combined to create healthy economic growth?

Key Terms

unemployment, p. 227

labor force, p. 228

unemployment rate, p. 228

labor-force participation rate, p. 230

discouraged workers, p. 231

underemployed, p. 231

labor demand curve, p. 233

labor supply curve, p. 234

natural rate of unemployment, p. 235

frictional unemployment, p. 236

structural unemployment, p. 236

real-wage or classical unemployment, p. 236

cyclical unemployment, p. 237

labor unions, p. 240

efficiency wages, p. 241

unemployment insurance, p. 242

Summary

LO 9.1 Explain how economists measure employment and unemployment.

To be considered unemployed, a person needs to meet three conditions: (1) be part of the working-age, civilian population; (2) not have worked in the previous week; and (3) be actively looking for work. Economists measure unemployment with the *unemployment rate*. This is the number of people who are unemployed, divided by the labor force.

The *labor force participation rate* is the fraction of the working age population that is working or looking for work. People who are not working but who are not actively looking for work—for example, students, homemakers, or *discouraged workers*—are not considered part of the labor force. Those, on the other hand, who are working jobs that don't utilize their skills or knowledge are considered to be *underemployed*.

LO 9.2 Explain how wage rates above equilibrium cause unemployment.

Like other markets, the labor market features a demand curve and a supply curve. The *total* demand for labor from all the firms in the economy is represented by the *labor demand curve*. On the whole, firms will want to hire more labor when wages are cheaper and less labor when wages are expensive, which means the labor demand curve slopes downward.

The total labor supply is represented by the *labor supply curve*. We would expect that people will be willing to supply more labor at higher wage rates and less labor at lower wage rates. This relationship gives the labor supply curve a positive slope.

Equilibrium in the market for labor is reached at the wage (price of labor) where the labor demand and labor supply curves meet. Unemployment results when the market wage rate remains above the market equilibrium; it is effectively a surplus of labor at the inflated wage rate.

LO 9.3 Explain why there is a natural rate of unemployment in an economy.

We think of the economy having a long-run natural level of unemployment. This *natural rate of unemployment* is the amount of unemployment that is unavoidable in a dynamic economy.

There are two reasons why we expect the economy to have some unemployment when everything else is normal: Some unemployment comes from *frictional* reasons, such as people changing jobs or locations. Some unemployment comes from *structural* reasons, such as government policies that affect how easily the wage rate can adjust. Structural unemployment also includes people who are unemployed because of technological development in the economy that results in a mismatch between the skills demanded by firms and the skills the labor force has.

LO 9.4 Explain why there is a cyclical component of unemployment.

There is also unemployment that is related to changes in GDP in the economy. When GDP is higher than normal, unemployment is lower than the equilibrium rate. When GDP is lower than normal, unemployment is above the equilibrium rate. This type of unemployment is called *cyclical unemployment.*

LO 9.5 Identify factors that may stop wages from falling to the equilibrium level.

Many factors affect the level of unemployment rate. Three reasons why the wage rate may not fully adjust to the equilibrium wage rate in the labor market are a minimum wage that is above the equilibrium wage rate, labor unions that negotiate a wage rate above the equilibrium wage rate, and *efficiency wages* (wages paid by firms, above the equilibrium wage rate).

LO 9.6 Describe the challenges policy-makers face when designing unemployment insurance and understand how this and related policies can affect rates of unemployment.

The design of the unemployment insurance programs is ultimately a balance of trade-offs. When benefits are not generous, losing a job can become a devastating financial hardship. When benefits are *too* generous, incentives to actively search for a job are diminished. In the United States, unemployment benefits last only a short time and pay only a fraction of people's average working wages, so as to minimize the incentive to shirk the job search.

Review Questions

1. During the 1960s societal norms regarding working women were changing, and many women who had been housewives began working outside the home. How would you expect this new norm to change the labor-force participation rate? What about the unemployment rate? **[LO 9.1]**

2. List at least five types of people who do not have paid jobs but would nevertheless *not* be considered unemployed. **[LO 9.1]**

3. Compare two countries, one that has unlimited unemployment insurance and one in which workers are eligible for 26 weeks of unemployment insurance. Explain one reason why the country with more unemployment insurance may have a higher equilibrium unemployment rate. **[LO 9.2]**

4. Suppose the president of a country comes to you to ask your advice. The country is currently at 8 percent unemployment, and the president wishes to reduce unemployment in the country to 3 percent. As an economist, you determine that the country's natural rate of unemployment is 5 percent. What advice would you give the president? **[LO 9.3]**

5. Innovation often requires "creative destruction," in which the new product or technology makes previous products or technologies obsolete. For example, when the personal computer was invented, typewriters became useless; hence, the personal computer "destroyed" the typewriter. This process of creative destruction often results in structural unemployment because workers who knew how to build and maintain the old products have skills that are no longer in demand. Do you think the government has a role in either limiting how often new products are created or in helping those workers who are displaced because of the new product? **[LO 9.3]**

6. Suppose the National Bureau of Economic Research (NBER) just came out with a report suggesting that the economy will soon dip into recession. How do you think the levels of frictional, structural, and cyclical unemployment will change as the recession begins? What will happen to the labor-force participation rate? **[LO 9.4]**

7. What happens to a country's levels of frictional, structural, and cyclical unemployment, as well as its labor-force participation rate, as a recession drags on for an extended period of time? **[LO 9.4]**

8. What happens to a country's levels of frictional, structural, and cyclical unemployment, as well as its labor-force participation rate, as a country begins to recover from a deep recession? **[LO 9.4]**

9. Give two reasons why it may be rational for a firm to offer wages above the minimum wage. **[LO 9.5]**

10. In France, labor laws typically made it very difficult or even illegal for firms to fire workers during economic downturns. How would these laws affect cyclical unemployment as well as frictional and structural unemployment? (Hint: Think about how these laws affect firms' decisions to hire workers in the first place.) **[LO 9.4, LO 9.5]**

11. Unemployment is often called a lagging or trailing indicator because unemployment tends to rise some time after the economy begins to slow down, and unemployment begins to fall again after the economy begins to rebound. In other words, unemployment trails GDP. Why do you think this might be the case? **[LO 9.5]**

12. The traditional goal of a government is to maximize its citizens' welfare. Given this goal, would you suggest getting rid of unemployment insurance? How would your answer change if the goal of the government is to maximize employment? **[LO 9.6]**

13. In the United States during regular economic times, the maximum length of time a worker can collect unemployment insurance is 26 weeks. During recessions, however, Congress often increases the length of time in which workers can collect benefits. During the recent financial crisis, workers could collect benefits for up to 99 weeks in some states. Comment on the advantages and disadvantages of this system. **[LO 9.6]**

Problems and Applications

1. For each of the following situations, is Rick Alexander (from the chapter-opening story) counted as employed, unemployed, or not in the labor force by the Bureau of Labor Statistics? **[LO 9.1]**

    a. Alexander is self-employed in his old job as a carpenter.

    b. Alexander moves to Florida and begins looking for work.

    c. Alexander feels discouraged looking for work and stops applying for jobs.

    d. Alexander starts looking for work again.

    e. Alexander starts work at a new job.

2. Consider the economy whose data appear in Table 9P-1. **[LO 9.1]**

    a. What is the unemployment rate?

    b. What is the labor-force participation rate?

TABLE 9P-1

Group of people	Number of people in group
Working-age population	100,000
Labor force	60,000
Unemployed	10,000

3. Table 9P-2 uses data for the year 2016, adjusted to be comparable to each other. All population values are in thousands.

    a. Fill in the blanks in the table. **[LO 9.1]**

    b. In part *a*, you should have found that the unemployment rates of the three countries differ significantly from one another. Suggest three possible reasons to explain why the countries might have different unemployment rates. **[LO 9.3, 9.4]**

4. Assume the equilibrium wage rate is $6. Draw a graph of the labor market to answer the following questions. **[LO 9.2]**

    a. When the government introduces a minimum wage of $5.50, does unemployment increase, decrease, or stay the same compared to unemployment at the equilibrium wage?

    b. When the government introduces a minimum wage of $6.50, does unemployment increase, decrease, or stay the same compared to unemployment at the equilibrium wage?

5. Assume that the labor demand equation for a fictional country is $L_d = 30 - w$, where w is the wage per hour worked and L_d is the number of workers demanded by firms. Assume also that the labor supply equation for that country is $L_s = 0.5(w)$, where L_s is the number of people willing to work. **[LO 9.2, 9.5]**

    a. Find the equilibrium wage and quantity of labor employed.

    b. At the equilibrium wage, how many people are unemployed?

    c. How would the number of unemployed change if the supply of workers increased?

6. Suppose a firm's labor demand equation is $L_d = 40 - 2(w)$ and the labor supply equation that it faces is $L_s = -20 + 3(w)$, where w is the wage per hour worked, L_d is the number of workers demanded by firms, and L_s is the number of people willing to work. **[LO 9.2, 9.5]**

    a. Find the equilibrium wage and quantity of labor employed.

TABLE 9P-2

Country	Working-age population	Labor force	Employed	Unemployed	Unemployment rate(%)	Labor-force participation rate (%)
Japan	110,849		64,460	2,160		
France		31,164		3,520		56.1
Germany	76,066	46,096			5.7	

b. The workers, thinking that their wages are too low, decide to strike. After tense negotiations, the firm decides to raise the wage by 50 percent. After the wage increase, how many people are unemployed?

7. Classify each of the following situations as either frictional, structural, or cyclical unemployment. **[LO 9.3, 9.4]**

   a. Maria has started looking for work after taking time off to have a baby.

   b. Juan left high school without graduating and can't find any jobs he is qualified for.

   c. Rohit had a job working on Wall Street but lost his job during the financial crisis.

   d. Adam has just arrived in a new city and is looking for work.

   e. Max wants to work as an air steward, but because the airline industry is heavily unionized there are very few jobs available.

   f. Jada has just lost her job in a web start-up that was affected by a downturn in the economy.

8. For each of the following situations, would the unemployment rate increase, decrease, or stay the same? **[LO 9.5]**

   a. A company begins paying efficiency wages above the equilibrium wage rate.

   b. The number of workers covered by union contracts falls.

   c. The government extends the duration of unemployment insurance.

9. Suppose a country has a 26-week limit on the duration that an unemployed person receives unemployment benefits. You collect some data and notice that workers in their 26th week of unemployment benefits somehow manage to find jobs at a much higher rate than other unemployed workers. What would this statistic tell you about the incentives involved with unemployment insurance? **[LO 9.6]**

10. Understanding that unemployment benefits give workers the incentive to not look for work until their benefits run out, suppose an economist suggested that instead of giving workers up to 26 weeks of unemployment benefits that end once the person finds work, a person who loses his or her job would just get a single big check for 26 weeks of benefits, regardless of how long the worker is unemployed. What are the advantages and disadvantages of this idea? **[LO 9.6]**

Endnotes

1. Rick Alexander's story is from Michael Luo, "Out of Work, and Too Down to Search On," *The New York Times*, September 7, 2009, p. A1, New York edition.

2. http://www.nytimes.com/2009/09/07/us/07worker.html?pagewanted=2.

3. Bureau of Labor Statistics: http://www.bls.gov/bls/glossary.htm#U.

4. http://www.nelp.org/news-releases/14-cities-states-approved-15-minimum-wage-in-2015/.

5. http://www.payscale.com/research/us/employer=mcdonald%27s_Corporation/Hourly_rate

6. Bureau of Labor Statistics, http://www.bls.gov/news.release/union2.nr0.htm, January 2016.

Economic Growth

Learning Objectives

LO 10.1 Calculate the growth rate of real GDP per capita, accounting for changes in price levels and population.

LO 10.2 Describe the relationship between productivity and growth and discuss the factors that determine productivity.

LO 10.3 Explain the difference between a country's level of income and its rate of growth.

LO 10.4 Use the growth accounting framework to describe how technology, labor, and capital contribute to economic growth.

LO 10.5 Assess the empirical evidence for and against convergence theory.

LO 10.6 Discuss policies that could promote growth and relate them to productivity.

LO 10.7 Explain how good governance and economic openness lay the foundation for growth.

WHY ECONOMIC GROWTH MATTERS

Between 2005 and 2015, a miracle occurred: Over 650 million people around the world rose out of poverty, cutting the number of the global poor by nearly half. These people moved from worrying about where their next meal was coming from to being able to worry instead about finding a better place to live or a more satisfying job.

What triggered this miracle? It wasn't a humanitarian intervention or massive government program. It was two little numbers: an annual (compounded) growth rate of average GDP per person of 8 percent for China and 5 percent for India.[1]

If you had traveled through those countries in recent years, you'd have found them buzzing with entrepreneurial spirit. Buildings and infrastructure sprouted like mushrooms. Highways roared with people and goods rushing between enormous cities. The bridge of new wealth connected millions of people to the Internet and a global consumer culture.

© Leung Cho Pan/Getty Images

High rates of economic growth have produced more than just tall buildings and smoother roads. The newly minted middle classes in China and India have cash to spend, buying the latest cell phones and flooding the roads with new cars. The middle class in China alone is bigger than the entire population of the United States. The bright lights of Shanghai and Mumbai also offer promise to millions of people who have migrated from poorer rural areas hoping to land jobs in factories or hotels, trading rural lifestyles for urban ones. Wages are rising, and poverty rates are plummeting.

It is easy to get excited by these transformations and to proclaim that we've found the solution to global poverty. But saying that economic growth is the solution to poverty is a bit like saying that brilliant medical research is the solution to curing diseases or that scoring lots of touchdowns is a good way to win a football game. Of course, it's important, but how do you make it happen? That's the hard part.

Leaders all over the world seek economic growth. It translates to wealthier, healthier, and better-educated citizens enjoying more comfortable lives. It also results in higher tax revenues for governments and enticing opportunities for investors. Sadly, we have no magic formula for economic growth. Decades of research have helped us see why some countries are rich and others poor. But history has also shown that it's not easy for policy-makers to translate this understanding into action.

The search for a recipe for economic growth captivates economists. It is simultaneously one of the most important and fascinating questions in economics, and one about which we're still learning. In this chapter, we will describe three aspects of the study of growth. First, we'll discuss how growth is measured and show the patterns that have emerged around the world in the last century. Second, we'll create a basic framework for understanding why growth happens, and how savings, capital, labor, and technology contribute to it. Finally, we'll dig into details on how public policy choices can affect growth.

Economic Growth through the Ages

Over the last 100 years, real GDP per capita in the United States has grown at an average rate of just about 2 percent per year. That might not sound so impressive compared to the 8 percent and 5 percent growth experienced, respectively, by China and India recently. In the context of history, however, it's revolutionary. In this section, we'll explore two reasons why this is so.

History of world growth

LO 10.1 Calculate the growth rate of real GDP per capita, accounting for changes in price levels and population.

Imagine you were living in 1800. Almost anywhere in the world at that time, income per person was not much different from what it had been a millennium earlier. The possibility of growth has always been around, of course, but very little of it actually happened until a century or two ago. Rapid economic growth is a modern phenomenon. 2

Look at Figure 10-1, which shows world population and income per person over the last 3,000 years. Historical records and archaeological evidence allow us to get a general sense of prices and standards of living in ancient days. Notice that for the first 2,800 of the last 3,000 years, very little was happening. The population was growing slowly, and the economy was growing just fast enough to keep up with the snail's pace of the population. The result was that real income per person barely changed at all.

Suddenly, in the 1800s, the nature of the global economy underwent a radical transformation. After staying about the same size for thousands of years, it started to grow. This growth was even more striking given that the world's population exploded at roughly the same time. The red line in Figure 10-1 shows real GDP per capita, calculated as if the entire world was one economy. The blue line shows world population growth. The figure shows that even though population grew at a historically fast pace in the twentieth century, real GDP per capita grew even faster.

FIGURE 10-1

History of world economic growth: Real GDP per capita, 1000 BC to AD 2000　For the first 2,800 years of this graph, real global GDP per capita was essentially constant. Then, in 1800, with the Industrial Revolution, incomes in Europe began to increase rapidly. In the last 50 years, real global GDP per capita quadrupled. Note that the numbers on the vertical axis refer to both real GDP per capita (calculated as if the entire world was one economy and deflated using PPP exchange rates) and to the number of people on earth—which rose to over 6 billion people (6,000 × 1 million) by 2000.

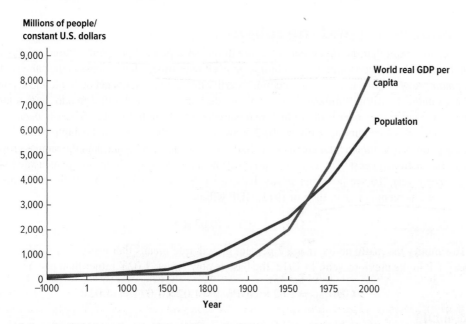

Source: http://www.j-bradford-delong.net/macro_online/ms/ch5/chapter_5.pdf.

The growth rate of real GDP per capita is typically the number we care about. It describes the change in actual purchasing power for each person. In order to get an accurate picture of the real GDP per capita growth rate, we need to subtract changes in both prices and population from the nominal GDP growth rate, as follows:

EQUATION 10-1

$$\text{Real GDP per capita growth rate} = \text{Nominal GDP growth rate} - \text{Inflation rate} -$$
$$\text{Population growth rate}$$

Just from glancing at Figure 10-1, you can see that the fast rise of GDP growth in the last few centuries means that nominal GDP must have grown much faster than inflation and population combined. As a result, the purchasing power of the average person in the world today is more than 30 times as high as it was 200 years ago. This represents a transformative change in the way people live. A growth rate like 2 percent may not sound revolutionary, but it is a big jump from what had been essentially zero growth for centuries before.

HINT

Growth rates usually compare the level of a variable in one year to its level the previous year (though growth rates can be calculated for other time frames too). To get a concrete sense of an annual growth rate, here's how to calculate the United States' real GDP per capita growth rate at the start of 2016: First, find the level of U.S. real GDP per capita in 2016 ($51,061 in January 2016) and the level in 2015 ($50,433 in January 2015).[2] Then subtract to find the absolute change, an increase of $628. The growth rate is then calculated as the absolute change between 2015 and 2016 expressed as a percentage of the level in 2015:

$$\left(\frac{\$628}{\$50,433} \right) \times 100 = 1.25 \text{ percent}$$

Compounding and the rule of 70

The second reason that the historical U.S. growth rate of 2 percent per year is more impressive than it sounds is that economic growth builds on itself over time. This process is the same as the *compounding of interest* in a savings account—earlier interest payments get added to the account and earn interest in turn. Similarly, a relatively modest annual growth rate can add up to a large change in the economy over time. In fact, real per capita GDP in the United States is *over seven times* what it was a century ago. Figure 10-2 shows this growth in real purchasing power.

Compounding results in total changes in GDP over time that are bigger than the annual growth rate would at first suggest. The key insight is that the base from which growth is measured gets bigger every year. To see how this works, let's call U.S. GDP in 1910 "Y." If the economy is growing at 2 percent per year, then in 1911, GDP will be:

$$\text{GDP}_{1911} = Y + (0.02 \times Y) = 1.02Y$$

To simplify the math, notice that a 2 percent growth rate means that every year GDP is 1.02 times GDP in the previous year. In 1912, the base is now larger, 1.02Y rather than just Y:

$$\text{GDP}_{1912} = 1.02 \times \text{GDP}_{1911} = 1.02 \times 1.02Y = (1.02)^2 Y$$

And, in 1913:

$$\text{GDP}_{1913} = 1.02 \times \text{GDP}_{1912} = 1.02 \times (1.02)^2 Y = (1.02)^3 Y$$

FIGURE 10-2

U.S. real GDP per capita, 1910–2015 (valued in 2009 dollars)   Since 1910, the trend of GDP has been overwhelmingly positive, with three exceptions. Two were caused by the Great Depression (in the early 1930s) and Great Recession (late 2007 to mid-2009). The other occurred toward the tail end of World War II (mid-1940s).

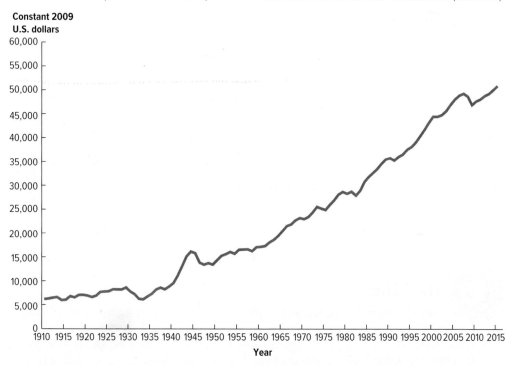

Sources: Louis Johnston and Samuel H. Williamson, "What Was the U.S. GDP Then?," *MeasuringWorth* (2016), https://www.measuringworth.com/usgdp12/.

Are you seeing the pattern? Because 1913 is three years after 1910, we find GDP in 1913 by multiplying the base 1910 GDP by one plus the growth rate three times—that is, by 1.02 to the power of three. If we generalize this formula, we can predict GDP per capita in any year, A. We start from year B and multiply by 1 plus the growth rate, as many times as there are years between B and A:

EQUATION 10-2 $GDP_{yearA} = GDP_{yearB} \times (1 + \text{Growth rate})^{(yearA - yearB)}$

Let's apply this equation to the 105 years between 1910 and 2015. In 1910, real per capita GDP in the United States was roughly $5,800 (valued in 2009 dollars). Plugging that amount for GDP_{yearB} into Equation 10-2, we calculate that real GDP per capita in 2015 would have been roughly $46,400 if the growth rate during that whole period had been a steady 2 percent per year:

$$\text{GDP per capita}_{2015} = \$5,800 \times (1 + 0.02)^{105} \approx \$46,400$$

It turns out that the actual real per capita GDP was $50,970 at the start of 2015 (valued in 2009 dollars), so the approximation of steady 2 percent growth was low, but not far off.

A different way to calculate the implications of steady growth is to use the *rule of 70*. It states that the number of years it will take for income to double at a given annual growth rate is approximately equal to 70 divided by the annual growth rate:

EQUATION 10-3 $\text{Years until income doubles} = \dfrac{70}{\text{Annual growth rate}}$

Thinking of growth in terms of "years to doubling" makes it easier to appreciate how small differences in growth rates can add up to huge differences in income over time. What if the growth rate in the United States increased from around 2 percent to about 3.5 percent? That might not sound like a big difference, but consider:

- At a growth rate of 2 percent, income doubles every 35 years. *5*
- At a growth rate of 3.5 percent, income doubles every 20 years instead of every 35.
- Over 100 years, income would have doubled five times instead of three.
- So, starting with $5,800 in 1910, instead of earning an average $46,400 by 2015 (at 2 percent growth per year), Americans would be earning an average of about $215,000—more than four times greater thanks to the 3.5 percent growth rate.

To see the effect that differences in growth rates can make, consider the incredible economic story of East Asia. Starting in 1960, four countries in Asia—Hong Kong, Singapore, Taiwan, and South Korea—managed growth rates of over 8 percent per year. That implies that real incomes doubled more than once every 10 years! In just 50 years, this impressive economic growth managed to vault many people in these countries out of poverty. For insight into the debate about why this "Asian miracle" hasn't happened elsewhere, see the Real Life box "What a difference 50 years makes."

Real Life

What a difference **50 years** makes: The story of Korea and Ghana

In 1960, Ghana and South Korea had similar levels of development. Both were quite poor, and most of their populations eked out livings on small farms. Ghana, however, had good prospects. Most economists thought it was poised to grow by at least 7 percent per year.

The consensus prediction for South Korea, on the other hand, was far less rosy. The first World Bank mission to the country called South Korea's growth plan "ridiculously optimistic"; it predicted sluggish growth.

Fast-forwarding 50 years, South Korea is now a major manufacturing force, making sophisticated, high-end electronics and cars. Its brands include Samsung, LG, Hyundai, and Kia. It is now a wealthy country, with a GDP per capita over $28,000.

Ghana's economy also grew, though much more slowly. But its population grew faster than South Korea's, so its average income per capita was actually *higher* in 1960 than in 2000. Today, Ghana is one of the richer countries in Africa, but it is much less well-off than South Korea. Ghana's GDP per capita in 2014 was a little over $1,400 per person. Over half of its workforce is still employed in the agricultural sector, either growing export crops such as cocoa or subsistence crops such as cassava and maize.

Why did Korea take off while Ghana failed to meet its early promise? The story is complicated, but an important part of it is that Ghana suffered years of political instability after 1960. Government intervention in the economy was heavy-handed and discouraged foreign trade.

South Korea, on the other hand, focused relentlessly on educating its citizens and encouraging people to save. The government gave firms generous incentives to export, including tax benefits and low-interest loans. South Korea's expanding manufacturing sector led it to an average growth rate of real GDP per capita of 5.4 percent in the half-century between 1961 and 2011.

The rule of 70 estimates that Korea doubled in size about every 13 years. Put another way, in the 50 years between 1961 and 2011, Korea doubled its income nearly four times. The result: The current generation of young adults in Korea have incomes that are about 13 times that of their grandparents, after adjusting for inflation.

Economists don't have a foolproof formula for creating growth miracles. But by studying how Korea grew and why Ghana didn't, we can get closer to a real understanding of economic growth.

Sources: http://siteresources.worldbank.org/DEC/Resources/84797-1275071905763/Lessons_from_Korea_Lim.pdf; http://countrystudies.us/south-korea/; http://www.nber.org/chapters/c8548.pdf; http://www.cimmyt.org/; http://economistsview.typepad.com/economistsview/2006/03/amartya_sen_dem.html; http://data.worldbank.org/indicator/NY.GDP.PCAP.CD.

✓ CONCEPT CHECK

☐ What was the overall trend of economic growth in the world before 1800? **[LO 10.1]**

☐ What is the rule of 70? **[LO 10.1]**

Determinants of Productivity

Growth may seem like an abstract concept, but it has a big impact on people's standard of living. If you happen to have been born in the United States or South Korea, for instance, you likely enjoy a standard of living much higher than that of your grandparents and great-grandparents. You are probably taller, healthier, better-educated, and more widely traveled and have more luxury and comfort in your life. Other regions of the world have grown much more slowly or not at all. As a result, in those regions people live in ways relatively similar to earlier generations.

What determines the dramatic differences between countries and their growth paths over time? In this section, we will build a framework to understand factors that determine the level of income in a country and the rate at which it grows over time. With this framework, we will have a basis for discussing the historical circumstances and policy choices that cause some economies to grow and others to stagnate.

Productivity drives growth

Imagine a single household—say, a family that lives away from others, on a farm in a remote place. The only goods available to this family are things its members can produce. If the family wants food or clothes or toys or a house, it will have to grow or make them. Suppose some family members learn to sew more quickly; they will make clothes more quickly and have more time left over to make toys for their children. Or suppose they build a plow that allows them to plant vegetables more easily, freeing up time and energy to build an extra room in their house. The total amount of goods they produce will increase, and so will their standard of living.

In fact, the *only* way that the family can consume more and enjoy a higher standard of living is to increase the amount each person produces. We call that output **productivity**. Productivity can be measured in various ways, but it's typically measured as output per worker.

productivity
output produced per worker

From Chapter 7, "Measuring GDP," we know that *output per person on a country level* is the same thing as *GDP per capita*. Just like the farm family, we can think of a country as a self-contained economic unit: It can earn and consume only as much as it produces. Thus, a country's income—like that of the farm family—depends on how productive its workers are.

Of course, hardly any family or country today consumes exactly what it produces itself. Typically, both sell some of the goods and services they produce. They then use the money they earn to buy goods and services that others produce. Still, the underlying relationship holds: The more a country produces, the more it can consume. In the short term, it can temporarily push consumption higher than production by borrowing money. But in the long run, debts have to be paid, and the only way to get to consume more is by producing more.

As a result, the standard of living in a country is driven by the average productivity of its people. *Increases in productivity per person* lead to *increases in per capita income,* which we call *economic growth.* So now the question is: What makes a country's people more productive?

Components of productivity

LO 10.2 Describe the relationship between productivity and growth and discuss the factors that determine productivity.

To answer the question of what makes people more productive, we'll go back to the enterprising farm family. What determines how many vegetables they can grow in a year? The answer depends on several other questions: How skilled and experienced are they at farming? How fertile is their land, and what is the climate like? Do they have plows and fertilizer? Do they have state-of-the-art computerized irrigation systems, or do they depend on rainfall? Do they use the latest high-yield seed varieties?

Most of us are not farmers. But the factors that determine our productivity as workers fall into the same categories: *physical capital* (like plows and tractors), *human capital* (farming experience), *natural resources* (land quality and rainfall), and *technology* (high-tech tools and crop varieties). Let's walk through each determinant to see how it affects productivity.

Physical capital

Most types of production require tools, and better tools allow workers to be more productive. A farmer with a sturdy horse-drawn plow will outperform a farmer with a shovel but won't do as well as his neighbor with a tractor. These are examples of **physical capital**, the stock of equipment and structures that allow for the production of goods and services. Elsewhere in the economy, examples of physical capital include a manufacturer's factory and machines, a cellular network's towers and cables, and so on.

We calculate the amount of physical capital in an economy by adding up the value of all tools, equipment, and structures. Every year, some new physical capital is added through investment (farmers buy new tractors). Likewise, some old physical capital wears out or becomes obsolete (old tractors stop working). Taking into account both new investment and the retirement of older capital, we can tell how much physical capital has been added to the economy on net.

Where does the money for investment in physical capital come from? It largely comes from the savings of ordinary households. You put away money in the bank, and the bank then loans funds to farmers and factories and cellular networks so that they can purchase new equipment. Thus, the *level of savings* in an economy can be an important determinant of investment in capital, and through that mechanism, a determinant of future productivity. In countries with low levels of savings, firms have trouble finding the money they need to invest in their factories and businesses. We will look in more detail at the relationship between savings and investment in later chapters.

Human capital

Having new machines is usually a plus for productivity, but only if workers know how to use them. **Human capital** refers to the set of skills, knowledge, experience, and talent that determine the productivity of workers.

Education is one of the main ways that we think about people building human capital. By taking an economics course, you are learning things that will make you more productive in the workplace. Human capital can also be acquired through training or job experience.

Human capital contributes to growth because it helps workers in the economy produce more with the same amount of physical capital. In other words, people can work smarter. A large increase in human capital is one explanation for the growth in the U.S. economy over the last 100 years. A century ago, the average person in America completed only around 8 years of

physical capital
the stock of equipment and structures that allow for production of goods and services

human capital
the set of skills, knowledge, experience, and talent that determine the productivity of workers

school; today, the average is more than 12 years of school. The average worker today knows more than the average worker at the start of the century and so will be more productive.

Countries with low levels of GDP per capita usually also have low levels of schooling. For example, the average person in Malawi or India has approximately 5 years of schooling. Helping people to invest in their human capital through better access to schools and job training is a priority for many developing countries.

Note that an individual's, or a nation's, human capital is not always improving—it can also become outdated or deteriorate. People who are unemployed for long periods of time can forget some of the skills that were valuable in the workplace, for instance.

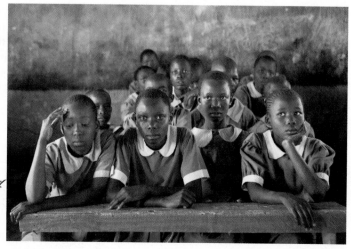

Schools around the world aim to build human capital. Here, a school in Kenya shows attentive students in a jam-packed classroom.
Courtesy of Aude Guerrucci

Natural resources

Natural resources are production inputs that come from the earth—lakes, mineral deposits, forests, and so on. Natural resources can be split into two categories: renewable or nonrenewable.

- *Renewable resources* can be replenished naturally over time. For instance, after cutting down a tree for lumber, you can plant another one to grow in its place. Likewise, when a hydroelectric plant harnesses the power of a river to generate electricity, it doesn't "use up" the river, which continues to flow. Of course, some things take longer to renew than others. The river renews immediately, but the trees take many years to replenish.

- Mineral deposits such as coal, oil, and gold, on the other hand, are *nonrenewable*. When you take them out of the ground and use them, they do not get replenished.

The availability of natural resources can account for some of the differences in economic development around the world. The United States has been blessed with a lot of fertile land, for example. Britain got a big boost from having easily accessible coal to power its manufacturing. But natural resources aren't everything. Japan and Switzerland are wealthy countries without an abundance of natural resources; Guinea and Kazakhstan are poor countries despite having many natural resources.

Technology

The word *technology* may conjure up the image of a sleek new consumer gadget. When we think of how technology contributes to productivity, though, we need to understand the term more broadly. Technology comes in all forms and sizes. It can be big developments such as the invention of the Internet or cell phones. It can also be seemingly small advances like a more efficient water pump for irrigating crops or an engine design that allows cars to travel further on the same amount of fuel.

Big or small, technology means that the same inputs will produce more outputs. In other words, countries with better technology will be able to produce more with the same amount of physical and human capital.

It is hard to overstate the importance of technology for understanding economic growth. Technology is fundamentally different from other factors of production, such as land, resources, capital, and labor. Whereas these other factors are in scarce supply and run into diminishing returns, technology can be shared relatively easily, with good ideas leading to even better ideas. A famous growth economist, Paul Romer of New York University, emphasized that ideas are like recipes: While the ingredients may be scarce, the instructions for combining the ingredients can be shared at low cost. Thus, if one country develops a better way to combine existing resources, that same idea can spread quickly to other countries and lead to faster economic growth worldwide.

One of the most striking examples of the power of technology is the transformation of agriculture in Asia starting in the 1960s. Scientists developed new varieties of seeds for crops like rice and wheat, which produced much higher yields than traditional seeds. These high-yielding seed varieties doubled the amount of food that could be produced on a plot of land. This "green revolution" not only erased the prospect of famine but also set the stage for the incredible overall growth that has occurred in Asia over the past five decades. We'll come back to this story later in the chapter.

Rates versus levels

LO 10.3 Explain the difference between a country's level of income and its rate of growth.

Imagine that you're driving a car and merging onto the highway, pressing the accelerator pedal to the floor. Your speedometer says you are doing 15 mph, then a second later 20 mph, then a second later 25 mph. Your *level* of speed is fairly low, but your *rate of change* is high. Now imagine you are on the highway and cruising at 55 mph. You are at a high *level* of speed, but the speed is constant—your *rate of change* is zero.

This analogy is useful for thinking about the differences between wealthy countries and fast-growing countries. Switzerland, for example, has high levels of physical and human capital and access to sophisticated technology. Consequently, it has high productivity and standards of living. Its current *rate* of growth is low, but it's starting from a high *level*. It's like the driver cruising along on the highway.

By contrast, China has lower *levels* of physical and human capital and less widespread access to the latest technologies. As a result, Chinese workers have lower productivity than Swiss workers, and GDP per capita in China is lower than in Switzerland. However, incomes are increasing very rapidly in China. They have not yet achieved the same level as Switzerland, but they are moving quickly in that direction. China is like the car merging onto the highway, not yet going as fast as the cars already on the highway, but with a high *rate of change*. Its level of speed is increasing all the time.

As we discuss policies that can influence future growth, the distinction between the *level of income* and the *rate of increase in income* is crucial. The factors that took a country to its current economic level may or may not be related to those that can lead to future growth. For instance, Kuwait has grown rapidly in the last few decades and enjoys high productivity and incomes. This growth was almost entirely due to its incredible natural endowment of oil. But Kuwait would be foolish to base its future economic growth strategy only on exploiting its oil reserves. The people of Kuwait might hope that there are untapped oil reservoirs hiding somewhere in the desert, but there's nothing they can do to make more oil than already exists.

Similarly, we saw in Chapter 7, "Measuring GDP," that increasing participation of women in the labor market partially explained U.S. growth rates from the 1970s to the 1990s. But clearly, as with Kuwait's oil, it would not be sensible to think you can grow an economy forever by encouraging more and more stay-at-home parents to get jobs or current workers to work longer hours. Sooner or later there will be no stay-at-home parents left, and no more hours in the day for people to work overtime. Such one-time changes in the economy can cause growth spurts that lead to higher income *levels,* but they cannot sustain a higher *rate of change* over time.

In contrast, improvements in technology *can* sustain high rates of change. Sure, when an inventor creates a new gizmo, that invention is a one-time

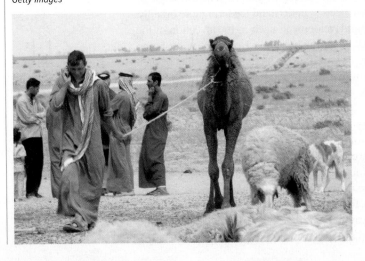

The spread of technology is a key driver of economic growth and can speed up rates of convergence. This Bedouin youth talks on a mobile phone as he leads a camel in southern Iraq.
© *Essam Al-Sudanie/AFP/ Getty Images*

change. If technology stops improving, the economy won't continue to grow. But often, improvements in technology lead to *more* improvements in technology. For example, computing capacity has approximately doubled every two years since the invention of computers, a phenomenon called *Moore's law.* People are constantly finding better and more effective ways to do things, and as a result, their productivity is continuously increasing.

Accounting for growth

LO 10.4 Use the growth accounting framework to describe how technology, labor, and capital contribute to economic growth.

Now that we've seen the main ingredients of growth, it's natural to ask which ones are the most important. It turns out that we can decompose (separate) the growth rate of output per person into the contributions of capital, labor, and technology. When we describe the determinants of output, we often use a *production function,* an equation that captures the relationship between the quantity of inputs and the resulting quantity of outputs.

Here, instead, we want to capture the relationship between the *growth rate* of inputs and the resulting *growth rate* of outputs. Economists call this *growth accounting.* In particular, economists use an equation like this:

EQUATION 10-4 Growth accounting equation

$$g_Y = g_A + \alpha g_K + (1 - \alpha) g_L$$

where the *g*'s with subscripts denote the percentage change in the variable indicated by the subscript:

g_Y = the growth rate of output

g_A = the growth rate of technology

g_K = the growth rate of capital

g_L = the growth rate of labor

α = the share of GDP that is distributed to the owners of capital

$1 - \alpha$ = the share of output that is distributed to labor

The growth accounting equation tells us that the growth rate of GDP is equal to the growth rate of technology plus the growth rates of capital and labor, weighted by their shares of output.

An important aspect of growth accounting is that it offers a way to estimate the importance of technology in economic growth. Output, labor, and capital are relatively straightforward to define and measure. In contrast, technology is hard to measure. It can take the form of new innovations in information technology, better management practices, or simply reduced government distortions. Measuring technology directly would therefore be close to impossible.

Growth accounting, however, provides an *indirect* route to measuring technology. Since we can directly measure the growth of output, labor, and capital, and we also have a rough idea how large the capital and labor shares are, we can simply compute the growth of technology as a *residual* in the equation above. Indeed, this residual is exactly what macroeconomists have in mind when they talk about technology—it's the unexplained part of economic growth!

As an example of how growth accounting works in practice, let's consider China's growth experience from 1978 to 2004, an era that generated the highest sustained period of growth on record. China's GDP grew at an average annual rate of 9.3 percent; employment grew at around 2 percent; capital grew at about 10 percent.[3] The capital share of output in China was about

40 percent during this period, while the labor share was around 60 percent. Substituting these values into our growth accounting equation (Equation 10-4), we can solve for the implied growth rate of technology:

$$0.093 = g_A + (0.4 \times 0.10) + (0.6 \times 0.02)$$
$$g_A = 0.093 - (0.4 \times 0.10) - (0.6 \times 0.02) = 0.041$$

Thus, even though China experienced a rapid increase in its physical capital stock over the 30 years since the beginning of the reform era, just about half of the total growth in GDP came from "technology." The quotes around "technology" are there to remind you that technology includes all changes that lead the economy to use inputs more efficiently; this includes the effects of reduced government distortions, for example, as well as new management practices and modernized factories.

Convergence

LO 10.5 Assess the empirical evidence for and against convergence theory.

Are poor countries doomed to stay poor, like cars poking along forever at 10 or 20 mph? Or does the fact that a country now is poor just mean that we are seeing it early in the development process, like a car moving slowly but accelerating toward highway speed? Will China and other low-income but fast-growing countries eventually reach a similar level of wealth to the United States and Switzerland? If they do, will they keep accelerating forever, or will they eventually see their rates of growth slow and settle in on the highway alongside the world's rich countries?

One classic model of economic growth suggests the "settling in" story is the correct one. This model relates to the idea of *decreasing marginal returns* to factors of production: Countries that start with very little physical capital will get a higher return from adding a unit of capital than will a country that starts at a higher initial level. This leads to the general hypothesis that countries starting at low levels of income (which correspond to low levels of capital) will tend to grow at much faster rates than those starting with high levels of income. Each additional unit of capital provides larger gains when you're coming from behind.

convergence theory
the theory that countries that start out poor will initially grow faster than rich ones but will eventually converge to the same growth rate

This idea is called **convergence theory** (or the *catch-up effect*). It says that poor countries will grow faster than rich ones, until they catch up and all countries "converge" to the same growth rate. The theory predicts that even if countries differ in their rates of savings, population growth, and other features, they will still converge to the same *growth rate,* although not the same *level of income.* In other words, countries that start out poor should initially grow faster than ones that start out rich but will eventually slow to the same growth rate.

In some ways, convergence theory fits the evidence from the real world. Figure 10-3 shows the differences between growth rates in countries around the world from 1990 to 2010. Looking at the map, you'll see that:

- Richer countries have mostly been growing slowly.
- Most of the fastest growth rates are occurring in some of the poorest countries. (However, you can also see plenty of poor countries on the map that have not been growing quickly, especially in Africa.)

Many economists think convergence theory explains the incredible growth of the East Asian countries. Those countries experienced very high marginal returns as they began to accumulate physical and human capital. They also were well positioned to take advantage of technologies and capital flows from wealthier countries.

In other places, however, convergence is clearly not happening. Most African countries started at levels of physical and human capital as low as East Asia's half a century ago, but they have

FIGURE 10-3

World GDP per capita growth rates, 1990–2010[*]   Over these 20 years, there has been a wide disparity in the rate of economic growth. This growth has been strongest in Southeast Asia, while the rate of economic growth in most of Western Europe has been sluggish.

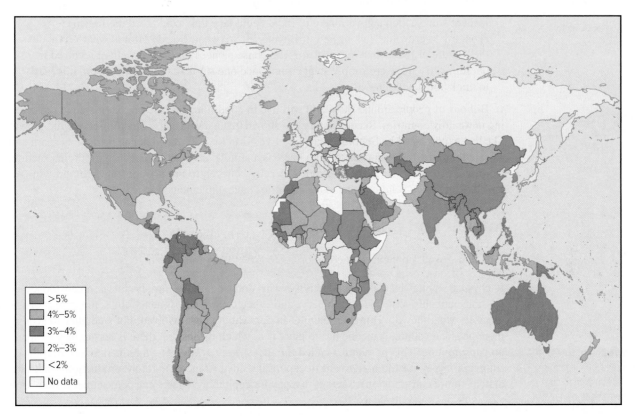

* In most of the former Soviet bloc, data start in 1991 after the fall of the USSR.
Source: World Bank, *World Development Indicators*, http://databank.worldbank.org/ddp/home.do.

not experienced the same growth spurt. In fact, many actually became poorer during the 1980s and early 1990s. Clearly, simply starting out poor is not a guarantee of achieving impressive growth rates.

The fact that the poorest regions of the world have tended to grow more slowly than the richest regions of the world suggests that world incomes have become more unequal over time. But that is true only if we take *countries* as our units of analysis. If we instead ignore countries and look at the distribution of *individual incomes* around the world, we arrive at a completely different picture of inequality. Because some of the fastest-growing countries in the world, such as China, India, and Indonesia, started out both relatively poor and populous, the world distribution of incomes has actually become more equal over time.[4]

To try to understand what allows some low-income countries to take off while others stagnate, we need to consider how public policy affects economic growth.

✓CONCEPT CHECK

☐ What are the main determinants of productivity? **[LO 10.2]**
☐ How are rates different from levels when talking about economic growth? **[LO 10.3]**
☐ How do economists measure the impact of technology on economic growth? **[LO 10.4]**
☐ What does convergence theory predict about growth rates? About income levels? **[LO 10.5]**

Growth and Public Policy

Nobel Prize winner Robert Lucas captured the fascination and sense of possibility that come with thinking about economic growth in this way:

> Is there some action a government of India could take that would lead the Indian economy to grow like Indonesia's or Egypt's? If so, what, exactly? If not, what is it about the "nature of India" that makes it so? The consequences for human welfare involved in questions like these are simply staggering: Once one starts to think about them, it is hard to think about anything else.[5]

Billions of people around the world still live in conditions that are unimaginable to those living in wealthy countries. Recent history has shown that a few decades of strong economic growth like that experienced by South Korea could transform their lives. What can be done to spark and sustain that growth? Unfortunately, no one has a simple answer to this question. In this section, we discuss some of the factors that are generally believed to promote or hold back growth. We also look at policy solutions that some countries have implemented successfully.

Investment and savings

LO 10.6 Discuss policies that could promote growth and relate them to productivity.

If physical capital increases productivity, why don't countries simply put as much money as possible into infrastructure, machinery, and other capital investments? In some cases, this is precisely what they do. However, there is an opportunity cost involved. For a country to acquire more physical capital, someone has to pay for it, which means that there is less money to spend on consumption. This problem is called the **investment trade-off**—a reduction in current consumption to pay for the investment in capital intended to increase future production (and, ultimately, future consumption). Savings that pay for capital investment can come either from within a country or from outside it.

investment trade-off a reduction in current consumption to pay for investment in capital intended to increase future production

domestic savings savings for capital investment that come from within a country; equal to domestic income minus consumption spending

Investment funds from within a country
Savings that come from within a country are called **domestic savings** and are equal to domestic income minus consumption spending. They can come from two sources:

- private households spending less than they earn or
- government revenues exceeding expenditures.

Savings rates vary enormously across countries, as Figure 10-4 shows. On one end of the spectrum, we have China, where the economy typically puts away a whopping 49 percent of GDP. In contrast, the United States saves just 18 percent, and households contribute a small share of that saving. In 2016, the U.S. household savings rate was just above 5 percent.[6]

Governments also can use tax revenues (or borrow money) to invest in physical capital. Governments often fund the underlying infrastructure that private companies rely on for their operations, such as roads, bridges, ports, and sewer systems. This infrastructure can have a major effect on growth. In many low-income countries, for example, even if farmers could grow more, it would be hard to get their goods to market because of poor roads. Many governments are currently investing heavily in communications infrastructure such as high-speed Internet, in the expectation that it will improve private companies' productivity.

foreign direct investment (FDI) investment when a firm runs part of its operation abroad or owns all or part of another company abroad

Investment funds from outside a country
Funds for capital investment can also come from outside a country. **Foreign direct investment (FDI)** is investment that occurs when a firm runs part of its operation abroad or invests in another company abroad. For example, when Toyota operates a plant in the U.S. state of Georgia, the

FIGURE 10-4

Gross savings rates among countries in 2014.   Savings rates vary a lot around the world. For example, China saves a whopping 49 percent of GDP, India saves 31 percent, and the United States saves 18 percent. Gross savings are calculated as national income less total consumption plus net transfers.

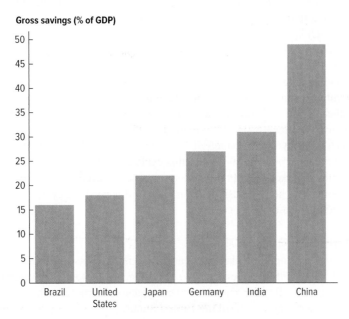

Source: *World Bank Indicators*. http://data.worldbank.org/indicator/NY.GNS.ICTR.ZS.

Japanese firm owns the machinery and buildings, even though the production takes place in the United States. Similarly, factories owned by U.S. firms on the Mexican side of the United States–Mexico border are an important source of FDI in Mexico.

Many governments actively work to attract FDI, hoping it will build up their capital stock when domestic savings aren't sufficient. Another benefit of FDI is that when foreign companies invest in local firms, they can transfer human capital to local managers and workers. Perhaps managers from the foreign country travel to oversee the investment. In doing so, they can train local staff or set up more efficient procedures.

However, FDI has its critics. Foreign firms with money to invest often have numerous governments competing to attract the investment. The firm can drive a hard bargain, demanding special tax breaks or legal exemptions that governments cannot easily afford. The transfer of knowledge or technology may also not happen to the extent some would wish, if foreign managers oversee operations without training up local talent. As a result, some argue that a policy of attracting FDI might not ultimately be as beneficial as it first appears.

Education and health

In rich countries, we take free basic education for granted. In many countries, however, schools may be few and far between, charge unaffordable fees to students, or simply provide very low-quality education. One of the major efforts of the Sustainable Development Goals—a collection of targets set by the United Nations to tackle aspects of poverty in low-income countries by 2030—has been to push countries to provide free elementary school education.

Free availability of high-quality public education for all children is one of the most important ways a country can increase its stock of human capital. Education teaches skills such as literacy, basic math, and communication—all essential to perform more than the most elementary jobs. High-quality education also builds the pool of scientists, thinkers, and entrepreneurs who develop new technologies and business models.

Using public policy to promote health can also contribute to growth. Workers who are in good health will be more productive and less likely to miss work days. Some economic benefits of improved health are less visible, especially in low-income countries. For instance, health economists have found that reducing vitamin and mineral deficiencies such as anemia (the result of a diet with not enough iron in it) and parasites such as worms can improve people's mental and physical energy. Treatment for such health problems increases the ability to focus, making it easier for children to learn in school and for adults to do their best at work.

It's hard to accumulate greater levels of human capital when health problems and lack of educational opportunities combine. Most of us would agree that we are more productive when we're working with other highly educated workers. In some places, like California's Silicon Valley, this creates a positive feedback loop in productivity: Talented computer programmers and business managers can multiply their productivity by working with other talented programmers and managers. In low-income countries, however, this cycle can work in the opposite direction: The productivity of skilled workers can diminish due to the lower average levels of skill of their co-workers. Public policy can help to push a country out of this negative cycle by improving public health services and the quality of education.

Technological development

A lot of research and development takes place at private institutions—in firms, private laboratories, and so on. However, public policy can also encourage technological development—through the educational system, funding for research and study, and tax structures that encourage firms to develop and adopt new technologies. In the United States, just under 3 percent of GDP is spent on research and development. Less than a third of that amount is spent by the federal government to support universities and research institutes. Most research and development spending is done by business.[7]

You might be wondering why the government should be involved in research and development in areas other than military spending and public works. Recall that technology is fundamentally about ideas, which once created can be adopted at low cost by others. This means that there is a positive externality associated with innovation: Part of the benefit associated with a firm's investment in new ideas goes to competing firms. As a result, there is a "free-rider" problem associated with innovation.

The economy as a whole would be better off with more innovation. But firms underproduce innovation because they care only about the direct benefits of innovation for their own bottom line. They do not care about the indirect benefits to other firms in the economy. The tendency to underproduce innovation creates a reason for the government to keep supporting research and development.

Advancements in technology can be fantastic, but they can also be fickle. The "green revolution," which introduced new agricultural technologies, was a rousing success in Asia but has been more complicated in Africa. The Real Life box "Green revolutions in Asia and Africa" provides details of this story.

Real Life

Green revolutions in Asia and Africa

In 1961, India was at risk of famine. The population was booming, and no more farmland was available. How would everyone be fed? Incredibly, by 1985 the specter of famine had all but disappeared, not only in India but across Asia. In just 25 years, crop yields doubled, easily outpacing the growth of the population.

This transformation in agriculture, called the *green revolution,* was the result of painstaking research and development funded by private charities such as the Rockefeller Foundation. It resulted in new crop varieties, such as strain IR8, or "miracle rice," developed in 1968 by the International Rice Research Institute in the Philippines. "Miracle rice" required more intensive fertilizer and irrigation treatments than traditional varieties but produced about double the amount of rice per plant.

Unfortunately, the green revolution did not reach Africa. While climate, soil, and growing conditions are fairly similar across much of Asia, they vary widely in Africa. The high-yielding varieties of rice and wheat simply didn't grow as well there. A variety of rice that doubles yields in most Asian countries may wilt in the drier climate of Ethiopia or be swamped in the equatorial rains of the Congo.

African farmers today mostly still farm as their grandparents did, and as farmers in Asia did 50 years ago, with little fertilizer and limited tools. Growing enough food in Africa requires the agricultural sector to employ a large percentage of the labor force. Many economists believe that this difference partly explains why Asia's economies have grown more quickly than Africa's in the last half century: When you don't need as many workers to grow food, they can do something else instead, such as work in factories in the city.

The search is now on for ways to make the green revolution work in Africa. The Bill and Melinda Gates Foundation and the Rockefeller Foundation are funding a regional approach that tries to tailor plant varieties and practices to local conditions. This new work may not be as immediate or dramatic as the Asian green revolution, but it may lead to innovations that put ample food in every bowl—and help Africa along the path to greater prosperity.

Laying the groundwork: Good government, property rights, and economic openness

LO 10.7 Explain how good governance and economic openness lay the foundation for growth.

Imagine that you live in a country where, if someone steals your truck, there is nothing you can do about it. The police won't help you, unless you bribe them. Even if you could get police help, it might take five years and a lot of money to prosecute someone in court. Would you still buy a truck? You might, if you thought that the potential benefits were high enough to outweigh the risk of losing your investment. But you'd certainly be less inclined to invest in trucks and other expensive capital goods than you would if you thought that your property would be protected.

This is just one example of the ways in which enforceable laws and effective, trustworthy government services are critical to a well-functioning economy. Most countries have mechanisms to punish those who violate the property rights of others and to enforce contracts between buyers and sellers. Institutions like police forces, courts of law, and government bureaucracies are meant to protect property, settle disputes, and provide a predictable legal framework in which people can make plans and agreements. However, these institutions are more effective and reliable in some countries than in others.

Stability in leadership and institutions is important, as is effectiveness. Would you want to build an expensive new factory if you thought there was a good chance of new leaders coming to power who might seize it? Would you risk investing in a business if the tax policies or laws that determine its profitability change from month to month?

Many economists believe that good government has a major impact on economic growth. The degree of government effectiveness can help us understand why some economies have grown rapidly and others have stagnated. How to improve government is a tricky question, though. It is challenging to design effective policies to tackle corruption, make courts more efficient, limit the powers of politicians, and so on.

Government policy also determines how open a country will be to trade. Firms often argue that governments need to protect them from competition by placing tariffs on foreign goods. However, the "Asian miracle" countries succeeded by combining industrial policy with "outward-oriented" policies to gear their economies toward exporting goods. Later in the book, we'll discuss free trade and why most economists believe that there are important gains to keeping economies open.

The juggling act

As with many things in life, there are *trade-offs* between different ways of promoting growth through public policy. Most governments—especially those in poor countries—can't pay for education *and* health *and* highways *and* better police all at the same time. Unfortunately, this is a vicious cycle: The richer you are, the better able you are to pay for things that will help you be even richer in the future. The poorer you are, the less able you are to pay for the things that can make you richer.

Earlier in the chapter, we noted the trade-off between current consumption and investment in physical capital, human capital, and research that will contribute to growth and to higher future income. The poorer the country, the tougher this trade-off becomes. It's harder for people who live close to the edge on a dollar or two a day to save a given amount of money or pay more taxes than it would be for wealthier people. This logic leads to the vicious cycle described above. If you can't afford to pay for a good court system or to invest in a tractor or a computer, you will find it harder to climb out of poverty. This "poverty trap" is one of the main justifications for foreign aid that provides loans or funding for infrastructure and human capital development.

Why don't countries take one element at a time—for example, focusing limited resources first on infrastructure, and then on education or health, and so on? Unfortunately, it's not usually that simple. Growth often requires concurrent improvements in many aspects of the economy. For instance, translating new technology into growth often requires a population with sufficient human capital to take advantage of it, and sometimes specific infrastructure.

Imagine a country trying to build an Internet-based economy. This would be difficult, if not impossible, if much of the population can't read, or if the electrical grid experiences regular blackouts due to insufficient power generation. Harnessing the power of the Internet to promote commerce, and thus growth, would require simultaneous improvements in literacy, computer skills, the power grid, a trustworthy postal service, and payment mechanisms.

Another trade-off that governments face is how much to sacrifice their natural environment in pursuit of economic growth. The What Do You Think? box "Should poor countries be as earth-friendly as rich ones?" explores this particular trade-off.

What Do You Think?
Should poor countries be as earth-friendly as rich ones?

During the European Industrial Revolution, factories spewed pollution into the atmosphere as they rolled out a steady stream of textiles, steel, and other goods. Power plants fueled by dirty coal dotted cities throughout Western Europe and eventually the United States. Miners and factory workers alike often died of lung diseases and other health problems associated with dirty air and unsafe working conditions. After many years of unchecked pollution, conditions got so bad that London suffered from chronic smog that would settle over the city for days, blotting out the sun. In 1952, one particularly severe smog episode killed over 4,000 people. In retrospect, the environmental and health consequences of Europe's industrialization seem awful. At the time, though, they were simply part and parcel of a massive increase in wealth and economic power.

In the past 50 years, technologies have been developed that allow firms to produce goods and energy with far less pollution. Low-income countries today don't necessarily have to go through the same painful arc that marked earlier industrial transformations. Despite this, China's economic explosion has been accompanied by smog and the release of toxic chemicals into rivers. Occasionally, actual explosions at factories have killed thousands of people and filled the atmosphere with pollutants. Why haven't firms in China chosen to use the new, cleaner technology now available?

There are two reasons:

- Acquiring clean technologies is not always straightforward, due to stringent trade policies or intellectual property laws.
- Even when these technologies are accessible, they may be very expensive.

The reason factories and power plants in Europe and the United States are now relatively clean is not because the new technologies are always cheaper than the older, dirtier methods. Rather, it's often because governments in those countries have introduced strict regulations requiring firms to mitigate their environmental impact and protect the health and safety of their workers and neighbors.

The questions for China and other low-income countries are:

- Do we want to introduce strict environmental laws, forcing companies to use expensive clean technology?
- Or do we want to grow our economy as quickly as possible by using cheaper ways of doing things, even if they are environmentally damaging?

Many in richer countries feel that fast-growing countries such as India and China should have to protect the environment by using the cleaner technologies now available. They point out that production in low-income countries is releasing vast amounts of greenhouse gases, which affect other countries, too. For example, even though China's economy is barely a third the size of the U.S. economy, China is already the largest producer of carbon dioxide in the world. The effects, through climate change, could be disastrous all over the world.

Low-income countries, on the other hand, counter that being forced to use the cleaner technologies would make their goods more expensive and less competitive in the world market. They argue that developed countries created the problem of climate change by releasing greenhouse gases during their own industrial revolutions. It's not fair, they say, to expect poorer countries to pay the penance. It's also not clear what the more "humane" policy is: We've seen that economic growth can decrease poverty and alleviate suffering, and stricter regulations likely mean slower growth and slower poverty reduction.

To help solve this impasse, the United Nations has launched a "Green Climate Fund." Starting in 2020, the fund will distribute $100 billion per year to low-income countries, partly to help them acquire and pay for cleaner technologies. The fund may help countries avoid some of the pollution associated with economic growth, but probably won't solve the whole problem.

WHAT DO YOU THINK?

1. Should all countries be held to the same environmental standards?
2. Do rich countries have a responsibility to help poorer countries acquire cleaner technologies?
3. Is it worth implementing cleaner technologies if it means slower growth?

Sources: http://www.reuters.com/article/2011/04/15/us-climate-fund-idUSTRE73E3WG20110415; http://www.cnbc.com/id/43139649; http://news.bbc.co.uk/2/hi/uk_news/england/2545759.stm;http://www.nytimes.com/2010/07/29/world/asia/29china.html; http://www.law.duke.edu/journals/dltr/articles/2009dltr001.html.

✓ CONCEPT CHECK

☐ What determinant of economic growth is influenced by domestic saving? **[LO 10.6]**
☐ Why do police protection and efficient courts matter for economic growth? **[LO 10.7]**

Conclusion

Economic growth can make the rich richer. It also is a powerful way to make the poor richer too. In this chapter, we looked at how we define and measure economic growth and why growth is so important. Because of compounding, even a small increase in the growth rate will have a large impact on the level of income in the long run. A country that is growing at 3.5 percent, instead of 2 percent, will end up approximately four times richer after 100 years.

In order to grow, a country needs to be able to put together the ingredients:

- savings that can be invested into physical capital,
- healthy and skilled workers,
- appropriate technology, and
- supportive public policies and institutions.

All governments face tough trade-offs: How much should the country invest in health, education, and infrastructure? How can the government create a secure legal environment for people to invest? The goal is a positive cycle in which people gain human capital, invent better technology, become more productive at their jobs, get richer and be able to afford more physical capital, and so on.

This process is not easy, but it is important. If policy-makers, businesses, and workers come together effectively to build the right environment for investment, their contributions can deliver a foundation for the prosperity of future generations.

Key Terms

productivity, p. 255

physical capital, p. 256

human capital, p. 256

convergence theory, p. 260

investment trade-off, p. 262

domestic savings, p. 262

foreign direct investment (FDI), p. 262

Summary

LO 10.1 Calculate the growth rate of real GDP per capita, accounting for changes in price levels and population.

The fact that growth compounds over time makes it hard to tell just from looking at the annual growth rate what the total effect on incomes will be. GDP growth rates are often stated without taking population growth into account and sometimes without taking inflation into account. To find the rate of real GDP growth, take the nominal growth rate and subtract both population growth and inflation growth rates.

National economic growth builds on itself over time. The result is that a relatively modest annual growth rate, like 2 percent, actually adds up to quite a large total

growth rate over time. The rate at which GDP increases incomes can be found through the *rule of 70:* To find how long it takes incomes to double within a country, divide 70 by the rate of real GDP growth.

LO 10.2 Describe the relationship between productivity and growth and discuss the factors that determine productivity.

The only way that a country can consume more and enjoy a higher standard of living is to increase its *productivity*— the amount it produces per worker. Productivity can be measured for any unit of labor, whether that unit is an hour of time worked or how much one worker produces; it is typically measured as output per person. The factors that influence labor productivity are physical capital, human capital, technology, and natural resources.

LO 10.3 Explain the difference between a country's level of income and its rate of growth.

There are two important distinctions to make in terms of economic development. One is about the *level* of well-being. Countries like the United States or Switzerland that have very high amounts of physical and human capital are said to be at a high level of development. The other distinction is about the *rate* of economic growth. While the United States may have a high level of development, the rate of growth in U.S. GDP is not nearly as fast as China's. Level matters because it tells how wealthy a country currently is. Rates matter because they tell how quickly a country is increasing its wealth.

LO 10.4 Use the growth accounting framework to describe how technology, labor, and capital contribute to economic growth.

The growth accounting framework is a way to explain the growth rate of GDP as the sum of the growth rate of technology plus the growth rates of capital and labor, weighted by their shares of output. The framework helps us see how much of growth is due to using more inputs (capital and labor) versus using existing inputs more efficiently (via technology).

While labor and capital are relatively straightforward to measure, it's much harder to measure technology. Fortunately, the framework gives a way to estimate the importance of technology in economic growth by calculating it indirectly as a residual. The evidence shows that technology (defined broadly) is often extremely important in explaining growth.

LO 10.5 Assess the empirical evidence for and against convergence theory.

Convergence theory predicts that countries that are starting at lower levels of income will grow at a faster rate than those starting at higher levels, until they catch up and converge to the same growth rate.

In some ways, convergence theory fits evidence from the real world. The four East Asian countries that experienced incredible growth since the 1960s started from low levels of physical and human capital but were well positioned to take advantage of technologies and capital flows from wealthier countries. However, most African countries had similar or even lower levels of physical and human capital than did East Asia half a century ago but have not experienced high growth rates.

LO 10.6 Discuss policies that could promote growth and relate them to productivity.

Countries face an investment trade-off, in which they must reduce current consumption to pay for the capital investment needed to increase future production. Funds to pay for capital investment can come either from domestic savings or from foreign direct investment (FDI) from outside the country.

A variety of policies can promote economic growth. Education teaches skills such as literacy, basic math, and communication, which are essential to perform more than the most elementary jobs. Education is also a way to develop the training and skills that countries need to be able to undertake technological research and development. Public health systems can also contribute to growth by increasing the portion of the population that is fit, healthy, and able to work. Public policy can also encourage technological development through the education system, funding for research and study, and tax structures that encourage firms to develop and adopt new technologies.

LO 10.7 Explain how good governance and economic openness lay the foundation for growth.

Enforceable laws and effective, trustworthy government services are critical to a well-functioning economy. The most important is the provision of property rights, giving people the ability to have control over the resources they own. Most countries have institutions and infrastructure that are at least partially designed to protect these property rights. Courts enforce the contracts between buyers and sellers. They also are responsible, through the criminal justice system, for punishing people who are accused of violating the property rights of others.

Review Questions

1. Explain why inflation reduces the real value of nominal GDP per capita. **[LO 10.1]**

2. When policy-makers discuss policies that encourage long-run growth in per capita real GDP, they often mention policies aimed at reducing the growth rate in the population. If effective, why might these policies improve long-run growth? Also, what are the potential costs associated with these policies? **[LO 10.1]**

3. Does the rule of 70 predict greater increases in the amount of income for richer or poorer countries when both have the same growth rate? Why? **[LO 10.1, 10.3]**

4. Explain why many rich countries are able to continuously grow, even though they already have very high levels of physical and human capital. **[LO 10.2]**

5. At a young age, would you rather have a large level of savings or a pool of savings that was increasing at a faster rate? **[LO 10.3]**

6. If a country's labor and capital grow at the same rate, is this likely to have the same impact on the growth rate of output? Why or why not? **[LO 10.4]**

7. Measuring the growth in technology directly is almost impossible. How does the growth accounting equation allow economists to calculate an implied growth rate for technology? **[LO 10.4]**

8. Using the growth rates for countries found in Figure 10-3, is there evidence that poorer countries in Africa and Asia are converging to the level of income found in Western Europe? Why or why not? **[LO 10.5]**

9. Southern states in the United States are, on average, poorer than northern states. Southern states also have higher growth rates in real GDP per capita, on average, than northern states. Use these facts to draw a conclusion about whether the theory of convergence is correct. What other factors should be considered? **[LO 10.5]**

10. Many believe that technology is very costly to create but cheap to transfer. For example, think of the personal computer: The technology underpinning the personal computer took a generation of time and a ton of money to create. However, now that the personal computer has been created, it is easy for others to purchase and reap the benefits. Given this insight, what do you believe will be the growth implications for the United States (traditionally more apt to create new technology) and China (traditionally more apt to adopt technologies created elsewhere)? **[LO 10.5, 10.6]**

11. How might low rates of saving in the United States limit the accumulation of physical capital? **[LO 10.6]**

12. Realizing that poor countries must solve many problems at once has shifted donors away from the idea of giving multiple small payments to the idea of a "Big Push." This Big Push entails giving a very large sum of money that could be used to fix multiple problems at once. In fact, the amount of money required might be so large that other countries might be the only ones who could afford the donation. What are the trade-offs associated with this idea? **[LO 10.6]**

13. How is it possible that Switzerland, a landlocked country with almost no natural resources, is one of the richest countries in the world while the Democratic Republic of the Congo, a huge country with vast deposits of many strategically important minerals, is one of the poorest? **[LO 10.2, 10.6, 10.7]**

14. Why could a free press be important for economic growth? (Think about the connection between the press and government.) **[LO 10.7]**

Problems and Applications

1. Fill in the blanks in Table 10P-1. **[LO 10.1]**

2. Equation 10-1 states that Real GDP per capita growth rate = Nominal GDP per capita growth rate − Inflation rate − Population growth rate.

   This equation is an approximation of the exact rate of growth of GDP per capita, and so it results in some errors when calculating this rate. However, the simplified equation both is easy to use and results in small error terms when inflation, nominal GDP growth, and population growth are low, and so it is a useful approximation. Table 10P-2 lists a fictional country's nominal GDP, real GDP, GDP deflator, and population over two years. **[LO 10.1]**

   a. Use your knowledge from Chapter 8, "The Cost of Living," to verify that the real GDP figures in Table 10P-2 are accurate.

   b. Calculate this country's real GDP per capita for both 2015 and 2016.

   c. Calculate the growth rate in this country's real GDP per capita between 2015 and 2016.

   d. Calculate the growth rates in the nominal GDP, GDP deflator, and the population.

3. For each growth rate below, use the rule of 70 to calculate how long it will take incomes to double. **[LO 10.2]**

   a. 4 percent.

   b. 7 percent.

   c. 2.5 percent.

   d. 10 percent.

   e. 3 percent.

4. For each part below, determine whether the following actions will increase or decrease productivity, and name the component of productivity that each affects. **[LO 10.2]**

   a. The local government builds a new school.

   b. Teachers in the new school hold classes for young students.

   c. A manufacturer installs robots on its assembly line.

   d. A research team designs a more efficient system of irrigation.

   e. A soda company discovers a new source of underground water that can be used to make its products.

   f. A professor writes a new and improved economics textbook.

   g. A large number of people have less access to health care.

   h. A worker receives on-the-job training to be a mechanic.

TABLE 10P-1

Country	Nominal GDP growth (%)	Population growth (%)	Inflation (%)	Real GDP growth per capita (%)
Svea	5	3		−1
Bonifay	2	1	0	
Chaires		2	7	4
Drifton	5	0	−1	
Estiffanulga	7		3	3

TABLE 10P-2

Year	Nominal GDP ($)	GDP deflator	Real GDP ($)	Population
2015	1,000,000	1.00	1,000,000	1,000
2016	1,050,000	1.02	1,029,412	1,005

TABLE 10P-3

Country	GDP per capita 2010 ($)	GDP per capita 2015 ($)
Boliv	3,664	4,592
Chi	4,102	7,519
Ghala	2,007	2,615
Artinia	10,860	15,854
Plazi	8,603	11,239

TABLE 10P-4

Country	Income per capita ($)	Real per capita GDP growth rate (%)
Ansonia	5,000	7.0
Trumbull	7,500	4.5
Shelton	10,000	2.0

5. Which of the countries shown in Table 10P-3 had the highest level of per capita income in 2015? Which had the highest rate of income growth from 2010 to 2015? Do incomes in these countries appear to be converging? [LO 10.3, 10.5]

6. In 2015 the median household income in Louisiana was approximately $45,000 per year, while the income per household in Massachusetts was about $69,000. However, suppose the growth rate of per capita real GDP in Louisiana is higher than in Massachusetts (3 percent versus 2 percent). [LO 10.3, 10.5]
   a. From the perspective of trying to maximize your income per capita, which state will have higher increases in income over the next few years?
   b. From the perspective of trying to maximize your income per capita, which state will have higher increases in income in the long run?

7. Will the three countries in Table 10P-4 converge to the same level of economic development given enough time? [LO 10.3, 10.5]

8. Indicate whether each of the following statements is true or false and explain your answer. [LO 10.4]
   a. Country A's labor share is 60 percent, Country B's labor share is 70 percent, and labor is growing at a rate of 3 percent in both countries. All else the same, Country B has a higher growth rate of output.
   b. Country A's labor share is 40 percent, Country B's labor share is 70 percent, and labor is growing at a rate of 10 percent in country A and 6 percent in country B. All else the same, Country A has a higher growth rate of output.
   c. Labor is growing at a negative rate in country A and a positive rate in country B, so country B must have a higher growth rate of output.
   d. Labor and capital are both growing more quickly in Country A than in Country B, so Country A must have a higher growth rate of output.

9. Calculate the implied growth rate of technology in each scenario in Table 10P-5. Assume labor's share of output is 70 percent and capital's share of output is 30 percent. [LO 10.4]

TABLE 10P-5

Scenario	Growth Rate of Output (%)	Growth Rate of Labor (%)	Growth Rate of Capital (%)	Implied Growth Rate of Technology (%)
A	3.0	2	2	
B	4.2	3	3	
C	3.0	1	5	
D	4.2	1	4	

10. For each of the following examples, state whether this activity would likely hinder or promote economic growth, and name a component of productivity each produces or reduces. **[LO 10.2, 10.6]**

   a. Not requiring students to attend school.

   b. Granting patents on new inventions.

   c. Building a solid infrastructure system.

   d. Allowing local rivers and streams to become polluted.

11. Policy-makers in the U.S. government have long tried to write laws that encourage growth in per capita real GDP. These laws typically do one of three things, as listed below. For each of the three points, name a law or government program with that intention. **[LO 10.6]**

   a. They encourage firms to invest more in research and development in order to boost technology.

   b. They encourage individuals to save more in order to boost the physical capital stock.

   c. They encourage individuals to invest more in education in order to boost the stock of human capital.

12. Name the type of institution that is responsible for promoting a stable environment for the economy regarding each of the following situations. **[LO 10.7]**

   a. Someone steals your car, but is caught.

   b. You claim that your employer violated the terms of your employment contract.

Endnotes

1. Calculated using the series at http://data.worldbank.org/indicator/NY.GDP.PCAP.CD.

2. https://fred.stlouisfed.org/series/A939RX0Q048SBEA.

3. Barry Bosworth and Susan M. Collins, "Accounting for Growth: Comparing China and India," *Journal of Economic Perspectives* 22, no. 1 (Winter 2008): 45–66, https://www.aeaweb.org/articles?id=10.1257/jep.22.1.45.

4. Xavier Sala-i-Martin, "The World Distribution of Income: Falling Poverty and . . . Convergence, Period," *The Quarterly Journal of Economics* 121, no. 2 (2006): 351–97.

5. Robert Lucas, "On the Mechanics of Economic Development," *Journal of Monetary Economics* 22 (1988), p. 5.

6. http://www.tradingeconomics.com/united-states/personal-savings.

7. http://www.nytimes.com/2015/05/20/business/economy/american-innovation-rests-on-weak-foundation.html; http://www.aaas.org/page/historical-trends-federal-rd; data from World Bank and Bureau of Labor Statistics.

Part Five

The Economy in the Short and Long Run

The three chapters in Part 5 will introduce you to . . .

a basic model of the entire economy. The preceding four chapters introduced the key economic concepts used to measure the health of the economy and how the economy changes over time. Now, we'll put the pieces together.

Chapter 11, "Aggregate Expenditure," focuses on the forces responsible for recessions and booms. The chapter develops a model of *aggregate expenditure,* which shows how an economy can get "stuck" producing below potential output. We build intuition without describing a complete model of the economy. To keep things simple, the chapter investigates what happens when the price level doesn't change in the short run.

Chapter 12, "Aggregate Demand and Aggregate Supply," introduces a more complete framework that describes the state of the national economy as a whole. All of the transactions in the economy—from the snack you bought on the way to class to the purchase of new computer servers by Amazon—can be represented by a single demand curve, called *aggregate demand.* On the other side, everything that firms produce is represented by a single supply curve, called *aggregate supply.* We can use these two curves, together, to investigate changes in the entire economy, through booms and busts. Aggregate demand and aggregate supply are the main concepts used in macroeconomics to provide fundamental insights into changes in the broader economy.

Using the aggregate demand/aggregate supply model, we can start to analyze how policy choices affect the national economy. Government decisions about taxes and spending make up *fiscal policy,* which is the focus of Chapter 13, "Fiscal Policy." The chapter compares the effects of taxes and government spending on the economy. It turns out that one dollar of government spending doesn't add just one dollar to overall GDP. Thanks to the effect of a multiplier, when the government spends money or changes taxes, the effect of the dollar gets magnified throughout the economy. If you understand the role of the multiplier, you're a long way toward understanding what policy can and can't do.

Aggregate Expenditure

Learning Objectives

LO 11.1 Identify the factors that affect the consumption component of aggregate expenditure.

LO 11.2 Identify the factors that affect the investment component of aggregate expenditure.

LO 11.3 Identify the factors that affect the government spending component of aggregate expenditure.

LO 11.4 Identify the factors that affect the net exports component of aggregate expenditure.

LO 11.5 Describe autonomous expenditure and outline the simplifications made in the aggregate expenditure model.

LO 11.6 Describe the difference between planned and actual aggregate expenditure and show their relationship graphically.

LO 11.7 Show how to find equilibrium aggregate expenditure when given the relationship between planned aggregate expenditure and actual aggregate expenditure.

LO 11.8 Explain the importance of the aggregate expenditure equilibrium model to understanding the behavior of the economy.

LO 11.9 Illustrate how any initial change in aggregate expenditure can have a multiplier effect on the overall level of aggregate expenditure.

THE BIG CRASH

In the fall of 1929, a famous economist, Irving Fisher, remarked, "Stock prices have reached what looks like a permanently high plateau." Unfortunately, Fisher could not have been more wrong. Shortly after Fisher's optimistic prediction, stock prices in the United States started plummeting, bottoming out in July 1932 at a level 90 percent below the high of September 1929. Millions of Americans lost their investments. Worse yet, the stock market crash was followed by a devastating drop in output, employment, and prices in the United States and around the world, known as the Great Depression.

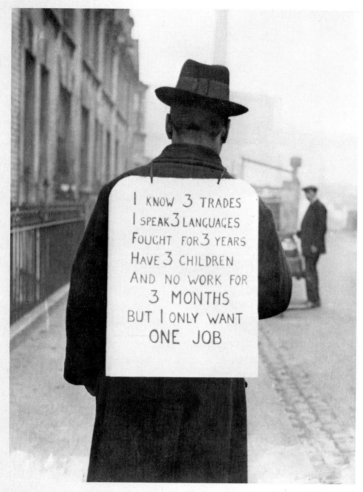

© General Photographic Agency/Stringer/Getty Images

Bill O'Reilly, a pundit on Fox News, recalls: "My parents were children during the Great Depression of the 1930's, and it scarred them. Especially my father, who saw destitution in his Brooklyn, New York, neighborhood: adults standing in so-called 'bread lines,' children begging in the streets."[1] The Great Depression started in 1929 and the worst part lasted through 1933, but it took over a decade for the economy to recover.

In contrast, the Great Recession of 2007–2009 was another sharp, global economic downturn, but it was shorter and less severe than what happened in the 1930s. As O'Reilly describes the biggest economic downturn since the Great Depression: "Fast forward to the severe recession of 2008, when millions of Americans lost jobs and equity in their homes. No bread lines, but much pain."[2]

Depressions and recessions are puzzling. People are *willing* to work at the prevailing wage, but they can't find a job. Firms can supply more output, but there simply isn't enough demand. Workers lose their jobs, machines run idle, inventories accumulate, and output falls sharply. A lot of people suffer.

It's no surprise that economists want to know why things go so wrong. More importantly, they want to know what policymakers can do to get an economy back on track. The classical economists of the day could not provide an answer—they assumed that markets would always reach equilibrium through increases or decreases in the relevant prices. They were like physicists who forgot to account for the role of friction in the mechanical transmission of energy.

In the 1930s, however, the British economist John Maynard Keynes (pronounced "canes") introduced price frictions into a model of the economy. That idea offered an explanation for downturns that focused on problems caused by declining aggregate demand, and it was revolutionary. Macroeconomists have now extended many of Keynes's original insights, and his basic ideas continue to help explain economic booms and busts in the United States and abroad.

In this chapter we'll use a simple model to explore Keynes's explanation for economic downturns. The model shows how it's possible for an economy to get stuck at a short-run level of output that lies below potential. In human terms, the model explains how widespread unemployment can persist, even when people are ready and willing to work. The model also points to practical solutions to help economies escape a recessionary rut.

The Components of Aggregate Expenditure

When economies face downturns, both spending and production fall. To understand that drop in spending, we need to start with the components of aggregate expenditure. Chapter 7, "Measuring GDP," showed that all activity in the economy can be summarized by gross domestic product (GDP), and one way of calculating GDP is by aggregating all expenditure in the economy. **Aggregate expenditure** can then be divided into four primary components of spending: consumption (C), investment (I), government spending (G), and net exports (NX).

If we use Y to denote aggregate expenditure, we can write the relationship simply as $Y = C + I + G + NX$. This tells us that everything that was produced must have been purchased by a combination of households, firms, the government, and foreigners. The equation is just an accounting identity. It doesn't depend on assumptions about the behavior of decision makers, and it can't tell us much about how the economy actually works.

To get further, we need to understand how the key players in the economy—especially households and firms—make decisions. With that knowledge, we can start to build a simple model of the economy. The model starts with a set of statements that we know to be true (like $Y = C + I + G + NX$). Then we'll use our understanding of economic relationships to make things more realistic. As Albert Einstein reportedly said, we're going to build a model that tries to "make things as simple as possible, but no simpler."

> **aggregate expenditure (Y)**
> the level of aggregate expenditure that consists of consumption, government spending, net exports, and actual investment by firms

Consumption

> **LO 11.1** Identify the factors that affect the consumption component of aggregate expenditure.

The starting point is *consumption*. Consumption makes up two-thirds to three-quarters of GDP in most countries. Because it accounts for such a large share, consumption accounts for much of the variation in aggregate economic activity.

You probably already understand the basics of consumption since you make consumption choices every day. You decide how much to spend on food, travel, entertainment, transportation, and housing. You also decide how much to save for later (that is, you choose how much *not* to consume now). Like most people making these choices, you likely consider four factors:

1. current income
2. wealth
3. expected future income
4. the interest rate on saving and borrowing

These basic factors are the building blocks of our model of consumption expenditures.

Current income

People who earn more tend to consume more. For example, most investment bankers live in nicer houses and drive fancier cars than college professors do. Of course, the exact relationship between earnings and consumption depends on the details: It matters whether your income will *always* be high or if it's likely to fall in the future. If you win the lottery this year, for example, you might save a big chunk of the winnings to spend later when your income goes back to normal. Alternatively, a young family may want to borrow to buy a house or car early on, especially if they expect that their future income will grow over time.

These details matter a lot when considering particular households. They matter much less when thinking about the *basic patterns* that hold across all households. When we think about households in general, we can streamline things by assuming that households simply consume a constant fraction of disposable income (income after taxes and transfers). This fraction is called

marginal propensity to consume (MPC)
the amount that consumption increases when after-tax income increases by $1

the **marginal propensity to consume**, abbreviated as MPC. If a household receives an extra $10,000 in disposable income, for example, and its marginal propensity to consume is 60 percent (MPC = 0.6), then the household will consume $6,000 (= 0.60 × $10,000) of the extra disposable income. The marginal propensity to consume plays a central role in the model of aggregate demand that we're developing.

Wealth

Wealth takes many forms. Examples of wealth include money held in savings and checking accounts; holdings of stocks, bonds, and mutual funds; and the value of houses. From those assets are subtracted the amount of any debt, such as credit card debt, mortgages (home loans), and student loans.

Wealthier households tend to spend more, so we assume that increased wealth leads to increased consumption (and decreased wealth leads to lower consumption). That should make sense. After all, higher-wealth households can afford to consume more for any given level of income. This is confirmed by the evidence: When the level of savings rises in an economy, aggregate consumption tends to rise as well. This occurs because households can dip into savings to fund consumption rather than being limited by their income. Indeed, changes in stock-market and housing wealth have driven some of the most dramatic movements in consumption in the past 20 years.

Often policymakers also want to know which households are likely to have a larger marginal propensity to consume. As we've noted, income and wealth matter. It is commonly assumed, for example, that poor households have a relatively high marginal propensity to consume out of income. Why? Because, by definition, poor households often do not have enough income. As a result, they are likely to spend a relatively big share of any income they receive. Recent research finds a surprising pattern: Some wealthy households also act like they're poor. To see why, read the Real Life box "The wealthy hand-to-mouth."

Real Life
The wealthy hand-to-mouth

The expression "living hand-to-mouth" means that you're spending all of your paycheck, with nothing left over to save. Not surprisingly, many poor families live hand-to-mouth. One implication is that, as a group, poor families have a high marginal propensity to consume out of disposable income.

But you don't have to *be* poor to *feel* poor. Economists from Princeton University and New York University found that some relatively wealthy people are living hand-to-mouth too. About a third of U.S. households are estimated to live hand-to-mouth, but only one-third of those are actually poor. The other two-thirds are relatively wealthy but still have to watch their budgets carefully.

These wealthy hand-to-mouth households are often young; many have assets that are tied up in forms that are hard to draw upon, such as a house or a retirement account, for example. As a result, they feel financially squeezed. They too have a high marginal propensity to consume out of disposable income.

This means that wealth alone is not a good predictor of the marginal propensity to consume—nor of how wealthy families feel. Figure 11-1 shows that the same pattern is even more pronounced in other countries. In each country, most people "living hand-to-mouth" are actually relatively wealthy.

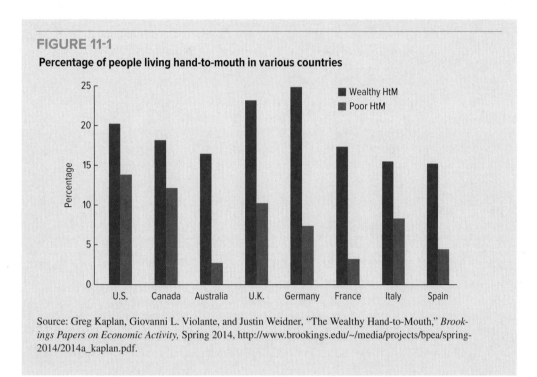

FIGURE 11-1

Percentage of people living hand-to-mouth in various countries

Source: Greg Kaplan, Giovanni L. Violante, and Justin Weidner, "The Wealthy Hand-to-Mouth," *Brookings Papers on Economic Activity,* Spring 2014, http://www.brookings.edu/~/media/projects/bpea/spring-2014/2014a_kaplan.pdf.

Expected future income

Most people try to keep their spending fairly steady even when their income rises and falls. (This is referred to as the desire to "smooth consumption" over time.) As a result, expected future income influences current consumption in much the same way that current income does:

- If you expect your income to rise in the future (specifically, expected future disposable income), you tend to be more willing to borrow or to dip into savings in order to fund a higher level of consumption today.

- Similarly, if you expect your income to be lower in the future, you tend to consume less now in order to save more for later.

As a result, there is a positive relationship between expected future income in an economy and current aggregate consumption.

The interest rate

The **interest rate** is also known as the price of money. For savers, it is the price received for letting a bank use money for a specified period of time. For borrowers, it is the price of using money for a specified period of time. Thus, the interest rate determines the financial return on saving and the cost of borrowing. The interest rate (specifically, the "real" interest rate, which is the interest rate adjusted for inflation) influences consumption:

- A higher interest rate generally encourages saving, which in turn decreases consumption.

- In the same way, a high interest rate discourages people from borrowing on credit cards and taking other loans to pay for purchases; this decreases consumption too.

Therefore, there is a negative relationship between the interest rate and consumption on an aggregate level.

Table 11-1 shows how increases in these determinants directly affect consumption. We can usually predict whether an increase in a determinant will increase or decrease consumption.

interest rate
the price of money, typically expressed as a percentage per dollar per unit of time; for savers, it is the price received for letting a bank use money for a specified period of time; for borrowers, it is the price of using money for a specified period of time

TABLE 11-1
**Determinants
of aggregate
consumption**

Increase in determinant	Effect on consumption (C)
Current income	Increase
Wealth	Increase
Expected future income	Increase
Interest rate	Decrease

Investment

LO 11.2 Identify the factors that affect the investment component of aggregate expenditure.

When you hear people talking about investing, they are often talking about buying and selling shares in the stock market. But when economists talk about investing, they often use the word "investment" in a more specific way. Economists use "investment" to refer to changes in capital—including changes in machines, structures, software, and even residential housing. The determinants of investment are thus the factors that change the benefits and costs of adding physical capital—specifically, expected profitability, the interest rate, and business taxes.

Expected profitability
Profit-maximizing firms, not surprisingly, make capital investments they think will increase profits. (And they avoid capital investments that they think will lose money.) When firms expect their projects will be profitable, they will invest more to grow their businesses. Therefore, there is a positive relationship between expected profitability and the current level of aggregate investment.

Not surprisingly, innovations that open up new spheres for profit usually spur high rates of investment in physical capital. For example, the information-technology boom of the 1990s was accompanied by a rapid increase in investment in the form of computer equipment and software.

The interest rate
One big way that businesses invest is by borrowing financial capital. The interest rate (again, the "real" interest rate, adjusted for inflation) can be thought of as the cost of borrowing. When the cost of borrowing decreases, the amount of borrowing increases. Therefore, there is a negative relationship between the interest rate and the amount of aggregate investment in an economy.

In fact, this relationship exists even if firms finance their investment by retaining earnings from their profits (rather than distributing them to shareholders). A lower interest rate reduces the returns that investors expect, which encourages firms to keep more funds for investment rather than distribute them.

In the same way, investment in housing is stimulated by a lower interest rate: When the interest rate is lower, it's less expensive for households to take out mortgages to fund home purchases. A lower interest rate generally results in an increase in mortgage borrowing.

(In practice, lenders may charge somewhat different interest rates, depending on the specific context. It's usually okay, though, to simplify by talking about "the interest rate," as a way to capture the role of interest rates in general.)

Business taxes
Business taxes reduce profits. Thus, when business taxes rise, firms have less incentive to invest. This dynamic creates a negative relationship between business taxes and aggregate investment in an economy.

Table 11-2 shows how increases in these determinants directly affect investment. We can usually predict whether an increase in a determinant will increase or decrease investment.

Increase in determinant	Effect on investment (I)
Interest rate	Decrease
Expected profitability	Increase
Business taxes	Decrease

TABLE 11-2
Determinants of aggregate investment

Government spending

LO 11.3 Identify the factors that affect the government spending component of aggregate expenditure.

Government spending is not like the other components of aggregate expenditure. It is different because the government chooses how much to spend based on beliefs about what citizens need (roads, schools, and the like). The government may also choose spending levels as a way to stimulate or restrain the economy. (That is, government spending is a tool of fiscal policy.) Therefore, in the short run, government spending is not directly affected by standard macroeconomic factors such as aggregate income, wealth, and the interest rate, so we take government spending as given in our model of aggregate expenditure.

Note that transfer payments to individuals are not included in government spending. Transfer payments include spending on unemployment insurance and Social Security benefits—payments the government makes to households without receiving any goods or services in return. Those transfer payments are often negatively correlated with aggregate income. For instance, more people tend to qualify for unemployment benefits during recessions (a time when aggregate income is relatively low and unemployment rises).

Net exports

LO 11.4 Identify the factors that affect the net exports component of aggregate expenditure.

The *net exports* component of aggregate expenditure is exports (the value of goods and services sold to foreign consumers) minus imports (the value of goods and services purchased domestically from foreign producers). The factors that increase net exports, therefore, are forces that increase exports and decrease imports. These forces are domestic income, foreign income, exchange rates, tastes for foreign goods, and trade policies.

Domestic income
Domestic income is the income earned by those living within a country. As domestic income rises, so does consumption.

- An increase in consumption generally leads to an increase in purchases of imports (along with increased purchases of goods and services produced domestically).
- When imports increase, net exports decrease (because imports are subtracted out in the calculation of net exports).

Thus, domestic income and net exports are usually negatively related.

Foreign income
Foreign income is income earned by those living outside a country. We just saw that increases in domestic income tend to increase the consumption of imports. Similarly, increases in foreign income tend to increase exports: As income increases in a foreign economy, citizens there increase consumption of goods from outside. The result is increasing exports to the foreign economy. Therefore, foreign income and net exports are usually positively related.

TABLE 11-3
Determinants of net exports

Increase in determinant	Effect on net exports (NX)
Domestic income	Decrease
Foreign income	Increase
Exchange rates	Decrease
Tastes for foreign goods	Decrease
Trade policies	Depends

real exchange rate
the value of goods in one country expressed in terms of the same goods in another country

Exchange rates

Exchange rates—specifically, the **real exchange rate**—are discussed in detail in Chapter 18, "Open-Market Macroeconomics." For now, it is sufficient to keep in mind that the real exchange rate is the value of goods in one country expressed in terms of the same goods in another country. Real exchange rates represent conversions between the cost of foreign and domestic goods that incorporates both currency exchange rates (that is, nominal exchange rates) and differences in foreign versus domestic price levels.

When real exchange rates increase, domestic goods get more expensive relative to foreign goods. That usually leads to an increase in imports and a decrease in exports. Since imports are subtracted out when calculating net exports, real exchange rates are negatively associated with net exports.

Of course, an economy has many real exchange rates, one for each country that it does business with. Therefore, it is helpful to think of a change in real exchange rates as the direction that the overall set of exchange rates moves on average.

Tastes for foreign goods

When tastes for foreign goods increase (when people find foreign goods more attractive than they did previously), domestic consumption expenditure shifts toward consumption of imports. This shift increases imports and, as a result, decreases net exports. Therefore, tastes for foreign goods are negatively associated with the level of net exports.

Trade policies

In part, the effects of trade policies are reflected in exchange rates and other macroeconomic variables rather than influencing the level of net exports directly. That said, trade policies can be analyzed on a case-by-case basis to determine whether they have a direct effect on net exports as well.

Table 11-3 shows how increases in these determinants directly affect net exports. We can usually predict whether an increase in a determinant will increase or decrease net exports.

Table 11-4 summarizes the determinants of all the components of aggregate expenditure. It's important to keep in mind that these relationships hold "all else being equal." Also, you should recognize that changes in macroeconomic factors can have both direct and indirect effects. For example, an increase in interest rates affects consumption and investment directly and also affects consumption indirectly because higher interest rates affect levels of wealth and expected future income.

Autonomous expenditure and simplifying assumptions

autonomous expenditure
expenditure that is independent of the current level of aggregate income in the economy

LO 11.5 Describe autonomous expenditure and outline the simplifications made in the aggregate expenditure model.

In the analysis that follows, we distinguish between sources of expenditure that depend on income and those that do not. **Autonomous expenditure** is expenditure that is not affected by

TABLE 11-4

Summarizing all determinants of aggregate expenditure

This chart summarizes Tables 11-1 through 11-3. It shows at a glance how increases in the determinants of aggregate expenditure directly affect all components of aggregate expenditure. We can usually predict an increase or decrease.

Increase in determinant	Effect on C	Effect on I	Effect on G	Effect on NX	Effect on aggregate expenditure (Y)
Domestic income	Increase	—	—	Decrease	Generally increase
Wealth	Increase	—	—	—	Increase
Expected future income	Increase	—	—	—	Increase
Interest rate	Decrease	Decrease	—	—	Decrease
Expected profitability	—	Increase	—	—	Increase
Business taxes	—	Decrease	—	—	Decrease
Foreign income	—	—	—	Increase	Increase
Exchange rates	—	—	—	Decrease	Decrease
Tastes for foreign goods	—	—	—	Decrease	Decrease
Trade policies	—	—	—	Depends	Depends

the current level of income in the economy. In general, consumption expenditure changes when aggregate income changes. But there is also some baseline level of consumption that is insensitive to income. After all, households need to consume some basics (basic food and housing, for example) even if they have zero income. This "basics" part is autonomous expenditure. This distinction will become important when we start graphing changes in aggregate expenditure.

In the previous discussion, net exports are also a function of aggregate income, so it follows that net exports would not be classified as autonomous expenditure. To simplify things and focus on the most important macroeconomic relationships, however, we will treat net exports as autonomous expenditure.

✓CONCEPT CHECK

☐ What happens to the level of consumption in an economy when interest rates decrease? **[LO 11.1]**

☐ What happens to the level of (planned) investment in an economy when businesses become more cautious regarding future profitability? **[LO 11.2]**

☐ Suppose that business taxes decrease in an economy. Which components of aggregate expenditure are directly affected? **[LO 11.2]**

☐ What happens to the level of government spending in an economy when the level of wealth in an economy increases? **[LO 11.3]**

☐ What happens to the level of net exports in an economy when other countries experience rapid economic growth? **[LO 11.4]**

☐ In reality, do net exports count as autonomous expenditure? What about in our aggregate expenditure model? **[LO 11.5]**

Aggregate Expenditure Equilibrium and the Keynesian Cross

The Great Depression of the 1930s was the longest-lasting economic crisis in U.S. history, so it's not surprising that economists have spent a lot of time trying to understand it. Millions of families lost their wealth; almost half of U.S. banks failed. At the worst point, one in four workers was unemployed. As the U.S. economy reeled, other parts of the world suffered too. International trade fell by a third. Economists couldn't figure out how to help get people back to work, and the United States remained in a downturn through the 1930s.

In Britain, the economist John Maynard Keynes made the case that insufficient spending was the main culprit. He argued that low spending could explain how economies got stuck in a pattern of output and income below their long-run productive capacity—that is, below potential GDP. Attention then turned to the components of aggregate expenditure described in the previous section. The questions were: How can aggregate expenditure be increased? And what will be the effect on the economy and unemployment?

Keynes's insight has had a lasting influence on policymakers and economists. "Keynesian" ideas were widely discussed (and often debated) during the 2007−2009 economic crisis, for example. Governments around the world have used Keynesian solutions to stimulate economies that had fallen into deep recessions. In this section, we show the core of Keynes's insight.

Actual versus planned aggregate expenditure

> **LO 11.6** Describe the difference between planned and actual aggregate expenditure and show their relationship graphically.

Keynes's big insight was that firms don't always produce the most they *can* at a given price. Instead, they produce what they can *sell* at a given price. So when demand is weak and prices don't fall, firms end up producing only what is demanded. The problem is that the economy could be producing more if prices adjusted. Because prices fail to adjust, the economy can get stuck below potential output. The way to see this is by looking at firms' planned and actual aggregate expenditure.

Sometimes firms are hit by surprises. That creates a difference between their planned and actual levels of investment:

- *Planned investment* is the amount that firms actively decide to put into new capital resources and inventory accumulation. Planned investment can differ from actual investment because unexpected changes in demand can cause actual inventories to be higher or lower than expected.

- *Actual investment* is the amount of new capital investment and actual inventory changes. Changes in inventories are included in investment, so when firms draw down existing inventories, actual inventory investment is negative. And when firms accumulate inventories, actual inventory investment is positive.

Keynes recognized that the difference between planned and actual inventories is a measure of unexpected slackness in demand. If actual inventories exceed planned inventories, the firms' managers must have anticipated higher demand than actually materialized. In an effort to cut inventories back down to planned levels, firms should then cut production and slow orders from other suppliers. We can summarize their decisions in Table 11-5.

As the first relationship shows, ending up with more actual inventories than planned is a signal that demand is weaker than anticipated. Firms then adjust by reducing production.[3] Over time, firms adjust to macroeconomic conditions such that planned and actual inventories align exactly (and there is zero unplanned inventory expenditure).

TABLE 11-5

How actual and planned inventories affect production decisions

Inventory relationship	Production decision
If actual inventories > planned inventories	Reduce production
If actual inventories < planned inventories	Increase production
If actual inventories = planned inventories	Maintain current production

Putting the pieces together, we can decompose **planned aggregate expenditure (PAE)**—the level of aggregate expenditure that consists of consumption, planned investment, government spending, and net exports—into two parts: One part depends on income and the other part depends on all other factors (real interest rates, wealth, and taxes). We can express those two parts in equation format:

EQUATION 11-1
$$PAE = A + bY$$

where

A = a constant that represents the autonomous sources of spending—those that are not directly influenced by income,

b = a positive coefficient that relates spending to national income, and

Y = national income.

In this equation, A accounts for a diverse set of factors, including real interest rates, financial and housing wealth, government spending, export demand, and taxes. In some versions of the model, b will simply be equal to the marginal propensity to consume (MPC). In more realistic versions, b might also capture the impact of income on net exports or the tendency for taxes net of transfer payments to rise and fall with income.

Figure 11-2 is a graphic representation of the planned aggregate expenditure equation. The sloped line is the **planned aggregate expenditure curve**. The intercept of the line at the *y*-axis is the level of autonomous expenditures, A. The slope, b, is the response of planned aggregate expenditure to changes in income.

planned aggregate expenditure (PAE) the level of aggregate expenditure that consists of consumption, planned investment, government spending, and net exports

planned aggregate expenditure curve planned aggregate expenditure as a function of actual aggregate expenditure, holding all other factors constant

FIGURE 11-2

Planned aggregate expenditure This figure shows planned aggregate expenditure as a function of income.

? POTENTIALLY CONFUSING

Aggregate expenditure. National income. National production. Total output. GDP. Y. What's the difference among these terms? None. For our purposes in this chapter, they are all the same.

In the "Production equals expenditure equals income" section of Chapter 7, "Measuring GDP," we showed that these concepts are equivalent. We get the same number for gross domestic product (GDP) whether we measure all the expenditure or the income in an economy. We showed then that

$$\text{National production} = \text{National expenditure} = \text{National income}$$

This is an important simplification, but it is also potentially confusing because there are many interchangeable terms. We have noted that national production and total output refer to the same thing. Further, GDP = Y, and Y also refers to national income—which is also aggregate expenditure, which is also national expenditure!

One important difference would arise if we consider international investment. Then, the national income of the United States includes the income of U.S. companies earned abroad (but it excludes earnings by foreign companies from sales in the United States). We discuss the implications of this consideration in Chapter 18, "Open-Market Macroeconomics."

In this chapter, however, we simplify by assuming that GDP = Y = National production = Total output = National expenditure = Aggregate expenditure = National income. To reduce confusion, we aim here to use Y (instead of GDP) and mainly discuss in terms of changes in "aggregate expenditure." Just know that all of these terms refer to the same thing.

Keynesian equilibrium

LO 11.7 Show how to find equilibrium aggregate expenditure when given the relationship between planned aggregate expenditure and actual aggregate expenditure.

Given our description of planned aggregate expenditure (PAE), we are now ready to develop Keynes's fundamental insight for how economies can get stuck producing less than potential output. Keep in mind that the *only* difference between planned aggregate expenditure, PAE, and actual output, Y, is the difference between planned and actual inventory investment.

Recall the production decisions relating to actual versus planned inventories:

- If actual inventories exceed planned inventories, then firms should cut production given the unexpected drop in demand.
- Conversely, when actual inventories fall short of planned inventories, firms get a signal that demand is higher than they expected; they should respond by increasing production.

Applying this mechanism to planned aggregate expenditure, we can see the effect our inventory relationships have on output, as shown in Table 11-6.

The last of these conditions characterizes what we call a **Keynesian equilibrium**—a situation in which planned aggregate expenditure is equal to actual aggregate expenditure. It is an equilibrium in the sense that firms no longer have a desire to change their output in response to a gap between planned and actual inventories.

We can depict the Keynesian equilibrium by adding to the diagram in Figure 11-2. The new diagram is shown in Figure 11-3 and, as before, has actual aggregate expenditure on one axis and planned aggregate expenditure on the other axis.

Keynesian equilibrium
a situation in which planned aggregate expenditure is equal to actual aggregate expenditure

TABLE 11-6

How actual and planned inventories affect output

Inventory relationship	Implication	Effect on Y
If actual inventories > planned inventories	Y > PAE	Decrease in Y
If actual inventories < planned inventories	Y < PAE	Increase in Y
If actual inventories = planned inventories	Y = PAE	No change in Y

We can find the Keynesian equilibrium by drawing an additional 45-degree line representing all of the points where planned and actual aggregate expenditure are equal, or PAE = Y. Such a line represents all of the possible equilibrium points. To find the particular equilibrium that emerges, we look at where the two lines intersect. (In the new figure, the $PAE = A + bY$ line is labeled PAE$_1$.) The intersection of the new PAE = Y line with the PAE$_1$ curve yields the unique equilibrium where planned aggregate expenditure is just equal to actual aggregate expenditure. We call this **equilibrium aggregate expenditure**.

In Figure 11-3, equilibrium aggregate expenditure is labeled as Y$_1$. As explained earlier:

- When planned aggregate expenditure (PAE$_1$) is higher than actual aggregate expenditure (given by the PAE = Y line), firms are surprised by the lower-than-expected inventories, and they respond by increasing production over time. (You can think of unplanned inventory investment as the vertical distance between the PAE = Y line and the planned aggregate expenditure line; just make sure that you get the sign right!) The increase in production in response to lower-than-expected inventory investment is indicated by the arrowheads to the left of Y$_1$ on the x-axis.

- When planned aggregate expenditure (PAE$_1$) is less than actual aggregate expenditure or output, firms are accumulating more inventory than planned, and they will decrease production in response. This is indicated by the arrowheads to the right of Y$_1$ on the x-axis.

These opposing forces, indicated by the two sets of arrowheads on the x-axis, drive the economy toward the steady state described earlier, which is the level of Y that brings planned and actual aggregate expenditure together.

equilibrium aggregate expenditure
the level of aggregate expenditure where unplanned investment is equal to zero, or, equivalently, where planned aggregate expenditure is equal to actual aggregate expenditure

FIGURE 11-3

The equilibrium level of aggregate expenditure

FIGURE 11-4

Nonincome determinants and changes in aggregate expenditure equilibrium

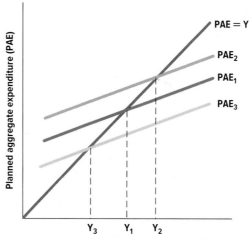

The equilibrium level of aggregate expenditure naturally depends on the levels of the non-income determinants of the components of aggregate expenditure—interest rates, government spending, taxes, and so on:

- Economic environments that correspond to higher levels of planned aggregate expenditure (for a given level of Y) have PAE curves that are higher up on the expenditure diagram.

- Economic environments that correspond to lower levels of planned aggregate expenditure (for a given level of Y) have PAE curves that are lower on the expenditure diagram.

For example, in Figure 11-4, planned aggregate expenditure curve PAE_2 corresponds to an environment with lower interest rates, more business optimism, or some other feature that increases PAE relative to curve PAE_1. In the same way, the planned aggregate expenditure curve PAE_3 corresponds to an environment with less government spending, higher exchange rates, or some other feature that decreases PAE relative to curve PAE_1. Not surprisingly, higher PAE curves result in higher levels of equilibrium aggregate expenditure, and lower PAE curves result in lower levels of equilibrium aggregate expenditure.

Output gaps

recessionary output gap
an output gap that occurs when equilibrium aggregate expenditure is below the level needed for full employment

inflationary output gap
an output gap that occurs when equilibrium aggregate expenditure is above the level needed for full employment

---

LO 11.8 Explain the importance of the aggregate expenditure equilibrium model to understanding the behavior of the economy.

Crucially, the model provides an explanation for how an economy can get stuck at a level of aggregate expenditure that is either below or above the full-employment level of output.

A **recessionary output gap** occurs when equilibrium aggregate expenditure is below the level needed for full employment. Graphically, a recessionary output gap is shown by the length of the red arrow in Figure 11-5. (Full employment output is given by Y_{FE}.)

Equilibrium aggregate expenditure can also be above the level needed for full employment. In those cases, an **inflationary output gap** occurs when the current level of output is above the level corresponding to full employment. Graphically, an inflationary output gap is shown by the length of the red arrow in Figure 11-6. (Full employment output is given by Y_{FE}.)

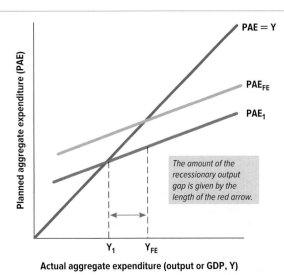

FIGURE 11-5

A recessionary output gap

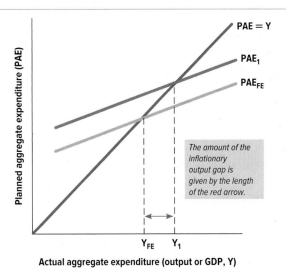

FIGURE 11-6

An inflationary output gap

The multiplier effect

LO 11.9 Illustrate how any initial change in aggregate expenditure can have a multiplier effect on the overall level of aggregate expenditure.

Another important insight that comes from the Keynesian model is that a change in autonomous expenditure (e.g., government spending) can have a *multiplier effect*. What does that mean? A **multiplier effect** is an increase in consumer spending that occurs when spending by one person causes others to spend more too, increasing the impact on the economy of the initial spending. The initial consumer spending ripples through the economy such that the overall change in output is larger than the initial change in expenditure.

To see the intuition behind the multiplier effect, consider what happens when you make a purchase: Let's say you hire a builder to construct a new deck for your backyard. The total bill is $5,000. This decision adds $5,000 to GDP, right? Yes, but that's not the end of the story.

Let's say that the builder decides to take her family on a two-week beach vacation, which she couldn't have afforded before you employed her to build your deck. The money she spends on her

multiplier effect
the increase in consumer spending that occurs when spending by one person causes others to spend more too, increasing the impact on the economy of the initial spending

vacation, including $3,000 on her family's hotel stay, also counts toward GDP. So, your decision to build a deck has added $8,000 to GDP, not $5,000. But that's still not the end of the story.

Thanks to the builder's stay at the hotel, the hotel owner feels able to buy a painting for the hotel lobby for $1,500. And so on. Your decision has sent ripples through the economy, increasing GDP by considerably more than the $5,000 you paid your builder. If you hadn't built the deck, none of this would have happened.

The multiplier effect arises because of an interaction between the consumers' response to changes in income and firms' reactions to the gap between planned and actual inventories. A positive marginal propensity to consume means that an initial change in government spending or consumption due to a change in taxes will have two effects: It will affect aggregate expenditure directly *and* it will start a cycle in which changes in expenditure cause changes in consumption, which in turn cause changes in expenditure, and so on. When this multiplier process finally comes to a halt, the economy has returned to a Keynesian equilibrium where unplanned aggregate expenditure is equal to zero, or, equivalently, where planned aggregate expenditure equals output.

Mathematically, with the help of a simple numerical example we can see how the multiplier effect works in our model. In particular, suppose that initially Y = PAE and then an increase in government expenditure causes PAE to increase above Y by $100. As a result, actual inventory investment is $100 less than planned inventory investment, and firms would respond by increasing output by $100. But the process doesn't stop there. Why? Because the increased output increases incomes by $100, and we know that b fraction of the increased incomes get spent, so that PAE is now $b \times \$100$ above Y. Firms again respond—this time by increasing output by $b \times \$100$. That increase then generates $b \times b \times \$100$ of additional consumption spending, so that firms once again find themselves increasing output, this time by $b \times b \times \$100$. This process continues, and eventually the gap between planned and actual aggregate expenditure shrinks to almost nothing.

The surprising result of the example above is that the final change in output will be larger than one-for-one. In the example, output changed according to:

$$\Delta Y = \$100 + b \times \$100 + b^2 \times \$100 + b^3 \times \$100 + \ldots = \$100 \times \left(1 + b + b^2 + b^3 + \ldots\right)$$

The sum in the parentheses is the sum of an infinite geometric series, which for $b < 1$ is simply equal to $1/(1 - b)$. Thus, the final change in output above is equal to

EQUATION 11-2 $$\Delta Y = \$100 \times \frac{1}{1 - b}$$

expenditure multiplier
the factor by which output increases in response to an initial change in aggregate expenditure

If, for example, $b = 0.8$, then $1 \div (1 - b) = 5$. So, the final change in output would be *five times* as large as the initial change in aggregate expenditure. The factor by which output increases in response to an initial change in aggregate expenditure is known as the **expenditure multiplier**.

The expenditure multiplier can also be seen graphically. The multiplier effect is illustrated by the fact that the distance between old and new equilibrium values of Y is greater than the distance between the corresponding old and new PAE curves. In Figure 11-7, the overall change in equilibrium aggregate expenditure is given by the length of the red horizontal arrow. Likewise, the initial change in planned aggregate expenditure is given by the length of the blue vertical arrow. The strength of the multiplier effect depends on the relative sizes of the two arrows.

The expenditure multiplier turns out to simply equal the length of the red horizontal arrow divided by the length of the blue vertical arrow. In the example given in the figure, the red arrow is longer than the blue arrow, implying an expenditure multiplier greater than 1.

The expenditure multiplier is a powerful idea in macroeconomics. As shown in the example above, the expenditure multiplier is critical in determining the impact of government spending on the economy. Knowing the size of the multiplier is important for economic policy. The

FIGURE 11-7

Overall change in equilibrium aggregate expenditure   The multiplier can be calculated as the length of the red horizontal arrow divided by the length of the blue vertical arrow. In the case drawn here, the multiplier is greater than 1.

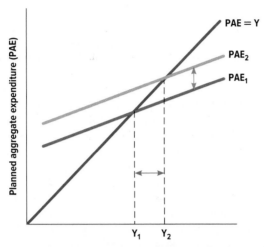

multiplier's size is an empirical matter, and it is a major subject of study. If the multiplier is large, even limited policy interventions can have big impacts.

The 2008 recession gives one example of how complex it can be to figure out how the multiplier effect works in the real world. Christina Romer of the University of California, who at the time was an economic advisor to the president, suggested a huge increase in government spending; other economists, such as Robert Barro at Harvard University, argued for tax cuts. The central focus of their debate was on the size of the multiplier for government spending. To see how this debate played out, read the Real Life box "The great 2009 multiplier debate."

Real Life

The great 2009 multiplier debate

Ask different economists about the size of the multipliers for government spending and tax cuts and you'll get different answers. Differing views on the size of the multipliers lead to disagreements between experts on how to design the best fiscal policy:

- On the optimistic end, the Congressional Budget Office predicted that the government-spending multiplier on "shovel-ready" projects in the 2009 stimulus bill, like building roads or schools, would be 1.5.
- More pessimistically, Robert Barro, an economist at Harvard University, argued that the government-spending multiplier was below 1. He thought that each dollar of government spending would add no more than 80 cents to GDP.

In the grand scheme of things, 1.5 may not sound that different from 0.8, but which figure you think is more accurate makes a huge difference to what economic impact you would expect from a policy to combat the recession. The difference in the expected impact of the 2009

(continued)

stimulus under a multiplier of 1.5 versus 0.8 is about $440 billion more in GDP increases and 4 million more jobs created.

Why is there such a large difference between different estimates of the multiplier? There are two big reasons. One is that the multiplier is determined by overall economic conditions. Suppose the government employs 100 workers to build a bridge at a time when the economy is doing pretty well and most of those 100 workers would have had little trouble finding other employment. In the worst case, the workers might actually get pulled into bridge-building from another, potentially higher-priority job. In that case, the impact of government spending on GDP would be much less than if those 100 workers had been sitting at home hoping for a job.

Second, economists hotly debate whether government spending has a positive or negative impact on private-sector investment. Some argue that stimulus spending will inspire confidence in the economy and encourage firms to invest more. This would increase GDP. Others counter that government borrowing may drive up interest rates. As the government increases its demand for money in order to finance its spending, all else equal, the cost of borrowing—i.e., the interest rate—will increase too. When faced with higher interest rates, firms may choose to invest less, decreasing GDP. This phenomenon is known as *crowding out*.

Taking these and other complicating factors into account, economists argue that different *kinds* of government spending and tax cuts will have different multipliers. Should the government invest in "shovel-ready" public works or put the money into widening the food stamp program? Would it be better to cut payroll taxes or corporate taxes? The answers to these questions lie in which programs have the highest multiplier.

Sources: https://www.cbo.gov/blog; http://online.wsj.com/article/SB123258618204604599.html.

✓ CONCEPT CHECK

- ☐ If planned and actual aggregate expenditure are always equal, what is the slope of the planned aggregate expenditure curve? **[LO 11.6]**
- ☐ What is the value of unplanned investment expenditure in an aggregate expenditure equilibrium? **[LO 11.7]**
- ☐ What important feature of the economy does the aggregate expenditure equilibrium analysis help to explain? **[LO 11.8]**
- ☐ Why can an increase in spending lead to a change in aggregate expenditure that is larger than the initial increase? **[LO 11.9]**

Conclusion

Keeping the economy running at capacity is one of the most important concerns of economics. A well-running economy doesn't just mean more production—it also generates income and jobs. But sometimes the economy fails to operate as well as it could. Our focus here has been on problems connected to aggregate demand.

In order to understand why aggregate demand and fiscal policy behave the way that they do, we developed a model of aggregate expenditure in the economy. We first outlined the drivers of aggregate expenditure and then used a simplified model to show how the drivers work. That helped show why even an economy with plentiful productive resources can still get stalled and not operate at its full potential.

The aggregate expenditure equilibrium model is the main building block for understanding the demand side of the macro economy. In the next chapter, we connect aggregate demand to aggregate supply to see a broader range of options available to policymakers.

Key Terms

aggregate expenditure (Y), p. 277

marginal propensity to consume (MPC), p. 278

interest rate, p. 279

real exchange rate, p. 282

autonomous expenditure, p. 282

planned aggregate expenditure (PAE), p. 285

planned aggregate expenditure curve, p. 285

Keynesian equilibrium, p. 286

equilibrium aggregate expenditure, p. 287

recessionary output gap, p.288

inflationary output gap, p.288

multiplier effect, p. 289

expenditure multiplier, p. 290

Summary

LO 11.1 Identify the factors that affect the consumption component of aggregate expenditure.

Other than the price level, there are a number of factors that affect the current level of aggregate consumption in an economy. Current income and consumption are positively related through the marginal propensity to consume. The levels of wealth and consumption are positively related. Expected future income and consumption are positively related. Interest rates and consumption are negatively related.

LO 11.2 Identify the factors that affect the investment component of aggregate expenditure.

Other than the price level, there are a number of factors that affect the current level of planned investment in the economy. Expected future profitability and investment are positively related. Interest rates and investment are negatively related. The level of business taxes and investment are negatively related. There is a relationship between the levels of saving and investment in an economy, but there doesn't have to be perfect parity between the two when government budgets aren't balanced and international trade is present.

LO 11.3 Identify the factors that affect the government spending component of aggregate expenditure.

The level of government spending on goods and services in an economy is an explicit policy choice and therefore is not directly determined by macroeconomic factors. That said, macroeconomic factors may enter into the policy discussion in an indirect fashion.

LO 11.4 Identify the factors that affect the net exports component of aggregate expenditure.

Other than the price level, there are a number of factors that affect the current level of net exports in an economy.

Domestic income and net exports are negatively related. Foreign income and net exports are positively related. Exchange rates and net exports are negatively related. Tastes for foreign goods and net exports are negatively related. Trade policies can have an effect on net exports, but the analysis of the relationship must be done on a case-by-case basis since increases and decreases are not always well defined.

LO 11.5 Describe autonomous expenditure and outline the simplifications made in the aggregate expenditure model.

Autonomous aggregate expenditure refers to expenditure whose level is independent of the level of current income in the economy. For the purposes of the equilibrium aggregate expenditure analysis, we assume that all categories of expenditure other than consumption are autonomous.

LO 11.6 Describe the difference between planned and actual aggregate expenditure and show their relationship graphically.

Planned aggregate expenditure is the sum of consumption, planned investment, government spending, and net exports, where planned investment is the level of investment in productive capital and strategic inventory accumulation that firms choose before aggregate expenditure is realized. Actual aggregate expenditure, by definition, is equal to aggregate output and income, and it is the sum of consumption, actual investment, government spending, and net exports. Actual investment includes not only planned investment but also unexpected investment in the form of accumulation of unsold inventory or divestiture of existing inventory. Graphically, the relationship between actual and planned aggregate expenditure results in an upward-sloping curve with a slope equal to the marginal propensity to consume.

LO 11.7 Show how to find equilibrium aggregate expenditure when given the relationship between planned aggregate expenditure and actual aggregate expenditure.

The equilibrium aggregate expenditure can be found by calculating the level of unplanned investment for various levels of output and finding the level of output where unplanned investment is equal to zero. Graphically, the level of output where planned and actual aggregate expenditure are equal can be found by drawing a 45-degree line on the planned aggregate expenditure diagram and finding the point where this 45-degree line intersects the planned aggregate expenditure curve.

LO 11.8 Explain the importance of the aggregate expenditure equilibrium model to understanding the behavior of the economy.

The aggregate expenditure equilibrium model is important because it shows how an economy can persist at a level of output that deviates from full-employment potential GDP. Specifically, the model explains how recessionary expenditure gaps can occur where equilibrium aggregate expenditure is below what is needed to sustain potential GDP. In addition, the model explains how inflationary expenditure gaps can occur where equilibrium aggregate expenditure is larger than what is needed to sustain potential GDP. Lastly, the model explicitly shows how the different parts of the model come together to create the multiplier effect of initial changes in aggregate expenditure.

LO 11.9 Illustrate how any initial change in aggregate expenditure can have a multiplier effect on the overall level of aggregate expenditure.

The determinants of the components of aggregate expenditure show that there is a circular relationship between current income and current consumption: Current income is a determinant of current consumption, but current consumption is also a determinant of current income. Therefore, any initial change to a determinant of aggregate expenditure is going to flow through to this consumption/income cycle. The result is an overall impact that is larger than the initial change. This overall impact can't be infinitely large, however, since the effect of the initial change on aggregate expenditure gets smaller with each iteration of the cycle.

Review Questions

1. What effect does an increase in current income have on current consumption? What effect does an increase in expected future income have on current consumption? **[LO 11.1]**

2. What effect does an increase in the interest rate have on current consumption? What effect does an increase in wealth have on current consumption? **[LO 11.1]**

3. How does a change in expected profitability affect aggregate investment? How does a change in business taxes affect aggregate investment? **[LO 11.2]**

4. How does a change in the interest rate affect aggregate investment? What if firms prefer to pay for investment spending out of retained earnings? Does a change in the interest rate still affect aggregate investment? **[LO 11.2]**

5. Does the amount of government spending in an economy respond directly to changes in aggregate income, wealth, or interest rates? Does it respond indirectly to changes in these variables? **[LO 11.3]**

6. What are government transfer payments? Are they included as part of the government spending component of GDP? **[LO 11.3]**

7. What happens to the level of net exports in an economy when income in that economy increases? What happens to the level of net exports in an economy when income in other economies increases? **[LO 11.4]**

8. You read in the paper that the dollar has strengthened in value relative to the euro. How is this change in the exchange rate value of the dollar likely to affect exports to Europe and imports from Europe? **[LO 11.4]**

9. Which components of aggregate expenditure do not directly depend on current income? **[LO 11.5]**

10. The investment category of GDP measures three different types of expenditures. What are they? Why is planned investment sometimes different from actual investment? **[LO 11.6]**

11. What causes a movement along the planned aggregate expenditure curve? What causes the planned aggregate expenditure curve to shift? **[LO 11.6]**

12. In a Keynesian equilibrium will the economy always be producing at its level of potential output? Why or why not? **[LO 11.7]**

13. Suppose planned aggregate expenditure is greater than actual aggregate expenditure. In this case, what do you think will happen to output over time? **[LO 11.7]**

14. Suppose the economy is experiencing a recessionary output gap. What has happened to planned aggregate expenditure? What might have caused this change? **[LO 11.8]**

15. Suppose that an increase in business confidence increases investment expenditure by one million dollars. How do you expect this increase in investment expenditure to affect equilibrium output? Will equilibrium output increase by exactly one million, more than one million, or less than one million? **[LO 11.9]**

16. Define the relationship between the expenditure multiplier and the marginal propensity to consume. If the marginal propensity to consume increases, what happens to the expenditure multiplier? **[LO 11.9]**

Problems and Applications

1. "People who earn more income tend to have higher levels of consumption spending, so the value of their marginal propensity to consume must be greater than that of lower income people." Do you think this is a true statement? Why or why not? **[LO 11.1]**

2. Do you think there is a predictable relationship between the business cycle and aggregate investment spending? Why or why not? **[LO 11.2]**

3. "During a recession more people qualify for unemployment insurance. This will increase the government spending category of GDP and help reduce the severity of the recession." Do you agree with this statement? Why or why not? **[LO 11.3]**

4. "When one country in the world falls into a recession, this tends to cause other countries to also fall into a recession." Do you agree with this statement? Why or why not? **[LO 11.4]**

5. For each of the following shocks, identify what component(s) of planned aggregate expenditure is/are directly affected and in which direction. **[LO 11.1, 11.2, 11.3, 11.4]**
   a. Tax rates increase.
   b. China experiences an economic boom.
   c. People become more optimistic regarding their future prospects.
   d. Congress decides to increase funding for education.
   e. German fashion designs become popular among celebrities.

6. Which of the following would be classified as an autonomous change to planned aggregate expenditure? **[LO 11.5]**
   a. Interest rates in an economy decrease.
   b. Current income in an economy increases.
   c. Domestic goods become more expensive relative to foreign goods.
   d. Congress decides to undertake an infrastructure repair project.

7. Consider the planned expenditure curve in Figure 11P-1. What is the level of autonomous expenditure in this economy? **[LO 11.5, 11.6]**

8. Draw a planned aggregate expenditure curve as described in the chapter. Then show what happens to

FIGURE 11P-1

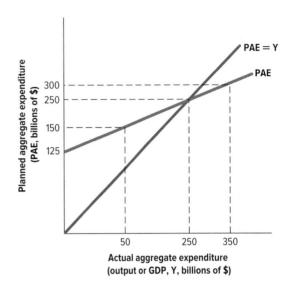

the planned aggregate expenditure curve in each of the following scenarios. **[LO 11.6]**
   a. Government spending increases.
   b. Business taxes increase.
   c. Aggregate income decreases.

9. Draw a planned aggregate expenditure curve for an economy where autonomous expenditure is $500 billion and the marginal propensity to consume is equal to 0.75. **[LO 11.6]**

10. Consider the data presented in Table 11P-1. **[LO 11.7]**
   a. What is the marginal propensity to consume for households in this economy?
   b. Based on the assumptions of our aggregate expenditure model, fill in the columns for planned investment, government spending, and net exports. What is this type of expenditure called?
   c. For each level of actual aggregate expenditure, calculate unplanned inventory investment.
   d. What is the equilibrium level of aggregate expenditure in this economy? How do you know?
   e. For each level of actual aggregate expenditure, label the future output tendency as "increase," "decrease," or "same" based on what you expect to happen to future output. What relationship does this categorization have to your answer in part *d*?

11. Suppose that an economy is at an aggregate expenditure equilibrium at an output level of $300 billion. **[LO 11.7]**

TABLE 11P-1

Actual aggregate expenditure or output (Y) (billions of $)	Consumption (C) (billions of $)	Planned investment (billions of $)	Government spending (G) (billions of $)	Net exports (NX) (billions of $)	Unplanned investment (inventory change) (billions of $)	Future output tendency
350	200	60	90	60		
400	220					
450	240					
500	260					
550	280					

TABLE 11P-2

Actual aggregate expenditure or output (Y) (billions of $)	Consumption (C) (billions of $)	Planned investment (billions of $)	Government spending (G) (billions of $)	Net exports (NX) (billions of $)	Unplanned investment (inventory change) (billions of $)
500	300	150	100	50	
600	350				
700	400				
800	450				
900	500				

a. Show this point on a planned versus actual aggregate expenditure graph.

b. Label a point on the planned aggregate expenditure curve where the economy will decrease its output next year. (To do this, pick a specific level of output that makes sense.)

c. Label a point on the planned aggregate expenditure curve where the economy will increase its output next year. (To do this, pick a specific level of output that makes sense.)

12. Consider the data presented in Table 11P-2. **[LO 11.7, 11.8]**

a. For each level of actual aggregate expenditure, calculate unplanned inventory investment.

b. What is the equilibrium level of aggregate expenditure in this economy? How do you know?

c. Suppose that planned investment increases by $50 billion. What is the new equilibrium level of aggregate expenditure in this economy?

d. What is the marginal propensity to consume in this economy?

e. What is the expenditure multiplier in this economy?

13. Consider the graph in Figure 11P-2, where the full-employment level of output is given by Y_{FE} and is the equilibrium level of aggregate expenditure for curve PAE_1. **[LO 11.8]**

a. Which planned aggregate expenditure curve will result in a recessionary output gap? Label the size of the recessionary output gap on the graph.

b. Which planned aggregate expenditure curve will result in an inflationary output gap? Label the size of the inflationary output gap on the graph.

14. Consider the graph in Figure 11P-3. **[LO 11.9]**

a. What is the expenditure multiplier in this economy?

b. What is the marginal propensity to consume in this economy?

FIGURE 11P-2

FIGURE 11P-3

15. In each of the following scenarios, describe and calculate the overall effect on aggregate expenditure. **[LO 11.9]**

   a. A recent stock market boom has increased household wealth by $20 billion, which increases consumption by $12 billion, and the marginal propensity to consume in the economy is equal to 0.6.

   b. Rising interest rates reduce domestic consumption by $4 billion and reduce investment by $7 billion, and the marginal propensity to consume in the economy is equal to 0.7.

Endnotes

1. Bill O'Reilly, "Welfare Nation," *Newsletter,* October 31, 2013, www.billoreilly.com/newslettercolumn?pid=41754.

2. Ibid.

3. When actual inventories are instead smaller than planned, it means that demand is stronger than anticipated. Then firms adjust by increasing production.

Math Essentials: Algebra and Aggregate Expenditure

Learning Objectives

LO E.1 Represent the components of planned aggregate expenditure algebraically and use these expressions to find equilibrium aggregate expenditure.

LO E.2 Illustrate the multiplier effect of aggregate expenditure using the algebraic form of the aggregate expenditure equilibrium.

In Chapter 11, "Aggregate Expenditure," we showed how to find the equilibrium level of aggregate expenditure by analyzing planned versus actual aggregate expenditure graphically. We can also solve for equilibrium aggregate expenditure algebraically if we make some assumptions about what functional form the components of aggregate expenditure take.

Using Algebra to Find Equilibrium Aggregate Expenditure

LO E.1 Represent the components of planned aggregate expenditure algebraically and use these expressions to find equilibrium aggregate expenditure.

The aggregate expenditure model that we developed in Chapter 11, "Aggregate Expenditure," implies that the functions for consumption, planned investment, government spending, and net exports depend on factors such as income, interest rates, and wealth. It is possible to include all of these factors in a model of the economy, but it helps to start by simplifying. We'll begin with a simplified model of the economy in which consumption depends only on disposable income plus a constant—the constant captures the roles of all other components of aggregate expenditure.

Consider a model economy, for example, represented by the following values for planned consumption, investment, government spending, net exports, and taxes net of transfers:

$$C = 0.75\,(Y - T) + 30$$
$$I_{planned} = 50$$
$$G = 100$$
$$NX = 30$$
$$T = 100$$

(To be closer to reality, think of these numbers as representing billions of dollars.) Note that the expressions for planned investment, government spending, and net exports are constant values. The expression for consumption, on the other hand, has not only a constant component but also a component that depends on the level of current income in the economy.

We can now combine the expressions to find planned aggregate expenditure:

$$PAE = Y_{planned} = C + I_{planned} + G + NX = 0.75(Y - 100) + 30 + 50 + 100 + 30$$
$$PAE = 0.75Y + 135$$

As stated earlier, the equilibrium level of aggregate expenditure is the level where planned and actual aggregate expenditure are equal. In algebraic terms, the equilibrium condition translates to the following:

EQUATION E-1 $PAE = Y$

We can solve this equation for Y by plugging in the expression we found for planned aggregate expenditure:

$$0.75Y + 135 = Y$$
$$0.25Y = 135$$
$$Y = 540$$

Solving the equation tells us that the equilibrium level of aggregate expenditure in this economy is $540 billion.

We can generalize this analysis by separating the components of planned expenditure into those that depend on output, Y, and those that do not. Let A denote all of the components of planned expenditure that do not depend on output, and let b denote the slope of the planned expenditure function against output. (In the previous example, $A = 135$, and $b = 0.75$.) The Keynesian equilibrium requires that planned aggregate expenditure equals output, or:

EQUATION E-2 $Y = PAE = A + bY$

We can now find the equilibrium level of aggregate expenditure by performing the same steps as before:

$$Y = PAE = A + bY$$
$$Y - bY = A$$
$$Y(1 - b) = A$$
$$Y = \frac{A}{1 - b}$$

Using this expression, we can find the equilibrium level of aggregate expenditure by simply plugging in the relevant values for the constant components of aggregate expenditure and the slope coefficient on income in an economy.

Using algebra to derive the expenditure multiplier

LO E.2 Illustrate the multiplier effect of aggregate expenditure using the algebraic form of the aggregate expenditure equilibrium.

One of the main purposes of the equilibrium aggregate expenditure model is to determine the overall impact of an initial change in a component of aggregate expenditure. Therefore, it makes sense to extend our algebra to analyze this impact as well.

Writing our equilibrium aggregate expenditure expression in changes rather than levels form gives the following:

EQUATION E-3 $\Delta Y = \frac{1}{1 - b} \Delta A$

As before, a $1 change in autonomous expenditure results in a $1/(1 − b)$ change in equilibrium aggregate expenditure.

Continuing the model economy used above, we can analyze the impact of a $10 billion increase in government spending by plugging the relevant values into Equation E-3:

$$\Delta Y = \frac{1}{1 - 0.75} \times 10 = \frac{1}{0.25} \times 10 = 4 \times 10 = 40$$

Note that many of the terms in Equation E-3 drop out because all changes other than the change in G are equal to zero. In this case, equilibrium aggregate expenditure increases by $40 billion, from $540 billion to $580 billion.

What if we instead considered a $10 billion decrease in taxes? Will this increase output by the same amount as the $10 billion increase in government spending described above? The answer is no. Each $1 reduction of taxes increases disposable income by $1, but only 0.75 times (which is the marginal propensity to consume) that increase in disposable income gets spent. Thus, the change in A is not $10 billion, but $10 billion times 0.75, or $7.5 billion. The change in output is:

$$\Delta Y = \frac{0.75}{1 - 0.75} \times 10 = \frac{1}{0.25} \times 7.5 = 30$$

But notice that as long as you correctly compute the change in autonomous expenditure A, you will always be able to find the change in output as the change in A times the multiplier. This means that there is a reliable way to solve for both the equilibrium value of output and the change in output due to a change in one of the expenditure components in just two steps:

1. Figure out the slope coefficient on income, b. In simple versions of the model, it will just be the marginal propensity to consume (MPC). But in other versions, it might reflect the MPC as well as factors like the tendency to consume more imports when income rises.

2. Sum up all the other components of aggregate expenditure that do not depend on income, which yields A. The multiplier will always equal $1/(1 − b)$. The equilibrium level of output will always equal A times the multiplier. And the change in output due to a change in one of the components of expenditure will always equal the change in the component times the multiplier.

✓CONCEPT CHECK

☐ Based on the model assumptions, which components of aggregate expenditure are represented by constants? **[LO E.1]**

☐ Algebraically, what is the equilibrium condition for aggregate expenditure? When the economy has reached this equilibrium, is it necessarily the case that output has reached potential? Explain. **[LO E.1]**

☐ Why does a $1 decrease in taxes have a smaller expansionary impact on the economy than a $1 increase in government spending? **[LO E.2]**

☐ The model economy in this section assumed that taxes net of transfers were a lump sum, with $T = 100$. Suppose instead that taxes net of transfers depended on income, so that $T = 100 + 0.1Y$. Solve for the expenditure multiplier in this case and say whether it is larger, smaller, or the same as the original multiplier. Provide a brief intuition for your answer. **[LO E.2]**

Problems and Applications

1. Consider the following components of the aggregate expenditure equilibrium model:

    $$C = 0.6(Y - 200) + 150$$
    $$I_{planned} = 175$$
    $$G = 200$$
    $$NX = 50$$

    Assume all model parameters are in billions of dollars. **[LO E.1, E.2]**

    a. What is the marginal propensity to consume in this economy?

    b. What is the level of taxes in this economy? (You can assume that the functional forms above are consistent with those described earlier.)

    c. What is the equilibrium level of aggregate expenditure in this economy?

    Now suppose that planned investment decreases by $25 billion.

    d. Find the overall change in equilibrium aggregate expenditure that results from this initial change by finding the new level of equilibrium aggregate expenditure and comparing this new level to the initial level.

    e. Again, find the overall change in equilibrium aggregate expenditure that results from the initial change, but this time use the changes formulation of the equilibrium aggregate expenditure expression directly.

Aggregate Demand and Aggregate Supply

"POP!" GOES THE BUBBLE

Home prices in the United States more than doubled between 2000 and 2007. Seeing that house prices were increasing, banks started making more mortgage loans, even to people who didn't earn enough to easily make their scheduled payments. The banks calculated that if these "subprime" customers got into trouble, the homes could be sold and the loans could be repaid from the profit.

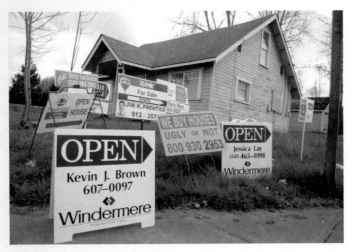
© Ty Wright/Bloomberg via Getty Images

Homeowners started feeling flush as they saw the value of their homes increase, and they started to spend on other things—a new car, a new kitchen, a holiday shopping splurge. In short order, the economy was heating up.

Unfortunately, the housing boom turned out to be an example of what is called an *asset-price bubble.* Bubbles happen when people buy assets for no reason other than that they think the price will go up. There are, of course, good reasons why you might pay a lot for a house—say, if you're willing to pay to get a house you like in the location you want. But during the housing boom, many people were willing to pay hefty prices simply because they believed prices would keep going up and they'd be able to sell for a profit.

But—inevitably—housing prices stopped rising. Between the end of 2007 and the middle of 2009, house prices fell by 25 percent. Banks found that many customers couldn't afford to repay the money they'd borrowed to buy their houses. Suddenly, the "subprime" mortgages that banks had been so eager to approve became a massive burden. Worse still, in many cases the houses were now worth less than the amount the bank had loaned, so even foreclosing and taking possession of the house wouldn't fill the gap.

Facing huge losses, banks tightened down on credit of all sorts. Now, homebuyers weren't the only ones finding that loans were scarcer and more expensive than before—businesses also began to find borrowing more difficult. Homeowners who had been happily spending on other things, confident that they could afford it because their houses were growing in value, suddenly got cold feet and stopped buying. This double whammy—the loss of cheap lending and a sharp decrease in consumer spending—hit businesses hard. The result was that GDP fell, unemployment rose, and the economy entered the period that some call the Great Recession.

How can we explain what happened to the national economy during this turbulent period? What is the connection between home prices, consumer spending, business invest-ment, and the overall health of the economy? In Chapter 11, "Aggregate Expenditure," we focused on issues specific to aggregate expenditure. In this chapter, we add more pieces. We will create a framework, called the *aggregate demand and aggregate supply model,* for understanding how the economy operates as a whole.

So far in this text we've looked at supply and demand in an individual market, for a partic-ular good or service. As macroeconomists, however, we need to think about *all* the goods and services in the economy. The aggregate demand and aggregate supply model is a way of add-ing up everything, leading to an "equilibrium" that describes the state of the national economy. We will use this model to understand how three important macroeconomic variables—output, prices, and employment—are determined and how they affect each other.

This bird's-eye view lets us see the economy from the perspective of policy-makers and businesspeople, who need to consider macroeconomic shifts and frame strategies to respond to them. When President Barack Obama began the first term of his presidency in 2009, the economy was already in deep trouble. One of the first challenges he faced was figuring out how the government should respond. In this chapter and the next, we'll see which policies are available to a president and how they can affect the national economy.

Tying It All Together

In recent chapters, we've developed tools for measuring the major features of the macroeconomy: output (GDP), prices, and unemployment. We also investigated aggregate expenditure. But these aspects of the economy don't exist in isolation. Instead, they are different faces of one big, complex system. You probably have some intuitive sense of how they are tied together in determining the health of the economy. For instance, when we say the economy is "doing badly," most of us have a mental picture of both falling production *and* high unemployment. Similarly, you might associate crashing or skyrocketing prices of important goods, such as houses or gasoline, with economic troubles.

In this chapter, we're going to build an economic model under that intuition. The model shows how the condition of the economy—described in terms of GDP and overall price levels—is really an equilibrium outcome. That equilibrium equates the total demand for all goods and services with the total supply. In some superficial ways, this will look like a microeconomic model of demand and supply. In the *macroeconomic* model:

- *Price* is the overall price level, calculated as a weighted average of the prices of all goods and services.
- *Quantity* is represented by GDP, the measure of the value of all goods and services produced by the economy.

However, new forces come into play when we start to *aggregate* (add up) demand and supply across many different goods and services.

The model of aggregate demand and aggregate supply shows how output, prices, and employment are all tied together as part of a single economic equilibrium. This allows us to see what happens when an event like the popping of the housing bubble or a natural disaster hits the economy, and why it is likely to affect all three measures. Using the same tools, we can see how a change in government policy—perhaps intended to counteract the effects of the bubble or disaster—will operate on the same system.

Aggregate Demand

This section will develop a picture of the demand side of the macroeconomy. The term *aggregate demand* describes the total demand for all goods and services in the economy. That means adding up demand across all of the individual markets for goods and services.

It might seem strange to add up quantities of completely different items—literally, adding apples and oranges—but, fortunately, we've already developed a tool for dealing with that problem. In Chapter 7, "Measuring GDP," we introduced the concept of GDP, which adds up all the goods and services in the economy by translating them into a common unit: market value. Thus, *aggregate demand* measures the total quantity of goods and services demanded in the economy, in terms of their market value.

The aggregate demand curve

> **LO 12.1** Show how the aggregate expenditure equilibrium model can be used to trace out the aggregate demand curve and understand why the aggregate demand curve slopes downward.

aggregate demand curve

a curve that shows the relationship between the overall price level in the economy and total demand

The **aggregate demand curve** shows the relationship between the overall price level and the level of total demand in the economy. When we graph aggregate demand, the price level is shown on the vertical axis, and output (or, equivalently, aggregate expenditure, Y, or GDP) is on the horizontal axis.

HINT

Remember from Chapter 7, "Measuring GDP," that aggregate expenditure is equal to output, and that Y and GDP reflect the same quantity. In Chapter 11, "Aggregate Expenditure," we put aggregate expenditure on the horizontal (*x*) axis. Since in this chapter we will bring together aggregate demand and aggregate supply, we will most often label the horizontal axis as "output"—which is equivalent to aggregate expenditure.

The aggregate demand curve slopes downward, just like the demand curves for televisions, haircuts, and any other individual good or service. But the reason for the similarity is not as obvious as it might seem. Here's the difference:

- When we draw the downward-sloping demand curve for televisions, for example, we assume that the price of all other goods is held constant. Thus, the demand curve shows the change in the quantity of TVs that are demanded when *only* TV prices drop.
- With *aggregate* demand, though, we can't change the price of one good and hold the prices of all the other goods constant. By definition, aggregate demand represents *all* goods, so we're interested in what happens when the prices of *all* goods go up or down—as measured by the price index, or inflation level.

So *why* does the aggregate demand curve slope downward? In Chapter 11, "Aggregate Expenditure," we learned how each of the main components of output—consumption, investment, government spending, and net exports—are affected by important economic variables. Now let's examine how each component reacts to changes in the *overall price level* of the economy. Keep in mind that we are interested in how the *real* values of these variables change in response to the price level (so we do not have to worry about a mechanical relationship between the price level and the nominal values of the expenditure components).

How price level changes affect the components of output

First, let's consider consumption. In general, changes in the price level will change the real value of people's wealth and income. A rise in the overall price level means that a given number of dollars won't buy as much in terms of real goods and services. Thus, increases in the overall price level reduce people's wealth, in terms of real purchasing power. When people are less wealthy, they reduce their consumption, creating a negative relationship between the overall price level and consumption spending. This relationship, called the *wealth effect,* gives us one way to explain the downward-sloping aggregate demand curve. As prices rise, people feel less wealthy and want to spend less, leading to a smaller quantity of goods and services demanded in the aggregate.

There's one important caveat to note: If wages increase exactly as much as prices increase, the purchasing power of those wages will stay the same. Many employers have a standard practice of increasing wages along with inflation. In that case, the wealth effect won't come into play. But the same can't be said for wealth that you have stored as cash in your wallet, in non-interest-bearing checking accounts, and in other dollar-denominated assets, which won't necessarily increase along with inflation. So, even when wages keep pace with increasing price levels, most people will probably still experience some reduction in real wealth, causing consumption to fall.

Next, let's talk investment. When prices rise, the interest rate—roughly speaking, the price of borrowing—also tends to rise. Higher interest rates make it more expensive for firms to borrow, which means they invest less in new factories and working capital. (We'll come back to this idea in Chapter 14, "The Basics of Finance.") The increased borrowing costs create an indirect negative relationship between the price level and investment spending.

Shifting to the next component, much of government spending is independent of the price level. Even when prices rise and fall, the government still needs to spend roughly the same amount on Social Security checks and salaries for government employees. Thus, the government spending component does not contribute to the downward-sloping nature of the aggregate demand curve.

Finally, we consider net exports. When prices in the United States increase, U.S. goods become relatively more expensive than goods from other countries, assuming that price levels stay the same in the other countries. As a result, we would expect imports into the United States to increase and exports to decrease. This means that when the price level increases, net exports (exports minus imports) should decrease. This means there is a negative relationship between the price level and net exports.

Graphing changes in the price level

We can show the effects of price-level increases on our aggregate expenditure diagram in Figure 12-1. In this figure, P_1 is the lowest price, so P_2 represents a price increase from P_1, and P_3 represents a price increase from P_2. Each price increase is represented by a downward shift of the planned aggregate expenditure line. To understand why, keep in mind that the aggregate

FIGURE 12-1

How price-driven shifts in planned aggregate expenditure trace out the aggregate demand curve

FIGURE 12-2

The aggregate demand curve

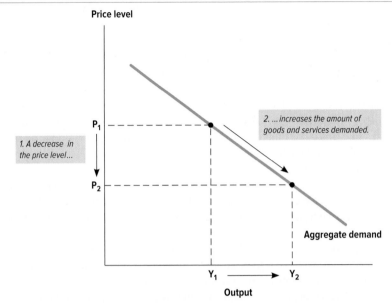

The aggregate demand curve shows the relationship between the price level and the quantity of output demanded by households, firms, the government, and the rest of the world. This relationship shows that as prices decrease, the quantity of aggregate output demanded increases.

expenditure line gives planned aggregate expenditure as a function of Y. Therefore, a downward shift represents a lower level of planned aggregate expenditure for each level of Y.

We can then use the equilibrium aggregate expenditure points to trace out the aggregate demand curve. As shown in the figure, we can plot the (Y, P) pairs that correspond to the equilibrium aggregate expenditure levels and price levels for each of the aggregate expenditure curves. We see, yet again, that the aggregate demand curve slopes downward.

What have we learned?

- There is a negative relationship between price level and national expenditure for three of the four expenditure components—C, I, and NX.
- There is no relationship between the price level and the fourth expenditure component—G.

When we put together this information, we get a negative overall relationship between the price level and aggregate expenditure or GDP. In other words, we end up with a downward-sloping aggregate demand curve, as shown in Figure 12-2.

Furthermore we have learned that every point along the aggregate demand curve corresponds to an equilibrium in the aggregate expenditure model from Chapter 11, "Aggregate Expenditure." One implication is that anything *other than a change in the price level itself* that leads to a different equilibrium in the aggregate expenditure model will cause the aggregate demand curve to shift.

Shifting the aggregate demand curve

LO 12.2 List factors that could cause the aggregate demand curve to shift.

Price changes generate movements *along* the aggregate demand curve. We saw that when the price level increases, for example, the wealth effect drives people to spend less, and overall output falls. However, the entire aggregate demand curve can also *shift* in response to *nonprice changes* in any of the four components of aggregate demand—consumption, investment, government spending, and net exports. Such nonprice changes move the entire curve to the left or right, making aggregate demand lower or higher at any given price level.

Big changes to the national economy can sometimes be described as shifts in the aggregate demand curve. Consider, for instance, the story of the housing bubble. People felt confident when housing prices were rising steadily until late 2007. Homeowners could see the value of their houses increasing, which made them feel significantly wealthier and more optimistic. They started consuming more, which made all kinds of firms throughout the economy also feel good about their future prospects. They started investing more.

The total effect of this boost in consumer and company confidence was to shift the aggregate demand curve to the right. Because confidence was high, people and businesses were willing to spend and invest more, increasing aggregate demand at any price level, as shown in panel A of Figure 12-3.

Unfortunately, that increase in housing prices turned out to be a bubble, which popped in late 2007. House prices started to fall, and people became worried that they were not as wealthy as they thought they were. This concern reduced consumer confidence, and people bought less. In turn, managers of companies became worried that they would not sell as many goods and services in the future, so they became less willing to invest. Together, this drop in confidence throughout the economy shifted aggregate demand to the left, as shown in panel B of Figure 12-3.

Confidence is a fuzzy concept, but as the example of the housing bubble shows, it can be critical to both consumption and investment:

- If people feel positive about their prospects for future income, they will be more likely to consume more.

- On the other hand, if people feel worried about losing their jobs or paying higher prices in the future, they will probably start consuming less and saving more for a rainy day.

FIGURE 12-3

Shifts in the aggregate demand curve

(A) A rightward shift of aggregate demand	**(B) A leftward shift of aggregate demand**
When the aggregate demand curve shifts out (to the right) due to an overall increase in consumption, GDP is higher at every price level.	When the aggregate demand curve shifts in (to the left), the opposite is true. At each price level, GDP is lower.

Much the same reasoning applies to firms:

- If businesses are optimistic about the direction of the economy, they will want to invest more in new factories, warehouses, and machinery.
- But if prospects for the economy start to look bleak, managers will be less interested in expanding and increasing capacity, and will invest less.

Increasing consumer and business confidence will therefore shift the aggregate demand curve to the right. Decreasing confidence shifts the curve to the left.

Some government policies, such as taxes and government spending, can also shift the aggregate demand curve:

- Cutting taxes on consumers is likely to increase consumption because people keep more of the money they earn and so are in effect wealthier. Increased consumption spending shifts the aggregate demand curve to the right.
- By the same logic, raising taxes can dampen the desire to spend by leaving consumers with less money. Higher taxes shift the aggregate demand curve to the left.

The government can also affect aggregate demand through its own spending:

- Government spending increases aggregate demand directly, through the "G" in the demand equation. (But as we'll see in detail in the next chapter, government spending can also have indirect effects on demand by encouraging more consumer spending.) In the face of a recession, government can increase spending in order to shift the aggregate demand to the right. For example, this strategy could mean the construction of federal highways, more spending for the military, or added spending for schools.
- If, instead, the government sharply cut its spending during a recession, it risks a decline in aggregate demand. In that case, the aggregate demand curve would shift to the left.

Table 12-1 shows examples of changes that can cause shifts in the aggregate demand curve. The middle column lists several factors that would increase aggregate demand, shifting the aggregate demand curve to the right. The right-hand column lists factors that would decrease aggregate demand, shifting the aggregate demand curve to the left.

TABLE 12-1

What causes the aggregate demand curve to shift?

Category	Increase (shift right)	Decrease (shift left)
Consumption	• High expectations about future income increase consumer spending. • Tax cuts increase consumer spending.	• Low expectations about future income lead to greater saving and less spending. • Higher interest rates discourage borrowing.
Investment	• Confidence in the future of the economy leads firms to expand their businesses. • A tax credit for small businesses inspires firms to buy new company cars.	• Firms cut back on spending in order to weather a recession. • Taxes on capital increase, leaving less money for investment.
Government spending	• Increase in government spending spurs spending after a recession.	• Decrease in government spending in response to concerns about increasing debt leads to less spending.
Net exports	• A new free trade agreement with Europe reduces most tariffs and other restrictions on U.S. goods. • Economic growth abroad in China increases demand for U.S. goods and services.	• Other countries increase their tariffs on U.S. goods, making the goods more expensive. • The dollar strengthens, making U.S. goods and services more expensive for international consumers, decreasing demand.

The multiplier and shifts in aggregate demand

LO 12.3 Explain how changes in government spending and taxes can have a multiplier effect on aggregate demand.

In Chapter 11, "Aggregate Expenditure," we saw that the *multiplier effect* means that each additional dollar of expenditure in the economy leads to more than one dollar of output. This principle has important consequences for economic policy.

Imagine that you're the president and you've just entered office. The economy is in a recession, and you are considering how to use economic policy to stimulate the economy and create jobs. Your economic advisors are divided over the best route to take:

- Some advise you to cut taxes. They reason that employees will take home more money and some of it will be spent, which will boost demand.

- Others advise you to increase government spending. Since millions are out of work, these advisors argue, the government should create jobs by spending on infrastructure projects. The income paid to newly employed workers will then flow into the economy as these workers in turn spend their new income on food, clothes, energy, and other things.

Both plans will stimulate the economy, but you want to ensure that you use government resources as efficiently as possible. Which policy gives you the "bigger bang" for the government's buck? First, let's consider the case of *stimulus spending,* as proposed by your second set of advisors. Suppose that government agencies buy new computers. Here's what happens:

- The government pays $500 million to the computer manufacturer. Immediately, this expenditure increases GDP by $500 million since government spending is one of the contributors to overall GDP.

- The computer manufacturer in turn uses the money to pay workers and make new capital investments, such as building a factory.

- The people employed to build the factory, in turn, spend money on goods and services elsewhere in the economy, and so on.

In the end, the $500 million injection of spending will increase GDP by $500 times the multiplier. In Chapter 11, "Aggregate Expenditure," we defined the expenditure multiplier as $1/(1 - b)$. If the marginal propensity to consume out of disposable income is 0.6, then $b = 0.6$ and the multiplier is $1/(1 - b) = 2.5$. Given a multiplier of 2.5, the stimulus spending would result in $500 million $\times$ 2.5 = $1,250 million in additional GDP.

Now imagine that, instead of spending that $500 million on new computers, the government decides to cut taxes by $500 million. The tax cut puts money in people's pockets, which they can use for consumption. The multiplier effect comes into play under this policy, too. This policy *seems* like it should have exactly the same impact as the direct increase in government spending, but that is not actually the case.

Again, the impact can be found by multiplying the initial spending increase by the expenditure multiplier. But note that in the case of the tax cut, the initial spending increase is not the full $500 million. Instead, because the marginal propensity to consume is less than 1, only a fraction, b, of the $500 million tax cut results in a first round of new consumption spending. Continuing to assume that $b = 0.6$, then the *initial* increase in aggregate expenditure with the tax cut is only $500 million $\times$ 0.6 = $300 million. This is less than the case of direct government spending, for which the entire $500 million was spent.

The tax cut still creates a multiplier effect, though. Because the expenditure multiplier is still 2.5, the total increase in output in the case of the tax cut would be $300 million $\times$ 2.5 = $750 million. More generally, each dollar *reduction* in lump-sum taxes will result in $b \times 1/(1 - b)$ additional dollars of GDP.

Note that you do not need to memorize two different formulas for understanding the impact of government spending versus tax cuts. As long as you correctly compute the initial change in aggregate expenditure due to the policy, you still multiply that change by the same expenditure multiplier. The only difference with tax cuts is that the initial change in expenditures is smaller (in absolute value) than the full change in taxes.[1]

When the economy is slumping because consumer confidence is down, politicians often try to get things moving again by asking people to spend more. When times are good, though, they give very different advice, as seen in the From Another Angle box "Save . . . no, spend!"

From Another Angle
Save . . . no, spend!

When Barack Obama started his first term as president in January 2009, U.S. households were feeling the pinch. Worried about the future, they had cut back on their spending and started to save more. On an individual level, it's a good idea to save in times of economic trouble. Unfortunately, though, the overall health of the economy is tightly linked with how much people spend. In fact, over 70 percent of total GDP in the United States comes from consumption spending. That's why, in a speech to Congress in 2009, in the middle of the Great Recession, Obama noted that the best path to recovery was for everyone to spend a little more:

> That's what [the stimulus] is about. It's not about helping banks—it's about helping people. Because when credit is available again, that young family can finally buy a new home. And then some company will hire workers to build it. And then those workers will have money to spend, and if they can get a loan too, maybe they'll finally buy that car, or open their own business. Investors will return to the market, and American families will see their retirement secured once more. Slowly, but surely, confidence will return, and our economy will recover.

Just five years previously, U.S. consumers had heard a very different message. In a 2004 speech, Federal Reserve Board Vice Chairman Roger Ferguson called on households to stop spending so much and start saving more. He explained that this saving would mean banks had more funds to lend to U.S. companies:

> Probably nothing is more critical to the long-run well-being of the U.S. economy than ensuring high rates of productivity growth. Productivity growth requires adequate levels of investment. While foreign saving is currently a feasible source of investable resources, it would be more economically advantageous in the longer run if we could raise the amount of household and government savings and close the gap between domestic investment and national savings.

Why would policy-makers give totally different advice, just five years apart? The U.S. economy had changed sharply in the time between the two speeches. In 2004, the economy was doing well. U.S. firms were eager to invest, which meant borrowing money, but because U.S. households were saving so little, investment funds from domestic sources were scarce. The logic was that if households would save more, banks would have more money to loan out, and firms would be able to make more investments to improve their businesses.

By 2009, though, the economy was in a rough spot. Consumers weren't spending very much. This lack of spending meant that firms were no longer as interested in borrowing to invest. If households could be persuaded to spend more instead of saving, the AD curve would shift to the right. In 2009 the logic was that when firms saw that demand was increasing, they would want to employ more people and invest again. Consumer spending would kick-start economic recovery.

In both cases, the aim of the advice was to improve the health of the economy. When times are good, saving makes sense as a way to help firms make needed investments to secure the future. When times are bad, extra spending can help move the economy out of a rut and toward recovery.

Sources: http://www.federalreserve.gov/boarddocs/speeches/2004/20041006/default.htm; http://www.whitehouse.gov/the_press_office/Remarks-of-President-Barack-Obama-Address-to-Joint-Session-of-Congress/.

✓CONCEPT CHECK

☐ What four components of spending make up aggregate demand? **[LO 12.1]**

☐ Is the relationship between price level and aggregate demand generally positive or negative? **[LO 12.1]**

☐ Would the construction of a new interstate highway by the U.S. Department of Transportation shift aggregate demand to the left or right? **[LO 12.2]**

☐ Does a decrease in consumer spending after a tax increase shift aggregate demand to the left or right? **[LO 12.2]**

☐ Why does a tax cut have a different multiplier effect than an equally costly increase in public spending? **[LO 12.3]**

Aggregate Supply

Now that we've described the demand side of the economy, we'll turn to the other side. *Aggregate supply* is the sum total of the production of all the firms in the economy. Production occurs when factor inputs—technology, capital, and labor—are combined to produce output.

The **aggregate supply curve** shows the relationship between the overall price level in the economy and total production by firms (output). The aggregate supply curve is similar to a market supply curve, with two key differences:

> **aggregate supply curve**
> a curve that shows the relationship between the overall price level in the economy and total production by firms

1. The aggregate supply curve represents production in the economy *as a whole* rather than just one good or service.
2. At the macroeconomic level, there is a difference between how the economy operates in the short run and how the economy operates in the long run.

Because of the difference between the short run and the long run, there are actually *two* different aggregate supply curves:

- One describes aggregate supply in the long run; it is called the *long-run aggregate supply curve (LRAS)*.
- The second describes how firms decide how much to produce in the short run; it is called the *short-run aggregate supply curve (SRAS)*.

We'll look at both in this section.

The difference between short-run and long-run aggregate supply

LO 12.4 Explain the difference between the short run and long run in the economy.

In order to understand the two aggregate supply curves, we need to explore the difference between the short run and the long run in the economy.

Short-run aggregate supply

The *short run* refers to the hourly, daily, or weekly decisions that firms have to make. If you're running a fast-food burger joint, short-run decisions include choices about how much beef and lettuce you want to order for the week or how many hours you want each employee to work. In choosing these inputs, you are essentially deciding how much food you want to produce.

In the short run, the aggregate supply curve slopes upward, as Figure 12-4 shows. This means that as overall price levels increase, firms are willing to produce more. Why is this so? Because the prices of final goods and services—like burgers—tend to increase more quickly than the prices of inputs. (Below, we explain why.) So, the burger joint is able to increase revenues faster than the increases in its costs. As a result, it is willing to produce more.

Why do prices of final goods and services increase more quickly than inputs? The key idea is that when the price level increases, input prices don't all increase immediately. Instead, some prices are "sticky," meaning that they adjust slowly in response to changes in the economy. Wages are a prime example. To understand why sticky wages cause the short-run aggregate supply curve to slope upward, think about a sudden increase in the price level. Firms are going to earn more revenue because the prices of their products are higher. However, wages don't adjust right away. In the short run, the burger stand can make higher profits because revenues have increased but labor costs haven't. Because of the sticky wages, firms will be prepared to hire new workers and produce more output.

But why should input prices be sticky, yet the prices of final goods can change instantaneously? Contracts or informal practices make wages and the prices of other inputs sticky. For instance, many firms reevaluate wages only once a year. Unionized firms typically have formal labor contracts that often determine wage levels for several years at a time. If an employee wants higher wages or an employer wants to implement a pay cut, they will have to wait until the next period in which wages are adjusted or when the present contract expires. Often, raw materials are supplied on the same basis. For example, a fast-food chain might have a contract with a beef supplier setting out how much it will pay for beef over the coming year.

Although contracts are common for input prices, the prices of final goods are rarely dictated by contract. It's not likely, for example, that a fast-food stand would ever get its customers

---

FIGURE 12-4

The short-run aggregate supply curve

In the short run, the aggregate supply curve reacts to price changes. This means that firms are willing to change how much they supply based on price.

to agree to a long-term contract that specifies how many burgers and fries they'll buy over a year. Instead, customers grab a burger whenever they're hungry, paying the price on the current menu. To change the price, the fast-food stand simply changes its menu. Although changing final prices isn't always easy, in general, we assume that final prices can change far more easily than input prices.

Long-run aggregate supply

Now let's look at the long run. The first thing to know is that *the long run is not a set amount of time*, like one year, two years, or 10 years. Instead, it is however long it takes for prices of inputs—such as wages, rent, and raw materials—to *fully adjust to changes in economic conditions.* In the long run, a burger stand can renegotiate the rent on its building, hire new employees, and negotiate new wages.

The adjustment process between the short and long run in macroeconomics differs from the adjustment process studied in microeconomics. In microeconomics, we focus on individual markets, and the key adjustment problem is one of quantities. Some costs are "fixed" because the quantity of an input cannot be adjusted in the short run; others are "variable" costs because the quantity used can easily be adjusted in the short run. For example, back to the burger stand, basic equipment like deep fryers and heat lamps are fixed costs in the short run. In the long run, new equipment can be purchased and installed. In contrast, the amount of beef used is more likely to be a variable cost, increased or decreased as weekly burger sales dictate.

In macroeconomics, the focus is on how long it takes for *prices to adjust through the whole economy,* rather than the flexibility of *quantities* within an individual firm. What happens to the shape of the supply curve in the long run? Let's return to our example of the fast-food stand. In the short run, the burger stand's owners are making extra profits because revenues have risen but costs have not. That situation can't go on forever. Since goods are now more expensive, fry cooks and cashiers are going to ask for higher wages. Input prices, which have been under contract, will increase when the contracts are renegotiated.

Once these input prices adjust, the burger stand no longer makes higher profits. Its revenues may be higher, but its costs also are higher. As a result, profits go back to where they were before the price increase. *This same process happens throughout the economy.* Once wages and input costs adjust to the new price level, the economy will go back to where it started.

In the long run, when input prices can adjust, our model says that changes in the prices of goods and services paid by consumers have no effect on aggregate supply. The long-run aggregate supply curve is a vertical line, showing that the same amount of output is supplied at *any* price level. Figure 12-5 shows an example of a long-run aggregate supply curve.

If it's not prices, what does determine the quantity of output supplied in the long run? The long-run aggregate supply curve represents *potential output* in the economy—the level of output possible if the economy is operating at full capacity. It may help to think of the long-run aggregate supply curve as a production function. The production function shows how society's natural resources, labor, and capital can be combined to produce the greatest output.

Changes in the long-run aggregate supply curve happen because something changes in the way that society's resources create output. Maybe there has been a new technological invention or the discovery of new resources, like a new oil reserve. The process of steadily pushing the long-run aggregate supply curve to the right—that is, increasing potential output—is the main driver of economic growth.

The economy does not always produce its potential output. Sometimes less output is produced, and sometimes more:

- When output is higher than potential output, the economy is in a boom.
- When output is below potential, the economy is in a recession.

We call these fluctuations around the level of potential output the **business cycle.** Figure 12-6 shows the business cycle for the United States over the past 50 years.

business cycle
Fluctuations of output around the level of potential output in the economy

FIGURE 12-5

The long-run aggregate supply curve

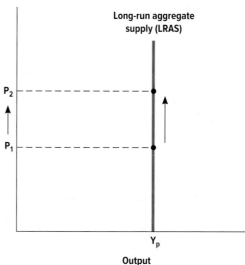

In the long run, the aggregate supply curve is fixed. Changes in the overall level of prices do not influence the level of output in the economy.

FIGURE 12-6

The business cycle

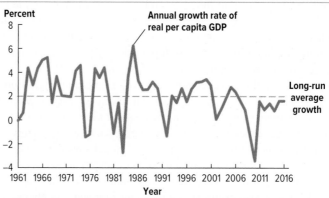

This graph shows the U.S. business cycle since 1961. Although the average real GDP per capita growth rate over this time is about 2 percent, the yearly average fluctuates quite a bit, with periods of expansion and recession.

Source: The World Bank Data, GDP per capita growth (annual %), http://data.worldbank.org/indicator/NY.GDP.PCAP.KD.ZG/countries.

You might be wondering: How can there ever be a boom? Using the model of aggregate demand and aggregate supply, how can short-run supply ever exceed the economy's level of potential output? It turns out that in the short run, production can be expanded beyond long-run potential by pressing all of the factors of production beyond their normal capacity. For instance, if firms ask workers to take on extra hours or run their factories around the clock, output can be temporarily pushed beyond the level of potential output.

To understand how this works, think about what happens at school during exam time. You may put in lots of extra hours to cram for a test. In doing so, you are operating beyond your long-run capacity for schoolwork. You may be able to study 18 hours a day for a few weeks before midterms, but that schedule is probably not sustainable over an entire semester. Cramming for exams racks up costs that wouldn't occur with a normal schedule. These include the stress that comes from worrying about final grades or the health costs of eating too much junk food, not getting enough exercise or sleep, and not having enough leisure time. Once exams are over, these costs will push you to return to a normal workload in the beginning of the next semester. In other words, you will go back to your potential output.

In the same way that you incur costs by operating above capacity during exam time, firms incur costs by operating beyond potential output in the aggregate supply and demand model. When the economy is below capacity, ramping up production is easy. Firms can hire workers who were unemployed and rent warehouses that were sitting empty. This isn't the case when the economy is operating at full capacity. Since wages and input prices are fixed in the short run, firms often have to pay current employees overtime to work longer hours, or hire workers who may not be fully qualified for the job.

Eventually, the intense demand for labor and capital when an economy is operating above capacity will drive prices upward. Hard-pressed workers will demand raises or leave to work for firms that are willing to pay them more money. As a result:

- input prices will increase,
- profits will shrink back to the original level, and
- supply will fall back to the long-run level.

The end result of this short-term boost in output is higher prices in the long run.

Shifts in the short-run aggregate supply curve

LO 12.5 Demonstrate a shift in the short-run aggregate supply curve and list factors that cause it to shift.

The short-run aggregate supply curve can shift—for example, if the costs of production change. Imagine that oil prices rise all of a sudden. Firms will feel the pinch. When oil prices rise, many firms will find that producing output is much more expensive. It's more costly for farmers to harvest and transport their crops, and transportation costs will make it more expensive to purchase the inputs that are needed for production. These changes shift the short-run aggregate supply (SRAS) curve to the left, as firms want to supply fewer goods at any given price level. Figure 12-7 shows this shift.

FIGURE 12-7

Shifts in the short-run aggregate supply curve

With an increase in the price of oil, prices increase for the same amount of production, so the aggregate supply curve shifts in (to the left).

POTENTIALLY CONFUSING

You may wonder at this point why a change in the world price of oil causes a shift of the SRAS instead of a movement along the curve. The reason has to do with the distinction between prices and costs. As oil prices rise, as we said, it's the increase in the *cost of inputs,* and therefore more costly production, that cause the SRAS to shift. An increase in the *cost of production* is different from an increase in the *price level:*

- An increase in the cost of production shifts the SRAS curve leftward, reducing the quantity of output produced at a given price level.
- In contrast, an increase in the price level itself—the weighted average of the prices of all goods and services we produce—would cause us to move from one point on the SRAS curve to another point on the same (unmoving) curve.

---

supply shocks
significant events that directly affect production and the aggregate supply curve in the short run

The short-run aggregate supply (SRAS) curve will also shift with other significant events that directly affect production—often called **supply shocks**. An example would be a major flood that disrupts the power grid and ruins crops.

Expectations about future input prices will also shift the SRAS. If firms *anticipate* that the price of oil, for example, is likely to increase, then suppliers will expect higher input costs in the future. This belief itself will reduce the quantity of goods supplied and shift the aggregate supply curve to the left.

Shifts in the long-run aggregate supply curve

LO 12.6 Demonstrate a shift in the long-run aggregate supply curve and list factors that cause it to shift.

In the long run, firms produce an amount dictated by available inputs, regardless of the overall price level. But that doesn't mean that the long-run aggregate supply curve never moves. Remember that the long-run aggregate supply (LRAS) curve is like a production function: A combination of land, technology, capital, and labor will produce a certain amount of output. Anything that affects the output possible using these factors will shift the LRAS curve, including new technologies, improved transportation systems, management innovations, and so on:

- The LRAS curve will shift to the right if the potential output of the economy expands.
- The LRAS curve will shift to the left if the economy loses productive capacity.

Consider the case of a new technology. When firms throughout the economy adopt a new technology, they can use the same amount of resources to produce more output than before. Historical examples include the power loom during the nineteenth-century Industrial Revolution and the Internet in the past 20 years. These innovations shift the LRAS curve out to the right, as illustrated in Figure 12-8.

The long-run aggregate supply curve also shifts with changes in the factors of production in the economy. For example:

- An increase in foreign investment will increase the capital stock of an economy. That will allow production to increase and will shift the long-run aggregate supply curve to the right.
- In contrast, if levels of investment are low and existing capital is not replaced as it wears out, we would see the opposite effect: Potential output decreases, and the long-run aggregate supply curve shifts to the left.

FIGURE 12-8

Shifts in the long-run aggregate supply curve

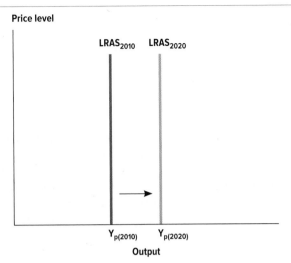

Price level

LRAS$_{2010}$ LRAS$_{2020}$

Y$_{p(2010)}$ Y$_{p(2020)}$

Output

With an increase in technology, firms can produce more goods with the same amount of inputs. This shifts the long-run aggregate supply curve, the potential output of an economy, outward (to the right).

TABLE 12-2

What causes the LRAS curve to shift?

A variety of factors can shift the long-run aggregate supply curve by changing the potential output in an economy.

Factor	Increases LRAS	Decreases LRAS
Technology	Technological innovation allows for greater production using the same amount of inputs.	A new law stripping away intellectual property rights reduces the incentive to innovate.
Capital	Foreign investment in factories and machines increases available capital.	Depreciation and wear break down capital.
Labor	Immigration increases the available supply of labor.	Aging population takes workers out of the labor force.
Education	Universal primary education gives everyone a chance to go to school.	Reduction of federal college grants makes it more difficult for some to go to school.
Natural resources	New energy sources allow factories to produce more with the same inputs.	Climate change permanently reduces the amount of land that can be farmed.

Table 12-2 gives some examples of changes that will shift the long-run aggregate supply curve.

Do the LRAS and SRAS always shift together?

Do the long-run and short-run aggregate supply curves always shift together? No. On one hand, everything that shifts the LRAS curve will also shift the SRAS curve. The reason is that the available factors of production and technology that determine the position of the LRAS will also drive short-run supply. For instance, the spread of the Internet in the past 20 years shifted both the LRAS and the SRAS.

However, the opposite is not true. Not everything that shifts the SRAS curve will also shift the LRAS curve. Specifically, *changes in expectations* about future price levels *affect only the SRAS curve.*

Before we discuss why this is so, it's a good idea to remind ourselves that although this situation involves the price level, it shifts the aggregate supply curve (a change in aggregate supply) rather than causing a movement along the curve (a change in aggregate quantity supplied). Why? Because we are focusing on *expected* changes in prices, not *actual* changes in prices. There must be an *actual* change in those prices to cause a movement along a curve, whether in the short run or long run.

Expectations about prices, on the other hand, are just guesses about the future. These expectations affect firms' production plans. Firms don't want to be caught unaware by changes in their costs. When they expect prices to rise at some future point, they also expect that workers will demand higher wages in order to keep up with the higher cost of living. As a result, firms reduce production at any given current price level, shifting the SRAS curve to the left.

Why don't changes in expected prices shift the LRAS curve? We can look at this in two ways. The first comes from our definition of the LRAS—as a representation of the production function, located at the economy's potential output. The only things that can shift the LRAS are those factors that affect how we produce, such as the amount of labor, capital, natural resources such as land, and technology. Expected prices aren't included in the production function, so they cannot cause the LRAS to shift.

The second way to think about this is to consider our definition of the long run versus the short run. In the long run, expectations are fully incorporated into economic variables such as the price level. Since our expectations are fully accounted for, no shift occurs.

No matter how we look at it, while all other factors we mentioned shift the SRAS and LRAS curves in the same manner, *changes in expected prices shift only the SRAS curve:*

- In only the short run, an expected increase in prices shifts the SRAS curve leftward.
- In the long run, these expectations are incorporated into the LRAS curve, and so we see no change at all.

Changes in expected prices will not affect the LRAS curve if they do not affect the number of workers, the amount of capital, or the amount of land and technology in the economy. In the long run, prices will fully adjust to take into account any changes in policies or expectations.

✓CONCEPT CHECK

- ☐ Why is the long-run aggregate supply curve vertical? **[LO 12.4]**
- ☐ What is the business cycle? **[LO 12.4]**
- ☐ Which way does the short-run aggregate supply curve shift when the cost of inputs decreases? **[LO 12.5]**
- ☐ Does the SRAS curve shift when the availability of land, labor, or capital decreases? If yes, in which direction does it shift? **[LO 12.5]**
- ☐ Does the LRAS curve shift when the availability of land, labor, or capital decreases? If yes, in which direction does it shift? **[LO 12.6]**
- ☐ How do changes in expected prices shift the SRAS? Why isn't the LRAS curve affected? **[LO 12.6]**

Economic Fluctuations

Now we have all the ingredients for a full model of the national economy: aggregate demand, short-run aggregate supply, and long-run aggregate supply. It's time to put them together.

Equilibrium in the national economy is the point at which aggregate demand equals aggregate supply. Short-run equilibrium is given by the intersection of the aggregate demand and short-run

FIGURE 12-9
A model of the macroeconomy

When the aggregate demand and supply curves are put together, we get a model of the entire economy. The intersection of these curves is the equilibrium, which represents a stable level of prices and output.

aggregate supply curves. In long-run equilibrium, the aggregate demand curve crosses the long-run aggregate supply and short-run aggregate supply curves *at the same point.* This means that prices are at expected levels and the short-run level of output is the same as long-run potential output. Figure 12-9 shows the macroeconomy in equilibrium: The intersection of the AD, LRAS, and SRAS curves gives the equilibrium price level and output.

A variety of shocks can push the economy out of long-run equilibrium. These shocks can shift either the aggregate demand curve or the short-run aggregate supply curve, causing the economy to shift away from potential output in the short run. In the long run, prices will adjust and the economy will return to its long-run equilibrium.

In reality, it's not always immediately clear whether a particular shock is shifting the aggregate demand or aggregate supply curve. In this section, we will show that supply-side shocks and demand-side shocks produce different implications for output and prices, which can help us to distinguish them.

Effects of a shift in aggregate demand

LO 12.7 Explain the short-run and long-run effects of a shift in aggregate demand.

Let's return to the example of the housing bubble. From 2000 to 2007, house prices were increasing, and people who owned homes felt that their wealth was increasing as well. Consumer confidence increased throughout the economy, and consumption rose. We saw earlier in the chapter that increased consumption shifts the aggregate demand curve to the right. How will an increase in consumption affect the economy in the short run and the long run?

Panel A of Figure 12-10 shows how the increase in consumption during a housing bubble affects the economy in the short run. When the AD curve shifts to the right, the short-run equilibrium moves from point E_1 (the intersection of the AD, LRAS, and SRAS curves) to point E_2 (the intersection of the new AD curve and the AS curve). Point E_2 shows the effect of the housing boom: Output was above the long-run potential level, and prices increased.

Point E_2 is an equilibrium point, but it is only a short-run equilibrium. How do we know this? *The long-run equilibrium is determined by the productive factors* in the economy, and this

FIGURE 12-10

The effect of an increase in aggregate demand

(A) Short run

(B) Long run

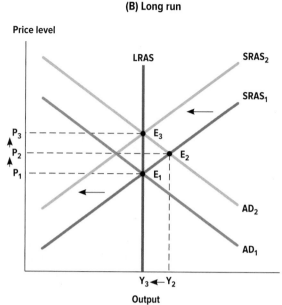

When people buy more as a result of increased consumer confidence, the aggregate demand curve shifts out. This results in a new short-run equilibrium at point E_2. At this new equilibrium, output and prices are higher.

As wages and prices increase due to the shift in aggregate demand, it becomes more costly to produce goods, so the short-run aggregate supply curve shifts to the left. This brings production back to its original level, but prices increase again.

increase in consumption didn't change any of the land, labor, or capital that was available for production. Therefore, we know that the LRAS curve hasn't moved.

How does the economy return to the long-run equilibrium? The SRAS curve has to shift again to restore the long-run equilibrium. As we'll see, this is where our model diverges from what actually happened during the housing boom. If the economy had come down naturally, wages and other resource prices would have started to increase gradually because of inflation, causing an increase in input costs for firms and therefore shifting aggregate supply. As contracts were negotiated and wages increased, the SRAS curve would have gradually shifted to the left until equilibrium was restored, as shown in panel B of Figure 12-10.

If you compare point E_1 to point E_3 in panel B of Figure 12-10—the movement from the initial long-run equilibrium to the new long-run equilibrium—you'll see that output didn't change, but the price level increased. So, the effects of an increase in consumption differ in the short and long runs:

- In the short run, absent any other changes, the effect of a shift in the AD curve due to an increase in consumer confidence will be to increase both prices and output.
- In the long run, the gains to output retreat, output returns to its former level, and the only change that is left is higher prices.

The economy is in an opposite situation when a negative shock shifts aggregate demand to the left, as shown in Figure 12-11. For example, suppose the economy is humming along at equilibrium. Then, all of a sudden, housing prices collapse. Consumer confidence falls, and consumption decreases, shifting the AD curve to the left.

In the short run, shown in panel A of Figure 12-11, output will be below the potential level of output. However, this change exerts downward pressure on prices. As prices adjust and inputs

FIGURE 12-11

The effect of a decrease in aggregate demand

(A) Short run

When aggregate demand shifts in due to a decrease in aggregate demand, the new short-run equilibrium moves to point E_2. At point E_2 both prices and output are lower.

(B) Long run

Lower prices of inputs make it cheaper for firms to produce goods so the aggregate supply curve shifts out. This shift restores the economy to a long-run equilibrium with the same original level of output, but with lower prices.

get cheaper, firms will increase their output—shifting the SRAS curve to the right, as shown in panel B. The new long-run equilibrium will be at the original level of output, but with a lower price level (point E_3).

If you compare point E_1 to point E_3 in panel B of Figure 12-11—the movement from the initial long-run equilibrium to the new long-run equilibrium—you'll see that output didn't change, but the price level decreased. So, the effects of a decrease in consumption differ in the short and long runs:

- In the short run, absent any other changes, the effect of a shift in the AD curve due to a decrease in consumer confidence will be to decrease both prices and output.
- In the long run, as prices adjust and inputs get cheaper, output increases to its former level, and the only change that is left is lower prices.

Table 12-3 summarizes the effects of a change in aggregate demand in the short run and long run. The key is this: Demand-side shifts change only the price level in the long run, while output eventually returns to its long-run potential level.

TABLE 12-3

Changes in aggregate demand in the short run and the long run

The impacts of a shift in demand can be separated into two main paths. An increase in AD will increase both prices and output in the short run. In the long run, only prices will be higher as output slides back to the original equilibrium level. The opposite is true for a decrease in aggregate demand.

Shift	Example	Short run	Long run
Increase in AD	Increase in government spending: increases G	Output increases Price increases	Output unchanged Price increases
Decrease in AD	Reduction in consumer confidence: reduces C	Output decreases Price decreases	Output unchanged Price decreases

Effects of a shift in aggregate supply

LO 12.8 Explain the short-run and long-run effects of a shift in aggregate supply.

The other type of shocks the economy can face is shocks to the supply side. Supply-side shocks may be either temporary or permanent:

- When such changes are temporary, only the SRAS curve will shift.
- When the changes are permanent, both the LRAS curve and the SRAS curve will shift.

Temporary supply shocks
Let's first consider a temporary shock. Suppose there is a year-long drought in the Midwest and a lot of corn is damaged. This shock will shift the SRAS curve to the left, as shown in panel A of Figure 12-12. The economy will move from its long-run equilibrium at point E_1 to the new short-run equilibrium at point E_2. Prices will be higher and output will be lower. How does the economy adjust?

A situation in which output decreases while prices increase is often referred to as *stagflation*—economic stagnation coupled with high inflation. Adjustment from this short-run equilibrium is not easy. A drop in wages would help, but employees are usually reluctant to accept lower wages. We say that wages are generally "sticky downward," meaning that it takes a long time for them to fall. Sticky input prices contribute to keeping the economy in this undesirable equilibrium.

When the economy is producing at a level less than the potential output and wages are slow to fall, firms will lay off workers; unemployment will be higher than its natural rate. If the unemployment rate remains high, wages will eventually begin to fall. As labor becomes cheaper, the

---

FIGURE 12-12

The effect of a decrease in short-run supply: A drought in the Midwest

A drought that destroys much of the corn crop will shift the short-run aggregate supply curve in. In the short run, prices will be higher, and output falls.

As the rainfall returns and wages fall due to increased unemployment, the short-run aggregate supply curve will slide out. This means that prices and output return to their original levels.

costs of production for firms will decrease. The short-run aggregate supply curve shifts back to the right, as shown in panel B. Eventually, costs will decrease to the point where the SRAS is back to its original level, and the economy will be back at its old long-run equilibrium (point E_1). In the long run, both prices and output return to their initial level.

Permanent supply shocks

Now let's think about a permanent supply shock. Instead of just a short-term drought, imagine that cataclysmic climate change makes it impossible to grow corn or anything else with yields similar to what farmers now get in the Midwest. Since the Midwest is integral to U.S. food production, there simply isn't enough other land to make up the difference. With a loss of one of the factors of production (in this case, land), the LRAS curve will shift to the left, as in panel A of Figure 12-13.

This change has effects in the short run as well. Corn grown in the Midwest is important in the production of goods throughout the economy. Everything from the cereal you eat for breakfast to the gas you put in your car likely contains some corn or product derived from corn. The increase in food and other prices means that the costs of production will also rise, shifting the SRAS to the left. The SRAS curve may not shift immediately to the new long-run equilibrium point. In the short run, the equilibrium may move only to point E_2 in panel A of Figure 12-13.

As long as prices are above the long-run equilibrium level, the SRAS will continue to shift to the left, as shown in panel B. This process continues until the economy reaches a new long-run equilibrium (at point E_3), with higher prices and a lower level of potential output.

FIGURE 12-13

The effect of a decrease in long-run supply: Climate change

(A) Short run

(B) Long run

With climate change, the impact to the economy is initially similar to what occurs with a shock like a drought. The aggregate supply curve shifts in. At the new short-run equilibrium, point E_2, prices are higher and output falls.

Since the effects of climate change are permanent, the long-run supply curve shifts to the left. With continually increasing prices, the short-run aggregate supply curve will shift to the left until it reaches the new long-run equilibrium at point E_3. At this point, prices are much higher and output lower than the original equilibrium.

Comparing demand and supply shocks

> **LO 12.9** Use the AD/AS framework to determine whether an observed change in output and prices was due to a demand shock or a supply shock.

The AD/AS model is a powerful tool for understanding overall economic conditions and figuring out how to formulate policy response to shocks. Successful economic policy hinges on being able to tell the difference between a demand and a supply shock. If you apply a policy designed to fight the effects of one kind of shock and it turns out to be the other, you could potentially make things even worse.

This section describes the two main challenges that arise when using the AD/AS model to analyze events in the economy:

- If you see a specific shock, can you tell which side of the economy it is going to affect?
- If you see a change in the economy, can you work backward to figure out what type of shock might have caused it?

First, think through whom a shock will affect and what role they play in the economy. For example:

- Higher oil prices are going to affect businesses that use oil to produce goods. This means that an oil-price change will be a shock to the *supply side* of the economy. Because the shock has to do with prices rather than real factors of production, it will affect only the *short-run aggregate supply curve,* and not the long-run curve.
- In contrast, if you see a shock that affects consumers or government spending, it is likely to affect consumption. It therefore will act on the *demand side* of the economy.

Table 12-4 shows some examples of demand and supply shocks. For each shock, think about (1) which group of people the shock will affect, (2) whether it is a demand-side or a supply-side shock, and (3) whether it is a long-run or a short-run shock.

When thinking in the other direction—when working backward from effect on the economy to figuring out the cause—there are clear predictions about how different types of shocks will affect prices and output; these give clues about what the main shock must have been. For example, when output falls in the short run, the cause could be either a reduction in aggregate demand or a reduction in short-run aggregate supply.

The two cases are shown in Figure 12-14 (which actually recalls panels from Figure 12-11 and Figure 12-12). By comparing the two panels of Figure 12-14, we can see very different effects on prices:

- The demand-side shock will reduce prices (panel A).
- The supply-side shock will increase the price level (panel B).

So, an economy in which output has decreased and prices have decreased would suggest a decrease in demand. On the other hand, an economy in which output has decreased and prices have increased would suggest that there has been a supply-side shock.

TABLE 12-4

Comparing demand and supply shocks

The first task to determine how an event will affect the overall economy is to decide whether it is a demand or a supply shock. This means figuring out whom the shock most affects and what their role is in the economy.

Event	What kind of shock?
Temporary increase in the price of oil	Short-run supply shock
Technological innovation	Long-run supply shock
Drop in consumer confidence	Demand shock
Sudden increase in immigration	Long-run supply shock

FIGURE 12-14

Different short-run impacts of decreases in aggregate demand versus aggregate supply When the economy experiences a decrease in aggregate demand, both prices and output decrease in the short run. But when the economy experiences a decrease in aggregate supply, prices rise and output falls in the short run.

(A) Decrease in aggregate demand

(B) Decrease in aggregate supply

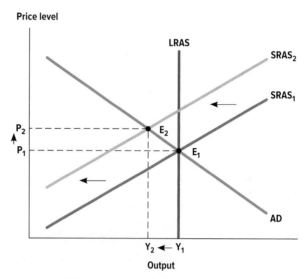

When aggregate demand shifts in due to a decrease in aggregate demand, the new short-term equilibrium moves to point E_2. At point E_2 both prices and output are lower.

A drought that destroys much of the corn crop will shift the short-run aggregate supply curve in. In the short run, prices will be higher, and output falls.

Sometimes, however, there can be a complex combination of overlapping shocks to untangle. For example, when the U.S. housing bubble popped in 2007, banks and other financial institutions faced large losses from the bad loans they had made. Their need to cover those losses and their growing pessimism about the economy made them less willing to lend to businesses. For firms, borrowing became harder and more expensive. The increase in the cost of doing business was a short-run supply-side shock; it shifted the short-run aggregate supply curve to the left. That was on top of the demand shock that happened when consumers reduced their spending after the housing bubble popped. The demand shock led to a further decrease in the level of output in the economy.

Demand-side and supply-side shocks can also differ in the long run:

- Demand-side shocks will cause a change to the price level in the long run since the short-run supply curve will shift in to restore the long-run equilibrium output.

- For a supply-side shock, there are no long-run changes to the price level. If the short-run supply curve initially shifts to the left, for example, prices will adjust to restore the long-run equilibrium.

We summarize the difference between supply-side and demand-side shocks in Table 12-5.

For an example of economic detective work to tease out whether shifts in supply or demand were responsible for observed effects in an economy, see the Real Life box "The Kobe earthquake and aggregate supply."

TABLE 12-5

Demand-side versus supply-side shocks

This table summarizes the impacts of a shock on the demand and supply sides of an economy. Each shock has a different effect on the economy in the long and short run.

Supply or demand?	Positive shock	Negative shock
Demand side	**Short run:** Output increases Price increases	**Short run:** Output decreases Price decreases
Demand side	**Long run:** No change in output Price increases	**Long run:** No change in output Price decreases
Temporary shock: Supply side	**Short run:** Output increases Price decreases	**Short run:** Output decreases Price increases
Temporary shock: Supply side	**Long run:** No change in output No change in price	**Long run:** No change in output No change in price
Permanent shock: Supply side	**Long run:** Output increases Price decreases	**Long run:** Output decreases Price increases

Real Life

The Kobe earthquake and aggregate supply

In January 1995, a large earthquake rocked the port city of Kobe, Japan. Many people lost their lives. Buildings and infrastructure were destroyed. The value of Japan's stock market dropped substantially. It was one of the most expensive natural disasters the world had ever seen, with a final damage bill equal to about 2.5 percent of Japan's GDP.

However, amazingly, only 15 months after the disaster, Japanese manufacturing was back to 96 percent of the pre-earthquake trend. How well can the aggregate supply and aggregate demand model explain the recovery of the Japanese economy?

George Horwich, an economist at Purdue, studied this question. The earthquake destroyed a large amount of capital, and so we would expect the short-run aggregate supply curve to shift to the left. This shift would push the price level higher and would reduce output, increasing unemployment. However, when Horwich looked at the data, he saw a different picture. Surprisingly, the price level was relatively stable, and employment was constant.

How can we match up those data with the predictions of the AD/AS model? There are two possibilities in Kobe: Either the aggregate supply curve shifted quickly back out again in the months after the earthquake or the aggregate demand curve shifted out.

We have a way to figure out what actually happened. If an increase in aggregate demand occurred, the price level would increase. But the data showed that the price level stayed constant, or even decreased. This suggests that there wasn't an aggregate demand response. Instead, Horwich argues, the aggregate supply curve shifted back out.

Although the damage in Kobe was significant, it seems that the Japanese economy was able to adjust to this very large shock in one part of the economy by rearranging how resources were used. In this process of adjustment, the aggregate supply curve shifted back out, returning the economy to its original position. The response to the Kobe earthquake tells us that the macroeconomy can sometimes adjust surprisingly quickly, even after large supply-side shocks.

Source: George Horwich, "Economic Lessons of the Kobe Earthquake," *Economic Development and Cultural Change* 48, no. 3 (April 2000), pp. 521–542.

✓ CONCEPT CHECK

- ☐ Will a positive demand shock lead to increased or decreased output in short-run equilibrium? What about in long-run equilibrium? **[LO 12.7]**
- ☐ How do prices and output change with a leftward shift in aggregate supply? **[LO 12.8]**
- ☐ How do changes in the price level help distinguish between a demand-side shock to the economy and a supply-side shock? **[LO 12.9]**

The Role of Public Policy

LO 12.10 Describe the policy options the government can use to counteract supply and demand shocks.

It can take a long time for the economy to fully adjust to demand and supply shocks, and waiting for adjustments often isn't comfortable for people who experience changing prices and unemployment. When the economy hits a recession, voters often call upon politicians to "do something." We will examine the role of government in the economy in more detail when we look at fiscal policy and monetary policy in later chapters. For now, we will consider just one channel through which the government can try to boost the economy out of a recession: government spending.

Government spending to counter negative demand shocks

Imagine that things are going badly in the economy: Newspapers are full of stories about falling home prices, mass layoffs, and factory closings. With the steady beat of bad news, consumer confidence decreases and consumption falls. These changes cause the aggregate demand curve to shift to the left, shown in panel A of Figure 12-15. Output and the price level decrease.

The government can try to counter this negative demand shock by increasing government spending. As we have seen, the effect of an increase in government spending is to shift the aggregate demand curve to the right. For policy-makers, the goal is to counteract the negative shock to aggregate demand with a positive one, and restore the curve to its original position.

This is not so easy to do. In practice, it can be hard to gauge the overall effect of government spending on aggregate demand. Even worse, it's rare to perfectly design government policy so that spending occurs at just the right amount to restore aggregate demand to its original level. Panel B of Figure 12-15 shows a case in which the policy is partly, but not entirely, successful: The increase in government spending shifts the AD curve only part of the way back to its previous position.

What about the long run? We know that for any demand-side shock, there can't be an effect on long-run output. According to our model, if the government did nothing, then eventually prices would adjust downward until output rose to its previous level. This occurs through changes on the supply side, as cheaper prices reduce the costs of production, shifting the aggregate supply curve to the right.

If, instead of doing nothing, the government increases spending to stimulate the economy, the end result will be slightly different. In this example, government policy was only partly successful, so the economy still has to adjust before reaching long-run equilibrium. The process of adjustment is still the same as before, except that, now, SRAS doesn't have as far to go as it did when the government hadn't acted. In the end, the long-run effect of the government's increase in spending is that the previous level of output will be restored, but at a slightly higher price level than if the government hadn't acted, holding all else constant. The result is that with a given income or wealth, people can buy less. This trade-off between increasing the speed of adjustment and allowing higher prices is a genuine challenge the government faces in setting policies to fight downturns in the economy.

FIGURE 12-15

Government response to a negative demand shock: The housing crash

(A) Housing-market crash

In a crash of the housing market, aggregate demand drops sharply, shifting the curve in. The new short-term equilibrium has lower prices and output.

(B) Government stimulus

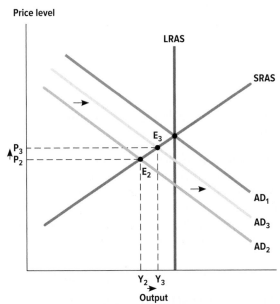

If the government increases spending in response to the housing crash, aggregate demand will shift back out. The new equilibrium is at a higher level of prices and output, but still below the levels under the long-run equilibrium.

Government spending to counter negative supply shocks

Now imagine a short-run supply-side shock: A terrible drought has reduced the corn harvest by 80 percent. The short-run aggregate supply curve has shifted to the left, as in panel A of Figure 12-16. The economy is now at point E_2: The level of output has fallen, and prices have risen.

In this case, policy-makers are in a bind. If they choose to do nothing, the economy will be stuck in a period of higher prices and lower output (stagflation). We'll talk more about the challenges of stagflation in Chapter 16, "Inflation." For now, imagine a period in which prices increase but with large amounts of unemployment and low output. It's a very hard situation to get out of. Remember that prices can be very sticky, especially when they have to adjust downward.

Instead of waiting for the aggregate supply curve to shift back out to the right, the government could choose to increase government spending in order to shift the aggregate demand curve. This action and effect are shown in panel B of Figure 12-16. With the shift in aggregate demand, the economy moves to a new short-run equilibrium at point E_3. While this shift solves the problem of low output and unemployment, it actually drives prices even higher.

In both examples, the long-run result of government intervention is higher prices at the same level of output. So, why would the government ever choose to intervene? One reason concerns the speed of the recovery. Without the increase in government spending, adjustment might have been a long and painful process. In addition, lower prices are not always a good thing. As we will see in Chapter 16, "Inflation," falling prices, called *deflation*, carry another set of challenges for the economy.

FIGURE 12-16

Government response to a negative supply shock: Extreme drought in the Midwest

(A) Drought shifts aggregate supply

Like before, a drought shifts the short-run aggregate supply curve in, which pushes the economy toward a new short-run equilibrium with higher prices and lower output.

(B) Government response

In response to the drought, the government increases spending, which shifts the aggregate demand curve out. Instead of falling back to the original equilibrium, the new long-run equilibrium is at a higher prices level.

The bottom line is that government spending is a *short-term* policy action that is often applied to address short-term demand shocks. Government spending is less effective in countering negative supply shocks, but political pressures can sometimes drive government action even when it's not a great solution.

✓**CONCEPT CHECK**

☐ What is the long-term effect on prices and output when the government counters a negative demand shock with an increase in spending? **[LO 12.10]**

Conclusion

In this chapter, we created a model of the whole economy. This model is relatively simple, yet ambitious. It helps us to understand what drives key macroeconomics outcomes such as prices, unemployment, and GDP.

The aggregate demand and aggregate supply model breaks the economy down into two sides. The *demand side* is composed of all the components of expenditure in the economy: consumption, investment, government spending, and net exports. The aggregate demand curve identifies the relationship between overall price levels and aggregate demand in the economy. On the supply side of the economy, the aggregate supply curve identifies the relationship between overall price levels and total production in the economy.

In the short run the economy responds to changes in the price level by increasing or decreasing output, so the short-run aggregate supply curve is upward-sloping. In the long run, production

---

is determined by the availability of inputs for production and the technology to convert inputs to outputs. In the long run, there is no relationship between the price level and output. The long-run equilibrium occurs at the intersection of the aggregate demand and long-run aggregate supply curves.

We used the model of aggregate demand and aggregate supply to understand the recession that engulfed the United States after the housing bubble popped in 2007, shifting the aggregate demand curve to the left. We also used it to understand the government's response, a stimulus package whose aim was to shift the aggregate demand curve back out and stimulate output and employment.

In the next chapter, we'll talk about policy responses to economic shocks in more depth and explore the different effects of spending versus taxes.

Key Terms

aggregate demand curve, p. 302

aggregate supply curve, p. 309

business cycle, p. 311

supply shocks, p. 314

Summary

LO 12.1 Show how the aggregate expenditure equilibrium model can be used to trace out the aggregate demand curve and understand why the aggregate demand curve slopes downward.

The aggregate demand and supply model captures the relationship between prices and output in the economy. It comprises two parts: the *aggregate demand* curve, which shows the relationship between the price level and total demand in the economy, and the *aggregate supply* curve, which shows the relationship between the price level and the total supply in the economy. The aggregate demand curve can be traced out by graphing how equilibrium planned aggregate expenditure changes as the price level changes. The aggregate demand curve is downward-sloping because consumption, investment, and net exports all decline when the price level rises.

LO 12.2 List factors that could cause the aggregate demand curve to shift.

Since the aggregate demand curve is derived from the definition of GDP—Y = C + I + G + NX—anything that affects any of the components of GDP will shift the aggregate demand curve. For example, if government spending increases, the aggregate demand curve will shift out; if net exports decrease, the aggregate demand curve will shift in. When the aggregate demand curve shifts, there will be a short-run change in output, but no long-run shift in output. The price level will change in both the short run and the long run.

LO 12.3 Explain how changes in government spending and taxes can have a multiplier effect on aggregate demand.

When the government increases spending, it sets into motion a series of additional rounds of expenditure in the economy. Each time aggregate expenditure increases, disposable incomes go up and households respond by spending more. The increased spending causes another round of increased aggregate expenditure, and the process continues. With taxes, the story is similar. A reduction in taxes increases disposable income, triggering a chain of higher spending, increased incomes, and further spending. There is, however, an important difference between the impact of taxes and government spending. Whereas government spending increases aggregate expenditure dollar-for-dollar in the first round of the multiplier process, a portion of the tax cut gets saved. Thus, the multiplier associated with a given dollar value of tax cuts will tend to be smaller than the multiplier associated with the same dollar increase in spending.

LO 12.4 Explain the difference between the short run and long run in the economy.

The aggregate supply curve is actually two different curves: a *long-run aggregate supply* (LRAS) curve and a *short-run aggregate supply* (SRAS) curve. The long-run aggregate supply curve shows what the economy can produce if all the factors of production are being utilized. This doesn't depend on prices, so the LRAS is vertical.

The SRAS is an upward-sloping curve between prices and output. There are factors that affect only the cost of production and do not change the amount of factors available for production. These changes will only shift the SRAS curve.

LO 12.5 Demonstrate a shift in the short-run aggregate supply curve and list factors that cause it to shift.

If the prices of *inputs* change, the entire aggregate supply curve will shift. Any change that makes production more expensive for firms will shift the supply curve in (to the left). Any change that makes production cheaper for producers will shift the aggregate supply curve out (to the right).

LO 12.6 Demonstrate a shift in the long-run aggregate supply curve and list factors that cause it to shift.

Anything that affects the output possible using these factors will shift the long-run aggregate supply curve. If the potential output of the economy expands, the long-run aggregate supply curve will shift out. If the production possibility frontier for the economy contracts, the long-run aggregate supply curve will shift in.

LO 12.7 Explain the short-run and long-run effects of a shift in aggregate demand.

When there is a positive shock in aggregate demand, prices and output increase in the short run. Eventually, input prices and wages catch up to the increase in the price level. The SRAS curve slowly adjusts to the right; in the end, this adjustment further increases prices while decreasing output. The final result is that output falls back to its original level, and prices are higher than they were originally. For a negative shock, the aggregate demand shifts to the left. Prices and output fall. The adjustment of the SRAS curve to the right brings output back to its original level, but prices fall even further.

LO 12.8 Explain the short-run and long-run effects of a shift in aggregate supply.

The aggregate supply curve is a relationship between total supply in the economy and price level. Anything that affects the factors of production or the level of technology will affect both the long-run aggregate supply curve and the short-run aggregate supply curve; this shift is a permanent supply shock. Anything that affects the prices of inputs or the costs of doing business will affect the short-run aggregate supply curve, but not the long-run aggregate supply curve; this shift is a temporary supply shock. When there is a temporary supply shock,

the price level and output change in the short run but not in the long run. For a permanent supply shock, both the price level and output change in the long run.

LO 12.9 Use the AD/AS framework to determine whether an observed change in output and prices was due to a demand shock or a supply shock.

In reality, we do not observe aggregate supply and demand curves shifting. Instead, what we see are changes in output and the price level. With the help of the AD/AS model, we can infer whether the changes in the economy were more likely to be caused by a shift in supply or demand and whether the shock was temporary or permanent. A situation where output falls and prices rise is likely due to a backward shift of the aggregate demand curve. If, however, output falls and prices rise, it's likely that the culprit is an upward shift in aggregate supply. Temporary shifts in demand and supply do not cause permanent changes in output and prices. Permanent shifts leave output unchanged, but they can lead to permanent changes in the price level. If, for instance, there is a permanent upward shift in the supply curve, long-run output will eventually return to potential, but prices will be permanently higher.

LO 12.10 Describe the policy options the government can use to counteract supply and demand shocks

Depending on the type of shock, the government can choose to increase or reduce government spending in response. The government often chooses to act because action is preferable to waiting for the economy to adjust after a shock. Shortfalls in aggregate demand can be corrected by increasing spending. The same is true of aggregate demand, although the government might want to be careful in this situation. Regardless of the shock, increases in government spending will produce higher prices in the long run.

Review Questions

1. Identify the four components of aggregate demand. Explain the relationship between aggregate demand and the price level. **[LO 12.1]**

2. The demand curves for individual goods are typically downward-sloping, due both to the substitution effect as well as to the income effect. Why does the substitution effect not affect the aggregate demand curve? **[LO 12.1]**

3. What is the relationship between the equilibrium level of aggregate expenditure in an economy and the aggregate demand curve? According to the aggregate expenditure equilibrium model, why does the aggregate demand curve slope downward? **[LO 12.1]**

4. What effect does rising business optimism and confidence have on the aggregate demand curve? What effect does falling optimism and confidence in business prospects have on the aggregate demand curve? **[LO 12.2]**

5. List several events that could cause a "demand-side" recession (i.e., a recession caused by a fall in aggregate demand). **[LO 12.2]**

6. Everything else equal, which will have a larger effect on aggregate demand and GDP: a $100 million reduction in taxes or a $100 million increase in government spending? Is everything else equal in practice? Why or why not? **[LO 12.3]**

7. Suppose the economy is in a recession and the president wants to stimulate production and create jobs. To do this, he has decided to increase government spending. Some of his economic advisors are suggesting the marginal propensity to consume (MPC) has a value of 0.9 and others are suggesting the value is 0.8. How will this difference in the value of the MPC affect the president's decision regarding the dollar amount of the increase in government spending? **[LO 12.3]**

8. Which typically can change faster: the components of aggregate demand or the components of aggregate supply? Explain. **[LO 12.4]**

9. Explain the difference between sticky wages and sticky prices. How do these two ideas explain the upward slope of the short-run aggregate supply curve? Why don't sticky wages or sticky prices affect the long-run aggregate supply curve? **[LO 12.4]**

10. List several events that could cause a "supply-side" recession (i.e., a recession caused by a fall in aggregate supply). **[LO 12.5]**

11. In the late 1990s, the United States experienced very high GDP growth, record low unemployment rates, and virtually nonexistent inflation. Based on the conclusions of the AD/AS model, what could explain this combination of good economic results? **[LO 12.5, 12.6]**

12. Why is long-run economic growth generally positive rather than negative? **[LO 12.6]**

13. Explain the mechanism through which the economy adjusts in the short run and the long run when consumer confidence falls. **[LO 12.7]**

14. Suppose a country is in the midst of an economic boom and is running large budget surpluses. The president suggests that due to the good economic conditions, the time is ripe for a large tax cut. What are the arguments for and against this position? **[LO 12.7, 12.10]**

15. Suppose a country is in the midst of a serious recession, with high unemployment and large government deficits. The president suggests that in times like this the government has the obligation to "tighten its belt" and cut spending since so many families around the country have to do the same thing. Do you agree with the president? Why or why not? **[LO 12.7, 12.10]**

16. Using the aggregate demand and aggregate supply model, explain the difference between a one-year drought and permanent climate change. What happens to the price level and output in the short run and in the long run for each type of shock? **[LO 12.5, 12.6, 12.8]**

17. A government official observes that there has been a short-run increase in the price level. Is it possible for her to determine whether this was caused by a demand shock or a supply shock? Why or why not? **[LO 12.9]**

18. A government official observes that there has been a long-run increase in the price level but no change in the level of potential output. Is it possible for her to determine whether this was caused by a demand shock or a supply shock? Why or why not? **[LO 12.9]**

19. Why does the government have a harder time counteracting shifts in AS than in AD? **[LO 12.8, 12.10]**

20. Whenever AD or AS shifts, putting the economy out of long-run equilibrium, AS has a natural tendency to shift in such a way as to bring the economy back into long-run equilibrium. If the economy always eventually comes back to long-run equilibrium, why would the government ever try to implement policies to bring the economy into equilibrium through government means? **[LO 12.10]**

Problems and Applications

1. Is there a negative, positive, or no relationship between the price level and the following components of aggregate demand? **[LO 12.1]**
   a. Consumption.
   b. Investment.
   c. Government spending.
   d. Net exports.

2. If the government cuts taxes, what components of aggregate demand are affected? **[LO 12.1]**

3. Consider the planned aggregate expenditure lines in Figure 12P-1. **[LO 12.1]**
   a. Suppose that the planned aggregate expenditure lines correspond to price levels of 100, 110, and 120. Which line corresponds to which price level?
   b. Use the information in the expenditure diagram to trace out the aggregate demand curve for this economy.

4. For each of the following shocks, say whether it is a demand-side shock or a supply-side shock. **[LO 12.2, 12.5]**

FIGURE 12P-1

a. Consumer confidence falls.

b. Government spending increases.

c. The price of foreign goods increases.

d. The price of oil increases.

e. A cyclone destroys manufacturing plants.

5. In the late 1990s, the U.S. experienced a technology boom. In part the boom was due to a revolution in communication technology that resulted in a massive expansion of the Internet; in part the boom was due to households and firms purchasing new computer equipment in anticipation of Y2K. What two curves of the model would be affected by these events? **[LO 12.2, 12.5]**

6. Suppose the marginal propensity to consume (MPC) is either 0.75, 0.80, or 0.90. **[LO 12.3]**

   a. For each value of the MPC, calculate the expenditure multiplier, or the impact of a one-dollar increase in government spending on GDP.

   b. For each value of the MPC, calculate the impact on GDP of a $250 million increase in government spending.

   c. Explain the relationship between the MPC and the impact of a change in government spending on GDP.

7. Suppose the marginal propensity to consume (MPC) is either 0.75, 0.80, or 0.90. **[LO 12.3]**

   a. For each value of the MPC, calculate the impact of a one-dollar decrease in taxes on GDP.

   b. For each value of the MPC, calculate the impact on GDP of a $250 million decrease in taxes.

   c. Explain the relationship between the MPC and the impact of a change in taxes on GDP.

8. Say whether the following statements are true or false. **[LO 12.4]**

   a. In the long run, prices don't affect output.

   b. In the short run, prices may affect output.

9. Say whether the following statements are true or false. **[LO 12.4]**

   a. If the prices of all final goods and services are sticky, then the short-run aggregate supply (SRAS) curve is horizontal at the given price level.

   b. If the prices of inputs and wages are not fixed by contracts, and instead adjust more quickly to demand and supply shocks, then the SRAS curve is more vertical.

10. "Fracking" is a newly invented technology that allows drillers to extract significantly larger quantities of natural gas from existing deposits than was previously possible. How is this discovery likely to affect the economy? (*Hint:* Think about whether this will have a short-run or long-run effect.) **[LO 12.5, 12.6]**

11. Throughout the nineteenth and twentieth centuries, the U.S. economy experienced frequent ups and downs, but over the past 200 years, the real GDP in the United States rose from roughly $8.2 billion to over $16.1 *trillion,* an increase by a factor of nearly 2,000 times. This growth represents a change in which curve? **[LO 12.6]**

12. Suppose that a statement by the chair of the Federal Reserve Board about the state of the economy causes a loss of consumer confidence. What will be the long-run impact on the economy if the government allows the economy to adjust without a policy response? **[LO 12.7]**

    a. Output will fall below its initial level in the long run and the price level will decline.

    b. Output will return to its initial level in the long run, but the price level will be lower.

    c. Output will return to its initial level in the long run, but the price level will be higher.

    d. Output will rise above its initial level in the long run and the price level will rise.

13. For each of the following situations, use an AD/AS model to describe what happens to price levels and output in the United States in the short run. In each case, assume the economy starts in long- and short-run equilibrium, and describe the appropriate shifts in the AS or AD curves. **[LO 12.7, 12.8]**

    a. A stock market crash reduces people's wealth.

    b. The spread of democracy around the world increases consumer confidence in the United States.

    c. The European economy crashes.

d. The United States enters into an arms race with China, resulting in a significant increase in military spending.

e. A revolution in Iran results in a significant reduction in the world's supply of oil.

f. Terrorist activities temporarily halt the ability of Americans to engage in certain productive activities such as transportation and finance.

g. Intel develops a new computer chip that is faster and cheaper than previous chips.

h. A summer of perfect weather in the Midwest leads to record harvests of corn, wheat, and soybeans.

14. For each of the following scenarios, say whether the shock was a demand-side shock, a supply-side shock, or a combination of both shocks. **[LO 12.9]**

a. The price level and GDP both fell. GDP then increased, but the price level fell even further.

b. In the long run, the economy had the same level of output but a higher price level.

c. In the short run, the price level increased, but GDP fell.

d. In the long run, GDP increased, and the price level fell.

e. In the long run, GDP increased, and the price level was constant.

15. In 2009, during the height of the U.S. financial crisis, real GDP fell 3.5 percent, and the Consumer Price Index fell from 215.3 to 214.9. Was this recession likely caused by a shift in aggregate demand or aggregate supply? **[LO 12.9]**

16. In 1974, GDP fell by 0.6 percent, and inflation increased from 6.2 percent to 11.0 percent. Was this recession likely caused by a shift in aggregate demand or aggregate supply? **[LO 12.9]**

For questions 17–20, use an AD/AS model to answer the following questions. In each case assume the economy starts in long- and short-run equilibrium, and show the appropriate shifts in the AS or AD curves.

17. Suppose a stock market crash reduces people's wealth. **[LO 12.7, 12.8, 12.10]**

a. Show what happens to price levels and output in the United States in the short run.

b. Suppose the government takes no action to help the economy. What happens to price levels and output in the long run?

c. Suppose, instead, the government decides to take action to help the economy. What action(s) would you recommend? Why?

d. If the U.S. government makes the appropriate policy response, what happens to price levels and output in the long run?

18. Suppose the spread of democracy around the world increases consumer confidence in the United States. **[LO 12.7, 12.8, 12.10]**

a. Show what happens to price levels and output in the United States in the short run.

b. Suppose the government takes no action to help the economy. What happens to price levels and output in the long run?

c. Suppose, instead, the government decides to take action to help the economy. What action(s) would you recommend? Why?

d. If the U.S. government makes the appropriate policy response, what happens to price levels and output in the long run?

19. Suppose a revolution in Iran results in a significant reduction in the world's supply of oil. **[LO 12.7, 12.8, 12.10]**

a. Show what happens to price levels and output in the United States in the short run.

b. Suppose the government takes no action to help the economy. What happens to price levels and output in the long run?

c. Suppose, instead, the government decides to take action to help the economy. What action(s) would you recommend? Why?

d. If the U.S. government makes the appropriate policy response, what happens to price levels and output in the long run?

20. Suppose a summer of perfect weather in the Midwest leads to record harvests of corn, wheat, and soybeans. **[LO 12.7, 12.8, 12.10]**

a. What happens to price levels and output in the United States in the short run?

b. Suppose the government takes no action to help the economy. Show what happens to price levels and output in the long run.

c. If the U.S. government reacts to the record harvests by increasing taxes or decreasing spending, what happens to price levels and output in the long run?

d. What is the problem associated with the government reacting to the record harvests by increasing taxes or decreasing spending?

Endnotes

1. The impact of increasing government transfers to households can be analyzed similarly to the impact of a tax cut.

Fiscal Policy

Learning Objectives

LO 13.1 Explain the difference between contractionary fiscal policy and expansionary fiscal policy.

LO 13.2 Explain how fiscal policy can counteract short-run economic fluctuations.

LO 13.3 Identify the time lags that complicate the formulation of fiscal policy.

LO 13.4 Discuss how stabilizers can automatically adjust fiscal policy as the economy changes.

LO 13.5 Describe the theory and evidence about Ricardian equivalence and what it implies for the effectiveness of fiscal policy.

LO 13.6 Describe how revenue and spending determine a government budget and how the U.S. budget deficit occurs.

LO 13.7 Explain the difference between the government deficit and debt.

LO 13.8 Understand how Treasury securities work and why people value them.

LO 13.9 Identify the benefits and costs of government debt.

FROM HOUSING BUBBLE TO GREAT RECESSION

By 2008, the warning signs were everywhere: Unemployment was increasing. Business confidence was down. The economy was at the start of a recession. What, if anything, could the U.S. government do to give the economy a boost?

The two political parties had different answers: Democrats argued that increasing government spending would kick-start the economy. To that end, they advocated for construction projects and other public investments, with the intention of creating badly needed jobs. Republicans argued that since times were tough, the government should tighten its belt, as individuals do when they face money problems. Their favored solution was to lower taxes, allowing people to keep a larger share of their income, to encourage people to spend more, boosting demand.

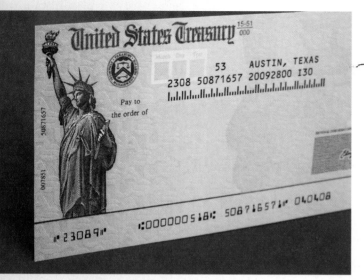

© karen roach/Shutterstock

In the end, both sides got a little of what they wanted. One of the first acts of newly elected President Barack Obama was to sign the American Recovery and Reinvestment Act of 2009, more commonly known as the "stimulus plan." That plan included both tax cuts and a sizable increase in government spending. Its total cost was nearly $800 billion—slightly more than 5 percent of U.S. GDP.

Despite the big sum spent, the recovery was slow. When economists looked back four years later (at the end of 2012), the economy had still not fully recovered. In the meantime, millions of people had lost their jobs and homes, and many businesses had closed. Things looked better after another four years (at the end of 2016). While the unemployment rate had hit 10 percent at its peak in 2009, by 2016 the unemployment rate had fallen to about where it was before the recession, under 5 percent. The increased spending and decreased tax revenues, though, had put the U.S. government further into debt. By 2012, the dollar value of the debt had climbed past 100 percent of GDP. In 2016 the debt was 104 percent of GDP.[1]

So, was the stimulus plan a success? We can't judge this simply by looking at what happened before and after it was signed into law. Instead, we need to ask: What *would have* happened if the stimulus plan had *not* been enacted? Or what would have happened if the government had chosen an alternative balance of tax cuts and government spending? Would the level of unemployment and the health of the economy have been better, worse, or just the same?

To answer some of these questions, we'll create a framework for thinking about how taxation and government spending affect the national economy, based on the aggregate demand and supply model you saw in Chapter 12, "Aggregate Demand and Aggregate Supply." By the end of this chapter you should be able to discuss the pros and cons of different policies in terms of their effect on both short-run economic fluctuations and longer-run issues such as the national debt. These questions have been hotly debated since 2007, as policy-makers tried to steer the economy out of the Great Recession, and they continue to have critical implications for the national economy today.

Fiscal Policy

fiscal policy
government decisions about the level of taxation and public spending

Each February, the U.S. president and Congress begin the process of deciding how much to spend on the varied functions of the federal government: how much to spend on building bridges, supporting the military, investing in medical research, and so on. At the same time, Congress decides how much money should be collected in taxes to pay for all of these things. Government decisions about the level of taxation and public spending are called **fiscal policy**.

Expansionary or contractionary

LO 13.1 Explain the difference between contractionary fiscal policy and expansionary fiscal policy.

Fiscal policy is more than just simple budgeting. Choices about how much to spend, how to spend it, and how to raise the necessary funds can have dramatic impacts on the economy. Recall from Chapter 7, "Measuring GDP," that government spending is one of the components of GDP. It is also part of the way we calculate the demand side of the economy in the aggregate demand and aggregate supply model:

$$\text{Aggregate demand} = C + I + G + NX$$

Fiscal policy affects the economy by increasing or decreasing aggregate demand. As we saw in the previous chapter, shifts in the aggregate demand curve translate into higher or lower output and price levels throughout the economy. Fiscal policy affects aggregate demand through two channels: government spending and tax policy.

Government spending *directly* affects the "G" in the aggregate demand equation (above):

- An increase in government spending will generally shift the aggregate demand curve out (to the right).
- A decrease in government spending will shift the aggregate demand curve in (to the left).

Government spending can also have *indirect* effects on the "C" (consumption) and "I" (investment) components of aggregate demand. These effects come through mechanisms called the *multiplier effect* and *crowding out.*[2]

The second channel through which fiscal policy drives aggregate demand is tax policy. This effect acts on aggregate demand *directly* through consumption, or the "C" part of the aggregate demand equation. It can also indirectly affect the other components, such as investment. Before anyone gets a paycheck, the government takes some money in taxes. Consumption therefore depends not on total income but, rather, on *disposable income*—what's left after taxes. How much individuals consume is related to their incomes:

- If the tax rate increases, workers will take home less disposable income, and we can expect them to reduce their consumption. As a result, the aggregate demand curve will shift in (to the left).
- If, on the other hand, the tax rate decreases, workers take home more money and will consume more. The decrease in the tax rate will shift the aggregate demand curve out (to the right).

We differentiate two types of fiscal policy. The first aims to increase aggregate demand, and the second is used to decrease aggregate demand. The term **expansionary fiscal policy** describes the overall effect of decisions about government spending and taxation intended to increase aggregate demand. Increased government spending and lower taxes both have expansionary effects: They shift the aggregate demand curve to the right, as shown in panel A of Figure 13-1. In contrast, the term **contractionary fiscal policy** describes the overall effect of decisions about government spending and taxation intended to decrease aggregate demand. Decreased government spending and higher taxes both have contractionary effects, shifting the aggregate demand curve in to the left, as shown in panel B of Figure 13-1.

expansionary fiscal policy decisions about government spending and taxation intended to increase aggregate demand

contractionary fiscal policy decisions about government spending and taxation intended to decrease aggregate demand

FIGURE 13-1

Expansionary and contractionary fiscal policy

(A) Expansionary fiscal policy shifts the AD curve to the right

Increasing government spending and lowering taxes are fiscal policies with expansionary effects, shifting the aggregate demand curve out to the right from AD_1 to AD_2. This has the effect of increasing output and price levels.

(B) Contractionary fiscal policy shifts the AD curve to the left

Decreasing government spending and raising taxes are fiscal policies with contractionary effects, shifting the aggregate demand curve in to the left from AD_1 to AD_2. This has the effect of decreasing output and price levels.

Policy response to short-run economic fluctuations

LO 13.2 Explain how fiscal policy can counteract short-run economic fluctuations.

One of the most important ways that policy-makers use fiscal policy is to try to smooth out fluctuations in the economy that might hurt consumers and businesses. In this section, we'll show how policy-makers use fiscal policy to counteract the effects of economic shocks through the aggregate supply and aggregate demand model.

In Chapter 12, "Aggregate Demand and Aggregate Supply," we saw how a shock like the collapse of the U.S. housing market in late 2007 can affect the national economy. The most immediate consequence of the steep drop in housing prices was that homeowners felt poorer. This response shifted the aggregate demand curve to the left. Panel A of Figure 13-2 shows the leftward shift of the aggregate demand curve, from AD_1 to AD_2. (If this figure looks familiar, it's because you saw a version of it before—as Figure 12-15, in a discussion of government response to a negative demand shock.) The decrease in aggregate demand caused the economy to produce below its level of potential output. The result was lower GDP (output) and higher unemployment, seen in panel A as a reduction in output from Y_1 to Y_2.

According to the AD/AS model, if nothing else happened, the economy would have automatically corrected itself—eventually. Wages would have fallen in response to unemployment, and lower production costs would bring other prices down. This response would cause the short-run aggregate supply curve to shift to the right until the economy returned to its original level of potential output level at Y_1. In the long run, output would have recovered to its previous level, with lower overall prices in the economy.

FIGURE 13-2

Effect of expansionary fiscal policy

(A) Initial market response to fall in AD

Initially, with a decrease in aggregate demand the AD curve shifts to the left. At the new equilibrium, prices and output are lower than before.

(B) Expansionary fiscal policy restores some AD

If the government decides to pursue expansionary fiscal policy, it will increase spending, which shifts the AD curve rightward (here, AD_2 to AD_3). The amount of the shift depends on the amount of spending. Here, the government's spending increases output and the price level, but not to their levels before the original fall in AD.

Why didn't lawmakers simply wait for this to happen? Because it could have been a painful and very slow process. The wage rate would have had to fall along with other prices; we saw in Chapter 9, "Unemployment and the Labor Market," some reasons why that might not happen quickly or easily.[3] When businesses fail and people lose their jobs, they want their government to do something about it. They don't want just to hear that the economy will work the problems out if they wait long enough. As economist John Maynard Keynes once said, "In the long run, we are all dead."

We'll show in this chapter that fiscal policy can have real effects on the economy even in the short run. Ideally, the government can counterbalance shocks like the collapse of the housing market, minimizing the damages to consumers and businesses without having to wait for the economy to correct itself in the long run. However, we'll also see that the government may not always be able to improve matters—it might even make things worse, for reasons we describe in the next section.

But if the government *is* going to act, for better or for worse, what should it do? Let's look at examples of both expansionary and contractionary policy responses.

Expansionary policy response

To counteract a decrease in aggregate demand like that caused by the 2007 housing-market collapse, the government can try to boost demand, either by spending more or taxing less. This kind of expansionary policy is often called "Keynesian," in recognition of John Maynard Keynes, who championed the strategy after the Great Depression of the 1930s.

The challenge is finding the dosage of fiscal policy that restores aggregate demand to its prerecession level. As shown in panel B of Figure 13-2:

- A completely successful stimulus plan would shift the AD curve all the way back from AD_2 to its original position, AD_1.

FIGURE 13-3
Effect of contractionary fiscal policy

(A) Economy overheats from too much AD

Price level

In an overheating economy, prices and output are above the long-run equilibrium in the economy.

(B) Contractionary fiscal policy lowers prices and output

Price level

In order to slow down the economy, the government can cut spending or raise taxes, shifting the AD curve leftward. When this happens, prices and output fall, although the economy is still above long-run equilibrium.

- If the stimulus is only partly successful, then it would move the curve only part of the way back, from AD_2 to AD_3. Even a partially successful stimulus may be better than nothing since it pushes the economy toward a better outcome (and the economy can continue adjusting toward the long-run equilibrium over time).

Contractionary policy response

What should the government do when the economy is suffering from the opposite problem—that is, when the economy is growing too quickly? People are often happy when the economy is booming, but government policy-makers worry that big booms can get out of hand. Implementing contractionary fiscal policy to slow down the economy is a lot like shutting down a raging party because you are worried that the guests might regret their choices in the morning. It can be the smart thing to do, even though there will be plenty of grumbling.

A surge in aggregate demand—like that caused by the housing market boom of the early and mid-2000s—increases output and the price level, as shown in panel A of Figure 13-3. Contractionary fiscal policy slows down the economy by cutting government spending or increasing taxes, shifting the aggregate demand curve back in to the left, as shown in panel B of Figure 13-3.

Real-world challenges

LO 13.3 Identify the time lags that complicate the formulation of fiscal policy.

Fiscal policy can seem like a golden solution: Why should any government wait for the economy to correct itself in a slow and painful way when it can do the work much more quickly? The analysis so far suggests that fiscal policy is a potent tool. After all, we saw in Chapter 12, "Aggregate

Demand and Aggregate Supply," that increasing direct government spending has a larger multiplier effect on output than a similarly costly reduction in taxes net of transfers. Looking at the math alone, it seems that there's a strong case for tackling a recession through government spending instead of tax cuts.

Unfortunately, it's not so simple. The analysis rests on some big simplifying assumptions that do not always hold. In the real world, things are more complicated. For instance, we've assumed that government spending doesn't *crowd out* (i.e., reduce) private-sector spending. As we show in greater detail in Chapter 14, "The Basics of Finance," one common form of "crowding out" happens when the government has to borrow in order to finance the extra spending. The government's borrowing tends to push interest rates upward, which then can decrease investment by the private sector. The decrease in private investment undermines the positive impact of government spending.

Even without this kind of crowding out, fiscal policy can be hard to get right. Fiscal policy choices often amount to no more than educated guesses, made without the benefit of all the relevant information. Furthermore, time lags between when policies are chosen and when they are implemented mean that sometimes it is too late to do any good.

To see some of the difficulties of implementing fiscal policy, imagine that the economy is a bus. You're the driver and it's your job to prevent the bus from stalling if it comes to an uphill section of road or from running out of control if it comes to a downhill section. You can step on the gas (in terms of the economy, use expansionary fiscal policy). Or you can step on the brakes (use contractionary fiscal policy). Sounds easy enough, right?

Now imagine that the windshield is blacked out so you can't see the road ahead. In addition, the speedometer indicates how fast you were going three blocks ago rather than how fast you're going now. Even worse, imagine that the bus is run as a democracy, so you also have to get the agreement of a majority of the passengers before you can hit the brakes or the gas, and they typically argue the matter for at least four blocks. Finally, once you actually hit the brakes or gas, it takes six to 12 blocks for that action to take effect.

This is how policy-makers can feel when deciding about fiscal policy. Lags in the policy-making process come from three main sources:

1. Understanding what the current economic situation is. *(You can't see out of the front of the bus, and the speedometer is three blocks delayed.)*

2. The process of deciding on and passing legislation. *(If the president is the bus driver, lawmakers in Congress are the arguing passengers.)*

3. The time it takes for the policy to affect the economy. *(Once you push the gas or the brakes, it takes several blocks until the acceleration or braking engages.)*

Information lag

The first issue involves an *information lag*. It might seem pretty clear that the economy is in a recession or boom, just as it might seem pretty clear from looking out of the back window of a bus that you've started to go up or down a hill. But it can take a long time to collect data that tell policy-makers about GDP, unemployment, and inflation. GDP figures, for example, are released every three months, and they report on economic activity that was happening three or four weeks before. These early numbers aren't always accurate, so it may be six months or more before the true figures are known.

Three to six months is a short time to register a trend in the overall economy. You certainly don't want to be the one who raises the alarm about a huge mountain up ahead of the bus, only to find that it was actually a tiny hill. It took an entire year's worth of data to trigger the announcement by the National Bureau of Economic Research that the U.S. economy was in a recession in 2008. By then, the economy had lost over 1 million jobs.

Just as it takes time to find out how bad things are, it also takes time to find out if the economy has reached the end of a recession. There will be news reports of companies hiring more workers, but it can take months to discover if this has translated into real gains for the economy. In both cases, policy-makers have to make important decisions for the future, but they only know where the economy was a few months ago.

Formulation lag

The second issue is *formulation lag*—the time it takes to decide on and pass legislation. First, a policy needs to be drafted and proposed in Congress, where it becomes a bill. The bill is first debated in the House of Representatives. If at least half of the representatives approve it, it then moves to the Senate. If a majority of the 100 senators approve, the president can sign the bill into law, or veto it, in which case the whole process has to start again. The 535 members of Congress can take a while to make up their minds: It was clear in September 2008, with the collapse of the investment bank Lehman Brothers, that the economy was in real trouble. But the stimulus act wasn't passed until after President Obama and a new Congress had been inaugurated in January 2009.

Implementation lag

The last hurdle for fiscal policy is *implementation lag*. Even after a policy has been proposed and passed, it may take time for it to take effect. It takes time for funds to be disbursed, employees hired, and materials purchased. Even tax cuts can take some time to kick in. In 2008, the government sent U.S. taxpayers a tax rebate as part of a first response to the recession, but it took three months to print and mail the 130 million checks. Even after receiving the checks, it took time for people to spend the money.

These three lags in the policy process—information lag, formulation lag, and implementation lag—make conducting good fiscal policy a tough endeavor. In fact, the lags may be so large that by the time the policy takes effect, the economy might have corrected itself, making the policy unnecessary.[4] In the worst case, the economy might even have started to face the opposite problem, making the policy actively harmful—like slamming on the brake when it turns out the bus is just starting to go uphill, or stepping on the gas when it's now going downhill.

For a timeline of all the delays involved in the 2009 stimulus, see the Real Life box "A timeline of the 2009 stimulus plan."

Real Life

A timeline of the 2009 stimulus plan

The U.S. economy went into recession in 2007, prompting the government to approve a stimulus plan. By 2011, most of the stimulus money had been spent, but not all. Why the delay?

Let's start with the *information lag*. Although experts now concur that the U.S. economy entered into a recession in December 2007, this designation did not become official until a year later, in December 2008. The earliest major response to economic troubles was the Economic Stimulus Act of February 2008, passed under the administration of George W. Bush, which gave a one-time rebate to taxpayers.

However, many people were not convinced that there were serious weaknesses in the economy until September 2008, when the investment bank Lehman Brothers went bankrupt. This bankruptcy prompted an emergency bill creating the Troubled Asset Relief Program (TARP) in October 2008 to stabilize the financial system. Congress then began work on a broader stimulus bill that was intended to help "Main Street" through a combination of tax cuts and spending on projects that could jump-start the economy right away.

The *formulation lag* was actually fairly short, compared with the time it often takes for politicians to agree on legislation. The first version of the stimulus bill, known as the American Relief and Recovery Act (ARRA), was introduced to Congress in January 2009. The bill was passed by both the Senate and the House at the beginning of February. One of President Obama's first acts in the Oval Office was to sign the ARRA into law on February 17, a month after he was inaugurated.

Then *implementation lags* came into play. The stimulus bill appropriated $524 billion in stimulus spending and $288 billion in additional tax cuts. Tax cuts are relatively quick to implement, but public works projects like bridge building take time to set up: First you need to decide where to build the bridge, then you need an architect to design it, and so on.

By the second anniversary of ARRA being signed into law, in February 2011, less than two-thirds of the stimulus money set aside for "contracts, grants, and loans" had been paid out. It took until the end of 2013 for spending and tax cuts to top $800 billion.

Did the stimulus work, despite these delays? We can't know for sure what would have happened if the stimulus bill hadn't been passed. When the University of Chicago Booth School of Business surveyed leading economists, 80 percent felt that the stimulus had helped to reduce unemployment (4 percent disagreed). The Congressional Budget Office (CBO) gives a relatively optimistic review: It estimates that in 2010, GDP was 1.5 to 4.2 percent higher than it would have been without the stimulus. The CBO also estimates that in the same period unemployment fell by somewhere between 0.7 percent and 1.8 percent thanks to the stimulus.

Were these short-term gains worth the billions of dollars in costs? About that, only 46 percent of the economic experts in the University of Chicago survey said yes.

Sources: http://money.cnn.com/2011/02/17/news/economy/stimulus_bill/index.htm; http://money.cnn.com/2009/08/04/news/economy/stimulus_spending/index.htm; http://www.cbo.gov/ftpdocs/121xx/doc12185/05-25-ARRA.pdf; http://articles.washingtonpost.com/2012-06-06/business/35462388_1_stimulus-work-package-of-temporary-tax-tea-party-caucus.

Policy tools—discretionary and automatic

LO 13.4 Discuss how stabilizers can automatically adjust fiscal policy as the economy changes.

The 2009 stimulus bill is an example of targeted, or *discretionary,* fiscal policy. This is policy that the government actively *chooses* to adopt. Even if there had been no stimulus act at all, though, fiscal policy would still have had some effect on the economy due to already-existing taxes and spending policies. These taxes and government spending that affect fiscal policy without specific action from policy-makers are called automatic stabilizers. Let's look at how both taxes and government spending act as automatic stabilizers.

automatic stabilizers taxes and government spending that affect fiscal policy without specific action from policy-makers

Taxes as automatic stabilizers

The income tax system is designed so that people pay higher tax rates as their earnings rise. It turns out that this feature of the tax system creates automatic stabilizers.

Income tax laws require you to pay a given percentage on each portion of your income that falls between certain ranges (often called "tax brackets"). For example, in 2016 single Americans paid the following rates:

- 10 percent in taxes on the portion of their income from $0 to $9,225
- 15 percent from $9,226 to $37,450
- 25 percent from $37,451 to $90,750, and so forth.[5]

Discretionary fiscal policy via taxes usually requires policy-makers to deliberately *change tax rates* owed on income. For example, a discretionary fiscal policy decision in the case above (tax rates in 2016) could have been for policy-makers to decide to raise the tax rate from 25 percent of income between $37,451 and $90,750 to 27 percent.

Automatic stabilizers work differently from that kind of discretionary policy. Even when the schedule of tax rates is completely unchanged, people can end up paying a different proportion of their income as taxes simply because as their income changes, they face different tax obligations. For instance, if you earned $35,000 in 2016, the highest tax rate you faced was 15 percent. But if instead you got a raise to $45,000 in 2016, you would have had to pay a greater proportion of your income as taxes in 2016 (compared to the situation without a raise) because part of your income would now automatically be charged at 25 percent.

Changing the tax rates through discretionary policy allows for active management of the economy. But the effectiveness of such policy can be undermined by information, formulation, and implementation lags. Automatic stabilizers are not affected by those lags. In addition, automatic stabilizers work to push the economy in the same direction that correctly timed and correctly formulated discretionary policy would. For example:

- When the economy is booming, people earn more and move into higher income ranges, so they pay taxes at higher tax rates automatically—without any new intervention from policy-makers. When that happens, the increased taxes that people have to pay put a slight check on overall spending. This slight check cools down aggregate demand by taking away dollars that might have otherwise been spent—just as would happen if policy-makers had intentionally increased taxes as a contractionary fiscal policy.
- When the economy is in a recession, people earn less and so automatically end up paying lower tax rates as they move to lower income ranges. The reduced taxes put more money in people's pockets, encouraging spending. This spurs aggregate demand slightly, just as would happen if the government had intentionally decreased taxes to implement an expansionary fiscal policy.

Government spending as an automatic stabilizer

Some aspects of government spending also work as automatic stabilizers. Unemployment insurance benefits and welfare programs such as food assistance and Medicaid have set eligibility criteria based on low income or unemployment status. Their effects reflect the health of the economy:

- When the economy is booming, fewer people are eligible for these programs, so government spending on them falls. With reduced government spending, the aggregate demand curve shifts to the left. This has a contractionary effect similar to discretionary policy that lowers government spending, reducing aggregate demand.
- In a recession, more people qualify for unemployment insurance and food assistance, so spending on those programs automatically rises. With higher government spending, the aggregate demand curve shifts to the right. This has an expansionary effect similar to discretionary policy that raises government spending, increasing aggregate demand.

In sum, when the U.S. economy hits a recession, fiscal policy *automatically* becomes expansionary: Average tax rates go down and spending on welfare programs goes up. In a booming economy, fiscal policy *automatically* becomes contractionary: Tax rates rise and welfare payments fall. The kind of *discretionary* stimulus bill approved in 2009 comes on top of these automatic effects.

Limits of fiscal policy: The money must come from somewhere

LO 13.5 Describe the theory and evidence about Ricardian equivalence and what it implies for the effectiveness of fiscal policy

Politicians often cut taxes in response to recessions. The idea is that people will spend more money when they have more cash in their hands. That spending, in turn, will raise business profits, create jobs, and help the economy recover.

But it's not always so simple. Those tax cuts don't come for free. The government will eventually have to find a way to make up for the lost tax revenue. That means either cutting an equivalent amount of government spending or, more frequently, raising taxes in the future.

What happens if people see that today's tax cuts just mean higher taxes tomorrow? In that case, people won't want to spend as much from their tax cuts, and the stimulus strategy will be less effective. This idea is known as *Ricardian equivalence.* This theory predicts that if governments cut taxes but not spending, people will *not* change their behavior. Why not? Because people realize that the government will have to borrow money to cover the financial shortfall created by cutting taxes. They realize that at some point in the future, they—or their children or grandchildren—will eventually have to repay the extra government debt through future tax increases. In other words, taxpayers understand that the money to maintain government spending must come from somewhere.

Knowja Test

Because taxpayers realize that the debt will eventually have to be repaid through future taxes, today's tax cut will feel more like a loan than a real windfall. According to the Ricardian equivalence theory, rational people should save what they receive rather than spend it today, in order to meet the financial obligation of future taxes. But if people save rather than spend, consumption does not increase, and the tax cut will be unsuccessful in increasing aggregate demand.

Of course, in reality, people may not be so rational and forward-looking. When they get a tax cut, they may go ahead and spend it (or part of it). If they do, Ricardian equivalence will fail to hold, and the fiscal policy *will* have the intended expansionary effect.

Nonetheless, the theory of Ricardian equivalence is a good reminder that people often respond to changes in government policy by adapting their behavior. Good policy has to take those responses and the unintended consequences that stem from them into account. In some cases, rational responses by individuals may be strong enough to make a well-intentioned policy fail. In practice, however, most people seem not to think about future tax increases when they open that envelope containing a tax rebate, as described in the Real Life box "Spending your stimulus check."

Real Life

Spending your stimulus check

In early 2008 it had become clear that the economy was ailing. President George W. Bush's administration took steps to address the problem with the Economic Stimulus Act, which sent taxpayers a "stimulus check"—a check that came in the mail, no strings attached, for the household to spend as it pleased. About 130 million households got checks, for a total of $100 billion across the nation. Individuals received between $300 and $600, and couples received twice that, plus $300 per child.

The government hoped that families would spend the checks, increasing consumption and shifting the aggregate demand curve to the right. But there was no requirement that people spend the money rather than just save it. In fact, the theory of Ricardian equivalence predicts that a rational family would save the rebate. This was the chance that the government took when sending out the stimulus checks.

What happened in practice? It turned out that families spent most of their windfall. They purchased cars and trucks and went back to the shopping mall. The average spending response amounted to between 50 and 90 percent of the value of the rebates. The increase in overall household spending did shift the aggregate demand curve to the right and helped stimulate the economy back toward its previous higher level of output.

(continued)

> In short, people did not respond in the way predicted by Ricardian equivalence theory—they spent a good chunk of the rebate, although not all of it. The economy wasn't out of the woods yet, but the tax rebate served its intended purpose as an early counterstrike against the contractionary effects of the recession.
>
> Sources: Jonathan Parker, Nicholas Souleles, David Johnson, and Robert McClelland, "Consumer Spending and the Economic Stimulus Payments of 2008," working paper, Kellogg School, Northwestern University, 2011, http://japarker.scripts.mit.edu/docs/PSJM2013.pdf; http://www.voxeu.org/index.php?q=node/1541.

Fiscal policy can be a powerful tool, enabling the government to counteract short-run fluctuations in the economy by increasing spending or cutting taxes. However, there is a catch: The government has to pay for all the roads and bridges and tax rebates somehow. Where does the money come from? It comes from taxpayers. If spending increases without a comparable increase in taxes, or if taxes are cut without a comparable decrease in spending, the government often goes into debt.

✓CONCEPT CHECK

- ☐ What are decisions about the level of government spending and taxation called? **[LO 13.1]**
- ☐ What type of fiscal policy increases aggregate demand? **[LO 13.2]**
- ☐ What are the three types of time lags involved in implementing fiscal policy? **[LO 13.3]**
- ☐ Are income taxes an example of discretionary or automatic fiscal policy? **[LO 13.4]**
- ☐ Why might citizens experience a tax cut more like a loan than a real windfall? And how would that affect fiscal policy? **[LO 13.5]**
- ☐ What does the evidence say about Ricardian equivalence? **[LO 13.5]**

The Government Budget

budget deficit
an amount of money a government spends beyond the revenue it brings in

budget surplus
an amount of revenue a government brings in beyond what it spends

We've seen why the government may want to influence the economy by changing the amount it spends or taxes. In practice this can require borrowing money. If spending is higher than revenue, which is the current situation in the United States and in most other countries, the government will have a **budget deficit**—an amount of money a government spends beyond the revenue it brings in. And although it happens more rarely at the federal level, it is also possible for the government to have a **budget surplus**—an amount of revenue a government brings in beyond what it spends.

When governments persist in running budget deficits year after year, the deficits can pile up over time. These accumulations are the *public debt*. In the remainder of this chapter, we'll discuss the government budget and the effect that public debt can have on the economy.

Revenue and spending

LO 13.6 Describe how revenue and spending determine a government budget and how the U.S. budget deficit occurs.

At a glance, how a government budget works is pretty simple: Money comes in as tax revenues and goes out through government purchases and transfer payments. (*Transfer payments* refer to payments from government accounts to individuals for programs, like Social Security, that do not involve a purchase of goods or services. As such, these payments are not reflected in GDP.) What's *not* simple about a government budget is the enormous amount of money involved.

Total U.S. government expenditure in 2016 was just under $3.7 trillion. The government took in, through tax revenue, approximately $3.2 trillion. The gap between revenue and spending—the budget deficit—was an incredible $439 billion.[6] The size of the deficit actually represents an improvement: In 2011, the U.S. government deficit was as high as $1.3 trillion. The last time the deficit had been that large as a percentage of GDP was during the run-up of spending on tanks and airplanes necessary to fight World War II.

It's important to keep in mind that government decisions about spending, income, and borrowing differ fundamentally from household decisions when it comes to recessions:

- When households face tough times, they usually think about belt-tightening and building up resources for a rainy day.
- When the government faces a downturn, it sometimes makes sense to *increase* spending and reduce taxes in order to stimulate aggregate demand.

Indeed, the government has a role in undoing the negative demand externality that occurs when households all "do the right things" for themselves (cut consumption), but which ends up reducing overall demand in the economy at a time when *greater* demand is in fact needed to help improve the economy.

The U.S. budget deficit

Figure 13-4 shows the U.S. budget deficit for the last 76 years. In almost every year since 1940 there has been a budget deficit. Deficits have been especially large in times of war, as government spending on the military increases. The amount of the budget deficit for 2015 was approximately $438 billion.

FIGURE 13-4

U.S. budget deficit since 1940   With the exception of World War II (the big upward spike in the 1940s comes from military spending), the U.S. budget was relatively balanced until about 1970. For a few decades afterward, there was a modest budget deficit. After a short period of surplus, the government again started running deficits due to tax cuts and, starting in 2008, efforts to spend the economy out of recession.

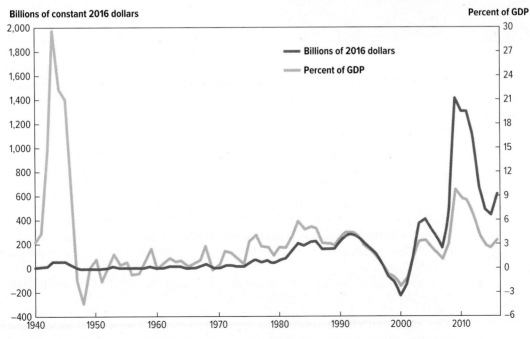

Source: White House Office of Budget and Management, Fiscal Year Budget Data, Tables 1.1 and 1.2, https://www.whitehouse.gov/omb/budget/Historicals.

Economists usually express the deficit as a *percentage of GDP* to emphasize the relationship between the deficit and the size of the economy. As Figure 13-4 also shows, during World War II, the deficit reached 30 percent of GDP. Much smaller spikes in spending corresponded with the 1990–1991 Gulf War and the period after September 11, 2001, when the wars in Iraq and Afghanistan were launched.

Spending increases can lead to larger deficits, but so can decreases in tax revenues. You may notice that the deficit was pretty high—on average 4 percent of GDP—during the 1980s, a time of economic growth and peace. This was due to changes on the revenue side of the government budget, as tax rates were lowered by President Ronald Reagan and the government took in less money. Recessions also tend to increase deficits, as can be seen in the sharp spike from 2007 onward. During a recession, government spending often increases as part of an expansionary fiscal policy, while revenues tend to decrease because people are earning and spending less.

✓ CONCEPT CHECK

☐ What is the term for when the government collects more revenue than it spends? **[LO 13.6]**

☐ Name three reasons why the budget deficit might increase during a recession. **[LO 13.6]**

The Public Debt

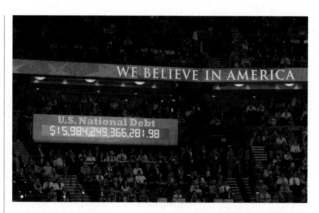

Since this photo was taken at the Republican National Convention in August 2012, the U.S. national debt has crossed the $19 trillion threshold, with little sign of slowing.
© *DW labs Incorporated/ Shutterstock*

Just a few blocks from the flashy billboards and dazzling displays of Times Square in New York City is a far more humble digital counter that keeps tabs on the debt incurred by the U.S. federal government. Every time the government runs a deficit, the **public debt**—the total amount of money that a government owes at a point in time—increases.

In the rare years when the government runs a surplus, the debt decreases. When the public debt decreased at the end of the 1990s, the clock's owner had to shut down the clock temporarily because he hadn't programmed it to be able to count backwards.

The upward trend soon resumed. The next time the debt clock had to be shut down, the reason was to add another digit as the debt passed $9,999,999,999,999. In 2016, the clock had rolled past the $19 trillion mark and showed little sign of slowing. This $19 trillion was the equivalent of almost $60,000 of debt per citizen.[7] Seymour Durst, who put up the NYC debt clock, said, "It'll be up as long as the debt or [New York City] lasts," adding, "If it bothers people, then it's working."[8] How bothered *should* we be about the size of the public debt?

Size of the debt

LO 13.7 Explain the difference between the government deficit and debt.

public debt
the total amount of money that a government owes at a point in time; the cumulative sum of all deficits and surpluses

In 1792, Alexander Hamilton convinced the only two banks in the country to lend the newly formed United States of America $19,608.61. This is the first known entry on the ledger of the country's public debt.

Although people sometimes confuse the terms *debt* and *deficit,* they are different, and the distinction between them is an important one:

- The *deficit* tells us how much the government revenues fall short of spending *each year.*
- The *debt* is the *total* amount that the government owes.

FIGURE 13-5

U.S. government debt since 1940   The total amount of U.S. government debt was held below $1 trillion through 1980 due to low yearly deficits. Afterward, the debt began to increase dramatically. As a share of GDP, the total debt decreased after 1948. Then government debt started to increase as a share of GDP, especially in 2008 due to large deficits.

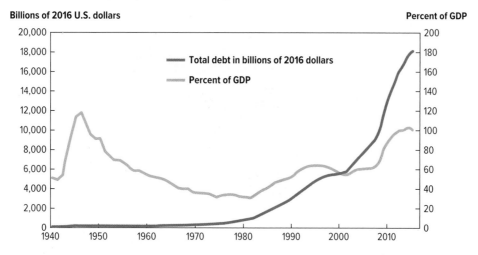

Source: White House Office of Management and Budget, Historical Tables, Table 7.1, https://www.whitehouse.gov/omb/budget/Historicals.

In other words, the debt is the cumulative sum of all deficits and surpluses.

Figure 13-5 shows the public debt since 1940, in real-dollar terms (green line) and as a share of GDP (peach line). This graph demonstrates the *cumulative effect* of the annual deficits depicted in Figure 13-4.

To see why it's useful to think of the public debt as a share of GDP, consider it in terms of personal finances. Which would you prefer:

- To be making $20,000 a year and owe $10,000 in debt?
- Or to be making $100,000 a year and owe $30,000 in debt?

In the second case, your debt is three times as large, but only 30 percent of your annual income. In the first case, your debt is smaller but amounts to 50 percent of your annual income. Even though you owe more in the second case, you'd be less worried about your ability to repay it.

Similar logic explains why debt as a share of GDP actually shrank between 1950 and 1980, even though in dollar terms the debt was going up: The economy grew quickly during these years, much faster than the growth in the debt. After 2009, in contrast, debt as a share of GDP increased quickly as the government spent money while the economy remained sluggish after the Great Recession.

Almost every country in the world has debt, some much more than the United States as a percentage of GDP. (Trivia: Only the nation of Brunei is debt-free, according to the International Monetary Fund.) Figure 13-6 shows the amount of debt owed by various countries. Four of them—Japan, Greece, Italy, and the United States—owe more than 100 percent of GDP.

How does the government go into debt?

LO 13.8 Understand how Treasury securities work and why people value them.

How exactly does government spending lead to debt? The process is more complicated than simply putting purchases on a charge card or getting a loan at a local bank. The government borrows money from people by selling **Treasury securities** (simply called "Treasuries" for short).

Treasury securities
debt-financing arrangements made by the U.S. government

FIGURE 13-6

Debt in various countries, 2013   There is a wide discrepancy in the amount of debt owed among countries. In 2013, Japan's debt was the highest in relation to GDP, at 242.6 percent of its GDP. Most countries have a level of debt that ranges between 20 and 80 percent of their GDP.

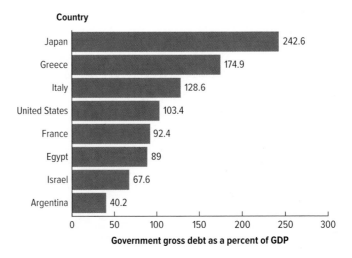

Source: International Monetary Fund, World Economic Outlook Database, http://www.imf.org/external/pubs/ft/weo/2015/01/weodata/index.aspx.

The details of Treasuries can be complex, but the basic idea is that the U.S. government accepts money from people with an obligation to pay them back by a certain date. Some Treasuries are short-term promises (the government will pay back the money after one month or one year); others operate on much longer time frames and don't get repaid for 30 years.

The shortest-term Treasury securities are *Treasury bills,* also known as *T-bills.* These are loans to the government that mature in less than a year. When you buy a T-bill, you're buying a promise that the government will pay you a set amount of money on a fixed date—for example, $1,000, three months from today. People bid for T-bills when they are issued, so depending on the state of the market for T-bills, you might pay, say, only $997 for this particular promise. The $3 difference is the equivalent of interest earned on a savings account. The return on these loans is usually quite low, but they are liquid (your money is tied up in the bond for less than a year). Most important, investors consider them to be very safe, and they thus appeal as a place to securely park money.

For longer-term investments, the government issues *Treasury notes* in 2-, 3-, 5-, 7-, and 10-year increments. When you purchase a Treasury note, every six months you receive an interest payment at a set rate. The return on 10-year Treasury notes is often cited as an indicator of the country's overall macroeconomic health. These notes pay more in interest than do T-bills, usually at a rate of about 3 percent for the 10-year note, since liquidity and interest paid are inversely related. (Chapter 14, "The Basics of Finance," addresses this relationship in more detail.) For those who are even more patient, the government offers its longest-term option: *Treasury bonds* mature in 30 years and pay a specified amount of interest every 6 months.

The big risk from investing in government securities is that inflation might eat away their value. For those worried about this risk, the Treasury offers *Treasury Inflation-Protected Securities (TIPS).* For TIPS, the original amount of the investment is pegged (tied) to changes in the overall Consumer Price Index (CPI), while the interest rate remains fixed. For example, if the original loan is for $10,000 with an interest rate of 3 percent, and inflation reaches 5 percent this year, the government would pay back slightly more than $10,800 ($10,000 plus the sum of the 3 percent interest rate and the 5 percent inflation rate). If the security were not inflation-protected, the government would pay back only $10,300.

FIGURE 13-7

The top seven foreign holders of U.S. debt, June 2015   In June 2015 the top seven holders of U.S. debt were Japan, China, banking centers (the Cayman Islands and Luxembourg), the United Kingdom, Canada, and Ireland. Due to the large export imbalance China and Japan have with the United States, together they hold just under a quarter of U.S. debt.

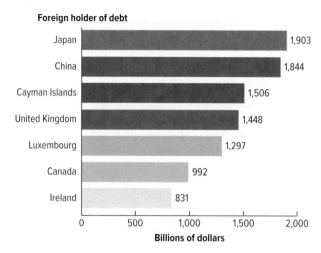

Source: U.S. Treasury, Report on Foreign Portfolio Holdings of U.S. Securities at End-June 2015, https://www.treasury.gov/press-center/press-releases/Pages/jl0469.aspx (June 2015).

Treasury securities are purchased as financial investments by individuals and by other governments and banks, both in the United States and abroad. Almost half of the privately held government debt is held by people who live outside the United States. Figure 13-7 shows the breakdown of U.S. debt holdings by country.

Why would people want to hold government debt? The main reason lies in the relative safety of the investment, especially when compared with other investments. When you invest in real estate, the housing market can crash. When you invest in a company's stock, the company can lose market value or go bankrupt. Governments can declare themselves bankrupt, too, and refuse to pay back money that people have loaned them. But investors generally believe that the odds of the U.S. government doing this are quite low, essentially zero. In the shakiest part of the Great Recession, investors flocked to short-term U.S. Treasuries to escape risks in the stock market and real estate market. Demand was so strong that for a while interest rates were negative, meaning that investors were willing to lose money in return for the safety of buying the debt of the United States.

Is government debt good or bad?

LO 13.9 Identify the benefits and costs of government debt.

In the summer of 2011, more than 100,000 people marched in the streets of Athens. They were protesting "austerity" measures that would cut government spending in the hope of taming Greece's astronomical debt burden. At 1.5 times the size of GDP, debt had become a serious drag on Greece's economy. (By 2015, Greece's debt had risen above 175 percent.)[9] However, most economists believe that *some debt* is necessary to the smooth functioning of government. What are the benefits and costs of government debt?

Benefits of government debt

There are two main benefits of government debt. The first is that it allows the government to be flexible when something unexpected happens. Hurricane Katrina, which devastated the Gulf

Coast in 2005, cost the U.S. government $105 billion, or almost 4 percent of government spending that year. If the choice is between borrowing to cover the costs of responding to an emergency or not responding at all, many people would say it's better to borrow.

The second benefit of debt is that it can pay for investments that will lead to economic growth and prosperity (and, presumably, higher tax revenues) in the long run. Just as you might decide to borrow to fund your college education because you expect it to lead to a better job and higher salary down the road, it can make sense for governments to borrow to invest in the education system or to construct roads and other infrastructure that will help the economy to grow more quickly.

Costs of government debt

On the other hand, there are both *direct* and *indirect* costs of government debt. The *direct cost* is the interest the government has to pay to the people it has borrowed from. Interest payments on the debt are substantial. In the past, interest payments on the U.S. debt have amounted to the fourth-largest budget expense, just behind spending on transfer payments (consisting of Social Security and means-tested transfer payments such as Medicare, the first- and third-largest budget categories, respectively) and defense (the second-largest budget category).

The direct cost of debt depends on the interest rate. If the interest rate increases, the government debt becomes more expensive to pay. The interest rate, in turn, depends on investors' confidence in the government's ability to pay back the debt. This can become a vicious cycle: If investors doubt that a government will be able to repay its debt, they will demand a higher interest rate before they are willing to lend to that government. That higher interest rate increases the burden of debt, making it even more doubtful whether the government can pay it back.

This self-reinforcing spiral of investor doubt and a higher interest rate has, in the past, forced defaults by some governments when they could no longer afford the direct costs. Although few people think there is a serious risk of this happening to the U.S. government, in 2011 the major rating agency Standard & Poor's downgraded its rating of U.S. debt from AAA to AA+. This downgrade implied some degree of doubt about whether U.S. politicians would be able to meaningfully tackle the tough choices required to shrink the ballooning amount of government debt.

There are also *indirect costs* of government debt. In some circumstances, government debt can distort the credit market and slow economic growth. We have already noted the possibility that government borrowing can *crowd out* private borrowing: When the government borrows money, it increases the demand for credit, and so increases the price of credit—the interest rate—in the wider economy. A higher interest rate increases the cost of borrowing for businesses that want to invest and for consumers who want to buy new homes or cars. (We describe this mechanism more extensively in Chapter 14, "The Basics of Finance.")

Finally, there is the question of who bears the burden of government debt. People today benefit when the government borrows to spend more on services or cut taxes, but people tomorrow will have to repay the loans. The costs of services are being kicked down the road to our children and grandchildren.

✓CONCEPT CHECK

- ☐ What is the difference between government debt and deficit? **[LO 13.7]**
- ☐ How do Treasury securities provide financing for the U.S. government's debt? **[LO 13.8]**
- ☐ What is one possible effect of government debt on the amount of private investment? **[LO 13.9]**

Conclusion

We started this chapter by looking at why the government might want to change fiscal policy to counteract economic fluctuations. When the economy is in a recession, expansionary fiscal policy—cutting taxes, increasing spending, or both, as with the 2009 stimulus plan—can increase aggregate demand and speed up recovery. Unemployment remained high even in the first years after the stimulus, but ultimately there is no way of knowing for certain whether it would have been even higher without it.

We also looked at how the government can borrow and how deficits lead to public debt. Debt adds to government flexibility, but it can be costly and slow down economic growth. It also raises questions about the fairness of expecting future generations to bear the burden of paying off the debt.

Governments have an alternative to fiscal policy when they want to influence the economy: monetary policy. Monetary policy works through the financial system, so before we get into monetary policy, we will cover the basics of finance in the next chapter.

Key Terms

fiscal policy, p. 334

expansionary fiscal policy, p. 335

contractionary fiscal policy, p. 335

automatic stabilizers, p. 341

budget deficit, p. 344

budget surplus, p. 344

public debt, p. 346

Treasury securities, p. 347

Summary

LO 13.1 Explain the difference between contractionary fiscal policy and expansionary fiscal policy.

Together, the level of taxation and government spending is called *fiscal policy*. We say that fiscal policy is either expansionary or contractionary.

Expansionary fiscal policy involves changes to fiscal policy that cause the aggregate demand curve to increase (shift out to the right). It is expansionary because it expands demand. Expansionary fiscal policy occurs because either government spending increases or the level of taxation decreases and is a response to recessionary conditions.

On the other hand, *contractionary* fiscal policy involves changes to fiscal policy that contract aggregate demand, causing the aggregate demand curve to decrease (shift in to the left). Contractionary fiscal policy occurs when government spending decreases or when taxation increases, and is a response to an overheating economy with the accompanying threat of excessive inflation.

LO 13.2 Explain how fiscal policy can counteract short-run economic fluctuations.

The government can use fiscal policy to counteract business-cycle fluctuations. When the economy is sluggish, the government can conduct expansionary fiscal policy to stimulate demand. This will lead to a faster recovery than without the fiscal policy. On the other hand, if the economy is overheating, the government can undertake contractionary fiscal policy to reduce

aggregate demand. This action also returns the economy closer to the long-run equilibrium level.

LO 13.3 Identify the time lags that complicate the formulation of fiscal policy.

Time lags can mean that sometimes a fiscal policy choice is too late to do any good. Time lags come in many forms. There are *information* lags (how long it takes to get the right information about the overall health of the economy), *formulation* lags (getting everyone to agree on the right policy), and *implementation* lags (how long it takes fiscal policy to have an effect on the economy).

LO 13.4 Discuss how stabilizers can automatically adjust fiscal policy as the economy changes.

To get around time lags, automatic stabilizers can affect fiscal policy without specific action from policy-makers. These features of government policy can automatically stimulate or slow the economy.

The tax system is designed so that people who earn more income should pay higher average tax rates. One consequence is that when the economy is booming, people move into higher income ranges, which means they automatically face higher tax rates. The automatically increased taxes have a contractionary effect by slightly checking overall spending and aggregate demand. When the economy is in a recession, people move to lower income ranges, which have lower tax rates. The automatically reduced taxes have an expansionary effect, encouraging spending and spurring aggregate demand.

Government spending can also work as an automatic stabilizer. When the economy is booming, fewer people are eligible for unemployment insurance benefits and welfare programs; government spending on those programs falls, reducing aggregate demand and having a contractionary effect. In a recession, more people are eligible for these programs and spending on them automatically rises, increasing aggregate demand and having an expansionary effect.

LO 13.5 Describe the theory and evidence about Ricardian equivalence and what it implies for the effectiveness of fiscal policy.

Ricardian equivalence predicts that if governments cut taxes but not public spending, people will recognize that the government will have to borrow money to cover the financial shortfall that's been created. People will then figure that, at some point in the future, taxes will have to go back up to repay the extra government debt incurred through tax cuts. Since people see that a tax cut today will just mean higher taxes in a few years (or maybe decades), they are reluctant to spend so freely after the tax cut. The theory says that, as a result, tax cuts will have no impact on spending: People will continue to save rather than spend, consumption will not increase, and the tax cut will be unsuccessful in changing aggregate demand.

Recent empirical evidence, however, shows that people do spend extra when taxes are cut, increasing aggregate demand. Ricardian equivalence is an important theoretical idea, but the data show it is not a good guide to predicting the actual effect of tax cuts.

LO 13.6 Describe how revenue and spending determine a government budget and how the U.S. budget deficit occurs.

The government budget includes all of the revenue it collects in taxes and all of the money it spends on government programs. When the government spends more than it collects in revenue, it runs a *deficit*. When it collects more revenue than it spends, it has a *surplus*. In most years, the government spends more than it collects in revenue. Deficits tend to increase during recessions and, more generally, when spending rises and tax revenues fall.

LO 13.7 Explain the difference between the government deficit and debt.

Deficits occur when annual spending is more than annual revenue. A surplus occurs when annual spending is less than annual revenue. The *public debt* is the total amount of money that the government has borrowed (but not yet repaid) over time. The debt and the deficit are closely related: The budget deficit tells us how much the government borrows each year, and the debt tells us the total that the government has borrowed and not paid back over time. In other words, the debt is the cumulative sum of all deficits and surpluses.

LO 13.8 Understand how Treasury securities work and why people value them.

The government borrows money from others by selling *Treasury securities*, which are debt-financing arrangements made by the United States with obligations to pay back the money over varying lengths of time (often for a year or less, but sometimes for as long as 30 years). Individuals, other governments, and banks, both abroad and in the United States, purchase Treasuries as financial investments. They are typically seen as relatively safe investments, and investors around the world flocked to these during the Great Recession and its aftermath.

LO 13.9 Identify the benefits and costs of government debt.

A deficit allows the government to spend more than its revenue. Allowing the government to run a deficit permits the government to respond to unexpected events and to undertake expansionary fiscal policy. However, there are also costs of running deficits. Interest needs to be paid on the debt, the government may not spend the money efficiently, and high government deficits may increase interest rates and thus reduce investment in the economy.

Review Questions

1. What is the best fiscal policy for a country suffering from high inflation? **[LO 13.1]**

2. If the government wants to reduce GDP by $500 million, should it increase or decrease its spending? Must it increase or decrease spending by exactly $500 million, some amount more than $500 million, or some amount less than $500 million? Would this be expansionary or contractionary fiscal policy? **[LO 13.1]**

3. President Obama said the following in November 2010 when announcing a two-year pay freeze for civilian federal employees: "After all, small businesses and families are tightening their belts. Their government should too." What do you think the intended effect of this policy would be, assuming the economy was in a recession at the time? Do you think it was the appropriate response? Why or why not? **[LO 13.2]**

4. If unemployment is high and spending is sluggish, what type of fiscal policy should be enacted? How would this be enacted via taxes? Via government spending?

What is the intended effect of this policy on aggregate demand? **[LO 13.2]**

5. "The problem with democracy," your friend tells you as you debate politics, "is the time it takes to get approval for every action the government takes. If the president didn't have to spend so much time arguing back and forth with Congress, policy wouldn't take so long to affect the economy." Is your friend right or wrong? What would your response be? **[LO 13.3]**

6. Explain the difference between tax rates and tax revenues, and how each is related to recession and policy enacted to counteract it. Do you expect to see tax rates rise or fall during recession? What about tax revenues? Explain your answer. **[LO 13.4]**

7. The government decides to reduce income taxes due to a recession in the economy over the past nine months. Will the reduction in income taxes boost spending in the economy? Why or why not? **[LO 13.5]**

8. Use the theory of Ricardian equivalence to explain why cutting taxes during a recession may not always be an effective expansionary fiscal policy. **[LO 13.5]**

9. Why have budget deficits been so high in the United States since 2007? **[LO 13.6]**

10. You hear on the nightly news that the president has vowed to decrease the nation's debt. "We'll have to buckle down and learn to do without, both the government and private citizens," he says. How can a nation lower its debt? How will the government and private citizens be affected? **[LO 13.6]**

11. A friend of yours looks at the state of the U.S. debt in 2011 and tells you, "Since the debt is so high, we must be running an incredibly large deficit every year." Is your friend's analysis valid? Why or why not? **[LO 13.7]**

12. Is it possible for a nation's government to run a budget deficit in some years but not have national debt? Explain your answer. **[LO 13.7]**

13. Explain the differences and similarities among Treasury bills, Treasury notes, and Treasury bonds. **[LO 13.8]**

14. Your friend thinks buying Treasury bills is riskier than leaving money in a savings account. You disagree. Who is right? **[LO 13.8]**

15. Taxpayers are clamoring for their government to be more responsible, and many strongly support a balanced-budget amendment. This would mean the country could no longer spend more than it takes in each year. Discuss the primary advantages and disadvantages of such a law. **[LO 13.9]**

16. Is government debt good or bad for the economy and the nation as a whole? Give one argument for each side of the debate. **[LO 13.9]**

Problems and Applications

1. Is each of the following policies an example of expansionary or contractionary fiscal policy? Explain your answers in terms of the effect on aggregate demand. **[LO 13.1]**

    a. The government slashes funding for the Environmental Protection Agency, without changing any other spending.

    b. The government raises taxes on households making more than $250,000.

    c. The government decides to fill gaps in Medicare by making it available to more people.

2. The economy is growing far too quickly, as high aggregate demand is causing inflation. What fiscal policy should be pursued in this instance—expansionary or contractionary? What will be the effect of the appropriate policy on aggregate demand? **[LO 13.1]**

3. Assuming that unemployment is high and spending is low, answer the following questions. **[LO 13.2]**

    a. Should the government pursue expansionary or contractionary fiscal policy?

    b. What will the appropriate policy do to the aggregate demand curve? Will the curve shift to the right or to the left?

    c. Through which component(s) of aggregate demand (C, I, G, or NX, or some combination of the preceding) will the change occur?

4. The diagram in Figure 13P-1 shows aggregate demand for New Caprica last year (AD₁) and this year (AD₂). If you were to advise the president of New Caprica on economic policy, how would you answer the following? **[LO 13.2]**

FIGURE 13P-1

a. How large is current output? How large is potential output? What is the difference, if any, between the two?

b. Is New Caprica in a recession or a boom?

c. Given your findings, should the president enact expansionary or contractionary fiscal policy, or no policy at all?

d. In which direction would the aggregate demand curve shift if the president used contractionary fiscal policy?

5. "Our fiscal policy was unsuccessful," an economic analyst says, "due to partisan bickering in Congress that delayed the passing of the appropriate measures and our failure to realize we were headed into recession until it was too late." What type of lags is the analyst describing? **[LO 13.3]**

6. Assume that the government in some nation intended to respond to low employment via fiscal policy. What type of policy would this require? Assume that this policy ended up having an undesirable outcome. How could this happen in terms of formulation and implementation lags? **[LO 13.3]**

7. Brenda earns $62,000 a year and pays an average tax rate of 15 percent. **[LO 13.4]**

a. Calculate Brenda's disposable income and the amount of tax she pays to the government.

b. Suppose a recession hits the economy and Brenda's income falls to $50,000 per year due to the fact that she is earning a smaller annual bonus. If she now pays an average tax rate of 12 percent, what is her disposable income and the amount of tax she pays to the government?

c. Calculate how much Brenda's annual salary and disposable income fell by due to the recession.

d. Explain how income taxes are an automatic stabilizer in this example.

8. True or false? If the amount of time a person is eligible for unemployment compensation is reduced from 26 weeks to 4 weeks, people will have an incentive to quickly find a new job. This occurs because unemployment compensation is an important automatic stabilizer for the economy. **[LO 13.4]**

9. Consider three countries. The first country runs small budget surpluses each year. The other two countries run large budget deficits each year. In one of the deficit countries the national debt-to-GDP ratio has been steady, whereas in the other deficit country the national debt-to-GDP ratio has been rising. Suppose each of these countries decides to reduce income taxes. Is

Ricardian equivalence likely to hold in all of these countries? Why or why not? **[LO 13.5]**

10. A country is in the midst of a recession with real GDP estimated to be $1.8 billion below potential GDP. The government's policy analysts believe the current value of the marginal propensity to consume (MPC) is 0.90. **[LO 13.5]**

a. If the government wants real GDP to equal potential GDP, by how much should it increase government spending? Alternatively, by how much should it reduce taxes?

b. Suppose that during the recession people have become less confident and decide they will spend only 50 percent of any additional income. In this case, if the government increases spending by the amount calculated in part a, will real GDP end up less than, greater than, or equal to potential GDP? By how much?

c. With the same decrease in consumer spending described in part b, if the government decreases taxes by the amount calculated in part a, will real GDP end up less than, greater than, or equal to potential GDP? By how much?

d. Why is it difficult for the government to predict exactly how a change in spending or taxes will affect GDP?

11. If in some year a nation's budget deficit is $9.56 trillion and government spending is $12.19 trillion, how much must it have earned in tax revenue this year? **[LO 13.6]**

12. "The government shouldn't borrow so much," your uncle claims. "Look at that national debt! It's no different from someone borrowing on credit cards they can't pay." **[LO 13.6]**

a. Is your uncle right?

b. How is government debt spending like someone borrowing on a credit card?

c. How is government debt spending different from someone borrowing on a credit card?

13. Econo Nation started 2013 with no national budget debt or surplus. By the end of 2013, it had a budget surplus of $304 million; in 2014, it had a budget deficit of $452 million; in 2015 it had a budget surplus of $109 million, and the amount of its budget deficit or surplus in 2016 is unknown. If at the end of 2016 Econo Nation's national debt totaled $50 million, did it run a deficit or surplus in 2016? How much? **[LO 13.7]**

14. "Though the national debt has increased, don't worry," the president says in a televised speech. "We will not have to pay these funds back to bond buyers." How is

this possible? How must the government have financed its debt in this case? **[LO 13.7]**

15. You buy a Treasury note for $1,000. Every 6 months you receive a payment of $40. **[LO 13.8]**

    a. What is the annual rate of return?

    b. What would be the annual rate of return if the payment was instead $30?

    c. What would be the annual rate of return if the payment was instead $45?

16. Your friend believes buying Treasury bills or Treasury notes will offer protection against rising inflation in comparison to buying stocks or mutual funds, because the rate of return on the Treasury bills and notes is known at the time of purchase. Do you agree? Why or why not? **[LO 13.8]**

17. Which of the following are examples of the negative effects associated with government debt? **[LO 13.9]**

    a. Increased interest rates.

    b. Increased taxes or lower spending in the future.

    c. Increased investment in the economy.

18. If the government could borrow as much as it liked with a 0 percent interest rate, would the government debt be cost-free? Explain your answer. **[LO 13.9]**

Endnotes

1. http://data.bls.gov/timeseries/LNS14000000 and http://www.tradingeconomics.com/united-states/government-debt-to-gdp.

2. The multiplier effect is described in greater detail in Chapter 11, "Aggregate Expenditure," and Chapter 12, "Aggregate Demand and Aggregate Supply." Crowding out is described in greater detail in Chapter 14, "The Basics of Finance."

3. In Chapter 16, "Inflation," we will also see that there are other reasons to be concerned about *deflation,* or falling prices in an economy.

4. It turns out that many recessions last less than a year. The official length of the 2007–2009 recession was 14 months. Of course, it's impossible to know how long the recession would have lasted without the government's expansionary policy.

5. www.irs.gov.

6. https://www.cbo.gov/publication/51110.

7. http://www.brillig.com/debt_clock.

8. http://content.time.com/time/business/article/0,8599,1850269,00.html#ixzz1OtKQCoQM.

9. http://blogs.wsj.com/briefly/2015/07/03/greeces-debt-the-numbers.

The Financial System and Institutions

The four chapters in Part 6 will introduce you to . . .

the financial and monetary systems and the institutions that make them work. In Part 6, we'll discuss everything from the traders on Wall Street to the humble dollar bill in your wallet.

Chapter 14, "The Basics of Finance," runs through the basics of financial markets and describes the roles that individuals and institutions play in them—including everyone from a family buying a first house to the traders making million-dollar bets on Wall Street. Financial markets connect savers and borrowers, helping money flow to the parts of the economy where it is the most valuable at any given time and allowing people to manage their money over time and minimize the risks they face.

Chapter 15, "Money and the Monetary System," is all about money. Money helps the economy operate smoothly. As a medium of exchange, it enables you to buy a pack of gum, a car, or an entire tropical island. It is more than just bills and coins, though. In the United States, the Federal Reserve is the main institution responsible for creating and managing the overall money supply. This power gives it a unique ability to steer the economy through good times and bad.

Chapter 16, "Inflation," covers the delicate relationship between inflation and unemployment. Policy-makers at central banks, like the U.S. Federal Reserve, have the task of controlling fluctuations in the value of money. They can also use the tools of monetary policy to influence the overall level of unemployment. With this power comes great responsibility: Recent history is filled with examples of how countries have suffered from inflation and unemployment caused by poor monetary policy.

Although financial markets usually run smoothly, there are times when the system fails to efficiently manage risk and fund new ventures. Investigating how financial systems break down provides unique insights into how they actually work. In Chapter 17, "Financial Crisis," we'll pick through the details of the worst financial crisis for generations: the problems that followed the 2007 crash in the U.S. housing market, which plunged the U.S. economy and others around the world into deep recession.

The Basics of Finance

Learning Objectives

LO 14.1	Define a financial market and describe the information asymmetry problems that can occur in them.
LO 14.2	Discuss the three main functions of financial markets.
LO 14.3	Describe the market for loanable funds, including the price of loanable funds, and differentiate between savings and investment.
LO 14.4	List the factors that affect the supply and demand of loanable funds.
LO 14.5	Understand how interest rates on loans vary with the length of the loan and the riskiness of the transaction.
LO 14.6	Describe why it is important for the financial system to intermediate between buyers and sellers, provide liquidity, and diversify risk.
LO 14.7	Differentiate between debt and equity and define the major types of assets in each category.
LO 14.8	Name the main institutions in financial markets and describe the role that each plays.
LO 14.9	Explain the trade-off between risk and return in financial assets and describe how risk can be measured.
LO 14.10	Give arguments for and against the assumption that markets are efficient.
LO 14.11	Describe why savings equals investment in a closed economy and how government spending and foreign capital flows affect the saving-investment relationship.

HENRY LEHMAN AND HIS BROTHERS

In 1844, Henry Lehman opened a dry-goods store in Montgomery, Alabama. At first, he sold groceries and basic supplies to local farmers. Soon, his brothers joined the firm, and the business began to expand. The Lehman brothers started acting as go-betweens for local planters, buying

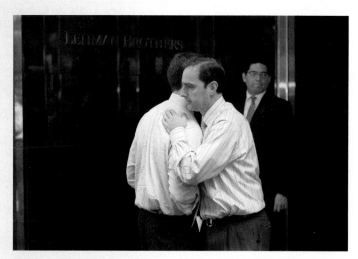

© Nicholas Roberts/AFP/Getty Images

their cotton and then selling it in more distant markets. Business boomed, and they opened an office in New York City, adding coffee and other commodities to their cotton brokerage. With its southern roots, the company was hard hit by the U.S. Civil War. At the end of the war, it regrouped and soon had a contract with the state of Alabama to help manage its finances and debt payments. By the end of the nineteenth century, the Lehman Brothers brokerage house had become one of the largest and most powerful institutions on Wall Street.

Lehman Brothers survived the Civil War, the Great Depression, World War II, an ill-fated merger with a rival, and the September 11, 2001, destruction of its headquarters, located just across the street from the World Trade Center towers. Despite all of that, on September 15, 2008, Lehman Brothers declared bankruptcy. The failure of such a large, long-standing, reputable firm was almost unimaginable. Global markets panicked. How could such a seemingly sturdy organization, which less than a year earlier had earned record profits, suddenly go broke?

The story of Lehman's collapse, the housing market crash that led to it, and the financial-system implosion and Great Recession that followed is one of the most fascinating economic tales of our time. To understand these events, we have to begin with an understanding of the financial system itself.

Traditional markets in goods and services are relatively straightforward—they help to match prospective buyers with those willing to sell. In comparison, *financial markets* can seem abstract and remote. What do they do? What exactly are Wall Street firms selling and on whose behalf are they selling it? How did old-fashioned cotton brokers like the Lehman brothers end up on Wall Street? Why do we have a financial system?

In fact, the basic purpose of financial markets is similar to any other market—they match people who want money to spend now (buyers) with people who want to save their money for later (sellers). In doing so, they also help people manage their money over time and protect themselves against risk. The *financial system* brings together savers and borrowers in a set of interconnected markets in which people trade a variety of financial products.

The basic premise of a financial market is simple, but actual transactions can be quite complex. Financial markets offer a wide variety of financial products, targeted to people with different investment or saving needs. Just as wholesalers and grocery stores mediate between farmers and hungry consumers, there are many different firms and institutions that mediate between savers and borrowers in financial markets.

Businesses, governments, nongovernmental organizations, and individuals depend on the financial system to achieve their goals. The system helps people get the money they need, in the right amount, at the right time, with as little uncertainty as possible. If you have a savings account, checking account, credit card, student loan, home mortgage, or car loan, then you benefit from access to financial markets. People tend to take these services for granted. But the global disruptions surrounding the Lehman bankruptcy showed just how valuable a well-functioning financial system is, and how much it matters.

In this chapter, we'll start by looking at the role of *financial markets* and the value they provide to savers and borrowers. We build a simple model of the market in which savers and borrowers participate. Then we look at the *financial system* from three angles: the functions it serves, the players involved in it, and the assets they trade. Finally, we'll look at some general features of financial products, like risk and return.

The Role of Financial Markets

The high-tech, elaborate dealings we associate with Wall Street are a relatively recent phenomenon, but basic financial markets existed at least as far back as ancient Greece. Money-lenders, based in temples, accepted deposits, changed money for travelers, and (as their name implies) made loans. A person's show of wealth went from precious metals, which were weighed, to coins stamped by the nation-state, which were counted. Stock markets we would recognize today first appeared in the seventeenth century. Why have financial markets been such a natural and useful institution in different societies throughout history? What do they do?

What is a financial market?

LO 14.1 Define a financial market and describe the information asymmetry problems that can occur in them.

In a **financial market**, people trade future claims on funds or goods. These "claims" can take many different forms:

- When you take out a loan, a bank gives you money now, in return for an agreement that you will repay the bank, with interest, in the future.
- When you buy stock in a company, you have a right to a share of any profits earned in the future.
- When you buy an insurance policy, you make regular premium payments, and the insurance company agrees to pay out, if and when something bad happens to you in the future.

financial market
a market in which people trade future claims on funds or goods

We'll talk about the details of these and other types of financial assets later in the chapter. The important thing to notice, for now, is that they are all agreements that allow people to move funds around, *from one time, place, or situation to another.*

The key idea behind financial markets is that, at any given time, the people who have spare funds are not necessarily the same people who have the most valuable ways to spend those funds. Financial markets allow funding to flow to the places where it is most highly valued at the moment. A well-functioning market makes everyone better off, by matching buyers and sellers who both have something to gain from a trade. In financial markets:

- Buyers are people who want to spend money on something of value right now but don't have cash on hand. Among the buyers in financial markets are families buying new houses, students paying for college, corporations building new factories, entrepreneurs starting new ventures, and often the government when it needs to finance public spending.

- Sellers are people who have cash on hand and are willing to let others use it, for a price. Sellers in financial markets are individuals, corporations, and government entities willing to forgo some spending right now in return for repayment down the road.

Information asymmetries and financial markets

information asymmetry
a condition in which one participant in a transaction knows more than another participant

An **information asymmetry** arises when one participant in a transaction knows more than another participant. You may have already encountered examples of information asymmetries in microeconomics. For example, the people selling used cars often know more about the quality of the cars than the people buying them. People buying health insurance, on the other hand, usually know more about their own health issues than the companies selling insurance. And so on. But perhaps nowhere are information asymmetries more prevalent than in financial markets: The people seeking loans tend to know more about the potential uses (and misuses!) of the funds than the lenders.

Information asymmetries are so fundamental to financial markets that they have essentially determined the structure of modern financial systems, with banks, stock markets, bond markets, and regulatory agencies restricting the activities of both borrowers and lenders. To get a sense of why information asymmetries are so important in financial markets, let's consider the two classic problems that arise when parties have access to different amounts of information: adverse selection and moral hazard.

adverse selection
a state that occurs when buyers and sellers have different information about the quality of a good or the riskiness of a situation, and this asymmetric information results in failure to complete transactions that would have been possible if both sides had the same information.

Adverse selection refers to a state that occurs when buyers and sellers have different information about the quality of a good or the riskiness of a situation, and this asymmetric information results in failure to complete transactions that would have been possible if both sides had the same information. For example:

- Mortgage borrowers might know that the actual market value of their house is much lower than the public assessment.
- Executives of a company issuing *stock* (an asset that represents partial ownership in the company) might know that the company is much closer to bankruptcy (in which case the stockholders would receive nothing) than could be judged based on public information.

In either case, the problem that arises is that market participants cannot "separate the wheat from the chaff"—that is, they cannot separate the reliable borrowers from the reckless or the genuinely promising company from the frauds. Without tight regulation on the provision of public information, adverse selection would lead to sharp decreases in the market prices of company stock (since investors would worry about drawing a bad apple) and higher interest rates on bank loans.

moral hazard
the tendency for people to behave in a riskier way or to renege on contracts when they do not face the full consequences of their actions

Moral hazard refers to the tendency for people to behave in a riskier way or to renege on contracts when they do not face the full consequences of their actions. It's an asymmetric information problem that arises once a transaction takes place. Once drivers have purchased car insurance, for example, they face smaller (financial) consequences of getting in an accident. As a result, they might be more likely to speed or try to pass other cars in risky situations.

In the financial context, moral hazard arises in almost all transactions. For example:

- When a borrower has secured a loan, he might be tempted to make riskier investments than promised in the loan agreement. The upside of the investment belongs to the borrower, encouraging the greater risk, while the downside is borne by the lender.
- A company might believe that the government is likely to provide support in the event of a financial crisis. In this case, taxpayers are providing the company with implicit

insurance against catastrophic risk. The company (which might be a bank or financial firm) might then take advantage of this "insurance" by engaging in riskier practices.

Sometimes the consequences of these information asymmetries are so severe that financial transactions are impossible. But more often, the participants find ways to limit the problems. Financial innovators (like Muhammad Yunus, the microfinance pioneer from Bangladesh described in Chapter 1, "Economics and Life") have been creative in developing new ways of banking that help financial markets overcome moral hazard and adverse selection (and, in the process, have helped millions of people get better access to banks).

Functions of banks and financial markets

LO 14.2 Discuss the three main functions of financial markets.

These days, financial markets are extremely complicated—so complicated that when Lehman Brothers fell apart in 2008, very few people really had the full picture of what was going on. But the origins of financial markets are not so complicated. It starts with a bank, savers, and borrowers.

Imagine a world without banks. People face a problem: The times when you need to spend money almost never match up perfectly with the times when you earn money. This problem crops up in a lot of different ways. Some mistiming is long term, reflecting the cycle of your whole life:

- You might want to pay for a college degree or a house or a car early in life, before you've had a chance to do much earning.
- You might want to earn more than you spend during your working years and then live on the savings during retirement.

Other types of mistiming are shorter term:

- You might earn a paycheck once a month, but you want to buy things in various places and times throughout the month.
- If you run a business (such as a farm), your revenues might come in during one season (harvest) but most of your expenses come in another (planting).

A bank helps to solve these problems: It takes in savings from people who are earning more than they're spending at the moment. It gives out loans to people who currently want to spend more than they earn.

Why do we need banks for that? Why not just stuff cash under your pillow as you earn it and lend to or borrow from family and neighbors as needed? In fact, that *is* the old-fashioned way of managing money. Even today, billions of people around the world don't have good access to modern banks, and they still rely on those simple methods. But for those who have access to them, banks—and, more broadly, financial markets, of which banks are one example—serve three main functions.

Intermediating between savers and borrowers

The first function is that a bank acts as an *intermediary* between savers and borrowers. Without a bank, you'd have to make the rounds every time you need a loan, trying to cobble together bits and pieces of savings from the people you know. If they don't happen to have savings at the moment, you might just be out of luck. That sort of bad luck isn't unlikely if the people you know are similar to you in some way. If they are about your age or work in similar jobs or farm the same crops, then they're likely to be short on cash at the same times that you are.

A bank connects you to a much wider range of people who might have savings when you need to borrow. It also saves you (and them) the time and effort of managing dozens of small, person-to-person transactions. A bank is an easy, one-stop clearinghouse for everyone, whenever they need to save or to borrow.

Providing liquidity

Second, a bank makes it easier to have access to cash when and where you want it. In the old days, people had to have cash on hand to be able to buy something. They had to carry heavy gold or silver coins around, and worry about having them lost or stolen. What's more, it was risky to let others borrow or invest your coins (even beyond the risk of not being repaid) because the coins wouldn't be available if you needed them back in a hurry. For instance, if you made a loan to your neighbor and then your child got sick, you might have trouble getting your coins back right away to pay the doctor. It was safer to keep some coins around, doing nothing, just in case they were needed. A bank lets people enjoy the benefits of *liquidity*—having cash easily available when you want it—without the downsides of holding cash.

Some of the liquidity benefits are logistical. With banks and the tools they provide, like ATMs, checkbooks, debit accounts, and credit cards, it's simple and inexpensive to have access to cash when you want it. And you don't have to worry about protecting your cash when you don't need it. The real value is that you can deposit your savings at the bank and feel reasonably sure that you will be able to withdraw them if a need comes up.

This works because there are many depositors at the bank, and it's very, very unlikely that all of them will need to withdraw their savings at once. So, the bank can keep just a small amount of cash on hand and can loan out most of the deposits, to be put to use in productive investments. The borrowers pay the bank interest on the loans and the bank can pay savers interest on their deposits—all without losing the benefits of liquidity for individual savers.

Diversifying risk

Finally, banks help savers and borrowers to *diversify risk*. Suppose that in the pre-bank system you made a big loan to your cousin, who wanted to open a store. If the store did well, you'd get paid back and everything would be fine. But if the store went bankrupt—as small businesses often do—you might be financially ruined. When you borrow and save on a person-to-person level, there's no getting around the risk involved in having a lot of your eggs in one basket, even if everyone is well-intentioned and trustworthy.

In contrast, a bank spreads your eggs around to many different baskets. Because the bank has a big pool of borrowers, the risk of everyone failing to pay back their loans at once is very small. A few borrowers will default on their loans, but most will repay, and no individual saver will have to bear the full burden of a failed investment.

In fact, it's not only banks that provide these benefits. The whole financial system—made up of many institutions, including banks, insurance companies, investors, stock exchanges, and government agencies—is designed to *intermediate* between savers and borrowers, *provide liquidity,* and *diversify risk*. We'll come back to these ideas over and over again throughout the chapter. In the next section, we look at how these buyers and sellers come together in a simplified type of financial market we call the "market for loanable funds."

✓ CONCEPT CHECK

☐ What is traded in a financial market? **[LO 14.1]**

☐ What are adverse selection and moral hazard, and how do they create problems in financial markets? **[LO 14.1]**

☐ What are the three main functions that banks, and the financial system in general, provide for savers and borrowers? **[LO 14.2]**

The Market for Loanable Funds: A Simplified Financial Market

Consider a whole country of people earning and spending. At any given time, some of them want to borrow and others want to save. How much do they want to borrow, and how much are they willing to save? If the amount people want to borrow is higher than the amount saved, what determines which loans get approved? Financial markets mediate the forces of supply and demand *by determining the price* at which the quantity of funds saved will be equal to the quantity invested.

Real-world financial markets involve many products, with different prices, targeted at different types of buyers and sellers. You can get the flavor of this variety just by browsing the business section of a newspaper or looking at the types of accounts and loans offered by any bank. We'll dig into some of this nuance later in the chapter. For now, let's simplify all saving and borrowing into one market, which we'll call the *market for loanable funds*.

Savings, investment, and the price of loanable funds

LO 14.3 Describe the market for loanable funds, including the price of loanable funds, and differentiate between savings and investment.

The **market for loanable funds** is a market in which savers, who have money to lend, supply funds to those who want to borrow for their investment spending needs. "Loanable funds" are the dollars that are on the table between them to be lent out and borrowed.

When talking about savings and investment, we have to be careful with terminology. Economists differentiate between savings and investment:

- **Savings** is the portion of income that is not immediately spent on consumption of goods and services.
- **Investment**, or, more properly, *investment spending,* refers to spending on productive inputs, such as factories, machinery, and inventories.

> **HINT**
> When people put money into a 401(k) account for retirement or purchase stocks, they often say they are "investing" the money. But to an economist, these are examples of *savings,* not investment.

Using the economists' definitions of savings and investment, we can build a simple model of the market for loanable funds. The supply of loanable funds comes from savings; the demand for loanable funds comes from investment.

Just as in any market, savings (supply) and investment (demand) are brought into equilibrium at the price at which the quantity supplied and the quantity demanded are equal. For sellers and buyers in the market for loanable funds:

- Saving is like *selling the right to use your money* for a time. The quantity of savings that people are willing to supply will depend on the price they receive.
- Borrowing is like *buying the right to use someone else's money*. The quantity of investment funding that people demand also will depend on the price they receive.

market for loanable funds
a market in which savers supply funds to those who want to borrow

savings
the portion of income that is not immediately spent on consumption of goods and services

investment
spending on productive inputs, such as factories, machinery, and inventories

interest rate

the price of money, typically expressed as a percentage per dollar per unit of time; for savers, it is the price received for letting a bank use money for a specified period of time; for borrowers, it is the price of using money for a specified period of time

For both savers and borrowers, the "price of money" is usually called the **interest rate**. It is typically expressed as a percentage per dollar per unit of time. Specifically:

- For savers, the interest rate is the price received for letting a bank use their money for a specified period of time.
- For borrowers, the interest rate is the price of borrowing money for a specified period of time. It is the price a lender charges a borrower for the use of funds until the loan is repaid. The interest rate determines the total amount that a borrower must pay back on a loan in addition to paying back the original amount borrowed (called the *principal*). For instance, if you take out a one-year loan of $1,000 with a 10 percent annual interest rate, you'll have to repay the $1,000 principal plus $100 ($1,000 × 0.10) in interest.[1]

Just as in any market, the intersection of the downward-sloping demand curve and the upward-sloping supply curve determines the equilibrium interest rate and quantity of loanable funds. The market for loanable funds is shown in Figure 14-1.

Why is the supply curve upward-sloping? This shape implies that the amount the population is willing to save increases as the interest rate increases. In markets for *goods and services,* the higher the price, the more people will find it profitable to supply the good. The relationship between price and quantity supplied in the market for *loanable funds* is essentially the same. The key is to realize that there is an opportunity cost of saving: Saving money means that you can't consume as much right now. People rationally calculate those trade-offs.

For example, if you save $100, you are trading off $100-worth of consumption now for the promise of getting some amount of money in the future. If the interest rate is zero, you will get just your $100 back. Some people will be willing to save even with zero interest—maybe they know they would rather consume $100 when they are retired than another $100 now. The higher the interest rate, the more people will find it worthwhile to delay their consumption in order to increase their future earnings. So, if you wouldn't save $100 in exchange for $101 a year from now, you might be willing to do it for $110. Even more people would save $100 if they were guaranteed to get $200 back in a year, and so on as the interest rate goes up.

FIGURE 14-1

The market for loanable funds

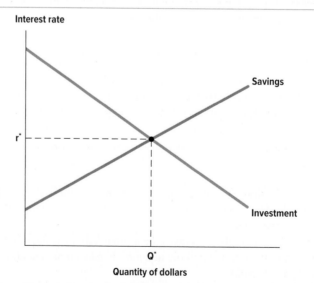

The typical market for loanable funds is at equilibrium at the point where the savings curve intersects the investment curve. From this point, one can determine the equilibrium interest rate (r*) and the amount of money traded in the market (Q*).

On the other side of the market for loanable funds, the demand curve is downward-sloping. This is because the cost of borrowing decreases as the interest rate decreases, making more and more investment opportunities worth the cost.

When deciding whether to borrow, firms or households that are contemplating an investment— say, building a factory or buying a new home—must first try to estimate the rate of return on that investment.[2] The *rate of return* describes the expected profit that the project will generate per dollar invested. The investment decision then becomes a matter of comparing benefits and costs:

- If the rate of return (the benefit of borrowing) is lower than the cost of borrowing, then the investor will lose money on net after paying back the loan. In that case, the investment probably isn't worth making.
- If the rate of return is above the interest rate, the investment will yield a profit, and it makes sense to borrow the money.

In the real world, there are a range of investment opportunities that offer different rates of return. As the interest rate rises, fewer and fewer of these opportunities will have a rate of return higher than the costs involved in borrowing, and so the quantity of loanable funds demanded will decrease. The result is the familiar downward-sloping demand curve.

Changes in the supply and demand for loanable funds

LO 14.4 List the factors that affect the supply and demand of loanable funds.

The underlying factors that determine how much people want to save and invest can change over time or differ from country to country. These determinants shift the supply and demand curves in the market for loanable funds, changing the quantity of funds supplied or demanded at any given interest rate. As a result, the equilibrium interest rate and quantity will change. In this section, we'll discuss some of the important underlying determinants of savings and investment.

Determinants of savings

Savings decisions reflect the *trade-off* people face between spending their income on consumption now and saving that money for later. The upward-sloping supply curve reflects the fact that as the interest rate increases, the value of saving relative to consuming increases. As the interest rate increases, people supply more savings.

However, factors other than the interest rate can also affect this choice. What are the underlying factors that determine how much people want to save at a given interest rate? Of course, many factors help determine individuals' choices about savings. In this chapter, however, we are concerned with factors that affect the economy on a macro level—issues that will cause the population of the country *as a whole* to want to save more or less. These factors can change over time within a country, but they can also help to explain differences across countries. The following are important factors that drive the supply of savings:

- **Wealth.** Studies show that richer households tend to save more of their income than others.
- **Current economic conditions.** When we think about how people's savings decisions respond to economic conditions, it's important to distinguish between *current* economic conditions and how current conditions might change expectations about the *future*. If expectations about the future don't change at all, then an economic downturn will generally decrease savings at a given interest rate. (That is, it will shift the supply curve for loanable funds to the left.) When times are bad and people lose jobs or have lower incomes, they will be less inclined to save and may even spend down past savings to pay for current expenses. In the recent recession, however, the savings rate actually went up. To explain this puzzle, we have to turn to . . .

- **Expectations about future economic conditions.** People often view a recession as a bad sign about how the economy will be doing in the future, as well as how it is doing at the moment. This expectation about the future can affect the savings rate: When people expect their income to be lower in the future, they will be more inclined to save, all else equal, to make sure that they have enough down the road.

- **Uncertainty.** When savers are uncertain about what the future holds, they are more likely to save extra as a precaution, just in case things turn out badly.

- **Borrowing constraints.** At any given interest rate, there will always be households and firms that would like to borrow at that interest rate but cannot. Banks and other lenders are typically willing to lend only to potential borrowers who have sufficient collateral (an asset that can be seized if the borrower is unable to pay) or sufficiently high expected incomes. When borrowing is difficult, households and firms are more likely to save to finance large purchases and investments. Borrowing constraints can change with loosening or tightening of regulations, changes in expectations about the future direction of incomes, and collateral values.

- **Social welfare policies.** Incentives to save at any given interest rate can be affected by public policies that determine the benefits people will receive if they lose their jobs, become sick or disabled, fall into poverty, or simply grow old. For instance, individuals in China may save more because they expect to bear more of the burden for their own health care and retirement costs in the future. In contrast, U.S. citizens expect to receive retirement benefits through Social Security and Medicare, reducing the need for some households to save. (Of course, tax contributions to Social Security could be thought of as forced saving for retirement—but that type of "saving" isn't counted in the savings rate.)

- **Culture.** Different cultures and traditions place varying weights on being frugal, showing your wealth through material goods, leaving an inheritance for future generations, and so on. These cultural expectations are difficult to quantify but at times help explain differing savings rates across countries.

A change in the underlying determinants of savings will shift the supply curve in the market for loanable funds. Imagine a change that makes people want to save less at any given interest rate. For instance, suppose people become more optimistic that the economy will be doing well over the next decade. Because they feel more confident that they will have jobs and earn plenty of money in the future, they become less concerned about saving now.

This change in expectations will shift the supply curve to the left, as shown in panel A of Figure 14-2. The equilibrium in the market for loanable funds moves up along the demand curve, to a new point with a higher interest rate and a lower quantity of funds saved and invested. In contrast, a change that increased the quantity people want to save at any given interest rate would shift the supply curve to the right, as shown in panel B of Figure 14-2. The new equilibrium would have a lower interest rate and a higher equilibrium quantity of funds saved and invested.

Diving further into the relationship between current economic conditions and expectations about future economic conditions, we can understand why average U.S. household savings rates *fell* dramatically when the economy was doing well through most of the 1980s, 1990s, and early 2000s, as shown in Figure 14-3. By 2005, households on average were hardly saving at all—the average savings rate was less than 2 percent.[3] Although we might think that good current conditions would make people willing to save more, it also made them optimistic about the future, which made them *less* inclined to save and more inclined to borrow. In addition, the strong economic times and housing boom meant that households saw an increase in their net worth, which further reduced saving. When the economy hit a big bump, the savings rate moved back up, starting in the depths of the financial crisis around 2008. This suggests that people took the recession as a negative sign about the future, and in response they saved more and borrowed less.

FIGURE 14-2

A change in the underlying determinants of saving shifts the supply curve for loanable funds

(A) Decrease in quantity of savings

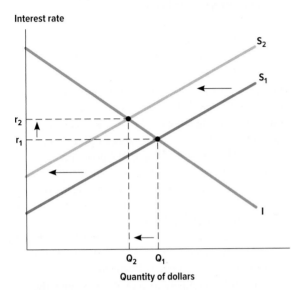

(B) Increase in quantity of savings

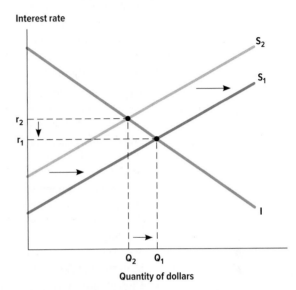

When the level of savings shifts dramatically to the left due to a change in one of the determinants of savings, the equilibrium interest rate is higher and the quantity of loanable funds in the market is lower.

When the level of savings shifts dramatically to the right due to a change in one of the determinants of savings, the equilibrium interest rate is lower and the quantity of loanable in the market is higher.

FIGURE 14-3

Savings rates in the United States since 1980 In the early 1980s, the savings rate in the United States was rather high, ranging from 8 to 10 percent. After this, the savings rate decreased steadily until it was about 2 percent in the mid-2000s. After the crash of the housing market in 2007, the savings rate jumped by about 5 percent.

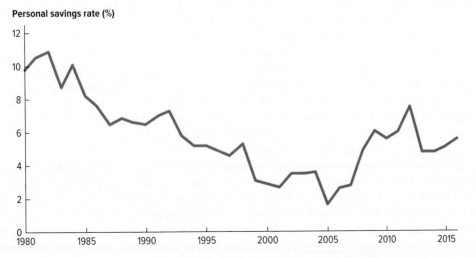

Source: Federal Reserve Bank of St. Louis, https://research.stlouisfed.org/fred2/series/PSAVERT#8eea7d87d8c09809d95.

Part 6 ■ The Financial System and Institutions

Determinants of investment

Investment decisions are based on the *trade-off* between the potential profits that could be generated by an investment and the cost of borrowing money to finance that investment. The downward-sloping demand curve in the market for loanable funds reflects the fact that as the interest rate increases, fewer and fewer potential investments will generate returns high enough to make the cost of paying back a loan worthwhile.

Just as on the supply side of the market for loanable funds, there are other factors that affect the demand for loanable funds. What underlying factors determine how much people want to invest at a given interest rate? They include:

- **Expectations about future profitability and future economic conditions.** Apart from the interest rate, the primary factor affecting the demand for loanable funds is expectations about the future profitability of investments made today. This view about future profitability usually goes hand in hand with overall expectations about future economic conditions. For example, in 2006, just before the Great Recession, the economy was booming and consumer demand was high, due in part to the thriving housing market. A booming economy can make investors eager to borrow money because they expect ventures like new companies, products, shops, and real estate developments to earn large profits. This expectation shifts the demand curve to the right, as firms want to borrow more at any given interest rate. The opposite was true once the housing market soured in late 2007. Since consumer demand was weak throughout the economy, there was little incentive to take out a loan to expand production or start a new business.

- **Uncertainty.** When investors are uncertain about the likely path of the economy, the demand for loanable funds will fall. Uncertainty especially reduces demand when it's costly to change investment strategies once fresh information arrives.

- **Changes in the government's budget deficit.** When the government borrows more, it increases the demand for loanable funds. This is simply because the total demand for loanable funds consists of both public and private demand.

These factors change the set of investment opportunities in the economy, increasing or decreasing the number of investments that are worth making at any given interest rate. For example, a change that increases the value of potential investments throughout the economy will increase the quantity of loanable funds demanded at every interest rate, shifting the whole demand curve to the right, as shown in panel A of Figure 14-4. As a result, the equilibrium will move up along the supply curve to a new point with a higher interest rate and higher equilibrium quantity of funds saved and invested. On the other hand, if investors are uncertain about the path of the economy, their desire to borrow will decrease, and this will shift the demand curve for loanable funds to the left, as shown in panel B of Figure 14-4.

Investment decisions are also affected by external forces that determine the *supply* of loanable funds and the level of the interest rate. At any given interest rate, there will be households and firms that would like to borrow at that interest rate but cannot. Banks and other lenders are typically willing to lend only to potential borrowers who have sufficient collateral or sufficiently high expected incomes. We noted above that borrowing constraints can affect saving decisions; much more directly, borrowing constraints reduce the supply of loanable funds. Borrowing constraints can change with loosening or tightening of regulations, changes in expectations about the future direction of incomes, and collateral values.

Earlier we discussed government borrowing, and how changes in the government's budget deficit can affect the demand for loanable funds. Some have suggested that when the government borrows more, it can *crowd out* private investment. **Crowding out** is the reduction in private borrowing that is caused by an increase in government borrowing. The government's increased demand for borrowing can shift the demand curve to the right, forcing up interest rates, as shown in panel A of Figure 14-4. This shift in the demand curve, in turn, increases the cost of borrowing and so reduces private investment. This kind of crowding out of private

crowding out
the reduction in private borrowing caused by an increase in government borrowing

FIGURE 14-4

A change in the underlying determinants of investment opportunities shifts the demand curve for loanable funds

(A) Increase in quantity of investment

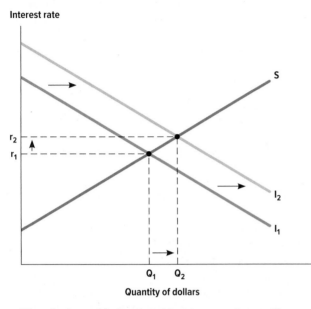

When the demand for investment increases, people are willing to invest more money at every interest rate. This takes the market for loanable funds to a new equilibrium, with higher rates and a greater quantity of loanable funds traded.

(B) Decrease in quantity of investment

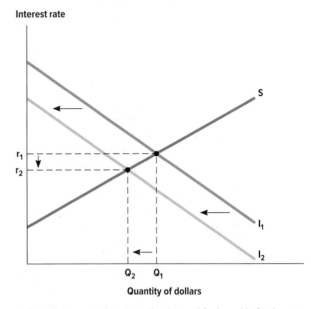

A weak economy decreases the demand for loanable funds. At every interest rate, people are less interested in making investments, fearing such investments will not work out. At this new equilibrium, the interest rate is lower, and the quantity of loanable funds traded is lower.

investment is always a fear when the government intervenes in the market. Evidence from the Great Recession suggests that crowding out was minimal then, but it is always a possibility that policy-makers need to take seriously.

A price for every borrower: A more realistic look at interest rates

LO 14.5 Understand how interest rates on loans vary with the length of the loan and the riskiness of the transaction.

The simple model of the market for loanable funds illustrates the basic relationships between supply and demand in financial markets. In reality, however, *there is no such thing as a single interest rate* that is paid by all prospective borrowers. Different borrowers pay different interest rates:

- An individual may have to pay a higher interest rate to borrow money than an established company would. Almost everyone has to pay a higher rate than the U.S. government.
- Also, the same borrower may also pay different rates on different kinds of transactions. For example, the interest rate will be less on a mortgage than on a credit card for a given individual.

How is the interest rate for a particular loan determined? Two basic factors drive differences in interest rates: length of time and degree of risk.

The first factor is the *length of time* the borrower has to repay the loan. The reason for this is not immediately obvious. Isn't a lender already being compensated for lending over a longer period by earning interest over that longer period? Only partially. Think of it this way: Lenders want to be compensated for the *opportunity cost* of being unable to get their money back quickly. When they lend money for 20 years at a fixed interest rate, they've tied up their money for that length of time; they must pass up any better investment opportunities and interest rates that could emerge in those 20 years. Since there's more uncertainty about potential future investment opportunities over a longer period of time, lenders generally want a higher interest rate to compensate them for the added opportunity cost when loans stretch over a longer period.

The second factor that drives differences in interest rates is the *riskiness* of the transaction. To understand why, ask yourself a simple question: To whom would you rather loan money—a stranger on the street or the local bank? Regardless of your answer, you probably had a simple criterion for deciding: Who was more likely to pay you back?

Lenders in the financial markets make this same calculation when they consider the likelihood that a borrower may default on a loan. A **default** happens when a borrower fails to pay back a loan according to the agreed-upon terms. If lenders think that a particular borrower might default, they will demand a higher interest rate to make it worth taking that risk.

Sometimes, loans are secured against an asset (called *collateral*), such as a house. If a borrower defaults on a mortgage loan, the lender takes ownership of the house as compensation for the loss. This explains why mortgages generally are made at a lower interest rate than credit card loans: If a mortgage borrower defaults, the lender can sell the house to get some money back (although usually not the full value of the loan). In contrast, credit cards aren't backed with valuable assets, so the lender's losses are higher if someone defaults.

The risk of a borrower defaulting on a loan is known as *credit risk*. It is measured against the **risk-free rate**—the interest rate at which one would lend if there were no risk of default. The risk-free rate is usually approximated by interest rates on U.S. government debt because the U.S. government is considered extremely unlikely to default. All other borrowers must pay higher rates to compensate lenders for the higher possibility that they will default.

The difference between the risk-free rate and the interest rate a particular investor has to pay is called the *credit spread* or *risk premium*. The difference can be quite large, both among investors and over time. The recession and financial crisis of 2007–2009, for example, caused credit spreads to rise dramatically, as borrowers of all kinds suddenly became more likely to default. Armed with data about the length of time of a loan and roughly how likely it is for the borrower to default, we can get an idea what price a particular borrower might face for a particular transaction in the market for loanable funds. In general, the longer the term of a loan and the more likely the risk of default, the higher above the risk-free rate will be the interest rate of that loan.

default
the failure of a borrower to pay back a loan according to the agreed-upon terms

risk-free rate
the interest rate at which one would lend if there were no risk of default; usually approximated by interest rates on U.S. government debt

✓CONCEPT CHECK

☐ What is another name for the price of money in the market for loanable funds? **[LO 14.3]**

☐ What are factors that can cause the supply curve to shift right in the market for loanable funds? **[LO 14.4]**

☐ In the market for loanable funds, which factors can cause the demand curve to shift right? **[LO 14.4]**

☐ Describe the factors that explain why interest rates on loans to households and firms are not all the same. **[LO 14.5]**

The Modern Financial System

Now that we've covered the basic *theory* of financial markets, we'll turn our attention to some key *realities* of the modern financial system. We've already noted that the idea of a single market for loanable funds is an oversimplification. In reality, people and firms face different interest rates based on the length and riskiness of their loans. The institutions that make up the **financial system** bring together savers, borrowers, investors, and insurers in a set of interconnected markets where people trade financial products. This section takes a more nuanced look at the role the financial system plays in helping people manage their money and risk. It also defines some of the most important types of products that are traded in the financial system and identifies the people and institutions that trade them.

financial system
the group of institutions that bring together savers, borrowers, investors, and insurers in a set of interconnected markets where people trade financial products

Functions of the financial system

> **LO 14.6** Describe why it is important for the financial system to intermediate between buyers and sellers, provide liquidity, and diversify risk.

At the beginning of the chapter, we saw how financial markets—banks, in particular—can help to fill three basic roles in the economy: *intermediating* between savers and borrowers, providing *liquidity,* and *diversifying risk.* In this section, we expand on these ideas and show how the *financial system as a whole* contributes to achieving them.

Matching up buyers and sellers: Intermediation

Imagine you want to borrow to start a small business. How are you going to get enough money together? You could go to everyone you know and ask them to lend you whatever amount they can afford. This approach won't necessarily fund your business unless you happen to know a lot of people with spare cash sitting around. But even if you managed to pull it off, the process of arranging and keeping track of all of those loans would be incredibly time-consuming and complicated.

The existence of banks lowers the *transaction costs* of the borrowing process. When banks exist, there is only one person you need to persuade to lend you the entire sum of money—the bank loan officer. This saves you—and the friends and family you'd otherwise be pestering for loans—time and money by replacing a lot of small, informal transactions with one big, professionalized one.

Various institutions act as **financial intermediaries**—they channel funds from people who have them to people who want them. A bank is one kind of intermediary. A different kind of intermediary is a stock exchange, which matches people wanting to buy ownership shares of companies with people wanting to sell those shares. This intermediation reduces transaction costs, by centralizing information about share prices and providing a broad and dynamic marketplace for transactions. The financial system offers savers and borrowers a wide set of interconnected markets in which to find financial intermediaries.

financial intermediaries
institutions that channel funds from people who have them to people who want them

Providing liquidity

A second critical function of the financial system is to provide liquidity. Earlier in the chapter, we talked informally about why people value liquidity. Formally, **liquidity** is a measure of how easily a particular asset can be converted quickly to cash without much loss of value. We say that an asset is *liquid* if it can be sold for cash quickly without much loss of value and is *illiquid* if it can't.

Consider two types of assets that many people own: cars and houses. If you needed cash quickly, which would you sell? A car is relatively easy to sell quickly. You can simply drive into a car dealership and ask the dealer to make you a cash offer. You won't get the best possible price, of course—but you'll get much of what the car is worth, in cash, right away. The house, on the other hand, is much harder to sell. You can't walk into most real estate agencies and expect a cash offer on the spot. The real estate agent will instead help you find a buyer, which can take time,

liquidity
a measure of how easily a particular asset can be converted quickly to cash without much loss of value

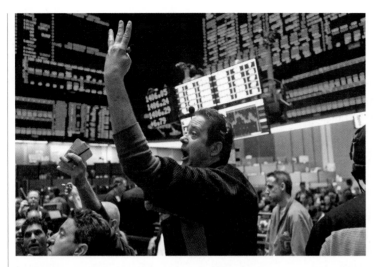

Financial intermediaries, such as the Chicago Board of Trade shown here, centralize information about prices and provide a marketplace for transactions.
© Tim Boyle/Bloomberg via Getty Images

and even then there are still mountains of paperwork and things that could go wrong.

In other words, the car is a more liquid asset than the house. Why is there such a difference in liquidity? Houses are more difficult to value and legally complex to purchase. Before you decide how much to pay for a house, you should do a thorough check of every part of it—make sure it doesn't have a leaky roof and that there aren't plans to build a waste-processing facility nearby. Cars are much easier to value. An experienced dealer can accurately size up a car from a peek under the hood. That's why there are car dealers fulfilling the role of liquidity providers but few equivalents in the real estate market. A *liquidity provider* is someone who helps make a market more liquid by being always ready to buy or sell an asset.

Various players in the financial system are liquidity providers, helping ensure that markets are liquid. The very structure of financial assets such as stocks and bonds (as we'll define and discuss below) also serves to increase liquidity. If you want to sell a share of company stock or a government bond, there is almost always someone in the financial system willing to buy it from you. Often that someone is your bank or your broker; it may also be a mutual fund or simply a large financial investor. We sometimes call these people *market makers*—they, in effect, "make a market" by being always ready to buy or sell, just like the car dealer.

Liquidity is important because it affects people's willingness to save. Savers generally want to know that their money will be there for them when they need it. If markets were not liquid, you couldn't count on being able to sell your assets quickly in order to get your money back. As a result, you'd probably be extremely cautious about lending money out for investment in the first place. That reluctance would reduce the supply of loanable funds, which would drive up interest rates, reduce the amount of investment, and lead to slower growth in the economy.

Diversifying risk

The third major role played by the financial system is that it spreads risk. Imagine that, as a saver, you could lend your money directly only to other individuals or companies. If the borrower defaulted, you would lose everything. If you lend your money to a bank, however, you know that the bank will pool your money with that of other savers and make thousands of loans to different borrowers. Some of those borrowers will default, but the bank won't lose everything at once, and neither will its savers. The bank has *diversified* the risk. **Diversification** is the process by which risks are shared among many different assets or people, reducing the impact of a particular risk on any one individual. The financial system helps share risk even more broadly than an individual bank.

Diversification is critical for the functioning of the economy. People are more willing to save money, and entrepreneurs are more willing to start new ventures, if they don't have to worry too much about the risk of losing everything.

diversification

the process by which risks are shared across many different assets or people, reducing the impact of any particular risk on any one individual

Major financial assets

LO 14.7 Differentiate between debt and equity and define the major types of assets in each category.

How does the financial system fulfill its roles of intermediation, providing liquidity, and diversifying risk? It does so by creating financial assets that can be bought and sold within the financial markets. There are far more varieties of financial assets than we could possibly cover in this text; we'll focus on just the major ones: equity, debt, and derivatives.

Equity

When you own part of a company and share in its profits, we say that you *have equity* in that company. Financial assets that represent this partial ownership are called *equities*. A "stock"—the financial asset you probably hear the most about—is the common name for an equity asset. The news media report figures from the stock market every evening, such as the Dow Jones Industrial Average, the Standard & Poor's (S&P) 500, and the Nasdaq. There even are television networks dedicated to following every move of these indexes.

What exactly are stocks? A **stock** is a financial asset that represents partial ownership of a company. If a company has issued 100,000 shares of stock, then the owner of each share (called a *shareholder* or *stockholder*) owns 1/100,000 of the company.

Why do companies issue stock? For one thing, issuing stock allows a company to raise capital without borrowing. Imagine a store owner who wants to expand her business by opening a new store but needs money to do so. She has two choices:

- She could borrow money from the bank, but she'd have to pay interest and pay back the loan even if the new store fails.
- Alternatively, the store owner may choose to sell some equity in her company. People who buy the shares of stock will become part owners of her company. As part owners, they take on the risk of losing money if the new store fails, and they expect a percentage of the profits if it succeeds.

Stock is also a mechanism for turning an illiquid asset (ownership of a company) into a liquid one (a share that can be sold on the stock market). Ownership of an entire business is not easy to sell. Just like buying a house, there are many complicated things that a potential buyer will want to understand beforehand. On the other hand, stock can be easily bought and sold in small, standardized increments on the stock market. A privately held company is an illiquid asset. In contrast, stock in *public companies*—so called because anyone can buy a share—is a liquid asset.[4]

Stockholders, as partial owners, are usually entitled to vote on certain aspects of how the company is run. They elect the board of directors, for example. Stockholders also are entitled to receive a portion of the company's profits, proportional to the size of their ownership stake, in the form of dividends. A **dividend** is a payment made periodically, typically annually or quarterly, to all shareholders of a company.

Debt

The main alternative to equity is debt. The most basic and familiar type of debt is a loan. A **loan** is an agreement in which a lender gives money to a borrower in exchange for a promise to repay the amount loaned plus an agreed-upon amount of interest. Banks make loans to individuals to make purchases like houses and cars, and they lend to businesses that want to make investments.

Making a loan is generally both less risky and less potentially rewarding than buying stock:

- A borrower might default on a loan. People who have loaned money to a company that goes bankrupt do have some protection: They have the first legal claim on that company's assets and will be paid as much as possible before stockholders earn anything.
- Buying stock in a company comes with a higher risk of losing everything if the company fails. But if the company does very well and earns huge profits, stockholders are usually entitled to a share of those profits. With a loan, no matter how successful the company gets, the lender will never receive more than the amount specified in the original loan agreements.

Like any other financial asset, loans can be bought and sold. Imagine that a bank lends you money to buy a house. You sign a contract, and you have a legal obligation to pay the loan back

stock
a financial asset that represents partial ownership of a company

dividend
a payment made periodically, typically annually or quarterly, to all shareholders of a company

loan
an agreement in which a lender gives money to a borrower in exchange for a promise to repay the amount loaned plus an agreed-upon amount of interest

at a specified interest rate by a specified date. The bank could then sell that obligation to somebody else. The buyer of the loan would pay the bank for the right to collect the money from you, according to the terms of the loan deal.

To make loans more liquid, they can be standardized into a more easily tradable asset, called a *bond*. A **bond** represents a promise by the bond issuer to repay the loan, at a specified maturity date, and to pay periodic interest at a specific percentage rate. Because of the set interest rate, bonds are often referred to as *fixed-income securities.* The owner of the bond (bondholder) is legally entitled to receive scheduled interest payments (called *coupon* payments). These coupon payment are generally paid every three or six months.[5] The bond owner also receives a final payment of the original loan amount for the bond (the *principal,* sometimes called the *face value,* of the bond) at the maturity date.

Bonds are issued in varying maturities. Corporate bonds typically have maturities of 10 to 30 years. Government bonds (issued by the U.S. Treasury, government agencies, and states and municipalities) generally range from one to 10 years. Governments and big companies often sell bonds as a way to borrow large sums of money, typically from a large number of lenders. Because bonds are standardized, it is easy for bondholders to sell them, making them a more liquid asset than regular loans.

Since a bond is essentially a loan, the basic risk-reward trade-off that applied to loans also applies to bonds: They are generally safer than stocks but also less rewarding. While returns can vary (and historical returns do not necessarily predict future returns), government bonds have historically averaged a real (inflation-adjusted) return of about 2 percent per year, while a broad index of stocks indicates a real return of nearly 7 percent per year over the same period.[6] Why might savers be interested in buying government bonds, with so much lower returns, instead of stocks? Because stocks are more risky. They can easily go down in value, whereas the government is very unlikely to default on a bond.

Wouldn't it be useful if there were a way to take nonstandard loans—say, loans to people to buy homes—and turn them into standardized, bond-like instruments that can be easily traded? It turns out there is such a process, called *securitization*. Securitization turns many loans into a single larger asset, thus reducing the risk to the lender of any individual borrower defaulting on the loan. Securitization became popular in the early 2000s. Financial assets of all types, from student loans to mortgage loans, were securitized to create liquid assets that would be appealing to a wide array of lenders. In Chapter 17, "Financial Crisis," we'll show how securitization played a starring role in the financial crisis that sparked the Great Recession and the fall of Lehman Brothers.

Despite its involvement in the financial crisis, debt is not bad when done right. As we've mentioned, debt is behind many of the transactions we take for granted. When you're able to drive off the lot with a new car, or a firm is able to build a new factory, it's likely that debt helped make those investments possible.

Derivatives

Stocks, loans, and bonds are examples of financial contracts in which one person or firm agrees to pay another a certain amount, under certain circumstances. If you get creative, you can come up with much more complex arrangements, based on the same fundamental idea. For instance, you can create a contract based on the future value of particular assets or goods, like mortgages, stocks, or the price of oil.

Financial contracts based on the value of some other asset represent a special category of financial assets, called **derivatives**. A derivative is an asset whose value is based on (or "derived from"—hence the term *derivative*) the value of another asset, such as a home loan, stock, bond, or barrel of oil.

The best example of this type of arrangement is a *futures contract.* The buyer of a futures contract agrees to pay the seller a set amount today based on the expected future price of some asset. For example, through a futures contract you could sell all or part of your farm crop in advance at

bond
a form of debt that represents a promise by the bond issuer to repay the face value of the loan, at a specified maturity date, and to pay periodic interest at a specific percentage rate

derivative
an asset whose value is based on the value of another asset

a set price. If the crop ends up being worth more than the contract price, the person you sold the futures to will be able to sell it for a profit. If prices fall, the buyer of your crop will lose out, but you will still get the contract price. In effect, you have managed your risk by transferring both good and bad risks about the future price of the crop to your contract partner. In general, derivatives are meant to transfer risk to people who are more willing to bear it.

Major players in the financial system

LO 14.8 Name the main institutions in financial markets and describe the role that each plays.

So far, we've seen the functions of the financial system and the major assets that get traded. We'll now look at four key players without whom there couldn't be a well-functioning financial system: banks and other intermediaries, savers and their proxies, entrepreneurs and businesses, and speculators.

Banks and other financial intermediaries

We've already mentioned that banks play a crucial intermediary role. Digging deeper, we can divide banks into two categories: *commercial banks* and *investment banks.*

Commercial banks are probably what you think of when someone says "bank." When you make a deposit at a bank or get a mortgage or student loan from a bank, you are interacting with a commercial bank. As well as being an intermediary between savers and borrowers, commercial banks help to create liquidity. The loans they make are relatively illiquid assets, typically taking years to be repaid.

Most savers, however, don't want their money to be tied up for years. How can banks "lend long" (make loans of long duration) while also "borrowing short" (using the money gained from deposits to make loans that allow them to be ready to give depositors their money back at short notice)? Crucially, banks assume that not all depositors will try to get their money back at once, so they keep on hand only a fraction of all deposits. If too many depositors want their cash back at once, the bank would run out of funds—a potentially disastrous situation known as a bank run. (We'll further explore the topic of fractional lending in Chapter 15, "Money and the Monetary System.")

Investment banks are part of what is commonly referred to as "Wall Street"—banks like Goldman Sachs and the now-bankrupt Lehman Brothers. These banks don't take deposits and they don't make loans in the traditional sense. Instead, they provide liquidity to financial markets by acting as market makers. They help companies issue stocks and bonds by guaranteeing to buy any that remain unsold (a process known as *underwriting*).

Most banks are either a commercial bank or an investment bank, but not both at once. This fact is due to a law passed in the 1930s, the Glass-Steagall Act, which banned banks from taking on both roles. However, Congress repealed this law in 1999, and a few of the largest banks—such as JP Morgan Chase and Bank of America—have taken on both roles simultaneously.

Savers and their proxies

Most savers don't approach financial markets directly. Instead, they operate through a *proxy*—that is, they give their money to someone else to decide whom to lend it to. These proxies include banks, mutual funds, pension funds, and life insurance companies. According to the Federal Reserve, by 2016 U.S. mutual fund companies held $13 trillion in assets, while life insurance and private pension companies held $15 trillion in assets.[7] (Remember that in economic terminology, buying assets like stocks and bonds is a form of savings, not "investing.")

A **mutual fund** is a portfolio of stocks, bonds, and other assets managed by a professional who makes decisions on behalf of clients. Savers entrust their money to mutual funds to save themselves the hassle of researching the thousands of stocks and bonds they could buy; instead, they let a professional make the decisions.

mutual fund
a portfolio of stocks, bonds, and other assets managed by a professional who makes decisions on behalf of clients

There are many different types of mutual funds. Two popular types are specialized funds and index funds:

- Managers of *specialized funds* try to beat the performance of the market by researching specific companies and picking stocks they believe will earn higher returns than the market average.
- *Index funds* buy all the stocks represented in a broad market like the Standard & Poor's (S&P) 500, with the goal of mirroring the same average return as the market.

Mutual funds charge a fee for their services that can be as little as a tenth of a percent of assets (such as with a simple index fund) or as much as 3 or 4 percent (in the case of a fund that spends a lot on stock research).

Pension funds are also a major outlet for individual savings. Usually linked to one's employer, a **pension fund** is a professionally managed portfolio of assets intended to provide income to retirees. Two main categories of pension funds exist:

pension fund
a professionally managed portfolio of assets intended to provide income to retirees

- *Defined-benefit* plans guarantee a fixed payout to employees who have met certain entry requirements, such as working a certain number of years with the company.
- *Defined-contribution* plans do not guarantee retirees a defined level of pension. Employees pay in a certain (defined) amount each year and their employers may match some portion of that contribution; the fund provides payouts that depend on how the stock market performs. The most common defined-contribution plan is the *401(k) plan,* in which contributions grow tax-deferred until they are withdrawn.

In the past, defined-benefit plans were the norm. Today, defined-contribution plans such as 401(k)s are much more common.

Life insurance policies are also a significant form of savings. The savings people put into these policies are called *premiums,* and as with mutual funds and pension funds, a professional decides how to use them in financial markets. Unlike mutual funds (from which you can take money out at any time) and pension funds (which you can access when you retire), life insurance policies pay out to your dependents only when you die.

These three proxies—mutual funds, pension funds, and life insurance policies—are by no means the only ways in which individuals can entrust their savings to a third-party manager. Other options include hedge funds, private-equity firms, and venture-capital funds. Still, surprisingly enough, the simplest approach may be the best, as outlined in the Real Life box "The incredible index fund."

Real Life
The incredible index fund

Entire TV networks dedicate their efforts to reporting the rise and fall of asset prices, from stocks to the price of gold. Bookstores are filled with advice on playing the stock market. If you're lucky enough to have money to put in the stock market, how can you make sense of this noisy information and find a way to outperform the market?

Maybe you shouldn't even try. Many savers have embraced *index funds,* such as the pioneering Vanguard Index Fund. Index funds, now offered by a wide range of financial companies, attempt to replicate the exact movements of a given stock market index such as the S&P 500, which is comprised of stocks in 500 leading companies.

Index funds have a big advantage over traditional, actively managed mutual funds: They cost much less to maintain. One reason for their lower costs is that index funds don't need to employ highly paid asset managers to research which stocks have the highest probability of "beating the market." Instead, the goal is to simply mimic the market average.

A second benefit of index funds is that they minimize the capital gains taxes that are owed when stocks are bought or sold. This occurs because the stocks that comprise an index like the S&P 500 don't change much, so there is much less buying and selling of stocks.

Perhaps you've spotted the most common objection to index funds: Professional fund managers point out that since index funds attempt to duplicate the exact movements of what is essentially the *average* performance of the market, they can miss out on large returns earned by specific subsets of the market. In the dot-com boom during the late 1990s, for example, the returns for some mutual funds that specialized in up-and-coming technological firms far outstripped the returns for index funds.

Who's right? Over the five-year period after it was created, the Vanguard Index Fund beat the returns of over 90 percent of actively managed mutual funds.

Sources: Richard A. Ferri, *All about Index Funds: The Easy Way to Get Started,* 2nd ed. (New York: McGraw-Hill Education, 2007); http://www.fool.com/mutualfunds/indexfunds/indexfunds01.htm.

Entrepreneurs and businesses

Entrepreneurs and businesses also are major players in financial markets because they are often looking to borrow money to finance their latest ventures. Strictly speaking, these are the people who engage in economic investment, often with the advice of specialized investment banks that channel savers' money to them. Without these borrowers, much of the financial system would simply cease to exist.

Speculators

The last group of major players in the financial system is speculators, who play a unique and controversial role in the financial system. A *speculator* is anyone who buys and sells financial assets purely for financial gain. You may ask what's controversial about that—aren't the other three key players we've considered (intermediaries, savers, and entrepreneurs) also out for financial gain? Yes, but what sets speculators apart is that they are neither a "natural" buyer nor a seller but are willing to play either role in an effort to make a profit.

There is fierce debate over whether speculators are good for the health of the financial markets, as summarized in the What Do You Think? box "Are speculators a good influence on markets?"

What Do You Think?
Are speculators a good influence on markets?

From 2006 to 2008, prices of many staple commodities, such as wheat and corn, practically doubled. The sharp increase in food prices was caused in part by the combination of a decrease in supply due to poor harvests and an increase in demand from people actually intending to eat the food.

However, some say that this combination of events does not explain all of the increase in commodity prices. Instead, they say prices were pushed up by increased demand from speculators, who saw the opportunity to profit by buying food and then selling it again at a higher price. Pope Benedict XVI, former leader of the Catholic Church, gave voice to a number of critics when he asked, "How can we be silent before the fact that food has become an object of speculation, or tied to happenings in a financial market that, lacking any certain rules and devoid of moral principles, appears to be still rooted to the sole object of profit?"

(continued)

How might speculators defend themselves against such comments? The main argument in favor of speculators is their role in price discovery—that is, they help markets to find the "correct" price for an asset, reflecting all available information. What might the price of wheat be six months from now? Because speculators are trying to earn a profit, they will spend huge amounts of research energy on understanding every nuance of this kind of question. Their goal is to figure out if they should be buying or selling wheat futures at the current price. Many believe that this is a valuable service, saving wheat farmers, bakeries, and grocery stores from needing to do this research themselves. Instead, they can be confident that the market price already reflects the best information available.

Others believe, however, that speculation actually has the opposite effect. They say that it causes prices to swing wildly away from the "correct" levels. Such swings magnify small fluctuations in the market and create potentially destabilizing bubbles and busts. Consider the housing boom of 2000–2007, which was driven in part by speculators buying houses in expectation that the price of real estate would continue going up. Critics argue that something similar happened with the prices of corn and wheat: Speculators bid up the prices because they expected the price to continue to go up, creating a self-fulfilling prophecy.

This sounds like a puzzle. If speculators research the market thoroughly, wouldn't they realize that wheat was overpriced and want to sell, thereby returning wheat to its correct price? Some say that's what happens. Others believe that speculators might still want to buy overpriced wheat today, if they're confident that the wheat will be even more overpriced tomorrow, and that they'll be able to sell again for a profit before the inevitable crash comes. The "correct" price will be found in the end, but perhaps only after a period of hysteria and a lot of damage to consumers and savers.

WHAT DO YOU THINK?

1. What benefits can speculators provide through their participation in financial markets?
2. Do you think speculators' incentives to discover the "correct" price for a good are aligned with those of "natural" savers and borrowers like farmers and customers? Why might their incentives sometimes be different from those of other players in financial markets?
3. Do you agree with the Pope that there are moral issues that go beyond economics involved in speculation in food prices? Why or why not?

Source: http://www.nytimes.com/2008/04/10/opinion/10thu1.html.

✓ CONCEPT CHECK

☐ Why is it important that the financial system provides liquidity? **[LO 14.6]**
☐ Which type of financial asset is included in the Dow Jones Industrial Average? **[LO 14.7]**
☐ Why would an investor wish to diversify his or her financial investments? **[LO 14.7]**
☐ What are the two different types of banks? **[LO 14.8]**
☐ What is a pension fund? **[LO 14.8]**

Valuing Assets

We've touched on one particular question a few times so far: *How do buyers and sellers in the market for financial assets reach agreement on the correct price?* We've already looked at how businesses balance the expected rate of return on an investment with the cost of borrowing. How do the suppliers of funds—that is, savers—decide whether to deposit money in a bank or to purchase stocks or bonds? And if they choose to purchase stocks or bonds, how do they decide what to buy? In this section, we'll explore some of the basic principles of *asset valuation,* which help savers make these decisions.

The trade-off between risk and return

LO 14.9 Explain the trade-off between risk and return in financial assets and describe how risk can be measured.

The basic trade-off in valuing any asset is between risk and return: If you face a high risk of losing your money, you're going to want the chance of a high return to make it worth taking that risk.

Figure 14-5 shows the historical risk and return profile for various major financial assets. As you can see:

- Cash and bond investments (both fixed-income and inflation-adjusted) are on the low-risk, low-return end of the spectrum.
- Stocks ("equities" of various types) are on the high end of the spectrum, both carrying a hefty amount of risk but generally also providing larger returns.

Different individuals have different appetites for risk: Some savers may prefer to keep their money in low-risk bonds. Speculators enjoy chasing high rewards at the risk of losing everything.

Diversification, market risk, and idiosyncratic risk

One way to manage risk is to hold assets like cash and fixed-income bonds that have low risk, but low return. Another way to manage risk but improve return is through diversification:

- If you put all your money in one company's stock and that company goes bankrupt, you've lost everything.
- If you buy stock in many companies, especially those in different industries, they're unlikely all to go bankrupt at the same time.

FIGURE 14-5

Risk and reward of various financial assets There is clearly a strong correlation between the expected risk and expected return in financial assets. Assets such as cash and fixed-income bonds carry very low risk and reward. At the upper end of the scale, financial assets in developing countries carry a return that is high, but they also are quite risky.

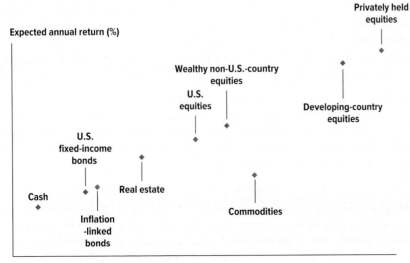

Source: http://www.nepc.com/writable/research_articles/file/2010_03_risk_parity.pdf/.

A *portfolio*—a collection or group of many different assets—will often have a higher return for a given level of risk than any individual asset could offer. To better understand how diversification works, let's look at two different types of risk that exist with financial assets.

First, **market risk**, also called *systemic risk,* refers to any risk that is broadly shared by the entire market or economy. An example would be the risk of unexpected inflation. Of course, some businesses will be more affected than others by unexpected inflation, but all businesses will face the consequences of the rising prices.

For this reason, market risk is harder to eliminate via diversification. For the case of unexpected inflation, one strategy to eliminate some of the risk is to buy inflation-linked bonds issued by the U.S. Treasury. The return to these bonds varies with inflation, so they hold their value even when prices rise without warning.

In contrast, **idiosyncratic risk** is unique to a particular company or asset. For example, the risk that a particular company will make a bad business decision, causing the value of its stock to fall, is idiosyncratic to that company. Idiosyncratic risks are the easiest to lower or even eliminate via diversification. If you buy stock in many different companies, it's unlikely that they're all going to fail at the same time.

A portfolio composed of many stocks succeeds in diversifying away idiosyncratic risks. As more stocks are added to the portfolio, idiosyncratic risk goes down without reducing the expected performance of the portfolio. Index funds are the natural extreme of diversifying to eliminate idiosyncratic risk: By investing in essentially all the stocks in the market, index funds achieve a very high level of diversification and face little to no idiosyncratic risk. A certain amount of market risk, just from having money in the financial market, remains in all portfolios and cannot be diversified away.

market (systemic) risk any risk that is broadly shared by the entire market or economy; also called *systemic risk*

idiosyncratic risk any risk that is unique to a particular company or asset

standard deviation a measure of how spread out a set of numbers is

Measuring risk

How is risk measured? The most commonly used measure of risk in financial markets is a simple tool borrowed from statistics: the standard deviation. The **standard deviation** is a measure of how spread out a set of numbers is.

In financial markets, the simplest way to measure risk is to look at the standard deviation of an asset's return over time. That means that we keep track of how much money it makes each day or month or year, and then measure how widely these numbers differ from period to period. For example:

- The stock market has historically returned about 7 percent per year after inflation *on average,* but the actual returns in a *particular* year have ranged anywhere from −80 percent to +120 percent. A 20–30 percent increase or decrease in any given year would not be particularly surprising.
- Government bonds, on the other hand, have historically gained about 2–3 percent per year after inflation on average. Rarely have they experienced more than a 10 percent gain or loss.

In other words, government bonds have a much smaller standard deviation—meaning they have much less risk than the stock market. Those historical figures don't necessarily give a good prediction of average levels of future stock prices, but they do show the bigger point: Higher average returns usually come with substantially higher risk.

Predicting returns: The efficient-market hypothesis

LO 14.10 Give arguments for and against the assumption that markets are efficient.

Imagine you were asked to pick the stock most likely to go up in value over the next year. How would you do it? There are three basic approaches you could take.

The first approach is through *fundamental analysis,* which involves trying to predict how much profit a company will make in the future and using that as a basis for calculating how much the company is worth now. Fundamental analysis is a fancy way of describing extensive research on an individual company: poring over financial statements, studying how the company is run, understanding the industry the company is in and who its competitors are, and so on. Specialized investment funds often employ hundreds of analysts to do such research.

Once we have a prediction of future profits, we can use interest rates to translate between the *present value* and *future value* of money. If you estimate the future value of the profits the company will make, you can translate it into the company's **net present value** (often abbreviated as NPV). Net present value is a measure of the current value of a stream of cash flows expected in the future. This tells you the "correct" price of shares in the company.

The second approach is called *technical analysis.* It ignores any attempt to predict future profits or calculate NPV or indeed to learn anything whatsoever about the stock in question. Instead you analyze the *past* movements of a stock's price to try to predict future movements; you look for patterns in the data that could point to what's going to happen next. This method is usually done with the help of highly sophisticated computer software.

This is all pretty hard work. Is there an easier way? Well, yes. Here's the third approach: Make a list of all the stocks, pin it to a wall, and throw a dart at it. Wherever it lands, that's your choice. This doesn't sound like a great plan, does it? But if many academic researchers in the finance world are right, this approach is often just as good as either of the first two approaches, as well as being a whole lot cheaper, quicker, and simpler.

The idea underlying this third approach is called the **efficient-market hypothesis**. It states that market prices always incorporate *all available information,* and therefore they represent true value as correctly as is possible. Both fundamental and technical analysis are ways of trying to outsmart the market; they work only if you find a stock whose current price is either higher or lower than the "correct" price. The efficient-market hypothesis (EMH) implies that finding incorrectly priced stocks is impossible. If prices already represent the best-possible information about the true value of a stock, then all stocks are already correctly priced, and so there is no additional information you can use to predict which stocks will gain value.

The intuition behind this idea is pretty straightforward. Imagine that careful observers of the stock market have information that a particular company will announce high profits tomorrow. Such an announcement generally causes a stock's price to rise, so it makes sense to buy the stock today in the hope of selling at a profit tomorrow. The effect is to drive up the price of the stock today, until it reaches the price expected for tomorrow. The expectation of tomorrow's announcement is now *priced in.*

So what will happen to the stock's price tomorrow? According to the efficient-market hypothesis, the stock's expected movements might go in any direction—described as a *random walk.* Any attempt to predict the price of the stock tomorrow is foolish: If there were any credible information out there that suggested the stock would go up or down, then the stock would already have priced it in. This brings us back to our dart-throwing plan: If you can't possibly predict stock returns, you might as well just pin a list of stocks on the wall and throw darts at them.

Not surprisingly, the efficient-market hypothesis isn't popular with the Wall Street brokers and analysts who are paid handsomely for their attempts to pick winning stocks. They argue that some analysts simply have better information than others or at least a better ability to put together all the complex pieces.

However, the number of people who have consistently outsmarted the markets over a long period is vanishingly small. The efficient-market hypothesis is exactly the reason why we should not be surprised that index funds consistently outperform actively managed funds. Neither type of fund beats the market on average, but actively managed funds charge higher fees that erode their net rates of return.

One argument against the efficient-market hypothesis is that occasionally the same financial asset can be traded at different prices in different markets. That's evidence that the market isn't

net present value (NPV)
a measure of the current value of a stream of cash flows expected in the future

efficient-market hypothesis
the idea that market prices always incorporate all available information, and therefore represent true value as correctly as is possible

arbitrage

the process of taking advantage of market inefficiencies to earn profits

efficiently using all its information. If you can manage to simultaneously sell that asset in one place while buying it in another, you can make a risk-free profit. The process of taking advantage of market inefficiencies to earn profits is called **arbitrage**. Some fund managers specialize in scouring different markets in search of arbitrage opportunities. However, it takes a huge amount of effort to spot these opportunities, and if you get the timing even slightly wrong, you can end up losing a lot of money. Given what we know about risk and reward, though, if you get the timing right, you can reap big rewards.

Bubbles

According to the efficient-market view, markets are rational, in the sense that asset prices incorporate all relevant information at any given point in time. There are times, however, when asset prices rise far above historically justified levels and then subsequently collapse, a phenomenon known as a *bubble*.

One of the earliest examples of a bubble was the Dutch Tulip Mania of 1634–1637. At the top of that market, a single tulip sold for as much as a house. More recent examples include the stock-market boom in the 1920s, the Internet bubble in the late 1990s, and the housing bubble that ended with the onset of the global financial crisis of 2009. (See Chapter 17, "Financial Crisis," for further discussion of some famous bubbles.)

What exactly is a bubble? Robert Shiller, one of the leading scholars in behavioral finance and a Nobel laureate, described a bubble as:

> [a] situation in which news of price increases spurs investor enthusiasm, which spreads by psychological contagion from person to person, in the process amplifying stories that might justify the price increase. This attracts a larger and larger class of investors, who, despite doubts about the real value of the investment, are drawn to it partly through envy of others' successes and partly through a gambler's excitement.[8]

Thus, bubbles in asset prices can be seen as social epidemics, in which the excitement surrounding rapidly growing asset prices infects people with a "bug" to buy in the hope of selling at ever higher prices. Since this process can't continue indefinitely, bubbles will eventually pop and prices will plummet, often causing severe economic damage in the process.

✓CONCEPT CHECK

☐ What is the general relationship between risk and return in financial markets? **[LO 14.9]**
☐ How does idiosyncratic risk differ from market risk? **[LO 14.9]**
☐ Is a stock that has a net present value lower than the current market price a good buy? **[LO 14.9]**
☐ What is the prediction of the efficient-market hypothesis? **[LO 14.10]**
☐ Does the possibility for arbitrage suggest that a market is efficient? **[LO 14.10]**

A National Accounts Approach to Finance

LO 14.11 Describe why savings equals investment in a closed economy and how government spending and foreign capital flows affect the saving-investment relationship.

Earlier in the chapter, we showed that when the market for loanable funds is in equilibrium, savings (supply) must equal investment (demand). This applies the microeconomic logic of market equilibrium to the financial system. We also can approach the analysis from a purely macroeconomic angle. By looking at savings and investment through the lens of the national income accounting method introduced in Chapter 7, "Measuring GDP," we can track the quantity of funds on a national level and separate out different sources of savings.

The savings-investment identity

Start by imagining a simplified economy with no government and no international trade. All transactions happen within the borders of the country, between its residents. How could the residents of our simple economy use the money they earn? They have only two possible uses for their income: They can *consume it* (spend it now) or they can *save it* (keep it for later). In other words, income is equal to the sum of consumption and savings:

EQUATION 14-1
$$\text{Income} = \text{Consumption} + \text{Savings}$$

In this simple economy, with no government or international trade, all savings are **private savings**—the savings of individuals or corporations within a country.

> **private savings**
> the savings of individuals or corporations within a country

Now, let's think about how people in this simple economy earn their income. Since there are no governments or foreign countries to interact with, they earn income only when other people in the country purchase goods or services from them. We can categorize all of these purchases as spending on *consumption* (things like meals, clothes, and cars) or as spending on *investment goods* (productive inputs like factories and machines). Income in the closed economy is equal to total spending, which is equal to consumption plus investment:

EQUATION 14-2
$$\text{Income} = \text{Consumption} + \text{Investment}$$

This result is related to the national accounts framework we developed in Chapter 7, "Measuring GDP."

Next, to relate savings to investment, we can put together Equations 14-1 and 14-2. Equation 14-1 says that consumption plus savings equals income. Equation 14-2 says that income also equals consumption plus investment. Putting the two together, we see that

$$\text{Consumption} + \text{Savings} = \text{Income} = \text{Consumption} + \text{Investment}$$

Since consumption appears on both sides of this equation, we can cancel it out and immediately see the *savings-investment identity:*

EQUATION 14-3
$$\text{Savings} = \text{Investment}$$

which is commonly written:

$$S = I$$

The savings-investment identity tells us that savings always equals investment in an economy with no government and no trade.

Private savings, public savings, and capital flows

Our simple economy is of course missing a large reality: government. When we add government to the picture, we also add taxes:

- If government takes in more through taxes than it spends, it can run budget surpluses. These government surpluses are another form of saving: The government receives income in the form of taxes and saves it by not spending it right away.

- On the other hand, if government runs a budget deficit (spending more than it takes in in taxes), it is *dissaving*. In that case, the government must borrow money from the rest of the economy in order to spend more than it collects in taxes.

> **public savings**
> the difference between government tax revenue and government spending

If we look at how much the government takes in through tax revenue and subtract what it spends, that difference is **public savings**. Mathematically, that's

EQUATION 14-4
$$\text{Public savings} = \text{Taxes} - \text{Government spending}$$

national savings
the sum of the private savings of individuals and corporations plus the public savings of the government

Adding public savings to private savings, we get **national savings**, which is the sum of the private savings of individuals and corporations plus the public savings of the government. When the government runs a deficit, national savings will be lower than private savings; the opposite is true when the government runs a surplus.

Now, there are *three* things that citizens of our simple economy could do with the income they earn: They can consume, save privately, or pay taxes to the government. We can show this by adding taxes to Equation 14-1:

EQUATION 14-5   Income = Consumption + Private savings + Taxes

There is also an additional way for citizens to earn income: They can sell goods and services to or receive benefits from the government. We can show this new income source as a variation on Equation 14-2.

EQUATION 14-6   Income = Consumption + Investment + Government spending

Just as we did before, we can put together these two ways of arriving at "income" (from Equations 14-5 and Equation 14-6):

$$\text{Income} = \text{Consumption} + \text{Private savings} + \text{Taxes} = \text{Consumption} +$$
$$\text{Investment} + \text{Government spending}$$

Canceling consumption from both sides, this reduces to

$$\text{Private savings} + \text{Taxes} = \text{Investment} + \text{Government spending}$$

Now, let's rearrange that equation to isolate investment:

EQUATION 14-7   Investment = Private savings + Taxes − Government spending

But we know (from Equation 14-4) that taxes minus government spending equals public savings. So, we can simplify further:

EQUATION 14-8   Investment = Private savings + Public savings

closed economy
an economy that does not interact with other countries' economies

open economy
an economy that interacts with other countries' economies

net capital flow
the net flow of funds invested outside of a country; specifically, the difference between capital inflows (investment financed by savings from another country) and capital outflows (domestic savings invested abroad)

And we know that national savings equals private savings plus public savings. Therefore,

$$\text{Investment} = \text{National savings}$$

In other words, national savings are equal to the total investment in the economy.

Note that we are still assuming no international trade. The identity between national savings and investment holds only in a **closed economy**—an economy that does not interact with other countries' economies.

The final piece of real-world complexity we need to add to our model is opening it up to international interactions. This is called an **open economy**. When money is allowed to move freely across borders, two different types of international financial transactions can happen:

- A *capital outflow* occurs when the money saved *domestically* (within the home country) is invested in another country.
- Conversely, a *capital inflow* occurs when savings from another country finance domestic investment.

The difference between capital inflows and capital outflows is **net capital flow**. A net capital inflow occurs in countries where investment is higher than national savings. In the opposite case, when national savings are higher than domestic investment, there is a net capital outflow.

For an *open* economy, national savings can be more or less than investment. But for the *global economy as a whole,* savings must be equal to investment. This means that any excess savings in one country have to be soaked up as investment elsewhere. In the From Another Angle box "Savings glut?" we evaluate this possibility in practice.

From Another Angle

Savings glut?

As children, we were often reminded of the virtue of saving. Many of us dutifully put our allowances in piggy banks, looking forward to blowing it all on a bigger and better toy or treat down the road.

For the past decade, though, people in the United States haven't been saving much. The government has, for the most part, run large deficits. Households save only a small percentage of their income on average. Many actually spend more than they earn, financing the difference by credit cards and loans. In addition, the country has long been running a sizable *current-account deficit,* meaning that it imports far more than it exports. All of these patterns suggest that people in the United States are spending way too much.

But could the problem be that other countries are *saving* way too much? This hypothesis, called the *global savings glut,* ties recent U.S. economic ills to high savings rates in Asia and Latin America.

When economies are open to cross-border capital flows, savings no longer have to equal investment within a given country. It's possible for a nation to save more than its firms and individuals want to invest. When that happens, these excess funds end up searching for the best returns in other investments around the world. Most of these funds end up in the United States, largely because it is seen as a safe place to invest. In fact, economist Kenneth Rogoff estimated that in 2007, a full two-thirds of excess savings in the world ended up invested in the United States.

This represents a huge sum of money. In the years before the 2007 financial crisis, net capital inflows—the amount of money coming in minus the amount the United States invested around the world—were around 6 percent of U.S. GDP. Ben Bernanke, the Federal Reserve chair at the time, argued that this large inflow of money kept interest rates low, which translated to cheap borrowing for Americans. Cheap borrowing enabled the housing boom during the mid-2000s, when people borrowed heavily to buy houses they wouldn't have been able to afford at higher interest rates.

Could the U.S. housing bubble really have been caused in part by industrious savers in Asia and Latin America? It seems hard to believe, but it's possible that this played a role.

Sources: http://www.federalreserve.gov/newsevents/speech/bernanke20110218a.htm; Kenneth Rogoff, "Betting with the House's Money," *The Guardian,* February 7, 2007, http://www.guardian.co.uk/commentisfree/2007/feb/07/bettingwiththehousesmoney.

✓CONCEPT CHECK

☐ What are the components of national savings? **[LO 14.11]**

☐ What is it called when the amount of capital leaving a country is greater than the amount going in? **[LO 14.11]**

Conclusion

In this chapter we've explored the basic framework of financial markets and the financial system: how buyers find sellers, how interest rates set the price of borrowing and the return on lending, and how the various players interact. We've also learned about a few of the major financial-asset classes and explored some of the ways that investors attempt to evaluate the risk and return potential of their investments.

You've seen that financial markets mostly operate like other markets. However, financial markets can sometimes behave in mysterious and opaque ways. We'll see more examples in Chapter 17, "Financial Crisis."

Now that we've covered the basics of how financial markets and the financial system work, it's time to look at the bigger picture: how the financial system fits into the overall economy. In the next chapter, we'll look at the origins of money and how the modern financial system is responsible for both creating and destroying money. We'll also learn about the people who oversee much of the financial system, including influencing the money supply, and how their actions affect economic growth in ways both enormous and subtle.

Key Terms

financial market, p. 361

information assymetry, p. 362

adverse selection, p. 362

moral hazard, p. 362

market for loanable funds, p. 365

savings, p. 365

investment, p. 365

interest rate, p. 366

crowding out, p. 370

default, p. 372

risk-free rate, p. 372

financial system, p. 373

financial intermediaries, p. 373

liquidity, p. 373

diversification, p. 374

stock, p. 375

dividend, p. 375

loan, p. 375

bond, p. 376

derivative, p. 376

mutual fund, p. 377

pension fund, p. 378

market (systemic) risk, p. 382

idiosyncratic risk, p. 382

standard deviation, p. 382

net present value (NPV), p. 383

efficient-market hypothesis, p. 383

arbitrage, p. 384

private savings, p. 385

public savings, p. 385

national savings, p. 386

closed economy, p. 386

open economy, p. 386

net capital flow, p. 386

Summary

LO 14.1 Define a financial market and describe the information asymmetry problems that can occur in them.

A *financial market* is one in which people trade future claims on funds or goods. Financial markets help ensure that the world's wealth is channeled to the individuals and organizations that can most effectively take advantage of it. A well-functioning financial market matches buyers and sellers as efficiently and effectively as possible. In financial markets, buyers are people who want to spend money on something of value right now but don't have cash on hand. Sellers are people who have cash on hand and are willing to let others use it, for a price.

An *information asymmetry* arises when one participant in a transaction knows more than another participant. Adverse selection and moral hazard are two types of information asymmetry problems of financial markets.

Adverse selection refers to a state that occurs when buyers and sellers have different information about the quality of a good or the riskiness of a situation, and this asymmetric information results in failure to complete transactions that would have been possible if both sides had the same information. *Moral hazard* refers to people's tendency, after a transaction takes place, to behave in a riskier way or to renege on contracts when they do not face the full consequences of their actions.

LO 14.2 Discuss the three main functions of financial markets.

Financial markets—including banks, which are one example—serve three main functions. First, they act as *intermediaries,* bringing together savers and borrowers in an easy, one-stop clearinghouse. Second, they provide the benefits of *liquidity*—having cash easily available when you want it—without the downsides of holding cash. Third, they help savers to *diversify risk* by providing funds to a big pool of borrowers. No individual saver will bear the full burden of a failed loan or investment.

> **LO 14.3** Describe the market for loanable funds, including the price of loanable funds, and differentiate between savings and investment.

The market for loanable funds is a hypothetical marketplace that brings together everyone looking to lend money (savers) and everyone looking to borrow money (anyone with investment-spending needs). The market for loanable funds clears at a price where supply and demand meet. This price is known as the *interest rate*. A key determinant of the supply curve for loanable funds is how much people decide to save. Economists differentiate between savings and investment: *Savings* is the portion of income that is not immediately spent on consumption, whereas *investment* is spending on productive inputs.

> **LO 14.4** List the factors that affect the supply and demand of loanable funds.

Many factors influence the supply and demand curves for loanable funds. Factors that determine how much people save include wealth, current economic conditions, expectations about future economic conditions, borrowing constraints, social welfare policies, and culture. Factors that determine investment decisions include expectations about future profitability and future economic conditions, borrowing constraints, and crowding out (reduction in private borrowing that is caused by an increase in government borrowing).

> **LO 14.5** Understand how interest rates on loans vary with the length of the loan and the riskiness of the transaction.

Two basic factors drive differences in interest rates: length of time and degree of risk. Lenders generally want a higher interest rate to compensate for the added opportunity cost when loans stretch over a long period and for taking on additional risk. The interest rate at which one would lend if there were no risk of default is the *risk-free rate* (generally approximated by interest rates on U.S. government debt). In the market for loanable funds, loans with longer terms and higher risks of default will have interest rates further above the risk-free rate.

> **LO 14.6** Describe why it is important for the financial system to intermediate between buyers and sellers, provide liquidity, and diversify risk.

Financial systems provide features similar to financial markets: intermediating between savers and borrowers,

providing liquidity, and diversifying risk. In financial systems, various institutions act as *financial intermediaries,* channeling funds from people who have them to people who want them. Intermediation in financial systems reduces transaction costs by centralizing information about prices and providing a broad and dynamic marketplace for transactions. Various players in the financial system are liquidity providers, helping ensure that markets are liquid. Some of these we even call *market makers* because they are always ready to buy or sell assets. The very structure of financial assets such as stocks and bonds also serves to increase liquidity. Liquidity is important because it affects people's willingness to save. Finally, the financial system spreads risk even more broadly than a financial market does: Savers can diversify into different savings products and across geographic areas; borrowers have access to loans from the funds provided by many more savers.

> **LO 14.7** Differentiate between debt and equity and define the major types of assets in each category.

The major types of financial assets are debt and equity. *Equity* is ownership in a company, and the most common form of such ownership is *stock*. As partial owners, stockholders are entitled to receive a portion of a company's profits, in the form of dividends, in proportion to the size of their ownership.

The most basic type of debt is a *loan*. *Loans* are an agreement between a lender and a borrower in which the lender lends money to the borrower in exchange for a promise to repay the amount loaned (the *principal* of the loan) plus an agreed-upon amount of interest. A *bond* is a loan that has been standardized into a more easily tradable and liquid asset. Bonds are a type of debt issued by corporations or governments as a way to borrow large sums of money. Stocks and bonds are liquid assets that are easily bought and sold in financial markets.

Financial contracts based on the value of some other asset represent a special category of financial assets, called *derivatives*. The best example of a derivative is a futures contract.

> **LO 14.8** Name the main institutions in financial markets and describe the role that each plays.

There are many different players in the financial market. There are banks, which can be divided into two categories: *commercial banks* and *investment banks*. When you make a deposit at a bank, or get a mortgage or student loan from a bank, you are interacting with a commercial bank. *Investment banks* focus on providing liquidity to the financial markets themselves, by acting as market makers, helping companies to issue stocks and bonds (a process known as *underwriting*).

Individual actors in the financial market have to operate through a *proxy*—they give their money to someone else to invest for them. These proxies include *mutual funds* (professionally managed portfolios of stocks and other assets), *pension funds* (professionally administered portfolios of assets intended to provide income to retirees), and life insurance policies (in which people pay *premiums* that pay out to dependents upon the death of the insured). Entrepreneurs and businesses are also major players in financial markets, as are speculators.

LO 14.9 Explain the trade-off between risk and return in financial assets and describe how risk can be measured.

In general, there is a direct relationship between risk and reward in the financial market. The riskier the investment, the higher its potential return. Typically, the investments with the lowest risk—and lowest return—are government bonds. Stocks are a considerably more risky investment, but also offer the possibility of higher returns. Two different types of risk exist for financial assets—*market risk* (risk that is broadly shared by the entire market) and *idiosyncratic risk* (risk unique to a particular asset or company). A *portfolio* of assets can help diversify away idiosyncratic risk; a certain amount of market risk remains in all portfolios.

In financial markets, the most commonly used method of measuring this risk is a simple tool borrowed from statistics: the standard deviation. The *standard deviation* is a measure of how far apart a set of numbers is in a distribution.

LO 14.10 Give arguments for and against the assumption that markets are efficient.

The efficient-market hypothesis holds that markets are *efficient*—that market prices incorporate all available information and, as a result, accurately predicting stock returns is impossible.

Supporters of the efficient-market hypothesis describe the expected movements of a stock as a *random walk,* a term from statistics that describes any variable (like the price of a stock) that moves in a completely unpredictable (random) way from one moment to the next. Those who argue against market efficiency suggest that some people simply have better information than others or a better ability to put all the complex pieces together to predict stock price. Occasionally markets have certain information inefficiencies that savvy investors, through *arbitrage,* can exploit to profit from the differences between prices in different markets.

LO 14.11 Describe why savings equals investment in a closed economy and how government spending and foreign capital flows affect the saving-investment relationship.

In a *closed economy,* one with no international trade, citizens can consume or save. The amount of savings within an economy is necessarily the amount of investment that can occur. Thus, savings and investment spending (the supply and demand of the financial markets) are always equal, a relationship called the *savings-investment identity.*

Review Questions

1. In financial markets, who are the sellers? Who are the buyers? **[LO 14.1]**

2. Identify the two types of information asymmetry defined in the chapter. What is the difference between them? **[LO 14.1]**

3. Explain why a country with poorly developed financial markets might have a hard time sustaining economic growth. **[LO 14.2]**

4. Is it savings or investment when Collins Inc. uses the proceeds from issuing bonds to purchase equipment needed to start a new product line? If Daisy buys some of the Collins Inc. bonds, is her purchase savings or investment? **[LO 14.3]**

5. When the real interest rate increases, what happens to the quantity of loanable funds supplied? What happens to the quantity of loanable funds demanded? **[LO 14.3]**

6. Why might a government want to encourage saving among its citizens? If the government enacts a successful policy aimed at encouraging saving, what would be the likely effect on the interest rate and the quantity of investment? **[LO 14.4]**

7. The government of a small country has enacted new regulations that make it more difficult to obtain a loan from a bank. How does this affect savings, investment, and the interest rate in the country? **[LO 14.4]**

8. Using the concept of default, explain why the interest rate on credit card debt is higher than the interest rate on a mortgage. **[LO 14.5]**

9. Your friend claims that there is no such thing as a risk-free interest rate because all loans are risky. Do you agree? Why or why not? **[LO 14.5]**

10. Is the stock exchange an example of a financial intermediary? Why or why not? **[LO 14.6]**

11. In a famous bet known as the Simon-Ehrlich wager, Paul Ehrlich bet that over the course of 10 years, the

prices of five commodities would be higher than they were at the start of the decade; Julian Simon believed the price of these goods would be lower. The loser had to pay the difference of the price from the starting point. What type of financial asset does this wager resemble? Why? **[LO 14.7]**

12. What is securitization? How did it contribute to the recent housing-market crisis? **[LO 14.7]**

13. How do economists generally define a bank? What kind of bank exemplifies this definition? Does an investment bank meet this definition? **[LO 14.8]**

14. What is an index fund, and why would a financial investor consider buying one? **[LO 14.8]**

15. Which is likely to have more risk, a government bond from a developing country or one from France? Which should have a higher return? **[LO 14.9]**

16. Define diversification and comment on how successful it is at managing market risk and idiosyncratic risk. **[LO 14.9]**

17. During the 1990s, securities related to technology and other dot-com firms experienced skyrocketing market prices, but around 2000 the market crashed. Was that crash an example that supports or offers evidence against the efficient-market hypothesis? **[LO 14.10]**

18. Describe the difference between fundamental analysis and technical analysis. Which, if any, does the efficient-market hypothesis suggest financial investors engage in? **[LO 14.10]**

19. Does the level of taxation in a closed economy have an impact on national savings? Explain. **[LO 14.11]**

20. Explain how a persistent government budget deficit can hurt a closed economy's ability to engage in economic investment. **[LO 14.11]**

Problems and Applications

1. For each scenario, indicate whether it is an example of moral hazard or adverse selection. **[LO 14.1]**

   a. You decide to buy a new car instead of a used car because you are worried about the quality of the used car.

   b. You sell your condominium because you fear there will be a large special assessment next year. There has been no official notice of an upcoming assessment.

   c. The owner of a company has just secured a new line of credit from the bank. He decides to change his business plan and open a second office in a foreign country.

   d. A firm that has purchased a large insurance policy becomes careless about setting the security alarm.

   e. A number of households find themselves owing more on their mortgages than their houses are currently worth. Some of them decide to abandon the house and walk away.

   f. The owners of a company suspect there will be more competition from foreign producers in upcoming years. They have just issued new shares of stock in their company.

2. The chapter discusses three main functions of a banking system. Classify each of the following by the function it best represents. **[LO 14.2]**

   a. Aaron can get cash out of the ATM at any time of day or night.

   b. Instead of lending all her savings out to one borrower, Barbara's bank makes the money in her savings account available to a variety of firms, with different characteristics and risk profiles, wishing to invest.

   c. When Charlie's car suddenly breaks down, he can quickly withdraw funds from his savings account to pay the mechanic and rent a car.

   d. Donna can get start-up funds for her new hair salon from a bank, instead of having to find people in her neighborhood willing to lend their extra money.

3. After graduating, you take an unusual job: consulting with the queen of a small, newly populated island in the middle of the sea. You've provided advice to her on matters related to government and the economy, and while she has taken your advice most of the time, she has so far turned down your suggestion to have a banking system. She claims that banks will make the economy more complicated and do little to make the lives of her subjects easier.

   Over the past several months, though, the queen has discussed with you several issues that have arisen in the newly formed economy. For each of the three quotes from the queen below, refer to one of the three functions of banks discussed in this chapter to explain how a banking system could help with the issue described. **[LO 14.2]**

   a. "When my subjects have money left over after spending, they want to keep it somewhere safe and earn some interest on it. But that's hard for most of them because they have no way of finding out who wants to borrow and whether it would be a good idea to lend to them."

   b. "My subjects are lucky that we have very little crime, so they can safely keep their extra money inside their houses and take only what cash they need for a day's spending. However, many of them have complained that if an emergency occurs when they're all the way on the other side of the island, they can't access their funds."

c. "Some of my subjects who are in the know about good borrowers have been making loans and earning interest. But lately there have been a couple of borrowers who defaulted on loans, and when they did, the lenders were totally out of luck. All that money just disappeared! And those bad experiences have made other potential lenders afraid, so that now borrowing and lending have dried up almost completely. If only there were some easy way for them to divide their savings among several different borrowers, they might feel safe enough to start lending again!"

4. Categorize each of the following as a type of savings or investment in the economic sense. **[LO 14.3]**

   a. You buy 100 shares of Apple Computer stock.

   b. You place part of your income in a mutual fund.

   c. A delivery service buys 1,000 new trucks.

   d. You put $1,000 in a certificate of deposit by giving money to the bank in exchange for a set amount of return.

5. Use the following words to fill in the blanks in the statements below about the market for loanable funds. *Choose from:* demanded, supplied; left, right; higher, lower. **[LO 14.4]**

   a. A change that makes people want to save less will shift the quantity of loanable funds ___ to the ___. The resulting new equilibrium in the market for loanable funds would be a ___ interest rate and a ___ quantity of funds saved and invested.

   b. A change that makes people want to save more will shift the quantity of loanable funds ___ to the ___. The resulting new equilibrium in the market for loanable funds would be a ___ interest rate and a ___ quantity of funds saved and invested.

   c. A change that makes people want to invest more will shift the quantity of loanable funds ___ to the ___. The resulting new equilibrium in the market for loanable funds would be a ___ interest rate and a ___ quantity of funds saved and invested.

   d. A change that makes people want to invest less will shift the quantity of loanable funds ___ to the ___. The resulting new equilibrium in the market for loanable funds would be a ___

interest rate and a ___ quantity of funds saved and invested.

6. Consider the market for loanable funds. Graphically illustrate the impact on the equilibrium interest rate and the equilibrium quantity of funds saved and invested in each of the following scenarios. **[LO 14.3, 14.4]**

   a. Due to slow growth in the economy, fewer workers are receiving pay increases and more workers are losing their jobs.

   b. The government decides to reduce the number of weeks a person is eligible for unemployment compensation.

   c. Numerous firms remain concerned about growth prospects in the economy.

   d. The government decides to reduce income tax rates, and this reduction leads to an increase in the size of the budget deficit.

7. You go to the bank and purchase a $1,000 certificate of deposit (CD). **[LO 14.5]**

   a. Who is doing the borrowing? Who is doing the lending?

   b. Which is higher, the interest rate paid on the 6-month CD or the 2-year CD? Why?

8. What does the risk premium measure? During a recession, what is likely to happen to the risk premium? **[LO 14.5]**

9. You have a sum of funds sitting in a savings account earning a modest interest rate of 3 percent. A good friend wants to borrow half of this sum, and he has agreed to pay you an interest rate of 5 percent. Should you lend your friend the money? Why or why not? **[LO 14.6]**

10. In your spare time, you help out with a magazine for high schoolers that focuses on current events related to economics and politics. While the magazine aims to be readable and entertaining, it also wants to use terminology correctly. Knowing that you've taken an economics class, the editor turns to you to look over a paragraph in a story focusing on the roles of saving and investment after the recent crisis in the housing market. Go through the following quotation and correct any errors in economic vocabulary, including an explanation for the editor about why the original was incorrect. **[LO 14.3, 14.6]**

    When Americans invest by buying securities such as stocks and bonds or putting money in a bank, they provide funds for firms wishing to engage in diversification by buying assets used to produce goods and services. Households with extra money left over after buying things they want or need consume by purchasing securities or putting their funds in savings accounts, and banks help transfer those funds to firms. By matching and working with these borrowers and lenders, banks act as a source of liquidity.

11. In each of following examples, name the financial product being described. **[LO 14.7]**

    a. A family borrows money to pay for a house.

    b. A new tech start-up offers investors the ability to purchase a small part of the company to raise needed capital.

    c. The U.S. government offers to pay investors a 3 percent return rate next year if they finance its debt today.

12. Evaluate each of the following statements and say whether it describes a loan, a bond, and/or a stock. **[LO 14.7]**

    a. It implies ownership in the issuing firm.

    b. Small businesses use these to raise funds for investment.

    c. This is also known as equity financing.

    d. We can think of this as a more liquid version of a loan.

    e. It pays some form of interest, and principal is paid at maturity.

13. Match each of the following players in the financial system with the financial product(s) they are most associated with. **[LO 14.8]**

    a. Commercial banks.   i. Stocks.

    b. Savers.   ii. Bonds.

    c. Investment banks.   iii. Loans.

14. Rank the following actors in financial markets by the level of liquidity they are providing. **[LO 14.8]**

    a. Entrepreneurs offering equity in their businesses.

    b. The Federal Reserve offering banks the chance to borrow short-term money through the discount window.

    c. Investment banks offering shares in mutual funds, which penalize you if you withdraw your money within 30 days.

    d. A bank offering you a no-minimum reserve requirement checking account.

15. Rank the following assets based on their expected return. Then repeat the exercise, this time ranking the assets based on their expected risk. **[LO 14.9]**

    a. Real estate.

    b. Commodities.

    c. U.S. equities (stocks).

    d. Cash.

    e. U.S. fixed-income bonds.

16. Evaluate whether the following statements are true or false. **[LO 14.9]**

    a. Risk is measured by looking at the expected value (average) of an asset's returns over time.

    b. Market risk can be minimized with a well-diversified portfolio.

    c. Idiosyncratic risk is unique to a particular asset, rather than to the market as a whole.

    d. A portfolio of well-diversified assets will often be less risky for the same level of return when compared to an individual asset.

17. "Listen," your buddy says. "Have you ever noticed that you can get the same type and size of tire for $30 cheaper in the next county over? I've got a way to make profits for years—we'll buy the tires where they're cheaper and bring them back here to sell." What is the term for the transaction your friend wants to make? Would the efficient-market hypothesis predict it will be as profitable as he says? Explain. **[LO 14.10]**

18. In each of the following examples say whether the market is behaving within the principles of the efficient-market hypothesis. **[LO 14.10]**

    a. The day after unrest in the Middle East, the source of supply for much of the world's oil, the price of oil falls.

    b. Investors find very few opportunities for arbitrage in the foreign exchange market.

    c. The Dow Jones Industrial Average, a major stock market index, changes in value by 5 percent for an entire week, even though very little economic news is released.

19. In 2015, U.S. government spending was $3.8 trillion, tax revenue was $4.5 trillion, GDP was $14.12 trillion, and total consumer spending was $10.5 trillion. If the economy has no exports or imports, what was the national savings in 2015? How much was public savings? How much was private savings? **[LO 14.11]**

20. A country's government has been running a deficit for the past few years. Suppose this country decides to increase its government spending. **[LO 14.4, 14.11]**

    a. Compare the impact of the increase in government spending in a closed economy and an open economy.

    b. Are you more likely to observe crowding out in a closed economy or an open economy? Explain.

21. Consider the U.S. market for loanable funds in a closed-economy model. Answer the following questions about each scenario. **[LO 14.4, 14.11]**

    a. The government starts offering a national savings bond to increase private savings, which pays a higher return than many other options available on the market. Which way will the supply of loanable funds curve shift? Will the interest rate increase or decrease? Will there be more or less borrowing?

b. Suppose the economy is now open. Due to rapid economic expansion in China, the Chinese government decides to invest in U.S. Treasury notes with some of its surplus. Which way will the supply curve shift?

c. A new computer software program is introduced into the market that offers businesses that purchase it promising returns on their investment. Which curve will shift? Which way will it shift?

d. The government reduces the capital gains tax, which taxes earnings on assets in the stock market. Which curve will shift? Which way will it shift?

Endnotes

1. For the moment, we are talking about the real interest rate. In Chapter 16, "Inflation," we'll talk about how the nominal interest rate can differ from the real interest rate when there is inflation; don't worry about that for now.

2. In Chapter 16, "Inflation," we will also see that there are other reasons to be concerned about *deflation,* or falling prices in an economy.

3. The savings rate is measured as the difference between disposable income and spending. The measure thus reflects how much money people put in the bank minus how much they borrow. Economists estimate that changes in how much people borrow explains much of the recent variation in the measured savings rate shown in Figure 14-3. See http://www.frbsf.org/economic-research/files/el2011-01.pdf.

4. Note that the word *public* in *public companies* indicates that ownership is open to the general public; it does not imply anything about government, as in the term *public*—government—*spending.*

5. In the past, bonds had actual coupons that bondholders would clip and return to the bond issuer in exchange for interest payments. Those coupons were quite different in purpose from the ones that people use to get price reductions on goods and services.

6. The average inflation-adjusted stock return in the 50 years between 1965 and 2015 was about 7 percent. A better measure of returns is the compound annual growth rate, which shows a gain of about 5.5 percent in the same period. If you're interested in looking further into data trends, you can try the stock market return calculator at http://www.moneychimp.com/features/market_cagr.htm.

7. https://www.federalreserve.gov/releases/z1/Current/accessible/default.htm.

8. Robert Shiller, *Irrational Exuberance,* 2nd ed. (Princeton, NJ: Princeton University Press, 2005).

Money and the Monetary System

Learning Objectives

LO 15.1 Describe the three main functions of money.

LO 15.2 Describe the characteristics that make something a good choice as money and distinguish between commodity-backed and fiat money.

LO 15.3 Explain the concept of fractional-reserve banking and the money multiplier.

LO 15.4 Describe M1 and M2.

LO 15.5 Understand the role of a central bank and discuss the idea of the Federal Reserve's dual mandate.

LO 15.6 Explain the tools the Federal Reserve uses to conduct monetary policy.

LO 15.7 Understand how monetary policy affects the prevailing interest rate and supply of money.

LO 15.8 Explain how expansionary or contractionary monetary policy influences the broader economy.

CIGARETTE MONEY

During World War II, millions of soldiers were captured and sent to prisoner-of-war (POW) camps. With no formal currency and little connection with the outside economy, the camps initially functioned with little more than an internal trading system: If a soldier had an extra bar of soap and really wanted a can of salmon, he would have to find someone who had a spare can of salmon and really wanted a bar of soap. Finding these kinds of trading possibilities sometimes worked, but it was time-consuming and inefficient.

Over time, a solution evolved: Prisoners began to use cigarettes as a common currency. A simple system of exchange with standardized prices developed: Cans of food could be bought for a set quantity of cigarettes, soap for another quantity.

Why did the prisoners start using cigarettes as money? To start with, they were a lot easier to carry around than bars of soap or cans of salmon. Unlike food, cigarettes didn't spoil. And

© Hulton Archive/Getty Images

there was a fairly stable supply. Cigarettes came into the camps in shipments of food and other supplies from the Red Cross humanitarian agency and were distributed among the prisoners.

Sometimes, though, there would be a sudden influx of cigarettes—say, if the Red Cross managed to send an extra shipment one week. Soldiers, having an abundance of cigarettes, would go on spending sprees. They would outbid each other to get the things they wanted. As you might predict, that bidding would send prices skyrocketing. Soldiers would then need a lot more cigarettes to buy a bar of soap.

But what would happen if war troubles caused the Red Cross to miss a few shipments? There would be a steady decrease in the number of cigarettes in circulation, as prisoners smoked them. Prices would plummet, and overall economic activity would fall, as trading slowed to a halt. Why would this happen? The reason is obvious if you think about it: With fewer and fewer cigarettes in circulation, and uncertainty about when the next shipment might arrive, cigarettes would become increasingly rare and valuable. This would give prisoners greater incentive to hoard rather than spend their cigarettes.

This unique system of money and trade was described by a British officer named R. A. Radford, who was captured by the Nazis and sent to a series of prisoner-of-war camps, where he remained until his rescue by Allied forces. After his return to Great Britain in 1945, Radford wrote a now-classic paper, "The Economic Organisation of a P.O.W. Camp." His paper showed that money—in whatever form it might take, even cigarettes—is an intrinsic part of any economic system.

The challenges that made World War II prisoners adopt cigarettes as their currency are the same as those faced in any economy. What is money? What functions does it serve and what problems does it solve? What makes a particular item (such as cigarettes) a good or bad choice for use as money? How does the supply of money influence the broader economy, and who controls the supply?

In this chapter, we'll see how and why money works in the economy. And we'll show how the tools of economics are being used to make sure the dollar in your pocket keeps its value.

What Is Money?

We all have an intuitive grasp of what money is—we use it every day. But what is it that separates the cash we hold in our hands from any of the other items we own that have value? Economies used to work on a system in which one person could trade a few eggs from her chicken for some milk from a neighbor's cow. Why did civilization long ago abandon that system for one based on the exchange of small pieces of precious metal? And how did sheets of printed paper come to substitute for that shiny metal and then give way to records kept in a bank's computer? To answer these questions, we'll need a more formal understanding of the functions money plays in society and what makes something good as money.

Functions of money

LO 15.1 Describe the three main functions of money.

How much money do you have? When asked that question, you might answer by counting just the cash in your wallet and maybe the amount in your bank account. You also might count the total value of your car (if you own one) or any stocks, bonds, real estate, or any other assets you may be fortunate enough to own. By most definitions, money consists only of what you typically use to buy something—which includes the cash in your wallet and the balance in your bank account, but not the stocks, bonds, real estate, car, or any other asset. More precisely, **money** is the set of all assets that are regularly used to directly purchase goods and services.

Money typically serves three major functions: it is a *store of value*, a *medium of exchange*, and a *unit of account*.

money
the set of all assets that are regularly used to directly purchase goods and services

A store of value

We say that money is a **store of value** because it represents a certain amount of purchasing power that money retains over time. To have $100 or $1,000 or $1 million is to have the ability to acquire a certain quantity of goods. Money stores value in the sense that if you put a $100 bill in a safe, you can expect to be able to purchase roughly $100 worth of goods when you take the bill out, whenever that is. The value won't be absolutely the same, of course—we'll learn more shortly about how changes in prices create changes in the value of money—but holding money is nearly always the most convenient way to hold onto wealth over time. If, by contrast, you stored all your wealth in bananas, you would lose most of that wealth quickly, as the fruit spoiled.

store of value
a certain amount of purchasing power that money retains over time

A medium of exchange

Of course, items other than money also generally store value pretty well, such as stocks and land. So we need to add to our list of money's functions its role as a **medium of exchange**—that is to say, the fact that you can use it to purchase goods and services. That is, you can make a transaction by exchanging your money for the goods or services you want to buy.

First, imagine a world without money, where the only way to acquire something you wanted would be to engage in **barter**—to directly offer a good or service (maybe your jacket or bike, or maybe the value of your labor) in exchange for some good or service you want. The reason barter is extremely inefficient is that you have to find someone who both has what you want and wants what you have.

Now add money to the world. Money makes life much easier because you need only find someone who wants what you have (say, your labor). You accept money in exchange for the labor because you are confident that, once you have money, the person who has what you want (say, groceries) will also, in turn, accept that money in exchange. There's no longer any need to find one person who fits both requirements.

Not surprisingly, an economy that uses money is dramatically more efficient than a society based on directly trading one good for another. Without money people and firms would

medium of exchange
the ability to use money to purchase goods and services

barter
directly offering a good or service in exchange for some good or service you want

have to search constantly for mutually agreeable trades. Using money reduces transaction costs immeasurably.

A unit of account

unit of account
a standard unit of
comparison

The final role of money is also important, though it is easily overlooked: Money provides a common **unit of account**—a standard unit of comparison. Imagine that you live in an economy without money and have to choose between two competing job offers:

- A farmer offers to pay you 12 big crates of eggs a week.
- A shoemaker offers weekly wages of a pair of fine leather shoes.

Which is the better option? It's hard to tell. But if one offered you $300 a week and the other offered you $400 for the same amount of work, you could easily compare the offers. By giving us a standard unit of comparison, money allows us to make more informed decisions.

What makes for good money?

LO 15.2 Describe the characteristics that make something a good choice as money and distinguish between commodity-backed and fiat money.

Now that we understand the functions played by money, we can ask a related question: What makes for good money? Economists differ on the exact answer, but two basic considerations offer a good starting point. Something makes for good money if it has *stability of value* and *convenience.*

Stability of value

We saw the importance of stability in our chapter-opening example, in which prisoners used cigarettes as a form of money. As long as shipments arrived predictably from the Red Cross, the value of a cigarette remained fairly stable. If there was either a sudden influx or a prolonged shortage of cigarettes, the functioning of the camp economy was disrupted.

Like cigarettes in the POW camp, the earliest forms of money were chosen primarily because they offered stability of value. These early versions of money generally took the form of a physical material that is durable and has *intrinsic value,* or value unrelated to its use as money. Goods that have intrinsic value will keep a more steady value; even if their value as money falls, the good is still useful to people for other reasons. Gold is the traditional example: In early societies, gold had intrinsic value because it was durable and people liked wearing it as shiny jewelry. That's still true today. The cigarettes in the chapter opener also had intrinsic value. After all, the reason the cigarettes were being shipped to the POW camp in the first place was that many soldiers smoked.

There is no reason, though, why money needs to have intrinsic value. A dollar bill has practically no intrinsic value: People don't typically eat it, smoke it, or wear it as a necklace. We accept dollar bills because we know that everyone else values them too. Wide acceptance comes largely from the fact that dollars have stable value.[1]

Convenience

How and why did we go from gold coins to dollar bills? Paper money is more *convenient.* Compared to paper money, gold coins are heavy and hard to use for small purchases. A solid gold coin weighing just one ounce would be worth over $1,300 at the time of this writing, making it hard to use to pay for a package of gum or a soda.[2]

Ultimately, as time goes on, technology allows for the development of more convenient forms of money. For an ingenious example of making money even more convenient in the developing world, read the Real Life box "Banking with a cell phone."

Real Life
Banking with a cell phone

Imagine you grew up in a small village in rural Kenya and moved to the capital city to find work. You want to send money back to your village to support your family, but how do you do it? Your village does not have a bank branch—the nearest is hours away. You could take a wad of banknotes back to the village yourself, but that would involve a long day's travel in a crowded bus. Or you could entrust the money to someone else who is traveling back to your village, but what if no one's going soon?

A Kenyan mobile phone company called Safaricom came up with a solution to this problem. It's called M-Pesa—the M stands for mobile, while *Pesa* is the local word for money. The system allows people to transfer money simply by sending a text message.

The process is amazingly simple. You go to an M-Pesa outlet (a small store usually located in the village marketplace) and deposit money into an account. This becomes your *e-float*, essentially an electronic representation of money. In this way, it's not all that different from a deposit at a traditional bank. You can then use a text message to transfer, say, $15 worth of e-float to the account of another M-Pesa user. (The transfer costs a small fee, but that's a much smaller transaction cost than the time and money of traveling back to the village.) The recipient then goes to the local M-Pesa outlet and withdraws the e-float as cash, paying another small fee.

With this ease of use, and the fact that M-Pesa outlets outnumber bank branches five to one, M-Pesa quickly became wildly popular. In 2015, M-Pesa had over 13 million active users—over 40 percent of Kenya's adult population. Annual transfers were equal to over 42 percent of Kenyan GDP. Three-quarters of M-Pesa members say they use their e-float accounts not just to transfer money but also to save money: Using an e-float account is safer than carrying cash and much more accessible than a traditional bank account. Safaricom has now introduced a product called M-Schwari that includes interest-paying savings accounts and greatly expands access to banking services in rural areas.

The system hasn't eliminated the need for cash since not everyone uses M-Pesa. Also, since there are small fees involved in sending money, sometimes it's better to use cash (depending on the amounts involved).

M-Pesa shows how new technologies can connect underserved areas and change the concept of money. Inspired by the success in Kenya, companies in over 80 countries—including the United States—are developing similar mobile banking systems.

Sources: http://siteresources.worldbank.org/AFRICAEXT/Resources/258643-1271798012256/M-PESA_Kenya. pdf; http://www.bbc.co.uk/news/business-11793290; http://www.safaricom.co.ke/personal/m-pesa/do-more-with-m-pesa/m-shwari; http://www.techweez.com/2015/05/07/ten-takeaways-safaricom-2015-results.

Commodity-backed money versus fiat money

The earliest forms of paper money could be converted at a bank into a specified amount of a named commodity. **Commodity-backed money** is any form of money—usually paper money—that can be legally exchanged into a fixed amount of an underlying commodity, generally gold.

In the United States, the dollar was commodity-backed for over 100 years, from shortly after the Civil War until 1971. Anyone who held dollar bills before 1971 could simply go to a designated "reserve bank" and exchange those dollar bills for a fixed amount of gold, whenever they wanted to. By law, the bank was required to make that exchange.

But what of the post-1971 world? If our money is no longer backed by the value of a commodity like gold, where does its value come from? What is it backed by? Well, it's backed by nothing—nothing tangible, at least. Instead, the U.S. dollar today is backed by "the full faith and credit of the United States government." In other words, the U.S. dollar has value only to the extent that people trust the U.S. government to keep using dollars and to keep their value

commodity-backed money
any form of money that can be legally exchanged into a fixed amount of an underlying commodity

fiat money

money created by rule, without any commodity to back it

roughly constant. The formal term for this type of money is **fiat money**. Fiat money is money created by rule, without any commodity to back it. (*Fiat* is a Latin term that roughly translates to "it shall be.")

When we say "to the extent that people trust the U.S. government," what exactly are we trusting it to do, or not do? Essentially, we're trusting the government to maintain a reliable system of money—in short, to not create lots of new money. Creating lots of new money would reduce the value of existing money—just as, in our chapter-opening example, an unexpectedly large shipment of cigarettes into the POW camp reduced the value of existing cigarettes.

✓CONCEPT CHECK

☐ What kind of exchange happens when people trade goods without using money? **[LO 15.1]**
☐ How are cigarettes a good example of commodity-backed money? **[LO 15.2]**
☐ What kind of money is the U.S. dollar? What kind was it 60 years ago? **[LO 15.2]**

Banks and the Money-Creation Process

We discussed how using actual gold coins in payment was eventually replaced by paper money that was backed by gold. We considered one obvious advantage of this: It's easier to carry around a piece of paper saying "10 gold coins" than it is to carry around 10 gold coins.

Here's another, less obvious, implication: Paper money made it possible for banks to *create money,* through a process called *fractional-reserve banking.* This is one of the most important, yet intuitively challenging, facts about our modern financial system. It's worth taking some time to make sure you understand it.

"Creating" money

LO 15.3 Explain the concept of fractional-reserve banking and the money multiplier.

The easiest way to understand how banks create money is to picture an economy making the transition from gold coins to paper money. To start with, imagine that you live in ancient times and all transactions are carried out using actual gold coins. How much money exists in the economy? That's an easy question to answer: It's simply the amount of gold.

Next, imagine that banking is invented, and now you're offered the chance to store your gold coins so you don't have to carry them around. When you deposit a gold coin in the bank, the bank gives you a piece of paper (a banknote) saying "one gold coin." At any time, you could go to the bank, give the bank back this piece of paper, and get a gold coin.

But you don't need to do this because merchants are happy to accept the banknote instead of the gold coin. They know that the note is as good as the coin itself. At any point they could take the note to the bank to get a coin. And people find it so much more convenient to use notes than lug around heavy gold coins.

Now put yourself in the bank's shoes (sandals): As a banker, you observe that on any given day, out of the 1,000 coins that are in your bank vault, people come in and ask for only 100 of them. The other 900 are just sitting there. Why not lend them out, charge an interest rate on these loans, and make a profit?

So, you decide to lend out the other 900 coins to people who want to use them to buy things— say, to pay workers to build a house. When the workers receive their coins as wages, the workers all decide to deposit them in the bank for safe keeping. For every coin they deposit, the bank gives them a piece of paper saying "one gold coin."

How much money is in the economy now? To answer that question, let's consider both the gold coins in the bank and the banknotes now available in the economy. As Table 15-1 shows, the bank again has 1,000 gold coins. But it has now issued 1,900 banknotes saying "one gold coin."

TABLE 15-1

Simple money-creation process

Gold coins in bank	Money (banknotes) in the economy
1,000 coins deposited in bank	1,000 banknotes issued in exchange for initial deposit
−900 coins loaned out (with 100 held in reserve)	
+900 coins that were loaned out and then deposited by workers	+900 banknotes issued in exchange for workers' deposits
1,000 coins in bank	**1,900 banknotes**

Because people are just as happy to trade banknotes as actual gold coins—and, thus, we can meaningfully consider the banknotes to be *money*—we can say that by making loans, the bank has *created money*. It has created 900 gold coins worth of money, to be exact. It did so simply by lending a portion of the money it had on deposit.

Money creation in today's economy

How does the money-creation process work in today's economy? Let's work through another simple example with the aid of some basic accounting tools.

Let's say that you walk into a bank with $1,000 in cash and you make a deposit. The bank takes your cash, puts it in a vault, and records $1,000 as your account balance. You can get your $1,000 back any time you ask the bank for it. Because of that fact, such deposits are called **demand deposits**—funds held in bank accounts that can be withdrawn ("demanded") by depositors at any time without advance notice.

From an accounting point of view, the $1,000 cash deposit represents two things for the bank:

- It is an *asset*—a resource the bank possesses.
- It also is a *liability*—an amount the bank owes. The bank owes you that amount and has promised that you can get your cash back at any time.

The primary way that banks earn money is by lending funds and collecting interest on those loans. So the bank wants to lend out as much of your $1,000 deposit as it (safely) can. As we saw in the example of the gold-coin bank, it's not necessary to keep on hand the total amount of the demand deposits. Instead, the bank decides to keep a certain amount on hand and to lend the rest. We call the cash that a bank keeps in its vault its **reserves**. In practice, modern banks keep reserves either as cash or as deposits at the Federal Reserve ("the Fed"), the U.S. government's central bank. As before, lending funds enables banks to "create" money.

The Federal Reserve requires banks to keep a certain proportion of their deposits as reserves. When expressed as an amount, it is called the **required reserves**. Of course, a bank can choose to hold more in reserves than the required minimum. Any additional amount, beyond the required reserves, that the bank chooses to keep in reserve is called **excess reserves**. As with the earlier gold-coin example, banks "create" money by lending funds not kept as reserves. When the reserve requirement is expressed as a fraction, is is called the **reserve ratio**. The reserve ratio is calculated as the amount of cash kept as reserves divided by the total amount of demand deposits. We'll assume throughout our discussion that the bank keeps a reserve ratio of 10 percent.

In the example above, we saw that the $1,000 cash deposit created both an asset and a liability for the bank. Financial accounting is based on the *basic accounting equation,* which says that assets must equal the total of liabilities plus owners' equity (the claim the owners of a firm have on assets):

$$\text{Assets} = \text{Liabilities} + \text{Owners' equity}$$

demand deposits
funds held in bank accounts that can be withdrawn ("demanded") by depositors at any time without advance notice

reserves
the money that a bank keeps on hand, either in cash or in deposits at the Federal Reserve

required reserves
the minimum fraction of deposits that banks are legally required (by the Federal Reserve) to keep on hand

excess reserves
any additional amount, beyond the required reserves, that a bank chooses to keep in reserve

reserve ratio
the fraction of deposits a bank must hold as reserves; calculated as the amount of cash kept as reserves divided by the total amount of demand deposits

Companies periodically report the balances of their assets, liabilities, and owners' equity in a financial statement called a *balance sheet*. One common form of a balance sheet is called the *account form* of the balance sheet; it mimics the accounting equation by showing assets on the left and liabilities and owners' equity on the right. We'll use that form to visualize the bank's transactions. In the example we work through here, we will assume owners' equity of zero. Thus, we will assume that for the bank, assets must equal liabilities.

Panel A of Figure 15-1 shows, in a simple account-form balance sheet format, what happens to the bank's assets and liabilities when you make a $1,000 deposit. The left-hand side shows the bank's assets—in this case, the $1,000 cash deposit. The right-hand side shows the bank's liabilities (the amount owed to you, the depositor)—in this case, the demand deposits of $1,000.

Now, let's see what happens when a new customer comes into the bank wanting to *borrow* $900—say, to purchase a new refrigerator. After completing the loan-approval process, the banker takes $900 in cash out of the vault and hands over the money to the customer as a $900 loan. Panel B of Figure 15-1 shows the bank's new situation: Because the loan is an asset for the bank, the bank still has $1,000 in assets: $100 in required cash reserves plus the loan of $900. The assets and liabilities both still total $1,000, though the composition of the assets has changed.

The bank has less actual cash on hand ($100 required reserves) than the total of its deposits ($1,000). Is this reckless on the bank's part? It's not, if you remember the thinking of our ancient bank that stored gold coins: Observing that only a small number of customers wanted to convert banknotes into coins on any given day, it was happy to keep only 10 percent of its coins in its vault and lend out the rest. In the same way, modern banks count on the fact that not all of their customers will try to withdraw cash at the same time.

Here's where things get even more interesting: The appliance store sells the refrigerator and gets paid $900 in cash. The store owner goes to the bank and deposits that amount in the store's bank account. Panel C of Figure 15-1 shows the bank's position now. It now has the following assets: the $100 required cash reserves, a loan of $900, and the new cash deposit of $900, for a total of $1,900. Demand deposits total the same amount. (The bank's assets equal its liabilities.)

FIGURE 15-1

How banks create money As the money comes in to the bank and then is lent out again, new money is created. In this example, by the time the money is lent out twice, the bank has created $1,900 from $1,000.

(A) Modern Bank

Assets		Liabilities	
Cash	$1,000	Demand deposits	$1,000
Total	$1,000	Total	$1,000

(B) Modern Bank

Assets		Liabilities	
Required reserves	$ 100	Demand deposits	$1,000
Loan	900		
Total	$1,000	Total	$1,000

(C) Modern Bank

Assets		Liabilities	
Required reserves	$ 100	Demand deposits	$1,900
Loan	900		
New cash deposit	900		
Total	$1,900	Total	$1,900

(D) Modern Bank

Assets		Liabilities	
Required reserves*	$ 190	Demand deposits	$1,900
Loans**	1,710		
Total	$1,900	Total	$1,900

*10% × $1,900
**90% × $1,900

After the new cash deposit, what happens to the required reserves? Let's say our modern bank keeps in its vault as required cash reserves 10 percent of what its customers have deposited. Experience indicates that that amount will be enough to cover day-to-day requests from its depositors for cash withdrawals.[3] With $1,900 in liabilities ($1,000 in the original deposit and the store owner's deposit of $900), the bank will now want to keep 10 percent of $1,900, or $190, required cash reserves in the vault. That means it will be happy to lend money up to the amount of $1,710 (90 percent of $1,900). The bank has already made loans of $900 and now lends another $810 to another customer in order to have lent a total of $1,710. This new situation is shown in panel D of Figure 15-1.

How far can this process continue? The bank will continue lending and taking deposits. Over time, the bank can end up creating as much as $9,000 in new loans. Why $9,000? Because you originally deposited $1,000, and the bank has to hold 10 percent of that (= $100) as required cash reserves. It then lends the rest, and eventually gets the loans back as deposits (assuming Modern Bank is the only bank in the economy).

Those deposits, in turn, create reserve requirements. By the time the bank has lent a total of $9,000, it can expect $9,000 in deposits—which creates a need for 10 percent of those deposits to be held as cash reserves too (= $900). The total sum of required cash reserves is thus $100 + $900. Thanks to your original $1,000 cash deposit, the bank has enough cash to cover that. But that's all the bank has in cash, so it can't lend more. With $9,000 in loans and $1,000 in reserves, there is no money left for new loans. Still, your original $1,000 has had quite a run: The bank has used it to create $9,000 in new money, effectively turning $1,000 into $10,000.

From one bank to an entire economy

So far, we have assumed that there's only one bank in the economy—everyone has to use that bank to borrow and save. In practice, of course, modern economies have many banks. The logic of the example still holds, though, if we think of the bank in our example as representing the *entire banking system:* The first deposit might be made into Bank of America, for example, and the next into Chase. The next might go to Citi. The key is that all money loaned out eventually gets put back into some bank within the banking system.

Let's round off our discussion with some formal terminology. In our example, the bank kept 10 percent of its deposits as reserves. If the reserve ratio were 100 percent (a situation known as *full-reserve banking*), no lending would have happened in the example. Your entire original $1,000 deposit would just sit in the bank's vault. If banks aren't lending, it would be very hard to get the money needed to buy a house or car. The entire financial system would grind to a halt.

Rarely if ever do we observe full-reserve banking. Instead, we have **fractional-reserve banking**, a banking system in which banks keep on reserve less than 100 percent of their deposits. (That is, the reserve ratio is less than 100 percent.) Fractional-reserve banking allows the bank to lend out a portion of the money deposited in the bank.

We call the ratio of money created by the lending activities of the banking system to the money created by the government's central bank the **money multiplier**. The size of the reserve determines the size of the money multiplier: As a simple approximation, we can calculate the money multiplier as $\frac{1}{R}$, where R is the reserve ratio.

fractional-reserve banking
a banking system in which banks keep on reserve less than 100 percent of their deposits

money multiplier
the ratio of money created by the lending activities of the banking system to the money created by the government's central bank

EQUATION 15-1

$$\text{Money multiplier} = \frac{1}{\text{Reserve ratio}}$$
$$= \frac{1}{R}$$

Thus, a reserve ratio of 10 percent (or, equivalently, 0.10) means the money multiplier is 10:

$$\text{Money multiplier} = \frac{1}{0.10}$$
$$= 10$$

With $1,900 in liabilities ($1,000 in the original deposit and the store owner's deposit of $900), the bank will want to keep $190 required cash reserves in the vault (10 percent of $1,900). That means it will be happy to lend money up to the amount of $1,710 (90 percent of $1,900)—the situation shown in panel D of Figure 15-1.

The bank has already made loans of $900 and now lends another $810 to another customer in order to have lent a total of $1,710. The approximation in Equation 15-1 works exactly as long as two things occur:

- People don't hold any money as cash outside the bank and
- Banks lend out as much as they can beyond what's legally required for them to hold as reserves.[4]

If either assumption fails to hold, the multiplier will be smaller than the approximation.

Ultimately, the system of fractional reserve banking is what makes possible the existence of banks as we know them. However, you may be wondering if there are big risks involved. What if too many customers turn up at the bank asking for their dollar bills at the same time? When that happens, a *bank run* occurs—the situation that arises from fear that the bank is in danger of running out of money. Read the Real Life box "Bank runs and the banking holiday" for some real-life examples.

Real Life

Bank runs and the banking holiday

In 2007, hundreds of panicked customers lined up outside branches of the British bank Northern Rock in a desperate attempt to get money out of their accounts. The media had just reported that Northern Rock had made big investments in financial products created during the U.S. housing bubble. Those investments were now nearly worthless, and the losses pushed the bank toward bankruptcy. Not surprisingly, customers suddenly wanted their money out of the bank.

British banking regulations at the time offered some protection to savers: The government pledged that customers wouldn't lose the value of their savings at Northern Rock, with a guarantee up to a limit of £35,000 (about $55,000). But many customers decided they'd prefer to withdraw their money immediately rather than risk it. About £2 billion of cash was withdrawn in just two days.

Bank runs are a problem because under a fractional-reserve system, banks don't hold enough cash to pay out more than a fraction of their depositors' money. Ironically, a bank run can *create* the very thing customers are afraid of—the bank going bust—even if their fears are unfounded. If enough customers demand their deposits back all at once, a bank will inevitably go bankrupt, no matter its initial condition.

The most important response to a bank run, therefore, is to try to reassure savers and create time for their panic to subside. During the Great Depression, in March 1933, the governor of Michigan feared that one of the largest banks in the state, the Guardian Trust Company of Detroit, was on the edge of shutting down for good. In order to keep the bank from failing, the governor took the drastic measure of stopping transactions at all of the 800 banks in the state, leaving people to get by on only the cash they had in their pockets. The move backfired. Far from quelling the panic, it only sparked greater concern. Many reasoned that if the banks could be saved only by preventing all transactions, the entire system must be in danger of collapse.

Word of bank trouble spread throughout the country, and bank runs threatened to spiral out of control, destroying people's savings and crippling the economy. In response, Congress quickly passed what became known as the "Bank Holiday," closing all banks in the country for four days (later stretched out to a week). Right before the banks were due to reopen, President Roosevelt talked to Americans through radio broadcasts known as "fireside chats" to explain what was going on. Furthermore, the Federal Reserve pledged to supply unlimited currency to banks that reopened, and so depositors essentially had 100 percent insurance on their deposits.

Amazingly, it worked. When the banks reopened, the panic had abated, and Americans replaced two-thirds of the money they had drawn out in the bank runs. The outgrowth of this holiday was the creation of the Federal Deposit Insurance Commission (FDIC) through the Glass-Steagall Act. It reassured savers that if their bank fails, the government will protect any deposit less than $100,000 (later increased to $250,000).

What happened to Northern Rock? After a second day of lines outside the bank's branches, the British government stepped in and announced that it would refund the entire value of customers' savings accounts if the bank went bust. The panic abated, and Northern Rock lived to see another day. (However, it lost so much money in the U.S. housing crash that the British government eventually had to take it over to keep it going.)

These experiences remind us that bank runs—widely thought to have been consigned to the history books—can still happen in today's economy.

Sources: http://www.nber.org/papers/w12717; https://www.bostonfed.org/-/media/Documents/education/pubs/closed.pdf.

Measuring money

LO 15.4   Describe M1 and M2.

Now that we know how money is created by the banking system, let's revisit our earlier question: How much money *is* there? If you are thinking to yourself, "That depends on what type of money you are asking about," you are exactly right. It is the job of the Federal Reserve to manage the **money supply**—the amount of money available in the economy—and the Fed provides the most common definitions of the money supply.

> **money supply**
> the amount of money available in the economy

The Fed classifies different types of money by their *liquidity*—that is, by how easy an asset is to convert immediately to cash without losing value. The most common classifications of money are the monetary base, M1, and M2:

- The **monetary base** is the sum of currency in circulation and reserves held by banks at the Federal Reserve.
- **M1** includes currency held by the public ("cash") plus checking account balances (demand deposits, which are not exactly cash but are readily accessible for most people).
- **M2** is broader still. M2 includes everything in M1 plus savings accounts and other financial instruments where money is locked away for a specified period of time. Since these forms of savings can't be accessed quickly without penalty fees, they are slightly less liquid than other forms of money. (Certificates of deposit are an example of a less-liquid form of money.)

> **monetary base**
> the sum of currency in circulation and reserves held by banks at the Federal Reserve

> **M1**
> definition of money that includes cash plus checking account balances

> **M2**
> definition of money that includes everything in M1 plus savings accounts and other financial instruments where money is locked away for a specified amount of time; less liquid than M1

All three are legitimate measures of the money supply. Which one we use depends on our goals. If we want to look at spending (liquidity), we use M1. If we want to look at savings, we would use M2. You can think of M2 as a measure of the "multiplied" money. Comparing it to the monetary base (the sum of currency and reserves) can give you some sense of what the money multiplier actually is at a given point in time.

Figure 15-2 shows that the money multiplier was relatively stable over time, until the huge change sparked by the 2008 financial crisis. At that point, the monetary base rose dramatically due to actions by the Federal Reserve to combat the financial crisis by adding to banks' reserves. But banks were nervous in the face of the crisis and reluctant to lend to others. As a result, there were relatively small increases in M1 and M2, despite the big expansion in reserves.

FIGURE 15-2

Monetary base, M1, and M2 over time

In nominal terms, all three measures of money steadily increased over this period of time, although the rate of increase of M2 sped up dramatically starting around 1995. The monetary base ("hard money") increased dramatically in 2008 as part of the effort to combat the financial crisis.

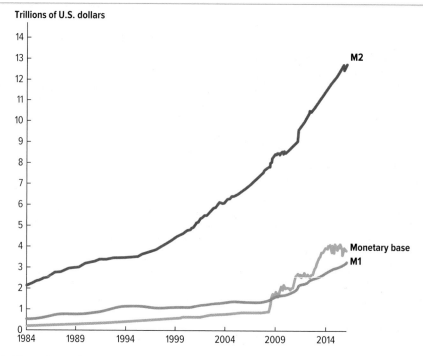

Source: Federal Reserve Economic Data, http://research.stlouisfed.org/fred2/ (accessed October 31, 2012, 2013).

At this point, you might wonder who decides how much money is going to exist. Obviously, based on our earlier discussion of money creation, the banks play a large role in M1 and M2. But who decides how much hard money there is to multiply in the first place? And who sets the required reserves ratio? We address these questions in the next section.

✓**CONCEPT CHECK**

☐ What is a reserve requirement of 100 percent called? **[LO 15.3]**

☐ How does the money multiplier create money in the economy? **[LO 15.3]**

☐ What type(s) of money includes demand deposits (amounts in checking accounts)? **[LO 15.4]**

Managing the Money Supply: The Federal Reserve

On October 24, 1907, the United States was in the middle of one of the most severe financial crises in its history. Tens of thousands of depositors were descending upon banks across the country, creating a bank run of such proportions that no one was safe. Even some of the largest banks were in jeopardy and struggling to survive day to day. In this flurry of activity, a single man took responsibility for the survival of the U.S. financial system: John Pierpont Morgan, president of J.P. Morgan & Co. and the most powerful banker of the time. With many banks already near collapse, at 1:30 P.M. on October 24th, news reached Morgan that the New York Stock Exchange was simply out of money. Even someone willing to pay 100 percent interest for a loan couldn't find a lender. Stock prices were plummeting. Absent any action, all stock on the exchange would become worthless.

With only a few hours to act, Morgan convened nearly every major figure in the U.S. financial world of the time—all of the leading bankers and industrial capitalists. Even the Secretary of the Treasury, George Cortelyou, came running to see if the most powerful banker in the country could save the U.S. economy from collapse. The system needed cash—lots of it. In the face of catastrophe, the U.S. government pitched in $25 million. John D. Rockefeller offered $10 million immediately and up to $40 million if extra funds were needed. By 2:30 P.M., Morgan had collected enough money to save the system.

The reliance on a single titan of industry to save the nation from collapse was a stark reminder that the nation was ill-prepared for crisis. Six years later, in 1913, President Woodrow Wilson signed the Federal Reserve Act into law, creating the Federal Reserve. Since then, the Fed has been the centralized institution responsible for coordinating the operations of the U.S. financial system.[5]

The role of the central bank

> **LO 15.5** Understand the role of a central bank and discuss the idea of the Federal Reserve's dual mandate.

Almost every major nation has a central bank. A **central bank** is the institution ultimately responsible for managing the nation's money supply and coordinating the banking system to ensure a sound economy. In the United States, the central bank is the Federal Reserve. Like any central bank, the Federal Reserve has two essential functions:

central bank
the institution ultimately responsible for managing the nation's money supply and coordinating the banking system to ensure a sound economy

- managing the money supply and
- acting as a lender of last resort.

Before we explain the two functions of a central bank, it may help to explain what a central bank *is not*. It is not the government's finance arm. In the United States, the financial operations of the government—collecting taxes, paying bills, issuing debt, and generally managing the nation's finances—are conducted by the Treasury Department. The Fed is responsible for deciding how much physical currency should be printed, but the printing itself is done by the Treasury Department's Bureau of Engraving and Printing. In short, the Treasury Department executes *fiscal policy,* while the Federal Reserve conducts *monetary policy.* Formally, **monetary policy** consists of actions by the central bank to manage the money supply, in pursuit of certain macroeconomic goals.

monetary policy
actions by the central bank to manage the money supply, in pursuit of certain macroeconomic goals

So, a central bank's most important function is to manage the money supply. A bit later, we'll learn more about the ways that the Fed does that. First, though, it's worth asking whether we in fact *need* a central bank to manage the money supply. Why not leave it to the private market to issue currency and control it? In principle at least, there is no reason why a privately issued currency should not gain wide acceptance. For more about one attempt to create a new currency, see the From Another Angle box "Is Bitcoin the currency of the future?"

From Another Angle

Is Bitcoin the currency of the future?

Some online communities have their own money: The simulation game Farmville 2 has "farm cash" and Second Life has "Linden dollars." Could virtual currencies ever take over from conventional currencies such as the U.S. dollar? In principle, it's a possibility. In practice, it's hard to imagine.

Think back to our discussion of what makes for good money. One of the most important features is stability of value. Why were people through the ages happy to store their wealth in

(continued)

gold? Because they thought it was unlikely that a huge new amount of gold would be discovered; such a discovery would slash the value of the gold they had. Why are people today happy to store their wealth in U.S. dollars? Because they are reasonably confident that the Fed will not suddenly decide to print trillions upon trillions of new dollar bills, thus rendering everyone's existing dollars near-worthless.

Who has the power to "print" money in virtual worlds? Ultimately, it's the people who run those worlds. Would you really be happy to hold your life savings in a virtual currency, trusting that those in charge would never decide to create huge amounts of new money? Most of us wouldn't be so brave (or, say some, so foolish).

In 2009, a mysterious programmer using the fake name Satoshi Nakamoto created a new virtual currency—Bitcoin—that proposed a solution to this problem: Nobody is in charge of the Bitcoin money supply. Instead, the supply of money increases at a rate predetermined by a mathematical algorithm.

In its early days, the value of a Bitcoin was a tiny fraction of a cent. Users of Bitcoins were a small community of computer enthusiasts. The first real-world purchase was made, for fun, by a Florida programmer named Laszlo Hanyecz, who paid 10,000 Bitcoins to get two Papa John's pizzas delivered. (He transferred the Bitcoins to another enthusiast, who paid in dollars.) Soon, Bitcoins attracted the attention of the media, and speculators started to buy them. Their value took off, and by June 2011 the value of a Bitcoin had soared to $27. The 10,000 Bitcoins that Laszlo Hanyecz had paid for his pizza just a few months previously would have been worth over $270,000 at those prices. "I don't feel bad about it," he claims. "The pizza was really good."

With Bitcoins worth so much, hackers started to look for ways to steal them out of users' accounts. In July 2011, an Internet site called Mt. Gox, which then handled 90 percent of all Bitcoin transactions, was hacked. Other security scares followed, and one user reported that his $500,000 worth of Bitcoins was stolen. The damage to the project's credibility saw the value of Bitcoins fall to around $3 at one point. The currency has experienced big price fluctuations over time. (By 2016 a Bitcoin was valued at about $575.)

Although the creator of Bitcoin, Satoshi Nakamoto, has disappeared without a trace, there are still plenty of enthusiasts for the Bitcoin project, working to bring the technology into the mainstream. Will the story of Bitcoin eventually come to be seen as just the first chapter in how new currencies rendered central banks obsolete? Or will it be just another online idea that didn't live up to all the hype? The Bitcoin saga shows that even in the digital age, we still need to take seriously the very old problem of how to maintain stable, trustworthy currencies.

Sources: http://www.wired.com/magazine/2011/11/mf_bitcoin/all/1; http://www.dailytech.com/Digital+Black+Friday+First+Bitcoin+Depression+Hits/article21877.htm; http://www.economist.com/blogs/babbage/2011/06/virtual-currency.

Another role played by a central bank is the *lender of last resort*. What does this mean? Think back to the story of J.P. Morgan, who almost single-handedly saved the banking system in 1907. When nobody else was willing to lend to banks facing a bank run, J.P. Morgan, along with others he rallied to the table, stepped in as lenders of last resort. They became the last line of defense before an imminent financial collapse. These days, that's the Fed's job. As we'll see in Chapter 17, "Financial Crisis," the Fed played exactly this role during the U.S. financial crisis in 2008.

How does the Federal Reserve work?

Now that you know what the role of a central bank is, let's look more closely at how the Federal Reserve—the United States's central bank—actually works. We will focus on two topics: the organizational structure of the Federal Reserve and the key principles that guide the Fed in its policy-making.

How the Fed is organized

The entity we popularly call the **Federal Reserve**, or Fed for short, is actually not one organization but an entire system. The Federal Reserve System consists of 12 regional banks and a seven-member Board of Governors that act as the central bank in the United States. The seven-member Board of Governors and its staff, based in Washington, DC, are responsible for the overall governance of the system.

Supporting the efforts of the Board of Governors are 12 regional Federal Reserve banks scattered in major cities across the country, as shown in Figure 15-3. These 12 banks conduct the day-to-day affairs of the central bank. Under them are the so-called *member banks,* which include most of the banks in the United States. These banks are considered to be members of the Federal Reserve System and are subject to its regulations.

The Board of Governors is made up of experts in finance, banking, and monetary policy who are appointed by the U.S. president and confirmed by the Senate for 14-year terms. In addition, the president appoints one member of the Board of Governors to be chair for a four-year term. The chair of the Federal Reserve is one of the most important economic positions in the United States, if not the world. The chair has significant direct control over the conduct of monetary policy by the central bank.

Each of the regional Federal Reserve banks, for their part, is led by a president. The regional presidents are generally selected from the banking and business community in the region. They are responsible for overseeing the day-to-day actions of the regional banks, including regulatory oversight and implementation of monetary policy.

In addition, five of the 12 regional bank presidents serve on the *Federal Open Market Committee,* or FOMC. Four of these regional presidents serve on a rotating basis; the president of the New York regional bank is always a member, emphasizing how important the financial

Federal Reserve ("the Fed")

the system consisting of a seven-member Board of Governors and 12 regional banks that act as the central bank of the United States

---

FIGURE 15-3

The Federal Reserve System   The Federal Reserve System is made up of 12 regional banks spread across the country, headed by the Board of Governors in Washington, DC.

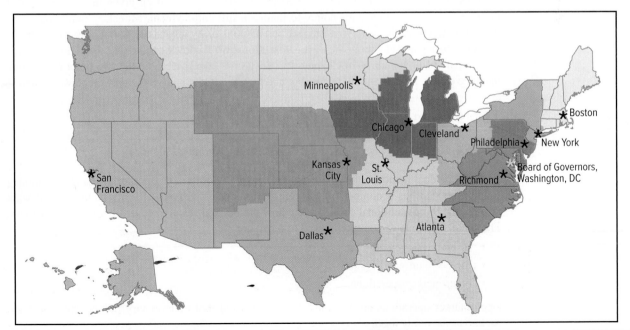

Source: http://www.federalreserve.gov/otherfrb.htm (accessed January 27, 2013).

Janet Yellen, a former business school professor at the University of California, was sworn in as chair of the Federal Reserve in February 2014.
© *Mark Wilson/Getty Images*

industry in the New York metropolitan area is to the nation's monetary and financial policy. The five regional bank presidents are joined on the FOMC by the seven-member Board of Governors (for a total of 12 members). The FOMC is the most important policy-making body of the Federal Reserve System. It carries full responsibility for setting the overall direction of monetary policy and guiding the money supply.

You may notice that for a governmental agency, the Federal Reserve has little connection with the rest of government. Though appointed by the government, the members of the Board of Governors enjoy the security of serving long terms, which helps them to be independent of politics. This is no accident. Politicians of all parties know the power of monetary policy. Giving the Fed a high degree of independence means that the Fed governors will not be as tempted by political pressure as someone with less independence. The Fed's independence, for example, makes it less likely to expand the money supply simply to make it cheaper for the government to repay its debt. In addition, knowing that technocrats rather than politicians are in charge tends to increase people's trust in the stability of the dollar.

How the Fed makes policy

dual mandate

the twin responsibilities of the Federal Reserve, to use monetary policy to ensure price stability and to maintain full employment

But what exactly does it mean to manage monetary policy for the benefit of the country? The Federal Reserve has twin responsibilities—what is commonly known as a **dual mandate**: The first part of this mandate is to *ensure price stability* and the second is to *maintain full employment.*

The first responsibility is what many think of when talking about monetary policy. It involves maintaining a stable money supply that meets the needs of the economy, while keeping prices relatively constant over time. For many central banks, this is as far as the mandate goes. (Maintaining price stability is, for instance, the only mandate of the European Central Bank, which manages monetary policy for much of Europe.)

In the United States, however, the Federal Reserve also has been given the second part of the mandate—to use monetary policy to maintain full employment. Monetary policy can have powerful effects on the economy. This second responsibility means using that power to keep the economy strong and stable. In the next few sections, we'll show how the Fed works to fulfill this second part of its mandate. In Chapter 16, "Inflation," we'll see how the two parts of the dual mandate can be fundamentally in conflict and how the Fed manages the tension between them.

Tools of monetary policy

> **LO 15.6** Explain the tools the Federal Reserve uses to conduct monetary policy.

To fulfill its dual mandate, the Fed manages the supply of money. In order to change the money supply, the Fed has a number of different options at its disposal. In this section, we'll walk through the three traditional ones to show how the Federal Reserve generally conducts business. These tools, from least commonly used to most, are

- reserve requirements,
- the discount window, and
- open-market operations.

Open-market operations are the most frequently used tool of monetary policy; the others are backup tools, rarely used.

Reserve requirements

Although it is seldom used, the most powerful tool available to the Federal Reserve is its ability to adjust the **reserve requirement**—the regulation that sets the minimum fraction of deposits banks must hold in reserve. The tool can have far-reaching effects, so policy-makers try to use it sparingly.

You'll recall that the reserve ratio a bank maintains is one of several determinants of how much money is available in the economy, and by extension how much lending occurs. If it wanted to, the Fed could even eliminate fractional-reserve banking altogether by mandating that banks hold 100 percent of their deposits in reserve, though that wouldn't be a very good idea.

Although changing the reserve requirement is a powerful tool, it is *too* powerful in most situations. Meaningfully controlling the money supply through reserve requirements would mean dramatically changing the amount of money banks are required to hold, an action almost certain to have significant and unpredictable consequences. Bank managers make their plans depending in part on a certain reserve requirement. Rapid change in the requirement would make it harder for them to manage their money. Rapid change also would have ripple effects throughout the entire economy, affecting the availability of credit and confidence in the banking system.

Despite the dangers of changing reserve requirements, some countries, most notably China, have used adjustments to the required reserve ratio as a primary tool of monetary policy (and have had mixed success). In the United States, changes to the reserve requirements are rarely used for policy unless there's a crisis. Think of changing the reserve requirement as a big shove; most of the time, monetary policy changes aim for more of a gentle push.

reserve requirement the regulation that sets the minimum fraction of deposits banks must hold in reserve

The discount window

The second tool used by the Fed is the discount window. The **discount window** is a lending facility that allows any bank to borrow reserves from the Fed. The interest rate charged for these loans is called the **discount rate**. The discount window is one of the Fed's primary tools for providing liquidity to the markets and acting as a lender of last resort. When a bank is in trouble (because of a bank run, perhaps), the discount window can be a guaranteed source of emergency funds.

Historically, although the discount window is key to the Fed's responsibility as lender of last resort, loans from the discount window are rarely used for monetary policy. The reason is that the discount rate has generally been somewhat higher than interest rates available in the market. As a result, banks tend to look elsewhere for loans. Because of that, any bank that makes use of the window opens itself up to significant speculation about its financial health. If the bank needs to borrow on unfavorable terms to stay alive, the thinking goes, it's likely that the bank is in trouble. Such stigma makes banks reluctant to use the discount window.

Sometimes, though, banks lack better options. The stigma of discount-window loans fell away during the 2008 financial crisis: Banks in desperate need of cash were forced to put aside their reputational concerns and turn to the only place willing to lend to them. In just one week in October 2008, banks borrowed $117 billion in emergency funds from the discount window.[6]

discount window the lending facility run by the Fed that allows any bank to borrow reserves

discount rate the interest rate charged by the Fed for loans of reserves through the discount window

Open-market operations

The final, most used, and most important tool in the Fed's traditional toolbox is open-market operations. **Open-market operations** are sales or purchases of government securities, by the Fed to or from banks on the open (public) market. The actual process is a bit more indirect than we'll present it here, but the ultimate end is the same: The Fed sells bonds to a bank or buys bonds from it. These transactions directly result in an increase or decrease in the money supply:

- Increasing the money supply: When the Fed wants to increase the money supply, it can purchase a bond from one of the large banks it trades with. The Fed pays for this purchase

open-market operations sales or purchases of government bonds by the Fed, to or from banks, on the open market with money it has on hand, which then translates into larger deposits and reserves in the commercial bank.

- Decreasing the money supply: On the other hand, if the Fed wants to decrease the money supply, it sells bonds, accepting as payment reserves from the buying bank. The Fed then effectively destroys the money it receives, which decreases the amount of the monetary base in existence.

How exactly do open-market operations affect the larger economy? This tool works two ways. The Fed can *buy* government bonds to pursue **expansionary monetary policy**—actions that increase the money supply in order to increase aggregate demand. When the Fed buys bonds from a bank, it pays for those bonds by increasing the bank's deposit in the Fed, which increases the bank's reserves. The bank can then lend more and set off a ripple effect that increases other banks' lending. This maneuver enables the Fed to increase the growth rate of the money supply and pursue expansionary monetary policy.[7]

When the Fed *sells* bonds to a bank, the bank pays for the transaction with money that it keeps on deposit at the Fed. The sale thus reduces the bank's reserves. This in turn reduces the bank's ability to lend. Through the multiplier effect, the reduction in lending sets off a ripple effect with other banks' lending and slows down the growth rate of the money supply. This is an important way to conduct **contractionary monetary policy**—actions that reduce the money supply in order to decrease aggregate demand.

Open-market operations have a couple of advantages over other tools of monetary policy. First, the transactions—the buying and selling of bonds—take place on a *daily* basis. Since the Fed commonly wants to make small adjustments rather than sweeping changes in the economy, the frequency of these transactions adds to this tool's flexibility. The ability to act on a day-to-day basis helps maintain the Fed's reputation for steady, credible policy.

The second advantage of open-market operations is that they affect the *federal funds rate,* the interest rate that banks charge when one bank makes a very-short-term (usually overnight) loan of reserves to another bank. The Fed uses this rate as a target in open-market operations, pushing it upward by selling bonds and pushing it downward by buying bonds.

The federal funds rate and money supply

The Federal Reserve rarely describes its policies in terms of changes in the money supply. Instead, it focuses on interest rates. Technically, the Fed announces a "target" for the **federal funds rate**—the interest rate at which banks choose to lend reserves held at the Fed to one another, usually just overnight.

Banks are required to maintain a certain level of reserves. Thus, when a bank finds itself short at the end of the day, it may choose to make up the shortfall by borrowing from another bank that has excess reserves. Since both banks have an account with the Federal Reserve, it is easy and safe to borrow money this way.

How does the Fed affect the federal funds rate? In contractionary policy, as we saw, the Fed sells bonds, taking reserves from banks as payment. This decrease in the supply of reserves pushes the federal funds rate upward. Why? By reducing the supply of reserves, the price of borrowing reserves rises, just as in the standard analysis of supply and demand in a market for goods. Other interest rates move in the same direction as the federal funds rate, so interest rates rise in general, discouraging spending on houses, cars, new machinery, and other things. Raising the federal funds rate thus helps meet the goal of contractionary policy—which is to slow the economy down.

A similar chain of logic applies to expansionary policy, in which the goal is to reduce interest rates to stimulate the economy. In expansionary policy, the logic works in the opposite direction: The Fed buys bonds, injecting reserves into the banking system, and lowers the federal funds rates.

The one caveat with expansionary monetary policy is that there is a natural limit to how low the federal funds rate (or any other nominal interest rate) can go. Since anyone in the economy

---

expansionary monetary policy actions that increase the money supply in order to increase aggregate demand

contractionary monetary policy actions that reduce the money supply in order to decrease aggregate demand

federal funds rate the interest rate at which banks choose to lend reserves held at the Fed to one another can always hold cold, hard cash, which offers a zero-percent interest rate, it is nearly impossible to push nominal interest rates on any other asset below zero. The natural lower limit on interest rates is known as the *zero lower bound,* and it has played a central role in the recent economic crises in the United States, Japan, and Europe.

These three tools—reserve requirements, the discount window, and open-market operations—comprise the traditional strategies of the Federal Reserve. We'll discuss examples of more unorthodox techniques in Chapter 17, "Financial Crisis." These innovations were used in the recent financial crisis to help shore up the entire financial system. Through use of such new policies, the Federal Reserve has rapidly adapted its toolkit to meet the changing demands of the global economy.

✓CONCEPT CHECK

☐ What is the name of the part of the Federal Reserve in Washington, DC, that oversees the Fed's operations? **[LO 15.5]**

☐ What is the dual mandate of the Federal Reserve? **[LO 15.5]**

☐ What is the most common tool that the Federal Reserve uses to conduct monetary policy? What makes this tool more appealing than the other two? **[LO 15.6]**

The Economic Effects of Monetary Policy

To understand why the Federal Reserve's control over the money supply is so powerful, we need a better understanding of the mechanism by which monetary policy affects the economy. Some economists, known as *monetarists,* argue that over the *long run,* monetary policy is irrelevant because prices will adjust to a high or low supply of money, without any change in overall economic output. (Consequently, monetarists say that "money is neutral.") However, most economists agree that in the *short run,* at least, the Federal Reserve's control over monetary policy allows it to combat recessions and cool an overheating economy. But how does this mechanism work?

Monetary policy primarily influences the economy through changes in the interest rate. Changes in the interest rate, in turn, affect the appeal of borrowing and lending, which can have significant impacts on the economy. In this section, we'll walk through the connections in this process as well as some of the challenges of implementing monetary policy.

Interest rates and monetary policy: The liquidity-preference model

LO 15.7 Understand how monetary policy affects the prevailing interest rate and supply of money

When the central bank increases or decreases the money supply, it changes the balance of money supplied versus money demanded. If the words "supply" and "demand" make you think about money in a market as depicted in the supply-demand graphs we've used so far, you're on the right track.

To understand how the relationships work, we first describe the nature of the supply and demand of money using an idea, first proposed by economist John Maynard Keynes in 1936, called the *liquidity-preference model.*

The demand for money
Economists use the term "liquid" to describe the ease of turning assets into cash. Cash is highly liquid by definition, and checking accounts (demand-deposit accounts) are nearly as liquid as cash. We need cash and easy-to-access bank accounts to be able to meet our daily spending needs. In other words, we have a preference for liquidity.

Government bonds, in contrast, are not very liquid. They have to be sold in order to generate cash for spending. Of course, government bonds have an important advantage over cash: they earn interest. The advantage of interest is weighed against the disadvantage of not being very liquid.

So, when the interest rate earned on government bonds is high, most people will try to hold more bonds and less cash. And when the interest rate on bonds falls, the advantage of bonds is reduced, making cash relatively more attractive. When you don't earn much interest on bonds, you may as well hold your money in cash and other liquid forms.

liquidity-preference model

idea that the quantity of money people want to hold is a function of the interest rate

This relationship is the central idea of the **liquidity-preference model**, which explains that the quantity of money people want to hold is a function of the interest rate. In this model, the money-demand curve slopes downward, showing a negative relationship between the interest rate and how much money is demanded. Why? Think of "money" here as cash—specifically, cash as opposed to other assets such as bonds that pay interest. (No matter how high interest rates are, though, you'll still have to hold onto some money to complete day-to-day transactions.)

On the whole, the liquidity-preference model means that people aren't going to demand much money when interest rates are high; they will demand more and more money as interest rates decrease. A change in the quantity of money demanded in response to a change in the interest rate is represented by movement along the money demand curve:

- When the interest rate rises, we demand a lower quantity of money, moving leftward along the curve.
- When the interest rate falls, we demand a higher quantity of money, moving rightward along the curve.

Not all changes in the quantity of money demanded result from movement along the demand curve. Some factors instead cause the demand curve itself to shift. One such factor is the price level in the economy. The demand for money in the United States is much higher today than it was 50 years ago, for the simple reason that almost everything is far more expensive today than it was then. Higher prices mean a greater need for money to meet the everyday needs of life, and that means more money demanded at every level of the interest rate. This increase in demand is represented by shifting the money demand curve to the right.

Increases or decreases in real GDP have a similar effect on money demand:

- Increases in real GDP—more production and income—mean more money is needed to purchase goods and services.
- Decreases in real GDP would have the opposite effect: With less activity going on in the economy, less money will be needed to purchase goods and services.

In addition to these economic factors, technological advancements can also play a role. Easier use of credit cards and greater availability of ATMs, for instance, reduce the demand for money. With these tools, people need to carry around far less cash in their wallets at any given time in order to make day-to-day purchases.

Money supply

In the simple version of the liquidity-preference model, the supply of money is considered to be set only by the Federal Reserve. Regardless of the interest rate, the Fed will ensure that there is a constant quantity of money supplied in the economy. As Figure 15-4 shows, this means that the money supply curve can be represented as a vertical line in the liquidity-preference model. It also means that the only way the supply of money can change is when the Fed does so for policy reasons.

Figure 15-4 shows the basic relationship between money supply and money demand in the liquidity-preference model. The point where the supply of money meets the demand for money (r^*) will determine the *nominal interest rate,* or stated price of money in the economy.

FIGURE 15-4

The liquidity-preference model

The liquidity-preference model shows the basic relationship
between money supply and money demand. In this model we
assume that the money supply is completely fixed by the Fed.
The money demand curve slopes downward as a function of
the interest rate. With high interest rates, people demand a
small quantity of money, but as interest rates decrease,
people demand more.

This simple model assumes that the Fed has complete control over the supply curve, but in reality an economy's money supply comes from a variety of sources. As the model currently stands, the Fed dictates the supply of the monetary base. Banks decide how much money is eventually created from the base money through the impact their lending decisions have on the money multiplier. As we'll see later, the Fed's ability to target the money supply and interest rates is not nearly as precise as this model suggests. Still, the assumption of a fixed money supply controlled by the Fed is useful for introducing the model.

Earlier, we discussed the tools the Fed has to adjust the money supply. These adjustments can be represented by shifts in the money supply curve, depending on whether the Fed wants to increase or decrease the money supply. Any actions that increase the money supply will shift the money supply curve to the right. These actions include decreasing the reserve requirement, decreasing the discount rate, or buying government bonds on the open market. In contrast, any actions that decrease the money supply will shift the money supply curve left. As you can see in Figure 15-5, changes in the money supply increase or decrease interest rates.

Knowing the slope of the money demand curve is important: The slope of the money demand curve determines how a change in the money supply will change the interest rate. If the quantity of money demanded is really responsive to changes to the interest rate (a flat, elastic demand curve), changes to the money supply will have a smaller effect on interest rates than if demand is less responsive (steeper, more inelastic). You can see this visually in Figure 15-6.

FIGURE 15-5

Shifts in the money supply curve and their effects on the interest rate

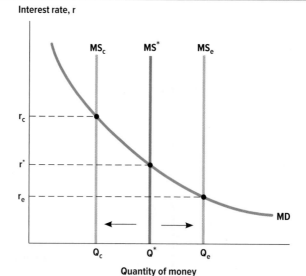

Shifting the money supply curve to the right (expanding the money supply) is called expansionary monetary policy (denoted with an e). The result is a greater amount of money in the economy, at lower interest rates. Shifting the curve to the left represents a decrease in the money supply. The result is less money in the economy, at higher interest rates.

FIGURE 15-6

The slope of the money supply curve affects the amount of change in the interest rate

(A) Elastic money demand curve

(B) Inelastic money demand curve

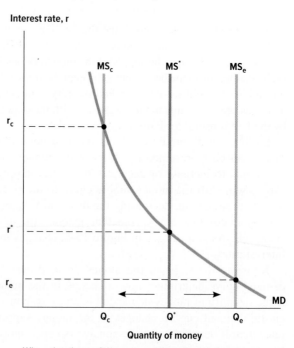

When the slope of the money demand curve is more elastic, changes in the money supply will have a smaller effect on interest rates.

When the slope of the money demand curve is more inelastic, changes in the money supply will have a greater effect on interest rates.

Interest rates and the economy

> **LO 15.8** Explain how expansionary or contractionary monetary policy influences the broader economy.

The liquidity-preference model explains how the Federal Reserve's actions can change interest rates. The Fed can cause interest rates to fall by increasing the money supply, or it can cause interest rates to rise by decreasing the money supply. But why does the Fed care about the interest rate? The answer is that the interest rate has important effects in the economy. Many of the large purchases we make—buying a house, a car, or an expensive appliance—are made using money we've borrowed. Likewise, corporations borrowing to make investments must also pay the price dictated by the interest rate.

Expansionary monetary policy

Changes in interest rates affect aggregate demand and supply in an economy: Lower interest rates make it cheaper to borrow money, and less rewarding to save money. At lower interest rates, people will spend on big-ticket items instead of save, further increasing the consumption part of aggregate demand. Monetary policy is thus an important way for policy-makers to respond to changes in the health of the economy.

For an example, let's say that the economy is in a recession. Aggregate demand is low. The economy is in a short-run equilibrium marked by sluggish output and lower prices. The Fed knows that lower interest rates would spur increased borrowing and spending—shifting the aggregate demand curve to the right. The Federal Reserve chairman announces that the Fed will lower the federal funds rate. So the Fed conducts open-market operations to increase the supply of money in the economy. This action is called *expansionary monetary policy.* As you can see in panel A of Figure 15-7, lower interest rates are the result of this action. It is important to keep in mind that the lower interest rates affect the rates of return on assets throughout the economy:

- When the Fed purchases bonds on the open market, it increases the demand for those bonds, drives up their prices, and therefore lowers their expected rates of return (since investors now have to pay more for the same stream of payments).
- Since investors no longer find Treasuries as attractive as before, they shift their portfolios toward other assets, like private stocks and bonds and real estate.
- This portfolio shift then increases the prices of the other assets in the economy and reduces *their* rates of return.

Thus, the Fed's decision to lower *an* interest rate—the federal funds rate—results in an economywide increase in asset prices and rates of return.

This increase in asset prices leads to what is known as the *balance sheet channel* of monetary policy. The idea is that a rise in asset prices causes firms and households to perceive an increase in their net worth. Then, when they feel an increase in net worth, they tend to increase spending. The causes of the additional spending differ for households and firms:

- In the case of households, the most important asset tends to be the house itself. For them, the balance sheet channel refers to spending out of an increase in housing wealth.
- In the case of firms, corporations tend to hold much of their business savings in the form of financial assets. When firms see an increase in their net worth due to increased asset prices, they are usually more willing to spend on new projects. They can use those larger internal savings to self-finance their investments. (Also, of course, the opportunity cost of using those funds is lower because the interest rate is lower.)

So, lower interest rates spur borrowing and spending. They also discourage saving. With increases in consumption spending and investment, aggregate demand increases. The aggregate

FIGURE 15-7

Expansionary monetary policy

(A) Expansionary monetary policy

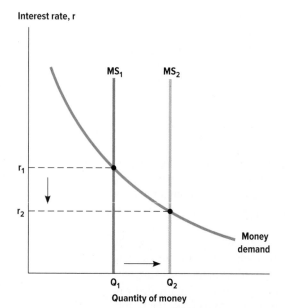

Expansionary money supply pushes interest rates lower and puts more money into the economy.

(B) Expansionary monetary policy and the AD/AS model

As a result people spend and borrow more, increasing aggregate demand. In this case, monetary policy was able to pull the economy out of recession.

demand curve shifts to the right as shown in panel B of Figure 15-7. Ultimately the effect is the same as that of the expansionary *fiscal* policy we discussed in Chapter 14, "The Basics of Finance." Both prices and output increase, taking the bite out of the recession.

Contractionary monetary policy

Conversely, what should the Fed do when the economy is booming, as it was in the housing bubble of 2006? Since the system was flush with cash, the aggregate demand curve was way to the right, and price levels were high. Output was also high, which made the decision of what needed to be done in this situation slightly tougher.

On the one hand, strong economic activity is obviously a good thing. On the other hand, it is possible for the economy to be operating beyond its means. When short-run output moves above long-run equilibrium, the price level will inevitably increase. Such increases in the price level are contrary to the central bank's mandate to maintain stable price levels. We'll go into this responsibility in more depth in Chapter 16, "Inflation," but for now, let's say that the Fed would be worried that these rising price levels would begin to adversely affect the economy.

When the Fed decides that the economy is a little too active—economists often call this "overheating"—it often moves to increase interest rates, as it did throughout the housing bubble. This increase in interest rates shifts the aggregate demand curve leftward, leading to lower prices and equilibrium output in the short run. That result, shown in panel B of Figure 15-8, is the effect of a contractionary monetary policy, shown in panel A of the same figure.

You'll note that we left both of these examples in the short run. In the long run, the economy will adjust to changes in the money supply, leaving only changes in the overall price level. This fact leads to one of the challenges facing the Federal Reserve: how to maintain stable price levels

FIGURE 15-8
Contractionary monetary policy

Contractionary monetary policy decreases the money supply, increasing interest rates.

Decreasing the money supply can cool down the economy when it overheats.

while also ensuring full employment. As you'll see in Chapter 16, "Inflation," these two goals are often in fundamental conflict.

Challenges and advantages of monetary policy

The examples of the use of monetary policy, above, show how policy can work in ideal cases. It is rare for the world to work so cleanly. When we discussed fiscal policy, we noted that policy-makers face practical challenges, such as time lags and imperfect information, when they try to make policy. The Fed faces the same problems as it seeks to steer the economy using monetary policy.

Although monetary policy usually does not take as long to implement as fiscal policy, a few months can pass before the Fed's actions start to have their desired impact. By that time, the state of the economy might have changed. A boost in the money supply could push the economy past the level of long-run equilibrium output, for example, and cause the economy to overheat. Even worse, the Fed could inadvertently contract the money supply just as the economy starts sliding into a recession. This mistiming of policy would make the ensuing recession even worse.

Even so, monetary policy does have advantages compared to traditional fiscal policy. The Fed does not have to wait for politicians to come to a consensus about the best policy to help the economy. Instead, the Fed Board of Governors and Open Market Committee typically meet every six weeks or so. They can, if necessary, change monetary policy then and there. Also, the Fed is made up of prominent economic policy-makers whose job is to make sure they fully understand the nuances of the overall economy in order to apply the right policy at the right time. It does not need to make specific decisions about spending and tax policy; it merely lowers or raises interest rates and lets the market determine spending decisions.

Benefits like these make monetary policy a vitally important weapon against low employment and excessive inflation.

✓CONCEPT CHECK

☐ What is the federal funds rate? **[LO 15.7]**

☐ What should the central bank do to fight low aggregate demand during a recession? **[LO 15.8]**

Conclusion

In this chapter, we've explored one of the most fundamental concepts in modern economics: money. We've looked at the roles money plays in the economy. We've also looked at how central banks and the private banking system interact to determine the size of the money supply. Finally, we've seen some of the tools the central bank has to manage the money supply and how those tools allow it to exert considerable influence over the broader economy.

This unique power gives the Fed (and central banks in other countries) incredible responsibility for the economy. As you'll see in the next few chapters, this responsibility usually comes down to two main tasks: keeping price levels stable and acting as a lender of last resort. The Fed is the last line of defense when a financial crisis threatens an economy.

Key Terms

money, p. 397

store of value, p. 397

medium of exchange, p. 397

barter, p. 397

unit of account, p. 398

commodity-backed money, p. 399

fiat money, p. 400

demand deposits, p. 401

reserves, p. 401

required reserves, p. 401

excess reserves, p. 401

reserve ratio, p. 401

fractional-reserve banking, p. 403

money multiplier, p. 403

money supply, p. 405

monetary base, p. 405

M1, p. 405

M2, p. 405

central bank, p. 407

monetary policy, p. 407

Federal Reserve ("the Fed"), p. 409

dual mandate, p. 410

reserve requirement, p. 411

discount window, p. 411

discount rate, p. 411

open-market operations, p. 411

expansionary monetary policy, p. 412

contractionary monetary policy, p. 412

federal funds rate, p. 412

liquidity-preference model, p. 414

Summary

LO 15.1 Describe the three main functions of money.

The three main functions of money are as a store of value, a medium of exchange, and a unit of account. Money derives much of its true importance from its role as a medium of exchange—from the fact that you can use it to purchase the goods and services you desire. Money is also important as a way to register the value of transactions.

LO 15.2 Describe the characteristics that make something a good choice as money and distinguish between commodity-backed and fiat money.

Money needs to have *stability of value* and *be convenient*. Items whose value varies from one day to the next will not be a good store of value, and so are not suitable as money. Money also needs to be widely accepted in order to fulfill its function as a medium of exchange. The earliest forms of paper money could be legally exchanged into a specific amount of a named commodity (generally gold), making it *commodity-backed money*. Since 1971, U.S. money has been *fiat money*, which is money created by rule rather than backed by a commodity.

LO 15.3 Explain the concept of fractional-reserve banking and the money multiplier.

Banks keep on hand a portion of the money deposited, in case depositors want to withdraw money. This money is known as the bank's *reserves*, and the ratio of the original deposit to the amount kept as reserves is the *reserve ratio*. If the reserve ratio were 100 percent (a situation known as *full-reserve banking*), no lending would take place; all deposits would sit in the banks' vaults, and the financial system would grind to a halt. *Fractional-reserve banking* allows a reserve ratio of less than 100 percent, enabling banks to lend a portion of the money that has been deposited. By means of that lending, banks "create" money. The ratio of money created by the lending activities of the banking system to the money created by the government's central bank is the *money multiplier.*

LO 15.4 Describe M1 and M2.

The Fed classifies different types of money by their *liquidity*—by how easy an asset is to convert immediately to cash without losing value. Cash and reserves physically held at the Fed are *hard money,* which can be used in transactions without delay. *M1* includes hard money plus checkable deposits (which are not exactly cash but are fairly readily accessible for most people). *M2* includes everything in M1 as well as things like savings accounts and CDs (certificates of deposit) that are generally harder to access immediately and so slightly less liquid than other forms of money.

LO 15.5 Understand the role of a central bank and discuss the idea of the Federal Reserve's dual mandate.

In any nation, the central bank's duties generally include maintaining the money supply and coordinating the banking system. In the United States, the central bank is known as the Federal Reserve—a system consisting of a Board of Governors and 12 regional banks. It has a dual mandate: to use monetary policy to ensure price stability and maintain full employment. Price stability means maintaining a stable money supply that meets the needs of the economy, while keeping the purchasing power of a dollar relatively constant over time by preventing destabilizing levels of price changes. Full employment can be affected through monetary policy to stimulate or cool aggregate demand.

LO 15.6 Explain the tools the Federal Reserve uses to conduct monetary policy.

The Federal Reserve has three tools to conduct monetary policy. The first is changing the *reserve requirement,* or the regulation that sets the minimum fraction of deposits that banks must hold. It is usually seen as a rather blunt tool—powerful but inappropriate for most day-to-day economic maintenance. The second is the *discount window,* a lending facility run by the Fed that allows any bank to receive cash in exchange for certain noncash assets like government bonds; the interest rate charged for these loans is the *discount rate.* The discount window is one of the Fed's primary tools for providing liquidity to

the markets and acting as a lender of last resort. The final and most-used tool is *open-market operations,* in which the Federal Reserve sells or buys government bonds in the open market. Use of this tool alters bank reserves and influences overall interest rates.

LO 15.7 Understand how monetary policy affects the prevailing interest rate and supply of money.

The *liquidity-preference model* explains that the quantity of money people want to hold (the demand for money) is a function of the interest rate, which the Federal Reserve controls. As the quantity of money supplied changes, the price of that money, reflected in interest rates, will change as well. Increasing the money supply (such as by buying government bonds on the open market) decreases interest rates. Decreasing the money supply (such as by selling government bonds) will increase interest rates.

LO 15.8 Explain how expansionary or contractionary monetary policy influences the broader economy.

Depending on the circumstances, the Fed may want to engage in either expansionary or contractionary monetary policy. *Expansionary monetary policy* involves lowering interest rates; the lower rates increase aggregate demand, helping to expand the economy. This action is generally taken in response to recessionary forces. *Contractionary monetary policy* involves raising interest rates, which shrinks aggregate demand and slows the economy; it generally is taken in response to inflationary forces.

Review Questions

1. Describe how money contributes to economic activity and allows for a more complex society than barter does. **[LO 15.1]**

2. Explain how cigarettes fulfilled the three functions of money in the POW camps during World War II. **[LO 15.1]**

3. Throughout time, metals such as gold have been popular choices for money across various societies. Explain why this might be, using our criteria for what makes good money. **[LO 15.2]**

4. On the Yap Islands in the middle of the Pacific Ocean, giant stone wheels, weighing as much as a small car, were used as currency. What were some of the likely problems with this currency? **[LO 15.2]**

5. Explain why keeping a reserve ratio of zero could be a very bad idea. **[LO 15.3]**

6. If banks keep 100 percent of deposits on hand as reserves, what would this imply about the reserve requirement and the multiplier? What would it imply about banks' ability to create new money? **[LO 15.3]**

7. Explain the role of base money and the money multiplier in the Federal Reserve System's enactment of monetary policy. [LO 15.4]

8. Give an example where depositors changing the way they hold assets could increase the M1 measure of the money supply while leaving M2 unchanged. [LO 15.4]

9. What is one key way in which the mission of the Federal Reserve differs from the mission of the European Central Bank? [LO 15.5]

10. What do we mean when we say that the Federal Reserve System is politically independent, and how might this independence be a good thing for the U.S. economy? [LO 15.5]

11. Explain why using changes in reserve requirements to conduct monetary policy is generally not a good idea for the United States. [LO 15.6]

12. Which tool of monetary policy is used most frequently by the Federal Reserve System? What makes this tool the best choice in most circumstances? [LO 15.6]

13. Are there any differences in the effects of fiscal policy versus monetary policy on aggregate demand in the short-run aggregate demand and supply model? [LO 15.7]

14. Describe the slope of the money supply curve in the liquidity-preference model. Are the assumptions behind the supply curve realistic? [LO 15.7]

15. Under the liquidity-preference model, how would the slope of the money demand curve affect the power of a central bank to conduct monetary policy? [LO 15.8]

16. Use the liquidity-preference model to explain how the Federal Reserve can react to the threat of exceedingly high inflation via monetary policy. Be sure to include the intended effect on the interest rate and quantity of money. [LO 15.8]

Problems and Applications

1. Determine whether each of the following would fulfill the three functions of money. If the item does not fulfill all three, name at least one function of money that it violates. [LO 15.1]
   a. Salt.
   b. The barter system.
   c. Baseball cards.

2. Imagine you own a lawn-mowing business. Identify the main function of money exhibited in each situation below. [LO 15.1]
   a. You swipe your debit card to purchase gasoline for your lawn mower.
   b. You stuff your earnings from mowing lawns into a piggy bank.

   c. You pay your friend Cornelius $5 to help you mow lawns.
   d. You calculate your net earnings for the year on your tax return.
   e. You determine how much value your new lawn mower has added to your business.

3. From 2004 to 2009 the country of Zimbabwe underwent hyperinflation, in which prices rise rapidly. The government began printing bills as large as 100 billion Zimbabwe dollars. Explain how this situation would have affected the characteristics of good money discussed in this chapter. [LO 15.2]

4. Suppose you live in a country perfect for growing tulips and governed by King Balthazar, who proposes that you use the tulips for your currency. After all, says Balthazar, they are widely accepted in the community, they've been valuable for years, and they are highly portable. If you were Balthazar's economic advisor, would you recommend using the tulips? If yes, list the traits of good money they satisfy. If no, list the trait(s) of good money they do not satisfy. [LO 15.2]

5. You decide to take $300 out of your piggy bank at home and place it in the bank. If the reserve requirement is 5 percent, how much can your $300 increase the amount of money in the economy? [LO 15.3]

6. Assume that $1 million is deposited in a bank with a reserve requirement of 15 percent. What is the money supply as a result? What would change if the government decides to raise the reserve requirement to 40 percent? [LO 15.3]

7. Say whether each of the following are types of M1 or M2, or both. [LO 15.4]
   a. Checkable deposits.
   b. Dollar bills.
   c. Money in your checking account.
   d. Money in your savings account.
   e. Certificates of deposit under $100,000.
   f. Traveler's checks.

8. Which of the following statements are true regarding the differences between M1 and M2? Check all that apply. [LO 15.4]
   a. M1 includes cash and reserves, whereas M2 does not.
   b. M2 represents a broader measure of the money supply compared to M1.
   c. Numerically, M1 is larger than M2.
   d. All items in M1 are more liquid than all items in M2.
   e. M2 includes savings deposits, whereas M1 does not.

f. Checking account balances are part of M2 but not M1.

9. The following quotation comes from remarks given by Ben Bernanke, former chairman of the Federal Reserve. The Federal Reserve has a dual mandate. Which mandate does the quote below refer to? **[LO 15.5]**

> The substantial ongoing slack in the labor market and the relatively slow pace of improvement remain important reasons that the Committee continues to maintain a highly accommodative monetary policy.[8]

10. Look back to the POW camps described at the beginning of this chapter. Who played the role of the central bank? **[LO 15.5]**

11. Which tool of monetary policy is most likely being described by each of the following statements? **[LO 15.6]**

a. It's the major way the Federal Reserve System enacts monetary policy.

b. This tool is good for emergency situations that require major, large-scale action.

c. This tool goes through the Federal Reserve's role as lender of last resort.

d. This tool is best for everyday monetary policy.

e. A major disadvantage of this tool is that it requires that banks want to borrow from the Fed.

f. Even if they aren't interested in buying, selling, or borrowing from the Fed, changes in this tool may inconvenience bank managers.

12. Name the monetary policy tool being used in each of the following examples. **[LO 15.6]**

a. The central bank buys government securities from banks.

b. The central bank raises the cost of borrowing money.

c. The central bank changes the amount of money banks must hold from their depositors.

13. The economy is in recession and the Federal Reserve wants to increase the money supply. Should it increase or decrease the following? **[LO 15.6]**

a. Reserve requirements.

b. The discount rate.

c. Purchases of bonds in the open market.

14. Using Figure 15P-1, answer the following questions. **[LO 15.7]**

a. Is this economy in recession, just right, or overheating?

b. What is the correct monetary policy in this situation—expansionary or contractionary?

c. What is the effect on prices of that policy—will they increase or decrease?

FIGURE 15P-1

15. What would happen to each of these components of the liquidity-preference model if the Federal Reserve decides to raise the reserve requirement? **[LO 15.8]**

a. Money supply.

b. Interest rates.

c. Quantity of money in the economy.

d. Money demand curve.

16. For each of the following situations, identify whether the Federal Reserve is likely to pursue an expansionary or a contractionary monetary policy. **[LO 15.8]**

a. The unemployment rate is at 0.5 percent.

b. The economy is experiencing record growth in GDP.

c. The unemployment rate is at 15 percent.

d. Inflation has reached 10 percent, a recent high.

e. A hurricane recently demolished a major city, causing a major recession.

Endnotes

1. This wasn't always the case: In the early days of the United States, there was no universal U.S. dollar; banks in each state produced their own currencies. In 1792 the United States started slowly phasing out the competing state currencies in favor of a standard form of money for the entire country. This was a critical decision in U.S. economic history.

2. http://www.jmbullion.com/charts/gold-price.

3. The bank has two reasons to hold reserves. First, the Federal Reserve *requires* the bank to hold a certain percentage

of deposits as reserves. It's simply the law. In the example, the Fed's reserve requirement is 10 percent. The second reason is that banks have to meet customers' needs for *liquidity,* independent of the banks' legal requirements to hold reserves. Sometimes banks find it strategic to hold extra reserves over and above the legal requirement. In the example here, the bank's legal requirement and its own judgment of customers' needs happen to coincide. So, for both reasons, the bank chooses to hold 10 percent of deposits as reserves.

4. In reality, some dollars might get held as cash rather than being deposited, but usually we're safe to ignore those very small amounts relative to the total, especially in the United States and other economies with well-developed banking systems. In some parts of the world today, however, much more money is held outside of banks and that fact would need to be taken into account.

5. Robert F. Bruner and Sean D. Carr, *The Panic of 1907: Lessons Learned from the Market's Perfect Storm* (Hoboken, NJ: John Wiley & Sons, 2007).

6. Binyamin Appelbaum and Jo Craven McGinty, "The Fed's Crisis Lending: A Billion Here, a Thousand There," *The New York Times,* April 1, 2011, p. B1, http://www.nytimes.com/2011/04/01/business/economy/01fed.html.

7. The Fed also buys bonds directly from the public–not just banks. Some of the money from the sales of those bonds gets put into banks as deposits. Those deposits increase the banks' reserves, and we see the same result as we do when the Fed buys the bonds directly from banks.

8. Speech by Chairman Ben S. Bernanke of the Federal Reserve at the New York Economic Club, New York, New York, November 20, 2012 ("The Economic Recovery and Economic Policy"), http://www.federalreserve.gov/newsevents/speech/bernanke20121120a.htm.

Chapter 16

Inflation

Learning Objectives

LO 16.1 Define inflation, deflation, headline inflation, and core inflation.

LO 16.2 Explain the neutrality of money.

LO 16.3 Describe and illustrate the classical theory of inflation.

LO 16.4 Explain the quantity theory of money and relate it to inflation and deflation.

LO 16.5 Analyze the economic consequences of inflation.

LO 16.6 Analyze the economic consequences of deflation.

LO 16.7 Describe disinflation and hyperinflation and explain the role of monetary policy in creating both situations.

LO 16.8 Understand why policy-makers favor a small amount of inflation over zero inflation.

LO 16.9 Explain the relationship between inflation, the output gap, and monetary policy.

LO 16.10 Explain how the relationship between inflation and unemployment is modeled by the Phillips curve and integrated into the non-accelerating inflation rate of unemployment.

A LAND OF OPPORTUNITY . . . AND INFLATION

The story is a familiar one: In the closing years of the 1800s, millions of immigrants sought out the promised land—a country rich in natural resources and with the highest standards of living in the world. These immigrants sought a new life in one of the world's great cities—a modern, cosmopolitan city where the blending of cultures led to vibrancy nearly unrivaled in the world. At its peak, nearly 50 percent of the city's residents were immigrants.

These immigrants were not greeted by the Statue of Liberty. They did not pass through New York's Ellis Island. They didn't set foot in Manhattan or anywhere else in the United States. Instead, they went to Buenos Aires—their promised land was Argentina. From the late 1800s

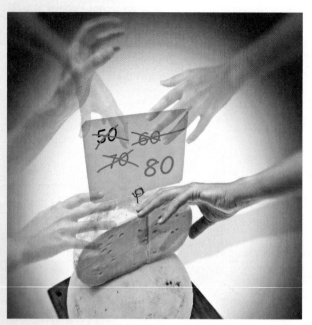

© Simon Chavez/dpa/Corbis

to the early 1900s, more than 5 million immigrants from across Europe arrived in Argentina, a country with seemingly limitless opportunity. In 1910, Argentina's per capita GDP was relatively high, four-fifths that of the United States.

In the century that followed, though, Argentina lagged behind economically. Its per capita GDP is now less than a third of that in the United States. What caused this divergence in fortunes? You could point to the political instability that led to a series of military coups and populist dictatorships. But dig a little deeper and you will find a common thread that came to define daily life in Argentina: steadily rising prices throughout the economy—in other words, out-of-control *inflation.*

More than almost any other country in the world, Argentina has struggled with rising prices. Over the past 75 years, Argentina experienced three separate *hyperinflations* (extremely long and painful inflationary periods). The worst of these, in the late 1980s and early 1990s, saw inflation peak at over 20,000 percent per year. (In other words, prices were doubling every month or two.) If this were to happen in the United States today, an iPod costing $100 at Christmas would cost $200 in February, $400 in March, and more than $20,000 by the following Christmas.

In between the periods of hyperinflation, Argentina has seen sustained high inflation unlike almost any other country in the world. In fact, the average annual inflation rate over the last 75 years is over 200 percent—a tripling of prices every year! Argentina has brought inflation down to about 25 percent per year recently—which seems modest compared to historical levels, despite being one of the highest inflation rates in the world.[1]

A century ago, Argentina seemed on the cusp of challenging the United States for supremacy in the Americas. Of course, the difference in inflation rates was not the only policy or geographic difference between the United States and Argentina. But it does help explain why that dream is gone. What is so damaging about inflation for a nation's economy? And why do most economists believe that its opposite—deflation—is even worse?

In the chapter on money and the monetary system, we saw how money creation and the supply of money can have an enormous impact on the overall economy, and in particular on interest rates. In this chapter, we will look at the topic of inflation from various angles—theories about changing price levels, inflation in its various forms, and the effects of inflation on monetary policy.

Changing Price Levels

The price level, and especially changes in it, is one of the most important concepts in macroeconomics. The economy is driven by billions of frequently changing prices. Some of these price changes matter for the economy more than others. There are a few key questions economists address: How should we summarize the most important price changes? What causes the price level to change? And how do changes in the price level affect the economy?

Measuring inflation

LO 16.1 Define inflation, deflation, headline inflation, and core inflation.

An overall rise in prices in the economy is called **inflation**. An overall fall in prices in the economy is called **deflation**.

As we saw in Chapter 8, "The Cost of Living," the U.S. government's Bureau of Labor Statistics (BLS) measures overall prices in the economy by creating a consumption basket designed to resemble the purchases of the average urban consumer. This measure of overall prices is called the Consumer Price Index (CPI). Measuring inflation or deflation is done by calculating the percentage change in the CPI ratio of the cost of the market basket to the cost of that basket in a base year. The BLS measures two inflation numbers:

- The measure of inflation that includes *all* of the goods that the average consumer buys is called **headline inflation**. It measures the changes in prices for the entire market basket of the average urban consumer.
- **Core inflation** is a measure of inflation that excludes goods with historically volatile price changes—energy and food. It is the BLS's official measure of changes in prices through the CPI. The reason to calculate core inflation is that changes in price levels due to goods with volatile prices might simply reflect shocks to individual product markets rather than any sort of economywide inflation. In 2015, for example, the price of gasoline dropped 27.3 percent, while core inflation rose by 1.7 percent.[2]

When economists are interested in the underlying rate of inflation in the economy, they often differentiate between headline inflation and core inflation. Figure 16-1 clearly shows how much more stable core inflation (as represented by the core CPI) is than overall or headline inflation (as represented by the CPI). Although headline inflation gives a more complete picture of how changing prices are affecting the average consumer, it's useful to subtract out food and gasoline if we want to get a better feel for underlying economic trends.

The neutrality of money

LO 16.2 Explain the neutrality of money.

When we say that the price level changes, what do we mean? To answer the question, it helps to think about what "output" really is. A country's GDP is simply an accounting of all of the purchases and sales that take place over a given period. In each transaction, somebody gives money to somebody else. All output, then, can be tied to the movement of money. But how do we measure that output?

It seems intuitive to measure output in terms of money, but this can become problematic. Imagine that the government were to simply add two zeros to every piece of money (automatically turning $1 into $100 and $100 into $10,000). Prices would jump, and the measured "value of output" in the economy would increase tremendously. But we would know that the real output, the goods and services traded, didn't actually change—only the numbers did. What we want to

inflation
an overall rise in prices in the economy

deflation
an overall fall in prices in the economy

headline inflation
measure of inflation that includes all of the goods that the average consumer buys

core inflation
measure of inflation that excludes goods with historically volatile price changes—energy and food

FIGURE 16-1

Running annual change in CPI and core CPI, January 2001–January 2016   The figure shows actual annual inflation rates, as represented by CPI (representing headline or overall inflation) and core CPI (representing core inflation). Core inflation is much more stable than headline inflation.

Sources: Federal Reserve Bank of St. Louis, FRED Economic Data: https://research.stlouisfed.org/fred2/series/CPIAUCSL# (CPI data) and https://research.stlouisfed.org/fred2/series/CPILFESL# (core CPI data).

measure is the output in terms of real, tangible goods and services: How many cans of soda or tons of steel were created by the country?

As you may recall from earlier chapters, we use the terms *real* and *nominal* to differentiate the quantity of tangible goods and services from the numbers associated with them:

- We call quantities measured in terms of real, tangible goods and service *real values.* They represent an accounting for the actual amount of something that is produced. That accounting is independent of how many pieces of paper with a certain number of zeros on it you would need to purchase that output.

- In contrast, values measured in terms of how much money it would take to purchase something are called *nominal values.*

We use changes in the *price level* to get from one to the other. In Chapter 8, "The Cost of Living," we described the concept of a *deflator*—the idea of using a price index like the CPI or the GDP deflator to adjust between nominal and real prices. These indexes allow us to convert nominal measures of output into real measures of output. In other words, they let us measure how much real stuff we get for our money. The **aggregate price level** is a measure of the average price level for GDP. In practice, it is measured by either the CPI or the GDP price deflator.

Now, back to the hypothetical: What if the government one day decided to add two zeros to the figure on every new and existing dollar bill (and added two zeroes to every financial

aggregate price level
a measure of the average price level for GDP; in practice, the CPI or GDP price deflator

account)? Doing this would essentially increase the money supply by 100 times. If nothing else changed in the economy, you can predict that a store-owner who previously sold a bottle of water for $1 would raise the price to $100; your $20 haircut would soon cost $2,000. And you would push for a raise from $10 an hour to $1,000 an hour in your job at the library. With that new wage, the change in the price of goods and services really wouldn't make much of a difference.

In this example, the change in the price level (prices and wages being 100 times higher than before) didn't dent your purchasing power because the *real* value of your money hasn't changed. When all prices (including wages) increase proportionately, what you could buy when you made $10 an hour is the same as what you can buy when you make $1,000 an hour. The change in the price level—that is, the change in the unit of measurement used to account for something— changed only *nominal* values, not real values.

This is the basic intuition behind what is called the **neutrality of money**—the idea that, in the long run, changes in the money supply affect nominal variables, such as prices and wages, but do not affect real outcomes in the economy. The underlying mechanism is described in the next section.

neutrality of money the idea that, in the long run, changes in the money supply affect nominal variables, such as prices and wages, but do not affect real outcomes in the economy

The classical theory of inflation

LO 16.3 Describe and illustrate the classical theory of inflation.

In Chapter 15, "Money and the Monetary System," we touched on the idea that the level of prices in an economy is affected by the quantity of money in an economy. It's time to explain formally how this process happens, using the *classical theory of inflation*. The classical theory of inflation illustrates the relationship between money supply, output (or GDP), and the overall level of prices. It also shows the neutrality of money in the long run.

Figure 16-2 illustrates the basic framework of the classical theory using the now-familiar aggregate supply and aggregate demand perspective. Suppose the economy is in long-run

FIGURE 16-2

Increase in the money supply under the classical theory of inflation

According to the classical theory of inflation, in the long run, increases in the money supply will lead to an increase in prices only; output will stay the same. In the short run, output and prices increase as aggregate demand shifts to the right. However, workers then begin to negotiate for a higher wage, which shifts the aggregate supply curve to the left. Output returns to the original level, while prices increase even more.

equilibrium at point E_1 in the figure. Short-run aggregate demand matches short-run aggregate supply, which matches the long-run potential aggregate supply of the economy.

➤ What happens if the Federal Reserve increases the money supply, as in expansionary monetary policy? The increased money supply will result in lower interest rates and higher levels of borrowing; in turn, aggregate demand will increase. As Figure 16-2 shows, aggregate demand shifts right, creating a new temporary equilibrium where the new short-run aggregate demand curve intersects the short-run aggregate supply curve and increasing output (real GDP). The economy is at point E_2.

We know from the idea of the neutrality of money, however, that this situation can't survive for long. Eventually, prices will rise in proportion with the increase in the money supply. In practice, this can take a little bit of time, since prices are relatively *sticky* (slow-moving). (For example, you don't get to renegotiate your wages immediately when prices go up; you have to wait until your contract is up for renewal or the time is right to renegotiate your wage.)

While it might take time for prices to rise, as long as money is neutral we know they will eventually tick upwards. The increase in prices, especially in nominal wages, in turn leads to a leftward shift in the short-run aggregate supply curve. Why? Because the higher input prices of labor and other goods used in production make it more expensive to produce a given level of output.

The economy eventually reaches a new equilibrium, indicated by point E_3 on the figure: Aggregate supply and short-run aggregate demand once again meet at exactly the level of the long-run aggregate supply curve, and real GDP has fallen back to exactly the point at which it started. (This point is often called *potential output,* a concept we'll explore later in the chapter.) In fact, the only difference is that now *the price level is higher*—reflecting the lower value of money due to the increased money supply. In other words, it will now take a higher number of dollars to buy a given good or service. (Again, think back to the effect of more cigarettes in the POW camp in Chapter 15, "Money and the Monetary System.")

The neutrality of money holds in many cases. But in extreme situations, such as the story of Argentina that we discussed in the chapter opener, the neutrality of money does break down. Extreme and sustained inflation can wreak havoc in the economy, leading to slower growth. At a minimum, stores would need to constantly reprice items. When prices change more rapidly, consumers and firms face uncertainty, and the cost of discovering (and updating) information about alternative prices rises.

It's important to emphasize that the classical theory of inflation describes a long-run equilibrium. Some economists have used the eventual neutrality of money to argue that the Federal Reserve can't meaningfully guide the economy through monetary policy. Others cite empirical evidence that suggests that there is considerable scope for the Federal Reserve to affect the economy in the short run through expansionary or contractionary policy. This is one reason our analysis may yield different answers in the short run versus the long run.

The quantity theory of money

quantity theory of money
theory that the value of money (and thus the aggregate price level) is determined by the overall quantity of money in existence (the money supply); it states that changes in the price level (inflation or deflation) are primarily the result of changes in the quantity of money

> **LO 16.4** Explain the quantity theory of money and relate it to inflation and deflation.

The classical theory of inflation is strongly connected to a related theory: the **quantity theory of money**. The quantity theory of money states explicitly that the value of money (and thus the aggregate price level) is determined by the overall quantity of money in existence (the money supply). Further, it states that changes in the price level (inflation or deflation) are primarily the result of changes in the quantity of money:

- An increase in the money supply leads to an increase in prices (inflation), as there are more dollar bills spent on the same number of goods and services.
- Likewise, a decrease in the money supply leads to a decrease in prices (deflation), as there are just as many goods and services but fewer dollars with which to purchase them.

The quantity theory of money depends on the velocity of money being relatively constant. The **velocity of money**, simply put, is the number of transactions a typical dollar is used in during a given period. If you buy a hamburger, some of the money you spent to purchase it goes to the waitress, another part goes to the cook, and yet another part goes to the rancher who raised the cow; some goes to the dozens of other suppliers who provided everything from the bun to the booth you are sitting in. In other words, your consumption spending is someone else's income, and that person can (and usually does) go on to spend at least part of that income on something else. Intuitively, the velocity of money is a simple concept. If the average dollar is spent five times a year, then the velocity of money for that year would be five.

velocity of money
the number of times the entire money supply turns over in a given period

We can mathematically calculate the velocity of money (V) as equal to the price level (P) multiplied by real output (Y), divided by the money supply (M):

EQUATION 16-1
$$V = \frac{P \times Y}{M}$$

For example, if an economy produces 1,000 units of output (so that Y = 1,000) with a price level of $1 (P = $1) and the money supply (M) is $500, velocity is

$$\frac{\$1 \times 1,000}{\$500} = 2$$

That means that over the course of the year, each dollar in the money supply was spent twice on average in order to generate $1,000 worth of output.

Rearranging Equation 16-1, we can see that the total amount of money in the economy (the money supply, M) multiplied by the number of times that money turns during the year (the velocity of money, V) must equal the nominal value of output (Y). If we now adjust this formula to incorporate the concept of real output and aggregate price levels, we can see that total money supply multiplied by the velocity of money is equal to the price level times real output. This is the **quantity equation** that underlies the quantity theory of money:

EQUATION 16-2
$$M \times V = P \times Y$$

quantity equation
the equation M × V = P × Y, which relates the money supply and velocity of money to the price value of real output

We've assumed that velocity is relatively constant. But is that true in practice? Figure 16-3 shows information on the velocity of money in the United States through history. As you can see, velocity has been relatively stable historically, though the recent financial crisis temporarily caused some significant changes. This means that real output (Y) will also not change in equilibrium (as long as the production process remains the same as well). Equation 16-2 implies that any increase in M (the money supply) has to eventually lead directly to an increase in P (the aggregate price level). Of course, a decrease in M would result in a decrease in P. In other words, increasing the money supply leads to inflation, and decreasing the money supply leads to deflation.

If the velocity of money were not relatively constant, then the quantity theory of money could not hold. With rapid increases or decreases in the amount of money changing hands in the economy, it would be possible for the money supply to double while people spend their money half as fast. Rather than increasing prices, as we would otherwise expect when the money supply doubles, the amount of money moving around in the economy would stay the same, and prices would stay roughly the same as well. As an example of this, the Fed increased the size of the monetary base quite substantially in an attempt to stimulate the economy following the 2007–2009 recession. If the velocity of money had not declined during this period (as shown in Figure 16-3), the result would have been far more inflation than was actually observed.

An implication of this theory is that deflation occurs if the money supply remains constant but real output increases. Logically, the effect is the same as if real output stayed constant and the money supply declined. As we saw in Chapter 15, "Money and the Monetary System," this relationship between output and the money supply is one of the main arguments against the gold standard. Barring a sudden discovery of gold, the supply of gold-backed money is

FIGURE 16-3

Velocity of M1 in the United States   For much of the early part of this graph, the velocity of money, reflected by the amount of money spent compared to nominal GDP, slowly heats up. After oscillating between six and eight times GDP in the 80s and early 90s, money velocity increases to over 10 times GDP at the height of the housing boom. The speed of money through the economy then slowed in the recession.

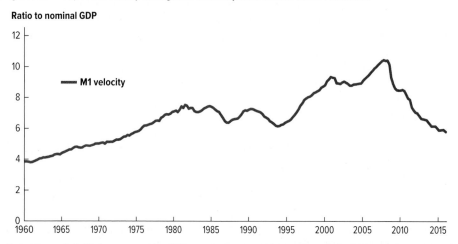

Source: Federal Reserve Bank of St. Louis, accessed from FRED economic data, August 2012, http://research.stlouisfed.org/fred2/.

relatively fixed. If M is constant, when the economy expands (that is, when Y increases), then either the velocity of money must go up or the price level must go down (or a combination of these two events will occur). And if velocity is relatively constant, then there is only one option: The price level must fall, a situation known as *deflation*. We will see in more detail later in this chapter why deflation can be extremely damaging to an economy.

The Where's George? website brings to life the idea of velocity. The site allows users to enter the serial number of a dollar bill and see where it has been (assuming other holders of that dollar have entered the bill). See the Real Life box "Where's George?" for more.

Real Life
Where's George?

Have you ever looked at a crumpled dollar bill and wondered where that piece of paper had been before it got to you? You might even have noticed a stamp on a dollar bill leading you to the Where's George? website (www.wheresgeorge.com). Now that you know more about how money works, you might find it interesting to see what happens there: Users track the adventures of millions of bills as they travel through the economy. Tracking those travels captures what economists mean when they talk about velocity.

The website works like this: Users input the serial number found at the corner of any U.S. bill. If the bill has already been entered on the site, you can see where the bill has been and how long it took for it to get around. If you are the first person to enter the serial number, the bill becomes part of the database that will record the story of that bill.

Statistics from the site can give a pretty interesting picture of who holds money in the United States. Overall, more than 263 million unique Georges have been added. The most bills are entered in California, New York, and Florida. This is not too surprising as these states are within the top five in total population.

The individual stories can also tell a lot about how money moves through the economy. The site records such statistics as the distance the bills traveled between being recorded in the site, which is also converted into a miles per day figure. Most bills travel about five miles per day on average.

One of the more intrepid Georges visited 14 cities in a 7,686-mile, four-year jaunt around the country that took it from the fast-food chain Whataburger in Tallahassee, Florida, to Aiken, South Carolina, via flashy Times Square and the hip streets of Portland, Oregon.

Most trips are far more mundane: 57 percent of the bills on the site travel only between 30 and 500 miles in the course of nine months. The website depends on users to add bills, and it has captured only a sliver of the 11.4 billion dollar bills in circulation. Still, the site reminds us that those crumpled dollars in your pocket might have already had some interesting adventures.

Sources: http://www.wheresgeorge.com/; https://www.federalreserve.gov/paymentsystems/coin_currcircvolume.htm.

Other causes of changing price levels

We've looked at how the quantity theory of money explains changes in price levels: Over the long term, any increase or decrease in the money supply—assuming that velocity and real output are held constant—will result in an increase or decrease in the price level. In addition, changes in the price level can also be created in a more temporary fashion by (1) the actions of the business cycle or (2) sudden supply shocks to a key resource in production.

We've actually discussed the changes in the price level resulting from the action of the business cycle many times before, in other chapters. Recall what happens in the aggregate supply and demand framework:

- When an economy goes through a boom, companies look to expand rapidly to meet rising demand and competition for scarce resources heats up. It becomes harder to find workers, leading employers to bid against each other for the best talent, increasing wages. This demand pulls prices higher, as too much money is spent chasing too few goods. This is *demand-pull inflation.*
- Of course, the opposite is also true. When economic activity is slow, fewer dollars are spent on the same amount of goods, pushing prices downward. This kind of demand-related deflation is relatively rare.

These two effects combine to create a rise in price levels during the boom periods and, potentially, a fall in price levels during busts. We'll explore the relationship between inflation and the business cycle, and in particular unemployment, in more detail a bit later.

The other type of change in price levels occurs when the price of any key input increases suddenly. Known as *cost-push inflation,* the rising cost causes firms to increase prices in order to maintain profits. A serious bout of cost-push inflation occurred in the mid-1970s in the United States when OPEC, the organization that controls most of the world's supply of oil, decided to cut the amount of oil they produced. Oil in its many forms is absolutely essential not only to the production of gasoline but also to many other goods, from corn to plastics. The shortage caused an increase in the price of oil, and the increase in the price of oil increased the prices of goods throughout the economy.

✓CONCEPT CHECK

- ☐ What is included in headline inflation that is left out of core inflation? **[LO 16.1]**
- ☐ Do changes in the aggregate price level change overall real output? **[LO 16.2]**
- ☐ According to the classical theory of inflation, will inflation increase or decrease if the Federal Reserve pursues expansionary monetary policy? **[LO 16.3]**
- ☐ What is the velocity of money? **[LO 16.4]**

Why Do We Care about Changing Price Levels?

At this point you may find yourself wondering why changes in the price level matter. After all, we've seen from the theory of money neutrality that the economy should adjust itself to different levels of nominal prices, leaving no change in overall output. So why be concerned about price levels?

As we'll see in this section, while the price level itself is immaterial, *changes* in the price level can have a big effect on economic behavior. We'll also see why many economists believe a modest and predictable level of inflation is a good thing, but high or unpredictable levels of inflation—and any level of deflation—are economically damaging.

Inflation

LO 16.5 Analyze the economic consequences of inflation.

We've defined inflation as an overall rise in prices (an increase in the aggregate price level). If the average price level rises 10 percent every year (that is, the prices of all the things in the economy go up by an average of 10 percent), we say that the economy is experiencing an inflation rate of 10 percent per year. The four panels of Figure 16-4 show inflation rates around the world in 1980, 1990, 2000, and 2010. Note that over the last four decades, the inflation rate has generally decreased.

Despite the generally decreasing inflation rate in the past four decades, inflation is always a threat. That makes it important to understand the costs of predictable inflation and the problems of unpredictable inflation.

FIGURE 16-4a

Inflation around the world (1980)*

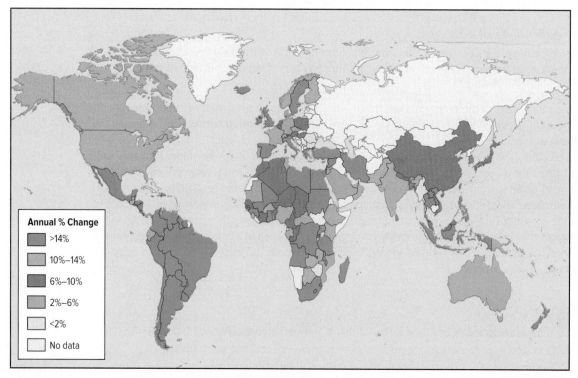

*National boundaries were slightly different in 1980, 1990, and 2000.

Source: World Bank World Development Indicators, 2012, http://data.worldbank.org/data-catalog/world-development-indicators.

FIGURE 16-4b

Inflation around the world (1990)*

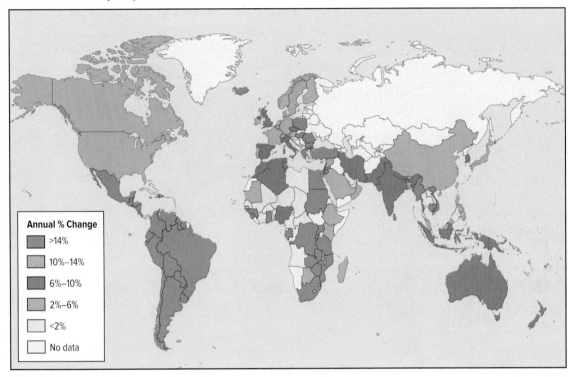

Annual % Change
- >14%
- 10%–14%
- 6%–10%
- 2%–6%
- <2%
- No data

FIGURE 16-4c

Inflation around the world (2000)*

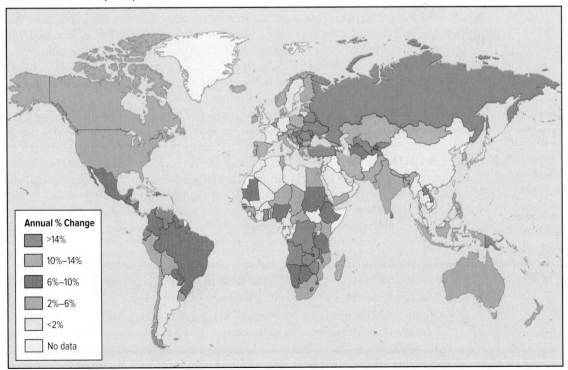

Annual % Change
- >14%
- 10%–14%
- 6%–10%
- 2%–6%
- <2%
- No data

FIGURE 16-4d

Inflation around the world (2010)

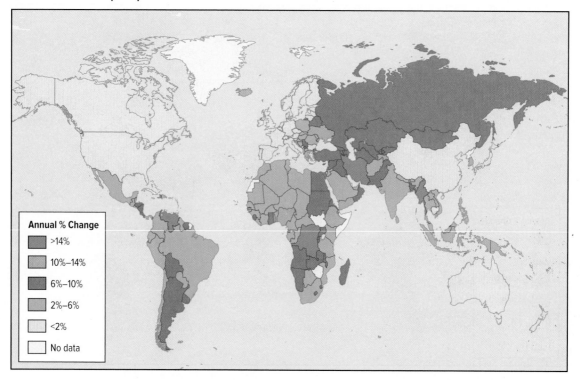

Annual % Change
- >14%
- 10%–14%
- 6%–10%
- 2%–6%
- <2%
- No data

Costs of predictable inflation

If money is neutral in the long run, why is it bad if prices go up? Won't the rest of the economy adjust to any price change? As we'll see shortly, arguably the most damaging economic consequence of inflation is the *uncertainty* it can create. Such uncertainty is increased when the amount or timing of inflation is *unpredictable*. But even if inflation is predictable—say, if you are sure that prices will go up by about 20 percent every year—it still imposes costs. We will discuss three types of costs that even stable and predictable inflation imposes on the economy: menu costs, shoe-leather costs, and tax distortions.

Menu costs refer to the costs of changing prices to keep pace with inflation. Such costs are measured in money, time, and opportunity. The term comes from the simple idea that for restaurants, changing prices likely means reprinting menus. Consider a company that runs vending machines and has to send someone out to reprogram every machine when it wants to raise the price of a can of soda. Even if a company has to update only a website, it takes some time and effort.

Inflation also imposes **shoe-leather costs** on the economy. That term refers to the time, money, and effort one has to spend *managing cash* in the face of inflation. Imagine you run a business that involves handling a lot of cash—a grocery store, say. You are likely to handle cash in different ways depending on how stable you think prices are:

- If you know prices are fairly stable, you will be relaxed about keeping cash on your premises if it's more convenient (and safe) to do so. If prices aren't going up much, you won't lose much buying power by holding the cash.

- But if you know prices are going up quickly, you will want to keep as much money as possible in an interest-bearing bank account. You'll earn at least a bit of interest to help offset the loss in buying power due to rising prices. In addition to other hassles, you'll likely waste a lot of time traveling back and forth to the bank to deposit and withdraw

menu costs
the costs (measured in money, time, and opportunity) of changing prices to keep pace with inflation

shoe-leather costs
the costs (measured in time, money, and effort) of managing cash in the face of inflation

cash—wearing out your shoe leather, hence the name. (And even though with online banking your actual shoes may not wear so thin, the time you spend transferring assets from one form to another could be spent in more profitable—and enjoyable—ways.)

The third type of cost that inflation imposes on the economy is *tax distortion* (also sometimes called *bracket creep*). This one is a bit more subtle than menu costs and shoe-leather costs but can be costly all the same. Tax distortions happen because tax laws take into consideration only nominal income—not what you can buy with it. It's easiest to show the consequences with an example. Let's assume that those who earn less than $60,000 a year pay a 10 percent tax on their entire income, and those who earn $60,000 or more pay a 15 percent tax on their entire income. If a family earns $50,000 a year, they pay $5,000 in tax to the government. But imagine that inflation is 20 percent per year and the family's income adjusts to exactly keep up with inflation. They now earn $60,000, but their purchasing power is unchanged. All the same, they now have to pay a 15 percent tax rate since they just entered the higher tax bracket. Their bill to the government has now increased to $9,000, and thus the tax system is essentially penalizing the family for inflation.

In theory, the government can adjust tax brackets for inflation. In practice this doesn't always happen. In the United States, the *alternative minimum tax* (AMT) is an example of a tax that often is subject to bracket creep. The AMT was designed to impose taxes on only very wealthy individuals. But because the cutoffs were not adjusted for inflation, millions of Americans who were not super-rich were eventually hit by the tax. In 2013, Congress created new rules that automatically adjust the AMT cutoffs for inflation.

Problems of unpredictable inflation

We've just considered three costs that occur even when inflation is stable and predictable. It turns out that even worse problems arise when inflation is *not* predictable.

In many businesses, the profit margin (the difference between the cost of producing a product and the amount it can be sold for) is less than 10 percent. If the company can't be sure whether the prices of the inputs used to make its product will go up by 5 percent, 10 percent, or 20 percent over the next year, planning becomes tough. Businesses become hesitant to invest in new ideas and to hire workers.

Uncertainty also lies behind a more complex "cost" of inflation, which occurs because changing prices affect interest rates. Here, there can be a redistributive effect, effectively transferring money either from savers to borrowers, or vice versa. To see how this happens, it might help to review the difference between *nominal* and *real* interest rates:

- The **nominal interest rate** is the everyday notion of the interest rate. It is the reported interest rate, not adjusted for the effects of inflation. For example, the percentage that the bank pays you for saving (or, if you're borrowing, the percentage that you pay the lender) is the nominal interest rate. Examples of the nominal interest rate can be found in the financial pages of a newspaper such as *The Wall Street Journal* or the *New York Times* or in a loan contract.

- The **real interest rate** is the interest rate adjusted for the anticipated effects of inflation. As we know, inflation means that each dollar becomes less valuable over time.

nominal interest rate
the reported interest rate, not adjusted for the effects of inflation

real interest rate
the interest rate adjusted for the effects of inflation

Since investors do not know, however, the exact inflation rate that will prevail over the duration of the transaction, they need to adjust nominal interest rates for the *expected* rate of inflation. When you're deciding how much to save, then, you need to look at two things that work in opposite directions:

- How interest will add to the value of your savings.
- How inflation will erode the purchasing power of each dollar in your savings account.

To know which effect is dominant—that is, whether the real value of your money will increase or decrease over time—you can calculate the real interest rate by subtracting the expected inflation rate from the nominal interest rate. Since both rates are typically stated as an annual percentage of the base level, the formula for calculating the real interest rate is simple:

EQUATION 16-3   Real interest rate = Nominal interest rate − Expected inflation rate

To see how important the difference between the nominal and real interest rates can be, look at Table 16-1. It shows an example of the same savings account with two different inflation rates. Suppose that in 2010 you had deposited $1,000 into an account with a nominal annual interest rate of 4 percent, keeping it there for five years. Here's what would happen with varying rates of inflation:

- If there is no inflation, then your real return is equal to the nominal interest rate. In that case you would end up with $1,217 in both 2015 dollars and 2010 dollars.
- If inflation runs at 3 percent per year over the five years, your real interest rate is only 1 percent (4% nominal interest rate − 3% inflation rate). Then, in 2015, you will still have $1,217 in 2015 dollars, but they are worth only $1,051 in 2010 dollars.
- If inflation is 5 percent per year, then your money actually loses value. The real interest rate is −1 percent (4% nominal interest rate − 5% inflation rate). You again end up with $1,217 at the end of the five-year period in 2015 dollars, but in this case it's worth only $951 in 2010 dollars.

Of course, the reverse situation applies to *borrowers*. Suppose you borrowed $1,000 in 2010 and agreed to pay it back at a rate of 4 percent interest. High inflation is now your friend: If inflation turns out to be 5 percent, then the real value of what you end up paying back is less than the amount you borrowed. That is good news for you!

In other words, when the inflation rate is higher than nominal interest rates (when *real* interest rates are negative), the value of both savings and debts decreases:

- Savers become worse off, as the value of what they have put in the bank becomes less valuable over time.
- Conversely, borrowers gain from inflation since inflation reduces the value of dollars; a loan made today will have a smaller value in real terms later. This debt will be easier to repay as its real value decreases.

Effectively, we can say that *high inflation redistributes wealth from those who save to those who borrow.* (We should note, however, that borrowers may eventually suffer if savers/lenders stop making loans entirely because of these losses.)

If inflation is predictable, then this redistributive effect need not happen. Even if inflation is high—say, 20 percent—savers will not lose out as long as banks offer nominal interest rates above 20 percent. However, changes in the inflation rate often come as a surprise, and it can take time for nominal interest rates to adjust. (Storekeepers cannot immediately change all prices, nor can employers immediately change wages.). And as we discussed earlier, there are other costs of inflation that apply even when its timing and amount are predictable.

TABLE 16-1

Real and nominal interest rates

Without inflation, the real and nominal interest rates are the same, so the interest rate you see is what you actually get. With inflation, the real interest you are earning is less than the nominal rate; if inflation is greater than the nominal interest rate, the investment actually becomes worth less in real value than the original investment.

Value in 2010 ($)	Nominal interest rate (%)	Inflation rate (%)	Real interest rate (%)	Nominal 2015 value ($)	Value in 2015 (2010 dollars)
1,000	4	0	4	1,217	1,217
1,000	4	3	1	1,217	1,051
1,000	4	5	−1	1,217	951

These same ideas about the economic consequences of inflation apply to governments that have taken on debt and need to repay it. The only difference is that a government can control inflation, at least to some degree, through monetary policy. A government may thus be tempted to slowly "inflate away" the amount of debt it owes. The pros and cons of such a strategy are discussed in the Real Life box "Inflating away the debt."

Real Life
Inflating away the debt

Picture this: You're the president of a country in an economic bind. Tax revenues are down. The prospect of economic growth is bleak. You face a growing government debt.

What do you do? You could cut government spending or raise taxes, but both of these options are destined to make you unpopular. Fortunately, your chief economic advisor has an idea: "Just print money! That can solve your debt problems," he says. "Printing more money would increase prices, and this increase in inflation would reduce the real value of the debt that is carried by the government."

Zimbabwe used this scheme when it found itself owing more money to foreigners and government employees than it could easily afford. To get out of the bind, the regime headed by Robert Mugabe decided to start printing Zimbabwean dollars. In 2006, the government printed 21 trillion Zimbabwean dollars (roughly $210 million U.S.) to pay off loans, and another 60 trillion (or $600 million U.S.) to pay civil servants.

Did the strategy work? In a sense, yes. The government's debts, denominated in Zimbabwean dollars, soon became almost worthless as inflation predictably spiraled out of control. Inflation in Zimbabwe reached an incredible *11 million percent* in 2008! However, such high levels of inflation caused utter chaos that crippled the Zimbabwean economy, leading to an unemployment rate of more than 80 percent.

Inflating away the debt is not always such a recipe for disaster. On a more modest scale, this strategy can have some success. In the 1940s, for example, the United States emerged from World War II with a debt-to-GDP ratio of 108.6 percent. In other words, all of the country's production for slightly more than a year would be needed to get rid of that amount of debt. According to economists Joshua Aizenman and Nancy Marion, thanks to inflation—which reached 14.4 percent in 1947—that ratio was cut by more than a third within a decade. In the meantime, the economy, buoyed by postwar economic activity, posted strong gains.

Even when the economy stays strong, inflation is not an ideal solution. Debt represents a promise made to lenders, and they stand to lose money if the government decides to print its way out of debt. In the end, nobody is going to want to lend money to a government that has a track record of inflating away its debts. Economist Alan Auerbach calculates that with the way debt is designed, inflation could wipe away only $5.4 trillion of the roughly $53 trillion budget shortfall projected for the United States over the next 75 years.

Still, it's easy to see the attraction of the idea: If you could simply print money to reduce the real value of your personal debts, wouldn't you be just a little bit tempted?

Sources: http://allafrica.com/stories/200602170023.html; http://economix.blogs.nytimes.com/2010/02/18/inflation-wont-solve-our-debt-problems/; http://www.nber.org/papers/w15562.

Deflation

LO 16.6 Analyze the economic consequences of deflation.

Inflation has a natural opposite: deflation. *Deflation* is an overall fall in prices (a decrease in the aggregate price level)—negative inflation, essentially. Periods of deflation occur far less often than inflation, and they generally occur in only the very worst economic circumstances. Deflation characterized the Great Depression of the 1930s, when aggregate prices in the United States fell by nearly half in a few years. More recently, Japan experienced a so-called lost decade of deflation in the 1990s, which continues to pose challenges for its economy.

Why is deflation such a problem? For one thing, it increases the burden of debt. As we saw in the discussion of the problems of unpredictable inflation, most loans are made in nominal terms: If you borrow $100 at an annual interest rate of 5 percent for one year, you will owe $105 at the end of the year. If the price level has gone down due to deflation, the *real* value of that $105 will be even higher. Since paying back loans eats up a greater part of what you can buy in real terms, consumption will decrease.

Of course, the flip-side is that if you are a saver in deflationary times, your savings will be worth more in real terms. In that case, won't savers spend more, given that deflation causes their savings to increase in value? Probably not. If people *expect* deflation, they will likely want to spend less. It's easy to see why: Suppose you expect prices to be 10 percent lower in a few months than they are now. Will you buy that new car now or wait a few months? The expectation that prices will fall explains at least in part why deflation can cripple an economy. In addition, companies that expect deflation to continue will be less willing to borrow money to invest. They expect the money they borrow will be worth more in real terms when they have to pay it back.

With consumption and investment both down, the net result of expected deflation is to *reduce the level of aggregate demand* in the economy. This, in turn, reduces prices, causing deflation to continue. This self-reinforcing cycle is referred to as a *deflationary spiral*, or deflationary trap.

As we saw in Chapter 15, "Money and the Monetary System," the risk of deflation is an argument against tying a currency to gold. Indeed, the pain caused by deflation was a major populist issue at end of the nineteenth century in America. Under the gold standard, prices were decreasing at the rate of 1 to 2 percent per year. This decrease consistently expanded the debts of borrowers, who were mostly poor farmers. At the 1896 Democratic Party convention, William Jennings Bryan railed against the power of the gold standard to the advantage of savers at the expense of borrowers, in what is now known as the "Cross of Gold" speech. He ended by saying, "You shall not press down upon the brow of labor this crown of thorns, you shall not crucify mankind upon a cross of gold."

Bryan instead advocated for returning to a bimetallic standard, in which silver and gold were both used as money. That change would have resulted in a substantial increase in the money supply and overall prices. This increase would have enabled farmers and workers to be able to pay off their debt more easily. In the end, Bryan's opponent, William McKinley, won the election and formally entrenched the gold standard as official policy of the United States in 1900.

Controlling inflation, or not: Disinflation and hyperinflation

LO 16.7 Describe disinflation and hyperinflation and explain the role of monetary policy in creating both situations.

Controlling inflation is a critical role of the Federal Reserve in managing the money supply, part of its dual mandate. When central banks succeed at controlling inflation, *disinflation* occurs. When central banks fail to control runaway inflation, *hyperinflation* occurs. Here, we look at both situations.

disinflation
a period in which inflation rates are falling, but still positive

Disinflation

Let's say the Federal Reserve wants to reduce inflation from 7 percent to 2 percent. If it succeeds, the result is **disinflation**, the term for a period during which overall inflation rates, while still positive, are falling. (Be sure not to get this concept confused with *deflation*, in which inflation rates are negative.) In general, disinflation is usually discussed in the context of the central bank (the Fed in the United States) aggressively trying to contain inflation via contractionary monetary policy.

In the United States, the Federal Reserve famously applied disinflationary tactics to slow the increase in prices experienced as a result of the OPEC oil embargo in the 1970s, when inflation hit about 10 percent per year. There were campaigns to avoid shopping at high-priced shops. A troop of Girl Scouts in Kansas hit the news when they pledged to fight inflation by keeping the price of their cookies the same as it had been two years before. Such efforts made little progress in reducing the ballooning inflation rate—until President Jimmy Carter appointed Paul Volcker as chairman of the Federal Reserve in 1979.

In a direct reversal of his predecessor's policies, Volcker advocated for "shock therapy" to gain control over the double-digit inflation. He bumped the official federal funds rate from 10 percent to 20 percent. Unsurprisingly, because the economywide rise in interest rates made it very expensive to borrow money, this increase in interest rates plunged the economy deep into recession. In protest, a group of farmers drove tractors onto C Street, in the heart of Washington, DC, and blockaded the main entrances of the Federal Reserve building. However, the shock therapy eventually worked. Inflation fell from 10.4 percent in 1981 to below 5 percent in 1983 and has stayed low ever since. Volcker's bold vision caused short-run pain, but it fixed the inflation problem in the long run.

Economists differ over how high inflation has to be before it becomes enough of a problem to merit such painful measures. Some countries have successfully coped with very high inflation (as much as 30 or 40 percent a year) for long periods of time without too much adverse effect on their economy. This is a high-risk situation, though: At such a high rate, inflation is extremely unstable, and it doesn't take much for an economy to slip further toward higher and higher inflation rates.

Hyperinflation

When inflation begins to spiral out of control, we say that a country is experiencing **hyperinflation**—extremely long-lasting and painful increases in the price level. Such increases are usually enough to render the currency completely valueless or close to it. This happened pretty quickly in Zimbabwe after the Mugabe regime started printing money to inflate away their debts in 2006.

In one of his first major involvements in public policy, John Maynard Keynes attended the meetings at Versailles that formally ended World War I. During these negotiations, Germany demanded, over the objection of Keynes, extensive reparation payments. Keynes left the Versailles meetings and returned to England to write *The Economic Consequences of the Peace* (1919). This popular work argued that the Versailles treaty demanded more in reparation payments from Germany than the German economy was capable of producing. Keynes predicted that it could lead to political and economic instability and the possibility of hyperinflation in Germany. Keynes's predictions materialized. While this was not the first or most severe hyperinflation experienced in Europe, it had far-reaching consequences: The resultant political and economic instability helped lead to the collapse of the Weimar Republic and the rise of Nazi Germany.

The worst hyperinflation ever recorded happened in Hungary in 1946. With the economy in ruins after World War II, and tax revenues covering only 15 percent of expenditures, the government began to print money to finance the gap. In January 1946, there were 16,500,000 *pengos* in circulation. By July 1946, there were 1,730,000,000,000,000,000. Prices were doubling approximately every 15 hours. Clearly, this situation was not sustainable. In August 1946

hyperinflation
extremely long-lasting and painful increases in the price level

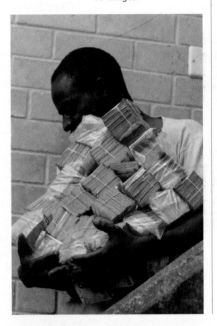

Imagine the complications of hyperinflation in daily life. This Zimbabwean man, at the height of the country's hyperinflation, is carrying enough money to buy some milk.
© Tsvangirayi Mukwazhi/ AP Images

To try to keep up with inflation, the Zimbabwean government kept printing bills in bigger denominations. Here is a 100-trillion dollar note—not enough to buy a gallon of milk.
© Finnbarr Webster/Alamy

the government abandoned the *pengo* and introduced a new currency, the *forint,* which is still in circulation today. By backing the new currency with gold, the government instilled confidence that it would not print huge amounts of forints.

Expectations can also perpetuate hyperinflation. In Brazil during the 1990s, prices rose in part because everyone simply expected them to keep rising. The increase was slowed only by an unorthodox plan that included an entirely fake currency. The story can be found in the Real Life box "A *real* plan—with fake currency."

Real Life

A *real* plan—with fake currency

In 1993, President Itamar Franco of Brazil appointed Fernando Henrique Cardoso to be the country's fourth finance minister within seven months. As the rate of turnover suggests, it was not an enviable job. Price levels in Brazil had been steadily rising for seven years, and the inflation rate was approaching 2,000 percent per year. If he wanted to keep his job, Cardoso had to tackle the hyperinflation quickly. No one had high hopes for his success, though. Cardoso was a professor of sociology, with little training in economics. Furthermore, years of failed efforts had convinced Brazilians that the hyperinflation was invincible to government efforts.

Cardoso sought help from an academic economist named Edmar Bacha, who had been debating with colleagues about how to tame Brazil's stubbornly high inflation. Observing that the traditional tactics used to fight inflation—freezes on prices and wages—had been unsuccessful, they proposed an elegant, if slightly unorthodox solution: Brazil would create a system of fake money, called "units of real value," or URVs for short.

The plan, dubbed *Plano Real* in Portuguese or "Real Plan," worked as follows: Cardoso required everyone in the economy—grocery stores, the government, retail outlets, and all other businesses—to quote prices in both *cruzeiros* (the Brazilian currency at the time) and URVs. Even contracts with promises for future payment had to quote the payment in URVs as well as *cruzeiros.* People would pay in *cruzeiros* but would always see the price in URVs as well.

Changing conversion rates would ensure that the URV price remained stable: If prices doubled, the conversion rate between *cruzeiros* and URVs would halve, so that prices in URVs would remain the same. The price shown on a pint of milk might increase from 1,000 *cruzeiros* to 2,000 *cruzeiros,* but the price in URVs shown alongside would remain the same.

How could this simple accounting trick possibly help to get inflation under control? The genius of the idea is that it tackled what economists call the *psychological inertia* of hyperinflation. As inflation rises and rises, and all government efforts visibly fail to reduce it, people simply get used to the idea that things can only get worse. Businesses raise prices merely because they expect that prices will keep rising. When enough businesses do this, it becomes a self-fulfilling prophecy. A vicious cycle ensues.

The *Plano Real* broke this cycle. Since prices in URVs were stable, people began to trust that they would *stay* stable. Once trust in the stability of URVs developed, the government simply traded out the untrustworthy *cruzeiros* for a new currency called the *real,* which is still in use today. The government explained that one *real* was worth one URV. Convinced through experience that URV prices were stable, people expected *real* prices to be stable as well. And because they *expected* prices to be stable, they were—relatively speaking, at least. In the first few years after the *real* was introduced, inflation fell to under 20 percent.

And what of Fernando Henrique Cardoso, whose job prospects as finance minister originally seemed so uncertain? A grateful nation promptly elected him president.

Sources: http://www.econ.puc-rio.br/gfranco/rptpd.pdf; http://uk.reuters.com/article/2011/07/02/uk-brazil-president-idUKTRE76119A20110702.

Why a little inflation is good

LO 16.8 Understand why policy-makers favor a small amount of inflation over zero inflation.

If deflation is bad and inflation is bad, then central banks must try to achieve perfect price stability with an inflation rate of zero, right? Wrong. In fact, for most central banks around the world, the preferred monetary policy is to promote modest positive inflation—something around 2 or 3 percent per year. Why do most economists believe it's better to aim for modest inflation than completely stable prices? There are three main reasons for this belief, which we discuss here.

The first reason to favor modest inflation over completely stable prices is that allowing for a little inflation reduces the risk of deflation. If the inflation rate tends to hover around zero percent, and the central bank miscalculates by making monetary policy too contractionary, the result would be deflation—which can have serious impacts on the economy. Keeping inflation at a modest positive level gives a central bank some leeway to make mistakes, without running the risk of tipping the country into a deflationary spiral.

Second, keeping inflation at a modest positive level leaves more room for the central bank to engage in expansionary monetary policy. To understand why, we can work through a simple example. Suppose that inflation is at a healthy 3 percent per year. Investors are going to want an interest rate that is at or above the inflation rate to ensure that the real rate of return they earn on their money is positive. For monetary policy, this means that the overall interest rate will likely end up somewhere at or above 3 percent. This gives the Federal Reserve some room to reduce interest rates before hitting the zero lower bound.

By contrast, if inflation was zero percent, nominal interest rates would be close to zero as well. In the case of a recession, a central bank would have very little leeway to further reduce interest rates in an effort to stimulate the economy. (This situation is sometimes referred to as a *liquidity trap*. It has been a major problem in Japan for more than a decade.)

In fact, during the latest financial crisis, Olivier Blanchard, the former chief economist of the International Monetary Fund (IMF), advised central banks to increase their inflation target from the traditional 2 percent to 4 percent. That extra room, he argued, could mean the difference between effectively fighting a deep recession and hitting the zero lower bound while the economy could still use some help from monetary policy.[3]

A third reason for having a positive inflation target is that the target makes it easier for firms to adjust real wages in the labor market in response to changing labor demand and supply conditions. Reductions in labor demand or labor supply result in reductions in the equilibrium real wage. If prices are stable, reducing the real wage requires employers to reduce the nominal wage; workers may respond to a 1 percent reduction in their nominal pay by reducing their work effort. But workers generally seem less bothered if they receive a 2 percent wage increase when there is 3 percent inflation. The effect is the same—a 1 percent reduction in income—but the cause of the reduced income seems different.

Furthermore, in cases in which there is a formal labor contract, nominal wages cannot be reduced during the life of the contract. With a low inflation rate, though, all that is required for firms to lower real wages is to increase nominal wages more slowly than the inflation rate. Thus, a low and stable inflation rate may help to "grease the wheels" of the labor market, allowing for more flexible real wages and more efficient labor markets.

✓CONCEPT CHECK

- ☐ Why would people at the highest income level not worry about bracket creep? **[LO 16.5]**
- ☐ Why do people spend less in the present when deflation is expected in the future? **[LO 16.6]**
- ☐ What is a reduction in the overall rate of inflation known as? **[LO 16.7]**
- ☐ Why would lenders favor unexpected deflation, while borrowers favor unexpected inflation? **[LO 16.7]**
- ☐ Why does the "zero lower bound" cause problems for macroeconomic policy? **[LO 16.8]**

Inflation and Monetary Policy

We've discussed the Federal Reserve's dual mandate in conducting monetary policy: maintaining price stability and ensuring full employment. Maintaining price stability is, of course, another way of saying that inflation rates should be consistently low. Ensuring full employment simply means that the economy experiences only frictional and structural unemployment and no cyclical unemployment.

The competing goals of the dual mandate

LO 16.9 Explain the relationship between inflation, the output gap, and monetary policy.

In practice, the goals of the dual mandate are often incompatible. To understand why, it helps to think about how inflation rates change through a typical business cycle. During a recession, inflation is typically very low. Why is that? During a bust, the economy is operating well below its potential. Economists refer to an economy's **potential output** as the total amount of output the country could reasonably produce if all of its people and capital resources (i.e., machines and factories and the like) were fully engaged. In practice, this means that only frictional and structural unemployment—no cyclical unemployment—occur.

potential output
the total amount of output a country could produce if all of its resources were fully engaged

The output gap and inflation

When an economy's actual output differs from its potential output at some point in time, we say that it is experiencing an **output gap**. An output gap can be negative or positive:

output gap
the difference between actual and potential output in an economy

- If output is below potential, then the output gap is *negative*. Resources—either factories or workers—are not being fully used. Workers are unemployed and factories are sitting idle, waiting for work.

- It is also possible for an economy to operate above capacity—with factories and workers not only fully employed but also working overtime. When an economy is working above capacity, we say that it has a *positive* output gap.

Figure 16-5 shows the historical output gap for the United States. For the most part, actual output has been below potential output (a negative output gap).

FIGURE 16-5

The output gap in the United States   The output gap registers the difference between the actual GDP and the potential GDP at full employment. For the most part, actual output has stayed below potential output.

Source: IMF World Economic Outlook database, http://data.okfn.org/data/core/imf-weo#data.

What is going on when an economy has a negative output gap? As we've said, a lot of resources are not being fully used. Workers are unemployed and factories are sitting idle. In other words, the economy is experiencing recessionary conditions. During recessionary periods, there is typically little threat of a rise in inflation (unless the economy is hit by an oil crisis or similar external shock). Low rates of inflation occur in part because there is so little demand for money in an economy experiencing recession: Borrowers, for example, are much less interested in taking out loans for big-ticket items during a recession since they are less confident in their ability to pay back the loans. Firms have little incentive to borrow in an effort to expand their businesses when overall demand for goods and services is low. Why produce if you don't assume there will be buyers for the output you make? As long as the supply of money stays the same, decreased demand causes the overall price level to fall.

But what happens when the economy is experiencing a positive output gap? With nearly everyone employed (and working overtime), hiring new workers can become very expensive. Employers have to compete for workers, who can eventually command higher salaries to switch jobs. Likewise, companies are competing to buy machines, factories, or other inputs to meet soaring demand for their products. That competition leads to a rise in the prices of those inputs as well. Rising prices across the economy, of course, mean inflation.

The output gap and monetary policy

As you can see, there is typically a strong relationship between the output gap and inflation. But what does this have to do with monetary policy? To answer that question, we'll have to go back to what happens when the Fed conducts monetary policy.

We'll start with *expansionary monetary policy.* In a recession, an output gap implies that employment is low. A central bank knows that it can fix this problem by engaging in expansionary monetary policy: It increases the money supply and lowers interest rates. As a result, borrowing may increase, which may then help the economy rebound. An increase in economic activity puts more people back to work, which fulfills the mandate: Prices have increased only a little bit, and employment is high.

But as you know, this is only a short-run equilibrium. The increased demand for goods and services will put upward pressure on prices. With an increase in the money supply, more money will be spent chasing the same amount of goods. The economy will eventually fall back to the long-run equilibrium. Employment will decrease, but prices will remain elevated. So what does a central bank do? It could continue to pump money into the economy in an effort to increase employment, but these gains will be short lived and inflation will worsen.

The opposite scenario occurs when inflation is above normal. When inflation is pulled high by demand, money in the economy is spent chasing a limited amount of goods. Firms want to buy machines and inputs in an effort to expand operations, while workers receive higher wages. In this case, employment is at full, or even beyond full, capacity. If a central bank decides that it needs to curb inflation, it will pursue *contractionary monetary policy:* It will reduce the growth rate of the money supply, to work toward a higher interest rate. As we described earlier, this action slows the economy. The higher interest rate makes borrowing more expensive, and firms slow investment. Although inflation decreases, the slowing of the economy increases unemployment. Eventually, though, as the economy adjusts to lower prices and we move into the long run, employment will return to full-output levels, leaving just the decrease in overall prices.

So, you can see that central banks, no matter how they conduct monetary policy, inevitably *affect only price levels,* with no lasting impact on employment in the long run:

- Attempts to stimulate the economy through expansionary monetary policy will increase the inflation rate.
- Attempts to slow the economy through contractionary policy will lower the inflation rate, and risk causing deflation.

The Federal Reserve has to navigate this trade-off carefully.

Inflation and unemployment

> **LO 16.10** Explain how the relationship between inflation and unemployment is modeled by the Phillips curve and integrated into the non-accelerating inflation rate of unemployment.

We've seen that there is a trade-off between inflation and unemployment in the short run, which poses a challenge for the Federal Reserve's dual mandate. Ensuring full employment is really another way of saying "keeping actual output near potential output." Fulfilling this mandate through expansionary monetary policy, however, risks violating the Fed's other mandate, that of price stability. How can the Fed calculate the best way to make this trade-off?

The Phillips curve

In 1958, an economist named A. W. Phillips plotted the change in prices against unemployment over a 95-year period in Great Britain. A distinct pattern emerged:

- As inflation ran higher, unemployment was low.
- When inflation was low, unemployment was high.

Phillips curve
a model that shows the connection between inflation and unemployment in the short run

The line showing that relationship is now called the **Phillips curve,** and it forms the basis of a model that shows the connection between inflation and unemployment in the short run.

Figure 16-6 shows the most basic form of the Phillips curve. The curve, based on hypothetical data, shows that if the central bank of this economy wants zero inflation, then it will have to accept 7 percent unemployment. If it wants to target a modest positive rate of inflation of, for example, 3 percent, then it will have to accept 4 percent unemployment. If it wants to get unemployment down as low as 1 percent, it will have to accept a rate of inflation of 6 percent. And so on.

This simple formulation fits our intuition about how the output gap—and, by extension, unemployment—relates to inflation. In general:

- High amounts of unemployment in an economy will coincide with low inflation.
- Higher amounts of inflation come with lower unemployment.

We can now further investigate this relationship using the aggregate demand and aggregate supply model in the short run, as shown in panels A and B of Figure 16-7. If the economy is

---

FIGURE 16-6

Hypothetical short-run Phillips curve for an economy

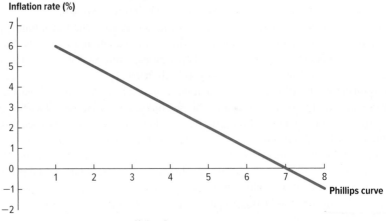

The short-run Phillips curve shows a direct relationship between the inflation rate and the unemployment rate. In an economy that is humming along, prices will increase at a faster rate, although unemployment will be low. As the unemployment rate increases, prices increase far more slowly.

FIGURE 16-7

Aggregate demand and the Phillips curve in the short run

(A) Aggregate demand and supply

(B) Phillips curve

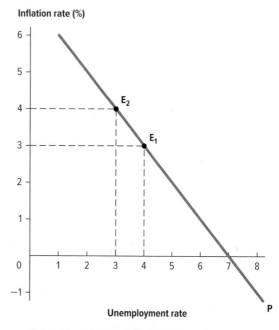

Panel A shows the result of two different aggregate demand curves. E_1 shows a short-run equilibrium with lower prices and output than point E_2 on a higher aggregate demand curve.

With more economic activity, point E_2 on the Phillips curve shows higher inflation and lower unemployment than point E_1, which represents the short-run equilibrium with lower economic activity.

at short-run equilibrium with 4 percent unemployment and 3 percent inflation, an increase in aggregate demand above expectations is going to cause the economy to be at a point higher and to the left on the Phillips curve.

However, this basic curve fails to consider an important factor: the role of *inflation expectations*. In any economy, people often come to expect whatever level of inflation has prevailed over the past few years. If inflation has been about 3 percent over the past few years, then the expectation of 3 percent inflation typically becomes "baked into" prices. If prices are rising by 3 percent per year, employees will expect raises of at least 3 percent as a matter of course, and 3 percent inflation becomes sort of a "default" for the economy.

Why does this matter? Let's assume that the economy represented in Figure 16-5 is hum- ming along at a *long-run equilibrium* of 4 percent unemployment and 3 percent inflation. Now imagine that the central bank decides to try to reduce unemployment, accepting a slightly higher inflation rate as a result: By expanding the money supply, unemployment falls to 1 percent and inflation increases to 6 percent.

So far, the central bank has achieved the results it hoped for. However, we know that the economy was in long-run equilibrium at 4 percent unemployment. And we know from Figure 16-1, earlier in the chapter, what happens if a central bank pursues expansionary monetary policy when the economy is already at long-run equilibrium: It can increase output (and, hence, reduce unemployment), but *only in the short run*. In the long run, output returns to its earlier equilibrium, and so do levels of employment.

Our hypothetical central bank finds that unemployment is now back at 4 percent, but inflation is now running at 6 percent. Effectively, by pursuing expansionary monetary policy when the

FIGURE 16-8

The Phillips curve responds to inflation expectations

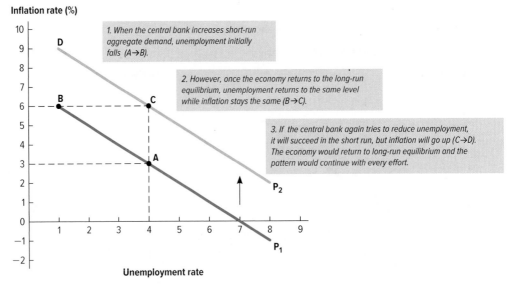

With preset expectations in the economy, the Phillips curve shifts upward by the amount of expected inflation. This means that the amount of inflation at any given amount of unemployment rises in the long run by the amount of expected inflation.

economy was already at long-run equilibrium, it has shifted the Phillips curve upward, as shown in Figure 16-8.

People in our hypothetical economy now *expect* inflation of 6 percent. What happens if the central bank, stubbornly, has another go at reducing unemployment to 1 percent? It will succeed in the short run, but as we can see from the new Phillips curve, inflation will go up to 9 percent (see point D). And in the long run, unemployment will rise again to 4 percent, but inflation will remain stubbornly at 9 percent because people will have adjusted their inflation expectations upward once again. Eventually, the central bank's efforts would simply spiral out of control, leading to more and more inflation and the unemployment rate never staying at the bank's goal in the long run.

Realizing this effect, economists proposed an improved version of the Phillips curve—one that also shows the long-run effect of changing inflation expectations. We'll now call the traditional Phillips curve the *short-run* Phillips curve. The new, improved version we call the *long-run* Phillips curve. Figure 16-9 shows both the short-run Phillips curve and the long-run Phillips curve for two different levels of inflation expectations. The two short-run Phillips curves in the figure tell us the trade-off facing monetary policy-makers between inflation and unemployment at any given time. The vertical line in the figure is the long-run Phillips curve, which is at 4 percent. This line represents the idea that in the long run in our hypothetical economy, it is impossible to get the level of unemployment below 4 percent.

To see why, we'll run through a story that we've told many times before: Let's say the economy is at 4 percent unemployment and the economy expands. In order to expand, firms need more workers, but with such a low unemployment rate, few workers are just sitting around looking for work. As a result, trying to hire more workers is going to be expensive. Wages—the price of labor—are prices, after all. With higher wages resulting from the increase in demand for labor, prices throughout the economy will increase. In Figure 16-9, the vertical line marks the lowest possible unemployment rate that will not cause the inflation rate to increase. Economists call this minimum level of unemployment the **non-accelerating inflation rate of unemployment** **(NAIRU)**. The NAIRU is sometimes also called the *natural rate of unemployment* or simply *full employment* (even though it's not technically 0 percent unemployment).

non-accelerating inflation rate of unemployment (NAIRU)
the lowest possible unemployment rate that will not cause the inflation rate to increase

FIGURE 16-9

The long-run Phillips curve

The long-run Phillips curve represents the fact that there is no trade-off between inflation and unemployment in the long run.

The NAIRU can change over time. Take, for example, the introduction of the Internet to job searches. This innovation reduced structural unemployment (and the NAIRU) on two fronts:

- It increased opportunities available to searchers. Before the availability of sites like monster.com and indeed.com (which allow you to search millions of job listings), job hunters had to scour local classifieds and attend job fairs. They essentially confined their searches to opportunities within a very narrow geographical range. With the Internet, that range has been greatly expanded.
- The Internet has also been a boon to employers. Today, a job posting on the Internet will be seen by more job seekers and bring forward a wider pool of high-quality applicants.

Both job seekers and employers have a wider range of opportunities, with an attendant reduction in the NAIRU.

In practice, calculating the exact NAIRU is difficult. It differs among economies and over time due to variations in the structural components of unemployment, the regulatory and competitive environment, and a multitude of other factors. As a result, it can be difficult to know whether an economy is truly at full employment at any given time—which is a challenge for Federal Reserve policy-makers looking to fulfill their dual mandate. Though we may not know the *exact* location of the NAIRU, we can fairly quickly determine if we are above or below it, though:

- If unemployment is below the NAIRU, inflation generally accelerates.
- If we observe involuntary unemployment rising, unemployment is above the NAIRU.

The Phillips curve and NAIRU in practice

To understand how the NAIRU and Phillips curve work in practice, we'll return to the story from earlier in the chapter of monetary policy after the OPEC oil embargo. When the oil embargo hit, the aggregate supply curve shifted sharply to the left. At that short-run equilibrium, prices were higher and output lower. Obviously, this combination was not desirable for policy-makers; it meant either permitting high rates of inflation, in order to keep unemployment in check, or slowing the economy even further in order to rein in inflation.

FIGURE 16-10

The Phillips curve winds upward

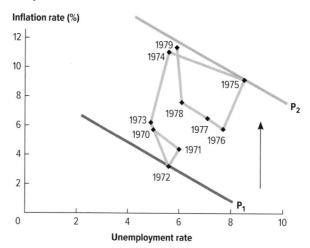

When the Fed tried to battle unemployment by allowing higher inflation, it eventually found that it had simply put the economy on a higher Phillips curve (P₂), as shown above.

During the 1970s, the Federal Reserve chose the first path. The Fed thought that unemployment was a greater danger to the economy than was inflation. The Fed even expanded the money supply to try to pick up the economy after the supply shock. As time wore on, inflation pushed higher and higher, but unemployment stayed relatively the same. You now know why: The economy had shifted to a higher Phillips curve. Since inflation was *expected* in the economy, further attempts to boost the economy simply pushed the trade-off between inflation and unemployment even higher.

By the end of the 1970s, inflation was running at double digits, with high unemployment. Figure 16-10 shows this adjustment upward toward higher Phillips curves, from an inflation rate of about 4 percent in the early 1970s to the double-digit rate by 1979.

When Paul Volcker became Fed chairman in 1979, he realized that shock therapy was needed to wean the economy off the expectation that inflation would continue to increase at relatively high rates. He employed the traditional tool used to fight inflation—Volcker decreased the money supply through increases in interest rates.

This blunt policy worked. Since people knew that the Fed was going to take a tough stand on inflation, expectations for price increases in the future evaporated. In just five years, the overall economy was in a position with a far more favorable trade-off between inflation and unemployment. In Figure 16-11 you can see the change in Phillips curves over this time period, resulting from a decrease in the inflation rate of about 14 percent in 1980 to a much tamer rate of about 4 percent in 1985.

The Phillips curve remains an essential tool for understanding how the Fed's dual mandate works in practice. Effectively, fulfillment of the mandate for full employment means ensuring that employment remains as close to the NAIRU as possible at all times. Pushing unemployment below that level all but guarantees that inflation will get out of control, violating the dual mandate by failing to maintain price stability. On the other hand, allowing unemployment to remain at a higher level than NAIRU would mean failing to maintain full employment, also violating the dual mandate.

The Fed's aim, then, is to keep unemployment levels near the NAIRU and inflation reasonably under control. As the story of the oil embargo shows, managing this trade-off is no easy task.[4]

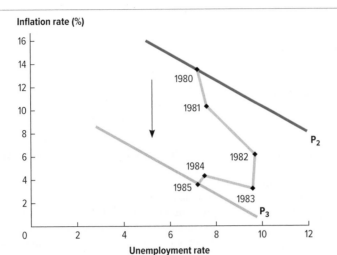

FIGURE 16-11
The Phillips curve adjusts downward

When Paul Volcker became Fed chairman, inflation was running above 12 percent. In the early 1980s, he led an effort to raise interest rates, thereby decreasing the money supply and bringing down inflation. By 1985, the economy was on a lower Phillips curve (P_3).

✓ CONCEPT CHECK

☐ What does it mean for the output gap to be positive? What will eventually happen if that occurs? **[LO 16.9]**

☐ What happens if unemployment is lower than the NAIRU? **[LO 16.10]**

Conclusion

In this chapter we've explored one of the most complex issues in economics: inflation. We've seen how mismanagement of the money supply can lead to runaway inflation, how even relatively modest inflation can have far-reaching consequences for healthy economies, and why deflation is a problem. We've also seen that expectations of inflation help determine whether savings will hold their value and whether it's a good time to borrow.

We've seen too that when people expect inflation to continue, those beliefs can, in themselves, perpetuate inflation. Thus, inflation can be a self-fulfilling prophecy. Getting runaway inflation under control thus requires the right monetary policy plus convincing people that inflation will indeed fall.

Key Terms

inflation, p. 427

deflation, p. 427

headline inflation, p. 427

core inflation, p. 427

aggregate price level, p. 428

neutrality of money, p. 429

quantity theory of money, p. 430

velocity of money, p. 431

quantity equation, p. 431

menu costs, p. 436

shoe-leather costs, p. 436

nominal interest rate, p. 437

real interest rate, p. 437

disinflation, p. 440

hyperinflation, p. 441

potential output, p. 444

output gap, p. 444

Phillips curve, p. 446

non-accelerating inflation rate of unemployment (NAIRU), p. 448

Summary

LO 16.1 Define inflation, deflation, headline inflation, and core inflation.

Inflation is an overall rise in prices in the economy. *Deflation* is an overall fall in prices in the economy. Economists measure inflation or deflation by calculating the percentage change in the CPI. This is the ratio of the cost of the market basket in a given year to the cost of that same basket in a base year. Two different measures of inflation are used: *Headline inflation* is the measure of inflation that includes all of the goods that the average consumer buys, while *core inflation* is the measure of inflation that excludes goods with historically volatile price changes (energy and food). The BLS's official measure uses core inflation because it is less likely to reflect shocks to individual product markets and more likely to show economywide inflation.

LO 16.2 Explain the neutrality of money.

Prices denote the nominal value of goods; the price level reflects prices when aggregated across the economy. The neutrality of money suggests that the money supply affects price levels throughout the economy, but in the long run has no effect on real variables in the economy, such as output. The neutrality of money implies that if the money supply suddenly doubled, nominal GDP would double as well, but real GDP would remain the same.

LO 16.3 Describe and illustrate the classical theory of inflation.

The classical theory of inflation describes the relationship between the money supply, output, and the price level. The theory argues that the money supply has no effect on output in the long run. However, it shows how adjusting the money supply can change output in the short run. If the Federal Reserve adopts expansionary policy, it could increase the money supply, shifting the aggregate demand curve to the right and causing output and prices to increase. The effect on the cost of production and anticipation that these high prices will continue causes the aggregate supply curve to shift leftward until it intersects the demand curve at the original level of output.

LO 16.4 Explain the quantity theory of money and relate it to inflation and deflation.

The quantity theory of money shows the relationship between the value of money in terms of the output we can buy and the quantity of it. Mathematically, the quantity theory of money indicates that the product of the velocity of money and the money supply (total spending) is identical to the product of the price level and real output (nominal GDP).

Changes in the quantity of money affect the price level. An increase in the money supply leads to inflation; a decrease in the money supply leads to deflation.

LO 16.5 Analyze the economic consequences of inflation.

Inflation is an increase in the price level in an economy. Over the long run, inflation is often caused by increases in the money supply. In the short run, it is more often a result of the business cycle. If inflation rates are unstable, they introduce uncertainty into the market, often causing a decline in output. Even a stable rate of inflation can impose costs on the economy, including menu costs and bracket creep.

LO 16.6 Analyze the economic consequences of deflation.

In contrast to inflation, deflation is a fall in the price level of an economy. Deflation is considered more dangerous than inflation. When prices are falling, borrowers have a more difficult time paying back their debts; deflation makes the debt more expensive over time, often causing borrowers to default. High default rates, in turn, lower prices, causing further defaults. A deflationary spiral often ensues, halting the economy.

LO 16.7 Describe disinflation and hyperinflation and explain the role of monetary policy in creating both situations.

When central banks succeed at controlling inflation, disinflation often occurs. Disinflation happens when inflation rates are positive but falling. A famous example of disinflation was Paul Volcker's efforts to stem inflation in the 1980s. When central banks fail to control inflation, hyperinflation can occur. Hyperinflation is an extreme rise in price levels. It can cause economic crisis and drastically reduce the value of a country's currency.

LO 16.8 Understand why policy-makers favor a small amount of inflation over zero inflation.

Although you might think that central banks want to achieve perfect price stability with an inflation rate of zero, most central banks around the world actually prefer modest positive inflation of around 2 or 3 percent per year. There are a few reasons for this. For starters, a little inflation reduces the risk of deflation, giving the central bank some leeway in case their monetary policy is too contractionary. Second, keeping inflation at a modest positive level leaves more room for the central bank to engage in expansionary monetary policy. Finally, positive inflation makes it easier for firms to adjust real wages in response to changing labor demand and supply conditions.

LO 16.9 Explain the relationship between inflation, the output gap, and monetary policy.

The central bank uses monetary policy to control inflation. Central banks prefer to keep inflation low but positive. When full employment occurs, the economy is said to be producing at its potential output, the total amount of output a country can produce if its resources are used efficiently. The output gap is the difference between potential and actual output. When the output gap is negative, inflation will decrease. Central banks will then pursue expansionary monetary policy by lowering interest rates, allowing inflation to rise and bringing back full employment. When the output gap is positive, inflation will increase.

LO 16.10 Explain how the relationship between inflation and unemployment is modeled by the Phillips curve and integrated into the non-accelerating inflation rate of unemployment.

This relationship between employment and inflation in the short run is modeled by the Phillips curve. The curve shows that a decrease in unemployment will be accompanied by an increase in inflation in the short run. The relationship does not hold over the long run, in part because of inflation expectations. If central banks pursue aggressive expansionary policy to reduce unemployment, inflation may spiral out of control. The level of unemployment at which inflation will remain stable is called the non-accelerating inflation rate of unemployment (NAIRU), or full employment.

Review Questions

1. What is the difference between the Consumer Price Index and the inflation rate? **[LO 16.1]**

2. What is the difference between core inflation and headline inflation? Why do economists calculate both types of inflation? **[LO 16.1]**

3. Your uncle comes to you with an investment idea. He tells you that the nominal GDP of Paradisia quadrupled over the past year and suggests that you invest there. Unemployment is at 20 percent, and inflation over the last year was 500 percent. Do you think it's a good idea

to invest? Draw on the neutrality theory of money to explain why or why not. **[LO 16.2]**

4. Why might we want to measure GDP in dollar terms? In output terms? How does the neutrality of money relate to your answer? **[LO 16.2]**

5. Suppose a country's currency is a gold coin. One day, speculators find a large gold mine, which doubles the supply of gold coins in the economy. What will happen to output in the short run? What about price levels? What will happen to output in the long run? What about price levels? **[LO 16.3]**

6. Explain how some analysts might use the short-run and long-run effects on the aggregate demand–aggregate supply model to argue that monetary policy can't affect employment in the long run. **[LO 16.3]**

7. Why might the velocity of money increase around the holidays? If the Federal Reserve wants to avoid inflation in those times, what should it do? **[LO 16.4]**

8. Use the quantity theory of money to explain how expansionary monetary policy can be inflationary. **[LO 16.4]**

9. Imagine you own an ice cream store in New York City. Write a brief note to your senators explaining two ways in which unpredictable inflation hurts your business. **[LO 16.5]**

10. Is inflation harmful only when it's unexpected? If yes, why? If no, name two costs that occur with even predictable inflation. **[LO 16.5]**

11. Your senators now claim that lowering prices would be good for everyone—"Who doesn't like lower prices, after all?" They tell you they plan to lobby for deflation. Explain why falling prices could lead to a bad situation. **[LO 16.6]**

12. When does inflation become hyperinflation? What causes hyperinflation? **[LO 16.6]**

13. What could have happened to prices and inflation in the years during and after the 2007–2009 recession if the government and the Federal Reserve had not intervened in the economy? How would this have affected the economy? **[LO 16.7]**

14. Are deflation and disinflation the same thing? Why or why not? **[LO 16.7]**

15. Would you expect nominal interest rates to be higher in countries that have higher target inflation rates? Why or why not? **[LO 16.8]**

16. Your friend claims that a target inflation rate of zero is a good policy because this will keep prices stable. You claim a positive target inflation rate is preferred because the country will be able to better avoid a liquidity trap. Who is right? **[LO 16.8]**

17. In the 1960s, policy based on the simple short-run Phillips curve worked better than similar attempts in the 1970s. How might better information availability have contributed to this result? **[LO 16.9]**

18. When we have a negative output gap, what is the proper monetary policy response in the short run? What are its intended effects on interest rates and employment? **[LO 16.9]**

19. Explain the effect contractionary monetary policy will have on the output gap, inflation, and unemployment if unemployment is currently at the non-accelerating inflation rate of unemployment. **[LO 16.10]**

20. Compare and contrast the effect of increased unemployment on inflation in the short and long run. **[LO 16.10]**

Problems and Applications

1. The price index values used to calculate headline and core inflation for 2012 through 2016 are found in Table 16P-1. **[LO 16.1]**

    a. Calculate the annual inflation rate for each series.

    b. Which series represents core inflation and which represents headline inflation? How do you know?

    c. Is there inflation or deflation in each year?

2. Determine whether each of the following events is likely to cause deflation, disinflation, no change in the price level, or inflation. **[LO 16.1]**

    a. A bubble in the biomedical industry just burst.

    b. A new technology is introduced into the economy, sparking an economic boom.

    c. The Federal Reserve conducts contractionary monetary policy.

    d. The Federal Reserve is successful at meeting its dual mandate of full employment and price stability.

TABLE 16P-1

Year	Series 1	Series 2
2012	132.00	122.00
2013	136.22	124.56
2014	138.26	126.68
2015	143.24	129.72
2016	144.81	131.79

3. Which of the following can be affected by the money supply in the long run? **[LO 16.2]**

    a. Nominal GDP.

    b. Real GDP.

    c. Inflation.

    d. Unemployment.

4. The average individual in a country earns an annual salary of $60,000, of which $24,000 is spent on housing, $10,800 on food, $10,800 on transportation, and $14,400 on other goods and services. Suppose the government in this country mandates that all salaries and the prices of all goods and services be reduced by 40 percent. **[LO 16.2]**

    a. How much does the average individual now earn?

    b. How much does the average individual now spend on housing, food, transportation, and other goods and services?

    c. What happened to the average individual's real salary?

5. To increase the self-esteem of dieters everywhere, powerful fashion designers lobby Congress to redefine "five pounds" as "one pound." Under this system, what would have previously been five pounds of bananas will now be one pound of bananas and a 500-pound gorilla would now weigh only 100 pounds. **[LO 16.3]**

    a. How much would someone who originally weighed 180 pounds now weigh as a result of this redefinition?

    b. Has there been a nominal change in the person's weight? A real change?

    c. How is this story similar to contractionary monetary policy via a decrease in the money supply in the long run? (*Hint:* Congress essentially shrunk the "pounds supply" by redefining the word.)

6. "Monetary policy is incredible," your friend says. "Just a little manipulation of the money supply and interest rates, and we end up at just the right price level and amount of output." Is your friend overstating the Fed's control over price levels and output? Why or why not? **[LO 16.3]**

7. Your dormitory Griffingate has appointed you central banker of its economy, which deals in the currency of wizcoins. Assume that the velocity of wizcoins in Griffingate is constant at 10,000 transactions per year. Right now, real GDP is 1,000 wizcoins and there are 2,000 wizcoins in existence. **[LO 16.4]**

    a. What will be the value of each of the variables that make up the quantity equation—M, V, and P?

    b. Now indicate how the other variables will respond to each of the following scenarios, taking each case separately and assuming that velocity remains constant.

  i. *Real GDP:* You increase the money supply to 4,000, and prices increase twofold.

  ii. *Price level:* Start with the initial values. Real GDP drops to 500 wizcoins, and the money supply remains constant.

  iii. *Real GDP:* Start with the initial values. Prices increase threefold because of a sudden scarcity of soda, and you decide to keep the supply of wizcoins constant.

  iv. *Real GDP:* Start with the initial values. You increase the money supply to 5,000 wizcoins, and prices rise by 350 percent.

8. Express the following relationships using the equation for the quantity theory of money. **[LO 16.4]**

  a. The money supply is given by nominal GDP divided by the velocity of money.

  b. The relationship of the money supply to the price level is the same as the relationship between real GDP and velocity. (*Hint:* Start by dividing the money supply by the price level.)

  c. Real GDP is given by the flow of money divided by the price level.

  d. The price level of an economy can be found by dividing the product of the money supply and its velocity by real GDP.

9. Identify whether the following individuals will be affected by bracket creep next year given the rates of taxation and levels of inflation found in Table 16P-2. **[LO 16.5]**

  a. Gabriela makes $9,500, and inflation is at 5 percent.

  b. Cooper makes $160,000, and inflation is at a record high of 20 percent.

  c. Shawna makes $140,000, and inflation is at 8 percent.

TABLE 16P-2

Marginal tax rate (%)	Income level ($)
10	0–10,000
15	10,001–30,000
18	30,001–50,000
20	50,001–100,000
23	100,001–150,000
25	150,001 and up

  d. Samuel makes $45,000, and inflation is at 6 percent.

  e. Marguerite makes $96,000, and inflation is at 6 percent.

10. Cookie Monster has decided to channel his love of cookies into a new business, "Me Want Cookies Inc.," a new partnership he has formed with Miss Piggy. They are considering different countries in which to start their venture and would like to rank the countries based on the inflationary environment. They decide to give a country 10 "menu-cost" points for each percent of actual inflation in the last year since inflation will cause their menu costs to increase. They also dislike unstable inflation, so they will give a country 20 "uncertainty" points for each percent difference in the actual inflation rate when compared to the projected inflation rate. Countries with the least total points will receive the highest rankings. Complete Table 16P-3 for Cookie Monster. **[LO 16.5]**

11. Jack recently took out a loan from Diane at an interest rate of 5 percent. Diane expected this year's inflation rate to be 2 percent and the real interest rate to be 3 percent. The loan is due at the end of this year. Complete

TABLE 16P-3

Country	Projected inflation (%)	Actual inflation (%)	Uncertainty points	Menu-cost points	Total points	Rank
Kermikopia	2	4				
Gonzoland	4	5				
Elmostan	7	8				
Oscaria	10	13				
Bertico	14	14				

TABLE 16P-4

This year's actual inflation rate (%)	Actual real interest rate (%)	Who benefits?
1		
4		
0		
−2		

TABLE 16P-6

	Year	Inflation rate (%)	Description
a.	1900	90	
b.	1901	80	
c.	1902	120	
d.	1903	40	
e.	1904	−2	

Table 16P-4, showing the real interest rate for each possible inflation rate. For each situation, determine whether the unexpected inflation level benefits Jack or Diane. **[LO 16.5]**

12. Assume the prices shown in Table 16P-5 are the prices of Big Macs in 2030, 2031, and 2032 and that changes in the price of Big Macs tend to closely keep up with inflation. For each of the four instances, determine the following. **[LO 16.6, 16.7]**

    a. The percentage changes in price levels between each consecutive year.

    b. Whether the economy was experiencing inflation, deflation, disinflation, or hyperinflation over each period. (Assume that inflation above 100 percent constitutes hyperinflation.)

13. Assuming that inflation above 100 percent is hyperinflation, categorize each of the inflation rates in Table 16P-6 as deflation, disinflation, inflation, or hyperinflation as we move from one year to the next. **[LO 16.6, 16.7]**

14. Suppose you live in Frigidia, a country near the North Pole that is experiencing hyperinflation. You work for a U.S. company that pays you a monthly income of $100 U.S. Today, you can exchange those dollars for frigids, the currency of Frigidia, at a rate of 1,000 frigids/dollar. You pay a monthly heating bill that costs

$10 U.S. Instead of paying the heating bill, you could simply burn Frigidia notes (which you can obtain in one-frigid denominations) at a rate of 1 million per month to supply heating. What would the exchange rate between frigids and U.S. dollars have to be for you to decide to burn bills instead of paying for heating? What level of inflation does this represent, assuming the real exchange rate remains the same? **[LO 16.7]**

15. "The problem wasn't having the wrong idea about interest rates," a sheepish central bank official says at a conference, "but rather not having the right idea about inflation rates." What does the official mean? How does the inflation rate affect the central bank's interest rate target, and how can a wrong prediction about inflation make monetary policy go awry? **[LO 16.7]**

16. In which scenario is monetary policy likely to be more effective? Explain. **[LO 16.8]**

    Scenario A—The inflation rate in the country has hovered close to zero for the last three years.

    Scenario B—The inflation rate in the country has averaged 3 percent for the last three years.

17. Consider a country that has experienced a decline in labor demand that results in a 2 percent reduction in the equilibrium real wage. **[LO 16.8]**

    a. If the inflation rate in the country has been at zero percent, what has to happen to the nominal wage to restore labor market equilibrium?

    b. If the inflation rate in the country has been at 4 percent, what has to happen to the nominal wage to restore labor market equilibrium?

    c. Do you think workers and employers would prefer to have a zero percent inflation rate or a 4 percent inflation rate in this case? Explain.

18. Determine whether the Federal Reserve would pursue contractionary monetary policy, expansionary monetary policy, or no change in policy in each of the following situations. **[LO 16.9]**

TABLE 16P-5

	Price in 2030 ($)	Price in 2031 ($)	Price in 2032 ($)
a.	1.00	1.02	1.03
b.	1.00	0.99	0.97
c.	0.01	0.05	1.00
d.	1.00	1.10	1.15

a. Inflation is 10 percent, above its average of 3 percent in the last several years.

b. The output gap is positive.

c. Unemployment is at a record high.

d. The economy is experiencing full employment.

e. The economy is on the brink of deflation.

f. A new technology causes output to surge.

19. Answer each of the following questions assuming the economy is experiencing a positive output gap. **[LO 16.9]**

a. Is inflation decreasing, increasing, or stable?

b. Is actual output greater than or less than potential output?

c. Is unemployment rising or falling?

d. Is the Federal Reserve more likely to pursue expansionary or contractionary monetary policy?

e. Is the economy likely experiencing an expansion or contraction?

20. Answer each of the following questions assuming the economy is experiencing a negative output gap. **[LO 16.9]**

a. Is inflation decreasing, increasing, or stable?

b. Is actual output greater than or less than potential output?

c. Is unemployment rising or falling?

d. Is the Federal Reserve more likely to pursue expansionary or contractionary monetary policy?

e. Is the economy likely experiencing an expansion or contraction?

21. Assume the Phillips curve is given by the simple equation $U = -I + 20$. The non-accelerating inflation rate of unemployment is 10 percent. If inflation changes to 15 percent, what will be the unemployment rate in the short run? What will it be in the long run? **[LO 16.10]**

22. Using what you know about the Phillips curve, determine whether the following quantities will increase, decrease, or remain the same. **[LO 16.10]**

a. Unemployment in the short run after an increase in inflation.

b. Unemployment in the long run after an increase in inflation.

c. Inflation in the short run after a decrease in unemployment.

d. Inflation in the long run after a decrease in unemployment.

Endnotes

1. "Argentina's Inflation Problem: The Price of Cooking the Books," *The Economist,* February 25, 2012, http://www.economist.com/node/21548229.

2. http://energy.gov/eere/vehicles/fact-915-march-7-2016-average-historical-annual-gasoline-pump-price-1929-2015; http://www.tradingeconomics.com/united-states/core-inflation-rate.

3. Bob Davis, "IMF Tells Bankers to Rethink Inflation," *The Wall Street Journal,* February 12, 2010, http://online.wsj.com/article/SB10001424052748704337004575059542325748142.html.

4. Marco A. Espinosa-Vega and Steven Russell, "History and Theory of the NAIRU: A Critical Review," *Economic Review* (Federal Reserve Bank of Atlanta), 1997, https://www.frbatlanta.org/-/media/Documents/research/publications/economic-review/1997/vol82no2_espinosa-russell.pdf.

Financial Crisis

Learning Objectives

LO 17.1 Describe the role of irrational expectations and leverage in the creation of financial crises.

LO 17.2 Discuss the causes of two famous historical financial crises.

LO 17.3 Trace the role of mortgage-backed securities and tranching in the rise of subprime lending.

LO 17.4 Analyze the factors that led to the housing bubble and rising levels of household debt.

LO 17.5 Explain how the collapse of the housing bubble created a credit crisis and subsequent contraction in output.

LO 17.6 Describe the monetary and fiscal policy responses to the financial crisis of 2008.

LO 17.7 Describe the different tools that can be used to stimulate the economy when interest rates are at the zero lower bound.

A FINANCIAL STORM

Guiding the economy is a bit like steering a massive cruise ship. Mostly the aim is to keep an eye on the latest data and navigate in the right direction. Every now and then the ship might need to speed up or slow down, but most of the time the job is just to keep things steady and steer forward.

Sometimes, though, ships run into huge storms, and all of a sudden the crew is fighting to keep the vessel afloat. The biggest recent *financial* storm for the U.S. economy started brewing in 2007 and reached full hurricane force in late 2008.

At 8:00 a.m. on a Friday in September 2008, Ben Bernanke, the chair of the Federal Reserve, joined Hank Paulson, the Secretary of the U.S. Treasury Department, for breakfast. They usually ate breakfast together once a week, but this morning was very different. Some of the country's biggest banks and financial companies were in desperate trouble. The firms had made risky bets about the future of the housing market, and now it was becoming clear how risky those bets were—and how badly they were turning out. What started as a simple breakfast turned out to be

© *Jack Guez/AFP/Getty Images*

the beginning of a week of tense meetings about how to save the economy from disaster.

Two days earlier, the investment firm Lehman Brothers announced that it had lost a staggering $4 billion on its bets. All weekend, officials at the Treasury and Federal Reserve scrambled to find a way to rescue Lehman, but the pieces didn't come together. Three days later, Lehman declared bankruptcy. Soon it became clear that Merrill Lynch, a major Wall Street Bank, also needed rescuing. So too did AIG, the insurance giant, and Washington Mutual, America's largest savings-and-loan bank. One crisis was leading to another, and related problems were intensifying in Europe. Within the month, the U.S. stock market was in free fall.

What started as a banking crisis was felt by people, rich and poor, across the country. Between 2007 and 2009, retirees saw the value of the stocks in their pensions collapse; investments built up over decades evaporated. Families lost their most valuable assets, their homes. All in all, household wealth was cut in half, and workers lost jobs, nearly nine million in all.

Over the next five years, the economy started coming back, the stock market began rising again, and companies created new jobs. But the effects of the 2007–2009 crisis are still being felt. This chapter tells the story of how the economy got into trouble and what economics teaches about tackling future crises.

Markets are a powerful tool for the efficient allocation of scarce resources. Financial markets are in many ways the purest expression of the market mechanism. Relatively free from government intervention, financial markets are a global marketplace in which sophisticated investors make billion-dollar decisions nearly every second of the day.

So, how can financial markets go so very wrong as they did in the 2007–2009 crisis? And why do the failings of financial markets reverberate through the broader economy? Developing an understanding of the common causes of financial crises has become an urgently important task.

In this chapter, we'll introduce a few of the basic concepts of financial crises. We'll talk about why things sometimes go wrong in financial markets and how those problems might be corrected. In particular, we will take a close look at the crisis that began in December of 2007 after the collapse of the housing market.

bubble
trade in an asset whose price has risen unsustainably far above historically justified levels

The Origins of Financial Crises

Financial crises often occur as the result of a financial bubble. As discussed in Chapter 14, "The Basics of Finance," a **bubble** involves trade in an asset whose price has risen unsustainably far above historically justified levels. The first recorded example of a financial bubble is a "tulip mania" that afflicted investors in Holland in 1636–1637. At the time, a single tulip bulb was worth more than a handful of diamonds. Investors paid incredible sums for bulbs, hoping to profit by selling later at even higher prices. After a few years, however, the mania surrounding tulips died out, and prices plummeted. Those who had invested in tulips lost fortunes.

This pattern has since been repeated many times. Prices go up and up and up, way higher than seems to make any rational sense, and then suddenly crash. Why does this happen? Two interconnected concepts lie at the heart of many financial crises: irrational expectations and leverage.

Irrational expectations

> **LO 17.1** Describe the role of irrational expectations and leverage in the creation of financial crises.

In Chapter 14, "The Basics of Finance," we talked about how financial markets are supposed to allocate funds efficiently. Ideally, they allow money to flow to the places where it is most highly valued at any given time. What's more, the efficient-market hypothesis says that financial markets should incorporate all available information, and so prices should represent the true value of an asset as correctly as possible. Where, in all of that, is there room for bubbles and crashes?

In reality, markets sometimes appear to be very irrational. The price of an asset can become inflated beyond the point where anyone can explain precisely why it should be so valuable. How does that happen? One hypothesis is that investors sometimes follow a "herd instinct," investing in something simply because everyone else is doing it. Investors are just people—albeit often well-informed people with a financial interest in making good investments. They can get caught up in the moment and act emotionally, just like anyone else. A bubble starts to inflate when investors become irrationally optimistic that an asset's price will continue to rise.

Where do irrational expectations come from? One possible explanation is a well-established cognitive bias called the *recency effect*. There is a basic human tendency to overvalue recent experience when trying to predict the future. When investors and speculators do this, it can lead to enormous miscalculations. For example, consider a company that enjoyed a spectacular few years of success: Apple Computer. In 2005, Apple's total profits were just over $1.3 billion. Then, it launched the MacBook, followed by the iPhone, and then the iPad. In 2010, Apple reported profits of more than $14 billion. That's a tenfold growth in profits over just five years.

With Apple's products still flying off the shelves, would an investor be justified in believing that Apple might continue its incredible run for another five or 10 or 15 years? After another five years of tenfold growth, Apple would be earning more than $140 billion a year. In 10 years, the company would be earning more than $1.4 trillion. By 2025, Apple would be earning $14 trillion annually—the current GDP of the entire United States! When you look at it that way, it becomes clear that there will come a time for Apple when future growth simply can't resemble past growth.

Although it's unlikely that anyone would project something quite that extreme, trends do influence our thinking. For example, in the housing markets, decades of rising house prices persuaded many Americans that it was inconceivable that they could ever fall. However, not all investors in a bubble are necessarily caught up in irrational expectations. Some may be aware that assets are overpriced but gamble on riding the rise in prices as close to the top as possible in the hope of selling at maximum profit, just before the inevitable crash. This high-stakes game is described in the From Another Angle box "Do investors rationally inflate bubbles?"

From Another Angle

Do investors rationally inflate bubbles?

On June 16, 2005, *The Economist* ran a story entitled "After the Fall." The magazine spelled out clearly why the fast-rising real estate prices around the world were a bubble that would burst, sooner or later:

> Throughout history, financial bubbles—whether in houses, equities, or tulip bulbs—have continued to inflate for longer than rational folk believed possible. It is impossible to predict when [housing] prices will turn. Yet turn they will. Prices are already sliding in Australia and Britain. America's housing market may be a year or so behind.

The question was not *if* the bubble would burst, but *when*? As it happened, housing prices in the United States stayed astronomically high for another two years after these words were written. Was this because house buyers had stubbornly plugged their ears to such warnings? Maybe. Or maybe speculators were continuing to buy real estate knowing that a crash would come but expecting that the bubble had a bit more inflating to do and hoping to maximize profits by selling at the peak price, *just before* the market came crashing down.

How do you make sure you get out just before the market goes into free fall? If the timing is off, investors can get their fingers badly burned. Fund manager Stanley Druckenmiller lost a lot of money by not selling soon enough during the bubble in tech stocks in the 1990s. He explained his mistake, using a baseball analogy, "We thought it was the eighth inning, and it was the ninth."

The problem is that no one knows exactly when the bubble will end. A bubble pops when a critical mass of investors decides that the time is right to sell. This causes prices to dip, and everyone who was sitting tight will rush to sell off as well, turning the dip into a plummet. If you haven't managed to sell before this moment comes, then you'll struggle to find anyone who wants to buy.

The existence of speculators practicing this sort of brinkmanship also complicates policy steps that could be taken to avert a crisis. If the bubble is being inflated by speculators who are poised to sell at the first sign of prices going into reverse, it might be impossible to prevent a gentle slowdown from turning into a crash landing.

Sources: http://www.princeton.edu/~markus/research/papers/bubbles_crashes.pdf; "After the Fall: Soaring House Prices Have Given a Huge Boost to the World Economy. What Happens When They Drop?" © The Economist Newspaper Limited, London (June 16, 2005).

Leverage

Irrational expectations help explain how prices get so inflated during a bubble, but we have to go further to understand why the crash is so damaging after a bubble bursts. One culprit is the extensive use of leverage, which multiplies the effect of gains and losses in financial markets. In finance, **leverage** is the practice of using borrowed money to pay for investments.

leverage
the practice of using borrowed money to pay for investments

The use of leverage means that a person or company can make an investment that is much larger in value than the amount they actually own:

- If the investment does well, you pay back the loan and get to keep the profits, which will be larger than what you would have earned if you could invest only the cash you had on hand.

- If the investment does badly, you still have to pay back the loan, and that can require digging deep into your own resources.

When financial markets are booming, leverage multiplies the gains; when they crash, leverage magnifies the losses.

On a personal level, people can leverage their funds through a "margin account." A margin account allows you to use your existing investments as collateral to either buy more financial assets or withdraw cash. For example, if you have $100 in an account that offers "2x" margin, you can effectively buy $200 worth of stocks even though you put in only $100. When stocks rise, you will earn twice as much profit, minus interest payments.

But what happens if the stock you bought goes down? Let's say it goes down 10 percent. If you did not buy on margin, your account value would go down to only $90. If you did buy on margin, however, you are going to lose $20, which would bring your account value down to $80. That doesn't sound so bad, but what if the stock goes down 50 percent? You would lose all your money since 50 percent of $200 is your entire original $100. If the stock goes down more than 50 percent, you could actually end up owing money to your broker!

In practice, brokers exercise a "margin call" to ensure that they don't lose money. If it looks like you are in danger of running through your money, the broker will force you to sell your stock and use the money to pay back the loan. Since this probably means selling at the worst possible time—just as the market is collapsing—this situation is both bad for you and potentially destabilizing for the market as a whole. A rapidly falling stock price can trigger a flood of margin calls, leading to massive sales of the stock, which pushes the price down even more.

Companies and banks can also leverage their funds. Such transactions can lead to losses on a much larger scale than personal margin accounts. For instance, an investment bank or hedge fund might use $5 million as collateral in order to buy a claim on $50 million worth of oil futures.[1] Gains or losses on that investment will be multiplied by the use of leverage in exactly the same way that they are on a personal level. If the value of the investment goes down by a lot, the company can end up owing more than it is able to pay. Just before it went bankrupt during the crash in 2008, Lehman Brothers investment bank was highly leveraged. Its total assets were valued at levels about 30 times the actual funds it owned, depending on exactly how one calculates it.

The amount of leverage a company takes on can be expressed in terms of the **leverage ratio**. That measure is the ratio of a company's assets to its equity, where equity is defined as the firm's assets minus its liabilities. In the case of Lehman Brothers, a leverage ratio of 30 implies that a 10 percent increase in the value of its assets would generate a 300 percent increase in the value of its equity.[2] This magnification of returns may sound attractive when we're considering positive changes in asset prices, but the logic also works in reverse: Small decreases in asset values can lead to catastrophic losses for highly leveraged institutions.

Leverage alone is not necessarily a dangerous thing—so long as it is limited and investors understand the risks well. Unfortunately, leverage combined with irrational expectations about a market can be a brutal combination. Imagine you believed that Apple would keep growing at 60 percent a year for the next decade, and borrowed heavily to leverage your investment. When the price of Apple stock inevitably fell back to earth, you would take a huge loss.

The two-headed monster of leverage and irrational expectations is at the heart of most financial crises.

leverage ratio
the ratio of a company's assets to its equity, where equity is defined as the firm's assets minus its liabilities

Two Famous Historical Financial Crises

LO 17.2 Discuss the causes of two famous historical financial crises.

Before we dive into a case study of the Great Recession, let's take a quick look back at how the twin dangers of irrational expectations and leverage have played out in two famous historical financial crises.

The South Seas Bubble
In the late seventeenth century, stock markets in England were in their infancy. In 1688, the East India Company made one of the first issuances of stock: Investors would be given a cut of the profits on a forthcoming voyage to India. By 1695, 140 companies were offering similar arrangements in London's Exchange Alley.

The South Seas Company took form in this new environment. The company was granted a government monopoly on trade between England and South America. Interest in the company's stock was intense. In just a single day, the price of South Seas Company stock rose from £130 to over £300. The company issued more stock, and the price jumped from £300 to £325 as investors used their existing stock as collateral to buy more. By June 1720, the bubble was in full swing, with stock of the South Seas Company trading at a price over £1,000 a share.

It was never entirely clear how the South Seas Company was going to earn enough profit to justify this fantastic share price. After all, there wasn't much trade between England and South America, which at the time was made up of colonies that were mostly controlled by Spain. The company depended on an agreement with Spain to be able to run trading ships, and Spain allowed it to run only one ship a year. Still, wild rumors circulated of the fabulous profits that would one day flow from the South Seas. Investors were caught up in the frenzy.

Con artists saw the high prices that investors were willing to pay for shares in the South Seas Company and decided to cash in on the frenzy. They concocted their own companies, which promised investors riches through fanciful schemes. One company claimed to be building a wheel of perpetual motion. Another famously invited investors to buy stock in "a company for carrying out an undertaking of great advantage, but nobody to know what it is." Eventually, the English Parliament realized the dangers and moved to regulate companies that traded stock publicly, through a law known as the Bubble Act.

Inevitably, sanity returned, and the price of stock in the South Seas Company plunged back to earth. Many investors were ruined. Sir Isaac Newton, the great mathematician and one of the investors, lost £20,000—the equivalent of about $5 million today. Kicking himself, Newton grumbled that he could "calculate the motion of heavenly bodies, but not the madness of people."

The Great Crash of 1929

The Great Crash of 1929 wreaked havoc on Wall Street—a loss the U.S. economy took 25 years to recover from.
© MPI/Getty Images

While the South Seas bubble could be considered the first financial crisis of the modern stock market era, the worst was arguably the infamous stock market crash of October 1929. This event led to the Great Depression, which wreaked havoc throughout the 1930s. Production slowed and unemployment in the United States exceeded 25 percent.

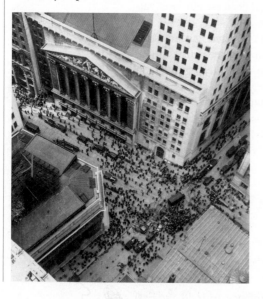

The Great Crash and resulting Great Depression had their roots in another bubble, a period of flashy exuberance known as the "Roaring Twenties." From 1922 to 1929, the total value of the stock market more than tripled, averaging an annual growth rate of over 18 percent. There was some foundation for this increase in share prices: U.S. soldiers, home from World War I, had boosted production with additional manpower. New technologies such as movies, radio, and mass-produced automobiles were causing widespread excitement. Many people began buying stocks on the margin.

If stock prices continued to rise, as many figured they would, buying on the margin could increase profits substantially. For most of the 1920s, that seemed a pretty good bet. Economist Irving Fisher infamously assured everyone that the stock market had reached a "permanently high plateau." Secretary of the Treasury Andrew Mellon stated on October 14, 1929, that there was "no cause to worry. The high tide of prosperity will continue."

Ten days later, the stock market fell apart. On October 24, 1929—"Black Thursday"—the leading index of stock prices dropped by 9 percent. Bankers tried to shore up confidence by buying up the stocks of large companies. But this buying couldn't stem the avalanche of selling as investors unloaded shares in an unprecedented, panicked sell-off. Once prices started to drop, everyone wanted to sell before the price dropped further. Of course, this rush of sales *caused* the price to drop further, making the panic a self-perpetuating problem.

On the following Monday, the stock market posted a loss of 13 percent. The next day, the market fell again by 12 percent. As more panic set in, the volume of shares traded reached a record-setting 16.4 million—more than four times the typical number.

By the time prices bottomed out in July 1932, 90 percent of the entire value of the stock market had been wiped away in just three years. It took until 1954—a full 25 years later—for the stock market to return to the peak reached in September 1929.

✓ CONCEPT CHECK

- ☐ Why does leverage exacerbate the effect of a financial crash? **[LO 17.1]**
- ☐ What is the name of the period of sluggish economic activity that followed the Great Crash of 1929? **[LO 17.1]**
- ☐ Why did the initial stock sell-off create further panic during the Great Crash of 1929? **[LO 17.2]**

The Great Recession: A Financial-Crisis Case Study

In the 1930s, Congress passed several laws intended to prevent similar crises in the future:

- The Glass-Steagall Banking Act of 1933 required the separation of investment and commercial banks.[3]
- The Federal Deposit Insurance Corporation (FDIC) insured bank deposits against possible bank failures, among other things.
- The Securities and Exchange Act of 1932 formed the Securities and Exchange Commission (SEC), which regulates the securities industry today.

These reforms contributed to a long period of relative stability in financial markets. For decades, the U.S. economy chugged along without a major financial crisis or contraction in output. It seemed that the stock market crash of 1929 might go down in history as the beginning of a new and more predictable era. Perhaps the global economy had moved on from the days of bubbles and panics. By the mid-2000s, this idea, sometimes dubbed "the Great Moderation," had support in the academic and policy-making community. Unfortunately, less than five years later, the global economy would again find itself in a major recession.

By 2008, we were in the midst of the greatest global economic downturn since the Great Depression. Industrial and financial giants from General Motors to Merrill Lynch were under threat of collapse. Millions of people saw their life savings evaporate as housing prices collapsed and markets around the world plummeted.

In this section, we'll explore the origins of the financial crisis and the extraordinary monetary and fiscal response from the world's governments, using the macroeconomics concepts we've explored over the last few chapters. We will focus on the United States—in many ways the epicenter of the crisis—but the global crash was not just the result of problems in the United States spreading to the rest of the world. Countries from Spain to Ireland and the United Kingdom also faced enormous challenges of their own that helped feed the global crisis.

In order to really understand how the U.S. economy collapsed so suddenly, we'll start by looking at some interrelated components of the U.S. economy: subprime lending, the housing and mortgage market, and the broader world of consumer debt.

Subprime lending

> **LO 17.3** Trace the role of mortgage-backed securities and tranching in the rise of subprime lending.

To understand the financial crisis that rocked the country in 2008, we have to start with the housing market. From World War II to the onset of the financial crisis—a period of more than 60 years—housing prices had never fallen across the entire United States. Housing prices on the whole had stayed steady, even when the rest of the economy went into recession. Buying a house was considered the safest investment anyone could make—a path to stability, wealth, and the American Dream. Even the federal government joined the bandwagon in promoting home ownership: It implemented policies ranging from tax deductions on home mortgage interest to government-created companies like Fannie Mae and Freddie Mac, which are intended to spread access to mortgage financing.

Yet some people still couldn't obtain a traditional mortgage loan—because of poor credit, low income, or job instability. Financial innovators opened a new path to home ownership through the growing availability of *subprime mortgages.* A subprime mortgage is a mortgage loan made to a borrower with a low credit score—that is, to someone who has a history of missing payments or otherwise struggling with debts. (The word *subprime* is in contrast to *prime* borrowers, who have better credit scores.) At first, subprime mortgages were seen as a triumph: They enabled even more Americans to pursue the dream of home ownership for the first time.

Why were lenders willing to lend to subprime borrowers? The loans, after all, are especially risky. Banks had long been wary of lending to subprime-rated borrowers. That all changed with the advent of securitization. **Securitization** is the practice of packaging individual debts, like mortgage loans or credit card debts, into a single uniform asset that can be easily bought and sold. In the late 1990s, investment banks began purchasing mortgages from the local banks that had created them. They, in turn, then packaged them as *mortgage-backed securities,* which were tradable assets made up of collections of individual mortgages, whose value was tied to the revenues of those mortgages.

> **securitization**
> the practice of packaging individual debts into a single uniform asset

Securitization of mortgages allowed *local banks* to reduce their exposure to risk by effectively selling their mortgage debt to investors. The investors got the revenues from mortgage payments, but if borrowers defaulted, the investors would experience a loss. For investors, the mortgage-backed security seemed to promise diversification: By combining many mortgages into one security, the risks specific to individual mortgages (called *idiosyncratic risk*) would be diluted. As a result, the combination of mortgages would have lower total risk than any individual mortgage. The reasoning was similar to that of a bank or insurance company pooling risks, as discussed in Chapter 14, "The Basics of Finance":

- If you make a single loan and the borrower defaults, you lose everything at once.
- If, however, you make 100 loans, it's very unlikely that everyone will default at once.
  A bank can take a thousand loans, estimate that *on average* 250 of them will default, and set prices so that it can still earn a profit on the total package.

An investor could go out and buy a thousand different individual mortgages to diversify risk. Doing that, though, takes time: It would involve scrutinizing each mortgage to guess how likely a particular homeowner is to default and ensuring that the thousand mortgages are not highly correlated. Instead, the mortgage-backed security was supposed to be a single, uniform asset that pooled risk while still being easy to buy and sell quickly. It allowed local banks to pass the risk involved in holding mortgage debts on to investors with higher risk tolerance.

Diversification is valuable, but the logic of pooling risks depends crucially on the degree to which the loans in the pool are correlated with one another. If for any reason the risks associated with a set of loans are highly correlated, then it is much harder to diversify away the default risk. (An example of high correlation of mortgage risk, for example, would be if many loans are issued to households who could make payments only if interest rates stayed low.) Worse yet, if investors are unaware that the underlying risks are in fact highly correlated, then they might unintentionally take on more risk than they want.

Some banks went one step further: They divided packages of debts into slices (called *tranches*), each with different risk and return characteristics. Packages of reliable, low-risk mortgages could be sold to more risk-averse investors; higher-risk subprime mortgages could be sold to risk-loving investors.

What was the point of this financial wizardry? It allowed local banks and mortgage companies to chase higher profits by making loans that they would have rejected as too risky in the past. Now they could sell those mortgages to investment banks, which in turn could chase profits by packaging them as mortgage-backed securities and selling them on.

Investors had such an appetite for mortgage-backed securities that local banks couldn't make loans fast enough. Real estate agents started pushing larger mortgages to customers, even to borrowers who wouldn't traditionally have been able to afford them. Some mortgage brokers cut corners in paperwork to be able to pump out more loans. By 2006, a full 20 percent of the mortgage market consisted of subprime loans, a category that barely even existed a decade before. The sudden explosion of subprime mortgages is shown in Figure 17-1.

The creation of the housing bubble

LO 17.4 Analyze the factors that led to the housing bubble and rising levels of household debt.

The sudden explosion of cheap and readily available mortgages encouraged people to buy bigger and better homes. A mortgage is a form of leverage—you make a down payment that is only a

FIGURE 17-1

Growth of the subprime loan market   This figure shows subprime mortgages as a percentage of all new mortgages from 2001 through 2007. Traditionally, new subprime mortgages comprised less than 10 percent of the total new mortgages in any given year. This changed in 2004, when the number of new subprime mortgages more than doubled as a share of new mortgages. Then, in 2007, the housing market collapsed, and lenders reacted by sharply reducing subprime loans.

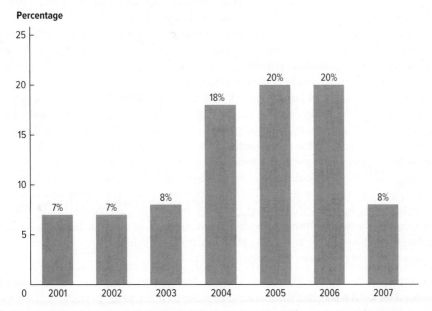

Source: *The State of the Nation's Housing*, Harvard University Joint Center for Housing Studies, 2008.

FIGURE 17-2

The housing bubble pops The chart shows the rapid increase of housing prices from 1999 to 2006. As you can see, prices peaked in early 2007 and then quickly plummeted. The bubble was large nationally (as seen by the national composite index, represented by the blue line), as prices doubled on average in the span of seven years. The bursting of the bubble is shown by the sudden decrease in housing starts, followed by a sharp reduction in price of houses.

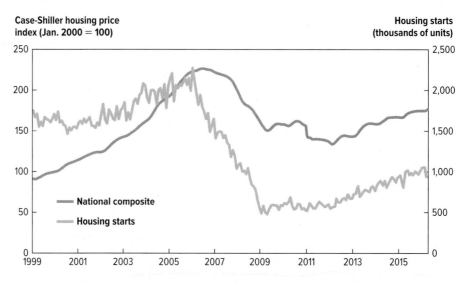

Sources: Price index data from FRED Economic Data, https://fred.stlouisfed.org/series/SPCS20RSA; housing starts data from U.S. Census Bureau, https://www.census.gov/construction/nrc/pdf/compsa.pdf.

fraction of the value of the asset (i.e., the house) that you are buying, and you borrow the rest. As down-payment requirements got smaller and loans got cheaper, many homeowners became more and more leveraged.

The frenzy of highly leveraged demand for houses was accompanied by a sharp run-up in housing prices. Figure 17-2 shows the rapid rise in U.S. home prices during this period and the number of *housing starts* (a term that means new home construction—an indicator of increasing supply in the housing market) in the same period. At the height of the real estate bubble, American homeowners were much like Lehman Brothers, with a very high ratio of home "value" to money actually paid. When housing prices stopped rising, however, millions of homeowners found themselves with payments they couldn't possibly make on highly leveraged housing properties.

Why did these loans get made? Economists continue to debate this question, but in many ways, the enormous run-up in housing prices was a classic bubble. People bought houses with the expectation that they would continue to go up in value. Banks began to offer special types of mortgages that allowed borrowers to defer payments for the first few years of the loan. Or they offered "teaser" interest rates that would increase to much higher levels a few years down the road. As long as home prices kept going up, borrowers would simply "refinance" their homes when the bills came. That is, they would use the new, higher value of the home as collateral to take out a new mortgage with friendlier terms. Banks and borrowers both got caught up in the moment. Convinced that housing prices would never go down, both agreed to incredibly risky loans.

Securitization encouraged the process by removing most of the risk from the lenders who created the original mortgage. This removal of risk from the original lender also may have contributed to misaligned incentives to properly assess risk:

- Investment banks on Wall Street relied on the local banks to assess each individual borrower. But local banks had the incentive to make as many loans as possible since they earned fees for each loan.

- Wall Street bankers made money not by ensuring local banks were making good loans, but by buying as many loans as possible, packaging them into mortgage-backed securities, and selling them to investors.

At some point up the chain, the people creating and buying complicated assets that were several steps removed from the original mortgage may not have fully understood what they were paying for.

Investors relied on the reassuringly high AAA ratings given to many of these assets by credit-rating agencies. However, the ratings agencies attracted business in part by keeping Wall Street happy. The ratings turned out to be much too optimistic. Politicians were driven by a vision of broader home ownership but failed to pay enough attention to the economics. The same tools that were intended to allocate funds and spread risk more efficiently made it difficult for everyone to stay fully informed; they diluted the incentive to do the research and to say no to bad risks.

Effects of the housing bubble collapse

LO 17.5 Explain how the collapse of the housing bubble created a credit crisis and subsequent contraction in output.

As housing prices continued to rise, consumers were simultaneously saving less and borrowing (and spending) more. Flush with the feeling of wealth from their inflated home values, many consumers used the value of their homes to secure loans and higher limits on their credit cards, taking on more and more debt to support their spending habits. In addition, consumers had become accustomed to *refinancing* their mortgages—paying off the existing mortgage and taking out a new mortgage based on the increased value of the home. Often the new mortgage was structured to result in lower payments (at least for a while), and often the appreciated value of the home enabled the homeowner to borrow some cash in the refinancing deal. These consumer responses to the housing bubble ultimately led to a credit crisis and a new equilibrium in the economy in which both prices and output had fallen.

Buying on credit

Personal debt levels in the United States had steadily been rising for decades, since the mid-1980s. As the housing market took off in the early 2000s and consumers began borrowing more, the growth in household debt accelerated rapidly, hitting a peak by the end of 2008. Figure 17-3 shows the historical trajectory of personal debt in the United States.

To understand consumer debt, economists look at a concept known as debt service. **Debt service** is the amount that consumers have to spend to pay their debts, often expressed as a percentage of disposable income. Over the two decades leading up the 2008 crisis, falling interest rates made borrowing—and therefore going into debt—much cheaper. Consumers could take on more debt without significantly increasing the amount of debt service they had to pay. Figure 17-4 shows the divergence between rising debt levels and relatively stable debt-service burdens. Unfortunately, that level of debt was sustainable only as long as interest rates remained low and home values remained high. Consumers would be facing serious trouble if anything unexpectedly went wrong—which is exactly what happened when the housing bubble popped.

debt service
the amount that consumers have to spend to pay their debts, often expressed as a percentage of disposable income

A domino effect toward reduced output

When housing prices stopped rising and began to fall in places like Nevada, Arizona, California, and Florida, consumers found themselves unable to refinance their loans. The housing collapse began in the subprime housing market. It was like a domino trail, in which the first domino that tips starts a cascading effect:

- Faced with impossibly high payments relative to their incomes, a massive wave of mortgage defaults occurred. Millions of people found themselves in *foreclosure:* Their homes

FIGURE 17-3

Historical personal debt trends in the United States   Since the 1960s, personal debt in the United States has almost doubled its share of GDP, from around 45 percent to about 80 percent of GDP today. During the financial crisis, personal debt was almost 100 percent of GDP.

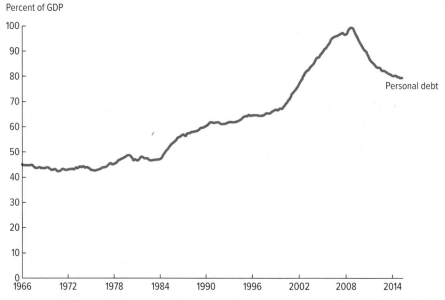

Source: FRED Economic Data, https://research.stlouisfed.org/fred2/series/HDTGPDUSQ163N.

FIGURE 17-4

Debt payments and total debt   This graph compares household financial obligations (which include payments during the year for mortgages, credit cards, property tax, and leases) and household debt (which is the total amount owed) as a percent of income. Despite the fact that household debt has risen considerably, nearly doubling from about 70 percent of total disposable income to just below 120 percent of disposable income, household payments on this debt have not increased very much, as low interest rates have kept the price of debt low.

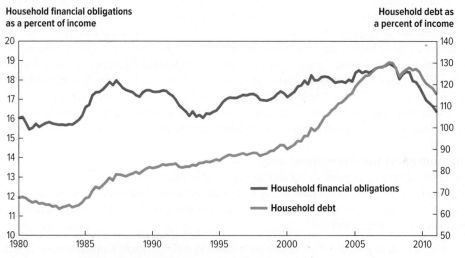

Source: Board of Governors of the Federal Reserve System, accessed on the FRED, updated June 8, 2012.

became the property of the bank when they defaulted on a mortgage loan. Often, the bank would then evict the homeowner and try to sell the house.

- The wave of foreclosed properties hit the market, creating a big increase in the supply of housing. The increase in supply depressed housing prices even further, leading to another wave of defaults.

- Consumers who had used second and third mortgages or borrowed in other ways to extract wealth from their homes suddenly found themselves "underwater," owing more in mortgage debt than their houses were worth. A vicious cycle of defaults and falling prices began; it would ultimately cause home values to fall by more than 50 percent in the hardest-hit areas.

As home prices fell, consumers were unable to refinance mortgages, and a cycle of defaults and falling prices followed, eventually engulfing the entire economy.
© *Anton Sokolov/123RF*

- Riskier real estate investments became worthless. Even the supposedly "safe," AAA-rated investments were badly affected. Banks lost trillions of dollars.

- Because of the opaque and complicated nature of mortgage-backed securities, it was difficult to tell which banks had been hit the hardest by the crash. As a result, the *entire* borrowing and lending engine of the economy ground to a halt. Nobody wanted to lend to anybody, in case they turned out to be a bad risk.

- Even the most venerable banks teetered on the edge of collapse. Large institutions and companies that had deposited money with Wall Street's banks began withdrawing their funds, leading to a run on bank assets. Two of the largest and most respected banks—Bear Stearns and Lehman Brothers—collapsed, and the rest were perceived to be at risk as well. Figure 17-5 shows the dramatic collapse in stock prices of the largest banks.

FIGURE 17-5

Stock prices of major banks   As a result of the housing boom, the financial sector performed well in the years leading up to the crisis. This ended when many of the banks announced that they held large amounts of toxic assets. Beginning in February 2007, prices began to fall. Come September 2008, prices of stocks throughout the financial sectors plummeted as the crisis hit.

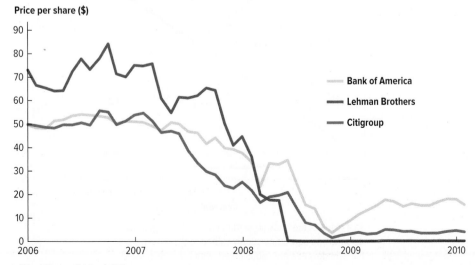

Source: Yahoo! Finance, October 4, 2011.

- Because banks were unwilling to lend, many businesses were suddenly unable to get access to credit for their day-to-day needs. Even simple tasks like buying inventory or taking delivery of a container ship full of imported goods became nearly impossible for many companies. Effectively, the aggregate productive capacity of the entire world was reduced almost overnight.
- The combination of increasing interest rates and pessimism about future economic prospects decreased investment spending: Businesses could no longer obtain credit to invest, and most would not have wanted to invest as the economy weakened anyway.
- Households found themselves struggling to pay back debts, and some faced reduced income and poor job prospects. The fall in home prices meant they were no longer as wealthy as they thought they were, and people reduced their consumption accordingly.
- With demand flagging, businesses had to cut back further. Some employees were laid off, and others saw their wages or hours cut.
- Lower incomes led naturally to lower spending and still more layoffs.

Figure 17-6 shows the combined impact of these forces: As a result of the housing-market crash, both aggregate demand and aggregate supply shifted to the left. The combined shifts put the economy at a new equilibrium, with dramatically reduced output. Prices fell because the effect of the leftward shift in the aggregate demand curve was stronger than the effect of the leftward shift in aggregate supply. The combined effect left the economy reeling.

It took barely two years for the bursting of a real estate bubble to tip the global economy into its worst downturn in over 75 years. Once housing prices collapsed and the bad loans in the financial system were revealed for what they were, it was only a matter of time before the convulsions on Wall Street led to job losses and economic pain on Main Street.

FIGURE 17-6

The financial crisis in terms of AD and AS

As a result of the housing-market crash, both aggregate demand and aggregate supply shifted to the left. This put the economy at a new equilibrium, with lower prices and dramatically reduced output.

The immediate response to the crisis

LO 17.6 Describe the monetary and fiscal policy responses to the financial crisis of 2008.

With the private sector reeling from the impact of the shifts in both aggregate demand and aggregate supply, many looked to the government to provide stability and ensure that the situation did not become even worse. We've talked about how the government can use monetary and fiscal policy to impact the economy. During the financial crisis, policy-makers used these tools to try to avert a catastrophic economic collapse.

With more banks failing each day, the goal of fiscal and monetary policy in 2008 was to "unstick" the frozen credit markets. Economists feared that any attempt to stimulate aggregate demand without first addressing the lack of supply would have been ineffective at best and dangerous at worst. It could potentially have led to **stagflation**—that is, high inflation despite low economic growth and high unemployment.

The challenges facing the financial system stemmed from the two fundamental issues of liquidity and solvency. The more pressing of the two was liquidity. There was great uncertainty about which banks were facing losses and which would most likely go bankrupt next. As a result, banks were not willing to lend to each other. The lack of liquidity meant that there wasn't enough money moving through the system to keep transactions going. Concerns about the amount of the liquidity in the market were reflected in interest rates: In the depths of the financial crisis, interest rates on even the most secure loans soared.

Addressing the liquidity problem fell to the world's central banks, and primarily to the U.S. Federal Reserve in its role as "lender of last resort." When a similar financial crisis shook the United States in the early 1900s, one man—J.P. Morgan—stepped in to act as the lender of last resort, averting a national financial collapse. Six years after that event, the Federal Reserve was created. In 2008, the existence of the Fed meant that the situation played out very differently. Shortly after Lehman Brothers' collapse, the Fed leapt into action: It offered nearly unlimited short-term financing to any bank that suddenly found itself short on cash. The European Central Bank and the Bank of England quickly followed suit, trying to help the financial system from seizing up completely.

Figure 17-7 shows the effect of this monetary policy response: a dramatic spike in the size of the Federal Reserve's balance sheet in September 2008. The Fed greatly expanded its

stagflation
high inflation despite low economic growth and high unemployment

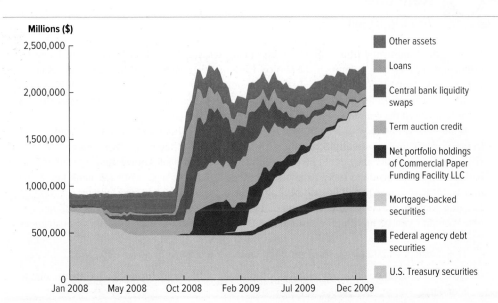

Millions ($)

- Other assets
- Loans
- Central bank liquidity swaps
- Term auction credit
- Net portfolio holdings of Commercial Paper Funding Facility LLC
- Mortgage-backed securities
- Federal agency debt securities
- U.S. Treasury securities

FIGURE 17-7

The Federal Reserve's balance sheet

Responding to the crisis, the Fed in fall 2008 doubled the assets on its balance sheet, over the span of just a month. Notice the rise in mortgage-backed securities beginning in early 2009, which the Fed began purchasing as a way to support the housing market.

Source: Board of Governors of the Federal Reserve System, http://www.federalreserve.gov/releases/h41/current/, updated July 5, 2012.

holdings of financial products, doubling the assets over the span of a month. The intent of the policy was to compensate for the loss of capital in the financial markets. By buying various assets, the Fed added nearly $1.5 trillion in new money to the U.S. economy. Even though you may not recognize every asset on the Fed's balance sheet, notice the rise in mortgage-backed securities beginning in early 2009, which the Fed began purchasing as a way to support the housing market.

At the same time, the U.S. Treasury began the difficult task of dealing with banks that had a solvency problem. "Solvency problem" is a gentle way of referring to banks that had lost so much money that they would inevitably go bankrupt. Hundreds of banks were allowed to fail during this period. However, certain banks were deemed **"too big to fail"**—that is, so large in terms of assets or customers or so historically important that banking regulators allow the bank to keep operating despite insolvency. The failure of one of these big banks carried the risk of causing a domino effect in the highly integrated financial system, causing widespread loss and credit seize-up.

Banks considered "too big to fail" were eventually bailed out through fiscal policy—that is, through increased government spending. The bulk of this effort came through the Troubled Asset Relief Program, commonly known as *TARP*. This program represented the first wave of the federal government's fiscal policy response to the crisis. The first wave invested more than $700 billion in failing institutions. The recipients ranged from major banks like Citigroup to insurance companies like AIG. General Motors and Chrysler, two automakers that were floundering in the weak economy, also received bailouts from the Treasury.

This one-two punch of monetary and fiscal policy averted a systemic collapse and brought stability to the global financial system. By shoring up the capital of the most heavily damaged banks and flooding the system with liquidity, the Treasury and the Federal Reserve worked together to restore the lines of credit within the economy.

Many officials argued that the bailouts were absolutely necessary to save the economy. Debate swirled around TARP as it made its way through government. Chief among the concerns was the fear that blanket bailouts would create a class of banks that *knew* they were considered to be "too big to fail" and so would continue to take unnecessary risks. This debate is covered in the Real Life box "Too big to fail?"

"too big to fail"
so large in terms of assets or customers or so historically important that banking regulators allow the bank to keep operating despite insolvency

Real Life
Too big to fail?

In 1984, the Continental Illinois Bank based in Chicago was headed for bankruptcy. The government and financial regulators had a choice: Either let the seventh-largest bank in the country fail and risk damages to the financial sector, or step in and provide it with the cash it needed to stay in business. In the end, the government decided to step in and save Continental Illinois because it feared the consequences of letting such a big bank fail.

What's the problem with a bank being "too big to fail"? Like any other firm, banks want to make profits but are usually constrained by the fact that if they make decisions that are too risky, there is a chance they could go bankrupt. However, if a bank knows the government will bail it out, the downside to risky behavior is reduced. If the risk pays off, the bank keeps the profits; if the risk goes bad, it doesn't bear all of the losses. This encourages greater risk-taking. Imagine going to the casino and knowing that if you lose everything, your parents will bail you out. Wouldn't you be more willing to gamble than if you had to bear all of the consequences yourself?

This "heads I win, tails you lose" problem creates a dilemma for government:

- On the one hand, the government doesn't want bank collapses to have negative effects on the economy.

- On the other hand, the government doesn't want to encourage risky behavior by bailing out banks whenever they get into trouble.

This dilemma came into sharp focus in 2008 when Lehman Brothers, the fourth-largest investment bank in the United States, faced bankruptcy. After many emergency meetings, the government ultimately decided *not* to bail out Lehman Brothers. That decision sent shockwaves through the financial sector. Many analysts had assumed that Lehman would be deemed "too big to fail." Though concerned about the consequences of a Lehman bankruptcy, the government decided it was more important to send a signal that it wasn't automatically going to help every bank that got itself into trouble.

The very next day, the insurance giant AIG was about to fail. This time, the government *did* step in to bail it out, to the tune of $85 billion. AIG was the country's largest insurer of commercial and industrial outfits. Policy-makers calculated that AIG could not go bust without inflicting extensive damage throughout the financial system.

Just a few weeks later, the Federal Reserve, together with the U.S. Treasury, put together TARP, essentially acknowledging that more banks were "too big to fail." As an illustration of how serious the situation had become, Ben Bernanke, chairman of the Federal Reserve, told politicians that the TARP was necessary because without it, "we might not have an economy on Monday."

Where does that leave banks today? Some have suggested that the solution to the "too big to fail" dilemma is to break up "too big" banks into smaller chunks. Those smaller banks could be allowed to fail without widespread damage to the financial system. Others argue that the "too big to fail" banks should be explicitly named and their activities more closely regulated, to reflect the risks that taxpayers are bearing.

As things stands, the dilemma remains: Any bank that faces going bust will have to wait nervously to discover if the government considers it to be more of a Lehman Brothers or an AIG.

Sources: http://www.nytimes.com/2008/10/02/business/02crisis.html; http://widerimage.reuters.com/timesofcrisis/.

The effect of the monetary and fiscal actions in the aggregate demand and aggregate supply model is shown in Figure 17-8, which builds from Figure 17-6:

- The Federal Reserve lowered interest rates to respond to the sharp reduction in the amount of credit available in the market:
- The Treasury through the TARP provided money in the market.

These two actions restored aggregate supply to its original level.

Once order was restored in the credit market, businesses were again able to finance their inventories and continue to grow their operations. This restoration pushed the SRAS curve back toward its original pre-crisis position. However, due to sluggish aggregate demand, output was still well below pre-crash levels (Y_1).

You might be wondering why all of that capital failed to stimulate aggregate demand. The short answer is that these programs did not have the same goal as traditional monetary policy conducted through the federal funds rate. Most of the offerings, instead, were used only by banks that faced problems getting the capital they needed to function normally—emergency programs for an extraordinary situation. So even as the financial sector stabilized, the United States found itself with the classic problem of most economic downturns: depressed aggregate demand.

FIGURE 17-8

Fed and Treasury intervention restores aggregate supply

The Fed and the Treasury both responded to the sharp reduction of credit available in the market. Their responses provided enough money in the market to spur aggregate supply and demand, although due to sluggish aggregate demand, output was still well below pre-crash levels (Y_1).

Stimulus at the zero lower bound

LO 17.7 Describe the different tools that can be used to stimulate the economy when interest rates are at the zero lower bound.

The policy prescriptions for fixing low aggregate demand are relatively straightforward:

- The Federal Reserve can pursue expansionary monetary policy, lowering interest rates to encourage borrowing and investment spending, which pushes the aggregate demand curve to the right.
- Alternatively, the government can engage in stimulus through fiscal policy, increasing aggregate demand through tax cuts or increases in government spending.

In fact, both routes were pursued in the 2007–2009 crisis. Congress and President Obama passed fiscal stimulus legislation intended to support demand. The Federal Reserve slashed the federal funds rate from a little more than 5 percent before the crisis to 2 percent. As demand stayed weak—even after stimulus spending—the Fed continued to cut the federal funds rate.

By 2009, the economy was in an unusual situation. Interest rates were near zero and the economy had still not recovered. Households were trying to pay down their debts; there was little desire to borrow for consumption—even when borrowing was essentially free. With consumption weak, businesses were in no mood to invest in expanding their productive capacity. With interest rates already at zero, it seemed as though monetary policy was out of ammunition. After all, the Fed couldn't lower interest rates below zero. What *could* it do?

quantitative easing
policies that are designed to directly increase the money supply by a certain amount

What came out of this impasse was a prescription for unorthodox monetary policy: quantitative easing. **Quantitative easing** involves policies that are designed to directly increase the money supply by a certain amount. As a policy, it contrasts with the more common practice of indirectly adjusting the money supply through interest rates. The Fed accomplished quantitative easing by purchasing long-term government bonds. The aim was to get more money into the economy. In all, the Fed purchased more than $1 trillion worth of long-term bonds with newly created money, thus adding $1 trillion to the money supply.

In choosing quantitative easing, the Fed wanted to avoid what happened in Japan after a housing bubble inflated in the 1980s and then popped. For years, the Japanese economy was weak, and deflation was a recurring problem. The Real Life box "Japan's lost decade" tells the story.

Real Life

Japan's lost decade

In the 1980s, Japan was one of the world's leading economies. In 1989, a real estate bubble threatened to destabilize the economy, and the Central Bank of Japan tried to gently rein in the price of housing by raising interest rates. The effect was dramatic: Housing prices fell 87 percent from their peak. This shock reverberated throughout the economy and ravaged the stock market. With the combined crashes in housing and the stock market, Japan lost the equivalent of three years of GDP, one of the largest peacetime losses of wealth in human history.

In response, the Japanese government and central bank engaged many of the traditional tools used to fight financial crises and recessions. They bailed out banks that were in danger of collapse. Banks got enough capital to keep them afloat, but it wasn't enough for normal day-to-day lending. These banks became known as "zombie banks"—banks that are nominally alive thanks to continued government bailouts but not able to play a useful role in the economy.

The government also embarked on an ambitious fiscal stimulus plan. Most of that spending went to building bridges and roads in rural areas. This stimulus also failed to improve the economy. Some argue the projects were ill-conceived. Others say the spigot of funding was turned off far too early to have a real impact.

In an especially drastic measure, the central bank dropped interest rates from 8 percent all the way down to zero. When that didn't work, the central bank said there was little else it could do—it had reached the *zero lower bound* on interest rates.

Japan's economy slipped into a downward spiral. Homeowners who had borrowed to purchase their houses when prices were high cut back on their spending so they could pay back debt. As a result, the economy became so weak that prices started to fall. The resulting deflation was incredibly damaging. Consumers held onto their money, knowing that they would be able to buy more in the future when its value increased. That reluctance to spend drove prices even further downward.

With these headwinds, the Japanese economy stayed stuck in neutral for two decades. What was originally known as the "Lost Decade" eventually became the "Lost Years." However, one economist who closely studied Japan's experience suggested that much of this stagnation was avoidable. The government could have let some of the zombie banks fail, continued stimulus spending, and tried alternative monetary policy measures, such as quantitative easing, to stimulate the economy.

Who was the economist who proposed these measures? It was Ben Bernanke, chairman of the Federal Reserve during the U.S. crisis.

Sources: http://www.nytimes.com/2010/05/21/opinion/21krugman.html; http://www.time.com/time/magazine/article/0,9171,1884815,00.html.

After the Fed's first round of quantitative easing, the overall money supply remained nearly unchanged. When the economy continued to stagnate, however, the Fed engaged in a second round of quantitative easing. The second round dramatically increased the overall level of the money supply. By mid-2011, the money supply stood at nearly $3 trillion, more than triple its level going into the crisis.

This enormous increase in the money supply was unprecedented. Critics feared that it would cause very high inflation. With the economy stagnating, however, the increase in the money supply led to only a slight increase in borrowing. Why did this happen? The money multiplier collapsed as banks were unwilling to lend and consumers and businesses were not very interested in, or capable of being approved for, borrowing. There is still debate about whether quantitative easing was successful in boosting demand. It appears, though, that the Fed's efforts at least prevented an outright fall in borrowing and lending, which would have further damaged an already weak economy.

✓ CONCEPT CHECK

- ☐ What is a subprime mortgage? **[LO 17.3]**
- ☐ Why did mortgage-backed securities lead to an increase in subprime lending? **[LO 17.4]**
- ☐ How did the 2007 financial crisis impact aggregate demand? **[LO 17.5]**
- ☐ What is the dilemma involved in deciding whether to bail out a bank that is considered "too big to fail"? **[LO 17.6]**
- ☐ Why would a central bank implement quantitative easing? **[LO 17.7]**

Conclusion

This chapter began with a simple question: Why do financial crises occur? Usually, financial crises arise from a combination of irrational expectations and leverage, which create bubbles that burst with dire consequences for the real economy. Crises have been around since the very first financial markets, as the example of the South Seas Company in the 1700s shows.

These forces surfaced once again when innovations in the subprime lending market led to a dramatic increase in home ownership and housing prices. When the real estate bubble burst in 2007, a financial crisis struck again, challenging economists' belief that economic crises had become a thing of the past.

Recent events show that we still have much to learn about the macroeconomy. Can we permanently moderate the business cycle? How will increasing global interdependency affect future crises? What can governments do to make financial markets work better? There are no quick and easy answers to these questions, but we are starting to better understand the complexity of the challenges. The unfortunate reality is that economies can collapse almost overnight, but they often take a lot longer to recover.

Key Terms

bubble, p. 460

leverage, p. 462

leverage ratio, p. 463

securitization, p. 466

debt service, p. 469

stagflation, p. 473

"too big to fail," p. 474

quantitative easing, p. 476

Summary

LO 17.1 Describe the role of irrational expectations and leverage in the creation of financial crises.

The existence of financial crises challenges the efficient-market hypothesis, showing that markets may not always accurately reflect all available information. Irrational expectations, often based on overly optimistic projections for the future, frequently lead to overvaluations of companies' stocks. Combined with leverage, irrational expectations can create or fuel financial crises.

LO 17.2 Discuss the causes of two famous historical financial crises.

The twin dangers of irrational expectations and leverage played out in two famous historical financial crises. The South Seas Bubble of the eighteenth century is one example: Unrealistic expectations about access to trade with South America led to dramatic overvaluation of companies and spawned fanciful investment schemes. Centuries later, the optimism and rush to invest in the stock market following the Roaring Twenties gave way to the Crash of 1929 and a decade of economic decline during the Great Depression.

LO 17.3 Trace the role of mortgage-backed securities and tranching in the rise of subprime lending.

Securitization in the market for mortgage loans created a wave of subprime lending. Investment banks packaged these loans into larger mortgage-backed securities, which pooled the risk of subprime loans and enabled more loans to be made. Eventually, banks began tranching these securities, dividing them into segments with different risk and return characteristics. This process allowed the banks to tailor mortgage-backed securities to their clients' investment needs. It also contributed to asymmetric information problems, which later contributed to the crisis.

LO 17.4 Analyze the factors that led to the housing bubble and rising levels of household debt.

Securitization of mortgage loans encouraged banks to offer more subprime mortgages, increasing demand for housing and pushing up prices. At the same time, homeowners found themselves with more wealth because the price of their homes had risen. Feeling wealthier, people increased their household debt, taking out more loans at attractive low interest rates, to pay for higher levels of consumption.

LO 17.5 Explain how the collapse of the housing bubble created a credit crisis and subsequent contraction in output.

Eventually, the housing bubble popped. Many subprime borrowers defaulted on their loans after teaser rates expired; home prices dropped, and banks found themselves with mortgage-backed securities worth a fraction of their original estimate. Many banks stopped lending and many failed; credit markets dried up. Businesses were no longer able to finance economic investments. Households, facing a negative shock to wealth due to depressed housing prices, began saving more and consuming less. Both aggregate demand and aggregate supply shifted to the left. At the new equilibrium, output was dramatically lower. Prices fell because the effect of the leftward shift in the aggregate demand curve was stronger than the effect of the leftward shift in aggregate supply. The economy entered a recession.

LO 17.6 Describe the monetary and fiscal policy responses to the financial crisis of 2008.

In response to the crisis, the federal government acted quickly to stabilize the financial system. The Federal Reserve, in its role as the lender of last resort, offered short-term financing to banks that couldn't access credit otherwise. This provided liquidity to the market, a crucial step in raising aggregate supply. The government also tackled solvency issues by bailing out several large banks through the Troubled Assets Relief Program (TARP). Once the crisis gave way to a contraction in output, the government used fiscal policy to increase aggregate demand by passing stimulus measures.

LO 17.7 Describe the different tools that can be used to stimulate the economy when interest rates are at the zero lower bound.

When the monetary policy hit the zero lower bound, the Fed undertook quantitative easing, designed to increase the money supply by a certain amount. In two rounds of quantitative easing, it directly purchased a total of $3 trillion in long-term government bonds, thus adding that amount to the money supply.

Review Questions

1. Your best friend comes to you for financial investment advice. She is wondering whether she should invest in (a) a sector of the economy that has been performing extremely well in the last five years relative to historical levels or (b) one that has been performing extremely poorly in the last five years relative to historical levels. What would you advise? How might irrational expectations affect your recommendations? **[LO 17.1]**

2. What is leverage, and how can it make an asset pricing bubble worse? **[LO 17.1]**

3. What causes a stock market bubble to form? **[LO 17.2]**

4. History suggests that all stock market bubbles will eventually pop and cause severe financial loss for many of those who purchased stock. Given this history, do you think that stock market bubbles will continue to occur? Why or why not? **[LO 17.2]**

5. Explain why it's possible for tranching to make investing in a mortgage-backed security more risky than investing in a single subprime loan. **[LO 17.3]**

6. Explain how a mortgage-backed security can increase loan availability to those with little credit or bad credit. **[LO 17.3]**

7. Explain the role that leverage played in the recent housing bubble. **[LO 17.4]**

8. How did government policies and asymmetric information problems make the recent housing bubble worse? **[LO 17.4]**

9. Many subprime borrowers entered into "adjustable-rate mortgages" with low teaser rates. These mortgages allowed borrowers to pay a low interest rate for the first two years on their mortgage, before the rate jumped to market levels. But the loan documents sometimes made it difficult for borrowers to understand that the rate would increase. Explain why this practice could lead to a bubble in housing prices. **[LO 17.5]**

10. How did the recent housing crisis affect the aggregate demand curve? **[LO 17.5]**

11. Imagine what would have happened if the Federal Reserve was not in place to act as a lender of last resort during the financial crisis. Absent government involvement, what would be the likely effect on aggregate supply? Why? What would be the likely effect on aggregate demand? Why? **[LO 17.6]**

12. As the Federal Reserve responded to the recent housing crisis, how did this affect its balance sheet? Can you think of what caused the balance sheet's size to change so much? **[LO 17.6]**

13. What is the "zero lower bound" that must be considered in monetary policy, and how can it cause problems in enacting such policy? **[LO 17.7]**

14. What is quantitative easing, and when might it be used? **[LO 17.7]**

Problems and Applications

1. Determine whether or not each of the following is an example of irrational expectations. **[LO 17.1]**

    a. The price of Amazon's stock rises after tech blogs reveal that the company plans to release a new tablet, rumored to be competitive with Apple's iPad.

    b. The CEO of a new start-up producing applications for tablets is quoted as proclaiming a new era of media, in which thirst for content will rise indefinitely as information becomes more and more convenient for people to digest. An economics blog continues the discussion a year later, discussing returns to investment that have never before been contemplated. Stock prices for media companies are consistently outperforming

historical levels by 50 percent and seem to be on a permanent rise.

    c. After an unusually cool summer, investors in Papa's Cool-Pops decide to sell, believing demand for frozen treats will never reach historic levels again because of the weather.

    d. The Justice Department reveals allegations against the CEO of a food and beverage company, alleging misconduct within the company. A trial could cost the company millions of dollars. The stock price falls by 5 percent by the day's end.

2. Ike, an investor, is considering opening a margin account and investing $1,000 in Mike's mutual fund. The terms of the account require that he pay back the amount he borrowed on the margin by the end of the year with 10 percent interest. Ike is trying to decide what level of margin he wants. For example, if he chooses an account at the level of 50 percent, the bank will let him borrow and invest an additional $500, or 50 percent of his original $1,000. Complete Table 17P-1 by filling in Ike's account value at the end of the year, given varying levels of the margin account and mutual fund performance. Assume that Mike's mutual fund will return 40 percent per year in a stellar market and 5 percent per year in a fair market, and that in a terrible market, it will lose 30 percent. **[LO 17.1]**

3. Consider a stock whose value increases across an 8-year period as shown in Table 17P-2. **[LO 17.2]**

    a. Calculate the percentage change in the value of the stock from year to year.

    b. Calculate the percentage change in the value of the stock across the entire 8-year period.

    c. Do you think this qualifies as a bubble? Why or why not?

4. Assume that a subprime mortgage involves a loan of $1,000 and is to be paid back in full with 30 percent interest after one year. **[LO 17.3]**

    a. Sometimes borrowers will not be able to pay off the entire mortgage or may default entirely. Calculate the final amount of money an investor earns under the payback rates shown in Table 17P-3. (Note that a rate of 130 percent means that the whole loan is paid off, plus the additional 30 percent of interest.)

    b. Assume investors are unwilling to invest in these loans unless the expected rate of return is 10 percent. Calculate the expected rate of return for this loan by adding up all of the products of the final value and the probability that that value will occur. Will investors want to invest in this loan?

TABLE 17P-1

Margin account level	Account value in a stellar market	Account value in a fair market	Account value in a terrible market
No margin			
60%			
100%			
150%			
200%			

TABLE 17P-2

Year	Stock Value ($)	Percentage Change
1	50.00	n/a
2	60.00	
3	75.00	
4	86.25	
5	103.50	
6	155.25	
7	248.40	
8	372.60	

TABLE 17P-3

Amount paid (%)	Final value	Probability
130		0.6
110		0.1
100		0.1
50		0.1
0		0.1

5. A single bank is considering two options: First, it can make a $200,000 mortgage loan for a customer with a 10 percent probability of default or, second, it can buy a $200,000 security representing a bundle of 100 mortgage loans, which break down as shown in Table 17P-4. You can calculate the weighted risk for each firm

TABLE 17P-4

Number of loans	Probability of default (%)	Weighted risk
40	3.0	40% × 3% = 1.2%
25	11.0	
15	1.5	
20	5.0	

category by multiplying the percentage of loans represented (for example, the first tier includes 40 loans, which is $\frac{40}{100} = 40\%$ of the total) times the probability of default on loans of that category. Do so for each type of loan, then add together the weighted risks to come up with an overall expected default risk for this financial investment. If the bank is willing to take on only projects for which the default risk is 6 percent or less, which option(s) should it choose? **[LO 17.3]**

6. Table 17P-5 shows hypothetical levels of average household debt and debt service payments in two years, 2010 and 2013. At what annual interest rate would consumers have had to borrow for the debt-service payments in 2013 to equal the debt-service payments in 2010, despite the increase in household debt? Assume households are paying only interest on their debt and not part of the principal. **[LO 17.4]**

TABLE 17P-5

	2010	2013
Household debt	$20,000	$80,000
Annual debt-service payments	800	?

TABLE 17P-6

Year	Household income ($)	Financial obligations ($)	Financial obligations as % of income	Household debt ($)	Debt as % of income
2011	35,000	4,000			
2012	38,500	4,200			
2013	42,000	5,000			
2014	45,250	6,200			

7. Table 17P-6 gives information on income and debt for a small nation for the years 2011 through 2014. The nation had average household debt of $34,000 at the end of 2010. Use this information to fill in the blanks. **[LO 17.4]**

8. Imagine that your personal finances are summarized by the account balances shown in Table 17P-7. Assume also that your decision to save is a function of your income and net worth. More specifically, assume that your savings each year will be equal to: $0.2I - NW$, where I is your income and NW is your net worth. **[LO 17.4]**

   a. If your income is $60,000, how much will you save this year?

   b. Assume the value of your house decreases by 20 percent. What is your net worth now? How much will you save?

9. If the rate currently payable on 10-year Treasury bonds is 4.8 percent and the risk spread is 2 percent, what is the average rate on other forms of commercial lending? **[LO 17.5]**

10. Which of the following policies were used in response to the latest financial crisis? Of those used, which are examples of monetary policy? Of fiscal policy? **[LO 17.6]**

    a. Aggressive controlling of inflation by raising interest rates.

    b. Providing short-term financing directly to small businesses to jump-start investment.

    c. Bailing out banks that have large amounts of risky mortgage-backed securities.

    d. Purchasing long-term bonds to increase the money supply.

    e. Raising the Social Security eligibility age by five years to encourage people to work.

11. Table 17P-8 shows the balance sheet of a bank in millions of dollars. **[LO 17.6]**

    a. What is the bank's net worth?

    b. Assume housing prices increase and defaults on subprime mortgages rise, causing the bank's assets in subprime mortgages to decrease from $500 million to $350 million. What are total assets now? What is the bank's new net worth?

    c. How far would the value of subprime mortgages have to fall to cause the bank to be insolvent (that is, for liabilities to be greater than assets)?

TABLE 17P-7

Assets		Liabilities	
Home	$100,000	Mortgage	$ 90,000
Checking account	15,000	Student loans	20,000
Car	10,000	Credit card	10,000
Total assets	$125,000	Total liabilities	$120,000

TABLE 17P-8

Assets (in millions)		Liabilities (in millions)	
Cash	$ 800	CDs	$2,000
Commercial loans	2,000	Savings accounts	1,500
Consumer loans	600	Long-term debt	1,000
Prime mortgages	800		
Subprime mortgages	500		
Total assets	$4,700	Total liabilities	$4,500

12. Japan's economic situation throughout its Lost Decade and beyond can be explained in terms of problems with monetary policy via interest rates. Explain what happened. Identify what Japan's central bank should have done. **[LO 17.7]**

13. Consider an economy with $10 billion in base money and a multiplier of 4. The money supply is currently $10 billion × 4 = $40 billion. Now let's say that the amount of base money rises by 50 percent, to $15 billion. How must the multiplier change for the money supply to remain unaffected by this change in base money? **[LO 17.7]**

Endnotes

1. *Futures* are standardized financial contracts that obligate the buyer to either buy or sell a specified amount of some asset at a particular price at a specific future date. There are two main motivations for buying futures. One is "hedging": Companies and individuals use futures contracts to reduce uncertainty about prices in the future. The other is "speculating": Other investors use futures contracts as a way to make bets on the direction of price changes—and, they hope, to make profits by betting correctly.

2. Holding liabilities constant, equity increases by exactly as much as assets. Since assets are 30 times the size of equity, a 10 percent increase in assets amounts to a 300 percent increase in equity.

3. This provision was effectively reversed by the Gramm-Leach-Bliley Act in 1999.

Part Seven

International Policy Issues

The two chapters in Part 7 will introduce you to . . .

the international financial system and development policy. Chapter 18, "Open-Market Macroeconomics," covers the *international financial system.* If you've ever traveled abroad and traded your dollars for another currency, you've participated in one part of the international financial system. Yet it goes much further than that. Anything that was originally produced internationally and imported into the United States was made possible by the international trade of money. In this chapter, we'll introduce the markets that make this trade possible. Like the domestic financial system, the international financial system is vitally important to the smooth operation of the U.S. economy. We'll describe how it works and where it can get into trouble.

Chapter 19, "Development Economics," turns to a large and pressing question: Why is the world filled with poverty amid so much wealth? This is one of the basic questions in *development economics.* We'll describe how understandings of economic development have changed over time. We'll review the current state of research and introduce promising new methods to rigorously evaluate policies and innovations that aim to reduce poverty. Finally, we'll give some examples of solutions that draw on ideas developed in this book—solutions that are making a practical difference in people's lives.

Throughout the text we've seen how economics sheds light on many questions, decisions, and policy issues. Some (such as tax policy) are more obviously about "economics" and some less so. We hope that in reading, you've learned how to apply the economic toolkit to help you solve everyday problems at home and investigate questions about the world around us.

Open-Market Macroeconomics

FROM FACTORY TO FIGURES

The Apple iPhone has been a runaway success. Since its release in June 2007 to the end of 2015, Apple has sold over 896 million phones around the world.[1] You might think of the iPhone as an all-American success story, given that Apple is a U.S. company. Technically, though, the iPhone counts as an import. That's because, like so many consumer goods, the iPhone's component parts are put together in a factory in China before the finished product is shipped to the United States.

© Qilai Shen/Bloomberg via Getty Images

The fact that the iPhone is considered an import means that every iPhone bought in the United States contributes to the trade deficit the United States has with China. In 2015, American consumers bought $483 billion worth of goods from China, while American firms sold only $116 billion worth of goods to consumers in China. The result is an astronomical $367 billion *trade gap* between what America is buying from China and what it is selling there. Mobile phone imports account for 2.3 percent of total imports from China, according to U.S. Census data for 2015. Two economists found that in 2010 iPhones *alone* contributed $1.9 billion to the U.S.–China trade deficit.

To see what this trade gap really means, imagine for a moment that China bought exactly as much from the United States as it sold to the United States. What would happen? Americans would convert $483 billion U.S. into the Chinese currency, the yuan, and use it to buy Chinese goods. In turn, Chinese people would use those $483 billion to buy American goods. Everything would balance out.

In reality, though, the Chinese use only $116 billion to buy American goods. So there must be $367 billion still sloshing around the Chinese economy. Presumably the Chinese don't just keep this money under their mattresses. Where does it end up?

Some dollars are spent or invested at home or abroad, searching for the best return. A lot of them end up being invested in U.S. government debt, which means the Chinese use the money to make *loans to* the U.S. government. Overall, the U.S. government has borrowed more than $1.6 trillion directly from Chinese investors by selling U.S. Treasury securities.[2] The web of international financial connections is something to think about the next time you see an iPhone.

What explains trade flows? How and why does the United States accrue debt to China? Why would China lend to the United States? What determines the rate at which dollars can be converted into yuan? This chapter will answer those questions by exploring international economics. We examine the flow of goods and money around the world and then discuss related shifts in the value of a country's currency.

By showing how to understand the macroeconomy in an international context, this chapter sheds light on important policy debates about exchange rates, trade balances, and capital flows across countries.

International Flows of Goods and Capital

International trade is not a new thing. More than 3,000 years ago, China was exporting textiles along the famed Silk Road to the Mediterranean and Persian empires. Spices were traveling from India to the Roman Empire along the Spice Route. The voyage of Christopher Columbus was inspired by the desire to find a quicker route to the riches of India. Today, modern communications and ease of transportation have allowed international flows of goods and capital to reach unprecedented levels: Consumers in Europe buy freshly cut flowers from Kenya, Americans dine on shrimp from Thailand, and Chinese utility companies ship in coal from Colombia.

In this section, we look at the different ways in which goods and capital flow around the global economy today.

Imports and exports

LO 18.1 Define the balance of trade and describe the general trends of U.S. trade.

First, let's look at some patterns of trade in the United States. Figure 18-1 shows trade flows over the last 50 years. You can see that both exports and imports have increased dramatically over this period as the economy has grown. In 2015, exports of goods and services were $2.3 trillion, or approximately 13 percent of GDP. Imports the same year were $2.8 trillion, or approximately 15.5 percent of GDP.

It is interesting to look at the flows in and out, but the number that economists care the most about is the net value of these flows. Called the **balance of trade**, it is the value of exports minus the value of imports. The balance of trade can be either negative or positive:

- If a country imports more than it exports, the balance of trade is negative. Economists call this situation a **trade deficit**. For nearly every year since 1970, the United States has had a trade deficit. In 2015, the trade balance was –$500 billion, or about 2.8 percent of GDP.

- If a country exports more than it imports, the balance of trade is positive. In that case, the country is said to have a **trade surplus**. Countries like Japan, China, and Germany run large trade surpluses. For example, the 2015 trade surplus in Germany was worth around 8.8 percent of its GDP.[3]

Figure 18-1 shows the total trade balance of the United States with all the other countries in the world. If you had to guess, which countries would you expect to be the main trading partners of the United States? Because trade requires transporting goods, which costs money, countries tend to trade with their neighbors. This holds true for the United States. Two of its biggest trading

balance of trade
the value of exports minus the value of imports

trade deficit
a negative balance of trade; a greater amount of imports than exports

trade surplus
a positive balance of trade; a greater amount of exports than imports

---

FIGURE 18-1

Imports, exports, and the balance of U.S. trade since 1960   Until 1980, trade by the United States was relatively balanced; imports were roughly equal to exports. Shortly thereafter, the amount of imports grew faster than the amount of exports, which led to a negative trade balance. Now, the trade deficit stands at $500 billion.

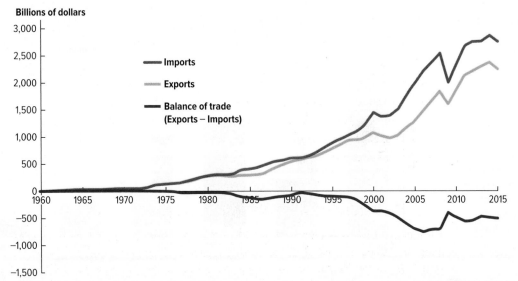

Source: U.S. Census Bureau, Historical Series: Annual Goods, Services, and Total Balance, Exports and Imports; https://www.census.gov/foreign-trade/statistics/historical/index.html.

partners are its neighbors: Canada to the north and Mexico to the south. In addition to being neighbors, trade has expanded because of the North American Free Trade Agreement (NAFTA), a pact that eliminates barriers to trade and investment among these neighbors.

Of course, as Figure 18-2 shows, not all trade partners are neighbors. In fact, the United States imports more goods from China than from any other country, including its neighbors Mexico and Canada. And the United States imports much more from China than it exports to it. This difference generates a negative trade balance with China that makes up about half of the total U.S. trade deficit for goods. As we go through this chapter, we'll examine explanations for the trade deficit with China. One factor is that Chinese products tend to be low in price. We'll also look at less-obvious factors such as the amount of savings in China and its exchange-rate policies.

We've seen how much the United States is trading and with whom—but *what* is it trading? As we described in Chapter 2, "Specialization and Exchange," there are *gains from trade* when countries specialize in producing particular goods and then trade with others to meet their other needs. Looking at trade statistics shows exactly where the gains from trade in the United States come from. Figure 18-3 shows the main categories of goods that the United States exports and imports, and the contribution to the trade balance for each category.

FIGURE 18-2

Major U.S. trading partners

Much of U.S. trade occurs with its closest neighbors, Canada and Mexico. However, the United States's biggest trading partner is China, even though it is far away. Trade between the United States and China consists mostly of imports into the United States.

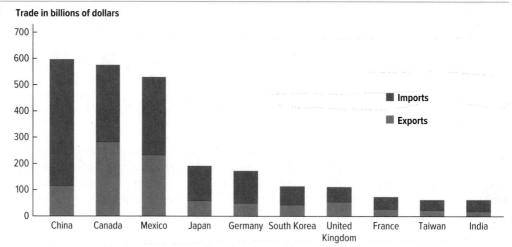

Trade in billions of dollars

Source: U.S. Census Bureau, Top Trading Partners for 2015, https://www.census.gov/foreign-trade/statistics/highlights/top/top1512yr.html.

FIGURE 18-3

What does the United States trade?

The United States imports a large amount of capital goods—things that are used to produce other goods—which also constitute the largest U.S. export. The largest difference between imports and exports is in the category of consumer goods, as the United States imports far more consumer goods than it exports.

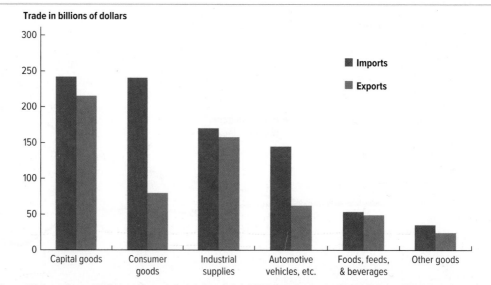

Trade in billions of dollars

Source: U.S. Census Bureau, U.S. Bureau of Economic Analysis News, July 6, 2016. Data for January through May 2016. http://www.bea.gov/newsreleases/international/trade/2016/pdf/trad0516.pdf.

The largest category of U.S. exports is capital goods—goods such as semiconductors and industrial machines. The United States exported $216 billion in capital goods in the first half of 2016. At the same time, it imported $243 billion worth of capital goods, mostly computers and telecommunications equipment. The balance of trade in capital goods was −$27 billion.

While the amount the United States imports and exports is pretty close for capital goods, consumer goods are dominated by imports—goods such as clothing, smartphones, pharmaceuticals, and toys. The balance of trade in consumer goods was nearly −$161 billion, with imports of about $241 billion and exports of about $80 billion for the first half of 2016. In fact, as of May 2016, the United States was running a negative trade balance in all categories. The "Foods, feeds, and beverages" category has the smallest trade deficit; the high value of U.S. exports of soybeans and corn, subsidized in part by the U.S. government, explains this.

Foreign investment

> **LO 18.2** Define portfolio investment and foreign direct investment.

Imports and exports are the most visible and straightforward aspects of international economics. Countries interact in other ways as well, including through investment. The investment when a firm runs part of its operation abroad or owns all or part of another company abroad is called **foreign direct investment (FDI)**. Foreign direct investment often makes economic sense for businesses—it helps broaden markets and can cut wage costs, for example. Some people object that such investment can encourage "sweatshops" abroad, where workers work for long hours under worse conditions than would be allowed in the United States. For a discussion of some of the issues surrounding foreign investment, see the What Do You Think? box "Are sweatshops good or bad?"

foreign direct investment (FDI) investment when a firm runs part of its operation abroad or owns all or part of another company abroad

What Do You Think?
Are sweatshops good or bad?

In 2001, an MIT graduate student named Jonah Peretti ordered a pair of sneakers from the NIKE iD service, which allows customers to personalize their shoes with a word of their choice. Peretti asked that his be emblazoned with the word "sweatshop." Nike refused, claiming that the word violated the NIKE iD terms and conditions because it was "inappropriate slang."

Peretti e-mailed back, with false innocence:

> After consulting Webster's Dictionary, I discovered that "sweatshop" is in fact part of standard English, and not slang. The word means: "a shop or factory in which workers are employed for long hours at low wages and under unhealthy conditions" and its origin dates from 1892. . . . Your web site advertises that the NIKE iD program is "about freedom to choose and freedom to express who you are." I share Nike's love of freedom and personal expression. . . . I hope that you will value my freedom of statement and reconsider your decision to reject my order.

Nike again refused, doubtless not wanting the bad publicity of someone walking around in a pair of "Nike Sweatshops." But Nike got bad publicity anyway when the e-mail exchange with Peretti went viral, sparking media coverage around the globe. Peretti had a pointed goal—to shame Nike for the use of "sweatshop" labor to make its shoes. (Nike, for its part, has since taken steps to improve labor standards and monitor conditions.)

Yet here is the irony: Although they are bad for publicity, it's not entirely clear that sweatshops are always such a bad thing. Economists, including Jeffrey Sachs of Columbia University,

(continued)

argue that some kinds of sweatshops are good for an economy. After all, the fact that people choose to work in sweatshops indicates that these jobs are better for them than their other options. Outside of working in the factories, the only alternative may be backbreaking agricultural work that pays even less than the low wages offered by sweatshops. By bringing people out of agriculture, sweatshops provide a source of relative financial security and contribute toward the growth of the economy.

Those who forwarded Peretti's e-mail exchange with Nike presumably felt uneasy with Sachs's argument. Critics of sweatshops think it's wrong that workers can toil for as long as 80 hours per week for what most Americans would consider a tiny wage. Often, it is not just that wages are low by U.S. standards. In addition, workers may be unknowingly exposed to hazardous chemicals and dangerous machinery. Such a problem could be a market failure due to information asymmetry if employees are not fully aware of the risks they are taking. Even where safety regulations exist, workers may be unable to report violations to local authorities without fear of retribution.

WHAT DO YOU THINK?

1. Why do rich countries tend to have stricter labor standards than poor counties? How do you think these labor standards developed?
2. If consumers feel uneasy about buying goods made in overseas sweatshops, should they support efforts to enact minimum wage and worker safety legislation all over the world? Why or why not?

Source: "Making Nike Sweat," Village Voice, February 13, 2001.

Of course, investment abroad doesn't have to be just in tangible assets such as factories. Often, investors also want to buy foreign financial assets, such as stocks or government-issued securities. We call this type of investment *foreign portfolio investment*. **Foreign portfolio investment** is investment funded by foreign sources but operated domestically. Portfolio investment allows investors to hold financial assets that deliver greater profit and reduce overall risk relative to financial investments available at home.

foreign portfolio investment investment funded by foreign sources but operated domestically

Portfolio investment can generally flow across borders quickly because it mainly involves transfers between bank accounts. When a country is small, the rapid movement of money across borders can easily overwhelm the country's financial markets. Foreign direct investment doesn't move as fast. You cannot just pick up a factory and move it across the border.

One of the largest portfolio investments comes from Chinese purchases of U.S. government debt. Part of the reason for this investment is that Chinese investors have a large reserve of U.S. dollars, so they want to buy assets that are U.S. dollar–denominated. Why do they have a large reserve of U.S. dollars? Because, as noted earlier, every time we buy Chinese goods, someone had to sell dollars in exchange for *yuan* to pay for these products. One option for what to do with all these dollars is to use them to buy U.S. Treasury bills.

net capital flow the net flow of funds invested outside of a country; specifically, the difference between capital inflows (investment financed by savings from another country) and capital outflows (domestic savings invested abroad)

When the total amount of foreign direct investment and foreign portfolio investment is tallied, we can find the net investment position of a country. The **net capital flow** is the net flow of funds invested outside of a country. Specifically, net capital flow is the difference between capital inflows and capital outflows:

- *Capital inflows* are investments financed by savings from another country. Countries that have a trade deficit have a *net capital inflow*.
- *Capital outflows* are domestic savings invested abroad. Countries that have a trade surplus have a positive *net capital outflow*.

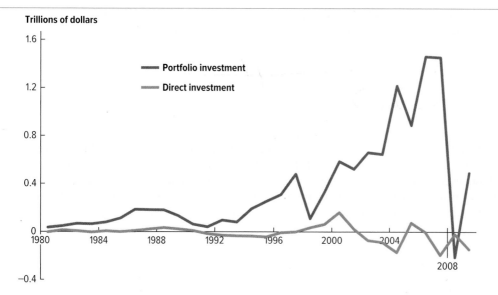

Trillions of dollars

— Portfolio investment
— Direct investment

Source: U.S. Bureau of Economic Analysis (accessed June 29, 2011).

FIGURE 18-4

Net capital flows for the United States

For a long time, portfolio and direct investment flows in the United States were small. Then, starting with the tech bubble, portfolio investment began to ramp up, blipped downward before the bubble popped, and then completely exploded in the housing bubble. The falloff from this crash was severe: In the span of one year, portfolio investment fell from $1.4 trillion to an outflow of $200 billion.

Figure 18-4 shows net capital outflow for the United States over 30 years. You can see that the capital outflow is broken down into the two types of foreign investment: direct investment and portfolio investment.

The trade in goods, services, and capital comprises trillions of dollars around the world. Keeping track of the trade balance and net capital flows helps organize these transactions. In general, the accounting for trade in goods and capital is known as the *balance of payments*.

Balance of payments

LO 18.3 Explain the connection between the balance of trade and net capital outflow.

How are countries like the United States able to sustain large deficits in trade? It turns out that trade in tangible goods and different types of capital must balance each other out, balancing trade deficits with capital surpluses. This is shown through the **balance-of-payments identity**, an equation that shows that the value of net exports equals the net capital outflow.

Recall the income-expenditure identity from Chapter 7, "Measuring GDP." The identity for a closed economy—that is, one with no imports or exports—looks like this:

$$Y = C + I + G$$

Remember also that in a closed economy, savings (S) equal investment (I). We have two kinds of savings in the economy: *private savings,* which is the money left over that households and businesses don't spend, and *public savings,* which is the money left over that the government doesn't spend. Thus, rearranging the variables in the income-expenditure identify, we find:

(1) $I = Y - C - G$

(2) $S = S_{private} + S_{public} = Y - C - G$

(3) $S = I$

What do things look like if we open up the economy and add in the variable of net exports? We get the typical equation for GDP, also known as the income-expenditure identity:

$$Y = C + I + G + NX$$

balance-of-payments identity

an equation that shows that the value of net exports equals net capital outflow

If we then rearrange the income-expenditure identity for an open economy, we get something that looks very similar to the equation above, except that savings equals investment plus net exports.

$$(4) \ I + NX = Y - C - G$$

$$(5) \ S = S_{private} + S_{public} = Y - C - G$$

$$(6) \ S = I + NX$$

Finally, assume that people can choose where they want to invest: They can invest in the home country; those investments we'll call I, as before. Or they can invest in the rest of the world; those investments we'll call NCO, which stands for "net capital outflow." The total amount of money that a country has to invest, its savings (S), must add up to I + NCO. Using this equation and (6) above, we find that net capital outflows to all other countries equal net exports to all other countries:

$$(7) \ S = I + NCO$$

$$(8) \ S = I + NX$$

$$(9) \ I + NCO = I + NX$$

$$(10) \ NCO = NX$$

The result—that net capital outflows equal net exports (NCO = NX)—is important and answers the question posed in the beginning of this section: *How are countries able to sustain large deficits in trade?* A country that exports more goods than it imports, like China, will necessarily also send out more capital than it receives. That's because China's high net exports must be balanced by high net capital outflows. The capital outflows allow countries to sustain trade imbalances for long periods of time. This idea may seem tricky, so let's work through a simplified example.

Let's assume that China and the United States are both initially closed economies; their savings equal domestic investment. Then, one day, a firm in the United States decides to buy a specialized battery made in China. The Chinese firm sends the battery to the United States, and the U.S. firm gives the Chinese firm a $100 bill.

What will the Chinese firm do with the $100 bill? It can do two things:

- Option 1: It can keep the money in America (for instance, by depositing it in a bank account in the United States, or buying bonds or stocks or financial securities in the United States).
- Option 2: It can buy something in America—say, a collection of economics books—and ship them back to China.

If the Chinese firm decides that it wants to keep the $100 in America, then it has made an investment in the U.S. economy. In other words, the *net capital outflow* from China to the United States is $100. The value of exports—the battery—from China to the United States is $100. Net exports are equal to net capital outflow.

What if, instead of investing the $100, the Chinese firm decides to use to it buy the books and import them back to China? Net exports for China are zero: The Chinese firm exported a $100 battery and imported $100 worth of books. Net capital outflow for China is also zero because the money earned from the batteries was used to buy books, rather than being invested in the United States. Thus, none of its money remains in the United States. So, for China, NX = NCO.

Now let's look at the same transaction from the U.S. perspective: In option 1, in which the United States has $100 of its currency owned by China, the U.S. net capital outflow is −$100. Because the U.S. firm bought the battery from China, the United States has net exports of −$100. Net capital outflow equals net exports for the United States as well.

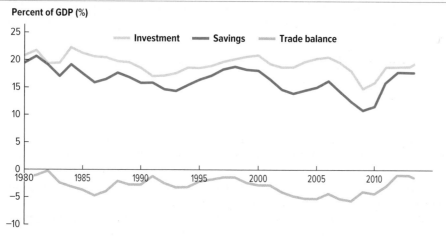

FIGURE 18-5

The equivalence of NCO and NX in the United States

The gap between savings and investment in the overall economy is shown by the trade balance. When investment is larger than savings, as it is in the United States, an economy will have a negative trade balance.

Sources: The World Bank, http://data.worldbank.org/indicator/NE.GDI.TOTL.ZS and http://data.worldbank.org/indicator/NY.GNS.ICTR.ZS.

What happens from the U.S. perspective in option 2? When the United States initially imported the battery, it had NX of −$100. But then it exported $100 worth of books, so NX became zero. No capital has been invested in or from China, so NCO is zero. For the United States, too, NX = NCO.

The balance-of-payments identity tells us that the net capital outflow of a country equals the value of its net exports. Figure 18-5 shows savings, investment, and net exports in the United States in recent years. Notice that the gap between savings and investment is almost exactly the trade balance. (There may be small differences, which stem from the complexities of measurement.) In general, savings equals investment plus net exports, as we saw in the equations above.

✓CONCEPT CHECK

☐ Which country is the United States's largest trading partner? **[LO 18.1]**

☐ What is portfolio investment? **[LO 18.2]**

☐ What is the relationship between net capital outflow and net exports in the balance-of-payments identity? **[LO 18.3]**

International Capital Flows

For the last three decades, seas of money have surged into the U.S. economy from abroad, in search of profitable investment opportunities. Why does capital flow into some economies and out of others? In this section, we'll develop a model to explain international capital flows.

Determinants of international capital flows

LO 18.4 Describe the determinants of international capital flows using the demand and supply for international loanable funds.

In Chapter 14, "The Basics of Finance," we developed a model of the market for loanable funds in a closed economy. In that model, the equilibrium interest rate was determined by the intersection of the domestic investment curve and the domestic savings curve—the demand and supply of domestic loanable funds.

How does this model change in an open economy? The basic idea is the same: There still is a demand for and supply of loanable funds. Exactly as before, the supply of loanable funds is the sum of national savings. Savings has a positive relationship with the interest rate. (That is, as the interest rate increases, savers will supply a greater quantity of loanable funds to the market.)

The demand for loanable funds (investment) comes from two sources:

- *Domestic investment* is the same as it was in the domestic market for loanable funds, when we considered the economy to be closed.
- *International investment* comes in two forms: capital inflow (when money from abroad is invested domestically) and capital outflow (when domestic money is invested internationally).

For the sake of this model, we will assume that all investment transactions occur through loanable funds. When we subtract capital inflows from capital outflows, we get *net capital outflows (NCO)*. This NCO plus domestic investment form the demand for loanable funds in the open economy. What does this demand curve look like?

We can start with the fact that domestic investment has a negative relationship with the interest rate. (That is, lower interest rates make it cheaper for firms to invest in equipment and factories.) Let's use that knowledge to think about the intuition behind how capital inflows and outflows will be affected by U.S. interest rates. Suppose the domestic interest rate declines:

- People in the United States will start to look overseas for opportunities to earn more interest on their money. The result will be higher capital outflows.
- Meanwhile, people overseas will be less keen to invest in the United States because of the lower returns, so there will be lower capital inflows.

Higher outflows and lower inflows both push *net* outflows in the same direction: *higher.*

Now suppose the interest rate goes up. In that case, the opposite happens:

- People in the United States will be more willing to keep their savings in the country; outflows will go down.
- At the same time, people overseas will send their financial investments to the United States in pursuit of better returns; inflows will go up.

Lower outflows and higher inflows both push net outflows in the same direction: *lower.*

When we put this result together with domestic investment, as shown in Figure 18-6, we get the combined I + NCO curve—which is the *demand for loanable funds in the open economy.* In the open economy, the equilibrium interest rate is found at the intersection of national savings and the combined I + NCO curve.

For a real-life example of the power of domestic investment and capital inflows, see the Real Life box "Iceland and the banking crisis." In 2007, banks in Iceland held $90 billion in their accounts, far more than the entire country's GDP. When these banks ran into trouble, the whole country was thrown into crisis.

Real Life

Iceland and the banking crisis

Iceland is a volcanic island in the North Atlantic Ocean, located between Greenland and the United Kingdom. The country is home to some 300,000 people, and until recently was best known as the home of the eccentric singer Björk. That changed in 2010 when a collapse of the banking sector in this quiet island nation nearly brought down the entire world economy.

Until the early 2000s, Icelandic banks were small and largely focused on catering to the basic financing needs of local citizens. Then Iceland deregulated its banking industry, and the country's banks expanded throughout Europe. This process was fueled by the Icelandic central bank's determination to control inflation by keeping interest rates high. We have seen that high interest rates lead to negative NCO (that is, a net *inflow* of capital).

Sure enough, money flowed into Iceland as savers from all over Europe rushed to deposit money in Icelandic banks. The banks grew bigger and bigger, creating leverage as they borrowed against the savings, and eventually amassing foreign debt of more than $90 billion, six times larger than Iceland's entire GDP. (All the money people deposited with them constituted foreign debt.)

As the financial crisis and Great Recession of 2008 washed up on Iceland's shores, all three of its major banks collapsed. Savers saw their savings evaporate. Could the government of Iceland have decided to bail out the banks to keep the wider economy from derailing? In theory, yes. But unfortunately Iceland's banks had grown so big that even the state couldn't afford to bail them out. Iceland had to ask the International Monetary Fund, the global agency responsible for helping to maintain international financial stability, to step in with emergency funds of $6 billion to keep the country's financial system functioning.

As the Icelandic economy shrank by more than 6 percent in 2009 alone, the British and Dutch governments undertook legal action to try to recover their citizens' billions in lost banking deposits. Not surprisingly, the people of Iceland reacted badly to the idea that their taxes should have to compensate British and Dutch savers. After all, ordinary Icelanders had little to do with the risky behavior of their nation's banks.

Icelanders vented their frustration at the politicians who had allowed this mess to happen by voting an absurdist comedian in as the new mayor of the capital city. His policy platform? "We should have this huge statue of Björk at the harbor like the Statue of Liberty." Sadly, the new mayor did not find the money to enact this plan.

Sources: http://www.nytimes.com/2010/06/26/world/europe/26iceland.html; debt statistics from the Central Bank of Iceland.

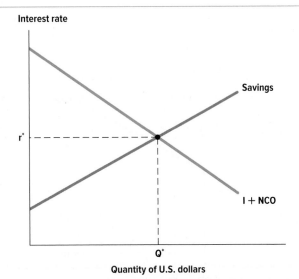

Interest rate

Savings

r^*

I + NCO

Q^*

Quantity of U.S. dollars

FIGURE 18-6

Expanded market for loanable funds

The market for loanable funds in the open economy is determined by both domestic and international investment as well as the amount of domestic savings. Domestic and international investment is reflected in the I + NCO curve. The interest rate is determined by the intersection of the savings curve and the combined investment + net capital outflow curve.

Effects of foreign investment

LO 18.5 Show how the international market for loanable funds can be used to explain events in the international financial system.

Using our model of international capital flows, we can begin to examine the impact of foreign investment—and understand why it's often economically beneficial. In short, foreign investment can

- Increase the GDP of the host country by giving it access to additional resources.
- Increase the GDP of the investing country by providing it with ways to earn higher returns on its capital.
- Make the world a more efficient place by moving capital from places with low returns to places with high returns.

To see how this works, imagine that financial troubles abroad trigger a "flight to quality," where investors suddenly find lower-risk U.S. government bonds more attractive as a safe haven for savings. Figure 18-7 shows what happens in this case. The shift in preferences toward investing in the United States means that the demand curve for loanable funds in the open economy will shift to the left, for two reasons. First, foreign investors are now more eager to purchase U.S. assets than they were before, so net capital outflows contract ($NCO_1 > NCO_2$). In addition, the existence of better investment opportunities in the United States means that domestic investors are also going to keep more of their money at home, which again contributes to the leftward shift of the loanable funds curve.

How does this contraction in net capital outflows affect interest rates, saving, and investment in the United States? The increase in demand for U.S. assets means that people are now willing to pay more for the same stream of payments (and investors are now paying more for the same asset), so the rate of return on these assets (that is, the interest rate) falls. The lower rate of return on financial assets makes saving less attractive for people in the United States, which can be seen

FIGURE 18-7

Effect of a flight to quality in the U.S. economy

If investors at home and abroad suddenly find lower-risk U.S. government bonds more attractive, the combined investment plus net capital outflow (I + NCO) curve shifts to the left. The result is a lower interst rate, more dollers invested in physical capital, and lower national saving.

FIGURE 18-8

Effect of an increase in the government deficit

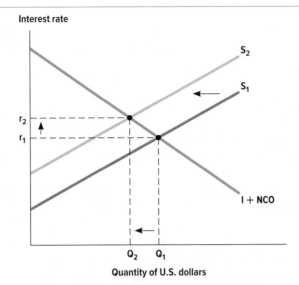

When the government spends more than it collects in revenue, it has to borrow money. This pushes the savings curve left, which results in an increase in the interest rate and lower quantity of investment.

as the leftward movement along the blue savings curve in Figure 18-7. However, the lower interest rate also makes it cheaper for firms to finance capital projects; as a result, investment demand increases. The increase in investment due to the lower interest rates helps explain why the quantity of loanable funds demanded does not fall by the full leftward shift of the I + NCO curve.

Investment is a key component of GDP, so the U.S. economy benefits when foreign investment increases. Foreign investors also benefit from better investment opportunities in the United States, adding to the GDP of their countries.

We can also examine the relationship between foreign investment and public savings. Doing so will bring us closer to understanding the trade imbalance between the United States and China. Recall that the savings curve for the economy reflects the sum of private and public savings. In order to see the connection, let's look at the case of a government budget deficit, which causes a decrease in public savings. When the government runs a deficit, the savings curve shifts to the left, as in Figure 18-8. When this happens, the new equilibrium interest rate is higher than before. With a higher interest rate, there is more incentive to invest in the United States. Less capital flows out and more capital flows in. Net capital outflow decreases and the quantity of loanable funds saved and invested in equilibrium drops.

Although net capital outflow is lower, the higher interest rate in the economy due to a decrease in savings instead means that there is a lower level of domestic investment. Foreign and domestic savings are used to finance the government budget, instead of being used to finance domestic investment. We say that the government deficit "crowds out" domestic investment; the higher interest rate reduces firms' investment in the economy.

As mentioned before, China funds much of the U.S. government deficit by buying Treasury securities. But where does all of that money come from? Ben Bernanke, a Princeton economist and former chair of the Federal Reserve, argues that China is simply saving too much.

Can a country save too much?

Saying that it is possible to save too much is like claiming that it's possible to eat too much broccoli. It's true only at the most ridiculous extremes. But perhaps China's saving rate is at that extreme. After all, it currently saves nearly 50 percent of its GDP! In comparison, the United

States saves only 18 percent of its total income.[4] High domestic savings can keep demand for local products low as people consume less. There are empty malls and vacant housing projects in China, simply waiting for customers to open their wallets. Saving too much can also lead to trade imbalances.

We mentioned this idea in Chapter 14, "The Basics of Finance," but now we have the tools to evaluate the effects of a "global savings glut." A growing propensity to save shifts out the savings curve, decreasing the equilibrium interest rate. Low interest rates in China relative to other markets encourage capital to flow abroad, raising net capital outflow—which explains why China has so much invested in the United States. The massive net capital outflow from China requires that large quantities of Chinese currency are exchanged into U.S. currency. The flip-side is the massive trade imbalance between China and the United States, which requires that large quantities of U.S. currency are exchanged into Chinese currency in order to buy the goods.

If this explanation of the trade imbalance is right, how could it be corrected? Consider a couple of possible solutions:

- One solution could be for China to reduce its savings levels and increase consumption. Imports should rise and exports should fall.

- Another solution could be for the United States to increase its own savings levels and spend a little less. The U.S. economy saves 18 percent overall, but the rate of household savings is low (usually less than 5 percent). The rate of government saving is actually negative (the government is running a budget deficit). If the United States were to increase its total savings, either because households or the government saves more, then capital outflow would increase from the United States, reducing the imbalance.

There's another story, however. Others, particularly politicians, suggest that the trade deficit between the United States and China stems from China's fixed exchange rate, an idea we explore next.

✓ CONCEPT CHECK

- ☐ Which two curves make up the international market for loanable funds? **[LO 18.4]**
- ☐ What is the difference between the closed- and open-economy versions of the market for loanable funds? **[LO 18.5]**
- ☐ Which way does the savings curve shift when the government reduces its deficit? **[LO 18.5]**

Exchange Rates

If you arrive in a foreign country with a pocketful of U.S. dollars, chances are you won't be able to use them locally. Most local shops and restaurants will require local currency, which you can get by exchanging your dollars at a bank or a specialized foreign currency dealer. The price at which the exchange happens is the *exchange rate*. Sometimes the exchange rate gives you lots of local currency for your dollars. Other times, the exchange rate requires you to give more of your dollars for the same amount of local currency. How does the market for currency work?

The foreign-exchange market

LO 18.6 Describe exchange rate appreciation and depreciation and understand their effects on trade.

The market for buying and selling foreign currencies is often referred to as the "forex" market, short for *foreign exchange*. Every weekday people engage in trillions of dollars of transactions around the clock. They trade dollars for euros or euros for Mexican pesos, for example.

Like any other market, in the forex market there are supply, demand, price, and quantity traded. And like any other market, the market for different currencies has a price, which is called the exchange rate. The **exchange rate** is the value of one currency expressed in terms of another currency. For example, in June 2016, one U.S. dollar—abbreviated USD—could be exchanged for 0.80 euro, 6.59 Chinese yuan, or 18.82 Mexican pesos.

13 **exchange rate**
the value of one currency expressed in terms of another currency

Exchange rates can be expressed in two ways: either in terms of the domestic currency or in terms of the foreign currency. When we examine the exchange rates between two nations' currencies, the exchange rates will be reciprocals of each other.

> **! HINT**
>
> Recall that the *reciprocal* of a fraction or ratio is just that fraction or ratio "turned upside down" or "flipped over": The numerator (portion above the fraction line) becomes the denominator (portion below the fraction line), and the denominator becomes the numerator. The reciprocal of $\frac{3}{4}$ is $\frac{4}{3}$, and the reciprocal of 2 (equivalent to $\frac{2}{1}$) is therefore $\frac{1}{2}$.

If 1 unit of domestic currency is worth 6 units of a foreign currency, then we can express this equivalently as the foreign currency being worth $\frac{1}{6}$ of a unit of the domestic currency.

In the real world, foreign exchange rates are often expressed in decimal form rather than fraction form, but the same idea applies:

- If \$1 is worth 0.80 euro, then 1 euro is worth \$1.25 (\$1 ÷ 0.80 = 1.25 \$/euro).
- If \$1 is worth 90 yen, then 1 yen is worth \$0.01 (\$1 ÷ 90 = 0.01 \$/yen).

From this point forward, we will express exchange rates *from the point of view of the United States, using the dollar as the domestic currency.* That means that exchange rates will be expressed in terms of *units of foreign currency required to "buy" one dollar.*

Of course, we could also look at things from the perspective of another nation—for example, from Japan's point of view. In that case, the yen would be considered the home currency, and exchange rates would be expressed in terms of the units of foreign currency—dollars, yuan, euro, and so forth—required to "buy" one yen. All concepts discussed in the chapter apply no matter which nation's point of view we assume.

You might wonder if discrepancies between the forex markets, located in so many places, might arise. Is it possible for a trader to make money by taking advantage of discrepancies in currency exchange rates? For example, could a trader convert dollars to pesos in a Mexican forex market, pesos to yuan in a Chinese forex market, yuan to euros in a European forex market, and euros back to dollars in an American forex market and end up with more dollars than she started with? This possibility is known as *arbitrage,* gaining financially by taking advantage of discrepancies in currency exchange rates. Yes, it is possible that money *can* be made on such trades. Because of that possibility, forex traders have sophisticated software constantly scouring information from the world's different forex markets to see if any discrepancies

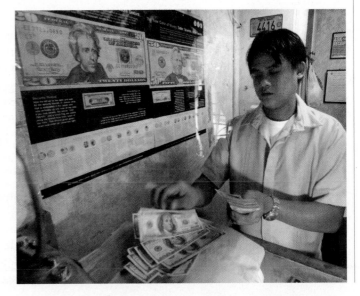

U.S. dollars can be used all over the world but need to be changed into local currency by currency exchangers. Sometimes this means a bank, and sometimes it is just a small shop, like this one in Manila.
© *Joel Nito/AFP/Getty Images*

exist. If they find them, they instantly trade the currencies until the discrepancy no longer exists. As a result, any opportunities for arbitrage are fleeting.

Another way in which speculators try to make money from forex is by betting on the direction that an exchange rate will move over time. The value of one currency relative to another can either increase or decrease. When the value of a currency *increases* relative to the value of another currency, we say that a currency experiences **exchange-rate appreciation**. When the currency appreciates, it can "buy" more of another currency. For example, if the U.S. dollar appreciates against the euro—say from 0.7 to 0.8 euro—the result is that one dollar can buy 0.1 more euro than before.

Who benefits when the dollar appreciates against the euro? The U.S. dollar can buy more goods that are denominated in euros, so people who have U.S. dollars and want to buy goods from Europe will benefit. For instance, American tourists in Paris will find that things are cheaper as the dollar appreciates against the euro:

exchange-rate appreciation
an increase in the value of a currency relative to the value of another currency

- A French hotel room with a nightly rate of 70 euros would cost $100 at an exchange rate of 0.7 euro per dollar: $\left[70 \text{ euros} \times \left(\frac{\$1}{0.7\,\text{euro}}\right) = \$100\right]$.
- After the dollar appreciates against the euro, and the new exchange rate is 0.8 euro per dollar, the hotel room would cost only $87.50: $\left[70 \text{ euros} \times \left(\frac{\$1}{0.8\,\text{euro}}\right) = \$87.50\right]$.

On the other hand, a U.S. company that sells DVDs in France will find that it has fewer customers:

- A $15 DVD would sell for 10.50 euros in Paris at an exchange rate of 0.7 euro per dollar: $\left[\$15 \times \left(\frac{0.7\,\text{euro}}{\$1}\right) = 10.50 \text{ euros}\right]$.
- After the dollar appreciates against the euro, and the new exchange rate is 0.8 euro per dollar, the $15 DVD would sell for 12 euros: $\left[\$15 \times \left(\frac{0.8\,\text{euro}}{\$1}\right) = 12 \text{ euros}\right]$.

exchange-rate depreciation
a decrease in the value of a currency relative to other currencies

In contrast, when the value of a currency *decreases* relative to other currencies, we say that a currency experiences **exchange-rate depreciation**. When the currency depreciates, it can "buy" less of another currency. In our example, when the dollar appreciates against the euro, logic tells us that the euro has *depreciated* against the dollar. Or imagine the U.S. dollar goes from being worth 6.5 yuan to 6 yuan. We say the U.S. dollar has depreciated—it now buys fewer yuan than it did before. Who's going to be happy if the dollar depreciates against the yuan? U.S. consumers will have to pay more for Chinese goods, which they won't like. On the other hand, U.S. exporters will have an easier time selling to Chinese consumers.

The exchange rate and net exports

Exchange rates affect nearly every dimension of international economics. The flow of goods is one example:

- When the U.S. dollar appreciates against a foreign currency, U.S. goods become more expensive to people abroad, and foreign goods become cheaper for Americans. As a result, we would expect *net exports to decrease.*
- When the U.S. dollar depreciates against a foreign currency, foreign goods become more expensive for Americans, and American goods become cheaper for foreign consumers. We would expect *net exports to increase.*

Does this expectation hold empirically? Figure 18-9 shows U.S. net exports plotted against an exchange-rate index. That index represents the average value of the U.S. dollar against its main trading partners. Just as we would expect:

- When the U.S. dollar goes up in value against other currencies, net exports tend to go down soon afterward. When net exports fall, the trade deficit rises. That's why we see that when the exchange rate rises (as represented by the "Real effective exchange rate index" line in Figure 18-9), the trade deficit will usually rise too.
- Similarly, when the U.S. dollar drops in value, exports tend to go up, which reduces the trade deficit. When the exchange rate falls, so will the trade deficit.

FIGURE 18-9

Trade deficit and the exchange rate in the United States   In the United States, there is a distinct relationship between the exchange rate (shown here relative to its 2010 level) and the trade deficit. When the exchange rate falls, the trade deficit decreases, although this effect operates on a lag, meaning that it takes time for trade to respond to changes in the exchange rate.

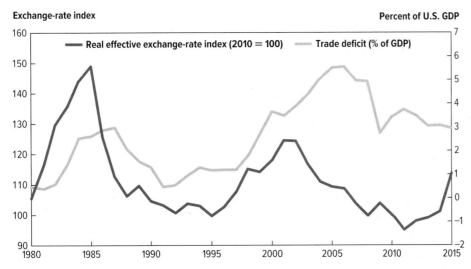

Sources: The World Bank, http://data.worldbank.org/indicator/NE.RSB.GNFS.ZS?end=2015&locations=US&start=1990 and http://data.worldbank.org/indicator/PX.REX.REER.

A model of the exchange-rate market

> **LO 18.7** Describe the determinants of demand and supply in the forex market.

The foreign-exchange market is a market like any other: There is demand for a currency and a supply of that currency. An equilibrium price and quantity are determined by the intersection of supply and demand. What determines demand and supply in the forex market?

Demand for foreign currency

Let's start with *demand.* Why would foreigners demand foreign currency?

The first determinant of demand for currency comes from *consumer preferences*—from foreign consumers, businesses, and governments that want to use the currency to buy goods or services in the domestic currency. For example, a British family might demand dollars to be able to vacation in Florida. A Japanese shop might demand dollars to import U.S.-made DVDs for sale to Japanese consumers. The Chinese government might demand dollars to be able to purchase financial assets such as U.S. Treasury debt.

The demand for dollars also depends on *interest rates,* both in the United States and abroad:

- High interest rates in the United States relative to overseas will attract foreign capital. These assets need to be paid for in U.S. dollars, so demand for U.S. dollars will increase.

- On the other hand, if foreign interest rates are high relative to those in the United States, demand for dollars will decrease as investors sell their dollars to buy foreign currency for investment.

The last key variable in determining the demand for a country's currency is the *perceived risk* of investing in that country against the perceived risk of investing in other countries. If investors feel confident about putting money into emerging economies such as Russia, Brazil, or

South Africa, they will invest more there, all else equal. If investors decide it is risky to invest in such countries compared to the United States, then more people will want to invest more in the United States, increasing the demand for U.S. dollars.

To make an investment, one has to have the right currency. Anything that motivates investors to invest in a particular country will therefore increase demand for the currency of that country.

Supply of foreign currency

What about factors affecting the *supply* of foreign exchange? The same three factors affect the supply: If the U.S. *interest rate* is low relative to foreign interest rates, financial investors holding U.S. assets will want to sell them and purchase foreign assets. Similarly, if investors' *confidence* in foreign economies increases, the supply of U.S. dollars will increase as investors sell off U.S. assets. Finally, *consumer preferences* also play a role. If U.S. consumers prefer foreign goods, they will sell their dollars to obtain foreign currency, increasing the supply of U.S. dollars in the forex market.

The equilibrium exchange rate

Panel A of Figure 18-10 shows how the supply of and demand for dollars determines the equilibrium exchange rate against any other given currency. The "price" of the currency is the exchange rate. As the exchange rate increases, the quantity supplied of dollars increases and the quantity demanded of dollars decreases

Panel B of Figure 18-10 shows how the equilibrium exchange rate in turn determines the level of net exports:

FIGURE 18-10

The foreign-exchange market in equilibrium

(A) Demand and supply

Like any other market, there is supply and demand for foreign currency. The quantity supplied of dollars increases as the exchange rate increases, and the quantity demanded decreases as the price of currency increases. The price of the currency is known as the exchange rate.

(B) Exchange rate and net exports

As the exchange rate from local to foreign currency decreases, the quantity of net exports decreases. With the lower price of goods, local goods will become attractive to foreigners, and foreign goods will be more expensive locally.

- When the price of dollars is high, foreigners will buy fewer goods from the United States and Americans will buy more goods from overseas. As a result, net exports are low and may even be negative.
- When the price of dollars is low, the reverse happens: It's cheap for foreigners to buy U.S. goods and expensive for Americans to buy foreign goods, so net exports will be high.

An example: Prius imports

Let's look at an example of how this model works in practice. When the Toyota Prius was released to the U.S. market in 2003, many people wanted to get their hands on the first mass-produced hybrid gas/electric vehicle. Because the Prius was manufactured by Toyota in Japan, U.S. dealers had to exchange dollars for Japanese yen to be able to buy and import Priuses. This led the supply curve of U.S. dollars to shift to the right. The exchange rate from the U.S. dollar to the Japanese yen fell as a result. The new equilibrium is shown in panel A of Figure 18-11.

What effect does the fall in the exchange rate have on net exports for the United States? As we have seen, the net export curve is a demand curve; it shows the demand for net exports at different prices (in this case, those prices are exchange rates). Just like a standard demand curve, shifts in preferences shift the net export curve. Actually, two shifts occur:

- When U.S. consumers decide they want to buy Priuses rather than cars made in America, this shift in preferences moves the net export curve to the left (because more imports mean fewer exports).

FIGURE 18-11

Increase in demand for Prius cars

(A) Foreign-exchange market

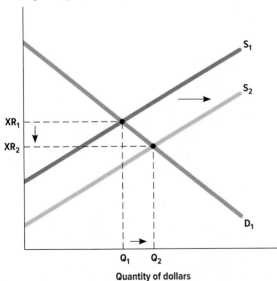

(B) Exchange rate and net exports

When the demand for Priuses shifts to the right, the supply of dollars at equilibrium increases as more people are trying to sell dollars in order to purchase yen. This shift increases the quantity of dollars traded, but lowers the exchange rate.

Since Americans are now importing far more cars, the net exports curve shifts to the left. At the same time the exchange rate falls. Depending on the size of these two changes, the quantity of net exports could be higher or lower than it was before; in this instance the two cancel each other out.

- However, something else is also going on at the same time: Because the value of U.S. dollars depreciated, U.S. exports became cheaper, which increased the quantity of net exports.

Panel B of Figure 18-11 shows the combined effects of these two shifts: The effects of a greater preference for Japanese cars are counterbalanced by the effects of the depreciation in the exchange rate. Depending on which effect is bigger, the quantity of net exports could end up being higher *or* lower than before the Prius was introduced. In this case, the graph depicts the effects as canceling each other out exactly.

Another example: A rising interest rate

Now imagine another scenario: The Federal Reserve decides to tighten monetary policy by increasing the interest rate. This increase is going to affect both the demand for and the supply of U.S. dollars:

- Because the return to investment is higher in the United States as a result of the higher interest rate, foreign investors want to buy U.S. foreign assets; the demand for U.S. dollars increases.
- At the same time, U.S. investors would rather invest in their own economy instead of buying financial assets abroad, reducing the supply of U.S. dollars.

As shown in panel A of Figure 18-12, these shifts will cause the exchange rate to appreciate. Nothing in this story will shift the net exports curve, however. Therefore, panel B shows that the higher exchange rate translates directly into a reduction in net exports.

FIGURE 18-12

Tighter monetary policy in the United States

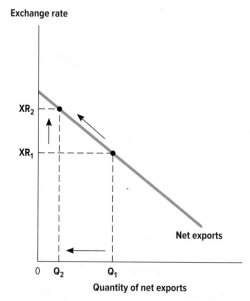

When the Federal Reserve tightens the money supply, the price of the dollar initially rises and supply decreases. Demand shifts out as well, and the price of the dollar rises and the quantity of dollars traded returns to the initial amount.

With an increase in the exchange rate of the dollar, the quantity of net exports falls, as U.S. goods are now more expensive for foreigners.

We can also look at the change in monetary policy in another way. We know that net exports equal net capital outflows (NX = NCO), so the higher exchange rate has also caused a reduction in NCO. In other words, it has caused more capital *inflows*. We know that there will be more capital flowing into the United States when interest rates go up, as foreign savers take advantage of the opportunity to get a better return.

Our model of the foreign-exchange market has shown us that monetary policy works on aggregate demand in two ways: reducing investment and reducing net exports. Remember, by raising the interest rate, the Fed is trying to cool off the economy. A higher interest rate makes borrowing more expensive, reducing investment. Increasing the interest rate also causes the exchange rate to appreciate, which reduces net exports. Because net exports are also part of aggregate demand, reducing net exports further reduces aggregate demand.

However, this result holds only in an open economy where the exchange rate is determined by the market. As we shall now see, some governments do not allow the market to determine the exchange rate for their currency.

Exchange-rate regimes

LO 18.8 Explain fixed and floating exchange rates.

The euro is used by 19 European countries, each of which previously had its own currency. Since many European countries are small, different currencies made life difficult. A 150-mile trip from Dusseldorf, Germany, to Brussels, Belgium, with a stop in Maastricht in The Netherlands, would require the use of three separate currencies—the German mark, Dutch guilder, and Belgian franc. Now, with the euro, tourists no longer have the hassle of exchanging money (and paying a commission to do so) every time they cross a border. Businesses that do a lot of trade with neighboring countries no longer have to worry about exchange-rate fluctuations changing the prices they have to pay for their inputs or will receive for their products.

There are also disadvantages, however. In being so tightly joined to other economies, the members of the euro zone give up some of their ability to conduct independent macroeconomic policy. Let's say that Germany has low unemployment: Wages are rising, and so are concerns about inflation. We know that to tackle inflation, a central bank would usually tighten monetary policy—that is, increase interest rates. Let's say at the same time Italy is experiencing *high* unemployment. There, a central bank would usually loosen monetary policy—that is, lower interest rates.

When Germany used the mark and Italy used the lira, these differing monetary policies would cause their currencies' exchange rates to change. In our example, the lira would depreciate and the mark would appreciate. The result? Italian products would become cheaper for other countries to buy, helping to boost aggregate demand in Italy and tackle unemployment. Meanwhile, just as we saw in the U.S. example presented in Figure 18-12, the appreciating German mark would help to reduce net exports in Germany, and also aggregate demand, easing the upward pressure on prices. However, when countries gave up their own currencies and joined the euro, they could no longer pursue their own monetary policies to tackle their specific macroeconomic situations.

You may be wondering why this isn't a problem among U.S. states. What if Wisconsin is experiencing high demand for labor and rising prices and wages, whereas Nebraska is experiencing high unemployment? The problem solves itself without any need for separate currencies and exchange rate changes: We would expect unemployed Nebraskans to move to Wisconsin in search of higher wages, and Wisconsin-based businesses to relocate to Nebraska in search of cheaper labor.

The difference with the euro zone is that, unlike people in Nebraska and Wisconsin, Germans and Italians speak different languages and have distinct cultures. In theory, Italian laborers can seek work in Germany and German businesses can relocate to Italy. But in practice it's not so easy—certainly not as easy as moving from one state to another in the United States.

Not all countries that share a currency are neighbors. In fact, Ecuador, a small country in South America, now uses U.S. dollars exclusively. The barriers seem even greater than between Italy and Germany: Ecuador and the United States are much farther apart geographically, and unemployed Ecuadorans don't have the legal right to seek work in the United States, as Italians do in Germany. Still, that hasn't stopped Ecuador from adopting the U.S. dollar as its currency, as the Real Life box "Dollarization: When not in the U.S. . . ." discusses.

Real Life

Dollarization: When not in the U.S. . . .

In 1998 and 1999, Ecuador experienced a wrenching financial crisis that caused the value of the Ecuadoran currency, the sucre, to fall by 50 percent in just two months. Within two years, 70 percent of Ecuador's financial institutions went out of business, sending shockwaves throughout the rest of the economy. When the crisis was over, the country's GDP, at $10 billion, was half of what it had been two years earlier.

Rather than try to reboot the sucre, the government decided to "dollarize"—to replace all sucres with U.S. dollars. This move immediately stabilized the Ecuadoran economy. In just three years, the annual inflation rate in Ecuador dropped from 20 percent to 2.7 percent.

However, dollarization has a drawback: It tied Ecuador's economy to that of the United States, for better or worse. In exchange for a stable currency and lower inflation, the government had to give up control of monetary policy. Ecuador's government cannot print U.S. dollars if the country's economy is in recession. Nor can it reduce the amount of U.S. dollars in circulation if it wants to cool an overheating economy. Only the U.S. Federal Reserve can do those things, and the Fed is not likely to take much account of Ecuador's macroeconomic needs when making decisions. If the U.S. economy is doing well while Ecuador is struggling, a contraction in the money supply would further damage the Ecuadoran economy.

Ecuador is one of 10 countries that have decided to dollarize. They have given up their own national currency and thrown in their lot with the United States in terms of monetary policy and exchange rates. Most of these countries are scattered throughout the Pacific (such as Palau and Micronesia) or Latin America (Panama and El Salvador, along with Ecuador). Although it is a rather dramatic step, for countries where inflation or financial instability is a persistent problem, the price of giving up control over monetary policy is one that's considered to be well worth paying.

Source: http://www.imf.org/external/pubs/ft/issues/issues24.

Fixed and floating rates

floating exchange rate
an exchange rate whose value is determined by the market

The dollar, euro, Mexican peso, and Japanese yen are all examples of currencies with a **floating exchange rate**. Their value is determined by the market, and the currency can be freely traded. The exchange rate of floating-rate currencies is set by the intersection of the supply and demand curves for foreign exchange, shown in panel A of Figure 18-13.

fixed exchange rate
an exchange rate that is set by the government, instead of determined by the market

Some currencies, however, have a **fixed exchange rate**—one that is set by the government, usually with reference to the U.S. dollar or some composite index of major global currencies. A fixed exchange rate can be fixed at a price that is above the market equilibrium rate or below the market equilibrium rate, as shown in panel B of Figure 18-13.

Why might a government decide to fix its currency's exchange rate? The thinking is similar to Ecuador's decision to dollarize. The theory is that a fixed rate allows for more predictability and stability. More stability helps attract foreign investment and gives businesses that depend on overseas trade more confidence to invest.

FIGURE 18-13

Floating versus fixed exchange rates

(A) Floating exchange rate

When the exchange rate is allowed to float, the market for foreign exchange will operate at the equilibrium price and quantity.

(B) Fixed exchange rate

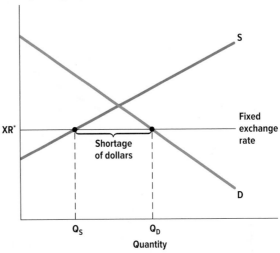

On the other hand, when there is a fixed exchange rate that is set too low, there is excess demand for the currency, which the government must cover by buying foreign currencies and selling the local currency.

How is a fixed exchange rate kept above or below market rates? To maintain a fixed exchange rate, the government needs to be prepared to intervene in the foreign-exchange market, either buying or selling foreign currency. For example, let's say that all of a sudden consumers develop a greater appetite for imported goods. If the exchange rate were allowed to float, the increased supply of local currency would push the exchange rate downward. When the exchange rate is fixed, though, the exchange rate is not allowed to depreciate. The government then has to step into the foreign-exchange market and buy up local currency to balance out the increased supply. Governments generally try to increase demand for their currency by using their own reserves of foreign currencies to buy the domestic currency.

> **HINT**
> Economists use a slightly different vocabulary to describe changes in the exchange rate when the exchange rate is fixed. Instead of saying that a currency depreciates, we say that it is *devalued* if the government lowers the level at which the fixed exchange rate is set. Likewise, instead of saying that a currency appreciates, we say that the fixed exchange rate is *revalued* if the fixed exchange rate is set higher.

Maintaining a fixed exchange rate can be tough. This is especially true when investors begin to doubt the overall health of an economy. Then investors will start to sell their investments, increasing the supply of local currency. To counter that, the government will be forced to spend large amounts of foreign reserves to prop up demand for its currency.

FIGURE 18-14

Speculative attack on the Thai baht

When a country suffers from a speculative attack, the supply of currency available shifts right. This lowers the equilibrium exchange rate even further, forcing the government to spend even more to defend the fixed exchange rate.

Some investors, called *speculators,* look for these kinds of situations. The moment that they begin to doubt the ability or the resolve of a country to maintain its fixed exchange rate, they will sell that currency, converting it into a different currency, like dollars. If they dump a lot of the currency quickly, they may cause the government to run out of its stock of dollars and other foreign reserves. If that happens, the government has to give up its efforts to maintain the fixed exchange rate. The value of the currency usually drops fast. At that point, the speculators come back in and buy the cheapened currency. They pocket a profit from having sold the currency at a high price and then buying it back at a low price. When this activity is happening, we say that a currency is experiencing a *speculative attack.*

In 1997, for example, the Thai baht came under intense speculative attack from investors. The Thai government had a fixed-exchange-rate policy; when the attack began, it needed to use foreign reserves to buy baht. The government spent more than $33 billion (about 90 percent of the country's foreign reserves) trying to protect the currency. It also increased domestic interest rates to encourage investors to keep money in the country. However, the attack continued, and the government eventually could not continue to defend the baht. The only choice was to untether the currency from the fixed exchange-rate system and let the baht float. Or, rather, sink: When the rate was allowed to float, the baht lost half its value.[5] We show in Figure 18-14 how a speculative attack on the currency puts pressure on the exchange rate.

Macroeconomic policy and exchange rates

LO 18.9 Describe why monetary policy is ineffective when maintaining a fixed exchange rate.

Now that we have outlined the difference between floating and fixed exchange rates, we'll look at monetary policy under the two exchange-rate regimes. Monetary policy is more effective *under a flexible exchange rate* than a fixed exchange rate because the flexible rate can affect two key variables: investment and net exports.

Imagine there's a recession and the Federal Reserve wants to increase the money supply to stimulate aggregate demand. The lower interest rates that follow this action will make investing in the United States less attractive. Since the return on investment is lower, demand for U.S. dollars will fall. At the same time, the supply of U.S. dollars will increase as investors sell their U.S. financial assets and look to buy assets abroad instead. Under a floating exchange-rate system, the exchange rate depreciates and net exports increase.

Figure 18-15 depicts what would happen if the exchange rate were fixed. Increasing the money supply would naturally cause the value of the dollar to fall. Since the government must maintain the exchange rate, however, it must buy its own currency in the foreign-exchange market. This purchase of dollars must be exactly the same as the increase of the money supply in order to maintain a fixed exchange rate. The end result is no change in the overall money supply, leading to a key point about fixed exchange rates: It is impossible to conduct monetary policy *and* maintain a fixed exchange rate.

Is the Chinese currency undervalued?

Our discussion of monetary policy and exchange rates leads us to the second explanation for the large trade deficit between China and the United States, which we mentioned at the beginning of this chapter. During China's great economic expansion, China maintained a fixed exchange rate, keeping its currency pegged at 6.5 yuan per dollar. This rate was *below* what the market would likely set. Why did China want to do that? Its goods would be cheap when measured in other currencies, so there would be lots of demand for Chinese exports.

The Chinese government keeps the yuan's value low by selling piles of yuan in the foreign-exchange market, and it uses a portion of those dollars to buy U.S. Treasury debt. The United States argues that China's currency is intentionally undervalued. The effect is to make China's exports more attractive to U.S. consumers and make it harder for U.S. companies to export to China. Chinese government officials, in turn, blame the trade deficit on U.S. government budget deficits and lack of savings.

FIGURE 18-15

Loosening monetary policy with fixed exchange rates

With a fixed exchange rate, monetary policy cannot be successful. When a country expands the money supply, the supply of currency increases and the exchange rate falls. Since this is unacceptable in a fixed exchange-rate regime, the government is forced to buy back the local currency on foreign markets, restoring the exchange rate.

Would a floating exchange-rate regime eliminate the trade deficit between China and the United States? If the Chinese yuan appreciated, Chinese exports would become more expensive and imports would become cheaper, and so the Chinese trade balance would fall. The effect on the United States's overall trade balance is not so straightforward, however. The United States would import less from China, but it is possible that consumers in the United States would instead choose to import from other countries.

Suppose the United States is right and China is undervaluing its currency to promote its exports. If having a low exchange rate is good for exports, we should ask, *"Why isn't everyone already doing it?"* Well, sometimes everyone does. This situation is known as *competitive devaluation,* or a currency war. It occurs when multiple countries are trying to boost their economies by lowering their interest rates. Of course, because the value of a currency is measured relative to other currencies, it's logically impossible for *all* the world's currencies to devalue simultaneously.

There are reasons why a government might not want to have an undervalued currency, though. For one thing, it means that savers tend to send their money to be invested overseas rather than domestically, just as much of China's savings end up in the United States. This may not be the best way to develop the domestic economy. A second cost is that an undervalued currency makes imported foreign goods more expensive. For example, an undervalued Chinese currency makes goods imported from the United States relatively more expensive for Chinese consumers.

The real exchange rate

> **LO 18.10** Describe the difference between the real and nominal exchange rates.

As we saw in Chapter 8, "The Cost of Living," it's not only currency exchange rates that determine the relative price of goods in different countries. Even after converting exchange rates, the exact same Big Mac might be more expensive in Switzerland than in the United States, and more expensive in the United States than in China.

nominal exchange rate the stated rate at which one country's currency can be traded for another country's currency

Up until now, we have been talking about the **nominal exchange rate**—the stated rate at which one country's currency can be traded for another country's currency. To really understand international trade, we also need to take into account the prices in two different countries by looking at the *real* exchange rate. The **real exchange rate** expresses the value of goods in one country in terms of the same goods in another country.

real exchange rate the value of goods in one country expressed in terms of the same goods in another country

To take a simplified example, let's consider only one good—an apple. Say that you can buy an apple in the United States for $1, and in China an apple costs 3 yuan. If the nominal exchange rate is 6 yuan per dollar, then the *real* exchange rate is 2. We'll provide a standard formula for calculating the real exchange rate in a few paragraphs, but for now, let's concentrate on the intuition behind this answer. Since $1 can be exchanged for 6 yuan, and 6 yuan can buy two apples (6 yuan/3 yuan per apple = 2 apples), the dollar that can buy only one apple in the United States can buy two apples in China. Note that our dollar "goes further" (buys more) in real terms in China than in the United States—you can buy twice as many apples with that dollar in China than in the United States.

Of course, people want to buy and sell more than apples. To calculate the real exchange rate properly, we need to look at *all the prices* in the United States and compare this total to *all the prices* in China. To do so, we need to look at the *price index* in both countries—the index that measures a typical basket of goods bought by a household. The real exchange rate uses the price level in each country to convert the exchange rate into a value that is in "real" terms. Similar to what we did with the apple example, to calculate the real exchange rate, we divide the price level at home by the price level in the foreign country, and then multiply by the nominal exchange rate. Mathematically:

EQUATION 18-1 $\text{Real exchange rate} = \left(\dfrac{\text{Domestic price level}}{\text{Foreign price level}} \right) \times \text{Nominal exchange rate}$

Note that the nominal exchange rate in this formula is expressed in terms of the foreign currency per dollar, as we've done throughout the chapter. So, for example, let's say that the price of a typical basket of goods in the United States (the domestic price level) is $100; in China it (the foreign price level) is 300 yuan. Further, let's assume that the nominal exchange rate expressed in terms of yuan per dollar is 6; in other words, 1 dollar can be traded for 6 yuan. With this information, we can calculate the real exchange rate to be 2:

EQUATION 18-1A

$$\text{Real exchange rate} = \left(\frac{\text{Domestic price level}}{\text{Foreign price level}}\right) \times \text{Nominal exchange rate}$$

$$= \left(\frac{\$100}{300 \text{ yuan}}\right) \times 6 \text{ yuan/1 dollar} = 2$$

The *real* exchange rate is another way of saying "the exchange rate adjusted for *purchasing power parity*," an idea we discussed in Chapter 8, "The Cost of Living." If there were parity in purchasing power—that is, if an apple cost the same in China as in the United States, after adjusting for nominal exchange rates—then the real exchange rate would be 1.

The same factors that complicate calculations of PPP also complicate calculations of the real exchange rate. Consumers in China purchase different kinds of goods than do U.S. consumers—more rice, for example, and fewer burgers—so it's not easy to compare price levels using typical baskets of goods. Still, the real exchange rate is a useful way of comparing how far your money will go in another country.

✓CONCEPT CHECK

- ☐ Does exchange-rate appreciation mean that the home currency gets stronger or weaker relative to other foreign currencies? **[LO 18.6]**
- ☐ When demand for a foreign good increases, what happens in the market for foreign exchange? **[LO 18.7]**
- ☐ How does the relative level of the U.S. interest rate affect the supply of foreign currency? **[LO 18.7]**
- ☐ What measurement gives the prices of the same goods in two different countries? **[LO 18.8]**
- ☐ Which variable can monetary policy affect under a flexible exchange rate that cannot be affected under a fixed exchange rate? **[LO 18.9]**
- ☐ What is another name for the real exchange rate? **[LO 18.10]**

Global Financial Crises

LO 18.11 Describe the role of the IMF and how financial crises are created by excessive debt and unsustainable exchange rates.

Although the international financial system works well most of the time, occasionally it falls out of order. In general, these crises can be labeled as one of two types: debt crises and exchange-rate crises. Throughout this section, you'll see how foreign direct investment and international flows can be fickle, which can destabilize economies when things go wrong.

The role of the IMF

Before working through some examples of disruptions in the financial system, we'll introduce the institution that is responsible for keeping the system together—the *IMF,* or *International Monetary Fund.* The IMF was created at the end of World War II. Although it's an international agency like the United Nations and World Bank, the IMF headquarters is in Washington, DC, a few blocks from the U.S. Federal Reserve headquarters and the U.S. Treasury Department.

Initially, when many countries had fixed exchange rates tied to gold, the IMF had the task of helping countries maintain their fixed rates. When countries ran into trouble maintaining their currencies, the IMF would step in and provide a loan to patch up a balance-of-payments deficit.

Now that most exchange rates are flexible, the IMF's role has changed. Today, the IMF often steps in as a lender of last resort, making loans to countries when private investors flee. The loans can help to stabilize the economy and keep fears from building on themselves. As the recent financial crises in Greece and Iceland show, international financial crises still occur, and the IMF is needed to help when things go wrong.

However, the IMF is not a magic solution for countries in need. Many IMF loans are made on the condition that the governments make certain policy changes. For example, a recipient country may be required to make efforts to reduce its budget deficit as a signal that it is committed to reform. In many cases, the IMF has been criticized for requiring economies to undertake contractionary fiscal policy and tighter monetary policy during the crisis itself. These policies usually depress the economy further and can exacerbate the crisis.

The role of the IMF and other global institutions is an area of ongoing debate. As globalization poses more risks of contagious collapse, how can the international system design institutions that will be able to prevent crises?

Debt crises

When countries need to finance their expenses, they often turn to international capital markets. The result is that a large share of government debt is often held by foreign investors. If those investors begin to worry whether the government will be able to repay the debt, the investors begin to move their money out of the country in a hurry. Why? If the government defaults, everyone who had invested in that debt stands to lose their money.

One such instance of investors losing confidence in the government's ability to repay debt occurred in Argentina in 2001. The setting for the debt crisis in Argentina started with heavy financing of a variety of industrial development projects during the 1960s and 1970s. The government then accumulated more debt in a war against the United Kingdom for control of the Falkland Islands.

As Argentina accumulated more debt, paying the interest on its debt formed a larger proportion of its budget. That wasn't the only problem, though. In an effort to curb inflation, Argentina had created a fixed exchange rate tied to the U.S. dollar, but the currency became overvalued. Domestic industry and large amounts of trade went to Argentina's neighbors, where products were cheaper. In addition, the financial crisis in Russia in 1998 made investors far more skeptical of investing money in "emerging markets" like Argentina. The combination of overvalued currency and loss in confidence raised interest rates, making it harder and more expensive to borrow more.

To try to stop the flight of capital, the government announced several attempts to reduce government spending. As you might have guessed, these promises were not kept. What followed was a painful economic spiral: Increased capital outflows from the country led to higher and higher interest rates. The increasing rates made debt payments more expensive, which created further government deficits. By 2001, the problem had spun into a full-on crisis, with bank runs and public protests. Unemployment came close to 20 percent. The government finally defaulted on its debt, unable to meet the increasingly high debt payments.[6]

We can analyze this scenario using the open-economy loanable-funds market set up earlier in the chapter. Figure 18-16 illustrates the stages of this debt crisis:

- When foreign investors started pulling their money out of the country, the net capital outflow curve shifted to the right.
- Interest rates then increased to r_2, which reduced investment. The higher interest rates also made the government's debt more expensive, and the government deficit increased.

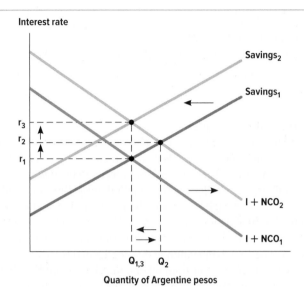

FIGURE 18-16
The Argentine debt crisis

Once investors got word that the Argentine government was in danger, they pulled their investments out of the country, shifting the combined investments and net capital outflow curve to the right, increasing the interest rate. This higher interest rate made the government debt more expensive, which decreased savings. This led to a further increase in the interest rate, and a repetition of the cycle.

- As the government deficit increased, this shifted the national savings curve to the left, increasing the interest rate again (to r_3) and reducing investment yet again.

Exchange-rate crises

Loss of confidence in a government's ability to defend an exchange rate can also spook investors. If a government devalues an exchange rate, it essentially represents a loss for those holding investments in the country.

With this in mind, we turn to the story of the Asian financial crisis. In the early 1990s, emerging economies in Asia—Thailand, Indonesia, Malaysia, the Philippines—received a lot of capital from global investors. The influx of investment contributed to a remarkable spurt of growth. With all that fresh capital, banks wanted to move money, and they started making loans to riskier entrepreneurs. Soon the signs of good fortune were fading. In Thailand, especially, most economic indicators started to create worries, and investors began pulling their money out of the country.

But the crisis didn't end there. Because the world is so interconnected, crises can easily spread in a chain reaction called a *contagion*. The virus imagery is fitting. When Thailand got into trouble, investors immediately became nervous about other countries in the area, regardless of their condition. Soon, fearful investors were pulling their money out of the surrounding countries as well, creating financial crises in those countries. In other words, the crisis was contagious.

After the financial fall of Thailand in 1997, speculative attacks spread to Indonesia, the Philippines, South Korea, and Malaysia. Like Thailand, each of these countries was unable to defend its fixed currency. Not surprisingly, their currencies rapidly depreciated once the fixed exchange-rate policies were abandoned and exchange rates were made flexible. GDP in these five countries fell about 10 percent between 1997 and 1998. The crisis lasted for about a year, and millions of people suffered. The overriding lesson of the Asian financial crisis was that the combination of fast-moving capital and fixed exchange rates can lead to devastating speculative attacks with the power to shake to whole continents.[7]

√ CONCEPT CHECK

☐ What is a lender of last resort? **[LO 18.11]**

☐ Why are fixed exchange rates vulnerable to speculative attack? **[LO 18.11]**

Conclusion

In this chapter, we opened up the national economy to understand how countries trade and invest with each other. When we add net exports to our GDP equation, we get an interesting result: The difference between what a country buys and sells is also equal to the level of foreign investment. In effect, if a country is buying more than it is selling, it needs to borrow money from abroad to pay for its imports. This important equality is called the *balance-of-payments identity*. The tight link between the trade balance and capital flows is the key to understanding issues such as the U.S. trade deficit and the U.S. debt with China.

We looked at two explanations for the trade deficit with China, which turn out to be different sides of the same coin. The first explanation is that the United States is not saving nearly as much as China and is relying on investment from other countries. From the balance-of-payments identity, we know that if foreign investment is high, then there must also be a trade imbalance.

The second explanation is that exports from China are artificially cheap because the Chinese currency is set at a price below what it should be—that is, below its market price. Cheap Chinese exports mean that the balance of trade is negative, and the United States needs to borrow money to pay for its spending.

In extreme cases, we saw how international debt and fixed exchange rates can tip countries into economic crises. As the world continues to become more and more interlinked, economic policy in one part of the world will have global effects.

Macroeconomics may seem more abstract than microeconomics, with lots of moving parts. Yet trade policy, government fiscal policy, monetary policy, and the decision of how to set the exchange rate affect the daily lives of every citizen, usually in ways that are hard to see.

In the concluding chapter, we will apply the lessons you've learned throughout the book to one of the most stubborn problems in economics—international poverty.

Key Terms

balance of trade, p. 489

trade deficit, p. 489

trade surplus, p. 489

foreign direct investment (FDI), p. 491

foreign portfolio investment, p. 492

net capital flow, p. 492

balance-of-payments identity, p. 493

exchange rate, p. 501

exchange-rate appreciation, p. 502

exchange-rate depreciation, p. 502

floating exchange rate, p. 508

fixed exchange rate, p. 508

nominal exchange rate, p. 512

real exchange rate, p. 512

Summary

LO 18.1 Define the balance of trade and describe the general trends of U.S. trade.

The *balance of trade* is the value of exports less the value of imports. It is also called *net exports*. Net exports respond to the value of the exchange rate: When the exchange rate is high, domestic goods are expensive and foreign goods are cheap, so net exports are low. When the exchange rate is low, net exports are high.

LO 18.2 Define portfolio investment and direct foreign investment.

There are two types of foreign investment. *Direct investment* is when a firm invests abroad with an active interest—for example, by building a factory and managing the factory. *Portfolio investment* is investment in financial securities, such as stocks or bonds, so that domestic residents still operate firms. Together, direct investment and portfolio investment give the net capital outflow of the country, a measure of the money a country invests outside its border.

LO 18.3 Explain the connection between the balance of trade and net capital outflow.

The balance of trade and net capital outflow are related through the balance-of-payments identity, which states that NX = NCO. This identity is an accounting identity: If a country has an imbalance of trade (positive net exports), it means that it has lent money to the rest of the world (positive capital outflow) to pay for these goods.

LO 18.4 Describe the determinants of international capital flows using the demand and supply of international loanable funds.

Net capital outflows are determined by the demand and supply for net capital outflow. The supply of net capital outflows is national savings less domestic investment. The demand for net capital outflow is determined by the domestic interest rate and the foreign interest rate. When the domestic interest rate is high, net capital outflow is low because foreign money flows into the country. When the foreign interest rate is high, net capital outflow is high because money flows out of the country to take advantage of high returns.

LO 18.5 Show how the international market for loanable funds can be used to explain events in the international financial system.

Various events can influence the international supply and demand for loanable funds. An increase in confidence in an economy will cut net capital outflows and lower the interest rate. A decrease in savings from an increase in the government deficit will shift the supply curve for loanable funds to the left, increasing the interest rate and decreasing net capital outflows.

LO 18.6 Describe exchange rate appreciation and depreciation and understand their effects on trade.

The *exchange rate* is the value of one currency expressed in terms of another currency. Exchange rates can be expressed in two ways: either in terms of the domestic (home) currency or in terms of the foreign currency. Exchange rates can appreciate or depreciate, as the currencies strengthen or weaken against each other.

LO 18.7 Describe the determinants of demand and supply in the forex market.

The exchange rate is determined by demand and supply for domestic currency. Demand and supply are influenced by preferences for domestic and foreign goods and services, the domestic interest rate, the foreign interest rate, and the perceived riskiness of domestic and foreign investment.

LO 18.8 Explain fixed and floating exchange rates.

A *fixed exchange rate* is an exchange rate that is set by the government, not the market. Usually fixed exchange rates are set to maintain a steady relationship with another stable currency. A government maintains a fixed exchange rate by intervening in the foreign-exchange market, by either buying or selling foreign currency. A *floating exchange rate,* on the other hand, is set by the market. Floating exchange rates are set by the intersection of supply and demand for foreign exchange.

LO 18.9 Describe why monetary policy is ineffective when maintaining a fixed exchange rate.

A fixed exchange rate necessarily means that monetary policy will not have an effect—any change to the money supply has to be counteracted by government actions on the foreign-exchange market to maintain the exchange rate. Monetary policy is more effective under a flexible exchange rate because the flexible rate can affect both investment and net exports.

LO 18.10 Describe the difference between the real and nominal exchange rates.

The real exchange rate is the nominal exchange rate corrected for the price levels in the domestic and foreign country. The real exchange rate is measured in terms of goods instead of currency. If the real exchange rate is 1, then a good can be exchanged in one country directly for a good in another country. If this is the case, we say there is purchasing power parity between the two countries.

LO 18.11 Describe the role of the IMF and how financial crises are created by excessive debt and unsustainable exchange rates.

Although the financial system works well most of the time, financial crises can occur. The IMF often steps in as a *lender of last resort* when this happens, making loans to countries when private lenders flee. However, this is not always an ideal solution. Crises exist because countries often turn to international capital markets to finance expenses, therefore meaning investors own the countries' debts. This can backfire if investors worry that the government won't be able to repay the debt or if they lose confidence in the government's ability to defend the exchange rate.

Review Questions

1. What happens to the U.S. balance of trade as oil prices rise? **[LO 18.1]**

2. Suppose a presidential candidate criticizes his opponent by saying his opponent's economic policies have made the dollar weaker and cost American factory workers their jobs. What would be your response? **[LO 18.1]**

3. Why would a company want to make a direct investment in countries where the company's home currency has higher purchasing power? **[LO 18.2]**

4. Part of the North American Free Trade Agreement (NAFTA) opened the Mexican stock market to U.S. and Canadian investors for the first time. How would this affect direct and portfolio foreign investment in Mexico? **[LO 18.2]**

5. If many factories that once made goods in the United States move to Mexico, what must also happen in order to correct the balance of payments in the United States? **[LO 18.3]**

6. Critics of NAFTA argued that opening our borders to free trade with Mexico would result in U.S. firms moving all of their factories to Mexico and the United States running large trade deficits with Mexico. Comment on the concerns of these critics using your knowledge of international trade and net capital flows. **[LO 18.3]**

7. Rating agencies rate countries on the perceived riskiness of investing in their economies. Standard and Poor's, one of the main rating agencies, downgraded the credit rating for U.S. Treasury bonds in 2011. According to this chapter, what impact should the downgrading have had on net capital outflows and interest rates? Why? **[LO 18.4]**

8. The interest rate on 10-year U.S. Treasury bonds just before Standard and Poor's downgraded the U.S. credit rating was 2.47 percent. One year later, the interest rate on these bonds had fallen to 1.60 percent. How can one explain this result that seems to contradict the findings of this chapter? **[LO 18.4]**

9. List three policies that a government could engage in that would reduce interest rates. (*Hint:* Look back to Figures 18-6 through 18-8.) **[LO 18.5]**

10. A country doubles its rate of saving. How is this likely to affect the equilibrium interest rate and net capital outflow? What is the impact on the trade balance? **[LO 18.5]**

11. Suppose the exchange rate value of the dollar depreciates. Who wins and who loses? **[LO 18.6]**

12. Suppose the exchange rate was 102 yen per dollar in 2014 and 110 yen per dollar in 2015. Did the dollar appreciate or depreciate? What about the yen? **[LO 18.6]**

13. Identify the main reasons why people convert one currency into another currency. **[LO 18.7]**

14. During a recession the central bank lowers interest rates. How does this affect the exchange rate and net exports? **[LO 18.7]**

15. A country has a fixed exchange rate. If world interest rates rise, what will the country have to do to maintain its fixed exchange rate? Has the fixed exchange rate become relatively more undervalued or overvalued? **[LO 18.8]**

16. Suppose that in response to a severe recession, a country with an overvalued currency and a fixed exchange rate moves to a floating exchange-rate system. Who are the winners and losers in this move? **[LO 18.8]**

17. A country operates under a flexible exchange rate system. When the central bank lowers the interest rate during a recession, how does this affect investment and net exports, and ultimately aggregate demand? What if the exchange rate was fixed instead? **[LO 18.9]**

18. What are the advantages to fixing the exchange rate at an undervalued level? What are the disadvantages? **[LO 18.9]**

19. Discuss what would happen to the real exchange rate between the U.S. and Australia if oil prices fell, which dramatically reduced the cost of transporting goods. **[LO 18.10]**

20. Is it ever possible for a country's nominal exchange rate to be depreciating while its real exchange rate is appreciating? Explain. **[LO 18.10]**

21. Foreign investors in a country become worried about the stability of the government due to its rising debt level. What do you expect to happen to the interest rate and the exchange rate value of the country's currency, assuming the country has a floating exchange rate? **[LO 18.11]**

22. Foreign investors in a country become worried about the stability of the government due to its rising debt level. How might the IMF help avert a financial crisis in this country? **[LO 18.11]**

Problems and Applications

1. Suppose total U.S. exports in the month of June were $122.9 billion and total imports from foreign countries were $192.4 billion. What was the balance of trade? **[LO 18.1]**

2. Suppose a country has total GDP $(Y) = \$10$ trillion, consumption = $7 trillion, government spending = $2 trillion, investment = $2 trillion, and taxes = $1.5 trillion. What is the level of net exports or balance of trade? What is the level of public savings? What is the level of private savings? What is the level of net capital outflow? **[LO 18.1, 18.3]**

3. In 2010, U.S. investors purchased $50 billion in foreign assets, and foreigners purchased $100 billion in U.S.

assets such as stocks and Treasury bills. In addition, U.S. businesses invested $150 billion in foreign factories and operations, while foreign companies invested $100 billion in U.S. factories and operations. What was the net capital outflow for the United States? **[LO 18.2]**

4. Define each of the following as direct or portfolio foreign investment. **[LO 18.2]**

   a. Nike (a U.S. company) builds new factories in Cambodia.

   b. A U.S. hedge fund purchases 30 percent of the shares of a Brazilian paper manufacturer.

   c. Mercedes-Benz (a German company) builds a new manufacturing plant in Alabama.

   d. Intel (a U.S. company) sets up a new call center in India.

   e. A British chocolate maker buys a smaller U.S. rival.

   f. Hilton Hotels (a U.S. company) builds a new resort in Hawaii.

5. Tom is stuck with his friends on an island that uses coconuts for currency, but they recently discovered Wilson's Island nearby. Tom's Island agrees to make only one transaction with Wilson's Island: It sells a fishing boat to Wilson's for 15 coconuts. Answer the following questions, assuming that yearly consumption on Tom's Island equals 500 coconuts and domestic investments in huts and farm equipment equals 150 coconuts. **[LO 18.3]**

   a. What are net exports for Tom's Island?

   b. What is the total national savings for Tom's Island?

   c. Suppose Tom's Island imports a volleyball net from Wilson's Island for 5 coconuts. What is the total national savings now?

   d. Now Tom purchases 1 coconut tree on Wilson Island at a cost of 10 coconuts. What is the balance of payments? (*Hint:* A coconut tree produces coconuts like a factory produces goods.)

6. Over the last five years, Portlandia's average income has risen and caused the supply curve of loanable funds to increase and shift right. **[LO 18.4, 18.5]**

   a. Would the domestic interest rate have increased or decreased?

   b. Given the change in the interest rate, would General Motors (GM) be more or less likely to open a Camaro plant in the country?

   c. If Portlandia hits a recession and interest rates fall, which way must the demand curve for loanable funds have shifted?

7. Describe what happens to the supply and/or demand curves for U.S. dollars under the following scenarios. In each scenario, does the U.S. exchange rate appreciate or depreciate, and what happens to the U.S. balance of trade? **[LO 18.6, 18.7]**

   a. A drought in Russia destroys the wheat crop, resulting in increased purchases of wheat from the United States.

   b. Bollywood movies become extremely popular in the United States, increasing demand for foreign movies.

   c. The U.S. government forces all government offices to purchase American-made computer products, instead of importing them.

8. Suppose there is major unrest in the labor market in the United States, making European investors nervous about investing in the United States. **[LO 18.6, 18.7]**

   a. Draw the supply and demand curves for U.S. dollars, and show the appropriate shift(s) in supply and demand for U.S. dollars associated with the labor unrest.

   b. Did the value of the U.S. dollar depreciate or appreciate?

9. A government has been running budget deficits for many years and decides to balance its budget. Explain how each of the following are affected under a floating exchange-rate regime. **[LO 18.5, 18.6, 18.7]**

   a. The interest rate.

   b. The exchange rate.

   c. The trade balance.

10. Suppose the new CEO for Apple Inc. decides to produce all the company's products in the United States instead of China. **[LO 18.7]**

   a. Which way will the supply for U.S. dollars shift?

   b. Which way will the demand for U.S. dollars shift?

   c. Does the value of the U.S. dollars depreciate or appreciate?

11. Suppose that in the United States last season's hot holiday gift was the iPad (which is made primarily in China), while this season's big gift is media content for the iPad (which is made in the United States). Determine whether there will be an increase, decrease, or no change for each of the following variables compared to last year. **[LO 18.6, 18.7]**

   a. Supply and demand for dollars.

   b. Exchange rate between the United States and China.

   c. Net exports for the United States.

   d. Net capital outflows for the United States.

12. In March 2009 the Canadian dollar was worth $0.78 U.S. In April 2011 the Canadian dollar was worth $1.06 U.S. What effect would this increase have on the trade balance between the United States and Canada? Why? **[LO 18.6]**

TABLE 18P-1

Exchange rate	USD	EUR	JPY
USD	1.00000	0.78230	81.200
EUR	1.27830	1.00000	103.796
JPY	0.01232	0.00963	1.000

13. Martha has $10,000 to invest in the foreign-exchange market. She's interested in trading U.S. dollars (USD) for euros (EUR) and Japanese yen (JPY). Using Table 18P-1, determine the arbitrage profit/loss Martha will make in each of the following scenarios. (*Note:* Any value less than $10 should be considered zero.) **[LO 18.6]**

   a. USD → EUR → JPY → USD.

   b. USD → JPY → EUR → USD.

   c. Now look up the current exchange rates among any three currencies. Show that there are no arbitrage opportunities for the three currencies you chose.

14. Some politicians argue for imposing trade restrictions in the hope that doing so will reduce the trade deficit of the United States. Assuming the United States has a floating exchange rate, answer the following questions regarding the impact of the trade restrictions. **[LO 18.7]**

   a. What is the impact in the foreign exchange market for dollars?

   b. What is the impact in the market for foreign currency (euros, yen, etc.)?

   c. What happens to the exchange rate of the dollar?

   d. What happens to net exports?

15. Suppose the U.S. economy slips into a recession. In response, the Federal Reserve cuts the federal funds rate in order to avoid unemployment. Consider what happens to the following under a floating exchange-rate regime. **[LO 18.8]**

   a. Domestic investment.

   b. Capital inflow.

   c. Capital outflow.

   d. Exchange rate.

   e. Net exports.

   f. Aggregate demand.

16. Reevaluate the previous problem assuming the U.S. economy follows a fixed exchange-rate regime. **[LO 18.8, 18.9]**

17. A country that has been operating under a fixed exchange-rate regime falls into recession. All attempts at using fiscal policy to lift the economy out of recession have failed. **[LO 18.9]**

   a. Can monetary policy be effective in this case? Why or why not?

   b. Should the country allow the exchange rate to float? Why or why not?

18. In Windsor, Ontario, a Big Mac from McDonald's costs C$4.16 (Canadian dollars), and across the border in Detroit it costs $3.54 in U.S. dollars. **[LO 18.10]**

   a. Suppose the nominal U.S. exchange rate with Canada is US$0.80 per Canadian dollar. Does purchasing power parity hold between the two countries?

   b. What is the purchasing power parity exchange rate for the United States?

19. Suppose the current U.S.–UK exchange rate is 0.63 pound (the pound is the UK currency) per dollar, and the aggregate price level is 170 for the United States and 140 for the UK. What is the real exchange rate? What does this real exchange rate mean in terms of the relative purchasing power of the dollar and the pound? **[LO 18.10]**

20. Imagine there are only two trading nations in the world. For each of the following scenarios, determine whether goods in one country will become more attractive relative to goods in the other country given their inflation rates and a shift in the nominal exchange rates. **[LO 18.10]**

   a. Inflation is 8 percent in the UK and 4 percent in Germany, but the UK pound–euro exchange rate remains the same.

   b. Inflation is 3 percent in the United States and 7 percent in Japan, but the exchange rate for U.S. dollars to Japanese yen increases from 70 to 80 Japanese yen.

   c. Inflation is 10 percent in the United States and 6 percent in Mexico, and the price of the Mexican peso rises from US$0.08 to US$0.15.

21. Over several years, foreign investors poured billions of dollars into a country due to its favorable growth prospects. They have now become concerned about the return on their investments because growth in the country is stagnating. As a result they are pulling their money out. Will this country be better able to withstand the financial crisis if it has a fixed or a floating exchange rate? Explain. **[LO 18.11]**

Endnotes

1. http://bgr.com/2016/04/06/iphone-sales-hit-one-billion-2016.

2. http://ticdata.treasury.gov/Publish/shla2010r.pdf.

3. http://www.ft.com/fastft/2016/05/10/german-current-account-surplus-swells-to-record.

4. http://data.worldbank.org/indicator/NY.GNS.ICTR.ZS.

5. http://fas.org/man/crs/crs-asia2.htm.

6. http://fpc.state.gov/documents/organization/8040.pdf.

7. http://fas.org/man/crs/crs-asia2.htm.

Development Economics

Learning Objectives

LO 19.1   Explain how the capabilities approach relates to economic development.

LO 19.2   Explain the relationship between economic growth and economic development.

LO 19.3   Describe how improvements to education and health can develop human capital.

LO 19.4   Explain the importance of institutions and good governance in development economics.

LO 19.5   Evaluate the role of industrial policy and clusters in development.

LO 19.6   Evaluate how migration and remittances promote development.

LO 19.7   Describe the aims of foreign aid, the role of poverty traps, the main institutions delivering aid, and criticisms of foreign aid.

LO 19.8   Understand how impact investing provides a new tool for creating social impact.

LO 19.9   Explain the need for impact evaluation and analyze the role of randomized controlled trials in measuring impact.

POVERTY AMID PLENTY

In the macroeconomics chapters, we've talked a lot about economic growth. But economic growth is not an end in itself. An economy can grow but still leave many people behind. Although the average level of real GDP per capita tripled in the second half of the twentieth century across the world as a whole, many people today still don't have enough resources for much of anything.

About 702 million of the 7.2 billion people on earth live on just $1.90 per day, the World Bank's measure of extreme poverty.[1] Billions more live on only slightly higher incomes. The depth and breadth of global poverty are not just a compelling humanitarian concern but also an economic puzzle: How can such poverty persist amid such plenty?

Some who have a more pessimistic outlook believe that poverty will always be a part of life. They point to a decades-long legacy of hopelessly failed bureaucracies and wasted foreign-aid budgets. Others who are more optimistic point to evidence of progress: Thanks to sustained

Courtesy of Robin Saidman

efforts by governments, nongovernmental organizations, and communities, many more children are attending school than even a decade or two ago. Infant mortality has dropped by half since 1960. Nine million more kids lived to celebrate their first birthday in 2006 than would have if the mortality rate had stayed at the 1960 level.

Impressively, such improvements have occurred even in places where average incomes failed to grow. So although growth is good in general, the poorest can do better even if there is little growth. Nor does lots of growth necessarily mean higher incomes for the poorest. In more technical words, overall growth and income for the poorest are correlated, but not perfectly.

So what can help the poorest lead better lives? One important step is improving access to markets and institutions that can expand opportunities and give more choices. Think of how you rely on a basic bank account to pay bills and save money. About half of the adults in the world live their lives without access to a bank. By expanding access to banks, millions would be helped to save, invest, and provide for their families. The same goes for access to improved markets for transportation, health care, education, and other basic services, backed by responsive legal and political institutions to maintain fair practices.

These are the issues taken up in the field of development economics, the topic of this chapter. Development economists tackle a series of questions that span several core economic issues: What makes some people—and some countries—richer than others? What makes others poorer? How can markets be made more efficient and wide-reaching in low-income countries? How should donors and investors choose among good options, given that resources are scarce?

In the first part of this chapter, we examine the relationship between economic growth and economic development. Then we look at the basics of economic development, taking a fresh perspective on some ideas we've encountered already in this book—human capital, good governance, investment, trade, and migration. In the final part of the chapter, we consider foreign aid—its history, the arguments for and against such aid, and how development economists are striving to understand what works.

Development and Capabilities

So far, we've talked a lot about economic *growth*. In this chapter, we talk about economic *development*. The concepts are intertwined, but distinct. Economic *growth* involves increases in GDP. However, GDP doesn't necessarily tell us much about what it's like to live in a country—its levels of inequality and poverty, what opportunities there are to better yourself if you're in the middle or at the bottom of the heap, how well basic institutions like courts and hospitals work, how many people can read and write, and so on. These are the kinds of things we're concerned about when we talk about economic *development*. Development economics looks beyond GDP growth to ask about the quality of life for all sectors of society. A helpful way to think about what matters comes from an idea called the *capabilities approach*.

The capabilities approach

> **LO 19.1** Explain how the capabilities approach relates to economic development.

The capabilities approach was developed by Amartya Sen, a Harvard professor who won the 1998 Nobel Prize in Economics. His idea provides a framework for economists to think about poverty, inequality, and human development. A **capability** is something a person is able to be or do. Examples of capabilities include being able to live a long and healthy life, have adequate food and shelter, get an education, speak one's mind, travel freely, live free of the fear of violence, be able to find secure and meaningful work, and be able to enjoy recreational and cultural activities.

capability
something a person is able to be or do, such as to engage fully in life, including having economic and political freedoms

In all, capabilities represent a vast spectrum of life—from basic survival and good health to self-expression and engagement in culture. Whereas economic growth focuses on expanding the economy, the capabilities approach to economic development instead looks to constantly improve what individuals can be and can do. Institutional and market failures restrict what people can do, and the restriction of capabilities often affects poorest citizens the most.

You might be wondering why we need a fancy new term like "capabilities" here. Aren't all of the things we've mentioned also simply things that increase utility? Why do we need to depart from the traditional economic framework of maximizing utility? Read the What Do You Think? box "Utility versus capabilities" for more on that question.

What Do You Think?
Utility versus capabilities

We have seen throughout this text that the idea of "maximizing utility" is the foundation of individual decision making in economics. It captures the idea that people want to obtain more of what gives them satisfaction. Can't we, then, simply use the *utility approach* to think about development? Why do we need to introduce the *capability approach* to establish the value of things like education and health and free speech? After all, aren't those capabilities also going to increase people's utility?

While the utility approach serves us well when thinking about how *individuals* make decisions, it may not guide us toward the best decisions for *society*. The early founders of the utilitarian approach, the philosophers Jeremy Bentham and John Stuart Mill, suggested that the best society is one that maximizes the collective utility of everyone in that society. Since then, other philosophers have argued that there are flaws in this idea. The capabilities approach addresses at least two of those flaws.

The first problem is that a simple utility-maximizing approach ignores the idea of fundamental rights. For example, what if slave owners received more utility from slave ownership than the utility slaves would get from being freed? Should society therefore allow slavery? Most people would say there are some rights, like not being enslaved, that are worth preserving even if it means accepting lower utility across society as a whole. As Sen says, "Happiness or desire fulfillment represents only one aspect of human existence. The capabilities approach attempts to fill the gap by looking at a much broader conception of life" (as quoted by Clark, 2011).

Second, simply trying to maximize utility ignores the *distribution* of that utility. Imagine that the president of an impoverished nation feels gnawing envy when he sees the presidents of

(continued)

richer countries flying around in private jets. His utility from owning a private jet is so great that it would outweigh the combined utility that citizens of a city would get from a new health clinic in their district. Should we, then, buy the president a private jet instead of improving health care? There seems to be something wrong with accepting this conclusion at face value.

On the other hand, by moving too far away from the utility approach, do we risk paternalistically giving the poor what we think they *ought* to want instead of what they really *do* want? In their book *Poor Economics,* Abhijit Banerjee and Esther Duflo tell of a man in a remote, dusty village in Morocco who, when asked by researchers what he would do if he had more money, said he would buy more nutritious food for his family. The researchers pointed out that he owned a television and a DVD player and asked why he'd bought these things when his family didn't have enough to eat. "Oh," he replied, "television is more important than food."

WHAT DO YOU THINK?

1. Should the World Bank and local governments be building bridges, schools, and clinics in low-income countries if citizens would rather have TVs?
2. Should development economists put more focus on capabilities or utility?

Sources: Abhijit Banerjee and Esther Duflo, *Poor Economics* (New York: Public Affairs, 2011); David A. Clark, "The Capability Approach: Its Development, Critiques and Recent Advances," http://www.gprg.org/pubs/workingpapers/pdfs/gprg-wps-032.pdf (accessed November 7, 2011).

Economic growth and economic development

LO 19.2 Explain the relationship between economic growth and economic development.

We saw in an earlier chapter that growth in countries such as China has slashed poverty rates. The average person in China now earns about $7,500 a year, compared with just $250 three decades ago.[2] Average levels of education and health have increased dramatically, too. That's not surprising. After all, when people have more money, you would expect them to spend more on improving their health and educating their children.

However, there is nothing inevitable about GDP growth improving health and education for everyone. For example, survey data show that in India, the rate of children suffering from malnutrition essentially didn't change over the span of two health surveys conducted in 1998 and 2005.[3] Clearly, it is possible for a country to experience strong economic *growth* without comparably strong economic *development.* There needs to be additional attention paid to policy mechanisms that can help to translate higher average incomes into improved capabilities for the poorest citizens.

What about the other direction of the relationship? Does economic *development* lead to economic *growth*? There are plenty of reasons to think it does. As we saw in Chapter 10, "Economic Growth," economists hotly debate the fundamentals of economic growth. There is general agreement, though, that those fundamentals include such things as property rights, the rule of law, and human capital. After all, an economy without healthy, educated workers is obviously going to have a hard time growing. We will turn now to considering in more depth some of the basic aspects of economic development.

✓CONCEPT CHECK

☐ What are some examples of capabilities? **[LO 19.1]**
☐ Does economic growth always lead to economic development? **[LO 19.2]**
☐ Why may improving the education and health of the poorest help those who are more well off? **[LO 19.2]**

The Basics of Development Economics

Knowing there's a difference between economic growth and economic development, let's return with a fresh perspective to some ideas covered in earlier chapters. As we look at how countries can promote health, education, and good governance—all questions central to development economics—remember that we can think of these policies in two ways: We can see them as putting in place the conditions for economic growth, and we also can see them as translating the fruits of economic growth into greater capabilities for people in society.

Human capital

LO 19.3 Describe how improvements to education and health can develop human capital.

Countries all over the world have witnessed dramatic improvements in health and education. This is especially true in Asia, and even countries in Africa that once lagged in health and education progress are now coming close to having all children in primary school. This is good news for both development and growth. Still, though, each year millions of kids die from diseases that could be prevented. These are improvements that could happen quickly and cheaply, but don't.

Health

Why do these improvements fail to happen? Part of the problem is that health care facilities don't exist in many parts of the world. In rural areas, especially, getting to a modern clinic may involve trekking on foot for miles. Another part of the problem is that even where clinics do exist, many people don't use them. Many choose instead to resort to home remedies and traditional village "doctors" who have little or no training in medicine but charge lower fees than those charged by modern hospitals and often are more attentive.

Recognizing this, countries around the world, ranging from middle-income Thailand to poorer Ghana, have started national health insurance programs. For a nominal fee, usually a couple of dollars per year, families can visit any national clinic or hospital to receive basic services. Still, often these national health care programs are not as effective as they could be. One study showed that in India, local health care workers were absent about 40 percent of the time on average. Even when the workers do show up, clinics sometimes run out of important drugs such as quinine (which fights malaria).

One study of health care clinics in Delhi, by Jishnu Das of the World Bank and Jeffrey Hammer of Princeton, found there were plenty of clinics available to poor households, but they provided much worse care than did private clinics in wealthier areas. It's not because the doctors were badly trained. Rather, Das and Hammer found that doctors serving poor patients often operated below their "knowledge frontiers"—the doctors provided care below the standard of their medical training. One study, for example, showed doctors in public clinics failing to ask even the most basic diagnostic questions when patients appeared to be having heart attacks. Why? Partly because doctors in private clinics receive a fee for their services, while in public clinics they receive a fixed salary. Doctors have a much higher incentive to get the treatment right when their income depends on customer satisfaction.[4] One of the challenges for development economists working in health care is to figure out a way to give doctors the right incentives when their own intrinsic motivation isn't enough.

Fixing these health care challenges can contribute greatly to economic growth as well as development. Well-nourished, healthy kids do better in school, making them more productive workers as adults. Epidemics that afflict young adults can have a profound impact on GDP. The AIDS epidemic alone has been found to lower growth rates by up to 1.5 percent per year throughout sub-Saharan Africa.

Is it first necessary to achieve economic growth to be able to fix health care challenges? Figure 19-1 shows the relationship between income measured in GDP per capita and life expectancy. As you would expect, people who live in countries with higher average incomes generally live longer lives. Still, the correlation is not exact. Compare Vietnam and Nigeria, for example. Nigeria has a slightly higher average income than Vietnam, but a baby born in Vietnam is expected to live about 22 years longer on average than a baby born in Nigeria. Clearly, it must be possible to improve health outcomes dramatically even without achieving strong growth in average incomes.

Education

As with health, the reasons for investing in teachers, schools, and books are related to both growth and capabilities:

- In terms of economic growth, educated workers are generally more productive: Each additional year of schooling is worth about 10 percent more in overall earnings over the course of a lifetime.

- In terms of capabilities, education can be seen as worthwhile in itself, as well as contributing to other capabilities. For example, more-educated women tend to make better decisions about family planning. Considerable data also indicate that more education tends to make a society more democratic and reduce its levels of inequality.

In 1999, 106 million children around the world were not attending school; by 2015, that number had fallen by more than half. Even countries without strong economic growth had made strong progress in school attendance. The abolishment of school fees is a major reason why

---

FIGURE 19-1

Income and life expectancy   Overall, the higher the income within a country, the higher the life expectancy of the citizens within the country. At lower levels of income, this relationship isn't perfect, however. Some countries have made strides in income without making much progress in development in life expectancy, while others have high levels of life expectancy despite low incomes.

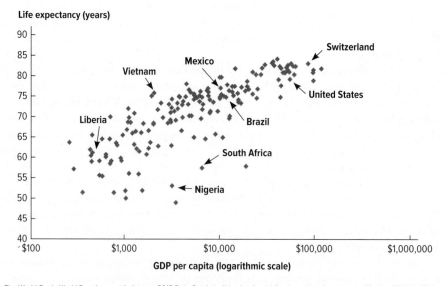

Source: The World Bank, World Development Indicators 2015 Data Set, http://databank.worldbank.org/data/reports.aspx?Code=SP.DYN.LE00.IN&id=af3ce82b&report_name=Popular_indicators&populartype=series&ispopular=y

more children are in school in a number of poorer countries. Even though the fees were usually small—about $30 a year—families living on just a few dollars per day simply could not afford them. Not surprisingly, when the fees were abolished, more kids went to school. In Kenya, for example, when school fees were eliminated in 2003, schools had to rush to find places for the 1 million more kids who enrolled around the country.

However, a sudden increase in students poses a new problem—crowded classrooms and over-burdened teachers. In some countries, there is only one teacher for 100 students. Development economists have recently started to pay more attention to the challenge of improving the *quality* of education. Even in middle-income countries such as Mexico, where all kids go to primary school, 91 percent of kids do not learn math well enough to be competitive on the international stage. The situation is worse for lower-income countries. One study in Ghana found that sixth-graders on average performed at the same level on a basic literacy test as one could achieve simply by guessing.

There are many ideas for how to improve schools. Recent research by development economists has made great strides in testing which approaches are more effective and which are not. To work with children lagging behind on basic math and reading skills, Innovations for Poverty Action tested a remedial education program in India, Kenya, and Ghana and found the program to be particularly successful. The approach included training women in the community to offer supplemental lessons to the students who were furthest behind in their learning. Other approaches, such as distributing textbooks, helped only the best students in the class. Providing parents with information about the quality of the children's schools had no effect at all.[5]

Institutions and good governance

LO 19.4 Explain the importance of institutions and good governance in development economics.

When we studied the determinants of economic growth, we discussed the importance of "good governance." Not surprisingly, good governance is also crucially important in economic development. Many basic capabilities rely on having a competent, well-intentioned government and good *institutions.* Economist Douglass North of Washington University in St. Louis (and co-winner of the 1993 Nobel Prize for his contributions to economic history) defines **institutions** as the humanly devised constraints that shape human interactions.[6] This definition includes *laws* enforced by the government as well as *cultural norms,* such as whether people see it as unacceptable to avoid responsibility at work, embezzle funds from your employer, cheat on your taxes, and so on. Stated informally, institutions are the "rules of the game" in a society.

institutions
the humanly devised constraints that shape human interactions

The term *institutions* is also commonly used to refer to government bodies (such as senates and ministries of education), development agencies (such as the World Bank), and international groups (such as the United Nations). According to North, to avoid confusion we should think of these as examples of "organizations" instead in development economics.

What exactly constitutes "good governance"? At first it seems like a highly normative question. Some think the best government is the smallest government, staying out of people's lives as much as possible. Others think that government should have its hand in many different sectors of the economy, all in the name of promoting stability, growth, and development. Most development economists agree that the most basic and important task of any government is to create a stable political system—one that ensures the important institutions of enforceable property rights and the rule of law.

Property rights and the rule of law

Say you'd like to sell a bucketful of apples. This will probably work just fine without your having to prove you actually own the apples. You set up shop at a market, someone gives you the cash, and you give them the apples. What if you want to sell a house or a field? Would you ever buy land if you didn't have clear proof that the person selling it is the owner? No, you would want to see the *title* to the land, a document that certifies ownership of property. In many countries, the system of *titling* (providing legal documents proving ownership of assets) is weak. Now imagine you own land and you want to use it as collateral for a loan—say, to buy a tractor so you can farm the land more effectively. Do you think the bank is going to lend you the money unless you can prove you own the land?

Hernando de Soto, a Peruvian economist and president of the Institute for Liberty and Democracy, says that that the weak titling system in Latin America results in "dead capital." Millions of people may have land or other assets, but without proper titles they are effectively unable to tap the financial power of those assets. Titles would allow owners to take out billions of dollars in loans that could be used productively to invest in starting new businesses or improving their farms. If only they had titles, De Soto argues, their capital could be put to better use—it could become "alive." The evidence supporting his claim is mixed, suggesting that titling may be important only if other conditions are in place too.

One of those conditions is the *rule of law.* There's no point in being able to prove you own something if the police and courts are corrupt or incompetent and won't help you if thieves take it away. The rule of law helps to create stability and provides a set of clear guides to govern transactions. Where crime is rampant and government unhelpful—or, worse, when a country falls into outright conflict—it's hard to sustain either economic growth or economic development.[7]

Is democracy necessary?

Studies indicate a link between economic growth and political stability. The correlation between economic growth and democracy is less clear. Many of the stories of sustained growth in formerly poor countries occurred under governments that were far from democratic. Just think of China. The tiny, landlocked East African country of Rwanda is another illustration: Over the last decade and a half, growth has averaged about 7.5 percent per year, and residents are provided with basic and almost universal health insurance. Despite this growth, journalists critical of the government are routinely jailed; political opponents are routinely harassed and barred from participating in elections. The current president, Paul Kagame, won the last election with 93 percent of the vote, achieved by keeping any serious opponents from getting on the ballot.

Rwanda shows that even a relatively autocratic government can promote economic development as well as economic growth. Despite its democratic shortcomings, the government often makes good policy. Anti-corruption laws are some of the strongest in Africa. Also, women are encouraged to participate in the political process—so much so that the Rwandan parliament is one of only two in the world in which women outnumber men (Bolivia is the other).

So if good policy and fair institutions do not require democratic elections, should we care about democracy? Amartya Sen's capabilities framework suggests that we should view democracy in its own right as an essential ingredient in improving lives and sustaining basic freedoms.[8]

Investment

LO 19.5 Evaluate the role of industrial policy and clusters in development.

We saw in Chapter 10, "Economic Growth," that investment is a key concern in promoting growth. Foreign direct investment is an important source of funds in many countries with low savings rates. Development economists debate the best way for low-income countries to deal with these flows of capital from overseas as well as the funds that come from domestic sources. *Industrial policy* has two traditional tactics: import substitution or export-led growth. It can also involve trying to promote a cluster of industries that share linkages through the economy, so that they can develop in unison—an idea called *clustering*. Let's consider these ideas in turn.

Industrial policy

South Korea's GDP per capita in 1960 was about twice the size of Brazil's. By 2015, it was more than four times the size.[9] What accounts for these different rates of growth?

One important difference is that South Korea successfully pursued an industrial policy. **Industrial policy** is an effort by a government to favor some industries over others. The hope of such a policy is that coordinated investments in a chosen industry will help the overall economy to develop and will spur growth in the long run. The tools at governments' disposal in pursuing industrial policy include trade barriers, tax breaks, subsidies, incentives for foreign direct investment, and investment in research. Traditionally, these tools have been used as part of two opposite philosophies of industrial policy: import substitution and export-led growth.

> **industrial policy**
> effort by a government to favor some industries over others

Import substitution is the practice of using trade policy to protect domestic industries until they are efficient enough to compete on the world market. Imagine you want to nurture a successful electronics industry in your country. But new electronics firms can't get off the ground because they have to compete with cheap imports from countries with well-established electronics industries. Why not impose temporary trade barriers to stop the cheap imports, allowing time for the domestic infant industry in electronics to grow big and strong enough to compete?

Unfortunately, import substitution has failed to work well in the real world. A couple of problems related to import substitution can contribute to such failure:

- Without the spur of foreign competition to drive down costs, an infant industry might never grow up. For years, the Brazilian government protected domestic computer makers, but Brazilian-made machines still cost double the price of an American or Japanese machine.

- Decisions about which industries to protect are frequently made on the basis of *political* connections rather than real *economic* considerations. Naturally, companies would like to have their industry protected from foreign competition. That desire encourages large amounts of "rent-seeking" behavior—firms attempting to influence politicians in the name of profits. Protective policies have often persisted long after they were expected to lapse, at great cost to the taxpayer.

Realizing the problems with import substitution, some Asian countries have gone another route: *export-led growth*. This involves investing heavily in an industry through tax breaks and export subsidies (government monetary support for exporters) with the aim of selling goods around the world. Rather than walling domestic markets off from international trade, export-led growth instead selects industries to push into the world market. Success depends on picking winners. The South Korean government, for example, has managed to do just that, supporting companies

South Korea is achieving export-led growth by favoring companies, such as Hyundai, that are succeeding in the world market.
© *Jean Chung/Bloomberg via Getty Images*

such as Samsung and Hyundai. As a result, South Korea made the jump from poor to rich over the course of five decades. Japan, Singapore, and Taiwan used similar strategies to create the so-called Asian miracle.

Unfortunately, export-led growth doesn't always work. The unexpected and unprecedented success of these Asian countries led to many imitators, but not all succeeded. International markets are fickle and competition can be fierce. While the benefits of picking winners can be huge, so can the costs if you end up picking losers.

Clusters

clusters
networks of interdependent firms, universities, and businesses that focus on the production of a specific type of good

As governments consider how to develop their industrial sectors, they often choose to focus on promoting not just one industry but *clusters*. **Clusters** are networks of interdependent firms, universities, and businesses that focus on the production of a specific type of good. Each part of the network is far less productive operating in isolation, so if governments can push each element of the cluster in unison, they should realize huge gains in productivity.

A successful example is Bangladesh's textile industry. Starting in the 1970s, the government made a concerted effort to develop a cluster around textiles. It ensured that complementary firms—such as those making fabrics and those sewing the fabric into clothes—were located in close proximity to minimize transportation costs. The government provided incentives for these firms to work together. Ready-made garments are now a multibillion-dollar industry in Bangladesh; in 2014–2015 they accounted for 81.6 percent of all the country's net export revenues.

Trade

World Trade Organization (WTO)
an international organization designed to monitor and enforce trade agreements, while also promoting free trade

In earlier chapters, we studied the benefits of international trade: When one country can produce a good more efficiently than another country, both can specialize in the industry in which they have comparative advantage and experience mutual gains. By opening up to foreign markets, countries gain access to a wide array of new products, save money through access to cheaper goods, and find new customers for their products. It's not surprising, then, that trade plays a major role in development economics.

In the last few decades, there has been great growth in free trade worldwide. Tariffs (taxes on imports) in low-income countries have fallen by more than 20 percent. Part of this change has been due to the efforts of the **World Trade Organization (WTO)**, designed to monitor and enforce trade agreements while also promoting free trade. But about two-thirds of the reduction in tariffs in the past 20 years comes from reforms by national governments changing their own policies or making agreements with each other.

Wealthy countries increasingly feel that trade can sometimes be a more powerful lever than aid to help poorer countries develop. In 2000, for example, the U.S. government initiated the African Growth and Opportunity Act, which gave preferential treatment to about 1,800 goods coming from Africa—especially goods like apparel and textiles, exempting them from duties and quotas. In 2005, aid donors began to offer "aid for trade" programs to fund initiatives in low-income countries that minimize barriers to trade and provide the infrastructure critical for imports and exports. While trade policy is often politically contentious, trade-related aid now accounts for over a quarter of official development assistance.

Migration

LO 19.6 Evaluate how migration and remittances promote development.

The prospect of a better life drives millions of people to move away from home to other cities, provinces, or countries thousands of miles away in search of opportunity. Research by economists Michael Clemens, Claudio Montenegro, and Lant Pritchett indicates that skilled workers in the

United States earn about 15 times more than workers with exactly the same skills in Nigeria.[10] It's hardly surprising, then, that according to the Gallup World Values Survey, 40 percent of those living in the poorest quartile of countries would like to emigrate (move out of their home country).

However, it's difficult to legally move to a high-income country. Every year, the U.S. Diversity Visa lottery randomly gives 500,000 people from low-income countries the chance to permanently immigrate to the United States. And every year, about 14 million people apply.[11] That's a 3.5 percent chance of admission—lower than admission rates to the most competitive U.S. colleges. Some of those who are unsuccessful are so desperate to find better-paying work that they set off on perilous journeys—crossing the desert to and from Mexico or taking a rickety boat from Africa to Europe—to try to enter a high-income country illegally.

As we saw in Chapter 9, "Unemployment and the Labor Market," in host countries such as the United States, the influx of immigrants can be a highly controversial issue. But when we look at migration from the perspective of countries of origin, it presents a variety of opportunities to promote development. One important consequence of migration is remittances (money sent home by migrants). As shown in Figure 19-2, remittances are a major financial flow in some countries. The largest overall recipients of remittances are China and India, which each gets more than $60 billion per year.

Overall, remittances have become a powerful force in the world economy, growing impressively even after accounting for inflation. In 1990, less than $50 billion in inflation-adjusted dollars was transferred. In 2014, this figure was over $590 billion.

In addition to the benefits from remittances, migrants often return home after a few years working overseas, bringing with them new ideas and skills that benefit their local economy. For

FIGURE 19-2

Remittances around the world　The top 10 countries in terms of remittances received are a diverse group. India and China are large countries, with many migrants abroad. The Philippines and Mexico are countries that have traditionally been associated with remittances. As the data for France and Germany show, remittances aren't strictly a flow from rich to poor countries.

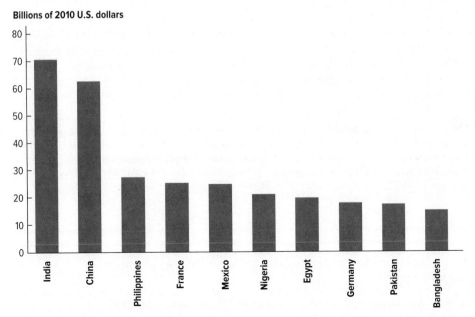

Billions of 2010 U.S. dollars

Source: The World Bank, 2014 data, http://www.worldbank.org/en/topic/migrationremittancesdiasporaissues/brief/migration-remittances-data

Michael Clemens, an economist at the Center for Global Development, and Lant Pritchett, author of the book *Let Their People Come,* the world has much to gain by loosening migration restrictions so that workers can more freely seek jobs in other places.[12] See the From Another Angle box "Trillion-dollar bills on the sidewalk?" for more.

From Another Angle
Trillion-dollar bills on the sidewalk?

In 2011, Alabama enacted HB56, a law punishing employers who hire illegal immigrants. After the law passed, tomato farmer Chad Smith found himself needing to hire Americans to pick his 85 acres of tomatoes. But picking tomatoes turned out to be hard, sweaty, poorly paid work, and most of his U.S. workers quit after just a couple of days. Without immigrant labor, Smith argued, his farm couldn't operate competitively.

This story illustrates why studies find that the available evidence often doesn't back up common concerns that immigration takes away jobs and drives down wages among the low-skilled. Often, immigrants do jobs that natives don't want.

On the flip-side, in the countries that migrants move away from, evidence suggests the shrinking labor supply pushes wages up as the supply of labor falls. One study estimated the effect of emigration from Mexico to be worth about an 8 percent raise for low-income workers who stay in Mexico. On net, then, research finds that more migration boosts incomes across the global economy.

From an economic-development perspective, there is another worry about migration: "brain drain." The workers who leave a country for better job opportunities naturally tend to be the most skilled. However, in a 2011 paper, John Gibson and David McKenzie concluded that lowering barriers to migration might actually *increase* the number of skilled workers in poorer countries. It makes sense, when you think about it: If workers in a low-income country know that it's possible to migrate, they may be more motivated to obtain crucial skills that would qualify them for jobs abroad. Not everyone in the end decides to move away—so the domestic economy ends up with more highly skilled workers as a result. This opens up the possibility of "brain gain" instead of "brain drain."

Economist Michael Clemens has done the math and found that removing just 5 percent of barriers to the movement of workers between countries has the power to lift income around the world by trillions of dollars. Overall, this 5 percent reduction would have more of an effect than removing all existing tariffs, quotas, and barriers to capital movement around the world. The impact of making migration easier could dwarf anything foreign aid can hope to achieve.

Sources: Dean Yang, "Migrant Remittances," *Journal of Economic Perspectives* 25, no. 3 (Summer 2011), pp. 129–152, http://pubs.aeaweb.org/doi/pdfplus/10.1257/jep.25.3.129; John Gibson and David McKenzie, "The Development Impact of a Best Practice Seasonal Worker Policy," Policy Research Working Paper, Impact Evaluation Series No. 48 (November 1, 2010), http://www.wds.worldbank.org/external/default/WDSContentServer/IW3P/IB/2010/11/30/000158349_20101130131212/Rendered/PDF/WPS5488.pdf; Michael Clemens; "Economics and Emigration: Trillion Dollar Bills on the Sidewalk," Center for Global Development Working Paper no. 264 (August 2011).

✓ CONCEPT CHECK

☐ What do development economists mean by "institutions"? **[LO 19.4]**

☐ What are the three types of industrial policy named in this section? **[LO 19.5]**

☐ What are remittances and how do they promote development? **[LO 19.6]**

What Can Aid Do?

Foreign aid has long been seen as part of economic development, although a controversial part. Taxes in many countries go to provide aid to the poor around the world. Many citizens in these countries also give money to private charities such as Heifer International, CARE, Save the Children, and church-based organizations. In fact, private donations are larger than the entire budget for official foreign aid provided by the United States.

Why is foreign aid often the central focus of development efforts? It has direct intuitive appeal:

- If people are poor, then surely money would help make life a little easier.
- Are children not going to school? Why not give families money so that they don't have to choose between work and school?
- Are roads full of potholes, making it costly and difficult to get to markets and jobs? Why not help governments build and repair them?

These donations can be very important, whether in easing hunger in famine-ravaged areas or providing funding to would-be entrepreneurs. The problem is how to make these funds go to the best uses. With many examples of misuse and waste, donating money often seems like a very unsure enterprise. Later in the chapter, we'll discuss how development economists are helping to discover what works—so that these donations can provide the most bang for their buck.

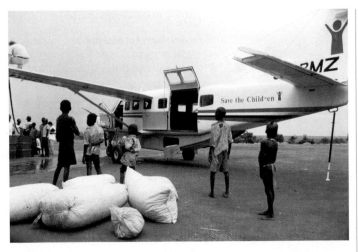

Children in Sudan look on as food and supplies are delivered by Save the Children, an international relief and development nonprofit organization.
© Mike Goldwater/Alamy

Perspectives on foreign aid

LO 19.7 Describe the aims of foreign aid, the role of poverty traps, the main institutions delivering aid, and criticisms of foreign aid.

Foreign aid got its start following World War II. In an unprecedented show of generosity, the United States distributed, as part of the Marshall Plan, $12 billion to help 16 European countries rebuild after the devastation of the war. In today's money (accounting for inflation between 1948 and now), the sum is the equivalent of over $100 billion. Of course, this aid wasn't entirely altruistic on the part of the United States. There was a good deal of strategic self-interest involved: It was seen as imperative to have strong European allies on the western borders of the Soviet Union.

Aid then shifted to the world's poorer regions. The 1947 Truman Doctrine pledged $650 million to help "free peoples who are resisting attempted subjugation by armed minorities or by outside pressures." In other words, the United States was willing to put forth money to spread development—and to try to halt the spread of communism. Russia, too, got involved in the aid business, trying to woo unaligned countries to join the communist bloc. During the "Cold War," a period of competition between the United States and Russia, many dams and bridges built in developing countries were the product of such altruism combined with political strategy.

The Cold War has been over since 1991. Yet foreign aid continues and is still largely dedicated toward building public goods. Public goods tend to be underprovided, considering the positive externalities they provide to the economy. This is especially true in countries that already lack means for collecting taxes and making capital investment. The result is a **financing gap**—the difference between the savings rate within an economy and the amount of investment needed to achieve sustainable growth. To plug that gap, a large fraction of aid

financing gap
the difference between the savings rate within an economy and the amount of investment needed to achieve sustainable growth

---

FIGURE 19-3

Official development assistance   In absolute terms, the amount of official development assistance (ODA) has steadily increased; over 50 years, the amount of money given by OECD countries in aid has tripled. Despite the 0.7 percent of gross national income (GNI) target set in the 1970s, the amount of ODA as a percent of the GNI has fallen and is not even half of this target.

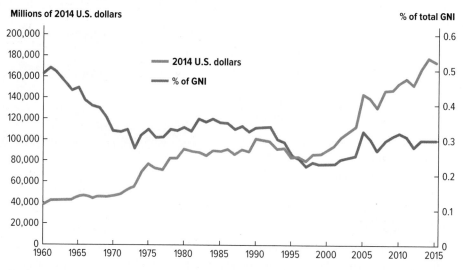

Source: Total flows by donor (ODA), http://stats.oecd.org/Index.aspx?ThemeTreeId=3#

goes toward building schools, health care systems, and infrastructure networks. For much of the history of foreign aid, the financing gap has been a driving force in decisions about how much to give.

In 2002, at the Monterrey Conference on Financing for Development, the leaders of the world's most industrialized countries made a major pledge: They would devote 0.7 percent of their gross national income (GNI, a combination of GDP plus net capital flow from abroad) to foreign aid, formally called *official development assistance* (ODA). For the United States alone, this pledge would mean at least $90 billion per year. Hopes were high for what that money could accomplish.

However, actual foreign aid budgets have fallen well below that goal. Of the 22 richest countries that made the pledge, so far only six have followed through to the extent promised. As of 2015, the United States devotes only about 0.3 percent of GNI to ODA, far below the 0.7 percent target and also below the average amount given by OECD countries. As you can see in Figure 19-3, the percentage has not been rising.[13]

Over the past 55 years, the amount given in aid has increased in dollar terms, but has fallen and leveled off in terms of aid *as a share of GDP*. Should the United States meet its pledge to give 0.7 percent? See the What Do You Think? box "Should the United States give more in foreign aid?" for more on this debate.

What Do You Think?

Should the United States give more in foreign aid?

In 2015, the U.S. government spent $31.08 billion on official development assistance, about 0.17 percent of the country's gross national income and less than 1 percent of the U.S. federal government's budget. In 2010, this number was even smaller. However, when the World Public Opinion survey asked U.S. voters in 2010 what portion of government spending they believe goes toward foreign aid, the average response was a full 25 percent. When the same voters were asked how much they thought would be "appropriate" to spend on international aid, the median answer was 10 percent—10 times more than we actually spend.

Does that mean most Americans would enthusiastically support candidates who promise to spend 10 times more on foreign aid? Not necessarily. According to a Pew Research Center poll conducted in January 2013, 48 percent of Americans would like to see foreign aid *reduced,* the largest share out of any of the other options presented. In comparison, just 24 percent of those surveyed would like to see cuts to the military and to domestic anti-poverty programs. Maybe most Americans feel at a gut level that however much the United States donates to the needy abroad, it's too much.

If the United States is one of the richest countries, does it have an obligation to be generous to less-fortunate countries? Ten percent of the U.S. budget would represent an incredible (and unrealistic) sum of money. A small increase in aid, however, could potentially have large effects. Aid advocates argue that many development programs can do a lot with relatively small increases in spending. The World Food Program, which provides badly needed food aid to areas of famine around the world, costs about $4 billion per year (which is a fairly modest cost given the size of aid budgets). Researchers estimate that a yearly investment of $7 billion would be enough to reduce the global prevalence of AIDS from 38 million cases to 1 million by 2050.

The other side of the argument centers on the idea that the United States should focus on problems at home first. As the United States faces growing public debt, it has to make tough decisions about which taxes to raise or programs to cut. Money spent on foreign aid could just as easily go toward addressing domestic problems. In March 2016, the U.S. government adopted a budget that cuts spending by over $3 trillion during a 10-year period in order to control the accumulating debt. This spending cut includes removing $2.5 trillion in funding from health care programs for low- to moderate-income people. Other cuts include $125 billion from the SNAP program (formerly knows as food stamps) and about $300 billion from other entitlement programs.

WHAT DO YOU THINK?

1. At a time when U.S. government programs are facing cuts, does it make sense to help provide health insurance in Tanzania, roads in Afghanistan, hospitals in Iraq, and agricultural development in Mozambique?
2. How should the U.S. government weigh (a) providing humanitarian assistance after natural disasters abroad versus (b) investing in the long-term development of poorer countries?

Sources: http://www.worldpublicopinion.org/pipa/articles/brunitedstatescanadara/670.php?lb=btda&pnt= 670&nid=&id; http://www.cbsnews.com/htdocs/pdf/poll_deficit_072909.pdf; http://www.washingtonpost.com/ blogs/federal-eye/post/whats-getting-cut-in-the-fy-2011-budget/2011/04/11/AFMIynLD_blog.html; http://www .people-press.org/2013/02/22/as-sequester-deadline-looms-little-support-for-cutting-most-programs; http://www .cbpp.org/research/federal-budget/congressional-budget-plans-get-two-thirds-of-cuts-from-programs-for-people.

Poverty traps and the Millennium Development Goals

Those who argue for ramping up foreign-aid budgets often assert that aid can help countries break out of poverty traps. A **poverty trap** is a self-reinforcing mechanism that causes the poor to stay poor. For instance, a poorly nourished and undereducated population is unlikely to have the energy or know-how to develop its economy. In the long run, it will struggle to earn enough to feed itself and educate its children. Foreign aid, the theory goes, can break this negative self-reinforcing mechanism and create a *virtuous cycle,* in which improvements build on improvements.

Some theories of economic development hold that escaping from poverty traps requires there to be simultaneous investments in a wide variety of sectors as well as improvement of institutions. One variant of this idea, championed by Columbia University economist Jeffrey Sachs in his book *The End of Poverty,* is known as the "big push."[14] The idea that concerted efforts in different sectors are necessary lay behind the United Nations' decision in 2000 to create eight *Millennium Development Goals.* These goals served as targets in all of the areas covered in Sachs's

poverty trap
a self-reinforcing mechanism that causes the poor to stay poor

"big push." The goals include establishing universal primary education and halving the number of people living on one dollar per day.[15] They were supposed to be achieved by 2015. Some were, and some were not. (Looking ahead, the United Nations agreed in 2015 on a set of 17 *Sustainable Development Goals* to meet by 2030.)

Of course, if a goal is not met, it doesn't mean the effort has been wasted. Even if universal primary education was not achieved by 2015, far more kids are going to school. As a result of this push, the number of children who were not in primary school fell from 100 million in 2000 to about 57 million in 2015.[16]

To showcase the "big push" idea, the United Nations and Columbia University's Earth Institute—headed by Jeffrey Sachs—together set up 13 "Millennium Villages," scattered around sub-Saharan Africa. The villages are intended to show what can happen with sustained and targeted investment. For $110 per person per year, new schools and clinics are built, sanitation improves, farmers receive improved varieties of seeds, and so on.

However, not everyone is convinced that such "big push" ideas are the right way for foreign aid to go. Critics argue that there is no guarantee the idea could work if rolled out globally, and it would be extremely expensive to try. They suggest other, cheaper ways to kick-start economic development, such as a focus on setting up better institutions or improving the quality of credit or insurance markets.

The major distributors of aid

How do governments of wealthy countries give their foreign aid? Much of it is channeled through national development agencies or sectors of foreign-affairs ministries. The *United States Agency for International Development (USAID)* serves this purpose in the United States. About $20 billion of the $31 billion allocated by the United States toward official development assistance funds USAID, which works to improve economic growth, trade, and agriculture, among other things.[17]

World Bank
a multinational organization dedicated to providing financial and technical assistance to developing countries

Other resources are channeled through international institutions. About $2.3 billion per year comes from the **World Bank**, a multinational organization dedicated to providing financial and technical assistance to developing countries. Formed in 1948 at the same Bretton Woods conference that spawned the International Monetary Fund, the World Bank is actually two development organizations:

- Much like a bank, the International Bank for Reconstruction and Development (IBRD) makes loans that are used by middle-income and creditworthy poor countries to finance a wide variety of investment projects.
- The International Development Association (IDA), on the other hand, more closely resembles what we think of as a traditional aid agency. From 2000 to 2010, IDA funded immunizations for 310 million children and clean water for 113 million. This work has continued since, on large-scale budgets that include $19 billion worth of commitments for the year ending June 2015.

United Nations Development Program (UNDP)
a global United Nations network that provides knowledge and resources to developing countries

Much development work is also conducted through a sprawling network of organizations under the **United Nations Development Program (UNDP)**—a global United Nations network that provides knowledge and resources to developing countries. In all, the UNDP is on the ground in 166 countries, operating a diverse set of projects, including everything from halting the spread of HIV/AIDS to developing democratic institutions. Within the UNDP, specialized organizations fund more targeted types of aid. The World Food Program, for example, spent over $4.2 billion in aid in 2015, 86 percent of which went toward fighting hunger in famine-ravaged areas, as part of its Emergency Preparedness and Response program.[18] Some government aid is also funneled through private, nonprofit organizations such as Heifer, CARE, and Save the Children.

Problems with foreign aid

With such a large system of aid, it's not surprising that not everyone is on board with the idea of doling out billions of dollars to poor countries around the world. It's not hard to find these critics—including some notable economists—who believe that aid can be inefficient and even counterproductive. Jean-Claude Duvalier, president of Haiti from 1971 to 1986, lived a fantastically lavish lifestyle while ordinary Haitians lived in intense poverty. Duvalier would regularly showcase Haiti's poor to international donors and then divert much of the resulting aid (one estimate is 80 percent) into his personal bank account.

Foreign aid is now tracked more carefully than it was in Duvalier's day, and agencies and governments now require a greater degree of accountability. But problems still persist. An intriguing insight was provided in 2011 when WikiLeaks, an organization that works to make classified documents public, released 250,000 classified cables from U.S. embassies. One of these cables revealed embezzlement and misplacement of funds from the UK Department for International Development (UK DfID) in projects around the world. In one example, almost $2 million given by the UK Ministry of Defense to "support peacekeeping" in Sierra Leone was instead embezzled by top generals in the Sierra Leone Ministry of Defense to buy plasma televisions and hunting rifles. In Kenya, the Ministry of Education admitted to losing $17.3 million worth of textbooks distributed through the "Free Education" program. In Uganda, officials managed to divert almost $27 million from an education fund.

Disappearing money may be one reason why, despite the spending of half a trillion dollars in ODA from 1970 to 1994, productivity growth in developing countries was essentially zero and economic growth not much more. Another big problem is that organizations such as the World Bank are not held accountable for what happens to funds once dispersed. Abhijit Banerjee notes the example of a World Bank computer kiosk program implemented in India, which the Bank trumpeted as a rousing success in its "Empowerment" sourcebook.[19] Many of these machines, however, were sitting uselessly in buildings that didn't have electricity or Internet connections. William Easterly, an economist at NYU who spent years working at the World Bank, argues that aid agencies typically have nebulous goals—such as promoting empowerment or economic growth or governmental reform—rather than being charged with completing a task that is specific and measurable. Without measurable goals, it's not surprising that organizations have little incentive to be sure that what they are doing actually works.

There are even stronger critics of aid than Easterly. Dambisa Moyo, in her book *Dead Aid*, argues that aid actually hurts the countries that receive it.[20] In many countries, aid is a substantial part of the budget. In Kenya, for example, aid averaged 10 percent of GDP from 1970 to 2010. Such large flows can have serious effects throughout the economy, notably crowding out domestic investment. When foreign aid flows in, it also has to be traded for local currency; that currency trade bids up the price of the local currency and hurts the competitiveness of the local export sector.

Aid can be particularly counterproductive when it involves trucking in goods for free or at highly discounted prices. Such aid is known as *goods-in-kind donations*. When aid agencies or governments distribute food, clothing, or other materials, they are giving goods in kind. To see the possible side-effects of well-intentioned donations, see the From Another Angle box "In Zambia, did the Steelers win Super Bowl XLV?"

From Another Angle

In Zambia, did the Steelers win Super Bowl XLV?

Before the confetti from Super Bowl XLV was swept away, the victorious players for the Green Bay Packers donned T-shirts emblazoned with the words "Super Bowl Champions." Of course, the Packers hadn't waited until *after* the game to have those T-shirts printed; instead, they had thousands printed beforehand, in case they won. So did the losing side, the Pittsburgh Steelers.

But as soon as the Steelers lost the game, their shirts became pretty much worthless. Who's going to buy a shirt that says the wrong team won? The NFL and a charity called World Vision

(continued)

came up with a solution: Instead of letting the T-shirts sit around, getting moldy in a warehouse, they could ship the T-shirts to Africa to give to the poor and needy.

Sounds great, right? Not if you're an African T-shirt maker. As it happens, T-shirts are not desperately needed in Africa. Africa has a solid homegrown and secondhand clothing market that supplies clothes at a fair price. Very few people go without T-shirts because they cannot afford them. An influx of Steelers T-shirts, instead of helping out, distorts the market: It hurts everyone from secondhand clothes marketers to local clothing makers, who obviously can't compete with free T-shirts.

That's not the only problem with the idea of shipping all those Steelers T-shirts to Africa. Shipping costs money. One particularly glaring example of this is the *One Million Shirts* campaign, started by a young entrepreneur. In order to cover the shipping charges for the one million shirts he planned to send to Africa, the founder asked for a dollar along with each shirt. While this sounds noble, the plan comes with a considerable opportunity cost. Is shipping unneeded shirts to Africa really the best way to spend $1 million? Would it be better to spend that money on, say, buying life-saving drugs or mosquito nets? In the end, the program was shut down after a firestorm of criticism.

The lesson is that it takes more than good intentions to solve the pressing issues of development. If good intentions were all it took, aid would have lifted everyone out of poverty long ago.

Sources: http://www.freakonomics.com/2011/02/15/what-happens-to-all-those-super-bowl-t-shirts-a-guest-post-by-dean-karlan/; http://www.nber.org/papers/w17456.pdf?new_window=1; http://www.time.com/time/world/article/0,8599,1987628,00.html.

Do these problems mean all aid should be stopped? Not necessarily. The lesson may be that more effort needs to go into improving the weak governments that embezzle aid or fail to use it productively. This idea was tested by economists Craig Burnside at Duke University and David Dollar, now at the U.S. Treasury Department. They found that in the decades of the 1980s and 1990s:

- Countries with sound fiscal, monetary, and trade policies and strong rule of law, combined with large amounts of aid, grew GDP at 1 percent.
- Countries with bad policy and high amounts of aid saw GDP shrink by 1 percent over the same time period.[21]

In fact, for countries with "bad" policy, aid was actually a detriment to growth. The example of Duvalier's Haiti at the beginning of this section suggests why: With aid flowing in to embezzle, Duvalier had little incentive to work to improve Haiti's economy because such improvements would reduce or eliminate aid.

The research behind the Dollar and Burnside study has been questioned (it turns out that more recent data do not show the same patterns). Nevertheless, their logic has spurred governments and aid organizations to think harder about links between aid and policy. In 2004, the United States created the Millennium Challenge Corporation to give cash to "worthy" governments. To qualify, these governments have to meet 17 requirements, including ruling justly, tamping down corruption, and maintaining a stable economy. So far, the Millennium Challenge Corporation has given out $11 billion in arrangements called "compacts" to 26 countries.[22]

Impact investing

LO 19.8 Understand how impact investing provides a new tool for creating social impact.

Most thinking about foreign aid has little to do with business. But businesses, after all, are extremely good at generating new products, producing at the right scale, marketing, and creating efficient supply chains. Those are the exact qualities needed to solve some of the toughest social and economic problems.

Private investors and institutions are supporting this new breed of socially minded businesses through an idea called impact investing. **Impact investing** involves investing money in firms to generate both financial and social returns. In some ways, it's an alternative to foreign aid, though in fact the two ideas can work together. The firms that receive the impact-investing funds are called "social businesses." They are involved in all kinds of endeavors from building cheap but effective private schools in the slums of Nairobi, to hospitals that serve the poor for free in South India.

The guiding idea behind impact investing is simple: Markets can be powerful tools to promote human development, but not if investors are interested only in a quick financial return.[23] Impact investors, who may be foundations, wealth managers, private managers, or nonprofit organizations, are willing to be more patient and take greater risks. They sometimes accept lower financial returns as long as they're convinced that their money is being used to create social change.

Solar-powered lighting makes things we take for granted in the United States, like studying at night and charging a cell phone, much easier to do.
© Mark Boulton/Alamy

One pioneering example of impact investing is the Acumen Fund, a "nonprofit global venture fund" that invests only in businesses that aim for social impact. Since its start in 2001, it has invested more than $101 million in health, housing, water, energy, education, and agriculture businesses across East Africa, West Africa, Latin America, India, and Pakistan. Among the firms supported by the Acumen Fund—to the tune of $1.5 million—is d.light design, which sells lanterns that produce light using solar energy. One out of four people in the world does not have electricity. The solar lanterns sold by d.light are a healthier solution than kerosene lanterns, which produce dangerous fumes.

Although the Acumen Fund's investments are a small fraction of the roughly $2 trillion in foreign direct investment that flows around the world each year, impact investing is growing quickly, particularly in Europe. Large banks are getting involved, as are universities: Colorado State University, for example, offers a Global Social and Sustainable Enterprise (GSSE) Master's in Business Administration. Stanford University's Entrepreneurial Design for Extreme Affordability class teaches students to design products to serve consumers at the lowest income level (and was the group that incubated the solar lantern behind d.light design).

impact investing
investing money in firms to generate both financial and social returns

How do we know what works?

> **LO 19.9** Explain the need for impact evaluation and analyze the role of randomized controlled trials in measuring impact.

There is no shortage of ideas for how to promote economic development. The Millennium Project, for one, offers 449 ways to reduce poverty. These ideas include hydrological monitoring systems, footpaths, road maintenance, electric power grids, women's empowerment initiatives, and industrial parks. But because resources are limited, governments and aid agencies have to make some tough choices about which policies would be the best in reducing poverty. In short, *how do we know what works?*

For most of the twentieth century, development efforts proceeded on a trial-and-error basis. Certain strategies were tried. If they seemed to work, they were kept; if they looked like glaring failures, they were scrapped. The trouble is, many of the failures weren't glaring enough. Often, aid agencies simply couldn't be sure whether a particular strategy had helped or hurt.

In recent years, some development economists have started to argue against charging forward with ideas that might or might not work. Instead they promote a more informed approach by rigorously evaluating the impact of development programs and policies.

Evaluations

Impact evaluation entails answering one seemingly simple question: How did people's lives change after a program or policy, compared with how they would have changed without it? This question would be easy to answer if everything else were held constant except the program or policy—but that's not the case in the complexities of the real world.

Consider the challenge of enrolling kids in school and ensuring they learn while they are there. To achieve those goals, there are many options and promising programs:

- For example, because schools in developing countries often have to make do with old, battered learning materials, one strategy is to provide students with better textbooks.

- Another strategy might be providing kids with school uniforms. Even when schooling itself is free, many schools require students to wear uniforms; when this is an expense that families cannot afford, their kids don't go to school.

At first glance, it seems as if it would be easy to evaluate efforts like these—just measure the test scores of kids in schools who receive the textbooks or the uniforms. If they're higher than before, great; if not, then back to the drawing board. Unfortunately, that type of evaluation is far from fool-proof. Beyond the question of whether the tests measure learning in a meaningful way, how do we know that the better test scores are not the result of something else? What if there's been an especially good harvest this year, so kids are learning better because they're no longer hungry while at school? In that case, we might be mistaken in thinking the textbooks are making the difference, and we'd keep pouring money into buying more textbooks when it could be put to better use elsewhere.

randomized controlled trial (RCT)
a method that randomly assigns subjects into control and treatment groups in order to assess the causal link from an intervention to specific outcomes

One way to avoid evaluation problems is by using **randomized controlled trials**, or **RCTs** for short. Randomized controlled trials randomly assign people into groups in order to focus on the impact of a particular intervention. Some of the stories told in this book, such as the one about giving out mosquito nets to protect from malaria (see the "Paying for bednets" box in Chapter 4, "Elasticity"), have been the result of such randomized controlled trials.

How could we use the idea of RCTs to know the true impact of providing more textbooks on test scores? We could select 100 similar schools and divide them into two groups of 50 at random. The first group doesn't get the textbooks; the second group does. If it's the textbooks making the difference, then schools in the so-called *treatment group* (the one that receives the textbooks) will do better than those in the *control group*. The key to the process is dividing the schools at random: The two groups should be similar on average before the study, so any factor other than the treatment itself should affect them equally. The RCT doesn't completely control for other variables that could possibly affect schools' performance, but it's a start.

Evaluations using the RCT method can give surprising results. It turns out if you want to boost school attendance, there's something you can buy and give out that's sometimes more effective than either textbooks or uniforms—deworming pills. Worms are tiny, parasitic organisms that cause chronic sickness that keeps kids out of school. The parasites were once common in parts of the United States, and they are still common in other countries. One study in Kenya found that, overall, a deworming program led to a 7.5 percent gain in primary school participation. Deworming pills are also far cheaper than textbooks or uniforms, costing just 50 cents per child per year. In comparison, the state-run *Oportunidades* (previously called *Progresa*) safety-net program in Mexico, which links cash benefits for families to activities such as getting kids vaccinated and sending them to school, costs many times this amount.[24] (Note that programs like Oportunidades also have other goals, not just increasing school attendance.)

Figure 19-4 shows the results from an RCT study of various programs intended to increase years of education. The figure shows that there is one intervention that is even more cost-effective than deworming. When researchers crunched the numbers of the program costs versus how effective they were at increasing school enrollment, they found that a very simple program scored highest. That program involves simply informing parents of the potential benefits of giving their children an education. Many of these parents in parts of the developing world may never have attended school themselves. Explaining the benefits of education turned out to be by far the most effective intervention, resulting in 20 extra "child-years" of education for every $100 spent.

FIGURE 19-4

Impact of programs intended to increase years of education   Evaluations allow researchers to compare the cost-effectiveness of various programs. Telling parents about the benefits of education ("Information on returns") was by far the most effective intervention, and resulted in 20 extra "child-years" of education for every $100 spent. Deworming is also very cost-effective. Although other programs were also effective at increasing schooling, they were not as cost-effective as the others.

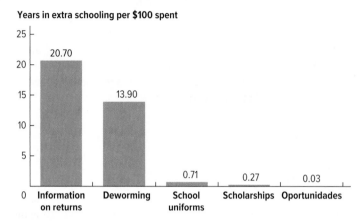

Source: https://www.povertyactionlab.org/policy-lessons/education/improving-student-participation.

Thanks to randomized controlled trials, policy-makers and program managers can more confidently channel resources to approaches that work and are cost-effective. Two organizations are dedicated to this research: One is the Abdul Latif Jameel Poverty Action Lab (J-PAL), founded by economists at MIT and Harvard. The other is Innovations for Poverty Action (IPA), a nonprofit organization started by Dean Karlan (one of the authors of this book). Many other organizations and researchers have followed their lead in using RCTs to investigate sectors as varied as microfinance, education, health, agriculture, charitable giving, corruption, and social capital. Thanks to rigorous evaluations, the remedial education program we described earlier in this chapter, for example, is now being scaled up in Ghana, with the aim of reaching thousands of schools.

This is not to say that these organizations have found the solution to global poverty. Like so many other tools, RCTs have challenges and limitations. Some questions, like the effect on economic development of changing monetary policy, simply can't be evaluated with an RCT. Even for those programs that can be evaluated, it's possible that the observed effects will change if the intervention is repeated on another continent or even in different areas of a country. And often it's hard to tell from an RCT exactly why the intervention worked or failed.

Still, using economic theory to help design experiments, and replicating experiments at different times and in different places, can be critical in moving knowledge forward. Along with other kinds of analysis, RCTs are helping to build knowledge, piece by piece, which is already pointing to some seemingly small interventions that can make large differences.

✓CONCEPT CHECK

- ☐ How do financing gaps justify foreign aid? **[LO 19.7]**
- ☐ How many countries pledged to participate in official development assistance? How many of them actually gave the amount promised? **[LO 19.7]**
- ☐ What are the Millennium Development Goals? **[LO 19.7]**
- ☐ Why might goods-in-kind donations cause problems for local producers? **[LO 19.7]**
- ☐ How does impact investing differ from foreign aid? **[LO 19.8]**
- ☐ What is a randomized controlled trial? **[LO 19.9]**

Conclusion

Although the work needed to put an end to global poverty may seem daunting, major strides have been made and continue to be made. Most obviously, decades of growth in the Chinese economy have lifted millions of people out of poverty. What worked for China was the product of a time and place that can't simply be bottled and shipped to other regions. Yet there are hopeful signs of improvements elsewhere, including Africa. Around the African continent, vigorously contested, democratic elections are taking place, and some countries are posting impressive growth figures.

Progress is being made through different mixes of good governance, aid, strengthened institutions, investment, and careful testing of what works and what does not among aid programs. While there is a long way to go, progress like this can promote the expansion of capabilities and help expand markets that truly work for the world's poor.

Key Terms

capability, p. 523

institutions, p. 527

industrial policy, p. 529

clusters, p. 530

World Trade Organization (WTO), p. 530

financing gap, p. 533

poverty trap, p. 535

World Bank, p. 536

United Nations Development Program (UNDP), p. 536

impact investing, p. 539

randomized controlled trial (RCT), p. 540

Summary

LO 19.1 Explain how the capabilities approach relates to economic development.

Development is a field of economics that studies the causes and nature of international poverty and human development. One way to think about development is known as the capabilities approach, developed by Amartya Sen. The goal of development is to increase human capabilities. There are many different types of capabilities, including very basic rights to health and education as well as other concepts like self-expression and reputation.

LO 19.2 Explain the relationship between economic growth and economic development.

The ideas of economic growth and development are similar but not identical. Economic growth can promote development. After all, when people have more money, you would expect them to spend more on improving their health and educating their children. There is general agreement, though, that the fundamentals of economic growth, including such elements as property rights, the rule of law, and human capital, will spark development.

LO 19.3 Describe how improvements to education and health can develop human capital.

By providing access to more and better schools and clinics, countries can develop human capital. Many countries are now mandating universal primary education and providing health insurance on the cheap to make great strides in basic human capital development. These efforts must be of high quality to be effective, though. Human capital is an important part of economic development, as it allows for more productive workers and greater economic growth. Improvements in human capital can also promote capacities development as people are able to lead more complete (better educated and healthier) lives.

LO 19.4 Explain the importance of institutions and good governance in development economics.

Development often takes root in places where there are strong institutions. Institutions are human-devised constraints that shape human interactions. In contrast, organizations are groups of people that act according to those constraints. Several institutions are important for development, including a strong system of property rights, the rule of law, and a government capable of implementing good policy.

LO 19.5 Evaluate the role of industrial policy and clusters in development.

Governments have turned to industrial policy in an attempt to favor some industries over others. Two popular types of industrial policy include import substitution and export-led industrialization. An alternative industrial policy is clustering, which promotes networks of interdependent firms, universities, and customers focusing on a specific type of good.

LO 19.6 Evaluate how migration and remittances promote development.

Every year, millions of people leave their home countries and villages to migrate in search of better-paying jobs. The money they send home to their families, called remittances, represents a large and growing financial flow around the world. As a result, governments and aid agencies work to make sure that these remittances best help the families back home escape poverty.

LO 19.7 Describe the aims of foreign aid, the role of poverty traps, the main institutions delivering aid, and criticisms of foreign aid.

Over the past 55 years, the amount given in foreign aid has increased in dollar terms but has fallen and leveled off as a share of GDP. Those who argue for ramping up foreign-aid budgets often assert that aid can help countries break out of *poverty traps*. Others suggest different ways to kick-start economic development, such as a focus on setting up better institutions or improving the quality of credit or insurance markets. Much of the foreign aid governments do give is channeled through national development agencies like USAID, or through global organizations like the World Bank and the United Nations. Although foreign aid can provide money needed to finance developments in infrastructure, clinic and school construction, and other important measures that simply would not happen without outside assistance, critics point to cases in which foreign aid has been a destabilizing force that was wasted at best, and destructive at worst.

LO 19.8 Understand how impact investing provides a new tool for creating social impact.

Most thinking about foreign aid has little to do with business. But private investors and institutions are supporting socially minded businesses through *impact investing,* which involves investing money in firms to generate both financial and social returns. Markets can be powerful tools to promote human development, and impact investors sometimes accept lower financial returns as long as they're convinced their money is being used to create social change.

LO 19.9 Explain the need for impact evaluation and analyze the role of randomized controlled trials in measuring impact.

Throughout history, ideas about how to spur development have mostly proceeded on a trial-and-error basis. Instead of wasting money on programs that may or may not work, economists have begun to evaluate the impact of various development programs. Impact evaluation tries to answer the question of how a particular program or policy changed people's lives. A *randomized controlled trial (RCT)* is one way to answer that question; it compares a treatment group with a control group to show the effect of a program.

Review Questions

1. Are capabilities and utility the same thing? If so, why do economists use two different terms for the same concept? If not, explain the difference, in terms of both their definitions and when each is best used in economic analysis. **[LO 19.1]**

2. Determine whether each of the following is true or false. **[LO 19.1]**
   a. The chance to see a musical is an example of a capability.
   b. The freedom to practice religion is not a capability because it is not directly related to economic development.
   c. Economists will make the same conclusions and recommendations using the utility-maximization approach as they will using the capabilities approach.
   d. The capabilities approach works better for analyzing what's best for society, while the utility-maximization approach works better for analyzing what's best for an individual.

3. Are economic growth and economic development the same? Why or why not? **[LO 19.2]**

4. Does economic growth lead to development? Or does the causation run the other way, with economic development leading to growth? Explain. **[LO 19.2]**

5. How can health and education work together to spur economic development? What does this imply about the best way to spend aid funds with the goal of increasing educational attainment in a developing nation? **[LO 19.3]**

6. Explain how better health care in a developing nation, such as increasing the number of immunized children, can have economic effects beyond fewer sick kids. **[LO 19.3]**

7. "I'm thinking about writing a paper for class on development economics," your friend tells you over lunch. "I'm going to focus on important institutions like government bodies and economic agencies." Is your friend using the term *institutions* correctly? Why or why not? **[LO 19.4]**

8. How can capital be considered "dead," and what do we mean by making this capital "alive"? **[LO 19.4]**

9. International trade is associated with economic growth and development—open economies tend to grow faster than closed economies, all else equal. Given this information, should a nation seeking to grow and develop faster use the method of import substitution or export-led growth? How would each of these two methods affect GDP through its net exports component? **[LO 19.5]**

10. Determine whether each of the following is an example of import substitution, export-led growth, or clustering. **[LO 19.5]**

    a. The government gives a $50 million grant to a leading university to work with car manufacturers and to research new ways to produce more fuel-efficient vehicles.

    b. The government gives $50 million to a domestic car company to subsidize its shipping costs to other countries.

    c. The government enacts a tariff on all cars imported from abroad.

11. How can emigration help the home economy in terms of income? Are the benefits of migration on income limited to those who actually migrate? Why or why not? **[LO 19.6]**

12. How does emigration affect wages and income in the migrant's country of origin? In the country the migrant immigrates to? **[LO 19.6]**

13. Say that the United States is considering giving direct aid to a nation run by a dictator known for his lavish lifestyle while the nation's citizens suffer through a terrible famine. What might be a problem with giving aid to this nation? Name at least one way to fix the problem. **[LO 19.7]**

14. What are goods-in-kind donations, and how can they hurt the economies they're meant to help? **[LO 19.7]**

15. How does impact investment differ from traditional foreign aid and traditional financial investment? **[LO 19.8]**

16. Explain briefly how you could set up an RCT to evaluate whether providing free breakfasts to elementary-school students helps them learn. **[LO 19.9]**

17. List three shortcomings of using an RCT to evaluate the success of a given economic program. **[LO 19.9]**

Problems and Applications

1. In a small town in the midwestern United States lives a drug dealer and manufacturer who supplies the illegal, addictive drug crystal meth. The drug dealer insists that making and selling the drug is what gives him the most satisfaction among any possible use of his time and resources. Using the utility-maximization approach, should he be allowed to continue supplying the drug? What about with the capabilities approach? Explain your answer. **[LO 19.1]**

2. Professor Bucks and Professor Liber are having a debate about the role of economic growth in contributing to economic development. Professor Bucks contends that economic growth is the only thing to consider in development, as people's utility is directly related to their income. Professor Liber agrees that income is directly related to development but says that there are other things to consider. Given what we've learned in this chapter, pick the option that is most correct according to the capabilities approach. **[LO 19.1]**

    a. Professor Bucks is correct because increases in income are the only way to measure economic development.

    b. Professor Bucks is correct because capabilities always increase when income does.

    c. Professor Liber is correct because income is unrelated to capabilities, which are the most important factor in development.

    d. Professor Liber is correct because income is related to development, but it is not the only contributor to capabilities.

3. Table 19P-1 shows the levels and annual growth rates of economic indicators for two countries, Nationavia and Countrystan. Assume these growth rates will remain constant for the foreseeable future. Use these data to determine whether each of the following statements is true, false, or indeterminable. **[LO 19.2]**

    a. The theory of income convergence (that national incomes in poor countries will "catch up" to those in wealthier countries) holds for Nationavia and Countrystan.

    b. Countrystan has higher levels of human capital than Nationavia.

    c. Inequality is greater in Nationavia.

    d. In 10 years, it's likely that Countrystan will have higher levels of human capital than Nationavia.

4. In Nation A, GDP per capita is $21,000 and is growing annually at a rate of 1.4 percent. The average citizen in Nation A lives for 51 years, and this figure is growing at 6 percent per year. Additionally, the average person in Nation A has 9 years of education, growing annually at

TABLE 19P-1

Indicator	Level	Growth rate (%)
GDP per capita—Nationavia	$50,000	3.1
GDP per capita—Countrystan	$30,000	3.0
Average years of education per capita—Nationavia	15 years	2.0
Average years of education per capita—Countrystan	5 years	8.0
Life expectancy—Nationavia	72 years	0.5
Life expectancy—Countrystan	56 years	1.8

5.1 percent, and 60 percent of Nation A's population is currently literate, growing at a rate of 2 percent.

In Nation B, GDP per capita is $40,000 and is growing annually at a rate of 0.8 percent. The average citizen in Nation B lives for 68 years, and this value is growing at 2 percent per year. The average person in Nation B has 10.5 years of education, increasing 2 percent annually, while 78 percent of its population is literate, a figure growing at 0.5 percent annually.

Which nation is experiencing more economic growth? Which is wealthier? Which currently has more capabilities for its citizens? And which is experiencing more economic development? **[LO 19.2]**

5. Imagine that you are the leader of a low-income nation. You have identified lack of access to health care as a major contributor to your nation's low income, and the United States has offered to help by providing funds to build more health clinics. Will this solve the problem? Why or why not? If it won't, what's one alternative to using these foreign aid dollars to build clinics? **[LO 19.3]**

6. While listening to the radio on the way to school, you hear a politician from a small, low-income nation say the following: "Over the last five years, there has been a 10 percent increase in the number of children attending school full time. We can expect to see these children grow up to be more productive workers because their human capital has increased." Is the politician's statement true, false, or somewhere in between? Explain your answer. **[LO 19.3]**

7. Classify each of the following as an institution or organization. **[LO 19.4]**
   a. The United States Agency for International Development, a U.S. government agency that channels aid abroad.
   b. The United Nations Development Program.
   c. The UN Declaration of Human Rights, an agreement among members of the United Nations regarding the rights of individuals.
   d. The United Nations.
   e. The Sarbanes-Oxley Act (SOX), which established rules for how publicly traded firms must report information in their financial documents.

8. A given nation has a good titling system, but theft of productive equipment is rampant, with few consequences for those who steal. What is the term development economists use for what's lacking in this economy? What effect will this lack likely have on economic growth and economic development? Give one way to improve the situation. **[LO 19.4]**

9. The small, landlocked nation of Wheatleyton is just starting to develop an agricultural sector. Firms in this sector appeal to the government to temporarily limit imports of agricultural goods from other nations with more experience and larger scale, resulting in import prices so low domestic firms can't compete. What is this desired policy called? What problems are associated with it, and how can we reduce them? **[LO 19.5]**

10. The small nation of Movieheim wants to develop a film industry. It is considering two options for doing so:
    Option A: Reimburse relocation expenses for firms and give tax breaks to acting schools, film studios, digital artists, etc., to encourage them to work together and share ideas.
    Option B: Make the purchase and exhibition of foreign films illegal for the next 10 years.
    What would development economists call each of these options? Which is more likely to encourage long-term economic development, and why? **[LO 19.5]**

11. Consider separately each of the following hypothetical scenarios about South Africa and answer the included questions. Assume in each case that medical school has an 80 percent success rate—in other words, 80 percent of people who attend medical school graduate and become doctors. **[LO 19.6]**
    a. No doctors are allowed to emigrate, and the number of people going to medical school is given by $D = 100,000 \times I$, where I is an index relating the income of doctors to those in other professions. If $I = 4$, how many students will go to medical school? How many more doctors will there be in South Africa?

b. The United States decides to offer visas for any doctors from South Africa. Additionally, I in the above equation changes to 10. Assume that 30 percent of doctors educated in South Africa immigrate to the United States. How many students will go to medical school? How many will become doctors? How many of those doctors will practice in South Africa, and how many will practice in the United States?

c. The United States decides to limit the number of doctors from South Africa who can obtain visas to no more than 10 percent of those graduating from medical school. Assume that I remains at 10. How many students will go to medical school? How many will become doctors? How many of those doctors will practice in South Africa, and how many will practice in the United States?

12. Table 19P-2 shows the size of various flows to developing countries in 2009 and 2010 in billions of dollars. **[LO 19.7]**

a. Rank each of the flows in 2010 as a percentage of ODA (official development assistance) in 2009, from highest to lowest.

b. Rank each of the flows in terms of their growth rates from 2009 to 2010, from highest to lowest.

13. The following equation provides an alternative calculation to determine a developing country's financing gap:

$$FG = (A \times g) - I_D$$

In this equation, FG is the financing gap; A is a variable that captures the country's starting income together with its ability to turn investment into growth (expressed in dollars); g is the targeted growth rate; and I_D is the amount of domestic investment currently in the economy. Assume that A = $50,000,000,000, g = 0.08, and I_D = $500,000,000, and answer the questions that follow. **[LO 19.7]**

TABLE 19P-2

Financial flow	Amount in 2009 (billions of $)	Amount in 2010 (billions of $)
Official development assistance	128	119
Foreign direct investment	510	573
Remittances	307	324

a. What is the size of the financing gap?

b. Assume that the population of the United States is 300 million. How much would each U.S. citizen have to pay to fill the financing gap?

c. What percentage of GDP per capita in the United States does your answer from (b) represent if GDP per capita is currently $45,000?

Now assume that the United States decides to donate the amount of the financing gap to the developing country as aid. Assume also that there are administrative and competitive costs associated with receiving aid. Specifically, 23 cents of every dollar spent on aid will go to administrative costs. Also, for every dollar received from abroad intended to be used for investment, 50 cents will be used for noninvestment purposes.

d. Calculate the real increase in investment dollars the aid from the United States will provide in the recipient country.

e. Calculate the new financing gap by subtracting the above from the financing gap you calculated in part (a).

14. The president of an organization specializing in foreign investment says the following at a shareholder meeting: "Our one-year program was a failure. We were hoping for a 6 percent return on our investment, but we got only 3 percent." Use the idea of impact investing to provide an alternative argument that the program was not a failure. **[LO 19.8]**

15. Table 19P-3 displays the results of a study on how to improve vaccination rates in a developing nation. The baseline numbers represent the rates of vaccination at the beginning of the study, while the endline numbers represent the rates of vaccination at the study's conclusion. Answer the following questions. **[LO 19.9]**

a. Which campaign(s) had a positive effect on vaccination rates in comparison to the control group?

b. Which campaign had the largest positive effect on vaccination rates in comparison to the control group?

c. Which campaign(s) had a negative effect on vaccination rates in comparison to the control group?

d. Which campaign(s) had no effect on vaccination rates in comparison to the control group?

16. Table 19P-4 displays the results of a study on how to improve vaccination rates in a developing nation. The baseline numbers represent the rates of vaccination at the beginning of the study, and the endline numbers represent the rates of vaccination at the study's conclusion. Rank the campaigns in order from most effective

TABLE 19P-3

Campaign	Vaccination rates (%)			
	Baseline, control	Baseline, treatment	Endline, control	Endline, treatment
Lectures	5	6	8	5
Free provision	5	4	8	8
Subsidy	5	5	8	10
Newspaper announcements	5	7	8	7

TABLE 19P-4

Campaign	Vaccination Rates (%)			
	Baseline, control	Baseline, treatment	Endline, control	Endline, treatment
Lectures	4	6	6	9
Free provision	4	7	6	8
Subsidy	4	5	6	9
Newspaper announcements	4	3	6	2

TABLE 19P-5

Campaign	Cost per person ($)
Lectures	10
Free provision	20
Subsidy	15
Newspaper announcements	5

to least effective. Then refer to Table 19P-5, which shows the cost per person of each campaign. Combining information from the two tables, rank the campaigns that resulted in an increase in vaccinations from high to low in terms of cost-effectiveness (based on treatment effect alone). **[LO 19.9]**

Endnotes

1. http://www.worldbank.org/en/news/press-release/2015/10/04/world-bank-forecasts-global-poverty-to-fall-below-10-for-first-time-major-hurdles-remain-in-goal-to-end-poverty-by-2030.

2. http://data.worldbank.org/indicator/NY.GDP.PCAP.CD.

3. http://blogs.ei.columbia.edu/2011/03/24/india-is-booming-so-why-are-nearly-half-of-its-children-malnourished-part-1/.

4. Jishnu Das and Jeffrey Hammer, "Strained Mercy: The Quality of Medical Care in Delhi," World Bank Policy Research Working Paper Series No. 3228 (2004).

5. Unpublished data from Innovations for Poverty Action.

6. Douglass C. North, "Institutions," *Journal of Economic Perspectives* 5, no. 1 (Winter 1991), pp. 97–112.

7. http://internationalpropertyrightsindex.org/introduction.

8. For evidence on the link between democracy and economic growth, see http://as.nyu.edu/docs/IO/2591/Development.pdf.

9. https://knoema.com/sijweyg/gdp-per-capita-ranking-2015-data-and-charts.

10. Michael Clemens, Claudio E. Montenegro, and Lant Pritchett, "The Place Premium: Wage Differences for Identical Workers across the U.S. Border," Center for Global Development Working Paper no. 148, July 2008.

11. https://travel.state.gov/content/dam/visas/Diversity-Visa/DVStatistics/DVApplicantEntrantsbyCountry%202013-2015.pdf.

12. Michael Clemens, "Economics and Emigration: Trillion Dollar Bills on the Sidewalk," Center for Global

Development Working Paper no. 264 (August 2011); and Lant Pritchett, *Let Their People Come* (Washington, DC: Center for Global Development, 2006).

13. The data in Figure 19-3 report *gross ODA,* which is the amount that the United States spends on ODA in a given year. Because the United States receives loan repayments from countries (due on loans made in previous years), the net outflow is smaller than gross ODA. Subtracting any loan repayments received yields *net ODA.* In 2015, net ODA provided by the United States was 0.17 percent of GNI.

14. Jeffrey Sachs, *The End of Poverty* (New York: Penguin Press, 2006).

15. http://www.unicef.org/publications/files/Children_and_the_MDGs.pdf.

16. http://www.undp.org/content/undp/en/home/librarypage/mdg/the-millennium-development-goals-report-2015.html.

17. https://www.usaid.gov/sites/default/files/documents/1869/USAIDFY2015DevelopmentBudgetFactSheet.pdf.

18. http://documents.wfp.org/stellent/groups/public/documents/reports/wfp284116.pdf.

19. Abhijit Banerjee, *Making Aid Work* (Cambridge, MA: MIT Press, 2007).

20. Dambisa Moyo, *Dead aid: Why Aid Is Not Working and How There Is a Better Way for Africa* (New York: Farrar, Straus and Giroux, 2009).

21. Craig Burnside and David Dollar, "Aid, Policies and Growth: Revisiting the Evidence," WB Policy Research Paper no. O-2834 (Washington, DC: World Bank, 2004).

22. https://www.fas.org/sgp/crs/row/RL32427.pdf.

23. Jonathan Morduch, "Not So Fast: The Realities of Impact Investing," *America's Quarterly,* Fall 2011, http://www.americasquarterly.org/not-so-fast-the-realities-of-impact-investing.

24. https://www.povertyactionlab.org/policy-lessons/education/improving-student-participation.

Guide
to Data Sources

Throughout this book . . . we've used data from a wide variety of sources to present theories on phenomena ranging from international aid to financial crises. Without accurate and timely data, we couldn't reliably say nearly as much about these issues.

Before recent advances in information technology, gathering data was much more cumbersome—and data sources were far less prevalent. Today, we have the opposite problem. The amount of data already collected is astounding. With so much data available, finding the right sources can seem like a challenge.

To help you dive into the real world of economics, we provide this guide to some of the most useful and widely used data sources for the economy. Since the quality of your data will have a big impact on the quality of any investigation in economics, you'll want to be sure you have the best data out there—and, more importantly, the correct data. Going to the right source can help you ensure that your data are from a trusted organization and up to date. (In the United States, the government is often the most reliable source.)

This short guide will introduce you to the sources that many economists use to answer thousands of different questions. In the sections that follow, we provide an overview of each source, including the organization's purpose and the data it hosts, and then we look at an example of how those data have been used. To gain experience using these sources, you'll need to explore each source on your own and learn how to manipulate the data as they appear on the site. To that end, we ask you to answer a few questions using the data you find.

National (United States) Data

Bureau of Economic Analysis (BEA)

http://bea.gov

Interactive database can be found at http://www.bea.gov/itable/index.cfm

The Bureau of Economic Analysis (BEA) is an agency within the U.S. Department of Commerce. Its mission is to promote "a better understanding of the U.S. economy by providing the most timely, relevant, and accurate economic accounts data in an objective and cost effective manner."

The BEA is one of the most widely cited sources for current economic news. Partly that's because it's responsible for publishing the granddaddy of all economic indicators, GDP. GDP is part of the National Income and Product Accounts, which give a broad overview of economic activity in the United States. The BEA publishes this information quarterly and houses historical data dating back to 1929.

A sample of the indicators you can find . . .

- GDP and its components
- Personal income and outlays
- Consumer spending
- Balance of payments
- Corporate profits
- Foreign direct investment

Note: When looking for information from the BEA (and other sources), be sure to look at the databases and not just the news releases. Only the databases will provide comprehensive information about the indicator over time.

TRY IT YOURSELF

√**APPLICATIONS**

Suppose you're an economic advisor to the president and are trying to gauge how well the economy is performing now in comparison to the last few years.

1. Find the historical database for seasonally adjusted real GDP and report the seasonally adjusted real GDP for the latest quarter available.
2. Use this same database to retrieve the quarterly data for GDP for the three most recent years in the database. Which quarter had the highest rate of GDP growth? Which quarter had the lowest? Graph these data over time.

√**PROBLEMS**

1. Does consumer spending in the United States tend to stay at the same levels throughout the year, or are there certain months in which it's higher than others?
2. Which countries have the most foreign direct investment in the United States? Where does the United States have the most foreign direct investment?

Federal Reserve Economic Data (FRED), Federal Reserve Bank of St. Louis

http://research.stlouisfed.org/fred2

The Federal Reserve Bank of St. Louis hosts FRED, a database of more than 82,000 U.S. and international economic indicators (time series) from 55 sources. It's the most inclusive, "one-stop shop" data source available for the U.S. economy.

The FRED website allows you to download, graph, track, and compare vast amounts of data covering a wide array of categories. Those include banking, business/fiscal, employment and population, exchange rates, financial data, foreign exchange intervention, GDP, interest rates, international data, monetary aggregates, prices, reserves and monetary base, U.S. regional data, and U.S. Trade and International Transaction data.

A sample of the indicators you can find . . .

- The federal funds rate
- Yield on Treasury bills
- Money supply

TRY IT YOURSELF

✓**APPLICATIONS**

Suppose you're an economist trying to examine how the Federal Reserve responds to various GDP growth rates in the economy.

1. Find the series for the monthly effective federal funds rate. (*Tip:* Use the search bar on the FRED home page.) What is the latest value for the effective federal funds rate? What was the value for the effective federal funds rate two years ago?
2. Now find the series for GDP growth. What is the average growth rate of annual GDP in the last two years?
3. Based on your answers to questions 1 and 2 (and lessons you learned from the macroeconomic chapters), do you think there's a relationship between the federal funds rate and GDP growth? If so, how would you describe that relationship?

✓**PROBLEMS**

1. What was the average personal savings rate in 1950? What is it today?
2. How much money is in circulation in the United States today, using M2?

U.S. Bureau of Labor Statistics (BLS)

http://www.bls.gov

The U.S. Bureau of Labor Statistics (BLS) is a government agency that is the primary source of statistics on employment and prices. Each month, it publishes an "Employment Situation Summary," which, among other statistics, gives an account of the number of unemployed people and the unemployment rate.

Labor statistics are of interest to a diverse crowd: from labor economists trying to understand the relationship between minimum wage and employment, to college graduates attempting to predict their employment prospects. Below is an example from the news that highlights the use of labor statistics.

U.S. Teens Struggle to Find Elusive Part-Time Jobs, Often Competing with Displaced Older Workers

AP; HARTFORD, Conn.—The economic turmoil that has left many Americans without work is having a disproportionate effect on teenage job-seekers, whose quest for entry-level positions often pits them against experienced older workers willing to take any job for a paycheck.

U.S. labor figures show the 2011 unemployment rate nationwide averaged just below 9 percent, but for job-seekers ages 16 to 19, it was almost 25 percent—the third consecutive year in that range, and with some cities recording rates far higher. . . .

Used with permission of The Associated Press. Copyright © 2013. All rights reserved.

A sample of the indicators you can find . . .

- Unemployment rate
- Consumer Price Index (CPI)
- Consumer spending
- Wages
- Worker productivity, workplace injuries, illnesses, and fatalities

TRY IT YOURSELF

✓ APPLICATION

Imagine you're advising a presidential candidate running against the incumbent. The candidate wants you to tell her about the employment situation, including specific information about whether certain parts of the population face higher unemployment rates than others do.

1. Find the latest Employment Situation Summary. When was it issued?
2. What was the unemployment rate for the last month? How did it compare to the unemployment rate for the month before that? Was it higher or lower?
3. Finally, look at the site's Table A-4, "Employment status of the civilian population 25 years and over by educational attainment." For the latest month available, what is the difference in the unemployment rate between those with a bachelor's degree and those without a high-school diploma?

✓ PROBLEMS

1. What is the highest rate of unemployment the United States has experienced in the past 20 years?
2. In the past 20 years, when did the Consumer Price Index have the fastest rate of annual increase?

Congressional Budget Office (CBO)

http://www.cbo.gov

The Congressional Budget Office (CBO) is a federal agency responsible for providing objective, nonpartisan analysis to assist Congress with budgetary decisions. Whenever you hear politicians argue over whose plan to improve the economy will cost more, it's a good bet that they'll mention a projection from the CBO. The Office is responsible for projecting the costs of government programs at the request of Congress. The CBO also provides regular reports to Congress on fiscal policy through the *Budget and Economic Outlook* and cost estimates of the president's budget through its *Analysis of the President's Budget.*

A sample of the indicators you can find . . .

- The federal deficit
- Federal spending
- Federal revenue

TRY IT YOURSELF

✓ APPLICATIONS

Imagine your professor has announced that the subject for a class debate is "Should the United States balance the budget?" You want to find the statistics that will back up your position.

1. Find the latest version of the *Budget and Economic Outlook* and navigate to the full document. Find the table titled "CBO's Baseline Budget Projections." What is the total deficit projected for this year in billions of dollars? What percentage of GDP does that represent?
2. According to the CBO's economic outlook, will the budget deficit increase, decrease, or remain the same over the next five years?

✓PROBLEMS

1. What is the projected shortfall in Social Security in 2050?
2. What is the projected budget deficit/surplus in 2025 as a percentage of GDP?

U.S. Census Bureau

http://www.census.gov

Interactive database can be found at http://factfinder2.census.gov/faces/nav/jsf/pages/index.xhtml

The U.S. Census Bureau is an agency within the Department of Commerce. The Bureau is responsible for conducting the United States Census, which attempts to collect very detailed information about all households in the United States every 10 years. These data provide a very clear picture of the changes and trends happening throughout America. In addition to the Census, the Bureau collects data every year through the American Community Survey and other sources.

A sample of the indicators you can find . . .

- Population
- Demographic information about households (age, sex, ethnicity)
- School enrollment
- Poverty
- Health insurance
- The number of businesses in a region
- The number of houses in a region

TRY IT YOURSELF

✓APPLICATIONS

Suppose you're a governor trying to determine whether your state's tax base will increase or decrease. As part of that effort, you want to know about population trends.

1. Find the two most recent population numbers for your state. How much did the population increase or decrease in the last decade?
2. Compare your state's population growth rate to the rate of population growth in the entire United States. Is the United States gaining population faster or slower than your state?

✓PROBLEMS

1. What is the state with the highest percentage of people living in poverty? With the lowest?
2. How many businesses are operating in your county?

International Data

The World Bank

http://databank.worldbank.org/data/home.aspx

The World Bank is an international financial institution that seeks to reduce poverty. As part of its efforts, it collects and analyzes statistics about economies around the world. Its World Development Indicators (WDI) are a widely cited source of statistics about development; its Global Development Finance indicators provide external debt and financial flows statistics for several countries. The bank publishes these two sources in an online database called the "World Data-Bank." The World DataBank catalogs indicators about a wide array of topics including income, education, health, gender, and the environment.

The World Bank's World Development Indicators are the most prominent source of data on development. Here's one example from economists at Yale, MIT, and Oxford who test the relationship between economic growth and human development.

Paths to Success: The Relationship Between Human Development and Economic Growth

Tavneet Suri, *MIT Sloan School of Management, Cambridge, MA, U.S.A.*

Michael A. Boozer and Gustav Ranis, *Yale University, New Haven, CT, U.S.A.*

Frances Stewart, *University of Oxford, Oxford, U.K.*

Accepted 26 August 2010. Available online 17 January 2011.

Summary

This paper explores the two-way relationship between economic growth (EG) and human development (HD). We develop panel data strategies to estimate the strength of these relationships and find that HD plays an essential role in determining growth trajectories (our measure of sustained growth). Not only is HD a final product in the sense that it measures basic human well-being but it is also a critical input into EG. Our findings illustrate the empirical relevance of endogenous growth, and are consistent with threshold effect models. Our results imply that successful policy requires an early focus on HD, not only because of its direct impact but also because of its feedback effect on sustaining EG.

Reprinted from *World Development*, Volume 39 Issue 4; Tavneet Suri, Michael A Boozer, Gustav Ranis, and Frances Stewart; *Paths to Success: The Relationship Between Human Development and Economic Growth*, pp. 506–522. Copyright 2011, with permission from Elsevier.

A sample of the indicators you can find . . .

- Government expenditure per student
- Urban population growth
- Real interest rate
- Net migration
- Gini coefficients
- Official development assistance

TRY IT YOURSELF

✓APPLICATIONS

Imagine you're an entrepreneur trying to start a global company and are looking for the best country in which to start it.

1. Navigate to the "Doing Business" database and select it. Under the "Country" drop-down, choose "Select all." Under the "Series" drop-down, scroll down to the data series called "Ease of doing business index." Select that series, and click on the small icon at the left to see metadata about the series, including a "Long definition" of the series. In your *own* words, what does the ease of doing business index represent?

2. Close the metadata window and open the "Time" drop-down, then choose "Select all." You should now have selected variables for Country, Series, and Time. Click on "Table" (at the top of the screen) to see your choices in table view. On the left-hand side of the page, switch to the "Layout" tab and set the options that will format your table with Country in rows, Series on the page, and Time in columns. Based on the latest available year in the table, what country has the highest ease of doing business? What country has the lowest?

3. What country made the most progress in the index from the earliest year available to the latest year available?

✓PROBLEMS

1. What country has the lowest literacy rate? What is that rate?
2. Which region in the world has the highest GDP per capita? The lowest?

CIA World Factbook

https://www.cia.gov/library/publications/the-world-factbook/index.html

Despite the sound of its title, the CIA's World Factbook is not a book for spies, filled with hidden facts about the inner workings of foreign governments. Rather, The World Factbook provides information on the history, people, government, economy, geography, communications, transportation, military, and transnational issues for 267 world entities. (Of course, spies could use it if they wanted to know any of that information.) If you're looking for the population of Armenia, or the percentage of people working in the agricultural sector in Vietnam, The World Factbook is the place to go.

The main advantage of The World Factbook is its ease of navigation. Whereas finding statistics on other sites is an exercise in sleuthing and patience, The World Factbook divides statistics by country and navigates like any other website—no databases to query here.

A sample of the indicators you can find . . .

- Maps of the major world regions
- Trade statistics
- Miles of paved roads

TRY IT YOURSELF

✓APPLICATIONS

Suppose your boss is looking at a few countries to invest in and wants you to put together a general country brief for each. Find and state the information detailed below for four countries: Bulgaria, Moldova, Romania, and Poland.

1. People and society
   a. Age structure
   b. Life expectancy at birth

2. Economy
   a. Labor force—by occupation
   b. GDP (purchasing power parity)
   c. GDP—per capita
   d. GDP—real growth rate
   e. GDP—composition, by sector of origin
   f. Exports ($ value)
   g. Exports—partners
   h. Imports ($ value)
   i. Imports—partners

✓ PROBLEMS

1. What is the size, in square miles, of Eritrea? Of Ethiopia?
2. How many miles of paved roads are in Poland?

The United Nations Statistics Division

http://data.un.org

Human Development Index can be found at http://hdr.undp.org/en/data/trends

UNdata is an initiative by the United Nations Statistics Division (UNSD) that brings together several data sources hosted by the United Nations. The United Nations collects statistics from its member states on a wide variety of topics. These include crime, education, energy, environment, population, and health, among others. Among its most popular indicators is the Human Development Index, a measure of general well-being calculated across countries. The Human Development Report Office within the United Nations Development Program hosts a site devoted specifically to this indicator. In addition to providing data on HDI, the site allows users to graph the data in simple and compelling ways, distilling complex data into concise graphs.

A sample of the indicators you can find . . .

- Quantity traded of commodity goods
- Gender inequality
- CO_2 emissions
- Foreign direct investment
- Prevalence of HIV

TRY IT YOURSELF

✓ APPLICATIONS

Suppose you're the head of a foundation with the mission to support governments and organizations trying to improve primary-school enrollment around the world. You want to know where to start your efforts.

1. Go to data.un.org, navigate to "The State of the World's Children" database, and view the data for "Net attendance ratio in primary education (NER)." Over what years are the observations given? What are the subgroups for the observations?
2. What country has the lowest attendance rate for males? What is it?
3. What country has the highest attendance rate for females? What is it?

✓ PROBLEMS

1. What is the most populous country?
2. What country receives the most development assistance?

Other Directories of Data

Google's Public Data

http://www.google.com/publicdata/directory

Google's Public Data site publishes several publicly available datasets in an easy-to-use way. The site continues to add sources; current sources include the U.S. Bureau of Economic Analysis, World Bank, World Economic Forum, International Monetary Fund, and the U.S. Bureau of Labor Statistics, among others.

The U.S. Government

http://www.data.gov/

The U.S. government has combined several government data sources into one site. This can be a good place to start if you know what category of data you need but aren't sure where to look for it.

Williams College Economics Department

http://econ.williams.edu/students/online-resources

The Economics Department at Williams College has provided links to many different data sources on one web page, to help students like you conduct research in several areas.

A

absolute advantage the ability to produce more of a good or service than others can with a given amount of resources.

absolute poverty line a measure that defines poverty as income below a certain amount, fixed at a given point in time.

accounting profit total revenue minus explicit costs.

administrative burden the logistical costs associated with implementing a tax.

adverse selection a state that occurs when buyers and sellers have different information about the quality of a good or the riskiness of a situation, and this asymmetric information results in failure to complete transactions that would have been possible if both sides had the same information.

agent a person who carries out a task on someone else's behalf.

aggregate demand curve a curve that shows the relationship between the overall price level in the economy and total demand.

aggregate expenditure (Y) the level of aggregate expenditure that consists of consumption, government spending, net exports, and actual investment by firms.

aggregate price level a measure of the average price level for GDP; in practice, the CPI or GDP price deflator.

aggregate supply curve a curve that shows the relationship between the over-all price level in the economy and total production by firms.

altruism a motive for action in which a person's utility increases simply because someone else's utility increases.

arbitrage the process of taking advantage of market inefficiencies to earn profits.

Arrow's impossibility theorem a theorem showing that no voting system can aggregate the preferences of voters over three or more options while satisfying the criteria of an ideal voting system.

autarky an economy that is self-contained and does not engage in trade with outsiders.

automatic stabilizers taxes and government spending that affect fiscal policy without specific action from policy-makers.

autonomous expenditure expenditure that is independent of the current level of aggregate income in the economy.

average fixed cost (AFC) fixed cost divided by the quantity of output.

average revenue revenue generated per product, calculated as total revenue divided by the quantity sold.

average total cost (ATC) total cost divided by the quantity of output.

average variable cost (AVC) variable cost divided by the quantity of output.

B

backward induction the process of analyzing a problem in reverse, starting with the last choice, then the second-to-last choice, and so on, to determine the optimal strategy.

balance of trade the value of exports minus the value of imports.

balance-of-payments identity an equation that shows that the value of net exports equals net capital outflow.

barter directly offering a good or service in exchange for some good or service you want.

behaving strategically acting to achieve a goal by anticipating the interplay between your own and others' decisions.

behavioral economics a field of economics that draws on insights from psychology to expand models of individual decision making.

bond a form of debt that represents a promise by the bond issuer to repay the face value of the loan, at a specified maturity date, and to pay periodic interest at a specific percentage rate.

bubble trade in an asset whose price has risen unsustainably far above historically justified levels.

budget constraint a line that is composed of all of the possible combinations of goods and services that a consumer can buy with her or his income.

budget deficit an amount of money a government spends beyond the revenue it brings in.

budget surplus an amount of revenue a government brings in beyond what it spends.

bundle a unique combination of goods and services that a person could choose to consume.

business cycle Fluctuations of output around the level of potential output in the economy.

C

capability something a person is able to be or do, such as to engage fully in life, including having economic and political freedoms.

capital manufactured goods that are used to produce new goods.

capital gains tax a tax on income earned by buying investments and selling them at a higher price.

cartel a number of firms that collude to make collective production decisions about quantities or prices.

causation a relationship between two events in which one brings about the other.

central bank the institution ultimately responsible for managing the nation's money supply and coordinating the banking system to ensure a sound economy.

choice architecture the organization of the context and process in which people make decisions.

circular flow model a simplified representation of how the economy's transactions work together.

closed economy an economy that does not interact with other countries' economies.

clusters networks of interdependent firms, universities, and businesses that focus on the production of a specific type of good.

Coase theorem the idea that even in the presence of an externality, individuals can reach an efficient equilibrium through private trades, assuming zero transaction costs.

collective-action problem a situation in which a group of people stands to gain from an action that it is not rational for any of the members to undertake individually.

collusion the act of working together to make decisions about price and quantity.

commitment device a mechanism that allows people to voluntarily restrict their choices in order to make it easier to stick to plans.

commitment strategy an agreement to submit to a penalty in the future for defecting from a given strategy.

commodity-backed money any form of money that can be legally exchanged into a fixed amount of an underlying commodity.

common resource a good that is not excludable but is rival.

comparative advantage the ability to produce a good or service at a lower opportunity cost than others.

competitive market a market in which fully informed, price-taking buyers and sellers easily trade a standardized good or service.

complements goods that are consumed together, so that purchasing one will make consumers more likely to purchase the other.

complete information state of being fully informed about the choices that relevant economic actors face.

compounding the process of accumulation that results from the additional interest paid on previously earned interest.

conditional cash transfer a program in which financial support is given only to people who engage in certain actions.

Condorcet paradox a situation in which the preferences of each individual member of a group are transitive, but the collective preferences of the group are not.

constant returns to scale returns that occur when average total cost does not depend on the quantity of output.

Consumer Price Index (CPI) a measure that tracks changes in the cost of a basket of goods and services purchased by a typical U.S. household.

consumer surplus the net benefit that a consumer receives from purchasing a good or service, measured by the difference between willingness to pay and the actual price.

consumption spending on goods and services by private individuals and households.

consumption externality an externality that occurs when a good or service is being consumed.

contractionary fiscal policy decisions about government spending and taxation intended to decrease aggregate demand.

contractionary monetary policy actions that reduce the money supply in order to decrease aggregate demand.

convergence theory the theory that countries that start out poor will initially grow faster than rich ones but will eventually converge to the same growth rate.

core inflation measure of inflation that excludes goods with historically volatile price changes—energy and food.

correlation a consistently observed relationship between two variables.

credit constraint inability to get a loan even though a person expects to be able to repay the loan plus interest.

cross-price elasticity of demand a measure of how the demand for one good changes when the price of a different good changes.

crowding out the reduction in private borrowing caused by an increase in government borrowing.

cyclical unemployment unemployment caused by short-term economic fluctuations.

D

deadweight loss a loss of total surplus that occurs because the quantity of a good that is bought and sold is below the market equilibrium quantity.

debt service the amount that consumers have to spend to pay their debts, often expressed as a percentage of disposable income.

default the failure of a borrower to pay back a loan according to the agreed-upon terms.

default rule a rule defining what will automatically occur if a chooser fails to make an active decision otherwise.

deflation an overall fall in prices in the economy.

demand curve a graph that shows the quantities of a particular good or service that consumers will demand at various prices.

demand deposits funds held in bank accounts that can be withdrawn ("demanded") by depositors at any time without advance notice.

demand schedule a table that shows the quantities of a particular good or service that consumers are willing and able to purchase (demand) at various prices.

depression a particularly severe or extended recession.

derivative an asset whose value is based on the value of another asset.

diminishing marginal product a principle stating that the marginal product of an input decreases as the quantity of the input increases.

diminishing marginal utility the principle that the additional utility gained from consuming successive units of a good or service tends to be smaller than the utility gained from the previous unit.

discount rate the interest rate charged by the Fed for loans of reserves through the discount window.

discount window the lending facility run by the Fed that allows any bank to borrow reserves.

discouraged workers people who have looked for work in the past year but have given up looking because of the condition of the labor market.

discretionary spending public expenditures that have to be approved each year.

discrimination making choices by using generalizations based on people's observable characteristics like race, gender, and age.

diseconomies of scale returns that occur when an increase in the quantity of output increases average total cost.

disinflation a period in which inflation rates are falling, but still positive.

diversification the process by which risks are shared across many different assets or people, reducing the impact of any particular risk on any one individual.

dividend a payment made periodically, typically annually or quarterly, to all shareholders of a company.

domestic savings savings for capital investment that come from within a country; equal to domestic income minus consumption spending.

dominant strategy a strategy that is the best one for a player to follow no matter what strategy other players choose.

dual mandate the twin responsibilities of the Federal Reserve, to use monetary policy to ensure price stability and to maintain full employment.

E

economic profit total revenue minus all opportunity costs, explicit and implicit.

economic rent the gains that workers and owners of capital receive from supplying their labor or machinery in factor markets.

economics the study of how people, individually and collectively, manage resources.

economies of scale returns that occur when an increase in the quantity of output decreases average total cost.

efficiency use of resources in the most productive way possible to produce the goods and services that have the greatest total economic value to society.

efficiency wage a wage that is deliberately set above the market rate to increase worker productivity.

efficient market an arrangement such that no exchange can make anyone better off without someone becoming worse off.

efficient points combinations of production possibilities that squeeze the most output possible from all available resources.

efficient scale the quantity of output at which average total cost is minimized.

efficient-market hypothesis the idea that market prices always incorporate all available information, and therefore represent true value as correctly as is possible.

elastic demand that has an absolute value of elasticity greater than 1.

elasticity a measure of how much consumers and producers will respond to a change in market conditions.

embargo a restriction or prohibition of trade in order to put political pressure on a country.

endowment effect the tendency of people to place more value on something simply because they own it.

entitlement spending public expenditure that "entitles" people to benefits by virtue of age, income, or some other factor.

equilibrium the situation in a market when the quantity supplied equals the quantity demanded; graphically, this convergence happens where the demand curve intersects the supply curve.

equilibrium aggregate expenditure the level of aggregate expenditure where unplanned investment is equal to zero, or, equivalently, where planned aggregate expenditure is equal to actual aggregate expenditure.

equilibrium price the price at which the quantity supplied equals the quantity demanded.

equilibrium quantity the quantity that is supplied and demanded at the equilibrium price.

excess reserves any additional amount, beyond the required reserves, that a bank chooses to keep in reserve.

exchange rate the value of one currency expressed in terms of another currency.

exchange-rate appreciation an increase in the value of a currency relative to the value of another currency.

exchange-rate depreciation a decrease in the value of a currency relative to other currencies.

excise tax a sales tax on a specific good or service.

excludable a characteristic of a good or service that allows owners to prevent its use by people who have not paid for it.

expansionary fiscal policy decisions about government spending and taxation intended to increase aggregate demand.

expansionary monetary policy actions that increase the money supply in order to increase aggregate demand.

expected value the average of each possible outcome of a future event, weighted by its probability of occurring.

expenditure multiplier the factor by which output increases in response to an initial change in aggregate expenditure .

explicit costs costs that require a firm to spend money.

exports goods and services that are produced domestically and consumed in other countries.

external benefits benefits that accrue without compensation to someone other than the person who caused it.

external costs costs imposed without compensation on someone other than the person who caused them.

externality a cost or benefit imposed without compensation on someone other than the person who caused it.

F

factors of production the ingredients that go into making a good or service.

federal funds rate the interest rate at which banks choose to lend reserves held at the Fed to one another.

Federal Reserve ("the Fed") the system consisting of a seven-member Board of

Governors and 12 regional banks that act as the central bank of the United States.

fiat money money created by rule, without any commodity to back it.

financial capital money saved by households that gets lent to firms for investment purposes and to governments to fund budget deficits.

financial intermediaries institutions that channel funds from people who have them to people who want them.

financial market a market in which people trade future claims on funds or goods.

financial system the group of institutions that bring together savers, borrowers, investors, and insurers in a set of interconnected markets where people trade financial products.

financing gap the difference between the savings rate within an economy and the amount of investment needed to achieve sustainable growth.

first-mover advantage benefit enjoyed by the player who chooses first and, as a result, gets a higher payoff than those who follow.

fiscal policy government decisions about the level of taxation and public spending.

fixed costs costs that do not depend on the quantity of output produced.

fixed exchange rate an exchange rate that is set by the government, instead of determined by the market.

floating exchange rate an exchange rate whose value is determined by the market.

foreign direct investment (FDI) investment when a firm runs part of its operation abroad or owns all or part of another company abroad

foreign portfolio investment investment funded by foreign sources but operated domestically.

fractional-reserve banking a banking system in which banks keep on reserve less than 100 percent of their deposits.

free-rider problem a problem that occurs when the nonexcludability of a public good leads to undersupply.

frictional unemployment unemployment caused by workers who are changing location, job, or career.

full information complete knowledge of the product being offered in the market.

fungible easily exchangeable or substitutable.

G

gains from trade the improvement in outcomes that occurs when producers specialize and exchange goods and services.

game a situation involving at least two people that requires those involved to think strategically.

game theory the study of how people behave strategically under different circumstances.

GDP deflator a measure of the overall change in prices in an economy, using the ratio between real and nominal GDP.

GDP per capita a country's GDP divided by its population.

Gini coefficient a single-number measure of income inequality; ranges from 0 to 1, with higher numbers meaning greater inequality.

government purchases spending on goods and services by all levels of government.

government-spending multiplier the amount by which GDP increases when government spending increases by $1.

green GDP an alternative measure of GDP that subtracts the environmental costs of production from the positive outputs normally counted in GDP.

gross domestic product (GDP) the sum of the market values of all final goods and services produced within a country in a given period of time.

gross national product (GNP) the sum of the market values of all final goods and services produced and capital owned by the permanent residents of a country in a given period of time.

H

headline inflation measure of inflation that includes all of the goods that the average consumer buys.

heuristic a mental shortcut for making decisions (sometimes in good ways, but sometimes not).

human capital the set of skills, knowledge, experience, and talent that determine the productivity of workers.

hyperinflation extremely long-lasting and painful increases in the price level.

I

idiosyncratic risk any risk that is unique to a particular company or asset.

impact investing investing money in firms to generate both financial and social returns.

implicit costs costs that represent forgone opportunities.

import quota a limit on the amount of a particular good that can be imported.

imports goods and services that are produced in other countries and consumed domestically.

in-kind transfer a program that provides specific goods or services, rather than cash, directly to needy recipients.

incentive something that causes people to behave in a certain way by changing the trade-offs they face.

incidence a description of who bears the burden of a tax.

income effect the change in consumption that results from a change in effective wealth due to higher or lower prices.

income elasticity of demand a measure of how much the demand for a good changes in response to a change in consumers' incomes.

income mobility the ability to improve one's economic circumstances over time.

income tax a tax charged on the earnings of individuals and corporations.

indexing the practice of automatically increasing payments in proportion to the cost of living.

indifference curve a curve showing all the different consumption bundles that provide a consumer with equal levels of utility.

industrial policy effort by a government to favor some industries over others.

inelastic demand that has an absolute value of elasticity less than 1.

inferior goods goods for which demand decreases as income increases.

inflation an overall rise in prices in the economy.

inflation rate the size of the change in the overall price level; the percent change in a price index such as the CPI from year to year.

inflationary output gap an output gap that occurs when equilibrium aggregate expenditure is above the level needed for full employment.

information asymmetry a condition in which one participant in a transaction knows more than another participant.

institutions the humanly devised constraints that shape human interactions.

interest rate the price of money, typically expressed as a percentage per dollar per unit of time; for savers, it is the price received for letting a bank use money for a specified period of time; for borrowers, it is the price of using money for a specified period of time.

inventory the stock of goods that a company produces now but does not sell immediately.

investment spending on productive inputs, such as factories, machinery, and inventories.

investment trade-off a reduction in current consumption to pay for investment in capital intended to increase future production.

K

Keynesian equilibrium a situation in which planned aggregate expenditure is equal to actual aggregate expenditure.

L

labor demand curve a graph showing the relationship between the total quantity of labor demanded by all the firms in the economy and the wage rate.

labor force people who are in the working-age population and are either employed or unemployed; people

who are currently working or who are actively trying to find a job.

labor supply curve a graph showing the relationship between the total labor supplied in the economy and the wage rate.

labor unions groups of employees who join together to bargain with their employer(s) over salaries and work conditions.

labor-force participation rate the number of people in the labor force divided by the working-age population.

law of demand a fundamental characteristic of demand that states that, all else equal, quantity demanded rises as price falls.

law of supply a fundamental characteristic of supply that states that, all else equal, quantity supplied rises as price rises.

leverage the practice of using borrowed money to pay for investments.

leverage ratio the ratio of a company's assets to its equity, where equity is defined as the firm's assets minus its liabilities.

liquidity a measure of how easily a particular asset can be converted quickly to cash without much loss of value.

liquidity-preference model idea that the quantity of money people want to hold is a function of the interest rate.

loan an agreement in which a lender gives money to a borrower in exchange for a promise to repay the amount loaned plus an agreed-upon amount of interest.

Lorenz curve a graphic representation of income distribution that maps percentage of the population against cumulative percentage of income earned by those people.

loss aversion the tendency for people to put more effort into avoiding losses than achieving gains.

lump-sum tax (head tax) a tax that charges the same amount to each taxpayer, regardless of their economic behavior or circumstances.

lump-sum taxes taxes whose levels do not change when income rises or falls.

M

M1 definition of money that includes cash plus checking account balances.

M2 definition of money that includes everything in M1 plus savings accounts and other financial instruments where money is locked away for a specified amount of time; less liquid than M1.

macroeconomics the study of the economy as a whole, and how policymakers manage the growth and behavior of the overall economy.

marginal cost (MC) the additional cost incurred by a firm when it produces one additional unit of output.

marginal decision making comparison of additional benefits of a choice against the additional costs it would bring, without considering related benefits and costs of past choices.

marginal product the increase in output that is generated by an additional unit of input.

marginal propensity to consume (MPC) the amount that consumption increases when after-tax income increases by $1.

marginal rate of substitution (MRS) the rate at which a consumer is willing to trade or substitute between two goods.

marginal revenue the revenue generated by selling an additional unit of a good.

marginal tax rate the tax rate charged on the last dollar a taxpayer earns.

marginal utility the change in total utility that comes from consuming one additional unit of a good or service.

market buyers and sellers who trade a particular good or service.

market basket a list of specific goods and services in fixed quantities.

market economy an economy in which private individuals, rather than a centralized planning authority, make the decisions.

market failures situations in which the assumption of efficient, competitive markets fails to hold.

market for loanable funds a market in which savers supply funds to those who want to borrow.

market power the ability to noticeably affect market prices.

market (systemic) risk any risk that is broadly shared by the entire market or economy; also called *systemic risk*.

means-tested the characteristic of a program that defines eligibility for benefits based on recipients' income.

median-voter theorem a model stating that under certain conditions, politicians maximize their votes by taking the policy position preferred by the median voter.

medium of exchange the ability to use money to purchase goods and services.

menu costs the costs (measured in money, time, and opportunity) of changing prices to keep pace with inflation.

microeconomics the study of how individuals and firms manage resources.

mid-point method method that measures percentage change in quantity demanded (or quantity supplied) relative to a point midway between two points on a curve; used to estimate elasticity.

model a simplified representation of the important parts of a complicated situation.

monetary base the sum of currency in circulation and reserves held by banks at the Federal Reserve.

monetary policy actions by the central bank to manage the money supply, in pursuit of certain macroeconomic goals.

money the set of all assets that are regularly used to directly purchase goods and services.

money multiplier the ratio of money created by the lending activities of the banking system to the money created by the government's central bank.

money supply the amount of money available in the economy.

monopolistic competition a market with many firms that sell goods and services that are similar, but slightly different.

monopoly a firm that is the only producer of a good or service with no close substitutes.

monopsony a market in which there is only one buyer but many sellers.

moral hazard the tendency for people to behave in a riskier way or to renege on contracts when they do not face the full consequences of their actions.

multiplier effect the increase in consumer spending that occurs when spending by one person causes others to spend more too, increasing the impact on the economy of the initial spending .

mutual fund a portfolio of stocks, bonds, and other assets managed by a professional who makes decisions on behalf of clients.

N

Nash equilibrium an equilibrium reached when all players choose the best strategy they can, given the choices of all other players. It is a situation wherein, given the consequences, the player has no regrets about his or her decision.

national savings the sum of the private savings of individuals and corporations plus the public savings of the government.

natural monopoly a market in which a single firm can produce, at a lower cost than multiple firms, the entire quantity of output demanded.

natural rate of unemployment the normal level of unemployment that persists in an economy in the long run.

net capital flow the net flow of funds invested outside of a country; specifically, the difference between capital inflows (investment financed by savings from another country) and capital outflows (domestic savings invested abroad).

net exports (NX) exports minus imports; the value of goods and services produced domestically and consumed abroad minus the value of goods and services produced abroad and consumed domestically.

net present value (NPV) a measure of the current value of a stream of cash flows expected in the future.

network externality the effect that an additional user of a good or participant in an activity has on the value of that good or activity for others.

neutrality of money the idea that, in the long run, changes in the money supply affect nominal variables, such as prices and wages, but do not affect real outcomes in the economy.

nominal exchange rate the stated rate at which one country's currency can be traded for another country's currency.

nominal GDP GDP calculation in which goods and services are valued at current prices.

nominal interest rate the reported interest rate, not adjusted for the effects of inflation.

non-accelerating inflation rate of unemployment (NAIRU) the lowest possible unemployment rate that will not cause the inflation rate to increase.

nonautonomous expenditure expenditure that changes as a result of the current level of aggregate income in the economy.

normal goods goods for which demand increases as income increases.

normative statement a claim about how the world should be.

nudge an implementation of choice architecture that alters people's behavior in a deliberate and predictable way without changing economic incentives much.

O

oligopoly a market with only a few firms, which sell a similar good or service.

open economy an economy that interacts with other countries' economies.

open-market operations sales or purchases of government bonds by the Fed, to or from banks, on the open market.

opportunity cost the value to you of what you have to give up in order to get something; the value you could have gained by choosing the next-best alternative.

output gap the difference between actual and potential output in an economy.

P

payroll tax a tax on the wages paid to an employee.

pension fund a professionally managed portfolio of assets intended to provide income to retirees.

perfectly elastic demand demand for which any increase in price will cause quantity demanded to drop to zero; represented by a perfectly horizontal line.

perfectly inelastic demand demand for which quantity demanded remains the same regardless of price; represented by a perfectly vertical line.

Phillips curve a model that shows the connection between inflation and unemployment in the short run.

physical capital the stock of equipment and structures that allow for production of goods and services.

Pigovian tax a tax meant to counterbalance a negative externality.

planned aggregate expenditure (PAE) the level of aggregate expenditure that consists of consumption, planned investment, government spending, and net exports.

planned aggregate expenditure curve planned aggregate expenditure as a function of actual aggregate expenditure, holding all other factors constant.

planned investment the amount that firms actively decide to spend on new capital equipment or strategic inventory accumulation.

positive statement a factual claim about how the world actually works.

potential output the total amount of output a country could produce if all of its resources were fully engaged.

poverty line See *absolute poverty line* and *relative poverty line*.

poverty rate the percentage of the population that falls below the absolute poverty line.

poverty trap a self-reinforcing mechanism that causes the poor to stay poor.

PPP-adjustment recalculating economic statistics to account for differences in price levels across countries.

present value how much a certain amount of money that will be obtained in the future is worth today.

price ceiling a maximum legal price at which a good can be sold.

price control a regulation that sets a maximum or minimum legal price for a particular good.

price discrimination the practice of charging customers different prices for the same good.

price elasticity of demand the size of the change in the quantity demanded of a good or service when its price changes.

price elasticity of supply the size of the change in the quantity supplied of a good or service when its price changes.

price floor a minimum legal price at which a good can be sold.

price index a measure showing how much the cost of a market basket has risen or fallen relative to the cost in a base time period or location.

price taker a buyer or seller who cannot affect the market price. In a perfectly competitive market, firms are price takers as a consequence of many sellers selling standardized goods.

principal a person who entrusts someone with a task.

prisoners' dilemma a game of strategy in which two people make rational choices that lead to a less-than-ideal result for both.

private benefits benefits that accrue directly to the decision maker.

private costs costs that fall directly on an economic decision maker.

private goods goods that are both excludable and rival.

private savings the savings of individuals or corporations within a country.

producer surplus the net benefit that a producer receives from the sale of a good or service, measured by the difference between the producer's willingness to sell and the actual price.

product differentiation the creation of products that are similar to competitors' products but more attractive in some ways.

production externality an externality that occurs when a good or service is being produced.

production function the relationship between quantity of inputs and the resulting quantity of outputs.

production possibilities frontier (PPF) a line or curve that shows all the possible combinations of two outputs that can be produced using all available resources.

productivity output produced per worker.

profit the difference between total revenue and total cost.

progressive tax a tax that charges low-income people a smaller percentage of their income than high-income people.

property tax a tax on the estimated value of a home or other property.

proportional/flat tax a tax that takes the same percentage of income from all taxpayers.

protectionism a preference for policies that limit trade.

public debt the total amount of money that a government owes at a point in time; the cumulative sum of all deficits and surpluses.

public good a good that is neither excludable nor rival.

public savings the difference between government tax revenue and government spending.

purchase price the price paid to gain permanent ownership of a factor of production.

purchasing power parity (PPP) the theory that purchasing power in different countries should be the same when stated in a common currency.

purchasing power parity (PPP) index index that describes the overall difference in prices of goods between countries.

Q

quantitative easing policies that are designed to directly increase the money supply by a certain amount.

quantity demanded the amount of a particular good that buyers will purchase at a given price during a specified period.

quantity equation the equation $M \times V = P \times Y$, which relates the money supply and velocity of money to the price value of real output.

quantity supplied the amount of a particular good or service that producers will offer for sale at a given price during a specified period.

quantity theory of money theory that the value of money (and thus the aggregate price level) is determined by the overall quantity of money in existence (the money supply); it states that changes in the price level (inflation or deflation) are primarily the result of changes in the quantity of money.

quota (imports) See *import quota*.

quota rents profits earned by foreign firms or governments under a quota.

R

randomized controlled trial (RCT) a method that randomly assigns subjects into control and treatment groups in order to assess the causal link from an intervention to specific outcomes.

rational behavior making choices to achieve goals in the most effective way possible.

rational ignorance choosing to remain ignorant when the opportunity costs of gathering information outweigh the benefits.

real exchange rate the value of goods in one country expressed in terms of the same goods in another country.

real GDP GDP calculation in which goods and services are valued at constant prices.

real interest rate the interest rate adjusted for the effects of inflation.

real-wage or classical unemployment unemployment that results from wages being higher than the market-clearing level.

recession a period of significant economic decline.

recessionary output gap an output gap that occurs when equilibrium aggregate expenditure is below the level needed for full employment.

reciprocity responding to another's action with a similar action.

regressive tax a tax that charges low-income people a larger percentage of their income than it charges high-income people.

relative poverty line a measure that defines poverty in terms of the income of the rest of the population.

rent-seeking the act of pursuing privileges that increase the surplus of a person or group without increasing total surplus.

rental price the price paid to use a factor of production for a certain period or task.

repeated game a game that is played more than once.

required reserves the minimum fraction of deposits that banks are legally required (by the Federal Reserve) to keep on hand.

reserve ratio the fraction of deposits a bank must hold as reserves; calculated as the amount of cash kept as reserves divided by the total amount of demand deposits.

reserve requirement the regulation that sets the minimum fraction of deposits banks must hold in reserve.

reserves the money that a bank keeps on hand, either in cash or in deposits at the Federal Reserve.

revealed preference the idea that people's preferences can be determined by observing their choices and behavior.

rise vertical distance; calculated as the change in *y*.

risk exists when the costs or benefits of an event or choice are uncertain.

risk pooling organizing people into a group to collectively absorb the risk faced by each individual.

risk-averse having a low willingness to take on situations with risk; when faced with two options with equal expected value, the one with lower risk is preferred.

risk-free rate the interest rate at which one would lend if there were no risk of default; usually approximated by interest rates on U.S. government debt.

risk-seeking having a high willingness to take on situations with risk; when faced with two options with equal expected value, the one with higher risk is preferred.

rival in consumption (rival) the characteristic of a good for which one person's consumption prevents or decreases others' ability to consume it.

run horizontal distance; calculated as the change in *x*.

S

sales tax a tax that is charged on the value of a good or service being purchased.

savings the portion of income that is not immediately spent on consumption of goods and services.

scarcity the condition of wanting more than we can get with available resources.

screening taking action to reveal private information about someone else.

securitization the practice of packaging individual debts into a single uniform asset.

shoe-leather costs the costs (measured in time, money, and effort) of managing cash in the face of inflation.

shortage (excess demand) a situation in which the quantity of a good that is demanded is higher than the quantity supplied.

signaling taking action to reveal one's own private information.

slope the ratio of vertical distance (change in *y*) to horizontal distance (change in *x*).

social benefit the entire benefits of a decision, including both private benefits and external benefits.

social cost the entire cost of a decision, including both private costs and any external costs.

social insurance government programs under which people pay into a common pool and are eligible to draw on benefits under certain circumstances.

specialization spending all of your time producing a particular good.

stagflation high inflation despite low economic growth and high unemployment.

standard deviation a measure of how spread out a set of numbers is.

standardized good a good for which any two units have the same features and are interchangeable.

statistical discrimination distinguishing between choices by generalizing based on observable characteristics in order to fill in missing information.

status-quo bias the tendency to stick with the current situation over other options, even when it is cheap to switch.

stock a financial asset that represents partial ownership of a company.

store of value a certain amount of purchasing power that money retains over time.

structural unemployment unemployment that results from a mismatch between the skills workers can offer and the skills in demand.

subsidy a requirement that the government pay an extra amount to producers or consumers of a good.

substitutes goods that serve a similar-enough purpose that a consumer might purchase one in place of the other.

substitution effect the change in consumption that results from a change in the relative price of goods.

sunk cost a cost that has already been incurred and cannot be refunded or recovered.

supply curve a graph that shows the quantities of a particular good or service that producers will supply at various prices.

supply schedule a table that shows the quantities of a particular good or service that producers will supply at various prices.

supply shocks significant events that directly affect production and the aggregate supply curve in the short run.

surplus (efficiency) a way of measuring who benefits from transactions and by how much.

surplus (excess supply) a situation in which the quantity of a good that is supplied is higher than the quantity demanded.

T

tariff a tax on imported goods.

tax incidence the relative tax burden borne by buyers and sellers.

tax wedge the difference between the price paid by buyers and the price received by sellers in the presence of a tax.

taxation multiplier the amount GDP decreases when taxes increase by $1.

time inconsistency a situation in which we change our minds about what we want simply because of the timing of the decision.

tit-for-tat a strategy in which a player in a repeated game takes the same action that his or her opponent did in the preceding round.

"too big to fail" so large in terms of assets or customers or so historically important that banking regulators allow the bank to keep operating despite insolvency.

total cost the amount that a firm pays for all of the inputs that go into producing goods and services.

total revenue the amount that a firm receives from the sale of goods and services; calculated as the quantity sold multiplied by the price paid for each unit.

total surplus a measure of the combined benefits that everyone receives from participating in an exchange of goods or services.

tradable allowance a production or consumption quota that can be bought and sold.

trade deficit a negative balance of trade; a greater amount of imports than exports.

trade liberalization policies and actions that reduce trade restrictions.

trade surplus a positive balance of trade; a greater amount of exports than imports.

tragedy of the commons the depletion of a common resource due to individually rational but collectively inefficient overconsumption.

transaction costs the costs incurred by buyer and seller in agreeing to and executing a sale of goods or services.

transfer payments Payments from government accounts to individuals for programs, like Social Security, that do not involve a purchase of goods or services.

Treasury securities debt-financing arrangements made by the U.S. government.

U

underemployed workers who are either working less than they would like to or are working in jobs below their skill level.

unemployment situation in which someone wants to work but cannot find a job in the current market.

unemployment insurance money paid by the government to people who are unemployed.

unemployment rate the number of unemployed people divided by the number of people in the labor force.

United Nations Development Program (UNDP) a global United Nations network that provides knowledge and resources to developing countries.

unit of account a standard unit of comparison.

unit-elastic demand that has an absolute value of elasticity exactly equal to 1.

utility a measure of the amount of satisfaction a person derives from something.

utility function a formula for calculating the total utility that a particular person derives from consuming a combination of goods and services.

V

value of the marginal product the increase in revenue generated by the last unit of an input; calculated as the output generated by an input (marginal product) times the unit price of the output.

variable costs costs that depend on the quantity of output produced.

velocity of money the number of times the entire money supply turns over in a given period.

W

willingness to pay (reservation price) the maximum price that a buyer would be willing to pay for a good or service.

willingness to sell the minimum price that a seller is willing to accept in exchange for a good or service.

World Bank a multinational organization dedicated to providing financial and technical assistance to developing countries.

World Trade Organization (WTO) an international organization designed to monitor and enforce trade agreements, while also promoting free trade.

Z

zero-sum game a situation in which whenever one person gains, another loses an equal amount, such that the net value of any transaction is zero.

index

Note: **Boldface** entries indicate key terms and the page numbers where they are defined.